PIMLICO

491

ISLAND FORTRESS

Norman Longmate was born in Newbury, Berkshire, and educated by scholarship at Christ's Hospital, where he was deeply influenced by an inspiring history teacher. After war service in the army he read modern history at Worcester College, Oxford. He subsequently worked as a journalist in Fleet Street, as a producer of history programmes for the BBC, and for the BBC Secretariat. In 1981 he was elected a Fellow of the Royal Historical Society and in 1983 he left the BBC to become a full-time writer.

Norman Longmate is the author of more than twenty books, mainly on the Second World War and on Victorian social history, and of many radio and television scripts on historical subjects. He has frequently been employed as an historical adviser by film and television companies.

ISLAND FORTRESS

The Defence of Great Britain 1603–1945

NORMAN LONGMATE

PIMLICO

Published by Pimlico 2001

2 4 6 8 10 9 7 5 3 1

Copyright © Norman Longmate 1991

Norman Longmate has asserted his right under the Copyright, Designs
and Patents Act, 1988 to be identified as the author of this work

First published in Great Britain by Hutchinson, 1991
Pimlico edition 2001

Pimlico
Random House, 20 Vauxhall Bridge Road,
London SW1V 2SA

Random House Australia (Pty) Limited
20 Alfred Street, Milsons Point, Sydney
New South Wales 2061, Australia

Random House New Zealand Limited
18 Poland Road, Glenfield,
Auckland 10, New Zealand

Random House South Africa (Pty) Limited
Endulini, 5A Jubilee Road, Parktown 2193, South Africa

The Random House Group Limited Reg. No. 954009
www.randomhouse.co.uk

A CIP catalogue record fo this book
is available from the British Library

ISBN 0-7126-6813-6

Papers used by Random House UK Limited are natural,
recyclable products made from wood grown in sustainable forests.
The manufacturing processes conform to the environmental
regulations of the country of origin

Printed and bound in Great Britain by
Mackays of Chatham PLC

CONTENTS

Maps in the Text

FOREWORD

With this volume I complete the history of the invasion of the British Isles, and of invasion attempts and alarms, between 55BC and 1945. The whole project has taken most of the eight years which have elapsed since I became a full-time writer in 1983. Approximately half that time has been taken up by research, including visits to most of the areas and often the specific forts mentioned.

I hope that in these circumstances I may be forgiven some personal recollections. The great Edward Gibbon, in a famous passage in his *Autobiography*, refers to being 'condemned during two years and a half to a wandering life of military servitude', while he was an officer in the militia during the invasion alarm of 1760-2, which I describe in Chapter 14. After an excellent account of his time under arms, Gibbon comments: 'The captain of the Hampshire grenadiers (the reader may smile) has not been useless to the historian of the Roman Empire.' My own 'military servitude' was twice as long, involving one year in the Home Guard and nearly four in the army, but I must similarly acknowledge that my experiences have also proved unexpectedly helpful in writing this book. It is not essential, in order to describe the deficiencies of a Sten gun, to have fired one, but it is certainly no disadvantage, and few military historians will, I think, have had the advantage I enjoyed during my military service of having attended a training course in army organisation.

My major problem, apart from the sheer volume of reading and vast range of subjects to be covered, has been the contradictions contained in the sources, which inevitably become worse the more authorities one consults, even over such basic matters as the number of men serving at a particular time, or the names of the ships sunk or damaged in a particular action. Where I have not been able to reach a definite conclusion on some disputed fact I have indicated this in a footnote. A constant annoyance has been the reluctance of so many writers to include an adequate number of dates, especially the *year* an event occurred. This fault, too, I have tried to avoid.

For much of the period covered by this volume variations in the spelling of surnames still occurred, and in these cases I have used what seems the preferred version with, the first time the name is mentioned, the alternatives in brackets. I have followed a similar practice over place-names, where standardisation came even later, and have also tried to identify their precise location, so often left vague in the original. As in *Defending the Island, From Caesar to the Armada*, to which this book forms the sequel, I have quoted from poems and other sources only when the narrative has reached the point when they were written. I have used throughout the pre-1974 names of the counties, but have 'translated' measurements and prices into their metric equivalents except in the case of tons, where there is little difference from the more recent 'tonnes'. In the earlier extracts I have occasionally retained the original spelling, but in general have standardised punctuation and the use of capitals (scattered in profusion, but inconsistently, through so many documents) to conform to modern practice.

A large number of people have assisted me in various ways, indeed of nearly sixty whom I approached only one failed to reply. The list that follows does not include most of those already mentioned in the Foreword to Volume I, but is otherwise comprehensive and I offer apologies to anyone inadvertently omitted.

Mr C.M. Tod of Whiteheads, estate agents, of Chichester, kindly gave me particulars of sale about No Man's Land Fort in the Solent, near Portsmouth; Messrs Vinder, Carew and Co., of Plymouth, were similarly helpful over Fort Picklecombe, as was Mr Richard Ashworth of Parker May and Rowden of London W.1 on the disposal of the former Royal Ordnance Depot at Weedon, and, on the same subject, Mr P.R. Waights of Daventry District Council. Mr Reg Curtis of Rochester provided me with much information on the Chatham defences of 1915-18 and put me in touch with Mr George Wilson, now of Ambleside, who provided me with a 'bricklayer's eye view' of the pillboxes on which he worked in Kent in the Second World War. I am much indebted to Mr Steve Goodhand, then an Assistant Keeper of Local History for the City of Portsmouth, who devoted two days to taking me round this important area, during which Lieut.-Commander H. Donnithorne, RN, kindly escorted me round the sites at Gosport now within the grounds of HMS *Dolphin*.

Many Museum curators and librarians and their staff gave generously of their time to help me and my acknowledgement is, wherever possible, to the individual concerned, though he or she may since then have moved elsewhere. On Dorset I am grateful to Mr A.M. Hunt of the Dorset Institute of Higher Education, Weymouth, and Mr Eric Reeson of the *Dorset County Post*, Dorchester; on the Fishguard landing to Mrs Joan Evans of the Public Library, Haverfordwest, and Mr D.G. Glover of the County Museum, Haverfordwest; on Hartlepool to Miss M.E. Hoban, Reference Librarian of the Hartlepool Central Library; on the London Defence Positions I am grateful to Ms Judith Blacklaw of the Ministry of Defence Library, to Mr P.E.R. Broadbent-Yale of the National Trust, Southern Region, at Dorking, and to Mr Malcolm Locock of the Box Hill Management Committee of the National Trust, who enabled me to visit the former forts now in its care; Mr Duncan Mirylees, of the Surrey Local Studies Library at Guildford, directed me to some items on the Battle of Dorking which I should otherwise have missed; on Newhaven, I was much helped by Mr Anthony Kemp of the National Coast Museum in that town; on the Portsmouth and Gosport area I was assisted by Miss Carol Bull of Fort Brockhurst, Gosport; Miss Denise Coutts of the Gosport Museum; Mr Tom King of the Museum of Naval Ordnance, Gosport; Mr A. King of the Central Library, Portsmouth; and Miss Sarah Peacock (now Mrs Sarah Quail) of the City Records Office, Portsmouth. On the bombardment of Scarborough Mr B. Berryman of the North Yorkshire County Library, Scarborough, was very helpful; so too, on Teignmouth and Devon generally, was Mr M.L.G. Maguire of Devon Library Services, Exeter. My research into the shelling of Whitby was assisted by Mrs Sandra Turner of the Whitby Branch Library, North Yorkshire; at Whitehaven Mr Harry Fancy, Curator of the Museum and Art Gallery, proved a mine of information on John Paul Jones's landing; and Brigadier D.F. Ryan of the Royal Artillery Institution, Woolwich, helped me track down an elusive but essential book. Mr. David Bennett of the Kent Defence Research Centre kindly supplied another hard to find title.

I owe a particular debt to the Fortress Study Group. The visits arranged as part of its annual conference have provided access to many of the important sites mentioned here which are normally closed and its members and ex-members form a panel of specialist knowledge on every aspect of fortifications history. I particularly acknowledge the help of: Mr David Barnes; Mr Anthony Cantwell; Mr David Clarke; Brigadier 'Jock' Hamilton-Baillie; Mr Ian Hogg; Mr Michael Powell; Mr Roger Thomas; Mr Victor Smith; and Mr Charles Trollope. I owe a special debt to Mr Peter Cobb; also to Mr Henry Wills, for patiently answering questions on his classic book *Pillbox*, which enabled me to get right what the official historian had got wrong. Details of this and of other books by the Group members mentioned above will be found in the Note on Sources.

A number of other private individuals have also assisted me. Miss Pat Burstall put me further in her debt by her research in Scarborough and by contributing information on cycling as it affected the Volunteers; Herr Karl Freudenstein, of Bonn, offered help with research on

German invasion plans. Mr John Robson, of Scarborough, suggested several sources on the events of 1914, including the excellent unpublished thesis by Ms Anne Walker, now of Rotherham, to whom I am indebted for lending me a copy; Mr and Mrs Terry Williams of West Hill, Ottery St Mary, suggested some material on the 'invasion' of Teignmouth and introduced me to the Devon and Exeter Institute in that city. Finally, I am grateful to Miss Sonia Anderson for reading the proofs with a vigilant historian's eye and to Mr Bryan Harris for invaluable assistance in editing the text.

June 1991   NRL

FOREWORD TO THE PIMLICO EDITION

For this new edition I have made a few minor corrections and updatings. (The Channel tunnel, for example, mentioned ten years ago as likely to be opened 'soon', is now an accomplished fact.) I am grateful to Mr Tim Allen for his comments on Chapter 36 and have incorporated a few small changes in my original text. Essentially, however, the present book is the same as that published in hardback in 1991.

June 2001   NRL

THE RATING OF SHIPS

Numerous references are made in the text to ships classed as 'first-rates' and the like. These terms were used throughout the sailing era to distinguish between various sizes of warship at first according to their size (see *Defending the Island*, p. 423), but later by the number of guns they carried. The scale varied at different dates but the following table shows the classification adopted around 1700. First- to fourth-rates were considered ships of the line, fifth- and sixth-rates were described as frigates.

Rate	Number of Guns
1	96–100
2	84–90
3	60–82
4	46–54
5	26–44
6	16–24

ACKNOWLEDGEMENTS

Grateful acknowledgement is made for the use of copyright material as follows: to Beaufort Publishing Ltd for Andrew Saunders, *Fortress Britain*; to Basil Blackwell Ltd for W.A. Speck, *The Butcher, The Duke of Cumberland and the Suppression of the '45*; to Frank Cass and Co Ltd for Arthur J. Marder, *The Anatomy of British Sea Power*, to Cassell plc for Winston S. Churchill, *The Second World War*, and Theo Aronson, *Kings over the Water*, to Columbia University Press for S. E. Koss, *Lord Haldane*; to Leo Cooper Ltd for Brian Bond, *Chief of Staff, The Diaries of Lieut.-General Sir Henry Pownall*; to Crabwell Publications for B.E. Arnold, *Conflict across the Strait*; to Croom Helm Ltd for Hugh Cunningham, *The Volunteer Force*: to Curtis Brown Group Ltd for Martin Gilbert, *Finest Hour, Winston Churchill 1939-1941*; to Terence Dalton Ltd for Frank Hussey, *Suffolk Invasion*; to Gill and Macmillan Ltd, Dublin, for Richard Hayes, *The Last Invasion of Ireland*; to David and Charles Ltd for Michael Moyniham (editor), *People at War 1914-1918*; to Faber and Faber Ltd for Sir Frederick Maurice, *Haldane*; to the Controller of Her Majesty's Stationery Office for Basil Collier, *The Defence of the United Kingdom*, T.H. O'Brien, *Civil Defence*, and extracts from Crown copyright documents in the Public Record Office; to David Higham Associates for Nigel Hamilton, *Monty, The Making of a General*; to Manchester University Press for Hew Strachan, *Wellington's Legacy* and A. Temple Patterson, *The Other Armada*; to Methuen and Co Ltd for F.W. Hirst, *The Six Panics and Other Essays*; to Oxford University Press for C.J.H. Bartlett, *Great Britain and Sea Power 1815-1853* (1963), Brian Bond, *British Military Policy Between the Wars* (1980). Arthur J. Marder, *From the Dreadnought to Scapa Flow Vol. I* (1972), P.G. Rogers, *The Dutch in the Medway* (1970), and Ronald Wheatley, *Operation Sea Lion* (1958); to Thames and Hudson Ltd for Charles Kightly, *Strongholds of the Realm*; to Yorkshire Regional Newspapers for extracts from *The Bombardment of Scarborough* in the Scarborough Evening News. In some cases it has proved impossible to trace a copyright-holder. Apologies are offered for any inadvertent breach of copyright and amends will gladly be made in any future edition.

ILLUSTRATION ACKNOWLEDGEMENTS

Aerofilms, Borehamwood: 4
Chas. Bowyer: 50
British Museum: 5, 6, 7
Carmarthen Museum: 15
Reg. Curtis: 44
e.t.archive, London N.W.1: 16, 24, 39, 46
Pauline Gough: 31
Illustrated London News: 28
Imperial War Museum: 42, 45, 47, 48, 49, 51, 52
Institution of Royal Engineers: 33
Kent County Council: 23
Mansell Collections: 8, 20, 21, 27, 34, 35, 36, 37
National Army Museum: 9, 12, 17, 18, 38, 40
National Galleries of Scotland: 11
National Maritime Museum: 1, 2, 3, 13, 14, 22, 32
National Portrait Gallery: 10, 25, 26
The National Trust: 41
City of Portsmouth Records Office: 29
Victor Smith: 19
Viner Carew Ltd, Plymouth: 30

BOOK 1
A NEW ENEMY
1603–1688

The Island and its Enemies

I

NO BORDERS BUT THE OCEAN

Now thou art all Great Britain and no more . . .
No borders but the ocean and the shore.

Samuel Daniel on the accession of James I, 1603

The sea had always been England's greatest source of danger from an invader. With the accession of James I to the throne, on Thursday 24 March 1603, it became the only one. The classic 'postern gate', or back door, into the kingdom from Scotland into Northumbria which had troubled the country's rulers since the days of Hadrian, and which, like him, they had tried, with little success, to block with fixed defences, was at last closed.

England's new sovereign was already a king. At 13 months old – he had been born in Edinburgh Castle on 19 June 1566 – he had become King James VI of Scotland. He was now 36 when, late on the evening of Saturday 26 March 1603, the news that he was now also King of England reached him at Holyroodhouse in Edinburgh.

As James made his slow, triumphal way south – he was to return to Scotland only once during his reign, despite a promise to revisit it every three years – he was warmly greeted everywhere, being entertained at Burghley House, in Huntingdonshire, with a 73-verse *Panegyric Congratulatory* by the poet Samuel Daniel:

> Shake hands with union, O thou mighty state!
> Now thou art all Great Britain and no more;
> No Scot, no English now, nor no debate:
> No borders but the ocean and the shore;

James himself ardently desired to see the two countries of which chance, or, as he believed, divine providence, had made him king, formally united under a single government and eloquently argued for it in his speech to the first Parliament of his reign, on 19 March 1604:

> Hath not God united these two kingdoms both in language, religion and similitude of manners, Yea, hath He not made us all one island, encompassed with one sea, and of itself by nature so indivisible as almost those that were borderers themselves on the late Borders,

3

cannot distinguish, nor know, or discern their own limits. These
two countries being separated neither by sea, nor great river,
mountain, nor other strength of nature, but only by little small
brooks, or demolished little walls, so as rather they were divided in
apprehension rather than in effect; and now in the end and fullness of
time united, the right and title of both in my person, alike lineally
descended of both crowns, whereby it is now become like a little
world within itself, being entrenched and fortified round about with
a natural and yet admirable strong pond or ditch, whereby all the
former fears of this nation are quite cut off.

In spite of James's eloquence, and the Shakespearean echoes of this
address, the nearest he could come to his dream of uniting the two
nations was to assume, without Parliament's consent, the title of King
of Great Britain, a term which henceforward passed into common use.
The two countries continued to have separate churches, parliaments
and legal systems, thanks to the deep English distrust of the Scots, who
it was feared might descend like a horde of greedy vultures on court
and country if the barriers between them were removed.

The reign of the first Stuart king began in high promise, with only
one disturbing sign. Although, like so many of his predecessors on the
throne of England, passionately addicted to hunting, James displayed
throughout his life a most un-regal, if not neurotic, fear of firearms and
explosives, perhaps because of his father's murder, after his house had
been blown up. Whatever the cause, this phobia was widely remarked
on. 'He is said to be personally timid and averse from war,' the Venetian ambassador reported in 1603. 'King James was the most cowardly
man that ever I knew,' confirmed Sir John Oglander, Deputy-Lieutenant of the Isle of Wight but often at court. 'He could not endure a
soldier or to see men drilled.'

James's preference for the company of his own sex also rapidly became obvious. 'He loved young men,' wrote Sir John Oglander,
'better than women . . . I never yet saw any fond husband make so
much or so great dalliance over his beautiful spouse, as I have seen
King James over his favourites.'

James's homosexuality, like that of Edward II before him, was to
have far-reaching consequences for the country's defence policy, but
initially he was condemned more for his obvious dedication to peace.
'He loved not a soldier, nor any fighting man,' noted a critical contemporary, and the royal motto, *Beati Pacifici*, Blessed are the Peace-
makers, earned more derision than admiration. 'At my coming here,
you are witnesses,' he told his first Parliament, 'I found the state
embarked in a great and tedious war, and only my arrival here, and by
the peace in my person, is now amity kept where war was before.' This
was true; in the summer of 1604 the hostilities with Spain which had

dragged on for nearly 20 years were at last wound up on probably the best terms available.

The realisation, following the peace with Spain, that no Spanish invasion on behalf of the old religion could now be expected, led to the best-remembered event of the reign, the plan for Parliament to be blown up on Tuesday 5 November 1605, creating such confusion that the Roman Catholic nobility could seize power. The conspiracy, frustrated by the capture of its leader, Guy Fawkes, the night before, reactivated the persecution of the Catholic 'recusants', who refused to practise the Protestant religion, and fear of the Papists, as potential supporters of a foreign invader, remained a potent factor in English politics for years to come.

James's assertion of the divine right of kings, which denied the ability of the pope to depose a sovereign, as Sixtus V had attempted, with the aid of the Spanish Armada and Philip II, to overthrow Elizabeth in 1588, had vast implications for the future, for it also excluded parliament from any effective part in government. 'As to dispute what God may do is blasphemy,' James told its members, 'so it is sedition in subjects to dispute what a king may do in the height of his power!'

The union of the two crowns had greatly simplified England's defensive problems. The costly garrison at Berwick could be disbanded and the Border castles allowed to dwindle into decay. Ireland, another area of seemingly endless expenditure, which in the last financial year before James's accession had cost £342,000 for military activities alone, had also apparently been tamed at last. A few days after the start of the reign the chief Irish rebel, the Earl of Tyrone, had surrendered, a year after the last Spaniards, who had been fomenting the outbreak, had left the country and on 4 September 1607 Tyrone, anticipating arrest, fled from Ireland to die in exile, nine years later, in Rome. Six counties in the north of Ireland – Tyrone, Donegal, Armagh, Coleraine, Cavan and Fermanagh – reverted to the crown and the systematic settlement in Ireland of loyal, i.e. Protestant, Scots and English families, the so-called Plantation of Ulster,* was now undertaken.

The Irish problem was to be solved by dispossessing its owners of their inheritance and replacing them with 'colonists' selected by the government in London, another policy that was to have lasting consequences. The same solution was adopted later in other parts of Ireland, notably Wexford and Longford, and occasionally a single place in England was entrusted with the occupation of a particular territory. Most of Coleraine was assigned to the City of London, its

---

* The famous name comes from James himself: 'We intend nothing with greater earnestness than the plantation of Ulster with civil men well affected in religion,' he wrote in 1609.

ruined 'capital' of Derry being renamed Londonderry, a name later rejected by many resentful natives.

For the moment the danger of invasion, whether of Ireland or of England, was slight. The new reign had hardly begun when the existing statutes requiring annual musters and the provision of horses and armour on a specified scale based on income were repealed. Some military training continued, but when, to the king's great distaste, he found himself called on to watch the militia from the Isle of Wight at their exercises he found consolation in paying close attention to the youngest youths. The Council, enlarged in size but with little real power since the king and his cronies decided on policy, issued the pious reminder in 1608 that 'Peace is best continued where there is ready and sufficient provision for war' and ordered musters to be held in the various divisions of each county on the same day to prevent the old abuses of the same man, or weapons, appearing in different places, but no county-wide turn-out was required and the incomplete returns suggest little effort in most places. One Lord Lieutenant warned in 1612 that 'trained bands' was a misnomer for the supposed cream of the militia in his area for their 'long vacation and rest' had robbed them of their former knowledge and discipline.

In the following year a new invasion alarm, regarded with some scepticism in the rest of the country, stirred the government into action. 'Talk of Spaniards invasion, buildinge of beacons in these parts and musteringe and shewinge armors,' noted one Northumberland landowner in his diary in the spring of 1613. His patriotism remained unstirred. 'I tooke up no horses,' he noted that November, when a full-scale muster of mounted men was held in an adjoining county.

An unwelcome consequence of Scotland having become a peaceful neighbour now became apparent. Traditionally not expected to provide men or horses to protect the South because of local needs the residents of the border counties proved unwilling to accept a share in national defence now that the situation had changed. The Bishop of Durham claimed that his men were as loyal and enthusiastic as those nearer London, but admitted that their equipment, dating from 1588 or even earlier, had suffered either from neglect or excessive cleaning. The Council, in London, was not impressed by the Durham gentry's plans to re-equip their men with the cheapest possible weapons and armour and thought their proposal to arm only every 30 or 35 men in every 100 with pikes (how the rest would be armed was not clear) inadequate. Other places, too, sought excuses for dragging their feet. The deputy-lieutenants claimed they were unfamiliar with the muster procedure but were incensed when the Lord Lieutenant refused to sign the certificate required by the Council in London that the county was in a state of readiness to resist an invasion. Nothing put the militia on their toes like a royal inspection, but James I's distaste for all things military meant that it was left to other members of his family to provide the necessary encouragement. Bristol was seized with martial fervour after Queen Anne visited it in 1613; enthusiasm for donning impressive uniforms, always the part of amateur soldiering which appealed most, reached such a pitch that the humblest private was said to resemble an officer. The government could also feel confident about the capital, where the trained bands, with in 1614 an establishment of 6,000, were supplemented by the members of a number of private military societies who met to be drilled at their own expense by professional instructors.

From 1613 onwards the government constantly pressed the counties to modernise the weapons issued to the militia. The only infantry weapons worth carrying, as current European experience had demonstrated, were pikes and muskets, the latter replacing the now obsolete calivers, to which they were superior in both performance and portability being, according to the official specification, three fingers' breadth shorter. In 1618 calivers were finally prohibited, and in 1620 the first real attempt to standardise weapons was made. A musket was henceforward – the rules did not apply to existing weapons – to be 4 ft [1.2 m] long, and large enough to take a bullet weighing approximately one eleventh of a pound [0.04 kg], but also acceptable were a bastard, or light musket, firing bullets weighing 14 to the pound [0.03 kg], and a petronel, with 17 to the pound [0.026 kg]. The bill laid down that swords should be 4 ft [1.2 m] long though one member protested that this was too short and that 'our men' in Ireland had 'quaked like a partridge [sic] under a hawke' on being confronted by the enemy's longer blades.

Supplying horsemen for the militia had always been the role of the gentry to whom, after 1608, the wealthier clergy were added, though not themselves expected to bear arms. Even counties where the foot were reasonably satisfactory constantly had to report an inadequate turn-out of horsemen, or even none at all. When they did muster, the numbers, or standard of equipment, were usually defective; Somerset, with 11 per cent reported as unsatisfactory in 1613, and Wiltshire, with 20 per cent, were probably far from the worst.

London provided a shining exception to a generally gloomy picture, due largely to its citizens' enthusiasm for artillery. The medieval prejudice which had led gunners to be considered inferior to true soldiers had disappeared; to belong to a privately financed artillery company was now a sign of social status. The first, and most famous, the Honourable Artillery Company, had been founded in 1537 and met at its headquarters in Bishopsgate in the City. In 1610 the 'Military Garden' was established, whose members drilled in St Martin's Field, near Charing Cross. These two institutions became, a contemporary observed, 'two great nurseries or academies of military discipline', and in 1611 they were joined by the Westminster Artillery Company, of which Henry, Prince of Wales, the king's dashing, military-minded, heir, then aged 17, became patron, though he, alas, died of typhoid in the following year. Before long a waiting list to join the society existed, the membership was doubled, to 500, and the movement had earned a place in English literature, both in the works of Ben Jonson, and Thomas Dekker's poem, published in 1616, *The Artillery Garden*.

In previous reigns the navy, as an actual or potential fighting force, had depended largely – in medieval times wholly – on the existence of a flourishing mercantile marine. Under James I the royal fleet declined while commercial shipping expanded. Everywhere could be seen the beginnings of that rich overseas trade which was to mark Great Britain's emergence as an international power and make essential a navy powerful enough to protect her merchant ships and overseas possessions. In September 1604, a few months after James's accession, the first fleet sent to the Far East by the East India Company, established in 1600, returned home after a voyage lasting two and a half years. In 1607 the first permanent English colony, in Virginia, was founded, and the first English depot was established on the mainland of India. In 1620 the Pilgrim Fathers made their epic voyage in the *Mayflower* to land at Plymouth Rock, Massachusetts. At ports all along the coast of Europe, in Scandinavia, in the Mediterranean, the red cross of St George or the white cross of St Andrew could be seen flying from the mastheads of English or Scottish ships; the Union flag combining the two, introduced by James in 1606, was reserved for British warships. Four hundred colliers engaged in the coastal trade plied up and down the North Sea and the Channel, being described by the king himself as 'the especial nursery and school of seamen'. The seafaring aptitude of the race was becoming famous. The Venetian agent, no mean judge, described the English as 'bearing a name above all the West for being expert and enterprising in all maritime affairs, and the finest fighters upon the oceans'.

Pursuing pirates was the perfect way to keep the navy in fighting trim but under James I it hardly existed. The whole defence of the south-west approaches rested on a single pinnace, the *Desire*, whose captain sadly acknowledged that he 'could neither catch nor fight' the troublesome intruders, and the port facilities at Plymouth were as yet inadequate to deal with the largest warships – even if any had been fit for action.

Neglect of the navy, the physical deterioration in its vessels and men and corruption in its management, were nothing new, but James I's pacific instincts discouraged the very type of bold, aggressive officer any successful fleet required. His first act when he came to the throne was to recall 'all vessels sent out with hostile intent' and as part of the peace settlement made with Spain in August 1604 all letters of marque licensing privateers to prey on Spanish shipping were withdrawn. 'After twenty years spent in the wars,' Sir William Monson, in command of the Channel squadron, told his Dutch opposite number, 'I was now become a watchman with a bill [i.e. weapon] in my hand to see peace kept and no disorder committed in the Narrow Seas.'

What brought a dramatic improvement was a change in James's fickle affections. His eye had now lighted on a new young man, George Villiers, the son of a Leicestershire knight, who arrived at court as a cupbearer in 1614, when he was 22, and only a year later was knighted and, most appropriately, made a Gentleman of the Bedchamber, subsequently being created successively Earl, Marquis and Duke of Buckingham. As a means of discrediting his bitter enemies, the Howard family, to which the Lord High Admiral, Lord Howard of Effingham, belonged, Buckingham secured an enquiry into the state of the navy, and the Commissioners of Enquiry's report, issued in September 1618, proved to be a landmark in the history of naval administration.

Although no accounts had been prepared for four years they calculated the average annual cost of the navy over that period at £53,000, more than Queen Elizabeth had spent in wartime, but of a fleet nominally of 43 ships only 27 were serviceable; the remaining 16 were either non-existent or too rotten to repair. The nation, it was discovered, was still paying £63 a year to maintain the *Bonaventure*, which had been broken up seven years before, £100 for the *Advantage*, burnt five years earlier, and another £60 for the equally ghost-like *Charles*.

The Commissioners undertook to put the navy back on a sound footing within five years, provided the reforms they suggested were carried out, and to support for this amount a navy of 30 seaworthy vessels, of an average of 570 tons, making the whole force, in tonnage at least, larger than when the navy 'was greatest and flourished most' under Queen Elizabeth. The plan was adopted. Buckingham became Lord High Admiral, James remarking with justice that he had not selected 'an old beaten soldier' but a young man he could trust, and Buckingham did indeed fill the post far better than the inept Howard, who was pensioned off.

Little was done to develop the ports and dockyards, and even less to improve the island's fixed defences, in the 22 years James I was on the throne. Ports which were primarily commercial might also when needed accommodate warships; here, too, a flourishing mercantile marine meant a stronger navy. The decline of the Cinque Ports, now partly silted up and used by few craft except small fishing boats, continued, though Deal served ships waiting for a favourable wind in the great anchorage of the Downs, the area of sheltered water, protected by the Goodwin Sands, which extended almost 4 miles [6.4 km] out to sea between there and Sandwich Bay, a few miles to the north. The small Sussex ports – Brighton, Shoreham, Chichester, Littlehampton – had as yet little significance, but Portsmouth, the last English port to suffer enemy attack, suffered a sad decline. The dry dock built by Henry VII was filled in and the town was said to be in 'a weak and ruinous condition'. The deep-water ports further west – Dartmouth, Plymouth and Bristol – fared better but the real growth in this period was in the Thames and the Medway. A dry-dock was built at Chatham in 1619, the only place where during James's reign the defences were actually strengthened. A new garrison of a captain and 20 soldiers was installed at Upnor Castle, which protected it, and the inadequate chain stretched across the river below it was replaced by a much more formidable barrier, consisting of the hulls of four ships and 16 former masts weighted down with 2 tons of iron. Other coastal defences were meanwhile neglected and in 1618 the castle at Southampton was actually de-commissioned and sold off, as too ruinous to repair.

In this generally dismal picture one bright spot remained; the nation's ship-designers and builders could still match and surpass the ships constructed by any of her rivals. Much of the credit was due to Phineas Pett, member of a famous ship-building dynasty deeply involved with the navy for nearly 150 years. Phineas was left almost destitute at 19 by the death of his father, a master shipwright at Deptford, in 1589, but he had been well educated, at Cambridge, and caught the eye of Lord Admiral Howard and, later, of James I. Pett was able to improve the design of the king's ships, giving them greater strength in proportion to their size while reducing the amount of timber required, and his *Prince Royal*, launched in 1610, was said to be the finest warship afloat. He survived the then prevailing corruption to see his son Peter succeed him at Chatham and become a naval commissioner like himself.

It was fortunate that there were, scattered here and there in positions of power, able and honest men like Pett for as the reign progressed it became increasingly clear that James's attempts to keep the peace in Europe, and to avoid damaging foreign entanglements, had failed. The central purpose of his diplomacy was to secure lasting peace with Spain, preferably through the traditional means of a dynastic alliance, and in 1620 he told the Spanish ambassador, 'I give you my word as a king . . . that I have no wish to marry my son to anyone except your master's daughter and that I desire no alliance but that of Spain.' Unhappily the wooing which, in 1623, followed merely left a legacy of ill-will. The young woman concerned declared that she would rather enter a nunnery than marry a heretic and the whole enterprise was bitterly unpopular in England where, it was believed, rightly enough, that the Spaniards saw the marriage as a first step towards reclaiming England for the faith and thus succeeding where Mary Tudor's Spanish husband, Philip, had failed. The would-be groom and his escort and adviser, Buckingham, came home not only without a bride but full of anti-Spanish sentiment, which the nation warmly shared. Parliament, usually so reluctant to incur expenditure on defence, was drunk with dreams of a naval war on the Elizabethan scale. The normally sober-sided Sir Edward Coke reminded the Commons that 'England was never richer than when at war with Spain. If Ireland is secured, the Navy furnished . . .' he boasted, 'we will not care for pope, Turk, Spain nor all the devils in hell.' 'Are we poor?' asked another respected member, invoking memories of Drake's conquests. 'Spain is rich. There [i.e. in Spain] are Indies. Break with them; we shall break our necessities together.'

Sensibly recognising the classic principle that England should not be simultaneously at odds with France and Spain, James now opened negotiations with Louis XIII for Prince Charles to marry Louis's sister, Henrietta Maria, giving a private undertaking that persecution of English Roman Catholics would cease. In June 1624 he made a treaty with the Dutch, undertaking to provide them with 6,000 soldiers for two years, a commitment which made war with Spain almost inevitable.

When King James I died, on 27 March 1625, at the age of 58, England was once again at war with Spain, as it had been on his accession, though no fighting had yet taken place. It was a war engaged in more out of habit than necessity. The real danger to Great Britain lay nearer at hand. Trade, not religion, provided the seeds of future conflict and here the Dutch, who would hardly have survived as a nation without past English help, were already proving far more dangerous rivals than the Spaniards.

2

THE MOST NECESSARY DEFENCE

For us islanders, it is most necessary to defend ourselves at sea.

Chief Justice Sir John Finch giving judgment in the ship-money case,
12 June 1638

The reign of Charles I, which was to end in tragedy, began in disappointment. The new king, aged 24, was a much more attractive figure than his father, courteous, sober, dignified and self-controlled. It was said that he had 'never violated a woman, struck a man, or spoken an evil word'. Unhappily he was almost as much under the thumb of the increasingly detested Duke of Buckingham as James I had been and both were blamed for the succession of military disasters which followed Charles's accession. An expedition to Cadiz, in October 1625, intended to repeat Drake's achievements of 40 years before, ended in humiliating failure.

The Cadiz venture, supposed to revive the glories of the Elizabethan age, had demonstrated instead Great Britain's military weakness and increased, instead of removed, the risk of invasion. The nation was, however, united more by dislike of Buckingham, and of King Charles's arbitrary rule, than by fear of the Spaniards. At a public meeting in Westminster Hall the citizens responded when threatened, if the Spaniards got ashore, with the loss of their 'goods, honour, wives, children and life itself', not with the expected donations to buy arms, but with cries of 'Parliament! Parliament!'

Parliament did in fact meet in February 1626 but after constant attacks on Buckingham was dissolved in June, after an ominous reminder from the king to its most recalcitrant members to 'remember that parliaments are altogether in my power for their calling, sitting and dissolution.' Meanwhile his marriage to Henrietta Maria, in June 1625, had failed to bring peace with her brother, King Louis XIII, and in March 1627, ignoring the classic English principle of not simultaneously alienating both her great neighbours, he found himself engaged in a naval war with France.

In January 1628 it was calculated in London that the country required a minimum of 100 ships to resist a joint Franco-Spanish invasion attempt upon England or Ireland, a highly realistic estimate; Louis XIII's chief minister, and the real ruler of France, Armand, Jean du Plassis, Cardinal Richelieu, the arch-enemy of the Huguenots, planned to have 80 ships ready to sail to Portugal – the starting point for the Armada – by April 1628, when a Spanish fleet, 20 strong, would join them. Even if this new armada did not materialise there was a very real danger of small forces evading the English patrols and landing somewhere on the coast, perhaps for short-term spoiling operations; the activities of the Barbary pirates, roving far and wide from their North African bases, and other privateers, had recently demonstrated how easily this could be done. The men of the Cinque Ports declared themselves 'miserably oppressed. [We] dare not,' they claimed, 'go about our voyages to Scarborough or Yarmouth or fish in the North Sea.' The Suffolk coast-dwellers reported ships 'fired or taken in their havens before our eyes', with, as a result, 58 others laid up in Ipswich alone; at Newcastle the coastal coal trade was said to be at a standstill. In some places traditional piracy had developed into major raids, with East Anglia, always regarded as a likely landing area for an invader, proving particularly vulnerable. At King's Lynn, in Norfolk, the dreaded 'Dunkirkers' were said to have landed to rob and burn, like modern Vikings, while in the adjoining county of Lincolnshire Dutch fishermen, with remarkable effrontery, had landed to dry and mend their nets. Early in 1628 the militia had been called out in Essex to repel an expected attack on Harwich by the Dunkirk desperadoes, though – luckily, as it turned out, since the defenders had proved to have too little powder, no bullets and weapons with a variety of bores – the expected landing had never materialised.

More important, however, than either ships or guns were men and they always came at the end of every queue. That February the discontent of those already mustered, or abandoned after earlier voyages, boiled over, and groups of ragged and hungry sailors deserted their ships and marched from Portsmouth to London to display their sad condition to the king and Lord Admiral. Some even attacked the latter's grand residence, Buckingham House, which lay between the Strand and the river, to be repelled by the Duke in person 'at first by promises and then sword in hand'. At Plymouth some of those already conscripted mutinied, and stormed the jail containing their previously arrested leader, only being beaten off by a force of soldiers, who left two sailors dead and others wounded. Similar disturbances occurred elsewhere.

Buckingham realised that a radical change in foreign policy was needed, so that England's enemies fought each other instead of uniting against her, but before he had been able to influence the king in this new direction, Buckingham himself was stabbed to death, in Portsmouth, on 23 August 1628 by a veteran of the Cadiz expedition who

blamed him, as did Parliament and the nation at large, for all the
country's recent ills. The London trained bands lined the funeral route
to prevent hostile demonstrations but the Venetian ambassador noted
even so 'some little noise' which sounded 'more like joy than commiser-
ation'.

There seemed, in 1628, a real, if not very immediate, prospect of invasion, as one of Buckingham's former subordinates, now Lord Wimbledon, Lord Lieutenant of Surrey and a future governor of Portsmouth, duly warned:

> The [greatest] danger of all is that a people not used to war believeth
> no enemy dare venture upon them. This kingdom hath been too
> long in peace – our old commanders both by sea and by land are
> worn out and few men are bred in their places, for the knowledge of
> war and almost the thought of war is extinguished. Peace hath so
> besotted us, that as we are altogether ignorant, so are we so much
> the more not sensible of that defect, for we think if we have men and
> ships our kingdom is safe, as if men were born soldiers.

In April 1629 peace was made with France, followed in November 1630
by the Treaty of Madrid with Spain. Neither war had achieved anything.

Raising money for foreign wars, or for the navy, required the cooperation of Parliament, with which the king was already at odds. Improving the trained bands, financed by the counties through a rate
levied on their better-off residents, was easier and from early on in his
reign the king supported an energetic campaign to modernise them,
partly with an eye to internal security, i.e. dealing with his political
opponents, though orders issued in 1626 referred to the danger of invasion and stressed that they emanated from the Council of War, not the
king or Buckingham personally. Charles's aim was to produce what
was described as an 'exact' or 'perfect' militia but, so lacking in native-
born veterans were most areas, that in February 1626 the government
brought over 84 experienced sergeants from the Low Countries, to
form a pool from which each county would draw two to four as required. The aim, as one Lord Lieutenant told his colonels, was to turn
out men with 'bodyes and mindes fitt for service' and great emphasis
was placed on physical fitness, exercise with bows, hammers and cud-
gels being recommended. In place of the casual attitude of the past
some men were now assembled for instruction every week, gradually
progressing into larger groups like companies for major exercises. As
the bands progressed in their training, the sergeants certified them
ready for service, while untrained men were sometimes mustered as a
reserve, to be equipped if need arose with privately owned weapons.
But bringing even a part-time army up to modern standards was expensive. Cheshire, for example, arranged to have a full-scale three-day

turn-out of the whole force, including training in making camp. The county's bill for tools, knapsacks, transport and other essentials was £4,000 even before buying new weapons.

The best-trained militia were in London, where the keenest volunteers must have achieved something approaching professional standards, as one commentator acknowledged in 1630:

> What hath effeminated our English, but a long disuse of arms . . .
> Though in a hard battell there would appeare a greate deale of difference betwixt an old beaten soldier . . . and a man of our traine bands
> of London: yet surely would the Londoner much sooner prove fit
> for a battell, then [i.e. than] the unexperienced countryman, even
> for that little use which he hath had of his armes in the Artillery Garden and Military Yard.

Although later in the reign everyone from 16 to 60 began to be summoned to musters, service in the militia normally began at 18, but the government encouraged cadet forces of young men below this age. At Lincoln Grammar School the pupils 'instead of childish sports, when they were not at their books . . . were exercised in all their military postures and in assaults and defences.' The school employed its own instructor, an ex-soldier, while the Free School at Chipping Campden went one better, possessing not merely muskets but even – surely a terrifying thought for their neighbours – some school artillery.

As in King James's reign, the government's chief difficulties everywhere came with the wealthier landowners who were rated to supply one or more fully equipped horsemen, armed with lances or, increasingly, pistols or carbines. Their mobility made them particularly useful against small parties of invaders. 'What good service we doe must be done at ye landinge,' noted Sir John Oglander, deputy-governor of the Isle of Wight, in 1627, recording his attempts that year to 'willinglie and voluntarilie rayse a hundred horse in owre Island, being ye beste thinge for owre defence'. He carefully listed those from 'The ladie Worseley' to 'Widdowe Rawlins' who might reasonably be expected to find a horse, and put himself down for two, but could only muster 700. Elsewhere, under less conscientious leadership, the response was far worse; of 40 members of one troop in Hampshire only ten actually appeared.

The complaint that amateur soldiering seemed to involve more drinking than training had been voiced since Tudor times and was to be heard again but according to Colonel Robert Ward's *Animadversions of War* in 1639 it was also interfering with the country's agricultural output. 'Now every moneth in the summer,' he alleged, 'they lose a day by reason of the training, and the greater part of the soldiers use to fall a-drinking after the training, and happily lose the next day also; and so in the moneths of June, July and August, which are busie times for

hay, and harvest, they lose three days or more.' His remedy was to replace the existing one day a month in the summer with 'foure dayes together in May' and 'the latter end of September, because harvest and
hoptime, for the most part is over, and wheat-seed not fully come', but
the suggestion does not seem to have been adopted.

For nearly forty years after 1603 the building of fixed defences stag-
nated. The art of fortification had never been much studied in England
and by around 1640 only Portsmouth and Hull had been provided with
reasonably modern defences, though, thanks to constant pressure
from Sir John Oglander, some effort had also been made to protect that
exposed salient, the Isle of Wight. In 1629 some of the gentry from the
island went to London to petition the king 'for moneyes to have owre
castells and fortes some amended, others where most neded requyred,
newe erected; and also for to have two places of retrayte, if so wee
should be beaten . . . Freschwater, for owre cattel, and ye mayne bodie
of our companies and Yarmouth for ye betterr sort of people.' The
king received the deputation courteously and referred them to the
Council of War who, Oglander recorded, 'told us wee were to [i.e.
too] fearful', but Oglander and his supporters persevered, sketching
out a modest scheme costing £3000, and were eventually successful. In
July 1632 two experts, 'who had bene longe employed by ye States of
Holland in making of ffortes and other fortifications' arrived on the
island, one an engineer, the other his 'maystor woorkeman'. Oglander
thought them 'both able men', though critical of the resulting fort at
Sandham, considering it too near the sea and with inadequate foundations, but it was in the event never to confront a foreign attacker; the
king's enemies lay nearer home.

It was the needs of national defence that caused the first major breach
between king and Parliament. In October 1634 the king issued the first
writ requiring the ports and coastal towns to provide ships and men for
the navy, or cash, known as ship-money, in lieu. Portsmouth, for
example, was required to supply one ship of 900 tons, manned by 350
men, one of 800 tons, with 260 men, four of 500 tons, with 200 men,
and one of 300 tons, and a crew of 150 – a substantial burden, but not a
new one. Only the City of London, required to send several fully
equipped ships to Portsmouth, protested, although they were earmarked for protecting the nation's commerce from pirates.

Charles's avowed aim, as well as clearing the seas of the pirates about
whom there had been so many complaints over the years, was to re-
assert the supremacy of England in the waters around its coast. As long
ago as 1336 Edward III had declared that 'The kings of England have
before these times been Lords of the English Sea on every side,'* and
successive monarchs since had attempted, with varying degrees of suc-

* See *Defending the Island, From Caesar to the Armada*, p. 261.

cess, to compel all foreign captains in the Narrow Seas to strike their flag and lower their topsails in salute when they encountered a naval ship.

The second ship-money writ was issued on 4 August 1635. It extended to the whole country, was to be based on personal property as well as land, and was at twice the rate of the previous year, being designed to raise £208,000. This represented no more than £1 for every 174,447 acres [70,600 hectares] of real estate in England and Wales, but the levy was fiercely resented and one Buckinghamshire landowner and MP, John Hampden, refused to pay, his name thereafter becoming a synonym for resistance to official oppression. Hampden, then aged 41, who had been at Oxford and then trained as a lawyer, had been in the past a consistent opponent of Buckingham and the king and was a cousin of another former MP and anti-royalist, Oliver Cromwell. A rich man, he could easily have paid the £1 levied on his Stoke Mandeville estate, one of several he owned, and he could hardly quarrel with the purpose of the Buckinghamshire assessment, which was to finance a ship of 450 tons, with a crew of 180 and fully found with rigging and ammunition, to be based at Portsmouth for 26 weeks 'to defend the dominion of the sea'. Hampden's lawyers based their case on the intrinsic illegality of the demand, and its dangerous implications. 'If,' they argued, 'His Majesty would have 20s, why not £20 and so on *ad infinitum*? The subject would be left entirely at the mercy and goodness of the king.'

While the case was still being tried a third demand for ship-money was made in October 1636, making clear that far from remaining, as in the past, a tax levied at long intervals in a national emergency it would become, in the words of the contemporary historian, Lord Clarendon, 'a spring and magazine that should have no bottom and an everlasting supply for all occasions'.

During the summer of 1637 a contingent of the notorious Barbary Corsairs known as the Salé [or Sallee or Sali] Rovers demonstrated the ineffectiveness of both the navy and the militia by a highly successful raid on the south-west coast. This time, however, retribution followed; later that year a detachment of the ship-money fleet under Captain William Rainborough sought out the Rovers in their lair, 110 miles [175 km] west of Fez on the Atlantic coast of Morocco and inflicted condign punishment upon them as well as liberating 300 prisoners. Nearer home, however, less was achieved, for the Dutch herring fleet was this year escorted by warships, whose commander refused to let the English vessels approach them, and Charles's admiral wisely avoided a direct confrontation.

In June 1638 came, at last, the final verdict in Hampden's case, the judges ruling by a seven to five majority that ship-money, even when charged annually, on inland towns and by the king's authority alone, was legal. The chief justice, Sir John [later Lord] Finch, who supported the decision, argued that national need, as interpreted by the king, out-weighed 'the liberties of the subject in his person and estate. For us islanders,' he summed up, 'it is most necessary to defend ourselves at sea.' But hostility to ship-money became more widespread and that year, although the assessment was reduced to £70,000, only a third of this – in contrast to the almost 100 per cent yield of earlier years – was actually paid.

During 1638 the gulf between the king and 'the Country Party', as his opponents were known, widened, following the signing by vast numbers of Scots of the National Covenant, pledging their support for the existing, Presbyterian church, and his attempts to impose an Anglican-style prayer book upon them by force had, by 1639, proved a failure. Here lay the seeds of far greater troubles to come, but 1639 also brought one more cheerful event, the launching of the pride of Charles's fleet, the largest and finest vessel so far built in England, the *Sovereign of the Seas*, later known as the *Sovereign, Royal Sovereign* and *Sovereign Royal*. The *Sovereign* mounted no fewer than 102 brass cannon, on three decks, said to have cost nearly £25,000, including what the contemporary writer Thomas Heywood described as 'murdering pieces, 10 pieces of chace-ordnance forward, and 10 right aft, and many loopholes in the cabins for musquet shot'.

In spite of this powerful addition to Charles's navy the ship-money fleet proved that autumn embarrassingly impotent. A Spanish fleet was blockaded while at anchor in the Downs and then, on 11 October 1639,* attacked by 100 Dutch warships under one of the first of their great seamen, Admiral Marten [or Maaten, or Martin] Harpetz [or Herbertson, or Harpurson] Tromp, in spite of the presence of a squad-ron of British ships, which, lacking orders from the king, did nothing.

As he sailed off the victorious Tromp mockingly lowered his flag in belated acknowledgement of Charles's claim to sovereignty over the Narrow Seas. An even more disastrous, though less public, rebuff fol-lowed. Taking advantage of Charles's preoccupation in Scotland, the Barbary pirates resumed their depredations on the British mainland, actually kidnapping and carrying off some 60 citizens from the Pen-zance area, while a force of 24 privateers from Dunkirk, with Spanish connivance, helped themselves almost at will to whatever goods caught their eye on the Kent or Sussex coast.

Not all the blame for these successive disasters rested on the king, though it was only just that, in claiming to be the sole source of authority in the state, he should be personally blamed for everything that went awry. The manifestly out-of-date idea persisted that the cost of defence should be a charge on the king's private purse, which was

---

* Not 'in November' as stated by Bowle p. 166, which gives a somewhat different account of this affair from the other sources consulted.

still not properly differentiated from the nation's annual budget. 'Wars belong to sovereigns and not to subjects', one Member of Parliament had declared back in 1628, while the public at large would have echoed the reaction of one taxpayer to the sailing of the ship-money fleet in 1638: 'What a foolery it is that the country in general shall be thus taxed with great sums to maintain the king's titles and honours! . . . I am £10 the worse for it already.'

In April 1640 Charles summoned what became known as the Short Parliament, for in May he dissolved it, after the Members had refused to vote the money for a new Scottish war but had instead complained again about ship-money and launched a general attack on absolutism. The City of London refused its financial support, the trained bands were mustered unwillingly, especially those from counties outside the North which regarded a war with the Scots as none of their business, and the campaign, of which Charles took personal command, ended in humiliation, leaving the Scots in possession of Durham and North-umberland. To get rid of them, the king had, much against his will, to secure his subjects' cooperation. In November 1640 what was to become known as the Long Parliament met. The gulf between its dominant, Puritan, party and the king rapidly became unbridgeable. In December 1641 the Commons proposed the Militia Bill, giving to parliament, not the king, the right to raise an army and navy and to appoint a lord-general and a lord-admiral to command them. Charles refused to accept it, declaring 'You have asked that of me . . . never asked of a king'. The breach which had begun over the financing of the navy was widened by an argument over the control of the other armed forces. Both sides now tried to secure control of the navy, the militia and key points such as Portsmouth, and on Monday 22 August 1642 the king formally raised his standard at Nottingham, calling on all loyal subjects to support him against those he labelled rebels, and the English Civil War began.

3

OUR ENGLISH WARS

For our English wars our English experience is as good as any.

Army chaplain recalling the Civil War, 1642-1646

No foreign intervention occurred during the Civil War in England, but the years of fighting which began in earnest in August 1642 demonstrated clearly how an invader might have been received had he landed. They also led to an unprecedented development in the military arts and England witnessed in a few months more sieges and stormings than it had in the previous six centuries. The country was soon as divided militarily as it was in sentiment, with the royalists controlling about half the total area of England and Wales. London was solid for Parliament, forcing the king to set up a rival capital at Oxford, which soon became a whole fortified region, surrounded by successive lines of defence, constructed under the guidance of King Charles's chief engineer, the Dutchman Bernard de Gomme, who was knighted for his services to his adopted monarch.

England when the war began contained no comparable expert on military engineering. The only supposedly trained force in the country was the militia, numbering in 1642 some 150-200,000, and both sides attempted to gain control of it. Over the years a vast amount of time and a fair amount of money had been devoted by the nation to developing the militia, its first, after the navy, and indeed last line of defence. Put to the test of actual fighting the militia proved, with one exception, to be useless. The exception was provided by the London trained bands, who became the backbone of London's defenders and a valuable mobile force at moments of crisis. Even the trained bands, however, were as conscious of their traditional rights as any members of the Saxon fyrd. They did, as a great concession, agree to march 100 miles [160 km] to the relief of Gloucester in 1643, but, as the parliamentary commander Sir William Waller complained, soon raised 'their old song of "Home! Home!"'

Both sides virtually created new armies from inexperienced volunteers, and, later, conscripts, then known as 'pressed men', aided by the

20

small numbers of officers and men who had served as professionals abroad. The parliamentary army at its peak achieved a strength of around 30,000, 5000 of them horsemen. The royalist forces were probably rather smaller but with a higher proportion of cavalry, who according to the military doctrine of the time were far more useful than infantry. The Cavaliers, as the king's army became known – a name derived from the Latin for 'horseman' – enjoyed from the first a large superiority in this respect. The Roundheads, however, as the parliamentary troops were nicknamed from the close-cropped hair style favoured by the Puritans, always possessed more artillery than their opponents and the means of manufacturing more. The whole iron industry of the Weald of Kent and Sussex, with its 27 furnaces and 47 forges, was under their control.

Finally the Civil War demonstrated the importance of the command of the sea in what was basically a land campaign, making clear that even if an invader did ever manage to get ashore in strength so long as an English fleet remained in being his position would remain insecure.

One question of interest to both soldiers and sailors had always been how effective naval bombardment was likely to prove against targets ashore and evidence on this point was now to be provided by the queen herself. Having, at the second attempt, arrived at Bridlington with a cargo of arms bought on the Continent – the first attempt had been frustrated by bad weather – the queen was roused at five in the morning by a salvo of cannon fire, from four ships, as she graphically described in a letter to her husband three days later, on 25 February 1643:

> One of these ships had done me the favour to flank my house, which fronted the pier, and before I could get out of bed, the balls were whistling upon me in such style that you easily believe I love not such music. Everybody came to force me to go out, the balls beating so on all the houses that, dressed just as it happened, I went on foot to some distance from the village, to the shelter of a ditch . . . but before we could reach it, the balls were singing round us in fine style, and a sergeant was killed twenty paces from me. We placed ourselves under this shelter, during two hours that they were firing upon us, and the balls passing always over our heads, and sometimes covering us with dust. At last, the Admiral of Holland [ie van Tromp, who had escorted the queen's ships to England] sent to tell them that if they did not cease, he would fire upon them as enemies . . . On this they stopped, and the tide went down, so that there was not water enough for them to stay where they were.

How effective either the royalist or parliamentary army would have been against a seaborne invader can only be a matter of speculation. The failure of Parliament's fleet to prevent Henrietta Maria's supply convoy from unloading safely and of Charles's few ships to stop Parliament reinforcing at will the ports it held were not encouraging. The accepted strategy if an enemy landed was to contain the initial lodgement with local forces while mounting a full-scale counter-offensive with the field army and militia, but the insuperable obstacle to delivering such a blow swiftly was lack of mobility. Even passing through friendly territory the best speed infantry could achieve was 13 miles [21 km] in a day, but the normal rate of progress was slower and, allowing for a rest day, to cover 70 miles [112 km] in a week was good going.

The chief reason for the slow progress, apart from the bad state of the roads, was that every foot soldier was heavily burdened with at least 60 lbs [27 kg] of weapons and equipment, often including a 'snapsack', or rucksack, containing up to a week's rations. The pikeman was further inconvenienced by his armour. In the end most pikemen discarded it, the need for speed in what was largely a war of movement outweighing the advantages of personal protection.

The infantry and cavalry in the parliamentary army were at first raised and organised much as among the royalists, the aim being to equip one third of the men with muskets and the rest with pikes to protect the musketeers while they were reloading. 'To trail a pike' was regarded as more honourable than carrying a firearm but it was, at 16 ft [5 m] long, so awkward to carry that, as one officer complained, 'some . . . in a windy day would cut off a foot, and some two, of their pikes, which is a damned thing to be suffered.'

Under the stress of war the musket was also improved. Commonly 4 ft [1.2 m] long when the Civil War began it had by its end often been shortened to 3 ft [0.9 m], making it possible to abandon the heavy rest, a length of tough wood with a fork at one end and a point at the other, used to support it while being fired. Even when the musket rest had vanished, the musketeer still had to carry a supply of lead bullets, each weighing up to 1¼ oz [35 g], in a pouch, though in action he usually kept one or two ready in his mouth. Each required a charge of about ¾ oz [21 g], divided into fine priming powder, carried in a 'touch-box', and coarser propellant, poured from a flask. To save time in loading, he was usually equipped with a dozen charges of powder already made up and transported in small tins or leather cases fitted to a bandolier slung over his shoulder, which in a high wind rattled noisily enough to drown the words of command and made surprise difficult to achieve. After dark a company of musketeers on the march was also easily detected by the 'link' of match, about 2 ft [0.6 m] long, lighted at both ends, which each man carried in his left hand.

A more reliable firing mechanism was provided with the introduction of the firelock musket, which steadily replaced the old matchlock during this period. The initial type, the wheel lock, where a spring was wound up by a key and then produced a spark by striking against a piece of iron pyrites, was rapidly overtaken by the snaphanse or flint-lock, where a flint made contact with a steel plate. This was one of those seemingly small inventions which made a vast difference on the battlefield. 'It is exceedingly more ready,' commented one writer a few years later of the improved weapon, 'for with the firelock you have only to cock and you are prepared to shoot, but with your matchlock you have endless motions.'

A well-handled musket could achieve a rate of fire of about one shot a minute,[*] with an extreme range of about 400 yards [366 m], but it was more commonly used at distances of 40 to 100 yards [37 to 91 m].

The traditional formation for musketeers had been ten deep, with each rank as it fired falling back to reload, but following the Swedish experience in the Thirty Years War this had generally been reduced to six ranks. These sometimes 'doubled up' to form three, which, with one kneeling, one stooping and one standing, could fire simultaneously. The shock effect was felt to outweigh the vulnerability of the musketeers as they reloaded, as the author of one contemporary military textbook explained:

> For thereby you pour as much lead in your enemies bosom at one time as you do the other way at two several times and thereby you do them more mischief, you quail, daunt, and astonish them three times more, for one long and continuated crack of thunder is more terrible and dreadful to mortals than ten interrupted and single ones.

The battles in the opening stages of the Civil War had often been casual, if not chaotic, encounters, but on 15 February 1645 the House of Lords finally endorsed proposals for what became known as the New Model Army, which consisted originally of eleven regiments of horse of 600 men each, 1100 dragoons, and 12 foot regiments, each 1200 strong, a total of 22,000. It provided for the first time proper support services in such neglected areas as medical care, and, in the quality of its leaders and the dedication and morale of its men, far surpassed all its predecessors, partly due to the fact that – another innovation – the men were, at least at first, decently and regularly paid. The New Model was the nation's first truly professional army. Permanently in existence, available to serve anywhere in the country, and financed by regular national taxation instead of by *ad hoc* levies on individual counties or communities, it provided for the first time an effective, regular means of national defence, though originally created to fight other Englishmen.

The English had, as mentioned earlier, no recent experience of siege

[*] Smurthwaite, p. 135. Young and Emberton, however, say, p. 36, 'a firing rate greater than one round every five minutes was not possible' while Firth and Fortescue offer no information on the point.

warfare or the art of fortification but both these deficiencies were now to be made good. During the next few years the country was to witness again the once-familiar ritual of challenges to surrender, elaborate sieges, heroic stormings – the going rate of bonus for parliamentary soldiers required to carry the assault ladders became 5s [25p] – and elaborate surrenders, though with a new addition: garrisons now marched out not only with flags flying but with the musketeers' matches lighted to show they were still able to resist.

The artillery weapons available to both sides were very similar and after a successful action often changed hands. The heaviest type, needed to breach the walls of such purpose-built fortresses as Warwick and Gloucester, held by Parliament, was the cannon royal, weighing 71.5 cwt [3.6 tons], which needed 16 horses and 90 men to move it, a vast, unwieldy weapon 8 ft [2.4 m] long, with a calibre of 8 inches [20 cm], with each 63-lb [28.6-kg] shot requiring a charge of 40 lb [18.1 kg] of powder. The ordinary cannon, 62 cwt [3.1 tons] in weight, with its 12 attendant horses and 70 men, was equally likely to find itself bogged down on the unmetalled roads of the time or on the sodden turf of some rainswept battlefield: British battles in every age seemed to be conducted in a downpour. It was even longer in the barrel, 10 ft [3 m], though smaller in calibre, 7 inches [18 cm], and firing a lighter, 47-lb [21.3-kg] shot, with a 34-lb [15.40-kg] charge. The demi-cannon and culverin, the next smallest pieces, were longer still, with 12-ft [3.6-m] and 11-ft [3.3-m] barrels respectively, a long barrel being necessary to overcome the innate inefficiency of seventeenth-century guns, with their poor quality powder.

The heaviest type of weapon used to bombard a town was the mortar, a short-barrelled, large-calibred gun which lobbed a heavy explosive shell, not merely a solid projectile, over the walls. The New Model Army had the use of at least one mortar, made of brass, weighing 10 cwt [500 kg], and delivering a shell from 12 to 14¾ inches [31-37 cm] in diameter. Some of these, bursting in the air 'in the midst of the castle, being open above', exposing the magazine to the risk of being blown up, brought about the surrender of Devizes in the autumn of 1645 within a week. The effect of being under mortar fire was vividly described by one of the garrison of Chester, which held out until February 1646:

> Our houses like so many splitting vessels crash their supporters and burst themselves in sunder through the very violence of those descending firebrands . . . Two houses in the Watergate skip joint from joint and create an earthquake, the main posts jostle each other, while the frighted casemates fly for fear.

Necessity generated invention. Like the coastal towns once plagued by French or Spanish raids, inland communities learned to defend themselves with whatever lay to hand. In Puritan Manchester, which lacked walls, chains were stretched across the streets to prevent cavalry charges while ramparts were being flung up; at Coventry the king's horsemen were halted by 'harrowes, carts and pieces of timber laid crosse waies on heaps'; at Bradford, the church tower, used by the defending snipers, was padded with 'large sheets of wool . . . so close to each other and so nigh the roof of the church, that it would be with difficulty for a ball to penetrate the steeple'; at Gloucester the one breach made in the wall by Charles's 'terrible engines of war' was filled with woolsacks, which proved remarkably effective in absorbing cannon fire.

London, the ultimate objective of every invader, was from the first solid for Parliament. Thousands of volunteers of both sexes laboured to construct a massive earthwork and ditch, 18 miles [30 km] long, which encompassed no fewer than 21 strongpoints, each blocking or controlling a major road into the capital. For the royalists Oxford was fortified at a cost of £30,000 and surrounded by a ring of defended localities. The city itself, already partly protected by two rivers, was further defended by a continuous wall of triangular-shaped bastions, built by Sir Bernard de Gomme according to the latest principles, which denied the attacker any possible dead ground.

A recurring nightmare in Tudor times had been that an enemy might secure a major lodgement on the coast of Cornwall, and cut off the whole south-west peninsula from the rest of the country,[*] and this possibility was now revived, in a new form, as Clarendon recorded, by the grandson and namesake of that great Elizabethan hero, Sir Richard Grenville of the *Revenge*, who 'cut a deep trench from Barnstaple to the south sea, for the space of nearly forty miles [64 km], by which, he said, he would defend all Cornwall, and so much of Devon, against the world.'

This romantic notion was never put to the test but England abounded in local leaders like Grenville who would have given any invader a hard time, and, even more important, in country houses which, converted into strongpoints under a resolute owner or determined wife, showed, during the Civil War, how easily an Englishman's home could literally become his castle. At Caldecote Hall, in Warwickshire, for example, a mere four men, aided by six women acting as loaders, held off Prince Rupert himself and 'when their bullets began to faile, they fell to melting all their household pewter, and having bullet moulds in the house speedily made more'. The little garrison finally succumbed to the danger of being burned out but only after shooting down 18 of the attackers, without loss.

Churches often provided ready-made forts and even the Anglican

* See *Defending the Island*, p. 492, on Sir Walter Raleigh's appreciation of this danger. On the *Revenge* see p. 484.

royalists readily made use of them as strongpoints, observation posts and sites for snipers. At Lichfield in Staffordshire the royalists centred their defences on the cathedral, strengthening the moat round the close to form their main line of defence, and mounting artillery in the main tower. A Roundhead officer described how Sir William Waller recovered Alton church in Hampshire from the royalists:

> The churchyard was full of our men laying about them stoutly, with halberts, swords and musquet-stocks, while some threw hand-granadoes in the church windows, others attempting to enter the church, being led on by Sergeant-Major Shambrooke . . . who in the entrance received a shot in the thigh.

This action ended dramatically with dead horses serving as barricades in the aisles and the royalist colonel dead in the pulpit; its evidence remains to this day in the loopholes in the church door and the bullet scars in the walls.

In many sieges the devices used would have seemed familiar to a medieval or even a Roman soldier. At Sherborne, the parliamentary commander ordered 'every soldier to cut his fresh fagot' and they advanced to the attack, each carrying his wooden stake, 'whereby in two hours time they had above 6,000 fagots with which to fill the trenches and throw stones and rubbish upon them'.

On 27 April 1646 Charles I escaped from Oxford to surrender himself to the Scottish army which he hoped, vainly, to persuade to change sides, and on 16 June he issued orders to surrender to the remaining places still holding out. Harlech did not do so until 13 March 1647, belated proof of the excellence of the castle-building of an even earlier monarch, Edward I.

The Civil War revealed that the nation, whose aptitude for naval warfare had long been recognised, could also, if put to it, make a respectable showing on land. An army chaplain summed up the value of these bloodstained years during 1646:

> Some men gain more experience in two years than others in ten, because they are more advertent and have better parts. And for our English wars our English experience is as good as any, and we have had more experimental service in these three or four years war in England, than falls out in other parts in a far longer time.

4

POWERFUL BY SEA AND LAND

Not only are they powerful by sea and land, but they live without ostentation.

French envoy reporting on the leaders of the Commonwealth, c.1649

'You have now done your work and may go play,' the captured commander of Charles's last army had told the victors in 1646, 'unless you will fall out among yourselves.' This proved a shrewd prediction.

The first Civil War was hardly over when it was followed by the second, as the Scots, in return for a promise from Charles I to introduce Presbyterianism, invaded England. After they had been defeated, the king was put on trial on charges of having entertained 'a wicked design . . . to introduce an arbitrary and tyrannical government' and having 'levied and maintained a cruel war in the land', and on 30 January 1649 was executed. The country was ruled for a time by a Council of State, answerable to Parliament, until in May 1649 it was formally declared a free commonwealth, or republic. In 1650 Cromwell became Commander-in-Chief of the army and the chief source of authority; in 1652 Parliament was suppressed; and in 1653 Cromwell became Lord Protector and, in effect, a benevolent dictator. The political history of these years is complicated and tortuous, but the basic situation was simple; if the Commonwealth and Protectorate were to survive they had, as much as any sovereign claiming to rule by divine right, to keep out invaders. This was all the more difficult since the invaders enjoyed the sympathy of a sizeable number of citizens, and claimed to be acting on behalf of England's true and legitimate ruler. Republicans dismissed him as 'that young man, the late king's son, Charles Stuart', but royalists venerated him as Charles II, claiming that he had automatically succeeded to the throne on his father's death.

The first real trouble came from Ireland but with the help of the Commonwealth navy, of which more will be said later, Cromwell was able to get an army safely across the Irish Sea and between August 1649 and May 1650 the Irish rising was suppressed by him with a ruthlessness at least as great as that of any previous royal expedition. A mass 'transplantation', or enforced transfer of suspect Irish to make room for more English, Protestant, settlers followed, in which, it was said, two-thirds of its land changed hands, leaving Ireland a permanently disgruntled neighbour on England's western flank. For the moment, however, the royalists' hopes of using it as a base for the reconquest of England lay in ruins.

A greater danger to the infant Commonwealth remained closer at hand. Charles II was proclaimed King of Great Britain, Ireland and – following the old, absurd fiction dating back to Henry V's time – France, in Edinburgh in February 1649 as soon as news of his father's death was received but the only English territory he actually controlled was the Scilly Isles and the Channel Islands, to which he returned in September 1649 en route, he hoped, to re-enter England via Ireland, a prospect to which Oliver Cromwell's success there decisively put paid.

Charles retained, however, considerable nuisance value, issuing letters of marque, the traditional licence to behave like a pirate, to French and Dutch privateers. Soon, as so often in the past, a state approaching undeclared war existed in the Channel, and in 1650 four of the infant colonies in the West Indies and North America proclaimed Charles II king and defied the home government. The Commonwealth was being forced to become an international naval power in order to preserve what had been achieved at home. By a pleasing irony, Parliament, between 1642 and 1652, continued to levy shipmoney – though it could argue that it now did so with proper legal authority, i.e. its own. (John Hampden, its great opponent, had died, sword in hand, at Chalgrove field in 1642.) The money was well spent. In naval matters as in military Parliament's officials were far more efficient and more honest than James I's and Charles I's, indeed the integrity of the nation's new rulers and their subordinates was one of the new government's great strengths. A hostile foreign observer, reporting to Cardinal Mazarin of France about this time, could not withhold his admiration:

> Not only are they powerful by sea and land, but they live without ostentation, without pomp, and without mutual rivalry. They are economical in their private affairs and prodigal in their devotion to public affairs, for which each man toils as if for his private interest. They handle large sums of money, which they administer honestly, observing a strict discipline. They reward well and punish severely.

The navy was now to reap the fruits of this enlightened management. With an income, in 1649, of around £2 million, compared to Charles I's a few years earlier, of £618,000, though much of it came from once-for-all fines and the sale of confiscated royalist land, the Council of State could afford to strengthen the navy and in the next three years it was doubled in size, by commissioning an additional 41 ships; some merchant vessels were also hired, giving England a larger fleet, approaching 200 ships, than it had ever possessed before.

While the great naval expansion programme was only just beginning, Charles, his hopes of recovering England via Ireland now dashed, was reluctantly looking towards the Scots as his new allies. On 13 February 1650 he left Jersey for Holland, where he met the Presbyterian ministers sent to negotiate with him. It was not a happy meeting. 'We find in you only lightness and vanity,' one of them told Charles bluntly, while to his counsellors the young prince confided: 'I perfectly hate the Scots, but I may have to give in to them.'

Charles's decision to come to terms with the Covenanters meant abandoning one of his most loyal supporters, James Graham, Marquis of Montrose, whom Charles I had appointed his lieutenant-general in Scotland. One of the founders of the Covenant movement, Montrose had fallen out with the ruling parties in Scotland and moved to the Continent, ending up in Sweden, where, in November 1649, a wealthy Scottish merchant provided him with a large quantity of arms and advanced him £13,500 to pay the motley army of soldiers of fortune, mainly Danish and German, he had assembled. Eventually, on 10 January 1650, he prepared to set sail from Gothenburg, with 1200 men, not a large force with which to regain a kingdom, but by no means negligible for Montrose was an able commander and natural leader, of whom his contemporary Bishop Burnet remarked that he lived 'as in a romance'.

Sailing from so far north made the risk of interception small but presented other hazards; having embarked on 10 January 1660 Montrose's ships were eight days later a mere two leagues [6 miles or 9.6 km] from the Swedish shore, trapped by the ice. In mid-February they set off again, on a shorter sea crossing, this time from Bergen in Norway to Kirkwall in the Orkneys.*

London lay 540 miles [870 km] as the crow flew from Kirkwall and at least double that distance as the soldier marched. It was the longest, most roundabout route ever contemplated by any invader. On 12 April 1650, he reached the mainland at John O'Groats, with fewer than 1000 men. While a messenger sent by Charles desperately sought to contact him, to tell him to abandon the expedition because of the prince's forthcoming deal with the Covenanters, Montrose, the most dedicated royalist in all Scotland, was leading his impressive little army along the coast to Sutherland, amid universal indifference; his hopes of a massive rallying of the Highlanders to the, for him, magic name of Charles Stuart proved unfounded. On 27 April 1650 the invaders were routed at the Battle of Carbisdale near the Kyle of Sutherland four

* I have followed Gardiner, Vol.I. p. 213, but Montague, p. 366, Ashley, p. 34 and Fraser, *Charles II*, p. 87, give slightly different and differing accounts, of the date Montrose and his troops landed.

miles [6.4 km] north-west of Kincardine, just inside the later county of Ross and Cromarty. The brave but hopeless adventure ended with Montrose being betrayed while in hiding and hanged in Edinburgh on 21 May 1650 with a placard recounting his misdeeds hung round his neck.

Three days later the king, who did not yet know for certain of his fate, set sail for Scotland to seek his throne with the help of Montrose's murderers. On 3 July 1650, while his ship lay at anchor off the mouth of the River Spey, on the north-east coast of Scotland, after an appalling 22 days at sea, suffering from contrary winds and escaping the ships of the Commonwealth navy only thanks to the fog, Charles swore his 'solemn oath in . . . allowance and approbation of the National Covenant'. He even undertook to accept Presbyterian worship and church government himself. 'I shall,' declared the supposed defender of the Anglican faith, 'observe these in my own practice and family, and shall never make opposition to any of these, nor endeavour any alteration therein.'

Charles was now, as a contemporary commentator put it, 'safely caught in the springe [i.e. the man-trap] of the Kirk', and forced to endure a wretchedly boring existence, spied on by his supposed subjects. The only entertainment, apart from golf, for which he did not care, were interminable sermons – he once had to sit through six in succession – and protracted graces before meagre meals. When urged to repent of his sins yet again as well as those of his 'idolatrous' (ie Catholic) mother, he grumbled sadly to a friend, 'I think I must repent me ever being born.'

While Charles was enduring his gloomy exile in Scotland, Parliament had been planning its counter-stroke. Cromwell was clear that the best way to deal with the threatened invasion from Scotland was by a pre-emptive strike. 'Your excellency,' he pointed out to Lord [formerly Sir Thomas] Fairfax, whom Parliament had appointed Commander-in-Chief, 'will soon determine whether it is better to have this war in the bowels of another country than our own.' But Fairfax was unwilling to launch an offensive war against Scotland; he now resigned his post and on 26 June 1650 Oliver Cromwell became by Act of Parliament Captain-General and Commander-in-Chief of all the forces of the Commonwealth. It was the natural climax to an outstanding military career, in which, never having heard a shot fired till the age of 43, Cromwell had outfought and outgeneralled professional soldiers with a lifetime of experience behind them.

He was 51 when he became the nation's chief soldier. 'By birth a gentleman, living neither in any considerable height nor yet in obscurity,' according to his own later account, he was the son of a minor landowner of Huntingdon and educated at the local grammar school before going up to Cambridge, where he did best in mathematics but, according to a royalist biographer, 'was easily satiated with study, taking more delight in horse and field exercise'. He studied law for a time at Lincoln's Inn before making a good and happy marriage, to the daughter of a rich city merchant who eventually bore him eight children, and returning to his native county to farm the land inherited from his father.

On 22 July 1650 Cromwell led his army of around 16,000 men across the Scottish border and eventually, after suffering heavy casualties from sickness – the weather was, as usual, appalling – found himself hemmed in between a larger Scottish army, holding the higher ground, and the sea just south of Dunbar, 25 miles [40 km] east of Edinburgh. The Council of War called by Cromwell that night were for getting away what foot they could by sea, as the English fleet lay just offshore, but Cromwell would have none of such faint-hearted counsels. Applying the same simple principle as in his last encounter with the Scots, 'to engage the enemy was our business', he insisted on a dawn attack, which in the grey early morning twilight of Tuesday 3 September 1650 took the Scots totally by surprise. The result was the greatest of all his victories, or, as Cromwell himself put it in his despatch to Parliament, 'one of the most signal mercies God hath done for England and His people, this war'. 3000 Scots were killed and 10,000 captured for the loss of a mere 20 English dead and 58 wounded.

On Christmas Eve 1650 Edinburgh Castle, which had held out long after the English had captured the city, finally surrendered. This dismal Christmas present for Charles was followed, however, by a happier New Year. On 1 January 1651 he was crowned King Charles II of Scotland and England, after a final bout of public repentance and sermon-mongering, in the cathedral at Scone.

Charles's personality, added to his famous Stuart name, was enough to make men ready to follow him to their deaths, and several times a week in the spring of 1651 he made the 35-mile [56-km] ride between the Scottish Parliament at Perth and the rapidly expanding army at Stirling. Here he inspected the troops wearing a homely 'soldier's dress' and told them that he, like they, had only one life to lose and would hazard it on the coming invasion of England.

The Scottish army began its long march – London lay 410 miles [656 km] away – on 31 July 1651 and crossed the border into England on 5 August. Charles was proclaimed King of England at Penrith in Cumberland, but the country failed to rise in his support and a small-scale supporting expedition from the Isle of Man which landed in Lancashire was rapidly defeated at Wigan. Charles eventually reached Worcester, the first city to declare for his father in the Civil War; the capital was now only 113 miles [182 km] away. But Cromwell, with the best of his subordinate commanders, had by now arrived, at the head of 28,000 men. On the anniversary of Dunbar, Wednesday 3 September 1651, they decisively defeated the 16,000 Scots and handful of English facing them in what Cromwell himself called 'as stiff a contest as ever I have seen'. Charles behaved with exemplary courage: 'Certainly a braver prince never lived,' testified one royalist officer. Only when dusk was falling, with 2000 of his followers dead and most of the rest facing capture, for the loss of only 200 Roundheads, was he persuaded to escape. Eventually everyone knew of the legendary sequel, how the 21-year-old contender for the English throne hid in an oak tree at Boscobel until on 15 October 1651, after a final hairsbreadth escape, Charles got safely away from Shoreham in Sussex, to France.

On the same day on which Charles had been defeated at Worcester a parliamentary fleet dropped anchor in the Downs. Its admiral, Robert Blake, was already showing the same dazzling talent for warfare at sea that Oliver Cromwell had displayed on land. Born in 1598, the son of a successful Bridgwater ship-owner, he had entered the family business on coming down from Oxford and gained some sea-going experience in its ships before the Civil War, before becoming a soldier and being entrusted with the defence of Lyme. Later he met Fairfax and Cromwell for the first time and clearly impressed them, for in February 1649 he was appointed one of the three Commissioners of the Navy.

From May to November 1649 Blake successfully blockaded Prince Rupert's fleet in Kinsale on the eastern coast of Ireland, enabling Cromwell's conquest to proceed unchallenged from the sea. When Rupert escaped to Lisbon, Blake was sent in pursuit. After keeping Rupert bottled up in the Tagus, though the Prince escaped in the fog when finally brought to battle in September, Blake virtually destroyed the royalist navy in a series of successful operations, and, for the first time, established England as a force to be reckoned with in the Mediterranean. 'God hath owned us in the midst of our implacable enemies, so that the terror of God is amongst them,' wrote one captain to the Admiralty Committee. 'The Spaniards are now exceeding kind to us.' One by one the countries of Europe, wherever their sympathies lay – the first was Catholic Spain – were sufficiently impressed by English sea-power to recognise the Commonwealth.

Parliament now had a navy strong enough to protect English interests and in October 1651, just as Charles Stuart was escaping back to France, Parliament passed the Navigation Act. Goods from outside Europe could under the Act only be imported into England in British ships and those from Europe only in such ships or those owned by the exporting country. The measure inevitably alienated the Dutch, who had become the great carriers of the seas, and their admiral, Maarten Tromp, was ordered to resist by force any British attempts to search Dutch ships to see if they were carrying foreign, usually French, goods.

Anticipating perhaps that new republic was no more likely to speak peace to republic than old monarchy had done, the Council of State had allocated £829,490 to finance the navy for 1652, more than double the previous budget of £376,000. This provided it, around the end of May 1652, with 99 ships available to defend the Channel, with another 29 further afield. The Dutch could muster 150 vessels, but they were mostly considerably smaller and less solidly built and more lightly armed. Tromp's flagship, an 800-tonner with 56 guns, was outclassed by no fewer than 20 English ships and most of his fleet was designed for in-shore work in shallow waters, not distant, deep-sea operations.

The Dutch began the war supremely confident of their ability to protect their merchant fleet, and meet any challenge the English might make. Tromp was the most acclaimed admiral of his time and had trounced the Spaniards in English waters a few years before, in 1639, while the royal fleet had not dared to intervene. Now, on 17 May 1652, he anchored with equal arrogance just off Dover, exchanging some musketry shots with the Castle before, on 19 May, he came into contact with Robert Blake's squadron, hastily summoned from off Rye. The Dutch force numbered 42 ships, the English 13, but Blake immediately demanded the customary salute, to which Tromp's reply was a broadside. After a four-hour fight, known as the Battle of Dover, the Dutch withdrew leaving Blake in possession of the scene and with two captured ships as prizes. The 48-gun *James*, his flagship, had taken more than 70 shots in her hull and masts but had lost only six men killed and 35 wounded.

The two countries were still officially at peace but war was formally declared on 8 July 1652. A minor inconclusive engagement, off Plymouth, followed on 16 August and on 16 September Admiral De With came close enough inshore to fire broadsides at two ships he had forced ashore near Dover, but was driven off by the guns of Sandgate castle, in a ship-to-shore duel. A full-scale encounter followed on 28 September known as the Battle of the Kentish Knock, after the strip of land just to the north of the Goodwin Sands and the North Foreland at the mouth of the Thames estuary. Blake's 35 warships, mounting from 100 to 10 guns, plus another 24 armed merchant vessels, fought for three hours against a Dutch fleet 64 strong but of inferior gunpower under Admiral De With. As Blake later wrote, 'The dispute was very hot for a short time, continuing till it was dark night.' De With summed up the engagement even more graphically: 'From about 3 o'clock in the afternoon, we saw nothing but smoke, fire and the English, until the sun went down.' The result was a decisive English victory which left three Dutch ships lost or captured, with an unrecorded number of dead but at least 2000 wounded; no English ships were lost. Thereafter De With was dismissed and, with their crews mutinous and unwilling to return to sea, the Dutch warships stayed in port.

The Dutch were in fact far from beaten. Tromp, highly popular with his men, was recalled, and on 21 November 1652 put to sea with a force which eventually totalled 450 vessels, and set course for Dover. On the afternoon of Tuesday 30 November 1652 the two admirals came in contact off Dungeness. Blake had 42 warships under his command, Tromp 78 and this time Tromp unquestionably came off best, sinking three English ships and capturing two more before continuing to escort the convoy he was protecting down Channel. The immediate sequel to Tromp's victory was the landing of a Dutch raiding party in Sussex which got clean away after seizing some cattle and sheep. Another group, of 60 men, put ashore in Kent, were all captured, after an energetic local commander, Colonel Nathaniel Rich, had cut off their retreat to their boats.

The Dutch victory at Dungeness led Parliament to appoint a commission of enquiry. Within two weeks it had produced recommendations for a whole series of reforms which now gave the Commonwealth a fleet comparable to the New Model Army, some of whose units were disbanded to release funds for the purpose; rivalry between the two services for the limited funds available for defence was henceforward to be a regular feature of English life. For the moment the army was the winner, being assigned £80,000 a month against the navy's £40,000.

Already, however, a new self-confidence and professionalism were becoming evident throughout the navy, as was evident in the letter which Blake and Deane addressed to the Speaker of the House of Commons on 12 February 1653, affirming their eagerness to 'hasten westward to wait for the return of the Dutch fleet'.

The next confrontation with the Dutch duly came off Portland on Friday 18 February 1653, the start of 'The Three Days' Battle', a ferocious fight over a wide area of sea between Portland Bill and Cape Gris –Nez involving about 80 warships on either side. The Dutch lost eight, the English one, but, thanks to Tromp's superb seamanship, he managed to get safely home nearly 100 of the 150 merchant vessels he was escorting.

The great victory at Portland was commemorated in a contemporary ballad which gave added currency to the still enduring legend that after the Battle of Dungeness Tromp had attached a broom to his masthead. The story appears first in a report from the frigate *Nonsuch*, at Portsmouth, which was published in the *Perfect Account* on 9 March:

> Their gallant Mr Tromp when he was in France [i.e. off the Isle of Rhe preparing to sail up the Channel], we understand, wore a flag of broom and, being demanded what he meant by it, replied that he was going to sweep the narrow seas of all Englishmen.

At home things were going less well for the English government. On

20 April 1653 the so-called 'Rump' of the Long Parliament was forcibly dissolved by Cromwell's troops, and authority passed to him personally, assisted by a ten-man Council of State. Meanwhile the Dutch war continued. On Thursday 2 June 1653 there came another English victory in the first Battle of the North Foreland or the Battle of the Gabbard, named after the Gabbard sands off Orfordness in East Suffolk. Tromp's consummate seamanship and the sandbanks off the Dutch coast saved the Dutch fleet from destruction but of his 95 ships 21 were lost, with 800 Dutch sailors dead and another 1400 taken prisoner; the English had got off far more lightly with 23 ships disabled, 126 men dead and another 236 wounded. 'I must say that the English are at present masters both of us and of the seas,' De With told the States-General and on 17 June 1653 a Dutch ship sailed up the Thames under a white flag to try to negotiate peace terms, though the war was to drag on for nearly another year, while in Amsterdam weeds grew in the streets, and 3000 houses stood empty.

The final, and decisive, battle of the First Dutch War, known as Scheveningen or the First Battle of Texel, was fought near the island of that name on Sunday 31 July 1653. Not only were at least 14 Dutch ships lost, with perhaps 4000 men, compared with two English ships and 500 men, but Tromp, attempting to break the stranglehold of the British blockade, was killed by a musket-ball, an irreplaceable loss.

On 4 December 1653 the new 'Barebones' Parliament, named after its most famous member, a Puritan leather-merchant called Praisegod Barebones [or Barebone or Barbon]*, dissolved itself, under some pressure, surrendering its powers into Cromwell's hands, and on 16 December 1653 he was formally installed in Whitehall as Lord Protector, 'having . . . been desired . . .,' as his inaugural oath explained, 'to take upon me the protection and government of these nations.'

The Protectorate, so different from anything which had preceded it, began under happy auspices. The First Dutch War ended in triumph in April 1654 with a treaty which secured the Dutch government's agreement to salute the English flag and to seek permission before their ships passed through the Straits of Dover. England's prestige had never stood higher, and her 160-strong fleet was now, for the first time, the most powerful in Europe. Between November 1654 and May 1655 Blake 'showed the flag' throughout the Mediterranean, being treated with increasing respect wherever he appeared and scoring a notable victory over the notorious Moorish pirates based at Porto Farina near Tunis.

In October 1655 Spain declared war on Britain, the causes of the quarrel being essentially the same as those which had caused trouble in the past. As the Spanish ambassador declared, 'To ask liberty from the

* Praisegod is said to have had a brother, Damned Barebone, short for 'If-Christ-had-not-died-thou-hadst-been-damned'.

Inquisition and free sailing in the West Indies was to ask for his master's two eyes.' Fortunately, as relations with Spain had deteriorated those with France had correspondingly improved, for Cromwell had most skilfully engaged in the traditional English diplomatic game of trying to play off one Roman Catholic power against the other. Underlying his efforts was the ever-present need to forestall any risk of a royalist invasion. Both France and Spain had recognised the Commonwealth, but, given the chance, any Catholic king was likely to support a fellow royal against a Puritan regicide.

For the moment, however, England seemed unchallengeable and it was a sign of her enhanced standing in the world when in July 1654 Charles Stuart was asked to leave France within ten days, though he was compensated by the arrears of the £6000-a-year pension previously promised him and a six-month advance on the next instalment. His future seemed unpromising. 'The king,' wrote his own future chief minister, Clarendon, 'is now as low as to human understanding as he can be,' and after travelling on horseback, as he had no carriage, through various countries, with his clothes and bedding accompanying him in 'a light cart', he eventually in March 1655, closely followed by Cromwell's agents, arrived at Middleburg in Zeeland to await a summons to England.

The rising planned for that month proved, however, a disastrous failure, and Charles went on to Louvain and Brussels where, on 12 April 1656 [2 April, by the Spanish calendar] he signed a highly satisfactory treaty with Spain. Following his usual principle of promising anything to regain his throne Charles undertook to restore to Spain all English possessions in the West Indies acquired since 1630, and, when he regained his throne, to suspend the laws against the Roman Catholics. His *quid pro quo* was the offer of 6000 Spanish troops to be provided so soon as he had secured a suitable port in England, though in fact most of the six regiments which Charles, with Spanish help, raised soon afterwards, were composed of émigré Englishmen, Irish and Scots. With the help of a second pension, this time from Spain, he now set up a new, and less impoverished, court at Bruges to wait for signs of a royalist revival in England.

These were slow in appearing. The failed rising of March 1655, already mentioned, which had brought Charles to wait hopefully near the Channel coast, had been followed by the division of England and Wales into eleven districts, each presided over by a major-general. This officer not only controlled the militia, but was also responsible for raising taxes to finance the new 'standing militia of horse', consisting of a troop of cavalry paid a small retainer to be ready for service at a day's notice, the force totalling nationally about 6000 men.

The rule of the major-generals proved highly unpopular and the excesses of the extreme puritans, who tried to exploit it for their own ends, went far to discredit the parliamentary cause. There was uni-versal relief when in December 1656 normal government was re-established. Meanwhile, abroad, the Commonwealth went from strength to strength. On 23 March 1657 Cromwell signed an alliance with France to supply troops and a fleet for a joint attack on the Spaniards in Flanders, with Dunkirk as England's share of the anti-cipated spoils. This was a revival of the old dream of protecting the island by an outpost on the far shore, which had seemed to disappear with Queen Mary's loss of Calais in 1558. Cromwell's Secretary of State predicted that Dunkirk in English hands 'would be a bridle to the Dutch and a door into the continent', but while the land operations were still in progress a new and dazzling success was achieved at sea when on Monday 20 April 1657 Robert Blake burst into the suppos-edly impregnable harbour of Santa Cruz de Tenerife in the Canary Islands and destroyed all 16 Spanish ships there, although, a vast loss, Blake himself died, worn out by his exertions, as his ship was entering Plymouth Sound.

For the royalists it was a bleak time. Between January and March 1658 one of Charles's most loyal and distinguished adherents, James Butler, Earl [later Duke] of Ormonde, bravely toured England as a royalist spy having dyed his fair hair black as a disguise, returning to Flanders to recommend a landing in East Anglia, near Yarmouth. The prince optimistically moved to Antwerp but, on 4 June 1658, a French army, including a large English contingent, routed a combined royal-ist and Spanish force. Half of Charles's small army was destroyed; the ships assembled to carry them were captured; and ten days later Dun-kirk surrendered and was duly occupied by parliamentary troops. Before the consequences could become apparent, however, on 10 Sep-tember 1658 far more sensational news reached Charles Stuart, as he idled his time away at Hoogstraeten in the Netherlands playing tennis – 'The devil is dead!'

The great Protector had died of a fever, at the age of 59, on 3 Septem-ber, and three hours later his eldest son, Richard, then 31, was pro-claimed Protector. He proved far too weak to bridge the widening gulf between Parliament and the army, and on 25 May 1659 abdicated as Protector, retiring into obscurity. England was now for practical pur-poses a military oligarchy, but still no upsurge of royalist sentiment occurred and the invasion which was to end the Commonwealth came from a totally different direction. General George Monck [later Duke of Albemarle], Commander-in-Chief of the Commonwealth army in Scotland, who was now 49 and had been a soldier all his life, became horrified at the near-chaos now developing in London, where the city was at odds with the army and the army with Parliament, and led his troops south to restore order. On 2 January 1660, like many an invader before him, Monck, a Devon man, crossed the River Tweed at Coldstream and advanced into England through the snow-bound north. Not a hand was raised against him, and soon after his arrival in London, on 3 February 1660, he apparently became convinced that only a return to monarchy could end the existing dissension.

On 4 April 1660, on Monck's prompting the king, as most men already regarded him, issued the Declaration of Breda, promising a pardon to all who had fought against him, except the regicides, and, subject to parliamentary approval, 'a liberty to tender consciences' in matters of religion. On May Day, one of the holidays against which the puritans had campaigned, the House of Commons formally invited Charles to re-assume the government. On 23 May 1660, he set sail from The Hague on the former *Naseby*, hastily re-christened the *Royal Charles*, and under perfect skies and across a calm sea made his way home. On Monday 25 May 1660 he landed at Dover, while the bonfires, intended to warn of an enemy's coming, blazed in welcome, and the massed cannon of the castle, built to repel an invader, roared out in triumph. The Kent militia, once the foremost of the nation's land defenders, lined his way along the classic invader's route from the coast to Canterbury and from Canterbury to Rochester, though the pretty maidens who scattered herbs in front of him were perhaps more to the king's taste. Everywhere he was cheered to the echo, until, as he wrote to his sister, 'My head is so prodigiously dazed by the acclamation of the people . . . that I know not whether I am writing sense or no.' On 29 May, his thirtieth birthday, King Charles II (as he was formally crowned a year later) rode in triumph into Whitehall to be welcomed by the Speakers of both Houses of Parliament. The 'invasion by invitation' was complete.

5

THE SOLE SUPREME COMMAND

The sole, supreme government, command and disposition of the militia, and of all forces by sea and land, is . . . the undoubted right of His Majesty.

Preamble to the Militia Act, 1661

Shortly after the Restoration Charles II put in hand the general demobilisation of the New Model Army. Parliament, by an act of 13 September 1660, voted £835,000 to meet its arrears of pay, plus a one-week termination bonus. The disbandment of this magnificent fighting machine occasioned regret even among royalists. 'They were certainly the bravest, the best disciplined, and the soberest army that had been known in these latter ages,' later commented the contemporary historian Bishop Gilbert Burnet, then aged 17. 'Every soldier was able to do the functions of an officer.'

Charles II had been deeply impressed during his enforced stay in France by Louis XIV's regular army, as Gilbert Burnet observed:

There was great talk of a design . . . to raise a force that should be so chosen and modelled that the king might depend upon it; and that it should be so considerable, that there might be no reason to apprehend tumults any more.

In the event England's new full-time, professional army was created by the purely negative decision not to disband certain regiments, at least for the moment, rather than by any positive intention.

Its birthday was Friday 23 November 1660, when Colonel John Russell, a 48-year-old royalist who had fought under Prince Rupert, was granted a colonel's commission to command the 1st Foot Guards. They were soon to acquire their first unofficial battle honours, on 6 January 1661, against a small group of 'Fifth Monarchy Men', religious-cum-political zealots with whom Cromwell had also had trouble.

Though numbering at most no more than 50, and led by a winecooper, Thomas Venner, they caused 'four files of musketeers', from the London trained bands, to flee in terror and subsequently 'beat the Life Guard and a whole regiment for half an hour's time', before being shot or rounded up.

Venner's rising confirmed Charles's conviction that a standing army was essential to his security and on 14 February 1661 the 2nd Foot Guards was formally created. It was based on the regiment of the New Model Army which George Monck had led into England from the Scottish village of Coldstream, hence its nickname of 'Coldstreamers'. Monck himself had already been created Duke of Albemarle and Commander-in-Chief. In the same month two regiments of horse were founded, each consisting of eight troops. The Life Guards were based on a force which had guarded Charles during his exile, and the Royal Horse Guards had performed the same office for Cromwell; they rapidly became known as 'The Blues' from the colour of their original uniforms.

A number of other regiments were established soon afterwards, usually named after the nobleman who formed and commanded each one – hence such titles as 'The Lord High Admiral's Regiment of Foot' and 'The Earl of Cleveland's Horse'. Many famous regiments claim to trace their origins back to this period, among them the Holland Regiment, which became the Third Foot, known as 'The Buffs' from the leather facings on their uniform, and Douglas's Foot, who became the Royal Scots. All told, 57 regiments were formed under Charles II, but many were later amalgamated or, being formed for a specific purpose, were short-lived.

In the first flush of post-Restoration euphoria Parliament expressly renounced any claim to a say in defence matters. The Militia Act of 1661, a misnomer, since it referred to full-time as well as part-time forces, was brief but pointed:

> Forasmuch as within all His Majesty's realms and dominions, the sole supreme government, command and disposition of the Militia, and of all forces by sea and land, and of all forts and places of strength, is, and by the laws of England ever was, the undoubted right of His Majesty, and his Royal Predecessors, Kings and Queens of England . . . both, or either of the Houses of Parliament cannot nor ought to pretend to the same.

Although the militia was often called out at times of public unrest, and was also employed during invasion alarms to dig trenches and watch the coast, the main force for defending the country was now the standing army. So hostile was the nation, after its recent experience, to the mere idea of military rule, that the force raised by Charles II was at first known as 'The Guards and Garrisons', a name which admirably reflected its two principal duties. 'The Guards', of which the nucleus, expanded as necessary, was formed by the four regiments already mentioned, cost around £122,000, a modest amount to pay for a regular army numbering some 6-7000 men, compared to Louis XIV's

16,000. The standing army in Scotland, however, 1200 strong, and in Ireland, with 7500, were in addition to the troops in England and Wales, and each enjoyed different rates of pay and conditions of service, though all three owed allegiance to the king personally as their Commander-in-Chief. 'The Garrisons', of which more will be said later, consisted of 28 essentially separate, locally based, detachments. They accounted for some £67,000, about 35% of the total military budget for 1661, though this total covered only the cost of the men and their personal equipment; the buildings and guns, a far bigger expense, were provided and maintained by the Ordnance Office, which was controlled by the Master-General of the Ordnance, not the Commander-in-Chief, and separately financed. The Guards and Garrisons together brought the total cost of defending the English mainland, excluding guns and fortifications, to just under £190,000.

Although during an invasion it would have provided an invaluable counter-attacking force, the army's most regular role was that of a national police force; as yet the maintenance of law and order rested in most places upon a single, possibly part-time, parish constable. The cavalry proved particularly useful for such duties. Groups of five or six troopers of the Royal Horse Guards would escort messengers transporting cash from the Navy Pay Office in London to the paymasters at Harwich and Portsmouth, or being sent by the Customs and Excise collectors in the country back to the capital. Transferring prisoners, breaking up 'seditious conventicles' such as meetings of Quakers and Presbyterians, protecting the press gangs recruiting men for the navy, or stopping deserters from coming ashore at Rochester and Chatham all fell to its lot. In Gloucestershire and Worcestershire the army was called on to destroy the tobacco which the locals were, in defiance of both the climate and the Customs, attempting to grow in their fields. In London it had the odd duty in 1668 of protecting the prostitutes around Moorfields from an attack on their brothels by the London apprentices; in 1676 some soldiers were assigned to play-going at a theatre in Dorset Garden 'to keep the peace there . . . so that no offence may be given to the spectators nor no affront to the actors'. In the same year troops were called out and rewarded 'for hindering the spreading of the fire in Southwark'; no one had forgotten the Great Fire of 1666 which had left most of the city of London in ruins.

The army's basic duty, that of maintaining order, though it was on such occasions placed under the control of the civil authorities, inevitably made it unpopular, but the most constant source of friction was the billeting of troops in public houses and private homes. Few barracks existed – no doubt had they been general there would have been complaints of the threat their segregated occupants posed to liberty – but hitherto billeting had affected only a few areas, and then only for short periods, as a foreign expedition was mounted or demobilised.

The existence of a standing army, spread in small detachments throughout the country, meant that far more people were affected. There were soon widespread complaints of householders not being paid for the food and accommodation they supplied or, even worse, being blackmailed into paying 5d or 6d [2-2½p] a night to soldiers to persuade them to go elsewhere. Eventually in 1679 the Disbanding Act declared the practice of compulsory billeting illegal and thereafter it ceased, though plans to build a barracks in Westminster came to naught.

Although supposedly promoted on merit, and only with the king's approval, officers had to buy both their initial commission and each successive step up in rank. As a captaincy in the Foot Guards could cost £1000 this was a heavy burden, and in contrast to Cromwell's time, when commissions were awarded on merit, service in the army became largely a rich man's diversion. Normally all an officer could expect when he retired was to be able to sell his commission, though all he was getting was his own money back.

Officers at least received what was known as Full Pay, though expected to find their own uniform and equipment. Other ranks had these provided but the cost was then reclaimed through 'Off Reckonings' of 2d [1p] a day leaving the ordinary private in theory with 8d [3p] a day, known as Subsistence Money, from which he had to feed himself. In practice further deductions were commonly made at source for food, billets and other items, so he received nothing like the gross amount and it was often paid in a lump sum months in arrears, when the temptation to indulge in a drunken spree might be irresistible. The ordinary dragoon was somewhat better off on 1s 4d [7p] a day, of which half was supposed to support his horse; in other cavalry regiments the basic trooper's pay was 2s 6d [12p], including his horse allowance. Sergeants, holding the highest rank to which an ordinary soldier could aspire and frequently left in charge while their officers were away, earned 1s 6d [8p] a day in the infantry, 2s 6d (less 1s 0d [5p] for the horse) in the Dragoons.

Soldiers now became a regular and familiar sight in many parts of the British Isles. In London the king was regularly escorted by his Life Guards, whose name explained their *raison d'être*. The Royal Horse Guards were, in 1665, established at Leyton, Bromley, Dartford, Uxbridge, Aylesbury, Thame and Salisbury, with one distant detachment at York. When other cavalry regiments were formed East Anglia, which offered ample stabling in the towns and was good horse country, became a favoured location, with units being stationed in most of the major towns, including Ipswich, Colchester – a garrison town since Roman times – Bungay and Beccles. Other regiments might be even more widely scattered and the Admiral's Regiment in 1665 had eleven companies in eight different locations, mainly traditional danger points on the coast: Hull, Landguard Fort near Felix-stowe, Harwich, Sheerness, Deal and Plymouth.

The standing army was kept up to strength, or expanded by new regiments being raised when required, by methods that soon became traditional. Recruitment was invariably to a specific regiment, normally from the county where its colonel, and probably the other officers who had obtained their commissions through his influence, had his home. If he were also a deputy-lieutenant of the county the first catchment area for new soldiers would be the local militia, but if more men were needed a small recruiting party would visit an area, collect a crowd, and, after a speech by the captain, sign on men for a bounty of 5s [25p], a practice known as recruiting by 'beat of drum'. The five shillings later dwindled to the 'king's shilling', by accepting which a man entered into a binding contract to join up. At times recruiters received 'levy-money' of £1 a head, supposed to reach the recruit, but largely retained by the captain if he could secure him for less. Service, if not for a specific campaign, was for life. Soldiers who survived the hazards of battle and the far greater risk of disease qualified by the end of the reign for a pension, financed by a contribution of 8d [3p] from each £1 of pay to the 'Invalid Fund'. This provided a foot soldier with one half, a horseman or dragoon with one third, of his ordinary pay. In the same year this scheme was introduced, 1684, the Royal Hospital Chelsea was opened for the 'relief of old, lame or infirm soldiers', financed from the deductions already mentioned and from a 1s [5p] in the £1 levy on the purchase price of commissions. The number of 'Chelsea Pensioners' rose rapidly from 100 to 400 a few years later.

The army had hardly been formed before it was being unfavourably compared with its predecessor. 'They go with their belts and swords, swearing and cursing, and stealing; running into people's houses, by force often times, to carry away something,' commented one former parliamentarian sourly, 'and that is the difference between the one and the other.' Significantly the name 'redcoat', coined in Cromwell's time when this garment was introduced as standard uniform, now often became a term of abuse.

Management of the army rested largely in the hands of civilians. The senior full-time official was the Secretary of War, who was not at this time a member of the government. His post, created on 28 January 1661, was at first filled by General Monck's former private secretary. The other permanent senior staff consisted of the Pay-master-General, the Judge-Advocate General, and the Commissary-General of the Musters, of whom more will be said in a moment, and who formed the link between the regular army and the militia. Operational command rested with the Lord General, but there was already a rudimentary, if very ineffective, intelligence organisation, headed by the Scoutmaster-General, responsible for the collection of information in the field, though not overseas espionage.

Because the army was spread so thinly and few units remained very long in one place, a major part of the work of the Secretary at War was the issue of Marching Orders. These involved planning the precise route and instructing officers to arrange accommodation and ensure that 'the soldiers satisfy their landlords for what shall be due unto them, and behave themselves orderly in their march'.

The orders left little to a commander's discretion. A typical march of four companies of Monmouth's Foot from near Brentford in Middlesex to Hull in 1678, a distance of 128 miles [205 km], envisaged an average journey of only 8 miles [13 km] a day, with 6d [2½p] a day per company for a cart to carry baggage, and the men allowed to rest one day in every four. The maximum distance covered was 15 miles [24 km], less than King Harold's forces, no doubt less heavily burdened, had achieved in 1066.*

Transfers between coastal stations, as from Berwick to Plymouth, were easier, as it had been found that an infantry company could be fitted conveniently into one of the recently introduced frigates.

The chief means by which army headquarters, already based in Whitehall, controlled its scattered empire was through the musters held six or seven times a year, where – as in the militia – the actual strength of every unit was checked and weapons and uniforms inspected. In between musters, with no real postal system in existence, orders reached the regiments, and returns reached Whitehall, via an 'orderly man' kept for the purpose at the Chequer Inn at Charing Cross, no doubt a much-sought-after posting.

The regiments were free to make their own arrangements over food, uniform and training, only matters concerning pay, movements and quarters being centralised. Already, however, each regiment had an adjutant, who handled the paperwork for his commanding officer, a name and idea borrowed, like the whole pattern of organisation, from France, and its quartermaster, who dealt with accommodation and food supply. He often acted also as provost-marshal, who enforced discipline, and every regiment also had its own chaplain and surgeon and a civilian regimental clerk or agent.

The Life Guards and the Royal Horse Guards were the elite units, protected by helmet and back and breast plates, and armed with short-barrelled flintlocks which could be fired from horseback. Other horsed regiments fought with sword and horse-pistols, 14 in [36 cm] long, apart from the humbler dragoons who carried muskets with their pistols. All the foot regiments still included pikemen but two out of three infantrymen now carried muskets. These were increasingly flintlocks, lighter, more reliable and with a more rapid rate of fire than the

* See *Defending the Island*, p. 155.

old matchlocks. The first to be so equipped was the Admiral's Regiment, conditions at sea being particularly unsuitable for matchlocks, but by 1678 the flintlock, or fusil – hence the name 'Fusiliers' for regiments armed solely with it – was coming into general use, though the matchlock survived for another two decades.

The time taken to load a matchlock often forced its owner to use it in close combat as a club and in one anti-Puritan operation in Southwark in 1670 the Coldstream Guards broke no fewer than 67 muskets in this way, as well as 27 pikes. The prescribed weapon for a musketeer in such situations was the bayonet, a double-edged blade on a short wooden shaft, which fitted into the muzzle of his firearm, thus converting it into a form of pike. These first bayonets prevented the weapon being fired, but in 1678 Charles rewarded two Englishmen for inventing the socket bayonet, which enabled it to be attached to a housing outside the barrel, though it was to be some time before the new weapon came into general use.

The other great change which affected the Foot was the addition to its armoury of the hand grenade, defined by one military historian as 'simply a small shell of from 1 to 2 inches [2.5-5 cm] in diameter, kindled by a fuse and thrown by hand'. On its first introduction in 1678 it was entrusted to the tallest men who could hurl it furthest, and they later formed a separate regiment distinguished by their height, the Grenadier Guards. During Charles II's reign no separate corps of field artillery existed, the field-guns being distributed among the battalions of infantry, while the heavy guns in forts were still the exclusive province of specialist gunners who had since late-medieval times enjoyed an almost civilian status. The gunners in each garrison were trained by the Master Gunner of England and selected from a small, elite pool. They received written instructions from the Board of Ordnance and were not subject to the orders of the officers commanding the army garrison. The Board of Ordnance was also responsible for supplying and keeping in repair all the hand weapons used by the rest of the army, and in 1685 it took over responsibility for the provision of field equipment, bedding, and picks and shovels from the quaintly named Office of Tents and Toils in Clerkenwell.

Communications on the battlefield had changed little for centuries. Orders were still conveyed by a drummer. The hautbois, a predecessor of the oboe, fashionable at Louis XIV's court, also enjoyed a vogue in British regiments, its shrill notes being supposed to cut through the noise of combat, while the Royal Scots in 1662 added a new terror to the battlefield by introducing a regimental bagpiper.

6

MISCHIEF IN THE MEDWAY

On the 28th I went to Chatham and thence to view . . . what mischief the Dutch had done.

> *John Evelyn, Diary, June 1667*

Cromwell had bequeathed to his successors a splendid fleet, well built and efficiently maintained, which the new sovereign ordered should be called the Royal Navy, in recognition of its special role in his restoration. Charles II had inherited 154 ships, most of them small: the total tonnage was only 57,463. Of these, 20 or 30 were prizes built by the Dutch, French or Spanish, almost all the rest having started life in the yards at Chatham and Woolwich supervised by the Pett family. He had always been fond of the sea and now appointed his brother, James, Duke of York, Lord High Admiral, assisted by a Navy Board of three, and later four, commissioners. One of them was the shipbuilder, Peter Pett. An official known as the Clerk of the Acts acted as the Board's secretary, and frequently as its chief executive. This was the post held by Samuel Pepys, relative and protégé of the newly created Earl of Sandwich. Pepys, now aged 27, was a good-natured, cultivated man, educated at St Paul's and Cambridge, and though he owed his appointment to nepotism he proved a dedicated public servant and is a uniquely valuable witness for the nine years, from 1660 to 1669, covered by his frank and highly readable diary.

The international situation faced by Charles II was little different from that which had confronted Cromwell. Faced by the same choice, between friendship with France or with Spain, Charles had opted for the former, though peace with Spain was formally proclaimed on 10 September 1660. Charles vastly admired Louis XIV, the famous 'sun king', and in 1661 married his sister Henriette to Louis's only brother, Philippe, Duke of Orleans, while in May 1662 Charles himself married the King of Portugal's daughter, Catherine of Braganza; he had given his negotiators a simple brief: 'I hate Germans or princesses of cold countries.' The real and continuing danger lay, however, from Holland. Pepys observed, in 1664, that most of the court, including the Duke of York, were 'mad for a Dutch war'. The City shared this view.

46

'The trade of the world is too small for us, therefore one must go down,' a Baltic merchant friend told Pepys that February.

On 22 February 1665 England declared war on Holland, and a contemporary ballad declared:

Dutchmen, beware, we have a fleet
Will make you tremble when you see't.

All told the navy now consisted of around 160 warships, mounting 500 guns and manned by 25,000 seamen. The Dutch could muster about 135 ships, mainly smaller and less well armed; only four carried more than 70 guns, half the number on the English side.

The war started promisingly. The Battle of Lowestoft, which began at 3 am on a perfect summer's day, 3 June 1665, about 40 miles [64 km] south-east of that port, saw the Dutch, unnerved by the blowing up of one of their ships, by 7 pm in full retreat, with the loss of at least 30 ships and perhaps 5000 men, against two English ships and 700 casualties.*

The Dutch, noted a jubilant sailor on board the *Monck*, 'began to turn their arses and run'. 'A greater victory was never known in this world,' rejoiced Pepys in his diary on 8 June but after Lowestoft little went right for the English. 'The Dutch War,' recorded Pepys gloomily on 31 December, 'goes on very ill, by reason of lack of money.' The new year brought more bad news. 'Yesterday,' wrote Pepys on 11 February 1666, 'came out the king's declaration of war against the French.'

After he had had a narrow escape in the Battle of Lowestoft, Charles forbade his brother, the Duke of York, to risk his life in action again and it was therefore Prince Rupert and the Duke of Albemarle who challenged the Dutch in the famous but bloody Four Days' Battle, which began on Friday 1 June 1666 18 miles [29 km] off the North Foreland and only ended on Monday the 4th after the contending fleets had reached Dunkirk. The final reckoning was uncertain but it was unquestionably a Dutch victory; they had lost from four to seven ships and 2000 men killed or wounded, the English about 20 ships and four times as many casualties, including two admirals dead and one captured.

After a battle in the Thames estuary on 25/26 July 1666, known as the St James's Day Fight or Orfordness, the English decided to carry the war to the enemy coast and on 8 August 1666 a small English squadron under Sir Robert Holmes destroyed two enemy warships and a vast fleet of Dutch merchantmen, variously estimated at 114 to 150 strong, sheltering behind the island of Terschelling, inflicting a million

* The secondary sources are even more contradictory than usual about the losses. See Ogg, p. 288, Boxer, p. 25 and Sanderson, p. 113 (whom I have mainly followed), for the various estimates.

pounds' worth of damage. The following day a landing party burned stores on the island itself and also destroyed a small, undefended, town. 'Holmes's Bonfire', achieved at the cost of a mere dozen English casualties, infuriated the Dutch, who professed to see in the Great Fire of London in the following month divine retribution on a gigantic scale. The Great Fire also, a little unfairly, increased discontent with the government in England. 'The people curse the king,' wrote one London woman at this time, 'wish for Cromwell and say "Come Dutch, come devil, they cannot be worse".' Charles himself, currently besotted (though by no means exclusively) by the most famous of his many mistresses, also came in for much whispered criticism. 'People say,' observed the woman just quoted, ' "Give the king the Countess of Castlemaine and he cares not what the nation suffers".'

More serious was the weakening of strength of the navy, and a decline in its morale, thanks to the old, tragic policy of under-funding. Pepys noted in his diary on 23 September 1666 that the Dutch war had cost in the past two years £3,200,000 of which 'above £900,000' was still owing. In the summer of 1665 there was a mass walk-out of rope-makers while in Portsmouth dockyard workers unable to pay their landlords were being turned out in the street. The worst treated of all were the sailors themselves. Ships were kept in commission because there was no cash available to pay off the crews, and from May 1665, when they did come ashore, they were either refused payment altogether and forced to join another ship to survive, or paid in the long-discredited 'tickets', redeemable only at the Navy Office in London. Inevitably the press-gang provided the only way to keep the navy manned. The ale-house was the traditional place for its raids, but churches were not immune and after the Four Days' Battle of June 1666 an eye-witness observed that many sailors swimming for their lives were dressed in their black Sunday best, which they had been wearing when seized.

Because of the damage inflicted on their trade the Dutch were eager to end the war but Johan de Witt [or De Witt], the 'Grand Pensionary', or chief minister, believed, in the words of a contemporary, 'the fleet . . . to be the best plenipotentiary for peace'. Back in June 1666 an attack on 'London's river' had been planned, but the idea had been discarded as too dangerous. Now, however, boldness was at a premium. De Witt, unlike his English counterparts, secured an adequate increase in taxation to finance the fitting out of a strong fleet, containing in this case 72 men-of-war, 12 frigates, 24 fireships and various ancillary craft, and a search began for English deserters and for Cromwellian refugees who knew the waters of the Thames.

The scale of the activity in the Dutch ports which began as soon as the winter's ice had cleared could not be concealed, as on 8 March 1667 an English observer at Rotterdam warned the government in London:

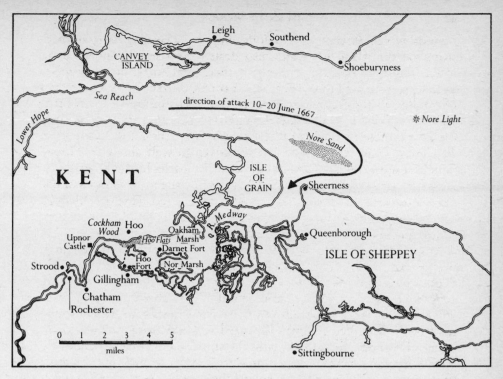

The Dutch in the Medway

The Estates preparations for warr goes [sic] on with might and maine and noe tyme is neglected in equiping the shipps, noe not soe much as Sunday, in soe much that the fflett will be out very tymely in the hand.

During April 1667 a small force of 20 Dutch ships had been sent to raid the Firth of Forth. It did little damage but achieved its main aim, to divert attention from the preparations now reaching their climax near the island of Texel and around Den Helder, at the tip of the adjoining promontory, which forms the western side of the then Zuider Zee, now the Ijsselmeer. Some 3-4000 soldiers had been assembled to go on board, along with a force of 'sea-soldiers', under the command of a colonel, Thomas Dolman, who had fought for the Commonwealth. One member of the English delegation at Breda wrote on 31 May 1667 to the secretary of Lord Arlington,* a leading member of the government, 'Certain it is they [the Dutch] have great business in hand, and I presume will very shortly attempt to execute it.'

Another correspondent from Amsterdam, a Frenchman who had bumped into two renegade Englishmen 'much in drink' on their way to join de Ruyter, described how they had boasted that the Dutch were

---

* Arlington was one of the five men known as the CABAL, from the initial letters of their surnames.

still seeking revenge for 'ye burning . . . of . . . ye houses in ye Schelling', i.e. 'Holmes's Bonfire', and that 'to their knowledge it was no hard matter to enter into severall English ports and burn and destroy all ye ships there in sight of either blockhouses or forts'.

All this intelligence was disregarded. On 1 June 1667 the Dutch fleet sailed south to Schooneveld, off the mouth of the Western Scheldt, to embark more troops, and from there on Tuesday 4 June 1667, a year to the day after the Four Days' Battle, Admiral Michiel de Ruyter, accompanied by Johan de Witt and his brother Cornelis de Witt, political representative with the fleet of the States-General, set course for England. That the Medway was a likely target for a Dutch attack was well understood, as the entry in Pepys's diary for 23 March confirms:

> At the office, where Sir W. Pen [Admiral Sir William Penn, one of the Navy Commissioners] come, being returned from Chatham, from considering the means of fortifying the River Medway, by a chain at the stakes, and ships laid there with guns to keep the enemy from coming up to burn our ships; all our care now being to fortify ourself against their invading us.

As so often in the past the weather now seemed likely to aid the English. When on the night of 5 June de Ruyter's fleet approached the North Foreland, at the most easterly tip of Kent, it was dispersed by a gale. No English ships were on hand, indeed there were none worthy the name in commission. 'The Dutch . . . have sent their fleet to sea,' the Secretary of State, Lord Arlington, confessed in a letter that day to the English ambassador in Lisbon, 'we having no strength to look them in the face.' This melancholy judgement was soon confirmed. On Friday 7 June the messenger bringing the Dutch terms for peace arrived at Dover from Breda and, as if on cue, at eight o'clock that evening the Dutch fleet, its order restored, anchored in the King's Channel, one of the main approaches to the Thames.

In London it was not a happy weekend. That Saturday morning the court and Admiralty learned of the arrival of the Dutch off the east coast, as Samuel Pepys records:

> Up and to the office, where all the news this morning is that the Dutch are come with a fleet of 80 sail to Harwich . . . After dinner to the office again, where busy till night. The news is confirmed that the Dutch are off Harwich . . . The king hath sent down my Lord of Oxford [Aubrey de Vere, Earl of Oxford, Lord Lieutenant of Essex] to raise the county and all the western barges are taken up to make a bridge . . . about the Hope, for horse to cross the river, if there be occasion.

The Hope was the stretch of water where the Thames makes a left turn below Gravesend Reach before turning due east past Canvey Island,

and on 9 June a squadron of Dutch ships, led by Admiral Willem van Ghent, put a landing party ashore on the island. Some barns and houses were burned down, some sheep killed to provide fresh meat, and then the militia appeared and the intruders withdrew to their boats.

In command of the English ships at Sheerness and in the Medway was a formidable, fighting Irishman, Sir Edward Spragge. In June 1667 the forces at his disposal were meagre, consisting mainly of fireships and ketches. He did possess one frigate, the *Unity*, stationed off Sheerness, and one large man-of-war, the *Monmouth*, but decided that these were too weak to challenge the Dutch on their own and therefore concentrated on getting the *Monmouth*, a likely prize, out of harm's way, ordering her to move up-river to a safer spot above the chain at Gillingham, after which 100 of her crew were to be sent down to Sheerness to oppose a possible landing. He also asked the Lord Lieutenant of Kent to send him the nearest regular troops, a Scottish regiment – later the Royal Scots – stationed at Margate, for the same purpose. Peter Pett, in charge at Chatham, was warned to keep two fully-manned guardships moored by the chain to deter any attack on it.

A whole series of mishaps, never satisfactorily explained, now occurred. The Scots at Margate, having been embarked on the night of Sunday 9 June, were then ordered ashore again, only a single company being sent to Sheerness, while the two ships bringing the men from the *Monmouth* both ran aground in the early hours of Monday morning, perhaps by intention, for all but 44 of the men on board promptly disappeared into the darkness.

Samuel Pepys's opposite number at Chatham, the 'Clerk of the Cheque', Edward Gregory, now deserted his desk to man a gun near Sheerness and witnessed the dramatic moment as the enemy fleet rounded the Nore Sand and turned towards the still unfinished fort:

> Being gott about the East End of the Nore, his headmost ships stood with us, and ahead of them a galliot hoy, sounding as we suppose, who came no sooner within shott of us, then wee obleidged him to a speady retreat, nor did the foremost man of war, though a great ship, care much for approaching us, after wee had placed a shott or two in him; thus wee began with them much about 5 in the evening, when their admirall now having gott the length of the Buoy, hove out his bloody flag att the topmast head, when immediately a ship of theirs . . . came boguing [bearing down] upon us and att her stern a fireship.

In spite of their warm reception the Dutch pressed on undeterred and as the rising tide enabled them to bring their guns into action against Sheerness the fort had to be abandoned, Gregory and his fellow gunners being rescued by the fast royal yacht the *Henrietta*. Their adventures lost nothing in the telling and during Sunday night alarming reports of the Dutch presence off Kent reached London. Monday morning, 10 June 1667, provided the start of one of the most eventful, rumour-ridden weeks the capital had ever witnessed. Samuel Pepys was in the thick of the excitement:

> News brought us that the Dutch are come up as high as the Nore; and more pressing orders for fire-ships. W. Batten, W. Pen and I to St James; where the Duke of York gone this morning betimes, to send away some men down to Chatham. So we three to Whitehall and met Sir W. Coventry, who presses all that is possible for fire-ships; so we three to the office presently; and thither comes Sir Fr. Hollis [i.e. Sir Frescheville Holles] who is to command them all in some exploits he is to do with them on the enemy in the river. So we all down to Deptford and pitch upon ships and set men at work; but Lord, to see how backwardly things move at this pinch, notwithstanding . . . the enemy's being now come up as high almost as the Hope.

Pepys was not impressed by Sir Frescheville Holles, any more than by the other fire-eating gallants who now, somewhat late in the day, appeared from all sides:

> Down to Gravesend, where I find the Duke of Albemarle just come, with a great many idle lords and gentlemen, with their pistols and fooleries; and the bulworke not able to have stood half an hour had they [i.e. the enemy] come up; but the Dutch are fallen down from the Hope and Sheel-haven as low as the Sheerness, and we do plainly at this time hear the guns play.

Unrecorded by Pepys, further developments had taken place that day almost within sight of him. The frantic waving of some of the residents of the Isle of Grain, between the Medway and the Thames, had revealed a Dutch landing there and around 5 pm that afternoon the attack on the Medway began in earnest as van Ghent's squadron sailed briskly on an incoming tide round Garrison Point towards Sheerness. The frigate *Unity* managed to get off one broadside before hastily retreating up the Medway, with her attendant fireships and ketches. All now depended on Sheerness Fort, which was still unfinished, and the recoil from the very first round fired by the 16 guns mounted in it wrecked their carriages. Seven were then brought back into action by wedging planks beneath the carriages, but that proved ineffective and the fortifications failed to protect the gun crews. After one man had been killed and another had had a leg and thigh shot off a rumour spread that no medical assistance was available and the morale of most of the rest, as often happened to unblooded troops in action for the first time, gave way. All but seven men abandoned their posts, one of this resolute remnant being the civilian Navy Board official who later sent Pepys an account of the affair. They could not hold the fort on their own, however, and, when they heard that a large force of Dutch troops had landed only a mile away, were forced to withdraw.

With the fort lost, the Isle of Sheppey, and its principal town, Queenborough, lay at the mercy of the Dutch, who were, according to the biographer of Admiral de Ruyter, sorely tempted to take revenge for 'Holmes's Bonfire' in the previous year. However they forbore, since 'they wished to act with greater generosity', leaving 'to barbarous nations this cruel way of waging war and visiting the sins of the guilty upon innocent people'.

An Amsterdam broadsheet, later that year, asserted that Queenborough was left untouched after the inhabitants had offered the Dutch 'a considerable sum' of money to leave it alone, though the borough archives contain no record of any such payment; a local historian later asserted that the mayor of Queenborough flew a white flag from the town hall, an event, if it did occur, unique in British history. It seems clear, at all events, that the invaders behaved with great restraint. The English and Scots troops later sent to re-occupy the island, ravaged through the empty houses far more destructively than the Dutch had done.

After Sheppey it was the turn of Sheerness town, which was bombarded by Dutch warships until 9 pm and then captured without resistance and, what was worse, with no attempt being made to destroy its valuable naval stores, as Cornelis de Witt reported that evening in a letter to the States-General, written, as he observed, 'From the *Agatha*, lying at the angle of the river of Chatham, before Sheerness Fort'.

> Our people found there an entire royal magazine, with very heavy anchors and cables and hundreds of masts. Our people took on board the ships as many of the cables, masts and round woods as they could, and they also acquired 15 heavy pieces shooting balls of 18 lbs [6.8 kg]. The rest was destroyed or rendered useless, and the magazine burnt. The damage done to the English at this island was estimated at more than four tons of gold.

In the early hours of Tuesday, 11 June 1667, the Duke of Albemarle had arrived in Chatham to take charge. According to his own, no doubt partial, report to the House of Commons, some time later, he discovered a state close to panic:

> I found scarce twelve of 800 men which were then in the king's pay, in his majesty's yards; and these so distracted with fear that I could have little or no service from them. I had heard of 30 boats, which were provided by the directions of His Royal Highness [ie the Duke of York]; but there were all, except five of six, taken away by those of the yards, who went themselves with them, and sent and took them away by the example of Commissioner Pett, who had the

chief command there, and sent away his own goods in some of them. I found no ammunition there but what was in the *Monmouth*, so that I presently sent to Gravesend for the [artillery] train to be sent to me.

The chief hope of keeping the Dutch out of the Medway rested on 'the chain', at Chatham, which already had, in 1667, a long history. In 1585, when war broke out with Spain, the first chain had been stretched across the river just below the newly erected Upnor Castle, but by 1667 it had been moved to between Hoo Ness and Gillingham. It was then about 350 yards [320 m] long, and Pepys, that June, 'caused the link to be measured and it was 6 inch and a quarter [16 cm] in circumference' so its weight must have been enormous. Pulleys at either end, housed in a crane-house, kept it taut, normally about 9 ft [2.7 m] below the surface, which meant that shallow-draught vessels, such as small fireships, might sail across it, and at 1 am on that frantically busy Tuesday, 11 June, Peter Pett had ordered a floating stage to be towed into position part-way across the river to enable the chain to be hoisted nearer the surface.

Later that night Albemarle presided over a meeting at Commissioner Pett's house at Chatham, at which, after a vigorous argument, Pett and the other dockyard officials were ordered 'at peril of their lives' to sink three further ships as near the chain as possible to provide a further obstacle should the Dutch manage to break it.

Tuesday had also been a day of preparation for the Dutch. Admiral van Ghent and his parliamentary 'minder' Cornelis de Witt had established their headquarters at Sheerness, from which a reconnaissance party was sent up the Medway. It returned with information about the rich prizes which lay moored between the chain in Gillingham Reach and Rochester Bridge, including at least 18 ships, among them the largest and newest in the Royal Navy, and two captured earlier from the Dutch. A small advance force was thereupon sent up the Medway to Mussel Bank, where they laboriously removed a blockship sunk earlier that day. By the time this was done the tide had ebbed, so, having cleared a passage for the main force, they anchored overnight.

At 6 am on Wednesday 12 June 1667 the Dutch squadron set sail from Sheerness under ideal conditions: an east-north-east wind and a flooding tide. The narrowness of the river, with shallows on either side, dictated their formation, in line astern, which meant that only a few ships at a time could bring their fire to bear on any single target, while the batteries on land could concentrate on any vessel within range.

The attacking fleet was soon spread out over perhaps 2 miles [3.2 km] of the River Medway, in a textbook formation: the advance guard frigates in front, followed by the small yachts, then the fireships and finally the main men-of-war, a total of some 20 warships. All were now held up by a single metal cable, until, as so often in naval battles, a single heroic incident transformed the situation. The former master of the 125-man, 40-gun *Vrede*, from Rotterdam, Jan van Brakel, was not merely in disgrace but under close arrest on board another vessel, the *Agatha*, for having, it was alleged, allowed his men to plunder the Isle of Sheppey two days before. Now he volunteered, if restored to his previous command, to draw the English fire while two fireships attempted to cross, or break, the chain. Cornelis de Witt, who, rather than Admiral van Ghent, seems to have been effectively in command, agreed and van Brakel skilfully sailed the *Vrede* from its position at the rear of the Dutch squadron, straight for the principal English ship left to protect the Gillingham end of the chain, the frigate *Unity*. With her 44 guns and 150 men she slightly outclassed the *Vrede* but many of the crew were Thames watermen pressed into service and they now seized their chance and abandoned ship, followed by as many of its regular complement as could get away. Sir Edward Spragge had prudently posted a boatswain from another ship in a longboat to prevent any deserters from the *Unity* getting ashore, but a longboat could not challenge a frigate and it now took refuge in a nearby creek. The resulting action of the *Unity* versus the *Vrede* hardly ranks as a glorious epic in the annals of the Royal Navy. For a total casualty list of five, including two dead, the *Vrede* captured the *Unity*, leaving the chain at the mercy of the Dutch. The first fireship in van Brakel's little task force, the *Susanna*, now charged it, without success, but the second, the *Pro Patria*, broke through and laid herself alongside the nearest English ship, the *Matthias*, moored on the Gillingham, i.e. Kent, side of the river and set her on fire, until she blew up with a loud explosion. It was unquestionably first blood to the Dutch.

The action now shifted to the Essex shore, where the *Unity*'s sister-guardship, the *Charles V*, successfully sank another Dutch fireship, the *Delft*, before being herself set on fire. Most of the demoralised crew took to the boats or simply jumped overboard; the rest, as van Brakel led an assault in person, climbing over the bows sword in hand, could not surrender fast enough. The English flag was hauled down and the total haul of English prisoners, with those already taken on the *Unity*, was raised to 56.

The powerful *Monmouth* was now towed higher up the river and after grounding, embarrassingly, while trying to negotiate the tricky bend into Upnor Road, was finally got into apparent safety in Chatham dockyard. The pride of the navy, however, the *Royal Charles*, still lay near the chain but only half rigged and the men ordered by Spragge 'on pain of death' to go aboard her simply disappeared as the Dutch approached. The *Royal Charles*, once the Cromwellian *Naseby*, which had brought Charles II back from exile and, with his brother aboard, had sunk the Dutch flagship at the Battle of

Lowestoft, was now to be captured without a shot being fired, as Pepys recorded ten days later, from an account by an eye-witness:

> The Dutch did take her with a boat of nine men, who found not a man on board her . . . and presently a man went up and struck her flag and jacke, and a trumpeter sounded upon her 'Joan's placket [ie petticoat] is torn'.

This tune, the words of which are now lost, was regularly played as a gesture of derision towards a beaten enemy,[*] and the sound of these mocking notes echoing across the waters of the Medway amid the swirling smoke through the roar of cannon and crackle of flames made a lasting impression upon contemporaries, underlining the extent of the nation's humiliation.

Further up the river was the *Sancta Maria*, a modern 70-gun ship previously captured from the Dutch which had run aground earlier that day and been abandoned. The Dutch now boarded the deserted vessel and, deciding it could not readily be re-floated, set it on fire. Their final success of the day came on land. So ferociously did they bombard the two batteries Albemarle had built to guard the ends of the now useless chain that the garrisons fled in panic and the remaining ships of van Ghent's squadron sailed past to anchor in Gillingham Reach. Van Ghent and Cornelis de Witt went aboard the chief prize to discuss their next move and from there de Witt sent his report to the States-General, with a new, and even prouder, dateline: 'In the *Royal Charles*, the 22 June [12 June, Old Style] 1667, about two in the afternoon, lying in the River of Chatham':

> Six of their ships, distributed in good order, lay before the chain. At the one end lay four, and at the other end two stout frigates which crossed the water. This notwithstanding, the Dutch, with more than mortal boldness, made an attack against all these dangers. Our people took the ship *Royal Charles*, fitted to bear 100 pieces of cannon and with 32 guns on board. Nothing more costly has been made in England . . . They also took the *Charles V*, which with two others of the largest ships, the *Matthias* and *Castle of Honingen* [ie the formerly Dutch *Sancta Maria*], are burnt. The chain was burst in pieces, and all within it destroyed or annihilated.

The position on Wednesday afternoon, 12 June 1667, as the light began to fade and the tide to ebb, was that the Dutch had captured three large vessels and burned two others for no significant loss. A mere mile [1.6 km] further up the Medway lay another broad stretch of navigable water, leading up to Rochester bridge. A mile or so above the bridge

[*] An even subtler insult may have been intended; 'placket' was sometimes a euphemism for 'virginity', though the *Oxford English Dictionary* does not acknowledge this usage.

the Medway rapidly narrowed, so that no further Dutch penetration, except by small boat, and, more important for the moment, no further retreat by the larger English vessels, was possible. In Chatham Reach, which stretched a mile and a quarter [2 kms] upstream from the town of Chatham, were moored the last of the navy's great ships, the *Loyal London*, the *Royal Oak* and the *Royal James*. Along its shores lay the navy's most important dockyard, with its stores, cranes and construction rigs. Despairingly, but no doubt correctly, Albemarle decided he could do little to save the ships, which were run aground in shallow water, and holes cut in the hulls to make it impossible for the Dutch to sail or tow them away. Almost all the smaller, less valuable ships were also run aground, but 16 were left to drift and three were scuttled, the *Katherine* below the New Dockyard, the *St George* opposite the ropeyard, and the *Victory* facing St Mary's Church, thereby obstructing the fairway in Dockyard Reach.

During Wednesday, unable to influence what was happening at the chain, Albemarle had concentrated on strengthening the defences of the dockyard. Boat-loads of stores and a company of soldiers were sent to Upnor and three new batteries were hastily constructed, one to cover the Old Dockyard against attack from the river, the other two to protect the New Dockyard, which lay a little below it. The 'train' of ten heavy guns from the Tower of London were mounted in a field in the New Dockyard and another 50, many removed from ships lying between the dockyard and Rochester bridge, were assembled to help cover the river. He had done well to get so much done, for the dockyard labour force was as disaffected as the seamen and, as he admitted to Parliament later, 'having no money to pay them, all I could do or say was little enough for their encouragement.'

In London it had been a strange day, with optimism giving way to gloom and gloom to panic. By evening the truth was known, as Pepys's diary for 12 June 1667 admirably records:

> And so home, where all our hearts do now ake; for the news is true, that the Dutch have broke the chain and burned our ships, and perticulerly the *Royall Charles* . . . And the truth is, I do fear so much that the whole kingdom is undone, that I do this night resolve to study with my father and wife what to do with the little that I have in money by me . . . So God help us, and God knows what disorders we may fall into . . . To bed with a heavy heart . . . full of fear and fright.

Albemarle, as described earlier, had done what he could during that dismal Wednesday to preserve the navy's remaining major ships by semi-scuttling them. Between them and the Dutch lay Upnor Castle, built specifically to resist just such an attack as now threatened it. Upnor had been erected between 1559 and 1567; before Elizabeth's time this stretch of the Medway had not been considered important enough to merit its own fixed defences. It had been kept in a reasonable state over the years, even though it had seen no action even during the Civil War, and the last major repairs had been completed as recently as 1653. It was, from its first conception, planned to command the river, with heavy guns mounted both on the projecting, angled bastion, which reached almost to the water's edge, and on the main building erected behind it. Although never one of the great fortresses of the kingdom it was a substantial, well-planned work, built almost entirely of stone, and now its hour had come.

Thursday morning, 13 June, dawned with not merely a Protestant but a positively Calvinist wind blowing from the north-east. By mid-day, when the tide was at last favourable, the wind had dropped a little, so it was two o'clock before the leading ships approached, to be greeted by a fierce bombardment both from Upnor and from Sir Edward Spragge's battery on the Chatham bank. De Ruyter, declaring 'I am going to see what our people will do!', had himself rowed forward in a longboat, accompanied by Cornelis de Witt, an example rapidly followed by van Ghent and his fellow admirals, and, thus encouraged, the men of the fireships rapidly set their vessels burning and laid them alongside the upper-works – all that was visible above water – of the *Loyal London*, the *Royal Oak* and the *Royal James* until all three seemed to be burning briskly. The men left aboard the English ships to protect them all fled, apart from one Scots officer on board the *Royal Oak* who died at his post, a distinctly unfashionable exercise that June. No one else followed this heroic lead but the Dutch encountered much more vigorous resistance than during their previous attacks, leaving them with 50 dead and an unrecorded number of wounded. This opposition, and the fact that they had used up all their fireships, deterred the Dutch commanders from venturing further up the river to attack the ships moored below Rochester Bridge, as Cornelis de Witt explained in his report that night to the States-General from 'The ship *Agatha*, lying at anchor in the river of Chatham, before the village of Gillingham, the 23 June [13 June old style] 1667.'

The Dutch were still masters of the Medway, but had already decided it would be foolhardy to venture any further and during the afternoon of Friday 14 June 1667 began to withdraw. The day's events were not yet, however, known in London, where a general expectation now existed of an attack up the Thames in force. During the weekend that followed, the full extent of the disgrace the nation had suffered, and the danger to which it was still exposed, began to sink in. 'People are ready to tear the hair of their heads,' wrote one Londoner on Saturday the 15th. 'We are betrayed, let it [i.e. the guilt] light where it will.' That weekend the government had issued its own version of recent events in the *London Gazette* of 16 June, which showed that in presenting damning facts in the most favourable light Charles's ministers were unsurpassed. The Dutch had, on the Wednesday, it claimed, only broken through the chain in Gillingham Reach after 'a stout resistance in which our men showed infinite courage, with considerable loss to the enemy', while the action on the Thursday now appeared to have been almost an English victory:

> They advanced with six men-of-war and five fireships . . . up towards Upnor Castle, but were so warmly entertained by Major Scot, who commanded there, and on the other side by Sir Edward Spragge, from the battery at the shoare, that after very much dammage received by them in the shattering of their ships, in sinking severall of their long boats manned out by them, in the great number of their men killed and some prisoners taken, they were at the last forced to retire, having in this attempt spent in vain two of their fireships . . . the *Royall James* and the *Loyall London*, . . . are much injured by the fire, but in probability may again be made serviceable, having been sunk before their [i.e. the Dutch] coming up.

What was really needed was a scapegoat. On Monday 17 June Peter Pett was arrested in Chatham, much to Pepys's alarm. Pepys was present at the critical enquiry into the disaster two days later, on Wednesday, 19 June 1667. That day, 19 June, the Dutch again demonstrated their control of English waters by landing for a second time on the Isle of Sheppey to round up sheep and other livestock. For hours they roamed across the fields totally unchallenged but fortunately for the local residents unofficial looting was forbidden and discipline was strict; some soldiers and sailors who had defied the order were dropped into the sea three times from the main-yard and also received 150 lashes apiece.

De Ruyter's ships now moved on up the east coast. 'This day,' Pepys recorded on Friday 21 June 1667, 'comes news from Harwich that the Dutch fleet are all in sight, near a hundred sail, great and small they think, coming towards them.' A week later Pepys's friend and fellow diarist, John Evelyn, travelled across the river from Deptford to Kent, to inspect the scene of the recent attack:

> On the 28 I went to Chatham, and thence to view not onely what mischiefe the Dutch had don, but how triumphantly their whole fleete lay within the very mouth of the Thames, all from Northforeland, Mergate, even to the buoy of the Noore, a dreadfull spectacle as ever any English men saw, and a dishonour never to be wiped off.

7

GREAT GUNS IN SUFFOLK

*I find all the news is the enemy's landing near Harwich and attacquing
Langnerfort and being beat off thence with our great guns.*

Samuel Pepys, Diary, *3 July 1667*

While King Charles's ministers were engaging in a face-saving witch-hunt and belatedly trying to make good years of neglect, the Dutch were justly cock-a-hoop. On Sunday 16 June the fleet had celebrated its recent victory with a service of thanksgiving, and the arrival of the richest prize, the *Royal George*, in Holland was the signal for public rejoicings there, with bells and firework displays. On Tuesday 25 June, while Samuel Pepys in London was lamenting the difficulty of getting an English fleet together, instructions reached Cornelis de Witt, with the victorious Dutch squadron at the mouth of the Thames estuary, that the success already gained should be followed up. While leaving the final decision to him, the States-General suggested that Harwich might be their next objective, followed by a sortie up the Thames itself, to Gravesend or even higher, to keep the English government in a state of alarm. Portsmouth, the Isle of Wight and Plymouth were all mentioned in letters to Cornelis de Witt but eventually opinion among the commanders on the spot hardened in favour of an attack on Landguard Fort, covering the entrance to the River Orwell, which marked the border between Suffolk and Essex. Behind Landguard lay the port of Harwich and a landing here was calculated to cause the same consternation along the east coast as the operations in the Medway had produced in Kent and the Thames estuary.

Landguard, on an exposed promontory two miles [3.2 km] from the nearest place of any size, Felixstowe, further up the Suffolk coast, had always been recognised as a vital but vulnerable point in the nation's defences. A *Survey of the Coast of Suffolk*, dated 13 December 1587, set out very plainly the reason why it might prove so attractive to an invader:

Langer Poynt we fynde to be a place of as great danger as any we have in this cowntie, so apt for the enemy to land at, as withowte helpe or use of boate, they may leape on land owte of their shippes. Beynge landed, the place serveth verye stronglie for the enemy to encampe him selfe, having there . . . space of playne and drye grownde. Two parrtes wherof ys defended by the sea and the other parte, by the coming in of the water at everye floode, ys alsoe devyded from the maine lande.

In June 1624 the Council of War had decided to build a new fort at Landguard and by 1627 it had a total of 62 guns of varying calibre, the largest a massive brass basilisk weighing four tons which could fire a shot weighing 60 lbs [27 kg]. The new fort was also intended to serve as a rallying point for the local militia.

The importance of the site was recognised during the Civil War, when it was held for Parliament, which kept it in much better order than the king had ever done. The ruling committee of Both Kingdoms described it in 1645 as 'that place of soe great concernment', an apt description, confirmed two years later by a report from the Surveyor General:

Landguard Fort (commanding the harbour at Harwich, accounted the most considerable haven to the northward) is raised to a point of land, shooting out from the mainland about a mile; the main sea not being above 20 or 30 yards [18-27 m] from the foot of the fort at low water, and not above 12 yards [11 m] at high water.

The chief danger to Landguard was always more from the elements than from armed attack. The sea was forever filling up the moat with shingle, or battering down its external bank, and even menacing the foundations of the walls themselves, while the damp sea breezes caused the drawbridge at the entrance on the landward side to rot and attacked the wooden platforms. Landguard had been well maintained during the Civil War but after the Restoration conditions deteriorated and on 20 May 1664 the Duke of Albemarle presented to the king 'a memorial for the better fortifying of Landguard Fort', which was followed in November by the approval of a new, and larger, establishment, consisting of two officers, five sergeants and corporals, four gunners or matrosses [i.e. assistant gunners] and some 90 rank-and-file soldiers, at a total cost of £1537 a year.

With the outbreak of war with Holland, early in 1665, and with France, in January 1666, the crucial importance of Landguard was recognised, two companies of 300 men and a troop of horse being sent there from Sudbury. Landguard protected the Gunfleet, the expanse of water about two miles [3.2 km] wide and 11 [17 km] long, stretching from the Naze, the promontory just north of Walton, almost to Bawdsey, beyond Felixstowe. Sheltered on the seaward side by a sandbank, the Gunfleet provided a natural anchorage of which the Dutch made frequent use, usually getting away unscathed. Early in July, however, after a fleet of 100 ships had installed itself there, the foraging party they sent ashore got more than it had bargained for, as a letter from Ipswich, dated 5 July 1666, made clear:

> 30 of de Ruyter's men in his boat landed on the marshes about Bard-sey [ie Bawdsey] for fresh meat for their general, but boat and men were all taken, as was some wine going to him.

Landguard was still in 1667 basically the same fort as had been completed 40 years earlier. By a nice irony it was probably designed by a Dutchman, Simon von Cranvelt, who was influenced by the then fashionable Italian school of military architects, as the pointed block-houses placed at the corners of the 500-ft [150-m] long sides suggest. A description exists, written in 1676:

> Landguard-Fort . . . was a handsome square fortification consisting of four bastions, viz at each corner one mounted with divers guns, those toward the sea being the largest; the entrance into it was over a draw-bridge, thro' a gate over which was their magazine; fronting the gate was a handsome brick building, in which the governor, when he was there, resided adjoining the south end of which was a neat chapel, in which the chaplain read prayers twice a week.

Landguard was armed in July 1667 with 59 pieces of ordnance: 18 culverins, 23 demi culverins, nine sakers, four minions and five three-pounders. The greatest danger to it, as with all coastal forts, probably lay in an attack from the land and large numbers of troops were stationed in the area. Their precise disposition is not recorded, but in the previous April, in addition to two companies of regulars at Landguard itself, four companies of the Lord High Admiral's Regiment were on call in Harwich and the Suffolk trained bands, under the Earl of Suffolk, camped on high ground near Walton to cover the low ground near the fort. The Earl of Oxford was in command of a force of cavalry, their role being to prevent an enemy landing on the Suffolk side of Orwell haven, if his ships should successfully get past Landguard.

Defence headquarters for the district had been established at Harwich around 13 June 'as the properest place to receive news and intelligence', and on 18 June a report arrived from Chelmsford, in mid-Essex, of three squadrons of ships observed from the steeple of Southminster church, 16 miles [26 km] nearer the coast, midway between the Crouch and the Blackwater estuaries, while from Aldeburgh, nearly 60 miles [96 km] away, on the Suffolk coast, people were already carrying their goods inland. Early next morning it was the turn of Lowestoft, 25 miles [40 km] due north, to sight the Dutch but they then turned back to anchor in the Gunfleet. On 21 June 1667 South-wold, between Aldeburgh and Lowestoft, reported 40 enemy ships in

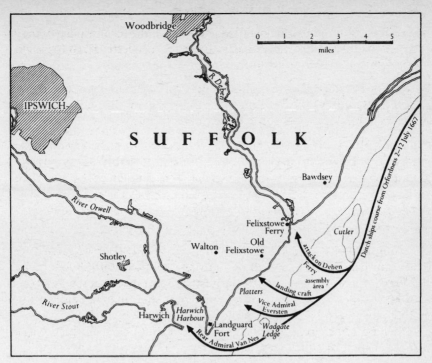

The Dutch in Suffolk

sight, and almost simultaneously Yarmouth [i.e. Great Yarmouth] in Norfolk was 'in a great fright' from a similar spectacle. 'The ranting Dutch have given some alarm to the Suffolk coasts', wrote one man from Norwich on 24 June, with notable understatement, people now being frightened by 'everything which had canvas about it'.

Around sunset on Friday 28 June 1667 de Ruyter's fleet, then at anchor near Sheppey, was joined by five troop transports sent from Holland, with an experienced land commander, Colonel Count van Hoorn, eight companies of troops and new instructions from the States-General, which plainly set out their objective:

> An exceptional service would be done for the state and considerable damage done to the enemy if the army and landing forces could become masters of the fort near Harwich by a determined attack by the ships on one side and the army on the other and with God's blessing the place be taken possession of.

At 4 am the following, Saturday, morning a conference of senior officers, presided over by de Ruyter and de Witt, was held on board the former's flagship, *De Zeven Provincien*, which agreed the operation should go ahead. A meeting of army officers was held at noon. Next day, at 8 am, the whole fleet weighed anchor and moved briskly north-wards. By 6 pm they were safely anchored in the Gunfleet and away to the north-east, in the Sledway, part of the network of deep-water channels which linked Harwich with the open sea.

Vice Admiral Sir Joseph Jordan, who commanded a small force of minor ships based in Harwich harbour – the strongest was only a 'sixth-rate' – had already made two brave but abortive forays against the Dutch ships moored offshore on their previous visit a week before. He now, on Sunday 30 June, made another attempt but found the tide 'too far spent' to enable him to engage the enemy. It was a time of great tension in Harwich as more and more Dutch ships arrived, until by 10 pm no fewer than 70 were assembled in the Gunfleet, while word arrived from London that they were expected to attack at any minute. Relief was all the greater when, having set off northwards at dawn next morning, apparently making for Landguard and Harwich, against an adverse north-west wind and unfavourable tide, they failed to turn towards the shore and disappeared into the darkness beyond Orford-ness.

The Dutch were later suspected of that oldest of military ruses, a mock retreat, to throw the defenders off their guard, but had in fact intended to carry out the attack on Landguard on Monday 1 July 1667, postponing it only because the wind was against them. They now instead anchored that night off Aldeburgh before describing a great loop and turning back on themselves, the wind having now changed to a more favourable, though far from ideal, light north-easterly.

The landing area had been carefully chosen, being about midway along the four-mile [6-km] stretch of beach, with rough vegetation behind, stretching from Landguard Fort on the invader's left to the River Deben on his right. Both these flanks were therefore protected by water and the beach itself was gently sloping shingle, with, at low water, patches of sand and exposed rock. There was at this point a break of about 700 yards [640 m] in the high ground which made up Felixstowe Cliffs, the nearest cliff face being set back from the water's edge. Two tracks gave access to the beach, one leading to the township of Walton and the road to Ipswich, the other to the village of Felix-stowe itself. These represented the main source of danger to the attacking forces but would be commanded by fire from the light guns in the bows of the landing barges, and could be sealed off by the first men to get ashore.*

The London Gazette later referred to 'about 3000 men' being involved in the operation, and one Dutch estimate spoke of 3800, but the actual number was around 1650, still by far the largest-scale enemy landing in England since 1066. The forces involved fell into three categories: those protecting the assault party, the assault party itself and the seamen who would ferry both ashore but would then if necessary take

* The invasion site can still be identified, the two access roads now being known as Fox-grove (formerly Middleton) and Maybush (then Wynyard or Vineyard).

up arms. The main body of infantrymen numbered 842, 20 of them officers, under the command of the apostate Colonel Thomas Dolman and the recently arrived Count van Hoorn, and was divided into 18 platoons, each containing both musketeers and pikemen. The marine detachment, specialists in amphibious warfare, consisted of another 408 men, including 12 officers, armed with flintlocks, under Lieut.-Colonel François Palm. The assault boats, consisting largely of small light-draught sailing vessels known as galliots and barges, would operate in pairs, each pair carrying a platoon, involving a force of some 400 sailors. One galliot master would carry ashore the engineer who would direct the attack on Landguard, along with 'fascines [i.e. bundles of brushwood to fill in ditches], 100 large axes, 100 pickaxes, 100 choppers, two bundles of fuses, six butter boxes filled with powder' and 'the available grenades'. These consisted of hollow metal spheres, weighing 2 lb [0.9 kg], four of which each grenade-thrower carried in a canvas bag. The orders laid down that 'In each group of twelve' within the assault party, 'there should be four accomplished grenade-throwers and some of them should carry scaling ladders and others should be armed with heavy axes, which would be used, with lengths of rope, to pull down and destroy any palisades that might be found.' Serious casualties were clearly anticipated for another galliot was assigned to carry in seven 'surgeons and appropriate medical stores' to set up a dressing station on the beach, while fighting was recognised to be thirsty work, orders being given 'to send another galliot with beer'.

Tuesday 2 July 1667 was a fine day, perfect for a landing. A Dutch admiral noted in his journal, 'At 11 o'clock it fell flat calm and very hot,' while a Dutch infantry captain recorded the start of the operation:

About midday all the ships from which our men were to be disembarked put a jack [i.e. a small flag] on the bowsprit, that being the sign that all was ready; after that Admiral de Ruyter put up a red flag at the fore and . . . they all rowed for the shore.

The force was landed in a single wave and, in spite of the weeks of anxiety and preparation, the Dutch achieved complete tactical surprise. Not a shot was fired as the barge carrying the marines' commander, identified by a blue pennant at its stern, grounded on the Suffolk shingle and Lieut.-Colonel Palm leapt ashore, rapidly followed by platoons 'of 36 soldiers, each led by a captain, a lieutenant or ensign with two sergeants', which formed up in parade-ground order on the beach with 'a distance of 150 paces between them'. Count van Hoorn, his barge marked by a white pennant, arrived almost simultaneously, his men being formed up to the right of the marines, and by 2 pm the assault equipment had been distributed and the whole force was split into three battalions and, apart from those told off to seal off the two lanes leading to the beach, making for its objective.

The Dutch land attack, like the earlier disembarkation, was cautious rather than dashing. Anthony [later Sir Anthony] Deane, master-shipwright at Harwich and one of the government's principal sources of local information, provided the definitive English account:

> [The enemy landed] at the bottom of Fillstow Cliffte in a plaine wheare they drew themselves in a boddy with a good stand of pikes. When they weare in this order they did with a good company get up the hill and lined the hedges and made good the way to the south end of the hill and at the bottom kept a reserve of about 600 men.

A scouting party had probably been sent out along the cliff top directly after the landing and this now returned with several prisoners, possibly the men manning the beacon, which they had duly lit. They were taken before Colonel Dolman and ordered to tell the truth about 'the strength of the contrey' under threat of death, but when they did so, stating that Landguard was protected by 60 guns and 800–900 men, were abused as 'lying English rogues'; their interrogators preferred the Dutch intelligence estimate of 'but ten or twelve guns and 100 men'. With a detachment holding the high ground behind the assembly area the main danger to the invaders lay to the rear, where a ferry crossed the River Deben. Beyond it lay a strong force of English horse and the White battalion of the Suffolk foot militia who had been hurrying back from the Aldeburgh area after following the Dutch fleet up the coast. They were now, most frustratingly, stranded on the wrong side of the river mouth at Woodbridge Haven, with the nearest bridge 16 miles [26 km] inland, at Woodbridge itself; the little ferry was inadequate to move such numbers quickly. Some cavalrymen were soon 'towing over their horse made fast to the vessels', and the Dutch believed that several hundred infantry were also got across, but 'the greater part remained on the other side of the river and . . . could not be shipped over for fear of our guns'. The attackers had in fact reacted quickly to the threat from the Bawdsey direction, for though the sea off Woodbridge Haven was too shallow for men-of-war, it was deep enough for lesser-draught boats which now, from guns mounted in their bows, kept up a brisk fire on the crossing point, effectively sealing off this source of reinforcements.

An essential part of de Ruyter's plan had been for his two subordinates, Vice Admiral Evertsen and Rear Admiral van Nes, to bombard Landguard from the sea while the infantry stormed it from the land. The intention was for the former, with his five men-of-war, to engage the defenders from the north, just inside the entrance to Harwich harbour, while another six, commanded by van Nes, close inshore on the other side of the promontory, fired on it from the south. They hoped to close to musket-shot range, i.e. 200 yards [180 m], at which their culverins, firing a solid 18-lb [8.2-kg] iron ball with a 'point blank' range of 460 yards [420 m], and a maximum one of 2650 [2.4 km], would have been lethal, but the waters around Landguard Point were shallow and inadequately charted, while the English had removed all the navigation marks and buoys. Cornelis de Witt described the result in his after-action report to the States-General the next day:

> We saw that the ships under Vice Admiral Evertsen, who were to engage the fort from the sea side, were lying far from the shore; and that those under the rear-admiral [van Nes] had not sailed inside the entrance. We decided with Lieut.-Admiral de Ruyter that we should be put on board these ships to get them closer in and inside the entrance. On coming to those under Evertsen it was found that they could not get nearer to the shore on account of the shallowness of the water, so that their shots could scarcely reach the fort. And on rowing to the rear-admiral, the pilot . . . declared that all the marks . . . had been cut down, so that he could not find the entrance, which was very narrow . . . The ships could not float any closer to the fort than a half cannon shot [i.e. about 1000 yards (900 m)] . . . None could make any impression on the fort.

Van Nes's own ship, the *Delft*, now ran aground, though later refloated, and the Dutch also discovered that, according to De Witt, 'the enemy had sunk four ships in the entrance to Harwich to prevent the States' ships getting in'. These blockships finally persuaded the Dutch that the original plan for the ships to keep Landguard under fire from both seaward and harbour sides while the troops attacked would have to be changed, as de Witt himself described:

> As we could not be of any further service there, it was agreed with Lieut.-Admiral de Ruyter that we should go in the barges to join the troops, which we found drawn up in battle order waiting for the men-of-war to sail inside the harbour. We reported to them that the ships were not able to sail inside the fort and it was decided that without further loss of time the soldiers, the marines and the sailors should attack the fort by land. The senior officers thought it advisable to leave a good number of foot at a certain pass for the protection of the boats and barges and also so that no horse would attack our men from the rear. When orders had been given for this the troops marched off in good order to the fort.

It was now about 4 pm, the time when the tide at Woodbridge Haven was beginning to turn and leave the Dutch rear exposed. Landguard Fort was probably about a mile [1.6 km] away when the final advance began, the 1000 men involved marching forward out of sight of the defenders below the slopes which followed the shore line. The original intention had been for three groups of 200 soldiers, plus 100 or so sea-

men, to attack the fort from the north, east and south after advancing
on it across Landguard Common, the platoons being supposed 'to
advance steadily on the fort as they fire', with an interval of six paces
between them. As usually happened in war, however, this tidy parade-
ground manoeuvre proved unattainable in practice and so much
smoke drifted inshore as the Dutch ships discharged their broadsides
that de Ruyter became concerned at the risk of harming his own
troops, and a pre-arranged signal was given for the bombardment to
cease. An English observer described the resulting scene:

> [They] made up to Landguard Fort with scaling ladders . . . of about
> 20 feet [6 m] or more, hand-grenadoes etc. They came briskly up
> with their cutleaxes drawne upon their armes; and their muskets;
> and came up close to ye fort; whose reception to them when dis-
> covered was as briske.

The Dutch advance had hitherto been 'under ffavor of the sea bancke'
and the troops proved reluctant to leave its shelter in the face of the
fierce fusillade of small-arms fire which greeted them. They duly returned fire but aimed high, 'rather against the firmament', as the
English eye-witness just quoted caustically remarked, 'than the fort'.
Another local informant confirms that the attack was now pinned
down:

> [The assault troops] got neare the fforte within pistoll shot, and
> when they had gott soe neare as they could they fired estreamely
> with theire small shott one the forte for halfe an howre, but neaver
> came over the banke at all, though about 4 of theire officers did do it
> and much urged theire ffollowing them up to the forte wall, yett
> they would not haveing a goode bank to ffrind [ie as friend].

Although one Dutch army captain later claimed that 'our men made
several charges against the fort' and some at least must have got close to
it, for one man suffered ultimately fatal wounds near the palisades protecting the ditch, the cries of 'Peace! Peace!' which the attackers
uttered, apparently calling on the defenders to surrender, can have had
little chance of being heeded. The Dutch nevertheless, according to
one English observer, successfully established themselves 'within car-
bine shot on two sides of the fort'. The first attempt to storm it was
probably made around 5 pm and not finally abandoned until around
5.45.

The English now began, belatedly, to bring their ships into action,
as De Witt described.

> On coming close to the fort the sailors advanced with their scaling
> ladders and their weapons. But the enemy fired on them with much
> grapeshot, chiefly from a galliot which was inside the [harbour] en-
> trance, which upset our people, principally the sailors, who threw

down their ladders and lay behind a rising.

Another eye-witness, Captain J.M. de Castillego, one of the landing party, now attended a conference on the beach to hear a report by those leading the assault on the fort.

> First, it appeared to be fortified with four good bastions or bulwarks, partly with earth and the rest with masonry with a good ditch.
>
> Secondly, it was fortified with a good covered way and counterscarp,* leaving those standing behind it in safety. The covered way was filled with men, who were well disciplined and alert and were faithfully keeping a lookout for us.
>
> On recognising this, Colonel Dolman called all the senior officers and captains to a council of war to consider whether it was possible to take such a well organised fort; and it was unanimously agreed that it was impossible.

It must have been a bitter blow to de Witt and de Ruyter, after their triumph at Chatham, to recognise that they could not take this second objective, and this may have prompted the second, and final, assault, much feebler than the first, which was launched around 5.45. By six o'clock it was all over and the Dutch troops were in full retreat, leaving behind 20 storming ladders† and, one Englishman noted, 'their hand-grenadoes and a case of very handsome pistols'.

Re-embarking a raiding party, with surprise lost, was even more dangerous than landing one and the situation on the beach near Landguard by the time Colonel Dolman's assault party rejoined Count van Hoorn's rearguard had, for the Dutch, changed for the worse. From around 4 pm the ferry route across the Deben had become progressively less in danger from Dutch gunfire as the falling tide forced the Dutch ships to withdraw further out to sea and one local observer recorded how 'the ffoote by 6 a clocke in the afternoone gott over, by which time the horsse', presumably having ridden round by Woodbridge, 'meet them on Fillstoe Cliffte', where there were soon 'geathered together about 1500 ffoot and 3 troups off horse'.

If the initial response of the defence had been slow the English troops had not let van Hoorn's rearguard stay unchallenged on Felixstowe beach, as one of the landing party described:

> They [the English] began with a furious fire upon them [the Dutch], trying to break through the pass and so to attack us from the front

---

* The counterscarp was the side of the ditch nearer to the attackers but may here refer to the ramparts, which were linked to the ditch by a covered way.

† One of these ladders, of 22 rungs, 18½ feet [5.6 m] long was retained as a trophy by the family of the fort commander and preserved in the church at Little Chart in Kent, which was destroyed by a flying-bomb in August 1944. See my book *The Doodlebugs*, p. 162.

and rear and then wipe us out. Our men [ie van Hoorn's] were in no great need of help but performed their duty courageously. There was much skirmishing and firing lasting for two hours, until the enemy began to withdraw, pursued immediately by our men, but they soon returned to their posts as further pursuit was dangerous.

The stout resistance put up by the Dutch at the moment when they were most vulnerable is confirmed by English witnesses. They point out that the Earl of Suffolk, who had arrived to take command, was unable to deploy his cavalry, and was harassed by light artillery. These 'drakes', described by a Danish observer as 'small metal pieces that could fire a three–pound [1.5-kg] shot', needed four men to carry them, but apparently at least two had been brought ashore. One of the government's informants, Silas Taylor, in charge of the naval stores at Harwich, described how with their help the Dutch effectively covered their withdrawal:

They spar'd about 4 or 500, releiv'd from ye main body (yt stood neare the place they landed with a strong body of pikes, which I plainly saw) to assault the forces above on the hill, and with them two or three drakes, with wch they maintain'd the lanes and hedges; soe that the Earle of Suffolke gott his ground of them in a manner but by inches, because his horse were excluded from the service.

Sunset fell around 7.45 and as the summer darkness deepened the Dutch disengaged and made their way down to the water's edge, waiting for the tide to refloat the small boats which had landed them:

About 9 of the clock all was silent and they drawn to their body about Filstow Cliff, their boats being on ground [i.e. aground] which caused them to stand . . . longer.

The Dutch infantry officer quoted earlier recorded the final stage of the operation with understandable relief:

The enemy made some alarms for us afterwards, but fighting was not so fierce as before. Nevertheless shooting continued until the evening at about 9.30, when we re-embarked . . . At about ten o'clock in the evening all were re-embarked and rowed out to the ships in the barges and the boats, leaving in the withdrawal not a single dead man, nor a wounded one, although the operation was carried out in sight of the enemy, who was on our tail to the last. And the Lord be praised, all got back safely on board, some of them having booty.

There had in fact not been much opportunity for looting, though, according to Ruyter's son, who was serving with the fleet, 'some silk clothes and coats' had been taken from a house and one captain admitted that some of the English dead had been stripped of their clothes.

This was not much to show for a day's fighting and de Ruyter's biographer, 20 years later, admitted that the Suffolk landing had proved a disappointment:

> The well led attack came to nothing with little loss; for in the whole fleet there were not more than seven killed and 35 wounded and the honour of the brave withdrawal sweetened the sorrow at the failure of their expectations.

These figures may not include the casualties suffered by the landing party, for Anthony Deane reported 'about the fforte 8 dead' and this excluded the main action near the landing area, while according to Silas Taylor 'several boats laden with dead men were seen . . . to put off from the shore'. Some Dutchmen were taken prisoner but their number is not recorded, nor, no less oddly, is that of the English killed or wounded, except among the defenders of the fort, where one man was killed and four wounded, including its commander, Captain Darell, struck in the shoulder by a musket ball. Happily he recovered, to be promoted to major and to have his leadership later commemorated by a well-deserved plaque:

> Captain Nathaniel Darell
> Governor of Landguard Fort
> 1667-1670
> A Dutch force attacked the
> Fort by sea and was entirely
> defeated by the garrison.*

The gallant galliot apart, the navy had done little to protect Landguard but at eleven o'clock on the evening of that fateful Tuesday Silas Taylor was still hopeful that the morning might bring the chance of revenge. During the following day, Wednesday 3 July 1667, people in London learned of the previous day's events, but they caused, in contrast to the earlier attack on the Medway, remarkably little alarm. Samuel Pepys dismissed them very briefly:

> I find all the news is the enemy's landing 3000 men near Harwich, and attacquing Langnerfort and being beat off thence with our great guns, killing some of their men and they leaving their lathers [i.e. ladders] behind them; but we had no horse in the way on Suffolk side, otherwise we might have galled their foot. The Duke of York is gone down thither this day, while the Generall sat sleeping this afternoon at the Council-table.

This was Pepys's only reference to the Dutch raid and John Evelyn,

---

* The plaque was still in place when I visited Landguard in September 1983. The fort was not then open to the general public, but was in process of being restored by the Felixstowe History and Museum Society. Landguard is now, not before time, a listed Monument in the care of the Department of the Environment.

who was in London that week, does not mention it at all, a lead, somewhat curiously, followed by most later historians.*

This was no doubt because the landing was, for contemporaries,
overshadowed by the earlier attack on Chatham and the realisation
that, then as later, what really mattered was less the army's successes
than the navy's failures. In contrast to events in the Medway the threat
to Suffolk and Harwich was also rapidly over. The correspondent
quoted earlier, writing at 5 am on Thursday 4 July 1667, was able to in-
form London that the Dutch had already weighed anchor and turned
back towards the south. By 6 am, two hours after sunrise, the Dutch
fleet, apart from the rearguard left in the Sledway to keep watch for an
English sortie out of Harwich, was under way on the ebb tide making
slow progress northwards.

During the morning a small boat containing about 40 men ran
ashore near Orfordness lighthouse, from which, according to a local
informant, 'about ten landed, peeped up and run aboard againe'. Later
that morning the Duke of York, who had travelled to Harwich overnight, was able to inspect the Dutch ships still in the Gunfleet and Sledway through a telescope, before going on foot over the recent battlefield and visiting Landguard on a morale-boosting tour which, Silas
Taylor observed, 'much comforted the people'.

Although the defence of Landguard had been a triumph, both for its
builders and its garrison, the suspicion was widespread that the Dutch
should not subsequently have been able to get away so easily, but, as
Anthony Deane recorded, the commanders concerned proved far
more energetic in justifying themselves than they had been on the
battlefield:

> To the Duke they make apollogies [saying that] if they would have
> got down the hill they would have don it, and to see whether it be
> soe the Duke himself have viewed every place and found ways they
> could have gon and they must needs know the country as well as
> himself.

The militia's officers meanwhile blamed *their* commander for its disappointing performance, and it was certainly true that they had been
expected to fight directly after an exhausting march and the demoralis-
ing experience of being under artillery fire at the Deben ferry. The
naval commissioner, Lord Berkeley of Stratton, appointed Lieutenant-General of Militia in Suffolk at the start of the crisis, had clearly
failed to be an inspiring leader and Anthony Deane, writing on 13 July,
recorded that 'The head officers of Souffoullke of the mellitia are whol-
ley disgusted at my Lord Berkely's power over them'. The authorities
in London seem to have demobilised it with extraordinary haste, con-

---

* The Landguard affair is, for example, ignored in the 779 pages of the definitive history
of the period, David Ogg, *England in the Reign of Charles II*.

sidering that the Dutch were still sailing up and down the east coast. The horse-militia had been discharged on 11 July and most of the foot, though four companies, plus 40 horse, were left at Landguard. The chief military result of the affair seems to have been a loss of faith in the militia by the government, and an increase of confidence in fixed defences. Following the Duke of York's visit, Harwich was, by 11 July, one correspondent reported, receiving 'an addition of strength, both in its lines and batteries' and the same day another informant told Pepys, 'The west syde of this towne is now allso a fortifying, every man's yard being a safeguard to himselfe and [the] towne.'

On 11 July also the English plenipotentiaries sailed from Deal for Breda, carrying Charles II's approval for the proposed peace terms. Even if de Ruyter knew this, however, he firmly kept to his last instructions, received on 5 July, and effectively kept up the pressure, not merely on East Anglia but all along the Channel coast. One squadron was left in the Gunfleet-Orfordness area to menace Harwich, where a new attack was expected; the Dutch, Silas Taylor aptly observed, regarded it as 'an aching tooth'. Another group of ships was posted off the North Foreland, on the far side of the Thames estuary, the two between them so effectively blockading the capital that the price of coal in London rose from 25s [£1.25] a chaldron [15½ cwt, 738 kg], to £6.10s [£6.50] forcing some bakers to stop production for lack of fuel. Meanwhile, just as in the now distant days of French and Spanish raids, the maritime counties were kept in a state of alarm, and reports of sightings of de Ruyter's fleet poured in to the Navy Board from towns as far apart as Dover, Portsmouth, Dartmouth and Plymouth. On 11 July 1667 there was a particularly fine example of an old-style invasion panic at Milford Haven, in south-west Wales, where the last successful invasion of Great Britain had taken place 170 years before.[*]

When 38 unidentified sail appeared offshore, 'The deputy-lieutenants', it was reported, 'caused the militia to arm, and a great number of men to draw to the waterside to defend the country . . . The county troops [of horse] with many young men riding as volunteers, were also ready.' Excitement mounted as the intruders moved into the haven and dropped anchor, only to give way to embarrassment when they were found to have on board nothing more dangerous than cows, bound for Ireland.

On Thursday 18 July the Dutch entered the harbour at Torquay and destroyed two small merchant ships, but by now every unfamiliar sail was being identified as hostile, as Admiral Sir William Batten coarsely observed, and Pepys recorded:

News came the other day so fast, of the Dutch fleets being in so many places that Sir W. Batten at table cried, 'By God! . . . I think

[*] See *Defending the Island*, p. 338.

the devil shits Dutchmen'.

At dawn on Tuesday 23 July the last Dutch ships sailed out of sight of Harwich making for the Thames estuary before a favourable north-north-east breeze, anchoring off the Nore to protect the line of retreat of van Nes's main force, which had itself sailed up-river for a final attack on the shipping in the Thames. The British government now hoped it might catch the main enemy force in a two-pronged attack, by Admiral Sir Edward Spragge, in command of the naval defence of the Thames and the Medway, and by Vice-Admiral Sir Joseph Jordan, sailing from Harwich. On 23 July, Jordan led his four frigates and 16 fireships out to sea; two other ships had to be left behind for, on learning of their destination, it was reported, 'ye 4th part of our best men tooke ye opportunity of theire heels and deserted'.

On Friday 26 July 1667 Jordan prepared to seize the best opportunity the navy was likely to enjoy to revenge its recent humiliation, but in the event he merely clutched it feebly. So poor had been the coordination between the two English commanders that when Jordan led his little force into the mouth of the Thames on a favourable flood tide and running well before a north-east wind, he mistakenly identified Spragge's squadron as a second enemy squadron and immediately attacked the few enemy ships anchored near at hand. They managed to get away and the rest immediately withdrew, while the crews on both sides behaved badly. According to an English pilot, 'all ye men in ye fregate which our fireships laid on board [i.e. alongside], skipped overboard, except fourty', instead of trying to fend it off, while the crews of some of the other fireships, equally unheroic, deserted at the mere approach of a Dutch vessel.

The runaway captains from Harwich were later put on trial and condemned to death, but reprieved, no doubt because on 21 July, shortly before that final, unnamed, skirmish*, peace terms had been agreed with Holland in the Treaty of Breda, though to allow time to notify all the ships at sea, hostilities were not to cease until 14 August.

In the intervening period Van Nes's ships were still lingering off the coast of Essex and Suffolk but on Sunday 28 July 1667 an English pilot on a purely peaceful errand was taken aboard the Dutch fleet's flagship, the *Admiral of Holland*, to hear the news of the Treaty of Breda and, as he reported in Harwich the following day, 'The men on decke [on] the Admiral stampt for the ship's company to come up and shouted for peace.' That day one of Pepys's correspondents wrote to tell him that the local waters were safe at last:

This day our late reputed enemy the Dutch weigh'd, the wind at W from the Gunfleete, and are gonn to the E. wards; we judge hear (per

* It might conveniently be known as the Battle of Sea Reach, the section of the Thames off Canvey Island between Southend and Thames Haven.

the discourse of the peace) [they] are gonn home.

De Ruyter and de Witt were still with their squadron off Plymouth, when, on 30 July, two English colonels rowed out to *De Zeven Provincien* with a report of the Treaty, to be entertained to drinks and sweetmeats, hospitality royally reciprocated a few days later with a present of English beef, salmon and fresh vegetables. On 26 August formal notification of the ending of the Second Dutch War appeared in the *London Gazette*, the arrival of peace being greeted with relief in both countries, but it was not until 5 October 1667 that Admiral de Ruyter's fleet finally dropped anchor at Hellevoetsluis, to a hero's welcome. A celebration banquet was held, gold cups were presented and commemorative medals struck.

Jubilation in Holland was matched by recrimination in England. No-one was under any illusion about the fact that the country had been soundly beaten and the blame for defeat was heaped on the unfortunate Commissioner of Chatham dockyard, Peter Pett, whose name provided a temptingly easy rhyme for Andrew Marvell's denunciatory verses:

All our miscarriages on Pett must fall:
His name alone seems fit to answer all . . .
Who all our seamen cheated of their debt,
And all our prizes who did swallow? *Pett.*
Who did advise no navy out to set?
And who the forts left unrepair'd? *Pett . . .*
Pett, the sea architect, in making ships,
Was the first cause of all these naval slips.

Peter Pett was officially dismissed as a Navy Commissioner on 7 February 1668, to retire into private life. Pepys and the rest of the Navy Board emerged with reputations unimpaired, thanks to his careful preparation and eloquent presentation of their case, when their turn came to be investigated, on 5 March 1668:

I began our defence most acceptably, and smoothly, and continued at it without any hesitation or losse . . . till half-past three in the afternoon, and so ended, without any interruption from the Speaker, but we withdrew. And there all my fellow-officers, and all the world that was within hearing, did congratulate me, and cry up my speech as the best thing they ever heard.

8

INTENDED FORTIFICATIONS

His Majesty . . . commanded me to repair to Portsmouth to set and stake out the new intended fortifications at Gosport.

Letter from Sir Bernard de Gomme, 12 February 1678

His painful experiences in 1667 at the hands of the Dutch reinforced Charles II's natural inclination to seek an alliance with France, whose culture, absolutist system of government and religion had always attracted him. On 22 May 1670, known only to a privileged group of ministers, England and France signed the Treaty of Dover, which committed them to a military alliance against Holland. The real heart of the treaty lay in its most secret clause:

> The king of England, being convinced of the truth of the Roman Catholic religion is resolved to declare it, and to reconcile himself with the Church of Rome as soon as the state of his country's affairs permit . . . The king of France . . . promises to pay to the king of England the sum of two million livres [£166,000] . . . [and] 6,000 troops for the execution of this design, if they should be required.

Charles II had *not* formally undertaken that his country would adopt Roman Catholicism, only himself, and much of the money he received from Louix XIV under this and later agreements was spent on the best guardian of England's independence, the navy. What had happened in the Medway also gave new impetus to his existing programme for strengthening the nation's fixed defences, which had begun shortly after the Restoration when he had appointed Sir Bernard de Gomme as his Chief Engineer. A Dutchman by birth, de Gomme had earned his knighthood as Engineer and Quartermaster-General in the royalist armies and though still, in 1660, only 40, already enjoyed immense authority in the fortifications field. Anything he suggested, complained a professional colleague a little later, 'was approved of, as from an oracle'.

De Gomme's first assignment was at Portsmouth, and in 1661 Charles II watched de Gomme pace out the sites for 'two halfe bastions towards the land side and two halfe bastions towards the water side', though these were apparently later scrapped; constant changes, usually to save money, were a feature of every fortress building programme in every age. A great deal was built, however, for though various works had been erected piecemeal over the years, de Gomme's scheme was the first both to provide a series of defences in depth within the harbour and to protect it from an attack from the land. To the east was Henry VIII's Southsea Castle, supposed to command the approaches from that direction, but to the west was the large Gosport promontory, with the wide curve of Stokes Bay on its north-west face, and stretching seaward between the harbour entrance and the Isle of Wight the large sheltered anchorage known as Spithead. De Gomme was the first to recognise that though the town and naval installations were all to the east of the harbour it was the open land to the west which was the most vulnerable spot.

On the Gosport side of the harbour entrance, on a small spot of land which became known as Blockhouse Point, de Gomme built a modest battery emplacement, finished in 1667. The next promontory on the Gosport side housed Fort Charles, constructed to a simple, almost classic, design, consisting of a two-storey stone tower, 60 ft [18 m] square and 27 ft [8 m] high. Another gun platform with parapets, about 140 feet [42 m] square, surrounded the tower. Finally an enemy ship faced a further challenge from Fort James, directly opposite the main dockyard. It was completed in 1679, about the same time as Fort Charles.

A recurring dream of those responsible for harbour defence was to shut out the enemy by means of a boom, which might perhaps double as a mooring for friendly ships. In October 1664 the authorities had placed an order for just such a chain at Portsmouth, 260 fathoms [474 m] 'for his Majestys shipps to ride by' but it had remained unfinished when they fell behind with their payments. After the disastrous incursion into the Medway, already described, the 10 fathoms [180 m] so far completed were dragged into position to block the harbour entrance, forming a formidable obstacle – each 3-ft [0.9-m] long link weighed 1½ cwt [76 kg].

After 1667 Portsmouth had for the moment to take second place, in defence priority, to Chatham and London. De Gomme was therefore diverted from strengthening the defences of Portsmouth to preparing plans for the construction of a major new artillery fort at Tilbury, some 20 miles [32 km] down-river from London, on the Essex side of the Thames. This had always been recognised as a strategically important point; the name itself derived from 'Tila's Fort' and it was here, where the river narrowed after the great right-angled bend between there and its mouth, that Elizabeth's army had massed to await the troops of the Spanish Armada.

Work, by fortification standards, began rapidly, in 1670, and so well was Tilbury Fort designed and constructed that successive improvements have left it basically unaltered to this day. It was primarily intended to harass enemy ships making their way up-river – half a mile [0.8 km] wide at this point – with its 50 heavy guns mounted in well-protected emplacements close to the waterline, but de Gomme had not neglected the danger of an attack from the land, such as the Dutch had launched in 1667, with conspicuous success, at Sheerness. He contemplated a defence in depth, in this case consisting of six successive lines, each covered by the guns of the next. Finally, while storming the main ramparts the attackers would be enfiladed by musket fire and by the heavy guns of the main fort firing 'grape', small bullet-like missiles packed into a shell, or 'canister', tins full of musket-balls. *

With the massive building programme at Tilbury well under way, de Gomme was able to turn his attention back to work on the Gosport Lines, designed to seal off the 'back-door' into Portsmouth, from where by 24 February he was able to report that he had 200 men at work. The main moat was 30 ft [9 m] wide and 11 ft [3.3 m] deep, the rampart, without its parapet, about the same height. Provision was made for ravelins, detached triangular-shaped bastions projecting into the moat, glacis, earth walls with a sloping face set outside the main fortifications to deflect shot over them, and a covered way, a sunken path where the sentry could walk in safety between the glacis and the moat.

The great weakness of the scheme, as de Gomme was well aware, was that it did not reach down to the shore to the south, and while work was still in progress he produced a revised plan to complete the Gosport Lines with an extension almost to the water's edge at Gilkicker Point, the tip of the promontory projecting into the Solent. It was to be left to later generations to complete this, but even in 1679 the lines represented a tremendous step forward, converting Portsmouth for the first time into an enclosed, fortified town.

Plymouth, lying between two rivers which combined to form the Sound, was even more vulnerable to seaward attack than Portsmouth. In November of the same year, 1665, that de Gomme began work at the latter town he received a royal warrant to build 'a new citadel' on Plymouth Hoe, the stretch of high open ground between the city and the sea. The Citadel, with its imposing baroque gateway bearing its royal founder's arms, and the large open space within its high walls, said to include Sir Francis Drake's bowling green, is still impressive today[†].

* For an admirably clear explanation, and illustration, of the layout at Tilbury see Kightly, pp. 190-1, from which the above details are taken.
† i.e. in July 1988, when I visited it during the Armada anniversary celebrations. At that time the supposed bowling green accommodated trophies from the Falklands War.

In 1671 Charles and James cruised down the Thames and round to Portsmouth and then transferred to an armed 75-ton cutter, the *Cleveland*, carrying a crew of 20, for the run to Plymouth on 17 July, reaching it next day. In 1683 the king again visited both towns, walking round the Gosport Lines and visiting Southsea Castle, which de Gomme had strengthened by reconstructing the dry ditch surrounding it and adding a glacis and covered way, as well as his royal master's arms over the entrance. This piece of architectural flattery, or the presence of the Duchess of Portsmouth, Charles's current mistress, clearly put the king in an amiable mood for he professed himself 'mightily pleased with all that is done, both there and everywhere'.

Underlying all the events of the latter part of Charles II's reign was the religious issue. Increasingly a substantial body of the nation, including men in high positions, distrusted what they regarded as the creeping Catholicism of which the court was the centre, linking with it a hatred of arbitrary power and of France. In accordance with his undertakings to Louis XIV Charles managed to engineer a new breach with Holland, sending to the Hague an envoy with the reputation of being '*le plus grand querelleur de la diplomatie britannique*' – 'the most quarrelsome individual in British diplomacy' – and instructions to make what were intended to be unacceptable demands. 'Our business,' acknowledged one English official candidly, 'is to break with them and yet to lay the breache at their door.' When the Dutch proved unexpectedly conciliatory Charles resorted to outright aggression. On 12 March 1672, a Dutch merchant fleet peacefully passing the Isle of Wight was attacked, without justification, by English warships, and on 17 March England declared war on Holland and began a joint attack on her on lines already agreed with France.

The degree of cooperation between the two countries was unprecedented. They were to exchange intelligence; French ships were to be repaired and refitted in British ports; and the French Vice-Admiral d'Estrées agreed to serve under the Duke of York. While, however, the French achieved considerable success in their operations against the Netherlands on land, attempts at amphibious operations, with the combined fleet escorting a landing force across the North Sea, foundered on the failure to defeat the Dutch fleet. At the Battle of Sole Bay, or Southwold, fought off the Suffolk coast on 28 May 1672, de Ruyter inflicted sufficient damage to prevent a seaborne invasion of Holland and fought the allies to a draw with heavy losses on both sides, the Dutch acknowledging the sinking of three men-of-war and heavy damage to seven others, with 1600 men killed or fatally wounded, the English seeing their best ship, the *Royal James*, blow up and suffering 2500 casualties in killed and wounded. On land things went very differently. The French armies invaded Holland at the end of May and achieved such success that the republic was overthrown, the de Witt

brothers, unfairly blamed for its failures, were murdered by a mob and
– an event of vast significance for the future – William, Prince of
Orange, aged 21, became, on 30 June, 'stadholder', or head of state, not
far removed from an absolutist monarch.

The campaigning season of 1673 began with the Dutch trying to repeat their success of six years before, and on 2 May they sailed into the
Thames estuary, planning to seal up the English fleet by blocking up
the Kings Channel, which leads from the Gunfleet off Harwich into the
area off Foulness and the Maplin Sands. Even the Dutch could not
cope, however, with the dense fog which came down and Prince Rupert was able to grope his way out through the shoals to the Nore and
drive them off. For the rest of the summer the English and French tried
to clear the way for an invasion fleet to be ferried across the North Sea,
but in three successive battles, on 28 May (First Battle of Schooneveld), 4 June (Second Schooneveld), and 11 August (the Texel, the fier-
cest and last battle of the Third Dutch War), de Ruyter, with inferior
forces, skilfully fended off the attackers, making effective use of the
treacherous flats and sandbanks which protected the Dutch coast. The
most lasting casualty of the summer's fighting was the Anglo-French
alliance. 'If the French . . . had obeyed my signall, and borne down
upon the enemy according to their duty,' complained Rupert after the
Battle of Texel, 'I must have routed and torne them all to pieces. It was
the plainest and greatest opportunity ever lost at sea.'

Anti-French and anti-Catholic feelings were now becoming inex-
tricably linked. During the Gunpowder Plot Day celebrations that
year the spectators were invited to shoot at a 'guy' dressed as a Frenchman, in addition to, as usual, burning the pope in effigy. Two weeks
later the royal family added to its unpopularity with the arrival of the
Duke of York's second wife, Princess Mary of Modena, from Italy,
widely believed by the British public to be the pope's daughter. The
Duke, a 40-year-old widower, thought the beautiful 17-year-old
would make a nice playmate for his eleven-year-old daughter, and
recorded, on 21 November 1673, that she 'had arrived at Dover and . . .
been wedded and bedded that same night'.

On 19 February 1674 the Third Anglo-Dutch War was ended by the
Treaty of Westminster, by which the Dutch agreed to salute the
English flag as a 'testimony of respect' rather than as a formal right, in
British waters, defined as stretching from Cape Finisterre to Norway.
A maritime treaty, agreeing to free commerce everywhere, except in
the East Indies, followed. The new policy of friendship with Holland
was endorsed in November 1674 when, much to Louis XIV's fury,
William of Orange married his cousin Mary, the 15-year-old daughter
of James Duke of York by his first marriage. She greeted her enforced,
dynastic, betrothal with tears, but William, a gloomy groom of 24,
consummated his marriage, as his new father-in-law had done, on the

wedding night, urged on by his uncle, Charles II, with cries of 'Now nephew to your work! St George for England!'

Anxiety over the succession was to have lasting consequences, for it led to the emergence in both Parliament and the country of two distinct parties. The Tories, placing loyalty to the crown above all else, were prepared to accept the rightful heir, Charles's brother, James, Duke of York, as the next king, although he was a Roman Catholic. The Whigs, fearful of royal tyranny and popery, favoured Charles's Protestant, but illegitimate, eldest son, James, Duke of Monmouth. The General Election of February 1679 was the first to be fought on party lines, which were to become a permanent feature of English politics and to affect attitudes to the armed forces and to spending on defence.

Growing distrust of the king led to a rapid cooling of the initial enthusiasm for entrusting the forces to his exclusive control. On 1 April 1679 MPs carried a motion reversing the decision of 18 years before, and 'Resolved that the continuing of any standing forces in this nation, other than the militia, is illegal; and a great grievance and vexation to the people.' The regular army continued in fact to exist, but in 1684 the sole remaining formation overseas, the garrison of Tangier, was brought back and incorporated in the home-based forces.

During this period, prompted more by anti-papist hysteria than any real cause, there were some minor invasion alarms. In 1678 rumours spread that a French army had actually disembarked in the Isle of Purbeck in Dorset, and in 1681 an even wilder story gained currency, that the Archbishop of Armagh was about to bring in French troops to secure Ireland for the Roman religion. Such excitements apart, the nation was by now again displaying its traditional indifference to the state of its defences. The fixed fortifications, recently modernised or extended, were often undermanned, and a source more of friction between the garrisons and the local population than of reassurance. At Landguard Fort there were constant quarrels between the resident governor and his officers and between both and the nearby residents.

Landguard, miserably situated on the exposed east coast, and with a tradition of uncomfortable living conditions and poor discipline, was particularly prone to such trouble, but far from unique. At Tilbury, the costly new fortress barring the way to the capital, a visitor in November 1679 found only 'a corporal and three files of musketeers'; at nearby Gravesend, it was observed, 'there was never a commissioned officer'.

Lacking their officers' opportunities, the other ranks found humbler diversions locally, and the garrison of Dover Castle became notorious for their marauding expeditions into the surrounding countryside. Mill ponds were dammed to collect fish for poaching, livestock were stolen and civilians who tried to intervene were physically assaulted, until a petition was sent by the desperate residents to the Privy Council seeking protection against the soldiers supposed to protect *them*.

9

DELIVERING THE KINGDOM

Declaration of James, Duke of Monmouth . . . now in arms . . . for delivering the kingdom from the usurpation and tyranny of James, Duke of York.

Proclamation read outside Lyme Regis Town Hall, 11 June 1685

On Friday 6 February 1685 Charles II died, at the age of 54, probably of kidney disease. At some time before his death he had honoured his long-distant promise to Louis XIV and been admitted into the Roman Catholic church. He had to the last insisted that the rights of his brother, whom he did not much like, must take precedence over those of his son, whom he loved, though observing shortly before his death that, 'I am afraid that when he comes to wear the crown he will be obliged to travel [i.e. go into exile] again.'

Despite these forebodings the reign of James II, now 51, began under promising auspices. If he lacked Charles II's attractiveness and easy charm he was, as all witnesses acknowledge, far more conscientious and industrious. A nobleman close to the king described him as 'The most honest and sincere man I ever knew . . . A great and good Englishman', while the Anglican Bishop Burnet summed up judiciously: 'If it had not been for his popery, he would have been, if not a great, yet a good prince.' And here, of course, was the rub.

The real threat to James II's peaceful succession was, as it had always been, Charles's eldest son, the Duke of Monmouth, originally named James Crofts, after his first guardian, and born, on 9 April 1649, when both his father and his mother, Lucy Walter, later Barlow, a well-connected Welsh girl then living at Hellevoetsluis in Holland, were aged 19. Charles always acknowledged him as his son and in 1663 made him Duke of Monmouth. That year Monmouth married a Scottish countess and took her family surname, Scott, and subsequently served in numerous senior positions, including that of captain-general of the royal forces. When his father died he was in exile in Holland but immediately contended, as he always had done, that he was the rightful heir to the throne, because, he claimed, Charles had been married to his mother.*

Almost all those around Monmouth urged the need for immediate action, before the Coronation, which in fact took place on 23 April, and to allow time for four months' campaigning before the harvest. Monmouth, an experienced, and naturally cautious commander, was doubtful. He would have preferred to wait till discontent against James had had time to take root. But his followers were impatient and 'The Duke of Monmouth,' one of them acknowledged, 'allowed himself to be overruled.' Monmouth's most difficult task was establishing a working relationship with the acknowledged leader of the anti-James faction, Archibald Campbell, ninth Earl of Argyll. A small, dark, intense figure, Argyll was Chief of the Campbell clan, devoted Covenanters who hated James II with the fierce loathing for which the clansmen were renowned. When Monmouth and Argyll met, on 6 April 1685, in Amsterdam they agreed on two roughly simultaneous expeditions. Argyll, it was decided, would not land in the Highlands but sail right round Scotland to come ashore on his ancestral lands, in the south-west lowlands, the area still known by his family name. Here he would be well placed for a move towards Glasgow and Edinburgh. Not more than six days after his departure Monmouth would set sail for Lyme Regis in Dorset and march across country to Taunton, the county town of Somerset, where he had many supporters and which he planned to make his temporary capital. From here, gathering strength as he went, Monmouth hoped to capture – or, rather, be warmly welcomed by – Bristol, before moving on with part of his army to Gloucester and thence into the Midlands and the North. Meanwhile the citizens of London were expected to come out on his side and detachments from both Bristol and Gloucester would be sent to assist them and take over the capital. Monmouth insisted at this stage that he was not seeking the throne, merely asking that his claims to it be examined and that he be permitted to protect the nation's religion against its new king, as the title he initially used, 'Head and Captain-General of the Protestant Forces of the Kingdom', implied.

A manifesto was now drafted for distribution once he had arrived which promised liberty of conscience, for both Roman Catholics and dissenters, annual parliaments, the restoration of city charters that James had abolished or tampered with, and a general increase in the authority of Parliament, an impressive list, well calculated to appeal to all who looked back nostalgically to the days of the Commonwealth. Monmouth's plans were betrayed to the British government by a courier but even without his perfidy James II's government would

---

* Monmouth's biographer, J.N.P. Watson, in *Captain-General and Rebel Chief*, p. 5 states: 'The inferences that such a marriage did take place are so convincing as to be almost conclusive', but Charles's biographers (eg Antonia Fraser pp.64-5) are sceptical. Watson's case is convincing, but the truth will probably never be known.

have had ample warning of what was in the wind. As Argyll's three ships, the *Anna*, the *David*, and the *Sophia* were loaded at Amsterdam at the end of April with 500 barrels of powder, arms and ammunition for the 8000 men expected to join him in Scotland, and the modest force of 100 who were to sail with him, they became aware of a party 'from the English Consulate with telescopes, watching them from a boat, which rowed round and round several times'.* On Saturday 2 May 1685 the same favourable east wind and calm sea that caused Argyll to set sail carried the traitor James Cragg, with his up-to-the-minute report, back to London.

The government had originally expected a single expedition, to the area now known as Argyll, and had assigned ships to watch the Firth of Clyde and the Kyles of Bute, but Argyll's little force first appeared at Kirkwall, on Orkney, on 6 May, when two men foolishly went ashore and were arrested. News of his arrival was then immediately sent to Edinburgh and when Argyll reached Dunstaffnage, about three miles [5 km] north of Oban he found the leading members of the Campbell clan, who should have provided his officers, already detained. He set up his standard none the less at Cambeltown (i.e. 'Campbell's town', an encouraging omen), and the traditional call to arms, a fiery cross, summoned loyal clansmen to assemble with their claymores, i.e. large swords, at the isthmus of Tarbert on Loch Fyne, almost at the head of which, 30 miles [48 km] to the north-east, was Argyll's ancestral home, Inveràry Castle.

Thanks to the government's precautionary measures and the mutual suspicions between the various clans, the response was poor, with only about 1800 men turning out instead of the 4000 or 5000 expected. Reluctantly Argyll agreed to send some of his scanty forces south-east to the coast of Ayrshire to try and muster support there, but the plan was frustrated by the presence of English warships and they ended up instead attacking Greenock, a fishing hamlet consisting of a single row of thatched cottages, about 15 miles [24 km] down the River Clyde from Glasgow. Here the first shots of the invasion were exchanged and the local militia briefly driven back, while the invaders seized some oatmeal. No one rallied to Argyll's flag, however, and the detachment withdrew to the Isle of Bute, about 20 miles [32 km] away by boat, where their leader had now made his headquarters. Further dissension about their next move followed, but eventually Argyll's original plan, for an advance on Inverary Castle, was accepted. An advance base, protected by guns removed from the expedition's ships, was set up on the island of Ealan Gheirrig, at the mouth of Loch Riddaw. Some English naval frigates now appeared but Argyll's council rejected his

* Watson, on whom I have drawn heavily for this chapter, refers, p. 203, to 'an expeditionary force of 100', but Ogg, *James II*, p. 145, says Argyll 'set sail with about 300 men'.

suggestion of a cutting-out sortie against them in small boats. He had no sooner ferried most of his men across the Loch into Dumbartonshire, however, than King James's ships forced the passage to Ealen Gheirrig, captured the now weakly defended stronghold, and seized all Argyll's ships – their sole means of retreat in the event of disaster – without a blow being struck. The morale of his own force crumbled when the news reached them, but, knowing that the best remedy was action, he now led them off on a march through the countryside between Loch Long and Loch Lomond towards Glasgow.

News of Argyll's landing was broken to Parliament by the king himself, in a speech on 22 May. It prompted a fierce outburst of loyalty, which took concrete shape in the voting to him of additional revenues worth more than £400,000 a year, so that James was never to be hamstrung for lack of funds as his brother had been. Past neglect had, however, left its mark on the navy. Only one ship, the unmartially named yacht *Kitchen*, could be spared to watch the Dutch coast and only two frigates could be mustered for home defence, though another ten were in harbour fitting out.

After Argyll's departure Monmouth completed his own preparations, being 'forced', one of his associates observed, 'to pawn all he had in the world' to scrape together the cash for four cannon, 100 muskets, an unrecorded number of carbines and pistols, 500 pikes, 500 swords and 250 barrels of powder. There were also, by way of uniform, '1460 helmets and suits of back-and-breast armour', and 'a good number of campaign coats, red laced with purple'. Monmouth's biggest purchase was a 32-gun, three-masted fifth-rater, the *Helderenberg* (or *Helderenburg* or *Helderenbergh*), which he bought for £5500 on learning of English naval patrols in the Channel. Two other vessels, a 200-ton fly-boat and 100-ton ketch, or pink, both laden with arms, made up his little fleet which carried, including the crew, around 150 men. It was a modest force with which to conquer a kingdom but the future Henry VII had succeeded with not so many more, relying, as Monmouth did, on recruits flocking in once he had landed.

Like earlier invaders the Protestant Duke had to wait for a favourable wind, but on Friday 29 May 1685 he finally boarded the *Helderenberg*, disguised 'in seaman's apparel, with great whiskers', as one of his officers later testified, and the following day the ships weighed anchor and set sail. 400 miles [644 km] away lay their destination, the coast of Dorset. Though his numbers seemed derisory Monmouth's expedition was by no means a forlorn hope. Young and energetic, with vast military experience, and unquestionably of the blood royal, he was a charismatic figure who had been almost idolised on his last progress through the West Country, in very different circumstances, only five years before. Crowds of thousands had turned out to shout 'God bless the Protestant Duke!'; he had, like a reigning monarch, touched a young girl for 'the king's evil' and she had been miraculously cured.

Although by 11 June Pepys had managed to scrape together 12 frigates to patrol the Channel, Monmouth's fleet got through undetected. After a rough passage in bad weather the ships halted briefly off the beach at Chideock, still a quiet, almost deserted spot, at dawn on Thursday 11 June 1685 while a long-boat ferried three of Monmouth's associates ashore to spread the news of his arrival and call out likely supporters in the area. The same boat brought back the unwelcome news that the Somersetshire militia had already been called out and that the Duke of Albemarle (i.e. the second Duke, son of General Monck, the first Duke) had gone to Exeter to muster the Devonshire militia. But it was too late for turning back and the invaders sailed on to Lyme, seven miles [11 km] away, which was reached around 9 am.

In a suit of royal purple, the silver star of a Knight of the Garter on his chest, Monmouth looked every inch a prince as he prepared to step on shore, where he knelt on the shingle of what is still called Monmouth Beach, just to the west of the Cobb, the long stone wall which encloses the harbour, to give thanks for his safe arrival. Then, drawn sword in hand, he led his 80 followers up the slope behind the Cobb and then round to the right into the town. 'We marched very well armed and clothed into Lyme in a military manner,' claimed one of Monmouth's closest associates, Lieut-Colonel Nathaniel Wade, formerly a Bristol lawyer and now commander-designate of the Blue Regiment, one of five into which the Duke planned to organise his troops. 'We were received by the shouts and acclamations of the people, the mayor being fled.'

The mayor was in fact riding hotfoot for Honiton and Exeter to raise the alarm, the local customs officers having set off to bear the news to London, while their fellow townsfolk lined the streets to shout 'A-Monmouth! A-Monmouth!'

During the day and long after dark 50 of Monmouth's tiny army guarded the approaches into Lyme while the rest unloaded his four cannon and the packing-cases crammed with muskets. A blacksmith broke open the door into the Town Hall, to use as a temporary armoury, while Monmouth set up his headquarters in the town's chief coaching inn, the George in Combe Street.*

By dawn the first 60 recruits had arrived, been issued with muskets and ammunition, and led off to the various outposts to be taught how to use them by the ex-Cromwellian officers who had landed with Monmouth; firing a flintlock musket was a complicated process which required hours of intensive drill and weeks of practice to make auto-

* Although Combe Street is still there the George was burned down in 1840. A plaque marks the site.

matic.*

The burliest volunteers, or those who proved slow in mastering the musket, were assigned to carrying pikes. No horses had been brought from Holland so a requisitioning party was sent out to round up suitable mounts from local farms and the gentry's stables. By noon on Friday 12 June, a scorching hot day, 50 had been brought in and 15 of these were soon engaged in the first skirmish of the campaign when a small troop was sent off towards the nearby town of Bridport, where the local constables were preventing men leaving to join Monmouth. The invaders encountered some horse militia, whom they charged without loss, killing two. It was first blood to Monmouth.

James II as yet knew nothing of these developments. He was roused at 4 am next day, Saturday, with the news borne by the Lyme customs men – who were rewarded with £20 apiece from the king's own hand – and immediately ordered Monmouth's known sympathisers in London to be rounded up. The London trained bands were called out; a £5000 reward was offered for the capture or killing of 'James Scott, late Duke of Monmouth', his title having been stripped from him, and it became a treasonable offence 'for anyone to say . . . that the late king was married to the late Duke of Monmouth's mother'.

The most important measures taken that day were the mobilisation of the West Country militia under the second Duke of Albemarle, and the issuing of orders to four troops of the Blues, two companies of the Royal Dragoons and five companies of a foot regiment recently returned from Tangier under Colonel Percy Kirke to move west to Salisbury. These last, known ironically as 'Kirke's Lambs', were already notorious for their brutality. On the following day, Sunday 14 June 1685, overall command of the force was given to Lord (John) Churchill [later first Duke of Marlborough], the 35-year-old son of Sir Winston Churchill, MP for Lyme. A 16-strong artillery train was assembled at the Tower of London, and instructions sent to Portsmouth for another, of eight guns, to be got ready.

In almost every invasion the initial advantage lay with the attacker, but rapidly passed to the defenders as they mustered their full strength. Monmouth's only hope of success was to retain the initiative and during the summer night of the 13th 400 of his foot, led by 40 musketeers and supported by 40 horsemen, secretly made their way towards Bridport, ten miles [16 km] to the east, which was strongly held by the Dorset and Somerset militia, numbering at least 1200 foot and 100 horse.

Most of Monmouth's men had never handled a weapon before but, aided by a thick mist, they achieved total surprise. The basic lay-out of Bridport, with its broad main street, intersected by another road half-

* For an excellent account of what firing a musket involved, see Chenevix Trench, pp. 128-9.

way along its length, where the Bull Inn still stands, has altered little since 1685. The militia officers sleeping in the Bull woke to find the intruders, who had charged in across the west bridge from the direction of Lyme, all about them, 'firing their guns and pistols very thick' and breaking down doors. The militia officers joined in, firing from the bedroom windows of the Bull, while their horses were soon adding to the confusion by 'running up and down the streets without riders'. Two militia officers were killed but others 'with much ado prevailed with their soldiers to stand' at the east bridge, where the fight was thickest.

Monmouth's men were now sadly let down by one of their officers, Lord Grey of Warke [or Werke, or Werk, late first Earl of Tankerville], given command on account of his title, which Monmouth hoped would attract other aristocrats to the cause.*

He had, however, been 'ordered to take the advice of Colonel Thomas Venner', a far better soldier who had been one of Cromwell's cavalry commanders, but his social inferior. Grey turned out to be concerned only to save his own skin and when two of his men were killed, led a disorderly and unnecessary retreat, as Nathaniel Wade observed:

> My Lord Grey with the horse ran and never turned face till they came to Lyme, where they reported me to be slain and all the foot to be cut off. This flight of Lord Grey so discouraged the vanguard of the foot, that they threw down their arms and began to run; but I bringing up another body to their succour, they were persuaded to take their arms again, all but such as ran into houses for shelter, which were never sixteen or seventeen.

Wade now made an effective, fighting withdrawal:

> I drew off my guards on the cross street and caused my men to retreat to the first bridge we had possessed at the entrance into the town and then, staying about half an hour, expected that the enemy would have attacked us, as we did them; not doubting, by an ambuscade of musketeers that we had near the bridge, to give them good entertainment; but they contented themselves to repossess the middle of the town, and shout at us out of musket-shot. We answered them alike, and by this bravo having a little established the staggering courage of our soldiers, we retreated in pretty good order, with twelve or fourteen prisoners, and about thirty horse.

It had been a respectable first battle, which had achieved its object, to

* Grey has a special place in parliamentary history, having allegedly secured the passage of the Habeas Corpus Bill through the House of Lords in 1679 by counting a fat peer as ten people. There was undoubtedly a miscount giving the Bill an undeserved majority of two. Grey's wife was widely believed to be, with his connivance, Monmouth's mistress.

give Monmouth's army self-confidence; it had, though heavily out-numbered, lost only seven men killed and 23 missing: mainly, no doubt, weaker spirits for whom one taste of gunfire had been enough. New arrivals, however, far outnumbered the deserters and by 3 am on Monday when, as a weary Nathaniel Wade recorded, 'we had orders to beat the drums', Monmouth's army had grown to 3000 men.

On Monday 15 June 1685 the rebels moved out of Lyme towards Axminster, a small town six miles [10 km] inland. Axminster was the obvious place to bar Monmouth's way to his likeliest destination, Taunton, and the road from Lyme was narrow and enclosed, lending itself to ambush, but, as Nathaniel Wade, now promoted to command the wounded Colonel Venner's regiment, recorded, the government forces missed their chance.

> After we had marched about two hours towards Axminster, we dis-covered, on one side, the march of the Devonshire forces; on the other, of the Somersetshire; to a conjunction, as we supposed, in Axminster . . . The Scouts of the Somersetshire forces had first entered the town, but on the approach of ours they retired. The Duke possessed himself of the town and seized on the passes re-garding [i.e. commanding the approach of] each army, which he guarded with cannon and musketeers; the places, by reason of the thick hedges and strait ways, being very advantageous for that pur-pose . . . The horse of the Devonshire forces advanced within half a mile [0.8 km] of our advanced post; but discovering that we had lined the hedges they retreated . . . So we drew off our parties from their posts, and encamped in a strong piece of ground on the other side of Axminster towards Chard, putting out very strong guards.

This was the militia's grand test; repelling an invasion and putting down a rebellion was precisely what it was intended for, but it failed lamentably. What happened at Lavington [presumably Market Lavington] near Devizes in Wiltshire was typical:

> We received certain information that the D of M's being at Lyme and presently after that a warrant for our foot soldiers to be that night at . . . Devizes; but I believe never did such confusion and dis-order appear. First the locks [on the muskets] being almost eat to pieces with rust. After this there was never a bullet mould to be had . . . and, if we had not thought of Laman [presumably a local resi-dent] by chance that possibly he might have one to make bullets for some of his guns, we must needs have sent them away without ammunition.

Seldom can men have gone to fight with less enthusiasm than the Lavington militia:

> Never I think were such fainthearted cowards seen, for they now

thought they were leaving their beloved bacon and ale and going on to certain destruction. Neither I think were some of their commanders more valiant, for Mr Noys, the lieutenant of our company, appeared amongst them with a white cap and a sad countenance, being taken extremely ill on a sudden. 'Tis said the king is sending some [regular] forces against them and I hope 'tis true, for if I may guess at other militia men by ours, three valiant rebels may beat three score of them.

Just what use those militiamen who had not already deserted or run away were likely to be was made clear on the night of Tuesday 16 June 1685 when to the beat of their drums the Taunton militia marched out of the town, not towards Chard, from which Monmouth was now advancing, but in the opposite direction, abandoning to him much of their arms and ammunition, which he badly needed; the stocks he had brought from Holland had long since been used up and most of his army were still armed only with pitchforks and flails, or home-made pikes.

The next day, Wednesday 17 June 1685, the government issued orders for the militia of Gloucestershire, Herefordshire and Monmouthshire to concentrate at Bristol, which it was anticipated would be the invaders' next target, but already it was becoming clear that it was going to require the regular army to deal with them. Meanwhile John Churchill, riding ahead of his infantry, reached Bridport with an advance guard of 300 horsemen, whose presence put new spirit into the recently defeated Dorset militia, before pressing on to Axminster. The bulk of Monmouth's army was meanwhile camped at Ilminster, five miles [8 km] from Chard and 12 [19 km] from Taunton. The following day, Thursday 18 June, he rode into Taunton with all the air of a monarch come to take possession of his kingdom, through streets crowded with people sporting sprigs of what became known as 'Leveller green'. Next day came a touching ceremony when the 27 little eight- to ten-year-olds of the Taunton Academy for Young Ladies, who had supposedly sacrificed their silk petticoats for the purpose, each presented Monmouth with an embroidered regimental banner, to be rewarded with a kiss.*

During the 19th 12 companies of the Foot Guards, and seven of the Coldstream, a total of about 1150 men, set out for a rendezvous with the Wiltshire militia and the new Lieutenant-General at Bath. Behind them trundled the main artillery train from the Tower, consisting of '16 large cannon with carriages, powder, ball, shovels, pickaxes and other warlike provisions'. Simultaneously a 'bye-train' of eight mainly

* These children's precocious political awareness was due to their headmistress, Miss Mary Blake, being related to Cromwell's famous admiral. She led her pupils to meet Monmouth carrying a Bible in one hand, a naked sword in the other, in the true Cromwellian tradition.

lighter guns – four iron 3-pounders and four brass falcons – set out from Portsmouth towards Sherborne, with another five companies of infantry, largely veterans from Tangier, under the command of John Churchill's brother, Charles. A total force of 1800 infantry and 26 cannon, preceded by 150 cavalry, was now on its way to the West Country, to reinforce the 400 horsemen and 300 foot soldiers of 'Kirke's Lambs' already mustered there against Monmouth.

That day the king also appointed a new Lieutenant-General as Commander-in-Chief of the anti-Monmouth operations, the former Louis Duras, Marquis de Blanquefort, now second Earl of Feversham. Feversham had learned his profession under his uncle, the famous Marshal Turenne, but Churchill, though promoted to brigadier as a consolation prize, was affronted at being demoted to second-in-command. 'I see plainly,' he commented, 'that the trouble is mine and that the honour will be another's.'

During Friday 19 June Churchill's and Monmouth's men came in contact for the first time, when two reconnaissance patrols, each about 20 strong, exchanged shots at the village of Ashill, halfway between Chard and Taunton. Monmouth's men, with their commander and three troopers dead and others wounded, came off worse and the rest fled back to Taunton.

On Saturday 20 June 1685 Monmouth had himself proclaimed king at the Market Cross in Taunton, a precautionary as well as a propagandist move, since under a statute of Henry VII, who had himself gained his throne in just such a manner, no one supporting a *de facto* king could be charged with treason. The unfortunate mayor and magistrates were forced to be present in their ceremonial robes to give the proceedings an air of legality, though one of Monmouth's officers told them bluntly: 'You must come out, gentlemen, or we'll run our swords through your guts.'

So many men flocked in to join Monmouth in Taunton that he was able to form a fifth infantry regiment, the Blue, commanded by a colonel who had travelled from London to assist him, to strengthen the existing Red regiment with an extra company of musketeers, and to form two more troops of horse, of 80 men each. The more recruits he attracted, however, the more acute became his shortage of arms and one of Monmouth's first acts as 'king' was to issue a royal warrant to the leading residents in all the surrounding villages 'to will and require you, on sight hereof, to search for, seize and take all such scythes, as can be found in your tything, paying a reasonable price for the same'. Ancient muskets and pikes were also in demand but it was the scythe that became the trademark of Monmouth's amateur army, about 200 men so equipped forming one company in each of his five infantry regiments. Primitive though it sounded, a scythe blade riveted to an 8-ft [2.4-m] staff was a formidable weapon, little shorter than an orthodox pike and better in hand-to-hand fighting than the standard musket with plug-bayonet.

Even the supply of scythes ran out, however, and ultimately about a quarter of Monmouth's 6000 troops were armed with clubs. He still had only the four small cannon brought from Holland, now drawn by teams of farm horses, and relied largely on oxen for transport, while the supporting services in which Cromwell's New Model Army had excelled were almost entirely lacking. One medical man who happened to be visiting Taunton at this time 'saw many miserably lamenting the want of chirurgeons to dress their wounds, compelled to expose wounded and fractured limbs to the violent agitation . . . of the carts'.

On Sunday 21 June, while John Churchill was listening to a sermon in Chard church on the text 'They who resist shall receive to themselves damnation', and waiting for the arrival later that day of Kirke's five companies of foot, only 16 miles [26 km] away by road and a mere 12 [19 km] across country, at Taunton, Monmouth was setting out on the second stage of his campaign. His objective was Bristol, a 43-mile [69-km] march away, 'capital of the West', a rich prize with the cash in its Customs House Monmouth needed to replenish his empty coffers; he had landed with no more than 90 guilders [£9] in his purse and the £400 he had 'borrowed' from the customs at Lyme was long since spent. His 7000 men travelled remarkably light with a mere 35 supply wagons, drawn by oxen and carthorses, and the four guns brought from Holland strapped on to ploughs, but even so spread out over three miles [5 km] of road.

Churchill's cavalry had so far been content merely to maintain distant contact with the rebel forces but there was another minor clash that day, near Langport, between two parties of about 20 horsemen, and on the following day, Tuesday 23 June, Monmouth moved on to Shepton Mallett and, not knowing that Feversham, hurrying ahead of his infantry via Newbury and Marlborough, had already got 200 of the Blues and Horse Grenadiers into Bristol, decided to make a dash for that city, crossing the River Avon by the bridge at Keynsham, midway between Bristol and Bath.

James II had already, on 21 June, issued orders that Keynsham bridge should be destroyed, but only some Gloucester militia had been left to guard the broken arch and they fled when a party of Monmouth's horse appeared, leaving the victors to collect planks and mend the breach. By 10 am on Thursday 25 June Monmouth's horse had crossed from Somerset into Gloucestershire and were forming up for an attack, when, more by chance than prior planning, one party of 100 troopers of the Blues charged into Keynsham from the Bristol direction, while 250 other horsemen swam the Avon below the town and rode in from the Bristol side. Fourteen of Monmouth's men were killed and many more wounded and morale – not least Monmouth's own – suddenly plummeted. Here was the second turning point in the campaign. Bristol was weakly held and the rebels vastly outnumbered its defenders, who could only get stronger as time passed, but Monmouth's nerve was gone. 'God forbid that I should bring such calamities as fire and sword on so noble a city,' he explained, suggesting instead an advance towards London through Wiltshire and Hampshire.

On Friday 26 June the balance of advantage in both strength and morale began to swing decisively towards the royalists. By the evening John Churchill and Percy Kirke arrived from the south-west, to join Feversham at Bath, bringing his strength up to about 2500 – only half Monmouth's, but all hardened, well-trained regulars. The artillery from London had not yet arrived but on Saturday 27 June Feversham paraded his men outside Bath and set off in pursuit of Monmouth, whose army was somewhat miserably encamped near the village of Phillips Norton, now Norton St Philip, nine miles [14 km] south-east of Bath, which had refused his summons to surrender.

Feversham was eager for battle and followed a simple strategy of continuing to advance until 'they had been shot att' as duly happened as his advance party of grenadiers came into contact with Monmouth's rearguard on the outskirts of Phillips Norton. 'The regiment being much superior in numbers,' recounted the commander of the Red, 'we fell with a good part of them into their rear; so that they were surrounded on all hands, save the left flank, by which way, through the hedge, many of them escaped.' The royalist horse, under Brigadier-General Churchill, effectively covered the infantry's retreat but many men were cut down in the hand-to-hand fighting which now developed. The battle had unquestionably been a victory for Monmouth with 100 royalist dead to his six, but he decided against trying to follow it up with a counter-attack.

During the night of Saturday 27 June, leaving camp fires burning behind them to deceive the royalist cavalry patrols, Monmouth led his army five miles [8 km] due south to Frome, marching across country on 'a miserable rainy night,' Colonel Wade recalled, 'up to the knees in dirt, almost to the destruction of our foot'. By 8 am on Sunday 28 June when the rebel army stumbled rather than marched into Frome, many of its members had lost their enthusiasm for war, while Monmouth himself, acutely aware of his failure to attract the country gentry, was in despair. Neither in London nor Cheshire had the expected rising occurred and now news arrived of the total collapse of Argyll's expedition to Scotland. After most of his supporters, as described earlier, had deserted him, Argyll had, around the end of May, advanced towards Glasgow, until he found his way barred by both militia and regulars at the River Leven. He managed to slip away in the darkness but, struggling to cross marshy moorland, his units became separated and some men deserted, leaving a mere 200 to reach the rendezvous at Kilpatrick [now Old Kilpatrick] on the Clyde. These survivors, realising that all was now lost, dispersed but on 18 June, just as Monmouth's first troops were entering Taunton, Argyll was captured near Inchinnan, eight miles [13 km] north-west of Glasgow. On the 30th he was executed at Edinburgh, under a sentence of death first passed four years earlier.

Monmouth now talked wildly of abandoning the whole venture but his Council of War, by a small majority, voted to carry on. On Monday 29 June, while Monmouth's army was still resting at Frome, James II announced that all who had taken up arms, except various named ringleaders, including Monmouth himself, would be pardoned provided they surrendered to a magistrate, or the royal army, within eight days. A report claiming that 'the country is rising for you' was enough to cause the Duke, on Tuesday 30 June, to march due west instead of east and that night the rebels camped outside Shepton Mallet; though with no funds to pay for billets or food and a royalist army known to be approaching, they were much less welcome guests than formerly. On Thursday 2 July Monmouth's army spent an uncomfortable night near Pedwell, about ten miles [16 km] south-west of Wells. Here a deputation arrived from Taunton begging Monmouth not to return there 'for that a siege would undoe them'. Many of Monmouth's formerly most ardent supporters now, in the words of one, 'came away intending to lay hold on the Act of Pardon', and it was a depleted army, probably no more than 400 strong, that Monmouth led back into a distinctly unenthusiastic Bridgwater on Friday 3 July.

From Frome Feversham had gone on to Shepton Mallet and that Friday marched through Glastonbury to Somerton, which was reached on Saturday 4 July. Tents arrived 'very seasonably' and on Sunday 5 July the royal army was able to set up camp in reasonable comfort at Westonzoyland, just over three miles [5 km] south-east of Bridgwater on slightly rising ground surrounded by a flat, peaty area known as Sedgemoor.

Monmouth now went through the motions of preparing Bridgwater for a siege, throwing up some earthworks on the approaches to it and, as one of his commanders recorded, 'sending warrants before to summon in the country people with spades and pickaxes' while in fact 'intending nothing less than to stay there'. The halt in the town was merely, the same source explained, 'to refresh our men and fix our arms, which were very much out of order'. After all-day discussions on Saturday with his Council of War its commander finally made up his mind on Sunday morning on his next move. He would 'take the formerly intended course into Shropshire and Cheshire' via Keynsham bridge, with a possible diversion to attack Bristol or Gloucester if the situation seemed promising.

With characteristic boldness, Monmouth rejected the alternative of merely slipping away in the darkness, a manoeuvre which, even if successful, would only postpone the inevitable confrontation with the royalist army. Instead he decided to take the initiative with a night attack, the type of operation in which he had always excelled, on the enemy camp.

Early on Sunday afternoon Monmouth led his senior officers up the spiral staircase to the top of the tower of St Mary's church to study through his telescope the disposition of the enemy forces three and a half miles [6 km] away. On descending he found awaiting him an expected messenger, a labourer sent by a local farmer, a keen Monmouthite.* This informant reported that the enemy foot were lying about sleeping, and perhaps drunk, on their scarlet coats, with the horse nowhere in sight. The guns were all concentrated on the southwest of the position, no sentries were visible, and a track running from the north into Westonzoyland seemed to be undefended.

The prospect of action showed Monmouth at his best. Having impressed on all his troops the need for total silence in the coming operation he issued orders that 'what man soever that made a noise should be knocked in the head by the next man'. At 11 pm, after a drumhead service on Castle Fields, Bridgwater, recently the scene of their last-minute training, Monmouth's army rode and marched off into the darkness, under the light of a full moon but shrouded in a timely moorland mist.

Monmouth's basic plan was bold and simple. He had ruled out the shortest, direct, route, which would have brought him up against the royal guns on the left of the enemy position, in front of Westonzoyland, and settled instead for a much longer, six mile [10-km] approach march, which would lead into the virtually unprotected right flank of Feversham's camp. Here his forces would split up, most of them bursting in upon the infantry, caught by surprise, it was hoped, in their tents or still struggling, half-awake, to answer the call to arms, while the rest of the rebels descended equally unexpectedly upon the royal commanders in Westonzoyland and their cavalry.

In overall numbers alone the two sides were not ill-matched.† Feversham had at his disposal about 750 horse, including the dragoons, 1900 infantry and 200 gunners, responsible to the Board of Ordnance, with 26 cannon. In reserve lay 3000 militia. Monmouth commanded about 600 horsemen, mainly untrained, 2980 foot and 30 gunners, for his three operational cannon, one having proved defective. Monmouth was probably Feversham's equal in experience and generalship,

* Various accounts of this episode are given in the secondary sources. I have opted for what seems the likeliest sequence of events.
† For an admirably clear statement of the Order of Battle of the two armies see Chandler, pp. 180-1.

but had a second-in-command of proven feebleness, Lord Grey, whom he refused to replace, while Feversham's deputy was the brilliant Lord Churchill.

Monmouth's men set off, as Feversham had expected, down the Bristol road, but at Marsh Lane, two miles [3.2 km] out of Bridgwater, while his 42 main supply wagons and the ineffective gun carried straight on, the ammunition wagons and all the fighting units swung right into Marsh Lane, the wagons, for greater mobility, being left on a small hill occupied by Peasey Farm, which was reached about midnight. The advancing columns went unnoticed by a patrol of the Blues making for Knowle Hill. Two watchmen from the village of Chedzoy, to which Monmouth had given a wide berth because of its fiercely royalist vicar, did spot the intruders but kept their mouths shut.

Monmouth's cavalry now moved to the head of the line, to be led across country by the Monmouthite labourer whose information that afternoon had set the whole operation in motion, but in a thick patch of mist he lost his way and hit the first obstruction barring their way, an eight-ft [2.4-m] wide water-filled 'cut' known as the Langmoor Rhine to one side of the crossing point called the Langmoor Stone. As he cast to left and right to find it the horsemen piled up behind him with their mounts slipping and neighing, a shot was fired, though whether 'by accident or by treachery' in the rebel ranks, or by an alert royalist trooper was never finally established.[*]

All surprise was now lost and, as the drums called the royal regiments to arms and the slow-match of the musketeers still armed with matchlocks lit the darkness with spreading pinpoints of flame, the first shots were exchanged as the captain of the picquet which had sighted the rebels obeyed his orders to 'fire and retire'. As he did so, his troop came into contact with Grey's cavalry, who, having splashed their way across at the Langmoor Stone at last, had been halted again by the Bussex Rhine. Uncertain of its depth or width Grey rode off, somewhat pointlessly, to the right, though one of his captains, who had fought under Cromwell, kept his head, found the regular crossing point, known as the Upper Plungeon, and led his 200 men across to fight vigorously with the three troops of Feversham's horse trying to hold it.

The time was now perhaps about 1.30 am on Monday 6 July 1685 and Lord Feversham, roused from his camp-bed in Westonzoyland, was carefully adjusting his full-bottomed wig and cravat in front of a 'paltry mirror' before taking command, a demonstration of coolness

* See Chandler, p. 60, on the possible alternatives. He attributes the 'accident' quotation to Daniel Defoe, who, on the evidence of the name 'Daniel Foe' appearing in a list of rebels later pardoned, is generally accepted as serving in Monmouth's army. He had unquestionably been intended for the dissenting ministry and was in 1685 aged about 25. His best-known work, *Robinson Crusoe*, was published in 1719.

later dismissed as being typical of a foppish Frenchman.

He ordered up his horse from the village to prepare to take the rebels in the flank, three troops of horse crossing the Bussex Rhine by the Lower Plungeon, the rest by the Upper. One returning patrol simply waded across in between them, as Grey could have done had he been bolder. Churchill had meanwhile led two of the foot regiments round behind the Guards to extend the right flank, from which the attack seemed likely to come, while in Middlezoy, a mile to the rear, the Wiltshire Militia were alerted and prepared to move forward in support. The royal guns were still positioned uselessly on the far left of the royal position and separated from their horses and handlers, billeted in Westonzoyland. The Bishop of Winchester, Peter Mews, now came to the rescue. Bishop Mews had lost an eye while serving with Charles I's artillery and was accordingly known as 'Old Patch' or 'The Bombardier Bishop'. He had driven over in his carriage to cast an experienced, if solitary, eye over Feversham's dispositions, and now enterprisingly harnessed his own coach horses to the wrongly sited guns, enabling two of the three batteries to be dragged into a new vantage point in front of the infantry to engage the main rebel forces across the Bussex Rhine.

Monmouth was now faced with what he had desperately hoped to avoid, a full-scale setpiece battle against a better-armed and better-trained force of regular troops, who heavily outnumbered him in horse and guns, though not in infantry. Most of these, however, with their scythes and clubs, could not be brought into action unless his musketeers could first establish superiority over the enemy regiments in a straightforward fire-fight and, probably about 2 am, the two sides settled down to shooting at each other across the Bussex Rhine, supported as the light improved – sunrise was about 4 am – by their cannon.

The rebel cannon did great execution against Dumbarton's Regiment facing it, for the glowing matches its men carried – the other musketeers were armed with flintlocks – provided an easy target in the darkness, and it was now that the royalist forces suffered most of their casualties. Had Monmouth's Yellow Regiment, with the Red in support, charged forward at this point, the Bussex Rhine being no real obstacle, Monmouth's men might still have started an uncheckable panic for in close-quarter combat in the darkness the outnumbered regulars would have lost their advantage, but by around 2.30 am the opportunity had gone. Now, as both infantry and cannon began to call for more ammunition, it was discovered that the men left at Peasey Farm to bring it forward had fled.

The balance of advantage now tipped decisively in favour of the royalists. John Churchill, seeing that the Scots of Dumbarton's Regiment were taking heavy punishment, ordered the two units on his left to march behind the royal line to the right flank of the position, to bring down fire on all three enemy regiments now in range. 'Old Patch' had meanwhile got the royal cannon into action and after silencing the much lighter enemy guns with some brisk counter-battery fire, using roundshot, the royal artillery was re-loaded with canister, small lethal balls packed into containers which burst among the enemy infantry with devastating effect.

Lord Feversham had at last arrived to take command and a little before 4 am, as it was growing light, he gave the order for the cavalry to charge. From right to left, they bore down upon Monmouth's infantry, already sadly cut about by cannon and small-arms fire. Watching closely, Feversham saw the enemy lines begin to waver as his horsemen burst upon them and a bitter hand-to-hand struggle began, giving most of Monmouth's pikemen their first chance to strike a blow since the start of the campaign. Eventually, however, Feversham saw the lines of the Green Regiment 'begin to shake and at last to waver' and unleashed his infantry, who swept forward over the Bussex Rhine, and charged forward with lowered pikes and with plug bayonets. Some of the rebels stood and fought where they died but many were forced backwards and John Churchill himself led a party of dragoons to cut down the enemy gunners, still guarding their now useless guns. Monmouth was already unbuckling his armour as he prepared for flight when Grey rode up to confirm his army was beaten. 'Nothing can stop those fellows,' the Duke agreed. 'They will run presently.' Soon the once-confident ranks, with their home-made weapons and simple faith in an unquestionably Protestant God, were shattered for ever and, wrote a contemporary, 'so dispersed that you could not anywhere see ten of their men living'.

By 7 am the last vestiges of resistance had ceased, but not the slaughter. 'Our men are still killing them in ye corne and hedges and ditches whither they are crept,' testified one soldier, sickened by the carnage, for most of the dead on the rebel side lost their lives after the fighting finished. One member of the Wiltshire Militia, which was left to clear up after the battle, put the number of bodies collected at 1384, but others were left 'unfound in the corn'. About 500 Monmouthites were taken prisoner, many of them wounded, and these were often treated with great cruelty. One man 'shot through the shoulder and wounded in the belly . . . lay on his back in the sun stripped naked for the space of ten or eleven hours', while 'a great crowd of soldiers came about him and reproached him, calling him "Thou Monmouth dog"'. He later died, after being shut up with 500 others, wounded and unwounded, in St Mary's church, Westonzoyland, where all the prisoners were left, unfed and uncared for, throughout a day and a night.

Monmouth himself, like his father after the Battle of Worcester, had fled from Sedgmoor in disguise, but, less fortunate than him, was captured ingloriously 'hidden in a ditch, covered with fern and bracken' in the village of Woodlands in Dorset, six miles [10 km] north of Wimborne Minster and 12 from the port of Poole and possible safety. He was beheaded, at the Tower, in circumstances of particular horror for the executioner sadly bungled the job, on Wednesday 15 July 1685, just one month and four days after the joyous landing at Lyme.

A few of Monmouth's leading supporters were pardoned on turning King's evidence, among them the ever resilient Lord Grey, who even had his title restored, but, contrary to the usual tradition, the rank-and-file rebels were treated with great severity. In the week following the Battle of Sedgmoor probably 100 prisoners were summarily executed without trial, and in the next five weeks many more fell victim to the brutal Colonel Kirke, who ordered his regimental drummers and fife players to strike up a tune as the victims struggled in their death throes so that 'they shall have music in their dancing'.

The chief instrument of the king's vengeance was the soon notorious Lord Chief Justice (George, first Baron) Jeffreys, 'The Devil in Wig and Gown', who was still only 37 when he arrived in Winchester on 25 August 1685 to begin the 'Bloody Assize'. At Dorchester, on Saturday 5 September, 29 men were sentenced in a single morning to the hideous death reserved for traitors. A week later, on 12 September, 12 rebels were duly hanged, drawn and quartered on the foreshore west of the Cobb at Lyme where Monmouth had landed. Mary Blake, whose pupils had embroidered banners for Monmouth's regiments, died in prison, the 'Maids of Taunton' themselves being spared on condition that their parents paid a £2000 a head 'ransom'. At the end of September Jeffreys returned to London, via Windsor, where he received the king's thanks and promotion to Lord Chancellor. In all, 1336 rebels had been tried in a mere nine days in court, of whom about 250 are believed to have been judicially executed and another 850 transported to virtual slavery in the West Indies.

What had seemed likely to be the most successful invasion since Henry VII's had ended in catastrophic failure, but it had left behind a legacy of hatred for the Roman Catholic religion and a widespread loathing for the whole Stuart dynasty. 'Those in the west,' commented one MP a few years later, when such things could safely be said in public, 'did see such a shambles as made them think they had a Turk rather than a Christian for their king.'

IO

INVASION IN GOOD EARNEST

He told me the Dutch were now coming to invade England in good earnest.

Lord Clarendon, *recounting conversation*
with James II on 24 September 1688

The suppression of the rebellion which followed Monmouth's invasion proved the high-water mark of James II's achievements, both as
soldier and statesman. In August 1685, the month after Monmouth's
execution, James inspected the ten battalions of infantry and 28 squadrons of cavalry he had assembled on Hounslow Heath, a mere 15 miles
[24 km] from Westminster. Such camps, designed to give experience
of life in the field and to accustom their commanders to deploying large
numbers of troops, became an annual event, involving 13-16,000 men.

James's real interest, however, was in the navy, and in September
1685 he visited Portsmouth, accompanied by both Samuel Pepys and
John Evelyn who was impressed by the new defences: 'Portsmouth
when finished,' Evelyn noted in his diary, 'will be very strong and a
noble key; there were now 32 men-of-war in the harbour.' Pepys was
still very much James's man, and for him, as Secretary of the
Admiralty, and for the navy, a golden age now began.

Much needed to be done. On paper the navy consisted of 179 vessels,
of which 120 were 'rated', the rest being lesser vessels, including fireships, yachts and a sloop, but in November the great Harwich shipbuilder, now Sir Anthony Deane, submitted to Pepys the report of a
recent inspection which revealed that only 37 of the 179 were immediately seaworthy. Every one of the 63 'ships of the line', the navy's
real fighting strength, needed urgent repair.

On New Year's Day 1686 Pepys laid Deane's dismal and alarming
survey before James II, at a 'solemn hearing', and subsequently, on the
king's instructions, Pepys submitted a radical plan for reform. This envisaged a three-year plan for totally overhauling the fleet and keeping a
permanent squadron in the Channel, as well as building some new
'fourth rates' and maintaining an establishment of 4000 men in winter
and 6000 in summer. All this, with efficient administration, could be
achieved for £400,000 a year, secured by regular payments from the

Customs, the one certain source of income. In April 1686 the King approved the plan and appointed a Special Commission for, in Pepys's words, 'the Recovery of the Navy', the most important Commissioner being Sir Anthony Deane. The existing members of the Navy Board were stripped of authority, and replaced by a group of Commissioners who undertook 'to apply themselves with the utmost thoroughness, diligence, efficacy and good husbandry' to the repair of the existing fleet, and to maintain 'a strict, methodical and perfect survey' of all stores. At the same time personnel matters were not neglected, the Commissioners being required 'to have a more than ordinary regard . . . to the recovering (as fast as may be) the lost discipline of the Navy and the encouraging and establishing of sobriety and industry' among all ranks.

The hated press gang remained; but, this apart, these energetic years left the navy transformed. On their appointment, in April 1686, the Special Commissioners had 'found nothing a'doing in the Yards'. By their dissolution, in October 1688, they had rebuilt 20 ships, fully repaired 69 others, and constructed three new 'fourth rates'. Incredibly, not a seaman, or dockyard worker, or contractor, was waiting to be paid. England could, if required, put to sea a fleet of 59 ships of the line, with the 'fourth rates', 'fifth rates' and 'sixth rates' bringing the total to 108; 26 fireships, 14 yachts and a number of smaller craft such as hulks and ketches, raised the overall strength to 173. This included the one new type of warship introduced at this time, the bomb-ketch or 'bomb', a small sailing ship carrying a wide-bore mortar which hurled, howitzer-like, an explosive shell at shore defences. The navy's manpower, though half was to be laid off during the winter, was put at 42,000 men, its fire-power at 6930 guns. As Pepys told the retiring Commissioners, 'I cannot but with great satisfaction reflect upon the condition you will be remembered to have left the navy of England in.'

All James II's achievements in strengthening the nation's defences were overshadowed by the religious issue. In October 1685, just as Deane and Pepys were beginning their reforming work, Louis XIV of France had repealed the Edict of Nantes, which since April 1598 had permitted freedom of worship to French Protestants. The brutal persecution which followed rivalled that of the notorious massacre of the Huguenots on St Bartholomew's Day, 1572, which had inflamed anti-Catholic feeling in England.[*]

Far from responding to the prevailing anti-papist mood James, in 1685, forbade the celebration of Bonfire Night. In the following two years he appointed a Roman Catholic as governor of Dover Castle, another as Commander-in-Chief in Ireland, a third, who provoked a mutiny by ordering mass to be celebrated on board the king's ships, as

---

[*] See *Defending the Island*, p. 420.

Vice-Admiral. He also expelled the Fellows of Magdalen College, Oxford, for refusing to accept a Roman Catholic President, and eventually, in 1688, caused the Archbishop of Canterbury and six other bishops to be prosecuted for challenging the king's right to give freedom of worship to both Catholics and dissenters.

While the victimised clerics were still awaiting trial news arrived, on 10 June 1688, that the queen had been delivered of a son. As James was 54, and it was six years since the queen, Mary of Modena, had borne a child, the Catholics proclaimed a miracle; the Protestants, more prosaically, alleged that the pregnancy had been false and that the baby, baptised James Francis Edward, had been smuggled into the royal bed in a warming-pan. If the child were genuine – as is now generally accepted – then he pushed aside from the succession the existing heir, Mary of Orange, daughter of James by his first wife, Anne Hyde, now married to the Protestant William of Orange. The country would then face the grim prospect of another Catholic king with, in all probability, an endless line of Catholic sovereigns thereafter. The acquittal of the seven bishops on 30 June 1688 provided an occasion for a popular demonstration against James, being received by cheers even by the troops again encamped at Hounslow, and that very day seven leading public figures signed a letter to William of Orange urging him to cross to England with an army large enough to depose its existing king before the end of the year.

William of Orange was, both in appearance and personality, no Monmouth. Exceptionally short and hunchbacked, with an unattractive face dominated by a hooked nose, he was in permanently poor health; he suffered from asthma, coughed constantly and never really recovered from a smallpox attack in his twenties. William dressed drably and smiled rarely; his beautiful 15-year-old bride, confronted with him just before their wedding in 1677, wept solidly for a day and a half. But 'Dutch William', as the English called him, had already by the summer of 1688, when he was 37, displayed many admirable qualities. The British ambassador had described him in his late teens as 'a most extreme hopeful prince' displaying 'good plain sense, with show of application if he had business that deserved it'. William enjoyed hunting and, when the day's work was done, drinking, but he was a devout Calvinist, and as Holland's Captain-General he had gained a substantial military reputation, his outstanding characteristic being caution.

William's preparations for the invasion of England were solid and thorough. Six English and Scottish regiments were in 1688 serving in the United Provinces, and these now formed the backbone of the expeditionary force assembled near Nijmegen, which was soon swelled by mercenaries recruited from all over Protestant Europe. Ultimately William commanded an actual strength, allowing for the usual shortfall on official establishments, of at least 12-13,000. This was a great deal more impressive than Monmouth's modest 200 but still inferior, by two or three to one, to the numbers at James II's disposal.

The plans for transporting and supplying this formidable army were the most elaborate to be drawn up since the days of the Spanish Armada. The collection of *matériél* was on a vast scale. The factories at Utrecht were kept busy day and night producing arms and the bakeries of Rotterdam turned out vast quantities of ships' biscuit. The final tally of stores included 10,000 pairs of spare boots, four tons of tobacco, 1600 hogsheads [84,000 gallons; 380,000 litres] of beer, 50 hogsheads [2625 gallons; 12,000 litres] of brandy, a mobile smithy, moulds for making coins and a printing press. As in every such operation, the horses were more troublesome to transport than the men, it being calculated that each of the 4000 being embarked would require 16 lbs [7.3 kg] of hay for ten days, amounting to a total of nearly 300 tons.

Shipping created the usual bottleneck in most invasions, but the Dutch excelled in all maritime matters and by the target date of 12 September (English style, i.e. 22 September in Holland), 225 transports, many of them of sufficiently shallow draught to get close inshore, had been assembled. William managed to collect an escorting force of 52 warships but, being fearful of what James's fleet might do to his unarmed troopships, urged caution on his naval commander, the naturally impetuous Admiral Herbert. 'He must,' William told his chief of staff and close friend, Hans Willem van Bentinck, 'avoid fighting as much as he can . . . This is no time to show bravery.'

James II always took the threat from across the North Sea seriously. On Sunday 26 August a conference of experienced seamen, attended by Pepys, was held at Windsor, at which it was decided to base the main fleet off the North Foreland in the more southerly of the two main channels leading into the Thames estuary, rather than in the Gunfleet off the Essex coast as Admiral Sir Roger Strickland, commanding the Channel fleet, favoured.

On 20 September 1688 James, visiting Chatham – in a letter to William of Orange he referred pointedly to 'the new batteries I have made in the Medway' – was recalled to London by the news that saddles, shovels and, sounding especially formidable, wheelbarrows, were being loaded on to the waiting ships at Hellevoetsluis. Three days later, on Sunday 23 September, an urgent message arrived from his ambassador at The Hague that William was beginning to embark troops. Next morning one of his ministers met James emerging from the royal bedchamber: 'He told me, the Dutch were now coming to invade England in good earnest. I presumed to ask if he really believed it. To which the king replied with warmth "Do I see you, my lord?"'

On 24 September James issued orders to George Legge, first Baron Dartmouth, Master General of the Ordnance, informing him that all the infantry regiments were being increased in size and giving detailed instructions about the provision of new and 'best-proof' armour for the mounted troopers. That same day Dartmouth, an Anglican, replaced the detested papist Strickland as commander of the Channel fleet. The Lord Deputy of Ireland was required to despatch four regiments of horse and foot to England, and ultimately about 5000 men were brought from Ireland, plus another 4000 from Scotland. James also called out the militia, but to little purpose for, as the Lord Lieutenant of Lincolnshire reminded the king on 27 September, the removal of the local gentry from such offices as deputy-lieutenant, during James's period of advancing Catholics, had left it in sad disarray, a verdict confirmed two days later by the Lord Lieutenant of Dorset. Few Protestants were keen to fight for a papist sovereign and though the Lord Lieutenant of Staffordshire assured the king's chief minister pointedly that 'several besides Roman Catholics will be glad to sell their lives as dear as they can in defence of his Majesty', Lord Chancellor Jeffreys was less optimistic. 'The Virgin Mary,' he observed privately, 'is to do all!'

On 27 September James announced a general pardon for political offenders, and on the following day issued a proclamation designed to appeal to his subjects' patriotism:

> We have received undoubted advice that a great and sudden invasion from Holland, with an armed force of foreigners and strangers, will speedily be made in a hostile manner upon this our kingdom; and although some false pretences relating to liberty, property, and religion, contrived or worded with art and subtlety may be given out . . . it is manifest . . . that no less matter by this invasion is proposed and purposed than an absolute conquest of our kingdom and the utter subduing and subjecting us and our people to a foreign power.

James explained in his proclamation that the writs summoning a new Parliament had been withdrawn because of the military situation, a reasonable enough excuse but one which his rival's counter-proclamation, issued on 30 September, exploited to the full.

> The last and great remedy for all those evils is the calling of a parliament, for securing the nation against the evil practices of those wicked counsellors, but this could not be yet compassed . . . those men apprehending that a lawful parliament being once assembled they would be brought to an account for all their open violations of law, and their plots and conspiracies against the Protestant religion.

William knew that the 'warming-pan' story of the substituted heir was nonsense, but when a throne was at stake one could not be too squeamish and the proclamation went on to assert that 'all the good subjects of those kingdoms do vehemently suspect that the pretended Prince of

Wales was not born by the queen'.

Realising how much harm his cause was suffering from the 'warming-pan' story James attempted to counter it, on 22 October, with an, in every sense, extraordinary meeting of the Privy Council in Whitehall at which 40 eye-witnesses, from midwives to ministers, swore on oath in front of the judges and Lord Mayor that the birth had been genuine. Lord Chancellor Jeffreys himself, coarsely and characteristically, testified that he had seen the new-born infant 'piping hot'. But an authentic Catholic male heir was even worse than a changeling (allegedly a miller's son) and few of James's subjects were reassured.

In purely military terms James was well placed to resist an invasion. Unlike his predecessors he had a large regular army officially numbered, with its Scottish and Irish reinforcements, at 40,117, though many troops were tied up in garrisoning forts at Hull, Yarmouth, Sheerness, Portsmouth, Plymouth and Bristol, and in small parties all around the coast and in garrison towns. These were designed to deal with the small forces William was expected to land at numerous points as a diversion, and to suppress 'evilly disposed persons' trying to raise support for the invaders. As for his likely destination, Scotland, Bridlington, Sole Bay and Essex all had their advocates, there being general agreement that the blow would fall on the eastern side of the country. In late August the Scots Guards, marching back from the usual summer camp on Hounslow Heath, were diverted to strengthen the garrison at Hull, to which more troops were also sent from other places inland, while the Norfolk militia were put on a state of readiness between 2 and 10 October, and Landguard Fort received an additional 100 men. Following the Dutch success there in 1667 Chatham and the Isle of Thanet were also well defended, but Monmouth's expedition suggested that William might make for the south-west and in the end, while keeping London well garrisoned, James placed his main striking force and strategic reserve on Salisbury Plain. Other troops were disposed to cover the coast of Kent and behind Portsmouth and Harwich.

In spite of his own naval experience James did not attempt to dictate Lord Dartmouth's strategy in intercepting the enemy fleet, declaring on 14 October that, 'He must govern himself according to the enemy's motions and as wind and weather will permit.' Dartmouth commanded 52 ships of the line, mounting 1876 guns, plus 17 fireships,* very similar in size to the force at the disposal of William of Orange.

On 24 October he moved his fleet from 'the buoy of the Nore' off the North Foreland to the other side of the Thames estuary, anchoring in the Gunfleet, south of Harwich. 'Sir,' he wrote proudly to the king that evening, 'we are now at sea before the Dutch after all their boasting, and I must confess I cannot see much sense to their attempt with

* Ogg, *England in the Reigns of James II and William III*, p. 214. Other historians give different figures.

the hazard of such a fleet and army at the latter end of October . . . Your statesmen may take a nap and recover, the women sleep in their beds, and the cattle, I think, need not be drove from the shore.'

Dartmouth's complacency was understandable in the light of the news reaching him from across the North Sea. William had begun loading stores as early as 12 September and the embarkation of troops, at various points along the coast, was completed on the 26th though, with the wind westerly and unfavourable, William did not join his fleet and set sail until Saturday 20 October (English style) after bidding a tearful farewell to his wife, whom he urged to marry again if he failed to return, but not a papist. Slowly the great armada, led by its 50 war-ships in two squadrons, with the long line of transports behind, made its way past the island of Goree and out through the mouth of the River Maas north-westward into the open sea. The whole force covered some 20 miles [32 km], with William's modest flagship, a 30-gun fri-gate, the *Brill*, near the front of the inner line of ships. Their destination was still uncertain for the wind, south-west by south, made it far easier to reach Yorkshire, the second choice of objective, than Admiral Her-bert's preferred target, the south-west. In the event the wind settled the matter for it veered back to the west and blew up into a gale, scattering the ships during the night of Saturday 20 October and forcing them to run for shelter to the nearest friendly port. By Tuesday, however, almost all had reached the new assembly point, at Hellevoetsluis, the only casualties being 400 horses, suffocated in their battened-down holds while their grooms were too weak from seasickness to attend to them. William himself, though badly affected by the same disabling condition, had managed to remain in command, and proved calm and resolute during the days that followed. 'There were few among us,' acknowledged Bishop Burnet frankly, 'that did not conclude . . . that the whole design was lost . . . Many that have passed for heroes, yet showed then the agonies of fear.' But William, as the fierce north-west gales whipped across the grey waters off the Dutch coast, kept his nerve. 'The worst loss,' he wrote after the expedition's ignominious return, 'is the time and the horses.'

Meanwhile in England spirits had soared among James's followers at the news of his enemy's false start. The British ambassador at The Hague – the two countries were still officially at peace – who employed two fishing-boats to watch William's fleet, had reported its departure on 20 October but it was not till the evening of 26 October that news reached Samuel Pepys at the Admiralty of William's setback. At 2 am on Saturday 27 October he dashed off a letter tactfully suggesting to Lord Dartmouth that he cross the North Sea to exploit the situation, but the admiral refused. 'The whole proceedings at this season,' Dart-mouth wrote to the king, 'looks like the advice of land men . . . Their growing mad shall not provoke me to follow their example.'

William of Orange was now watching the weather-vane of the nearest church, as William the Conqueror, another autumn invader, had once done, and at last, on Tuesday 1 November (English style) he again led his fleet out of Hellevoetsluis towards the open sea. Next day, while it was moored offshore, a final Council of War was held on board the *Brill* to hear a last-minute report about the disposition of James's army and a firm decision was taken, although the wind was north-westerly, to make for Dorset or Devon. Two days earlier, on 30 October, Dartmouth, confident as ever, had reported to James, 'I have scouts abroad and I believe it is impossible for us to miss such a fleet,' but miss it they did. 'Three good sailing frigates and brisk men' were watching the Dutch coast and two yachts, off Friesland and Heligoland respectively, with a third as long-stop somewhere near the Goodwin Sands, but the frigates were dismasted, and the yachts blinded, by bad weather. They failed to observe either William's departure or the crucial change of course, following a shift in the wind, which he made while about 80 miles [128 km] off Spurn Head at the mouth of the Humber. The whole great fleet turned sharply round so that it was soon sailing almost due south, past Norfolk, the Gunfleet and the North Foreland, towards the Straits of Dover, within a mere 15 miles [24 km] of the main English fleet. Dartmouth, somewhere off Harwich, woke at daybreak on Saturday 3 November (English style) to find himself totally outmanoeuvred, with 13 enemy warships, guarding the western flank of the invading armada, visible on the horizon, pressing steadily southward.

By midday, off the North Foreland, William was debating whether to change his plan and make a sudden strike up the Thames to London, but he rejected the idea and instead redeployed his ships into the most impressive pattern to overawe, or encourage, those on shore. In bright sunshine and in splendid visibility, the invaders sailed, around 1 pm, from the North Sea into the Narrow Seas, while musicians played, guns fired salutes and long pennants streamed in the breeze from the Dutch mastheads, bearing the slogans William had made his own, 'For liberty and a free parliament' and 'For the Protestant religion'.

Once through the Straits, somewhere off Dungeness, the invaders turned almost due west and by dawn on Sunday 4 November 1688 were off the Isle of Wight and close to Portsmouth. This was James's strongest fortress, and William again decided against a landing, though by Dutch reckoning it was his thirty-eighth birthday and his wedding anniversary, both with propagandist possibilities.

Lord Dartmouth was still 100 miles [160 km] behind when, at dawn on Monday 5 November 1688, with the wind obligingly veering to the south, William of Orange's fleet sailed, totally unchallenged, into Torbay. Soon afterwards the early morning fog cleared and in bright sunshine the commander of William's footguard led a party of grenadiers

ashore on to the sands of the village of Brixham in Devon. They were
followed by the rest of the infantry, then the cavalry, the whole force
being ashore within 24 hours. William himself landed on the first afternoon and at a thanksgiving service on the beach made his only
recorded joke, remarking to Bishop Burnet, who rejected this Calvinist doctrine, 'Well, Doctor, what do you think of predestination
now?'

That night, which William spent on a mattress on the floor of a
fisherman's hut, it rained heavily and next morning his troops set off
along muddy lanes towards Exeter, paying for any provisions they
needed, though the country people pressed cider and apples upon them
and shouted 'God bless you!'

News of William's landing spread slowly; the alarm beacons had not
been lit for fear of attracting sympathisers to his banner. But as early as
7 November 60 gentlemen from Buckinghamshire were seen riding
westward through Oxford, under the command of a Whig politician
and minor poet, Thomas [later first Marquis of] Wharton, while
another pro-William group, including some professional soldiers,
were already assembling in Gloucester. So far, however, the principal
sign of his gathering support was the mania for the tune *Lilliburlero*
which now swept the country. The words, credited to Thomas Wharton, were poor stuff but the tune was a catchy one and *Lilliburlero* later
became a popular marching song and is still played frequently today.*

On Friday 9 November 1688 William entered Exeter. Its citizens
gave a tumultuous welcome to the modest force of four battalions of
infantry, two cavalry regiments and the units of English refugees,
which he led through its streets, although the mayor refused to cooperate and the Bishop of Exeter fled hotfoot to London, to be rewarded
with promotion to the Archbishopric of York. During the two weeks
William spent at Exeter he was joined by the first of a flood of important supporters, including some senior officers from the garrison at
Portsmouth, parts of three royal cavalry regiments, and even the
loathsome Percy Kirke, who had fallen out with his royal master and
brought with him 200 officers and men. Meanwhile, on 15 November,
a diversionary rebellion had broken out in Cheshire and rapidly spread
to Derby and Nottingham, which became the main Orangist headquarters outside London. The rebels' possession of Chester was also
strategically important, since it was the main port through which
James might have brought in reinforcements from Ireland, the only
troops on whose loyalty he could rely.

While his kingdom was collapsing around him, James II stayed in

---

* I share G.M. Trevelyan's view that 'It has less than no merit as literature' (*England under
the Stuarts*, p. 369 fn). The words can be found in Kenneth Baker, p. 221-2. The tune
could until recently be heard daily on the BBC World Service.

London, torn between the rival fears that if he left the capital it might rise against him and that if he did not soon join his troops he might have no army left to command. On Saturday 17 November he finally took the road westwards, reaching Salisbury on the 19th, but was incapacitated for the two following days by a severe nosebleed, and the surgeons' blood-lettings which followed left him visibly enfeebled. As wind and rain howled round the Bishop's Palace where he lay helpless, his adversary was on the march. On 20 November the first blows were exchanged in what had so far been a bloodless campaign, when a party of Dutch infantry, 25 strong, sent ahead of the main army into Somerset to buy horses, were intercepted by 120 cavalrymen of the Life Guard; the Dutch did well to get away with nine dead and six men taken prisoner, having killed four of the horsemen and wounded two more. The next day, Wednesday 21 November, having learned that the commander of Plymouth, the Earl of Bath, was about to declare for him – he did so publicly on the 24th – William began his advance towards London, confident that his rear was safe; Plymouth, only 40 miles [64 km] to the west, had contained 1000 royal soldiers; now it became a naval base for the invaders.

The English navy remained totally inactive. Lord Dartmouth and his flag officers had, with incredible feebleness, advised the king there was no point in their trying to interfere now the Dutch were ashore. On 12 November James nevertheless ordered his commander to attack the enemy wherever he found him, but Dartmouth sheltered in the Downs on the plea of bad weather and then, during a half-hearted foray towards Torbay, ended up, thanks to unfavourable winds, at Alderney. 'The Channell,' he declared despondently, 'is harder working than any Battle.' Finally, by 19 November, he had assembled 22 ships off Brixham, but, confronted by the much larger Dutch fleet, simply turned tail. The best navy England had ever possessed had lost the will to fight.

William spent the night of 22 November at Honiton, and that day the 'capital' of the north, York, declared for him, followed soon afterwards by the main northern garrison towns, Hull and Carlisle, and then Scarborough, where the Castle had been stripped of its 100-man garrison who had gone to join the field army. On Friday 23 November 1688 William established his headquarters in fiercely Protestant Axminster, while 56 miles [90 km] away James II was holding a Council of War at Salisbury. This was the moment of decision if William was to be held, as Monmouth had been, within the south-western peninsula, for Salisbury lay near the centre of the 60-mile [96-km] line between the Severn and Southampton Water and Bristol, the furthest point reached by Monmouth. Lord Feversham was, however, suffering badly from lack of up-to-date information about William's movements. He was afraid to send out troops of horse to reconnoitre in case they went over to the enemy, while deserters from the enemy army, the other source of intelligence, were wholly lacking. James on his arrival at Salisbury had contemplated a brisk advance westwards to contain the invaders. His army, with some 30,000 men on Salisbury Plain alone, outnumbered William's by two to one, and James also possessed a reserve of 8-9000 garrison troops who could be recalled to join the field forces. By now, however, he was depressed, and content to leave the initiative to the invader. He decided to withdraw eastwards to the line of the Thames, which would be held on a 20-mile [32-km] front from Marlow to Chertsey, concentrating his troops at Windsor, near the centre of the position, Staines and Egham. Feversham himself was to remain with the cavalry at Reading, with the not very heroic role of using his horses to eat up all the local forage before William's cavalry arrived. Instructions were sent to a regiment near Bristol to break down the same bridge at Keynsham which Monmouth had briefly held, but the troops were recalled before the order could be implemented. Thus Bristol, too, was left for the invader to occupy at leisure, which he duly did on 2 December 1688, giving William yet another naval base and securing his western flank.

John Churchill, Feversham's second-in-command, had, on 23 November, advised against the withdrawal towards London, but that night he himself deserted, leading numerous officers and 400 cavalrymen into William's camp at Axminster. About the same time Princess Anne, James's second daughter by his first wife and hence William's sister-in-law, a close friend of Churchill's wife, deserted her father, making a not very romantic exit through the door used for the discreet emptying of her lavatory. So distrusted was James that wild stories circulated alleging, 'The Papists have murther'd her', but she soon turned up at Nottingham to join the Orangists. His daughter's desertion hit the king hard. 'God help me!' he lamented, 'my own children have forsaken me!'

Meanwhile William was steadily advancing, through Crewkerne, Sherborne and Wincanton, to Salisbury, which he reached on 4 December. Although the weather was seasonably bitter, and William was soon suffering from a bad cold, the march took on increasingly the character of a triumphal progress rather than a military campaign. His infantry were now established on the Berkshire Downs between Great Bedwyn and Little Bedwyn and moving down into the Thames Valley; troops of horsemen had pushed well ahead to Newbury, Abingdon and Reading, where the second skirmish of the campaign took place. It proved a disaster for the royalists. When a Dutch cavalry unit launched an attack on 50 Irishmen holding the bridge over the Thames the English horse and Scottish foot assigned to support them remained inactive and, it was recorded, 'never a man drew sword but went civilly to make room for the prince's forces'. On 7 December, after crossing Salisbury Plain unchallenged via Collingbourne Kingston near North Tidworth, William settled with relief into the Bear Inn at Hungerford, still a comfortable hotel, to plan the final stage of the campaign.

James still held Portsmouth, Tilbury and the Tower of London and possessed an army several thousand strong whom, on 6 December, he reviewed in Hyde Park, but the heart had gone out of the royalists, and not least the king himself, and on 8 December his commissioners met William at Hungerford to open peace negotiations on the basis of each side staying where it was while free elections were held. This was merely a delaying tactic while James completed his preparations to go into exile for on 10 December he sent his wife, disguised, in the best Stuart tradition, as an Italian laundress, to France with his infant son.

'My affairs are, as you know, in so desperate a condition that I have been obliged to send away the queen and the prince . . . ,' he wrote to Lord Dartmouth that night. 'Having been basely deserted by many officers and soldiers of my troops and finding . . . that the same poison is got amongst the fleet . . . I . . . therefore have resolved to withdraw till this violent storm is over.' In the early hours of the following morning, 11 December, the king burned with his own hands the writs summoning a new parliament, and, leaving Whitehall by a secret staircase, threw the great seal into the Thames as he crossed it at Vauxhall. (He made a hash even of this petulant gesture; five months later the great seal was recovered by a fisherman.) By nightfall he was on board ship near Faversham in Kent, waiting for a favourable tide to carry him down river en route for France.

By now organised resistance had ceased. Lord Dartmouth had already gone over to William, to avoid bloodshed, and on that same fateful Tuesday Lord Feversham, having formally disbanded the army, wrote to William to offer his personal surrender. Excitement increased next day when 'Bloody Jeffreys' was caught at Wapping, trying to get away disguised as a seaman. He narrowly escaped being lynched and was imprisoned in the Tower, where he died of natural causes soon afterwards. Already the homes of known Catholics, like the Spanish ambassador, had been attacked by the mob and darkness on 12 December ushered in 'Irish Night', with the public in an uproar awaiting an influx of throat-cutting Irishmen. Lord Dartmouth's wife, still in London, sent to her husband at Portsmouth a vivid, if oddly spelt, account of the deteriorating situation:

Lord Chanseler is prisoner in the Tower . . . indeed this town as bin mighty unquiat since the king's departure, by pulling the chappels down and houses of papists and ambassadors, so that everybody is in great frights, and wish for the Prince of Oringe's coming to quiet things.

On 14 December William reached Windsor, where he learned that, to everyone's deep embarrassment, James, by pure chance, had been detained unrecognised by a group of vigilantes hunting for Catholic priests while he waited to catch the tide, and on Sunday 16 December he returned to London in something approaching triumph, welcomed by crowds eager to see law and order re-established. James II, Part II was, however, to prove shortlived. William moved on, unopposed, to Sion Park in Chiswick, on the western edge of London, and at 2 am on Tuesday 18 December James was woken by a delegation from William which told him he must be ready to leave that morning. It was agreed, after some discussion, that he should go to Rochester, from which, it was tacitly understood, he would be allowed to escape to France, and around 11 am on a dismally cold and wet winter day, King James II was rowed down river towards brief captivity and ultimate exile.

It was already growing dark when, inconspicuously and by back streets, William III arrived at St James's Palace to take possession of his kingdom. It was a gloomy start to the new reign and, in his absence, sympathy for the deposed king was already beginning to make itself felt when, to universal relief, on 22 December he embarked at Rochester to land, after a stormy snow-bound crossing, at Ambleteuse in France on Christmas Day (English style; 4 January 1689 new style).

On 29 December an assembly of former Members of Parliament invited William to act as a 'caretaker' ruler until a national 'convention' – not a parliament, since there was no king on the throne to summon one – could meet to settle the nation's future. This duly met on 22 January to declare the throne vacant since, it was resolved, 'It hath been found by experience to be inconsistent with the safety and welfare of this protestant kingdom to be governed by a popish prince,' and to offer the throne jointly to William and his wife. Both had declared they would accept it on no other terms, William refusing, in a famous phrase, to become his 'wife's gentleman usher'. The king, it was well understood, would be the real sovereign. On 12 April 1689 King William III and Queen Mary II were crowned in Westminster Abbey, like those other successful invaders, William I and Henry VII, but after a campaign remarkable for being almost bloodless. A little later Parliament voted £600,000 to repay the Dutch the cost of the invasion, though this was some 13 per cent less than the £678,000 actually spent.[*]

It was the first time that the cost of an invasion has been so precisely quantified and marked a tidy beginning to a new era in English history.

[*] Baxter, p. 250. Carswell, pp. 244-6, puts the overall cost, from 6 October to 31 December 1688, as £1,028,000.

BOOK 2
FROM LOUIS TO NAPOLEON
1689–1815

The Invaders 1685–1745

II

GOOD SUCCESS IN IRELAND

At the moment all depends on good success in Ireland.

William III to Lord Portland, 7 February 1690

What soon became known as 'The Glorious Revolution' was to shape England's defence policy, and affect her place in the world, for at least the next century. That James would attempt to recover his lost throne seemed inevitable, especially since he had taken refuge in France. Immediately on his arrival, Louis had installed the exiled Stuart in a palace at St Germain-en-Laye, where he lived in a far more impressive style than most royal exiles. Louis described James as 'the best fellow in the world' and was distinctly smitten by his wife, Mary of Modena, though the French were puzzled that, as a beautiful woman of 30, she should be faithful to a husband 26 years her senior. James would probably have been content to live quietly for a time but both Mary and Louis were insistent on immediate action and his chief remaining ally in the British Isles, Richard Talbot, Earl of Tyrconnel, Lord Deputy and Commander-in-Chief in Ireland, wrote urging him not to settle into comfortable inactivity in France when Ireland offered a kingdom of his own 'plentiful in all things for human life'. Men were not lacking in Ireland but Tyrconnel needed both money and arms, specifying his requirements as 500,000 crowns [£125,000], 16,000 muskets and 12,000 swords. Over supper on 20 January 1689 (English style), Louis persuaded James, who would have preferred to begin the recovery of his lost throne via Scotland, to respond to Tyrconnel's plea, offering a handsome contribution in money and arms plus five experienced officers to help train the raw Irish troops and a diplomatic adviser, formerly French envoy at the Hague.

James sailed from Brest on 24 February 1689 with 25 ships and landed at Kinsale, about 15 miles [24 km] from Cork, on the southern coast of Ireland, on Tuesday 12 March. He was the first English king (as Irish Catholics still considered him) to visit the country since Richard II in 1394 and when he entered Dublin on 24 March, with his old friend, Tyrconnel, whom James had created a duke, riding before him, he received a rapturous reception, with bells ringing, girls in white scattering flowers in front of him, and the clergy carrying the host in a monstrance. Dublin Castle, like most things in Ireland, was somewhat dilapidated, but here he set up his new court.

Ireland in March 1689 presented a mirror-image of the situation in England. By James's landing in mid-March the Protestants had been forced to abandon most of their strongholds and soon after his arrival they gave up Dungannon, 35 miles [56 km] west of Belfast, and Coleraine, a seaport on the north coast, which succumbed to an Irish force under a French commander. That left two places in 'enemy' hands. One was Enniskillen, on an island in the River Erne, which offered the only crossing point between Connaught and Ulster; the other was Londonderry, or Derry as Catholics called it, a major port four miles [6.4 km] from the mouth of the River Foyle, near the centre of the northern coast of Ulster. It was strongly protected by walls completed in 1618 and occupied by the descendants of the Scottish Presbyterians 'planted' there earlier in the century.

James decided to concentrate his efforts on subduing Londonderry, but in the end had to ride back, damp and disappointed, to Dublin, where, on 26 April, as he wrote in his memoirs, 'he found the arms not arrived from Cork, Kinsale or Waterford; and that in the arsenal nothing had been done for preparing of tools'. While he was struggling to put things right, and to organise the manufacture of cannon, of which his vast, mainly barefoot, army was desperately short, a large French convoy of 24 ships of the line and ten fireships docked at Bantry Bay, near Cork, bringing welcome supplies and reinforcements.

James's private quarrel with William now became irretrievably caught up in the greater feud between England and France. William's navy had failed dismally in not intercepting James's convoy on its way from Brest in March and now the Comte de Châteaurenault [or Château Renault] had made the same voyage unchallenged, only being brought to battle on Wednesday 1 May 1689, as he prepared to leave his anchorage. Admiral Herbert, who had emerged with credit from William's invasion of England, had hastily assembled a squadron at Portsmouth to pursue the French but now, with 17 ships of the line and three bomb-vessels, one of their earliest appearances on the maritime scene, found himself outnumbered. The French lost about 40 men, the English about 80, and only a quarrel between the French commanders prevented a disaster. When James was told that the French navy had beaten the English he commented patriotically, 'It is the first time then,' while William, as a face-saver, created Herbert first Earl of Torrington.

Bantry Bay was the first engagement of the Anglo-French war officially declared by William on 7 May 1689; Holland had already begun hostilities in February, the start of that great international effort to prevent Louis XIV dominating Europe which was to be William's main preoccupation till his death and to shape English naval and military policy for years to come. For the moment the immediate danger to William lay in Scotland, which was still an independent country, with no longer the same king as England. A Convention, similar to that in England, which met in Edinburgh on 14 March 1689, eventually decided to offer William the throne, though many Scots, especially the chieftains in the Highlands where the old religion remained strong, still regarded James II as their king, and others, not necessarily Catholic, saw in the dispossessed Stuarts the best hope of regaining Scotland's lost independence. Hence Jacobitism, the belief that James II and his heirs were the rightful rulers of Scotland (and possibly England as well) took far deeper root in Scotland than England, where it soon became the mere dream of a few impractical romantics. In Scotland the new dedication to 'the king over the water' found its first solid mani-festation on 18 March 1689, when one of the most famous of Scottish noblemen, and the ablest soldier in the country, John Graham of Claverhouse, led his troop of horse out of Edinburgh and in April raised James's standard in Dundee. 'Bloody Claverse' as his enemies described him, 'Bonny Dundee,' as his admirers and a later poet im-mortalised him,* with his 'long dark curled locks' and 'melancholy haughty countenance', was one of those colourful, charismatic leaders who lend authority even to a bad cause.

Dundee had received a commission from the deposed James II as his Commander-in-Chief in Scotland, and fled into the Highlands to gather support among the clans. They assembled, on 18 May 1689, in Glen Roy [or Glenroy] in Inverness-shire, near the hamlet of Roy-bridge [or Roy Bridge], which is about ten miles [16 km] north-east of the site of the future Fort William.

Early in June 1689 Edinburgh Castle, which had been held for James, surrendered, but Blair Castle, at Blair Atholl in Perthshire, eight miles [13 km] north-west of Pitlochry, had now declared for the Jacobite cause. Perched above the main route which runs alongside the River Garry through the mountains separating southern Scotland from In-verness, it commanded the link between the Highlands and the Low-lands, giving a vast strategic advantage to whomever held it. Both sides now hastened towards it, Dundee with a single troop of horse, 2500 'irregulars' on foot and 300 supposedly trained soldiers from Ire-land, Major-General Hugh Mackay, William's newly appointed Com-mander-in-Chief in Scotland – he had commanded the English and Scottish contingent in the 1688 campaign – with 3000 infantry, eight troops of cavalry and dragoons.

On the afternoon of Saturday 27 July 1689 the two armies came face

---

* i.e. Sir Walter Scott. For the text of 'Bonnie Dundee' see Baker, p. 225.

to face at the Pass of Killiecrankie, about midway between Pitlochry and Blair Castle, where the road ran through a narrow valley beside a deep gorge. As Mackay emerged from the Pass he saw Dundee's army approaching down the valley, just ahead of him, and hastily deployed his troops on the slopes on his right flank, 'a ground fair enough to receive the enemy,' he later wrote in his memoirs, 'but not to attack them'.

Half an hour before sunset Dundee's Highlanders swept down upon Mackay's troops, following the natural curve of the ground and charging headlong through the enemy front. Before William's men could reload, or fix their old-fashioned plug-in bayonets, the enemy were upon them, fearsome in their kilts and ferociously wielding the dirks, claymores and broadswords that had always been the clansmen's favoured weapons. When Mackay launched his cavalry at the attackers' flank to try to restore the situation, they were caught up in the rout of the demoralised infantry, now stampeding from the field, while the victorious Highlanders pressed on unchecked until distracted from killing by the chance of plunder as they reached Mackay's baggage train. Dundee himself was fatally wounded while leading the final victorious charge, thereby becoming a legend, one of 600 casualties among the Jacobites. Mackay fell back on Stirling, having lost three-quarters of his men on the battlefield or through desertion.

Following Dundee's death the Jacobites suffered a series of defeats, the last, and decisive one, on 1 May 1690, at Cromdale in Moray, about 30 miles [48 km] east of Inverness. Organised resistance to William in Scotland ceased, though the last clans did not formally submit for another 18 months.

While Bonnie Dundee was establishing in Scotland the Jacobite tradition of romantic failure a different legend was being born in Ireland, that of 'No surrender', the slogan adopted by the Protestant defenders of Londonderry. The fight to hold Londonderry began heroically when, in an episode still commemorated today, the 'apprentice boys' barred the gates but the governor, Robert Lundy, proved a broken reed, if not a covert traitor, recommending that the citizens surrender and actually sending away two regiments despatched to the town's relief. He was driven out, with most of his officers, on 17 April, but the first attempt to relieve Londonderry from England failed. On 19 April 1689 the siege had begun in earnest, with the arrival of French troops outside the walls. A boom was now built across the River Foyle which connected it, via Lough Foyle, with the open sea, and the 30,000 citizens began a long ordeal by privation and disease, in which many thousands died, while enemy bombs plunged down upon the town. The population, though reduced to eating cats and dogs, fought back, however, so long as their ammunition lasted, with 16-pounder [7.3-kg] and 24-pounder [11-kg] cannon, continuous musket fire and frequent sorties and on 30 July an expedition led by General Kirke rammed the boom; the following day, as the first stores were being unloaded, the siege was abandoned, having lasted 105 days. Simultaneously, Colonel William Wolseley, landed by Kirke to organise the loyalists around Enniskillen, totally defeated, on 30 July 1689, a much larger force at Newton Butler, 15 miles [24 km] south-east of Enniskillen, capturing its commander. James had now failed to seize either of the main Protestant strongholds in Ireland and could clearly not feel secure till they had been subdued.

The presence of the deposed Stuart sovereign, and of French officers and troops, in Ireland posed a continuing threat, however, to William III which he could not simply ignore, and in August 1689 he sent another large army there, under a 74-year-old Huguenot general, Frederick Herman, first Duke of Schomberg. Half of Schomberg's force perished through disease, the autumn rains being appalling even by Irish standards, without a shot fired against them.

William, who was already bored by court life in London and still found spoken English hard to follow, decided he must go to Ireland and take command in person. 'He understood that better,' he was reported as saying, 'than how to govern England.'

The king's arrival in Belfast on 25 June was greeted with bonfires, followed by a warm welcome wherever he went. William was visibly more relaxed than at home. 'The country is worth fighting for,' he remarked as they marched through Louth towards Drogheda, at the mouth of the River Boyne, where James's army was preparing to make its stand. On 29 June 1690, described as 'excessive hot', William's army camped behind the hills on the north bank of the Boyne, while James's troops occupied the other bank.

James was up at 1 am on Tuesday 1 July 1690, in immaculate uniform decorated with star and garter, ready for the battle to decide who should rule England. It was to be fought with far larger armies than on similar occasions in the past: about 36,000, with superior troops, cannon and equipment on William's side, about 25,000, some of them first-class French troops but mainly ill-trained, poorly equipped Irish, on that of the man the English called 'the late King James'.

Schomberg dismissed William's plan, to force the river crossing, as too dangerous but the normally cautious king overruled him. The scene that followed was one of the most dramatic in the history of warfare and destined to live, like the defence of Derry, in Irish Protestant annals. In bright sunshine and intense heat the Dutch Guards, ten abreast, led by their massed drums, deployed out of a narrow valley between the hills and plunged into the river, to wade across, sometimes up to their necks in water, under heavy fire, emerging with ardour undimmed, to storm the enemy breastworks. 'My poor Guards! My poor Guards!' William was heard to exclaim as, with their foot beginning to give way, the Jacobite horse charged three times to restore the situation, forcing some of the attackers back into the river. Old General Schomberg was killed there; so was another of William's commanders. William himself survived, riding straight through a line of 40 grenadiers in a trench, who coolly stood to fire their muskets at him. Soon the Jacobite infantry were in full flight, with William himself leading the pursuit across seven miles [11 km] of countryside, where many stragglers died amid the dykes and hedges, though quarter was, on his order, given to all who asked for it. It was after ten when the long day ended, the king having busied himself visiting the wounded, including those from the enemy army; he had, it soon appeared, decisively won the Battle of the Boyne for the loss of 500 men; James's casualties were put at 1600.

James had meanwhile reached Dublin, blaming the Irish, whom one eye-witness had described as 'like sheep flying before the wolf', for his defeat. His only hope now, he believed, was a direct invasion of England from France and he moved on almost at once to Kinsale, where a French frigate was waiting to take him to Brest. He landed on 10 July (English style) and went on to find Paris *en fête* celebrating the supposed death of William III; sadly, James knew better.

William himself rode into Dublin on Sunday 6 July, and, wearing the crown of Ireland on his head, attended a thanksgiving service in Christ Church cathedral. He did not return to London until early September, leaving his subordinates, especially John Churchill, recently created first Earl of Marlborough, to complete the subjugation of Ireland. 'No officer living who has seen so little service as my Lord Marlborough is so fit for great commands,' commented William prophetically after the 40-year-old general had, in the autumn of 1690, rapidly captured Cork and Kinsale.

In May 1691 a new French general reached Limerick, with further arms and other supplies, but in August the Duke of Tyrconnel died, and on 3 October 1691 an uneasy peace was restored to Ireland by the Treaty of Limerick. Under its terms any soldier who wanted one was offered a free passage to France. The 11-12,000 who accepted were greeted by James on their arrival in Brittany at the end of 1691. They formed, in theory, a private army of his own, for though Louis XIV paid them they were organised into regiments under Irish officers, but William preferred to have them confronting him openly on the far side of the Channel rather than lurking, disaffected, in his rear on the other side of the Irish Sea.

While William III had been occupied in Ireland the French had been active in the Channel. The new Earl of Torrington faced his first challenge on 21 June, when a French squadron 75 strong, with 6 frigates and 20 fireships, was sighted off the Lizard, moving up channel as if to blockade the Thames. Late on 29 June 1690, having so far evaded battle, he was ordered by the government to engage the enemy, being goaded into action by a message from the queen herself: 'We apprehend the consequences of your retiring to the Gunfleet to be so fatal, that we choose rather that you should, upon any advantage of the wind, give battle to the enemy.'

On the morning of 30 June 1690, with 360 miles [573] away near Drogheda, William III and 'the late King James' prepared to fight the Battle of the Boyne. Torrington, with a fleet of 58 English and Dutch warships, backed by a favourable wind, reluctantly engaged a French fleet of 77 sail under Admiral de Tourville [Anne Hilarion de Constantin, Comte de Tourville]. Torrington's mishandling enabled the enemy to drive a wedge between the English and Dutch ships and by 1 pm the former were in shameful retreat, a disaster only being averted when the wind suddenly changed, though Torrington did not drop anchor until safely within the Thames. Only one warship and some fireships had been lost but during Tuesday 1 July Torrington had to burn five more ships of the line, mounting from 72 to 50 guns, to prevent their falling into enemy hands, leaving Louis XIV master of the Channel.

The Battle of Beachy Head was recognised as a national disgrace and Torrington, in spite of his earlier services, was court-martialled, though acquitted.[*] The news of his defeat caused a panic. John Evelyn, writing on 6 July, reflected the national mood:

> The whole nation now exceedingly alarmed by the French fleet braving our coast even to the very Thames mouth; our fleet commanded by debauched young men, and likewise inferior in force, giving way to the enemy, to our exceeding reproach; God of his mercy defend this poor . . . nation.

The familiar routine of anti-invasion preparations was soon well under way. Trinity House was ordered to remove the navigation buoys from the Thames estuary; the militia in the south-western counties was called out, seriously disrupting the bringing in of the harvest; Essex, Buckinghamshire and Bedfordshire between them raised 22 troops of cavalry who occupied Hounslow Heath; while the foot from Kent and Surrey were mustered at Blackheath. The bonfires of the beacon chain were again built and guarded. The City of London raised a loan of £100,000, which was gratefully accepted; an elderly duke volunteered to emerge from retirement to lead the fleet, an offer which was declined.

While England was in the grip of anti-invasion fever James was desperately urging Louis XIV to seize a unique opportunity. He well

* See Sanderson, pp. 31-2, for a concise account of the battle and Ogg, *James II*, p. 354, on contemporary reaction. Aubrey, p. 50, however, cites several authorities, including Mahan, who consider Torrington was unjustly criticised.

understood that the real defence of his former kingdom lay in sea-power and that, with the fleet beaten and the king and field army away in Ireland, there would never be a better chance to get an expedition across the Channel. But Louis XIV was not to be persuaded. The Battle of the Boyne had shaken his confidence in James's value as an ally and his admirals were well aware of the difficulty of maintaining a large fleet in the Channel, with no port east of Brest able to accommo-date their large ships whatever the state of the tide and wind, while the English fleet had a choice of harbours from Plymouth to Chatham, and of splendid natural anchorages from Torbay, via Portland, the Downs and the Nore, to the Gunfleet, usable in any weather.

During July 1690, demonstrating the French command of the Nar-row Seas, small landing parties were put ashore on the Sussex coast to put up posters urging local residents, and especially army and navy officers, to support their former king, a somewhat pointless propa-ganda exercise, but a much more serious incursion followed. The accounts are, as usual, contradictory, but according to the fullest account* de Tourville next despatched nine of his ships back to Brest to collect additional troops, who were to be transported across the Chan-nel in shallow-draught galleys, collected from the Mediterranean, with a mere two feet [0.6 m] of freeboard between waterline and deck.

Although they carried ancillary sails, the galleys' principal means of propulsion was 50 or 60 oars, each manned by five or six galley-slaves – criminals, captured Moslems or, worst of all in English eyes, Hugue-nots – with 336 rowers required for every 155 soldiers carried. The French were so proud of introducing these alien craft to unaccustomed northern waters that they struck a special medal to commemorate their proposed use, at which English sailors laughed aloud. They had, how-ever, smiled too soon. On Monday 21 July 1690 a huge fleet put at 111 sail appeared off Portland in Dorset, but de Tourville instead sailed on, appearing next day in Torbay, opposite the fishing hamlet where Tor-quay now stands.

At sunset, however, after a day sunning themselves on deck, in per-fect invasion weather, and with not an English ship or soldier in sight, the French weighed anchor and left, leaving the news of their presence to be spread by beacons and horsemen all over Devon and Cornwall.

Five miles [8 km] away by sea, but nearly twice as far by road, lay the small fishing town of Teignmouth, consisting of about 40 houses, clustered round a Norman church, and with a wide, gently sloping shingle beach, where today a broad promenade overlooks stretches of firm sand. Here, early on the morning of Wednesday 23 July 1690, the French fleet anchored offshore, while a stream of large oar-powered

* i.e. by Hozier, Vol. I, p. 308.

galleys carried about 1000 soldiers ashore, in a procession as orderly as on an exercise.[*]

All the occupants of Teignmouth had fled as the French came ashore and the 500 horse militia which assembled on Haldon [or Halden] Hill, some two miles [3.2 km] behind Teignmouth, simply watched as the invaders tore down the thatch from the cottages before setting them on fire. Others looted the communion plate from the church, mockingly dressing themselves in the despised Anglican vestments, before that building, too, caught fire, bringing the walls crashing to the ground. Some fishing smacks in the harbour were also burnt.

Still the English did nothing. By the first evening 16–17,000 men had already been mustered on Haldon Hill and other reinforcements, including 7000 tin-workers from Cornwall, were on their way, but the Lord Lieutenant of the county, the Earl of Bath, who arrived to take command, was an experienced regular officer and was not prepared to risk sending the militia against Louis XIV's troops. Had the French attempted to move inland he would, it seems likely, have fought a defensive battle on ground of his own choosing, but after a few days, with not a shot fired on either side, the French re-embarked and de Tourville sailed home with his fleet intact.

It was an inglorious episode in English history, little remembered since, and regarded at the time less as a disgrace than as a deliverance. Queen Mary had mixed feelings about her countrymen's humiliations. 'I think,' she remarked, 'it has pleased God to punish them justly, for they really talkt as if it were impossible they should be beaten.' John Evelyn made little of the episode. 'The French domineering still at sea,' he recorded on 3 August 1690, 'landed some souldiers at Tinmoth in Devon and burned some poore houses.' Ten days later the earlier panic had subsided. 'The French fleete returned to Brest and from our coast,' he noted on 13 August, 'the militia of the trained bands, horse and foot, which were up [i.e. mobilised] throughout England now dismiss'd.'

After the signing of the Treaty of Limerick in October 1691 the risk of an invasion via Ireland was slight, but unrest continued in Scotland, with whose problems William III had no sympathy; he is said to have remarked that he wished it were a thousand miles away. He was content to leave matters there to his Secretary of State for Scotland, Sir John Dalrymple, Master [later Earl] of Stair, who offered a pardon to all those chiefs who would swear allegiance to the new king by New Year's Day, 1692. Owing, however, to a series of accidents, including bad weather, the head of one small clan, Macdonald of Glencoe, a wild valley in Argyllshire, was late in taking the oath, and those on the spot

[*] Foord and Home, p.345. But Aubrey, p.55, says 2800 and that the French re-embarked after only five hours on shore, having captured three guns and taken seven prisoners. His version differs in many respects from the much fuller account of Hozier, I, pp.311-16.

seized the chance to make an example of him and pay off some private scores. In the early hours of Sunday 13 February 1692, Captain Campbell, from a clan hostile to the Macdonalds, along with 120 of his soldiers, whom the Macdonalds had been entertaining for the previous fortnight, suddenly fell upon their hosts and butchered them, shooting Macdonald himself in the back and killing nearly 70 men, women and children. Worse atrocities had occurred in Scotland, but 'the massacre of Glencoe' was taken up by the government's critics, and has remained a convenient stick with which to stir up nationalistic sentiment ever since.[*]

Louis XIV was in 1691 persuaded by James to support a new attempt by the deposed monarch to regain his throne. He was given not merely men but the specialist help of a French general, Marshal Bellefonds, who was to command the expedition on land, and an intelligence and political adviser, François de Bonrepaux, who had served recently as French ambassador in England. These now formed, with the former king, a three-man invasion committee to plan the military operations while shipyards from Brittany to Provence, and factories in Toulon and Brest, were turning out the shipping, munitions, clothing and harness needed. James's original idea was for a short sea crossing from Ambleteuse near Calais, where he had landed at the start of his exile, and from here he proposed a descent on Kent. Dover was to be captured first, then Rochester, the invaders seizing its naval stores and ships; its occupation would, James believed, discourage the English seamen whose homes and families were there from further resistance. From Rochester the Irish-French army would march on London. James planned a diversionary landing in Scotland and Major-General William Buchan was sent to Dunkirk with such few troops as he had been able to assemble to sail direct to Aberdeenshire.

Once Louis's advisers were involved these grandiose plans gave way to more realistic ones. The diversionary attack towards Scotland was dropped and the new objective for the main force was now Torbay, which appealed to James because William of Orange had landed there and to the French because of de Tourville's successful raid on Teignmouth, which had revealed the weakness of the local defences. The new target date was April 1692 and the main assembly area lay directly behind the Baie de La Hogue, where the Irish troops who had come to France under the Treaty of Limerick had disembarked.

A fleet of 80 ships was assembled at Brest under de Tourville, who was to be joined off Ushant by others sailing from Rochefort and Toulon, but in the event neither force was ready on time and when de Tourville sailed on 2 May he had only 37 ships, excluding fireships,

* The site is still wild and rugged and perhaps best viewed in wretched weather, as when I visited it in April 1989. It now contains an excellent Visitors Centre, run by the National Trust for Scotland.

under his command, though seven more arrived later.* Their role was to clear the Channel of the Dutch and English fleets, before returning to escort across the invasion army in its transports. Too late, on 12 May, the French learned that the Dutch fleet had already joined the English. A fast ship was sent to recall de Tourville but fog in the Channel delayed it and the French prepared, all unknowing, for a battle in which they would be seriously outnumbered.

William III was, as usual, absent on the Continent and the forces which Queen Mary had at her disposal to repel James were far fewer than those available to James himself five years before. They totalled only some 10,000 regulars, perhaps 3000 of whom were needed to hold the 38 fortified strongholds in the country, particularly Plymouth, Portsmouth and Tilbury. Most of the available forces were concentrated between the south-east coast and London, with a major camp on Portsdown Hill, behind Portsmouth. There were also the militia, who were duly called out, and the usual routine of beacons and watchers was set in motion. Little was done to protect the south-west.

The nation's real shield was the navy. Louis was told that it was substantially smaller than in the previous year, but in fact the allied fleet assembled at Portsmouth consisted of 63 English ships and 36 Dutch, with a combined fire-power of 6736 guns, plus 38 fireships; the French, moving up-Channel from Brest, could muster 44 warships with 3240 guns and 38 fireships.† On Wednesday 18 May 1692 Admiral Edward Russell (later Lord Orford) put out to sea and at 4 am next day, Thursday 19 May, one of his frigates reported the enemy in sight. At 10 am, with the French heavily outnumbered but enjoying the weather gauge, as a 'small gale' was blowing from the south-south-west, some miles off Cap Barfleur, at the north-east point of the Cotentin peninsula, de Tourville, who had no faith in the proposed invasion, led his ships towards the enemy. A fierce battle followed, lasting until around 4 pm when a thick fog descended. The Anglo-Dutch fleet pursued the beaten French as they withdrew and the Battle of Barfleur now merged with the Battle of La Hogue [or La Hougue] by which name both are sometimes known. During Friday 20 May and Saturday the 21st the fierce chase continued, during which some of the French ships were scattered all over the Channel; a few, like the Spanish Armada before them, only escaped by sailing right round the British Isles. Fifteen ships of the line, caught by the flood-tide, were carried into the unprotected bays of Cherbourg and La Hogue, where,

* Aubrey, pp.83-4. Hozier, I, pp 321-2, Ogg, *James II*, pp.367-8 and Sanderson, p.29, all give different figures.
† Ogg, *James II*, p. 368. Aubrey, pp.175-79, however, provides a detailed list which names 56 English and 26 Dutch warships, plus smaller vessels, and 44 major French ships. See also pp. 180-82 for a useful appendix explaining how ships were rated and the range of the various types of cannon.

on Sunday 22 May, Russell at last caught up with them. De Tourville's flagship, the *Soleil Royal*, and two other large vessels were promptly burnt and next day Russell turned his attention to the remaining 12, every one of which, during the night of 23/24 May 1692 and the following morning, was destroyed by the English fireships or by small raiding parties. With them burned the transports and troopships waiting to carry James's army to England. James himself, watching from the shore with the rest of his 'invasion committee', could not restrain his admiration as he watched his last hope of regaining his throne go up in smoke. 'Ah!' he observed, as he had done at Bantry Bay, 'None but my brave English could do so brave an action!'

La Hogue re-established England's mastery of the Channel and ended the immediate risk of invasion. On 28 December 1694, vindicating her husband's foresight in having himself made joint sovereign, Mary II died, but William III now went on to rule alone, with no dispute over the succession. The hopes of the Jacobites came to be centred on James's offspring, who were agreed on all sides to be enchanting children: Louise Marie, born in June 1692 after the great disappointment of La Hogue, whom James himself nicknamed 'la consolatrice', i.e. his 'Solace' and – the real threat to William and his heirs – the so-called Prince of Wales, James Francis Edward, the 'warming-pan baby' whose birth, on 10 June 1688, had really cost James his throne. The young James was, at seven, nicknamed 'The Blackbird' because of his dark hair and eyes, but was fair-skinned and unmistakably his father's son. Pictures of the royal family in exile, with their dogs, were soon circulating in both England and Scotland, the start of an enduring cult.

Louis XIV and his admirals had, meanwhile, after the Battle of La Hogue, licensed numerous 'corsairs' to make a nuisance of themselves in the Channel and North Sea, some of whom, actually held naval rank and had guns – up to 50 or 60 in the larger ships – lent them by the French navy. These licensed pirates were often outstanding seamen, and the most famous, Jean Bart, son of a Dunkirk fisherman, became a legend, if not a hero, on both sides of the Channel. He became a great favourite at Versailles, where he demonstrated his tactics by breaking through a line of courtiers by the use of his fists and elbows. In 1692 Bart took more than 100 prizes into St Malo within a year and in the following year, with three frigates from Dunkirk, he made three destructive raids into the North Sea, spreading panic as far as Newcastle.

On 21 September 1697 the long war with France was ended by the Treaty of Ryswick [or Rijswijk], to which Spain and Holland were also signatories. It contained a most important provision, the formal recognition by Louis XIV that William was King of Great Britain *par la grâce de Dieu*, i.e. with divine approval, and an undertaking not to give aid to any of William's enemies, but this undertaking did not extend to William's successors; here lay the seeds of future invasion attempts.

The English Parliament, somewhat ungratefully, used the restoration of peace to revive all its old objections to a standing army and eventually forced the king to get rid of all but 10,000 of his 30,000 troops, £350,000 a year being voted for the remainder, considered the minimum needed for home defence. Separate establishments were provided for Scotland and Ireland. Half-pay was to be granted to disbanded officers, to enable them to be recalled if necessary. In December 1697 a civil list of £700,000 a year was established, which, for the first time, distinguished between money provided for defence purposes and that for the other expenses of government. The most important innovation of the reign, however, was the Mutiny Act, first passed in 1689, which provided a legal basis for military law, and, since it had to be passed afresh each year, acknowledged, by implication, that a standing army had come to stay.

Not surprisingly, in view of the dangers and discomforts of a life at sea, the navy could still only be kept up to strength by the press gang, but the public did their best to obstruct the activities of the pressmaster, as one, writing from Hull on 13 May 1694, made all too clear:

> My trouble has increased mightily every day for want of places to secure my men . . . And the people here consisting generally of seamen, neither I nor the pressmasters can be safe from . . . curses; and not a house that I know of that would not receive a fugitive and shut the door on him . . . I prevailed with the gaoler (the sheriff denying me) to take some of the seamen that I thought most dangerous [i.e. the likeliest to try to escape] a week ago, and, notwithstanding the strength of the place, from a turret . . . four men slipped away by a cord in a minute . . . Now a pressmaster dare scarce carry an impressed man through the streets . . . I might as well be desired to drive twenty foxes to market.

In 1700 Parliament passed the Act of Settlement, laying down that if Anne died without any surviving children, as now seemed highly likely, the throne should pass to her nearest Protestant relative. It was a prudent precaution, for the former James I's death, on 5 September 1701, was followed only six months later by that of William III, who died after a fall while riding, on 8 March 1702. The Jacobites abandoned their customary toast to drink, with grim humour, to 'the little gentleman in the velvet coat', the mole whose burrowings had caused the king's horse to stumble.

12

A POPISH PRETENDER

This crooked disciple pretends he will bring
A Popish Pretender, whom he calls a king.

Verse on the Earl of Mar's rebellion, September 1715

Queen Anne was 37 when she came to the throne, a plump, somewhat dumpy woman, more likely to inspire affection than passionate devotion, but immensely conscientious and unshakeably Anglican. 'As I know myself to be entirely English . . .' she told Parliament in March 1702, three days after her accession, 'there is not one thing you can expect or desire of me which I shall not be ready to do for the happiness or prosperity of England.' Her husband, Prince George of Denmark, was a large, hard-drinking, notoriously dull ex-soldier, of whom Charles II had observed, 'I've tried him drunk and I've tried him sober but there's nothing in him.' George was merely the queen's consort and by his death in 1708 had left no mark on English history.

Within a few hours of becoming queen Anne wrote to the Dutch States-General setting out the basis of her policy. Like William III, she would, she declared, support 'all measures which it will be necessary to take in preserving the liberty of Europe and reducing the power of France to its just limits'. On 4 May Parliament endorsed the declaration of war on France and Spain, thereby becoming involved in the War of the Spanish Succession, which had followed the attempts of Louis XIV to instal his grandson on the throne of Spain, and his invasion of Holland. Louis joked that he must be getting old 'when ladies declare war against me', but it proved an ill-judged jest.

Apart from one major attack on a convoy off Kent in 1706 the French were content to rely on their privateers to menace English shipping and it was the achievements of her army that formed the great glory of Anne's reign. No major developments in military technology occurred but, significantly, in 1704 pikes were finally phased out, and in 1706 a musket and socket-bayonet became the standard small-arm. The British infantry, firing a heavier bullet – 16 to the pound against the French 24 – than their enemies, and trained to do so rapidly, by platoons instead of in cumbrous ranks, now achieved a mastery of the battlefield that was the envy of continental commanders. So, too, was the success of John Churchill, Earl of Marlborough, whom Anne in December 1702 created a Duke, an almost unprecedented honour normally reserved for the sovereign's sons, a promotion which he rapidly justified by a series of brilliant victories, from Blenheim in August 1704 to Malplaquet in September 1709. From 1702-1711 he was also simultaneously Captain-General and Master-General of the Ordnance, responsible both for commanding the nation's armies in the field and for its land defences against invasion.

It was largely the desire to create a diversion away from Flanders for Marlborough and his triumphant armies that led to new plans for a Jacobite invasion of the British Isles. Louis XIV had promised the dying James II in September 1701 to recognise James's son as 'King of England, as he surely will be' and the 13-year-old boy was that month duly proclaimed in France as King James III of England and VIII of Scotland. In the spring of 1705 Colonel Nathaniel Hooke [or Hookes], an Englishman who commanded a regiment in the French army, was sent to Scotland to spy out the land. He received little except somewhat vague offers of support but early in 1707 went back to Scotland, this time returning to St Germain with a formal invitation to 'James III and VIII' to reclaim his kingdom. 30,000 men would, James was assured, rise to support him, provided he came with at least 5000 French troops and arms for the whole Scottish force.

The government in London was kept well informed of what was happening and the rebellion might never have got off the ground but for the effects of the Act of Union of the Two Kingdoms of England and Scotland, which came into effect on 1 May 1707. Although the two countries retained their distinctive systems of law and church government, they had henceforward 'one and the same parliament, to be styled the Parliament of Great Britain', common citizenship, a common currency and the same taxes. Article II laid down that if Queen Anne failed to leave an heir the succession should pass to a relatively distant claimant,[*] 'the most excellent Princess Sophia, electress and duchess dowager of Hanover, and the heirs of her body being Protestants'.

The Act of Union stirred up the latent nationalism even of non-Jacobite Scots. Three out of four, it was said, were now Jacobites. 'Different interests, differing parties, all join in a universal clamour,' wrote Daniel Defoe from Edinburgh on 9 August 1707, 'and the very Whigs declare openly they will join with France or King James or anybody rather than be insulted, as they call it, by the English.'

Late in February 1708 news reached England of a French fleet being assembled at Dunkirk to carry 12 battalions of infantry, plus artillery,

* Sophia's mother was James I's daughter, Elizabeth, the exiled 'Winter Queen' of Bohemia.

to Scotland and having, like his father before him, been presented by Louis XIV with a jewelled sword as a good-luck present, on Thursday 26th (English style) James Edward Stuart reached that port, having issued a proclamation denouncing Queen Anne as a usurper. 'The Old Pretender', as he is commonly known, although at this time still only 19, was a tall, dark figure, said to resemble Charles II in appearance, though not in character, for he was cold, reserved and prematurely pious, carrying candles in religious processions. His health was poor, for he suffered constantly from a malarial type disease, quartan ague, which left him feverish and weak. To this was now added, untimely as his father's nose-bleed at Salisbury, a bout of measles. The young James bore up bravely, although having to be carried about his flagship wrapped in blankets. 'My courage is so high that it will uphold the weakness of my body,' he declared in a letter to his mother from Dunkirk. 'I hope that when I write to you again it will be from the palace at Edinburgh.'

On Thursday 4 March 1708 (English style) the queen informed the House of Commons of the expected invasion, and a powerful English fleet, 64 strong, plus frigates and fireships, under Vice-Admiral Sir George Byng, was sent to take station off Dunkirk. Adverse weather conditions, however, caused it to withdraw into shelter and while it was away the French fleet, consisting of eight sail of the line and 24 frigates under Admiral de Forbin, managed, on 8 March, to get out to sea unintercepted. By the time Byng got back to Dunkirk the birds had flown. James had won the first round, though, suffering agonies of seasickness, he was in no mood to celebrate, while Admiral de Forbin, in an excess of caution, stood so far out to sea that they overshot their intended destination, Leith in the Firth of Forth, and instead made their landfall 60 miles [96 km] north of Aberdeen and 150 [240 km] from the real objective. By the evening of 12 March they were opposite Crail. De Forbin now turned back, but a French frigate, sent into the Forth to contact supporters on shore, failed to receive any response and with the appearance on 13 March 1708 of Admiral Byng's 28 ships on the horizon, de Forbin, not the most heroic of commanders, hastily stood out to sea. James, having pleaded to be allowed to land and take his chance, was, much against his will, whisked back to France, having merely glimpsed his intended kingdom through the mist and rain.

Before de Forbin could get all his ships away Admiral Byng managed to open fire, and captured one, the *Salisbury*, with 400 French soldiers aboard. Three of de Forbin's remaining ships made a brief appearance in the Moray Firth, about 45 miles [72 km] east of Inverness, where they landed a foraging party, but with these exceptions not a Frenchman set foot on what, since 1707, could properly be called British soil. Though all de Forbin's fleet, except the *Salisbury*, got home safely the men on board suffered heavily from sickness, the final casualty list being put at around 4000, a high proportion of those taking part. As James himself came ashore, pale and exhausted, he was greeted by cries of 'Vive le roi!' but it was evident that what might, copying later usage, be called 'The '08' had been a disastrous failure.

The queen's popularity soared still further when, on 9 April 1713, she was able to announce to Parliament the final signature, two days before, of the Treaty of Utrecht, restoring peace to Europe and bringing to Great Britain such solid benefits as the destruction of the fortifications of Dunkirk and the retention of Gibraltar as a British possession. The French also agreed to acknowledge Anne's right to be queen of England and to expel the Old Pretender from France. Few wars can have achieved so much and, as one MP wrote from Westminster on 4 April 1713, 'In the churches the bells, in the streets the bonfires, and in the windows the illuminations, proclaimed the joy of the people.'

The nation had rejoiced too soon. On 8 June 1714 the Electress Sophia of Hanover, who had been expected to succeed Anne, died suddenly, and on 1 August 1714 so did Queen Anne, aged only 49. The throne now passed to Sophia's son, a 54-year-old German, who automatically became King George I of England, the founder of a new dynasty, the Hanoverians. His right to the throne was distinctly tenuous; there were said to be 57 people, if Roman Catholics were included, with a better claim. He was clearly far more remote from the succession than William III, or at least his wife, had been but he was a Protestant and he duly landed at Greenwich on 18 September 1714, with two mistresses in tow, both very plain. (They became known to his subjects, from their poor but different figures, as 'The Maypole' and 'The Elephant and Castle'.) Although conscientious, the new king was a dull, uninspiring figure, rather below middle height, with heavy features, an awkward manner and very little command of English; German was his preferred language but state papers were translated for him into French.

Louis XIV duly carried out the letter of the Treaty of Utrecht by forcing the self-styled James III to move into Lorraine, technically a separate province, 100 miles [160 km] from Paris, but James II's widow still resided at St Germain, a centre for Jacobite intrigue, from which messages were carried to England by French diplomatic couriers. The pro-Stuart exiles were greatly strengthened early in the new reign by the arrival of two formerly powerful new allies. Queen Anne's former chief minister, Henry St John, Viscount Bolingbroke, who had been ousted from office by a Whig on George I's accession, arrived in Paris that spring, to be followed in August by another influential figure, James Butler, Duke of Ormonde, who had succeeded Marlborough as Captain-General and had contemplated leading a military rebellion against the new king. Soon afterwards they became respectively the Pretender's Secretary of State and one of his leading generals.

The British government's intelligence system on the Continent was, as always, first-class. Bolingbroke found himself spied on as he travelled from Paris to Lorraine to see the increasingly unappreciative Pretender, and his letters, with their easily-deciphered substitutions – 'Lady Mary' for 'England', 'Nelly' for Scotland – intercepted. The British ambassador in Paris, John Dalrymple, second Earl of Stair, a former general who had served as an ADC to Marlborough, soon revealed a natural talent for espionage. 'Stair has his spyes in every quarter and even att the first posts on the several roads,' complained one irate conspirator, but often their work was easy for, as Bolingbroke observed, the most secret plans were a subject of gossip 'among women over their tea'.

The planning of the new invasion was nevertheless more realistic than for any previous attempt. There were to be diversionary rebellions in Scotland and the north of England, supported perhaps by spontaneous risings in other areas like the already restive Midlands, but the main effort was to be in the south-west, centred on Bath. Bristol and Plymouth were to be secured by local sympathisers and then James was to arrive somewhere on the south coast, to lead a march to London. By mid-July, thanks to the vigilance of Lord Stair, the British government had ample indication of what was afoot.

During the summer a fleet under Admiral Byng was despatched to keep watch on the Channel ports and early in September it appeared off Le Havre, where, Lord Stair had reported, some seven or eight ships had been hired under a false name and loaded with 10,000 'stand of arms', i.e. muskets and ammunition sufficient for that number of men. The Duc d'Orléans refused Stair's demand to hand over the ships and their contents to Byng but did agree to unload the weapons and remove them for safe keeping to a French arsenal, a notable diplomatic triumph.

On 9 September 1715 Bolingbroke wrote to James's leading supporter in Scotland, John Erskine, sixth (or, under another reckoning, eleventh) Earl of Mar, to convey this and other bad news, but if he intended to discourage any immediate action he was too late.

Mar was a 40-year-old former Secretary of State for Scotland who, dropped from office by George I, had turned Jacobite, making his house in London a centre of the anti-Hanoverian conspiracy before, in August 1715, sailing from London on a collier to Newcastle and thence to Elie in Fife. He now invited eight fellow earls and other leading noblemen to join a 'hunting party' at his castle, Kildrummy, near Braemar, 50 miles [80 km] west of Aberdeen. The assembled guests well knew they were after bigger quarry than hare or stag and at the small town of Kirkmichael, Mar, on Tuesday 6 September, formally proclaimed James King of England, Scotland and, as tradition required, France, a poor return for all the help the Bourbons had given to the Jacobite cause.*

The rising in Scotland provoked an outburst of loyalty amid King George's English supporters, including at least one set of verses denouncing the rebel leader:

This crooked disciple pretends he will bring
A Popish Pretender, whom he calls a king,
For which both himself and his master may swing;
Which nobody can deny.

The Jacobites had planned to follow the proclamation at Braemar by seizing Edinburgh Castle, which would have got the rebellion off to a flying start, for with the Castle gone the city would almost certainly have been captured. The night chosen for the attempt, Friday 9 September 1715, was suitably dark and stormy but, as so often, Scottish throats had imbibed too freely, Scottish tongues had wagged too readily and the raiding party, scaling the walls in the darkness, were driven off or captured. The securing of Edinburgh Castle was to have been announced by the firing of three cannon from the ramparts, the signal for a chain of beacons to carry the news to Braemar, 70 miles [112 km] to the north, but in the end the rising went ahead without this symbolic success.

The main fear of the government in London was still of a rash of insurrection spreading across England. Sentries in all the major towns now kept watch for suspicious-looking strangers, checkpoints were mounted at crossroads and a round-up of suspect gentry in Cumberland and Westmorland left many whose loyalty was doubtful safely lodged in Carlisle Castle.

Two suitably romantic leaders, who escaped in time, now emerged, the 26-year-old third Earl of Derwentwater, a grandson of Charles II by one of his mistresses, who had been brought up with the Old Pretender at St Germain, and become a major landowner in Westmorland, and Thomas Forster, an MP for Northumberland.

On Thursday 6 October 1715 Derwentwater and Forster, with a mere 60 horsemen, occupied Rothbury in central Northumberland, a small market town about 27 miles [44 km] north of Newcastle and about 14 [23 km] from the Scottish border. They moved on to Warkworth, on the coast, where Forster was now more or less elected to the post of James's general in England, though he and his followers knew little of the art of war, being described by one observer as 'fox hunters armed with dress swords'. He was, however, a Protestant, and now duly proclaimed King James III as King of England, the first such ceremony on English soil.

* The secondary sources are contradictory even about the date and place of this important event. I have followed Leadam, p. 246, as to date, and Imbert-Terry, p. 174, as to the place.

On Monday 10 October 'General' Forster's little army reached Mor-
peth and were joined by some well-off Scots, riding their own horses,
from across the Border, swelling their numbers to 300 but, lacking
arms, Forster was unable to accept the volunteers who flooded in offering to serve as infantry. Had he pressed on he might none the less have
taken Newcastle, which contained many Jacobite sympathisers, but
while he dallied, turning aside to Hexham, 15 miles [24 km] west of the
city, the Newcastle magistrates called out the militia and trained
bands, mobilised a force of 700 tough keelmen, who worked on the
lighters in the harbour, patched up the ancient city wall, though they
lacked cannon to defend it, and bricked up the gates. Forster now withdrew to Rothbury, which he reached on 19 October.

The bulk of Mar's forces were still with him at Perth and his total
force was now perhaps 10,000 strong; the Duke of Argyll, in command
of George I's army in Scotland, had no more than 4000. Instead of
making use of this superiority in numbers, however, Mar seemed
determined to throw it away by constantly dividing his army. One
detachment was sent on westwards to attack Argyll's home, Inverary
Castle, on Loch Fyne, 65 miles [104 km] west of Perth, but the attempt
failed. About the same time, Mar sent his best soldier, Brigadier-
General William Mackintosh [or Macintosh], to make a second
attempt to seize Edinburgh, but this was also unsuccessful. Eventually, after a series of confrontations in which both sides seemed
curiously reluctant to come to blows, Mar's and Argyll's main armies
were left uneasily eyeing each other at Stirling, while Mackintosh,
around 22 October, joined up at Kelso in Roxburghshire, on the River
Tweed, a mere five miles [8 km] short of the Border, with 'General'
Forster's English rebels, forming a combined force of around 2100
men, of whom 600 were well-armed cavalry. Here a series of councils
of war revealed that the Highlanders did not want to cross the Border
into England, while Forster's Northumbrians were more interested in
reclaiming England than Scotland for King James. By 1 November
1715, when Forster at last led his depleted army across the Border
towards Penrith, most of the disgruntled Highlanders had gone home.

James and his immediate circle had always regarded Scotland as a
sideshow and while Mar, Mackintosh and Forster were engaging in
their bloodless manoeuvring in the north, he had despatched the Duke
of Ormonde [or Ormond] to make another attempt in the south-west.
Sailing with about 50 men in mid-October, Ormonde had an uneventful passage from Normandy to Torbay, but failed to see any signs of a
rising there and thereupon returned to St Malo. Here, on 28 October,
he met James, who agreed that he, James, should go to Scotland to try
and exploit the rebellion there, while Ormonde should make one more
attempt on the West Country. Ormonde duly did so, but this time a
storm drove him back to France, and he got into St Malo just as an

English squadron arrived to blockade it.

While James was making preparations for his voyage the English rebels scored their first real success. On 2 November 1715, General Forster, who had now received a commission from the Earl of Mar appointing him Commander-in-Chief of the Jacobite forces in England, led his somewhat reluctant army through Longtown and Brampton towards Penrith, though the Highlanders with him had cheered up, and become noticeably more loyal, on being promised the handsome pay of sixpence [2.5p] a day. The whole horse militia of Westmorland and northern Lancashire, and all the militia of Cumberland, were drawn up in front of the little Lake District town, under the chief local landowner, Lord Lonsdale, and with 10,000 men they easily outnumbered the rebels, but a mere sight of Forster's advance guard was enough and the whole body fled in terror, leaving the field littered with horses and arms. Lord Lonsdale had to take refuge in his castle at Appleby while Forster captured the town and, via Kendal and Kirkby Lonsdale, marched on into Lancashire.

This was a strongly Catholic area and about the campaign there was now an almost holiday quality. 'The gentlemen soldiers,' it was recorded, 'dressed and trimmed themselves in their best clothes, for to drink a dish of tea with the ladies of this town,' who 'appeared in their best rigging'. If Lancaster, with its castle and harbour, could have been garrisoned for James it could have provided a connecting link with France, but Forster could not spare the men and had to press on south, through wretched weather and along increasingly miry roads.

The rebels' immediate objective was the bridge at Warrington, from which they proposed to swing west and seize Liverpool, an important prize. Preston, at the mouth of the River Ribble, lay roughly halfway between Lancaster and Warrington, and Forster's horsemen reached and occupied it on 9 November, to be followed a day later by the slower-moving infantry. Four barricades, three of them protected by cannon, were built at the ends of the main streets, and 200 or 300 men posted at the bridge over the River Ribble, but no defences were built there.

The task of dealing with the mainly English force of rebels commanded by the M.P. Thomas Forster had been assigned to General George Carpenter, a highly experienced cavalry officer. He had been drawn away to Newcastle by a false report but was now, unknown to the Jacobites, hurrying back towards them, while Carpenter's subordinate, General Sir Charles Wills, another successful career soldier, spent 11 November assembling at Wigan, 15 miles [24 km] away, the troops previously distributed all over Lancashire. On the morning of Saturday 12 November 1715 he suddenly advanced on Preston with six regiments of cavalry and one of foot. The rebels on the bridge rapidly fell back but the troops manning the street barricades were made of sterner stuff and beat off Wills's men, killing and wounding 76 for 42 casualties of their own.

Next morning, Sunday 13 November 1715, General Carpenter reached Preston with three regiments of dragoons and blocked off the rebels' only escape route, towards Liverpool. Forster, without consulting his officers, sent to Carpenter to ask for terms, though the Scots threatened to kill him and fight on. 'The poor man,' a contemporary recorded, 'had little to say but that he was sorry for what he had done, and wept like a child.' On Monday 14 November Carpenter reluctantly accepted the lachrymose Forster's capitulation 'at discretion', i.e. unconditionally.

What followed was tragic, if predictable. The recent recruits from Lancashire were allowed to go home, but about 1300 others were taken prisoner, four officers on half-pay being shot as deserters and 150 of the more prominent civilians being led through London, amid mocking shouts from the crowd, with arms tied behind their backs and preceded by – a final gesture of contempt – a man carrying a warming-pan. Young Lord Derwentwater was later beheaded, but Thomas Forster escaped from prison to France, where he died in exile.

Before news of the collapse of the invasion of England had reached the Earl of Mar in Scotland he, too, was facing military defeat. On the night of Saturday 12 November, just as Forster, 180 miles [290 km] away at Preston, was fighting off General Carpenter, he faced Argyll at Sheriffmuir, a large open space six miles [10 km] north of Stirling. On the bitterly cold morning of Sunday 13 November 1715 the two armies were woken respectively by bagpipes and trumpets. The Jacobites, with 800 horse and 6300 infantry, easily outnumbered Argyll's 960 dragoons and 2200 foot soldiers. The opposing sides took up conventional formations, initially two miles [3.2 km] apart, in two lines, with the cavalry on either flank in both. The Highlanders were eager to get to grips with the enemy and, after an opening volley of musketry, charged forward to attack Argyll's right, only to be taken in the flank by his dragoons. Resisting stubbornly, the Highland units were pushed back through a 180° arc for nearly two miles [3.2 km] and driven across the River Allan, while the Jacobite right forced Argyll's left to retreat towards Stirling. Eventually, as the winter darkness descended, the fighting ceased, both sides boasting of a victory, though as Argyll re-occupied Sheriffmuir the following morning[*] he had the better claim to have won.

The respective casualty figures are, as usual, uncertain. Modern research suggests 600 dead on both sides, with the Hanoverian forces suffering most of them.[†]

[*] Smurthwaite, p. 198. Leadam, p. 258, says he returned at 7 pm on the 13th.
[†] Smurthwaite, p.198. But Leadam, p. 258, says, 'Argyll lost 600 killed, wounded and prisoners; the rebels considerably more.'

Even in the south of England it was an exceptionally severe winter. Conditions in Scotland were far worse and with Argyll now securely holding the Forth, ruling out any hope of a fresh advance southwards, many of Mar's Highlanders simply went home.

So far 'King James III and VIII', for whom all this sacrifice was being made, had not yet set foot in either of his kingdoms. He now travelled in disguise from St Malo on 18 December 1715, to Dunkirk, from where, after a six-week wait, he was at last able to set off on a small eight-gun 200-tonner, for Scotland. After an appallingly rough five-day voyage the self-styled monarch was unable to land, as intended, at Montrose in Angus, because of the presence of a suspicious-looking vessel, and had to sail on for a further 60 miserable miles [96 km] to Peterhead, beyond Aberdeen. Here, with no one to meet them, he had to be carried ashore through the icy sea by the captain, more dead from seasickness than alive,* to make his wretched way to Glamis, Dundee and – 100 miles [160 km] to the south of Peterhead – Perth, still held by Mar's troops.

On 29 January 1716 Argyll, assisted by one of Marlborough's favourite staff officers, General William Cadogan, who had brought with him to Scotland the 6000 Dutch troops who had swollen the Hanoverian army, began his advance on Perth where that same night the rebels decided on a retreat towards Dundee. By then James had, somewhat unwillingly, been persuaded by Mar and a few of his leading supporters that it was his duty to preserve the dynasty by making his escape. From Montrose, on 3 February 1716, he wrote a final despairing appeal to the French regent seeking immediate help, but the following day he sneaked out of the back door of his house, just as his father had left Whitehall nearly 30 years before, taking Mar with him, having appointed a new Commander-in-Chief in Scotland, Lieutenant-General Alexander Gordon. Two French ships were waiting at Montrose. By the time the remnants of his army learned of his flight he was well on his way to Gravelines.

His followers now escaped as best they could. Some made hazardous, roundabout trips to join the Pretender via the Orkney Islands and Norway, but the government's vengeance on those who could not get away was relatively restrained. Twenty-six officers were sentenced to death, three peers, including Derwentwater, were executed; of the rank and file 700 were sentenced to seven years' transportation to the West Indies. The heaviest punishment fell on the areas that had supported the rebellion. '[There was],' recorded one Jacobite, 'nothing but an entire desolation from Stirling to Inverness. The Dutch have not left a chair, nor a stool, nor a barrel, or a bottle . . . undestroyed and the English troops were very little more merciful.'

* Aronson, p. 95. The engraving allegedly showing James's arrival, like that purporting to show William of Orange's landing at Torbay, is a work of the imagination.

So long as the Old Pretender remained at large an invasion of England or Scotland continued to be an ever-present possibility. During the summer of 1716, a sensitive time since 1 August marked the anniversary of King George's alleged usurpation of the throne, considerable unrest occurred in London where taverns associated with the Whigs were attacked by mobs which would break up the premises but leave enough of the stock undamaged to drink the health of 'James III'.

James had to take what comfort he could from such events, for with the failure of 'The Fifteen' his prestige in Europe had been greatly diminished, and the Duke of Orleans even threatened to arrest him if he did not leave France. James settled briefly in the papal city of Avignon before, as a result of British government pressure, he was obliged to move on to Italy. Conscious that he needed an heir, James now acquired a wife, having instructed the envoy sent to find him a suitable bride that she should not be 'too horrible'. He ended up in fact with a high-spirited beauty, the Polish princess Clementina Sobieska, who was smuggled out of Austria and across Europe in the most romantic circumstances, although George I ungallantly offered a £10,000 dowry to any other suitable candidate who would marry her first.

After James's ignominious arrival back in France in February 1716, the international situation had changed dramatically. As Elector of Hanover George I had been at war with Charles XII of Sweden, one of the outstanding soldiers of his time, since October 1715 and England now became involved due to the frequent presence of an English fleet in the Baltic, which the Swedes were inclined to regard, as the English did the Channel, as a private sea of their own. Along with 'The king over the water!' James's supporters now began to toast 'The gallant Swede!'

The British government took decisive steps to disrupt any threat from Sweden. On 2 April 1719 Sir George Byng sailed from the Thames to blockade, or if necessary to attack, the Swedish ships gathered at Karlskrona, on the south-east coast of Sweden, in the Baltic, and Gothenburg [or Göteborg] on the west coast, at the head of the Kattegat, facing the northern tip of Denmark, 500 miles [800 km] from the nearest British port, Peterhead. (Karlskrona, since no canal yet linked the Baltic and the North Sea, was at least another 300 miles [480 km] distant.) The Swedes, however, took shelter within their fortifications; the invasion, if ever planned, had, it appeared, been called off and in August 1717 the arrested Swedish ambassador was exchanged for the English envoy resident in Sweden, who had been detained in a tit-for-tat reprisal.

In November 1717 Byng and his ships returned home, to counter another, far more threatening, invasion plot now being hatched by a far older enemy of England, Spain. This once mighty state was now again becoming a major power in Europe, thanks less to its nominal ruler, Philip V, than to his prime minister, Cardinal Giulio Alberoni. Exploiting other nations' internal difficulties was Alberoni's speciality and he eagerly encouraged the Pretender in order to make trouble for England. In August 1717 Alberoni began trying to persuade Charles XII of Sweden and Czar Peter the Great of Russia to sink their differences in return for a present of £100,000 from the Pretender, to pay for their armies to restore him to his throne.

On 17 December 1718 England declared war on Spain. That month the Earl (or by Jacobite reckoning Duke) of Ormonde visited Spain, at Alberoni's invitation, to be followed by two other leading Jacobites, George Keith, the tenth Earl Marischal, who had commanded the cavalry at Sheriffmuir, and his brother James, known as Marshal Keith, who had also taken part in that campaign. The Spanish Cardinal and the three Scottish soldiers rapidly worked out a plan for a new invasion of Great Britain, to be based, as intended in 1715, on a two-pronged assault. Ormonde was to make another attempt on the West Country, being promised by the Spaniards 5000 infantry, 1000 cavalry, ten cannon and arms for the 15,000 English Jacobites expected to rally to the cause. He would sail from Corunna with ten men-of-war and 19 frigates, as well as the Pretender himself. Meanwhile the Keith brothers, with three frigates, would cross from San Sebastian to Scotland, with six companies of Spanish troops and arms for 2000 local recruits.

Such lack of success had greeted all of James's earlier attempts that loyal Englishmen had dubbed him 'Old Mr Misfortune', but when invited to leave his luxurious refuge in the papal state of Urbino for yet another amphibious expedition, this time courtesy of Cardinal Alberoni and Spain, he did not hesitate. The Duke of Mar, unwelcome in Scotland following his much-criticised flight after 'The Fifteen', was employed as a decoy, leaving Rome with a large retinue, by way of Florence, and by the time the imposture had been discovered the real Pretender had, on 8 February 1719, himself left Rome undetected, the start of a journey which, had the stakes not been so high, would have belonged to the realm of farce. In Marseilles he was laid up with his familiar fever; at the Iles d'Hyères, near Nice, he found himself obliged to dance with the proprietress of a rough tavern to avoid embarrassing enquiries about his identity, while as always when the Stuarts set sail, the weather was appalling. It was not until 27 March that he reached Madrid, to be given a flattering reception, as if a reigning monarch, by Philip V, before hurrying on to Corunna, where he arrived on 17 April.[*]

The Spaniards had put about a cover story that the fleet assembled at Cadiz was being made ready to sail to Sicily and Ormonde was forbid-

---

[*] Aronson, p. 108. But Lenman, p. 65, says 17 March, which seems unlikely.

den to go near the port; he was to be picked up from Corunna. The original intention had been for the expedition to sail on 10 February but the usual bad weather made this impossible and Ormonde became progressively more reluctant to leave, suspecting that all hope of surprise had now been lost. James, when he finally reached Corunna, was to remain there until a successful lodgement in England had been made.

The British government was well aware that another invasion was being planned. The Jacobites used a simple cipher in private correspondence – a reference to Frederick being attached to Patricia, for example, meant that Mar was still loyal to James – but this presented little difficulty to the British code-breakers, as one Jacobite warned another:

> In this art they are skilful to perfection . . . And they spare no cost; there are proper officers for every part, and there is one reader and decipherer has £500 a year pension, besides other perquisites . . . Whenever they let a letter pass, it is only to encourage and watch for the answer.

On Saturday 7 March 1719 (English style) the Spanish invasion force, consisting of 5000 men, plus some horses and with food and water for a month, sailed from Cadiz in 25 transports, escorted by only five weakly armed warships which would have been outnumbered and out-gunned if they had encountered either of the British squadrons. They had so few experienced seamen on board that an English prisoner was released from his chains to take the helm of one vessel during what was said to be the worst storm for 20 years. The ships soon lost sight of each other and for three days were tossed violently about while cannon, horses, weapons and even food were thrown overboard to lighten them. One by one, from about 5 April, their supplies depleted, badly damaged, often without masts and rigging, and with exhausted crews, Alberoni's armada crept into any ports its captains could find. James got to Corunna, where the whole force had been supposed to rendezvous and pick up Ormonde, in time to see the last battered casualties arrive, grateful perhaps that, so soon after his own recent sufferings in the Mediterranean, he had been spared this further ordeal. All now depended on the landing in Scotland, originally intended only as a diversion, though few who remembered James's disaster-prone record can have felt very optimistic about it.

On Sunday 8 March 1719 (English style) the Earl Marischal, George Keith, at around 26 the youngest of James's commanders, sailed from Los Pasajes [or Pasjes] Bay, near San Sebastian, with two frigates, carrying 327 Spanish soldiers and one influential Scottish nobleman, William Mackenzie, fifth Earl of Seaforth, who had been involved in 'The Fifteen'. After an eventful journey to Stornoway on the Isle of Lewis in the Outer Hebrides, off the north-west coast of Scotland, he was joined by his younger brother, aged around 23, James Keith, who had travelled through France to Paris like a military Pied Piper, collecting Jacobites as he went, before embarking on a little 25-ton ship at Le Havre to sail round the west coast of Ireland.

The invaders assembled at Stornoway were now divided by a bitter quarrel over whether or not they should move on to the mainland, only ended when one of the Earl Marischal's supposed subordinates, William Murray, Marquis of Tullibardine, suddenly produced a commission granted to him two years before by James which appointed him Commander-in-Chief of all his forces in Scotland. The Earl Marischal, who had supposed himself to be in charge, immediately yielded his position to Tullibardine, though retaining command of the ships which had brought them there.

The change of leader meant a change of plan, for the Earl Marischal had agreed with Alberoni, before setting out, that the expedition would march at once on Inverness, to await there news of Ormonde's proposed landing in England. Tullibardine, far more cautious, was reluctant even to cross to the mainland and when they did at last set sail they suffered the usual Jacobite bad luck. Adverse winds carried them not to Kintail, from which they could have got within a few miles of Inverness by water, but to the shores of Loch Alsh, a sea-water inlet separating the Isle of Skye from the south-west tip of Ross and Cromarty. Here they established themselves in a former clan stronghold, the island castle of Eilean Donan, at the point where Loch Alsh divided into Loch Long and Loch Duich, the latter giving access, via Glen Shiel, Glen Moriston and Loch Ness, to the route to Inverness.

Eilean Donan provided a strong, almost impregnable, base, the invaders still enjoyed the advantage of surprise and Inverness, supposed to be lightly held, lay a mere 56 miles [90 km] away, but, after several days of indecision, Tullibardine lost his nerve completely and proposed a return to Spain. He had, however, reckoned without the Earl Marischal, who, as naval commander, had sent their two frigates back empty, without consulting his Commander-in-Chief. The little party, under a 'general' with no faith in the enterprise and with an 'admiral' lacking ships, was irrevocably committed to going on. A garrison of 45 Spaniards was left behind in the castle, to guard the bulk of their weapons and supplies, while the rest prepared to advance eastwards. The operation, likes others before it, depended on local recruits pouring in and the Spaniards had provided both officers and men to form a nucleus for rapid expansion. The total establishment, of 327 regular soldiers, included 24 companies, of 12 men each, to serve as a cadre for the expected flow of Highlander recruits, along with 19 officers, ranging in rank from a lieutenant-colonel, with six captains, lieutenants and ensigns respectively. The response, however, as news of the invaders' arrival spread, was disappointing. 'Not a thousand men appeared,' the Earl Marischal summed up, 'and even those seemed not very fond of the enterprise.' The navy, which had failed to catch the invaders en route, now struck the first counter-blow against them. On Sunday 10 May 1719 three warships subjected Castle Eilean Donan to a fierce bombardment which left gaping holes in its walls and the small garrison, in their alien white and yellow uniforms, surrendered, in the most gratifying fashion, to a few boatloads of English sailors, who seized the rebels' stores and blew up the old fortress. No way of retreat, and no safe base, now remained for the remaining Spaniards and their Scottish allies.

After the rising of 1715 the British government had made a somewhat half-hearted attempt to tame the Highlands. Small numbers of Highlanders had been recruited to serve as scouts and guides and installed in four fortified barracks, each with a garrison of 30. These were not expected to withstand a regular siege, but the walls were loopholed for muskets, with two turrets at the corners sited to cover the intervening area with fire, to enable a casual attack by armed clansmen to be held off until help arrived. The four were sited at Inverlochy, later Fort William, at the south end of Loch Ness, the future site of Fort Augustus, Bernera, on Glenelg Bay, about 32 miles [51 km] north-west of Fort William, and Ruthven near Dalwhinnie in the central Highlands, 35 miles [56 km] south of Inverness.

None of the four played any part in the 1719 invasion, and the real centre of British power in the Highlands was Inverness, where Major-General Joseph Wightman was in command of some 130 Highlanders, 120 dragoons and about 850 foot soldiers, including four companies of infantry from Holland. Wightman was a sound and cautious general. Having marched from Inverness along the side of Loch Ness he waited for a day in the hope that more pack-horses would turn up, but when none were forthcoming left behind most of his supplies and provisions, though his men were still heavily burdened as they crossed the mountains in search of the enemy; roads in the Highlands, and local sources of supply, were almost non-existent. At around 4 pm on Wednesday 10 June 1719 he found the invaders barring his way at Glenshiel [or Glen Sheil], between Loch Cluanie and the head of Loch Duich, about 21 miles [34 km] north-west of Invergarry, which is itself 35 miles [56 km] south-west of Inverness. The Jacobites were protected on their right by the River Shiel and on their left by a cliff. With the two sides more or less equally matched in numbers, and Wightman's horse unable to deploy effectively, Tullibardine was well placed to achieve a modest victory. Wightman began the action with a bombardment by his four Coehorn [or Cohorn] mortars, light support weapons which hurled grenades, and then attacked uphill. In this initial skirmish his men suffered badly with some 20 killed and 120 wounded, while the rebels, well dug in, had only a single casualty.*

But the bursting grenades set the heather on fire, forcing the Highland right to withdraw, and after a brisk fire-fight lasting some three hours the whole Jacobite line took to its heels. They had now suffered around 100 casualties, and next day a council of war agreed that the Highlanders should disperse to their homes while the Spaniards, conspicuous in their white and yellow uniforms, should surrender. The idea of marching them the length of the British Isles, to Plymouth, as a propaganda exercise, was not pursued. In the end, though England was still at war with Spain, they were, on 27 October, put on board ship at Leith and sent home. The Keith brothers and the other leaders of the rebellion managed, as was traditional after such affairs, to escape to the Continent while Cardinal Alberoni, the driving force behind the whole affair, fell from power that December and became, like James himself, an exile in Italy.

'Old Mr Misfortune' found consolation for his latest failure by marrying his 17-year-old bride, on the very day they met for the first time, 2 September 1719. Their home, the Palazzo Muti, a large, gloomy house off the Via del Corso, not far from the papal palace, now became the international headquarters of Jacobitism. It was a red-letter day for his supporters everywhere when, on 31 December 1720, a son was born to James's new young wife, in the presence of no fewer than 100 cardinals, ambassadors and other important witnesses; clearly the charge of being a 'warming-pan' changeling was not going to be laid against Charles Edward. The infant was at once created Prince of Wales, to indicate that in Jacobite eyes he was the real heir to the throne of England, and the Young Pretender was soon to become universally known as Bonnie Prince Charlie.

Even after two Jacobite invasions had failed the Highlands remained in a more or less permanent state of lawlessness. Finally, in July 1724, George I sent one of his ablest officers, Major-General [later Field Marshal] George Wade to investigate the situation. In December 1724 Wade reported that of the 22,000 fighting men who, he estimated, might be raised in the Highlands, 12,000 were active or potential Jacobites, some with hidden weapons, and that the best way to keep them in check was with independent companies of loyal Highlanders, under their own Whig but Gaelic-speaking officers. To enable them to police such a large and inaccessible area he recommended the building of a number of new fortresses, to be linked, by road and water, for rapid reinforcement. Wade's plan was immediately accepted and by the summer of 1725 he was back in Scotland with a new appointment, that of

---

* Hozier, I, p. 463. The sources as usual disagree. Lenman, p. 70, writing in 1986, states that 'roughly a hundred men were killed or wounded on each side', which is irreconcilable with Hozier's figures for the opening phase. Smurthwaite, p. 200, says 'Jacobite casualties had been few' but says nothing of Wightman's.

Commander of the Forces in North Britain.

The easiest part of the scheme was the raising of the six companies of 70-110 men each, increased in 1739 to ten, and as a concession to national sentiment the new units were allowed to wear the kilt; its dark tartan, of blue, green and black, soon gave them a distinctive name: the Black Watch. The second part of Wade's work was repairing Edinburgh Castle and Fort William, at the western end of the Great Glen which runs diagonally from Inverness right across Scotland and forms a natural barrier separating the northern third of the country from the rest. At Inverness Wade built a new fort on Castle Hill, Fort George, a name later transferred to a much stronger building north-east of the town. Roughly mid-way along the Great Glen line, between Loch Lochy and Loch Ness, at Killiehuimen, Wade replaced the existing minor fort with a new, much stronger one, finished in 1742. To enable it to keep in touch with Fort George he built the 30-ton *Highland Galley*, capable of carrying 60 soldiers or 20 tons of supplies and, he claimed, 'seldom above three or four hours in her passage'. She was not primarily a warship but did carry eight 'patteroes', anti-personnel guns which fired a lethal scattering of stones. Wade also rebuilt the existing barracks at Ruthven and Bernera, already described, and over the next ten years or so a total of more than 30 other forts to protect his new, Roman-style, network of roads.

Like the Romans, Wade built wherever possible in a straight line, going over hills rather than round them. The roads were exceptionally wide, 16 ft [4.9 m], and solidly built. First a trench to hold the foundations was dug out, then large stones, broken up by gunpowder if necessary, were moved into position, followed by smaller ones, smashed by sledgehammer, then at least two feet [0.6 m] of gravel, delivered by cart, which was pounded into place by shovels and the soldiers' boots. When the ground was marshy, brushwood and timber provided a 'raft' for the first layer of stones. Almost all the work was done by manual labour alone and the order which Wade sent to Edinburgh Castle in 1726 for '94 shovells, 82 pickaxes, 42 spades, 3 iron crows' is typical and could have been repeated many times over.

The road-builders' diet, mainly cheese and biscuits, was monotonous, but for the average soldier if the beer supply was adequate everything was all right and Wade met the problem of a lack of local supplies in a typically sensible way, as he reported to London in 1733:

> In . . . the Highlands . . . their [*sic*] was no other drink for the soldiers than brandy and spirits; which rendered them incapable of performing their work, for remedy of which the officers did provide utensills and stores for brewing and did supply them therewith.

The men needed their beer. The working day was ten hours long, sometimes starting at 3 am, and the expected rate of completion was one and a half yards [1.4 m] a day, though, with extra inducements two yards [1.8 m] or even more could be achieved. The results were remarkable. As early as July 1728 Wade was able to report: 'I am now with all possible diligence carrying on the new road for wheel-carriages between Dunkeld and Inverness, of about 80 English measured miles [128 km]', but it was 1731 which saw the creation of his masterpiece, the road from Dalwhinnie to Fort Augustus, in the middle of the Great Glen. The problem here was not the distance, only 28 miles [45 km], but the intervening ridge of high ground, which rose to a height of 2500 feet [760 m], and the River Spey, across which he built his first double-arched bridge, 180 feet [55 m] long; another four single-arch bridges were required elsewhere on the route. It was the Corrieyairack [or Corriearrack or Carriearrack] Pass, however, the narrow, winding route along which the road would have to run, which presented the real challenge. This required 18 traverses, short stretches of road linked by sharp bends, with beyond it a ravine. In spite of six weeks of unceasing rain Wade was, by October 1732, able to write, 'I still hope in a fortnight to pass the Coriarick Mountain in my coach', and sure enough by the end of October the road was finished, 'made through a part of the country,' as he justly claimed in his report to the Treasury, 'that was scarcely passable for man or horse . . . now made as easy and practicable for wheel carriages as any road in the country'.

The completion of the Corrieyairack road – it was also the end of the road-building season for that year which ran from April to October – was made the occasion of a notable celebration, here described by an eye-witness:

> Upon entering into a little glen among the hills . . . I heard the noise of many people, and saw six great fires, about which a number of soldiers were very busy . . . An officer invited me to drink their majesties' health . . . It being the 30th October, His Majesty's birthday, General Wade had given to each detachment an ox-feast and liquor; six oxen were roasted whole, one at the head of each party. The joy was great, both upon the occasion of the day, and the work's being completed, which is really a wonderful undertaking.

All told, between 1726 and 1737 250 miles [400 km] of road were built in the Highlands. The backbone of the system was the 60-mile [96-km] road along the Great Glen linking Fort William and Fort George, to build which vast quantities of solid rock had to be blasted away along the eastern side of Loch Ness. The fords at first included were later replaced by some 40 bridges, many of which still stand, and many miles of the original road were in use until only a few years ago.*

After Wade's departure in May 1740 further extensions were made to the road network, especially between 1743 and 1760, under the

* In April 1989, when I visited this area, much of the original road was still visible.

direction of his former Inspector of Roads, Major William Caulfeild. These included a new, 30-mile [48-km] section from Dumbarton to Inverary on Loch Fyne, near the head of which the weary soldiers inscribed a stone providing its name, still in use: 'Rest and be thankful'.

Even the death of George I, in June 1727, while en route to Hanover, did not lead to a new Jacobite invasion and he was succeeded, without any public disturbance, by his 43-year-old son. George II resembled his undistinguished father in appearance, in character and in his strong preference for Hanover. Dull, physically unattractive and solidly Germanic, the new king was hardly the sovereign to arouse his subjects' patriotic enthusiasm, and that in the opening years of his reign no invasion attempt occurred was due largely to his chief minister, the all-powerful Sir Robert Walpole. Walpole was not deceived when, in 1738, Jacobite MPs argued in the House of Commons that since their cause was clearly dead the regular army could be reduced. He replied that an army of 5-6000 men might still successfully evade the Royal Navy and descend anywhere on the coast, so that the nation needed a minimum of 18,000 under arms, one-third to protect London, another third distributed throughout the country to crush any supporting rebellions, and the final third to provide a strategic reserve – an admirable analysis of the problem.

The Old Pretender could at any time become a menace if taken up by England's enemies. Constant friction between the two nations at sea led, on 23 October 1739, to the British government declaring war on Spain, the resulting conflict being known as 'The War of Jenkins's ear'; Robert Jenkins was the master of a British ship who had had his ear cut off by a Spanish officer during a search. The new war led in turn to a breach with France, and during 1740 the British government became seriously alarmed at the simultaneous assembling of a French fleet at Brest and a Spanish one at Ferrol [or El Ferrol], Spain's chief Atlantic base, 12 miles [21 km] north-east of Corunna.

The 1740 invasion scare revealed some serious weaknesses in the nation's defences. Only 80 of the Royal Navy's 124 ships of 50 guns or more had proved fit for service, fewer than the 40 Spanish and 50 French ships of the line, and both in seaworthiness and weight of gunfire the best French and Spanish ships out-classed the finest English vessels. The war brought, however, a number of naval victories and 1740 saw the first performance of *Rule Britannia*, which soon acquired the status of a second national anthem.

The navy's real weakness, as always, lay in manning. During 1740 the First Lord of the Admiralty, with Walpole's support, tried to carry a bill to create a national register of sea-faring men from which suitable recruits could be sought in time of crisis, but it was denounced by the Opposition as being akin to slavery and thrown out.

The army at the start of the war with Spain probably had somewhat poorer officers and somewhat better quality Other Ranks than the navy. George I had tried, but failed, to end the pernicious practice of the purchase of commissions, which encouraged officers to recoup what they had spent by making what profit they could on clothing and feeding their men or through claiming the pay for ghost-like soldiers who existed only on the nominal rolls. Each regiment still tended to be regarded as almost the private property of its colonel and until 1753 was usually known by his name. The army suffered from separate ministers or officials being responsible for plans of campaign, billeting, pay, stores, engineering and artillery matters and movements, this last being designed to keep the military firmly under civilian control, and for similar reasons, instead of being billeted together, units were scattered over as many as six villages. A proposal to build more barracks was rejected by Parliament in 1739 on the grounds that 'the people of this kingdom have been taught to associate the idea of barracks and slavery'.

Curiously enough, the same MPs who opposed the building of barracks never objected to the press-gang nor to the occasional use of conscription to keep the army up to strength. In 1739 (and, later, in 1763) Acts were passed empowering the justices 'to raise and levy such able-bodied men as have not any lawfyl calling or employment . . . or do not make use of any lawful means for their support and maintenance, to serve as soldiers'. Each of these enforced recruits was consoled with a bounty of £1, a similar amount being paid 'to the constable or other officer' who had rounded him up.

The first permanent companies of artillery, to replace the basically civilian gunners hired *ad hoc* when required, had been formed, on Marlborough's advice, in 1716, and in 1727 their number was increased to four and they were united as the Royal Regiment of Artillery. This, in 1741, acquired its own base and training school, the Woolwich Academy, still the home of the Royal Artillery today. By 1761 the artillery consisted of 31 field companies, totalling 3200 officers and men; the former, unlike their infantry and cavalry colleagues, did not have to purchase their commissions but were appointed and promoted solely on merit, and the British artillery was soon recognised as the best in the world. A corps of Military Engineers, formed in 1717, had by 1751 attracted only 61 officers, and the first school of military engineering, set up in 1741, was very slow to rival the success of Woolwich. From the beginning, however, the engineers, like the artillery, were free of the incubus of purchased commissions.

In February 1742 Robert Walpole was created Earl of Orford and resigned. John, Lord Carteret [later Earl of Granville], who succeeded him, was under no illusions about France, which he identified as 'the enemy always aiming at our destruction'; periods of peace with her he considered 'only an intermission of hostility'. His attitude was justified

when, during 1743, the French government again began to give active
encouragement to the Old Pretender. James Edward, 57 that June, had
lost his taste for active campaigning, but on 23 December 1743, a week
before his elder son's twenty-third birthday, James issued a Declaration of Regency, uncompromisingly dated 'In the forty-third year of
Our Reign', passing on the claimant's torch to his son.

'Bonnie Prince Charlie' had been a strikingly attractive and charm-
ing child and he lost neither characteristic as he grew older though he
lacked both his father's scholarly bent and his younger brother Henry's
piety. ('Cardinal York', as he became known, was a fervent believer in
the Stuart cause and eventually called himself Henry IX, but plays little
further part in the invasion story.) His father considered Charles 'extreme backwards' and chided him for his 'aversion to all application'
and his reluctance 'to cultivate the talents which Providence has given
you'. But from Rome the British agent sent a warning while Charles
was still a boy: 'Everybody says that he will be in time a far more
dangerous enemy to the present establishment of the government of
England than ever his father was.'

Although France and Great Britain were technically at peace, constant clashes occurred between their forces both on sea and on land.
The French reacted by opening negotiations with the Jacobite exiles in
Paris, who responded with the usual optimistic accounts of the prospects for an invasion. Thus encouraged, the French began to assemble
in November 1743 an army, variously estimated at 6-10,000 strong,[*] at
Dunkirk, under the command of Marshal Maurice Saxe [or de Saxe],
one of the ablest generals in Europe.

The French had, like the Old Pretender, lost faith in the strategy of
the roundabout approach via Scotland or the south-west of England
and now planned to land at Maldon in Essex, a mere 42 miles [67 km]
from London.

Late in 1743 a messenger was sent to alert James in Rome, and at
dawn on 9 January 1744 Charles left the Palazzo Muti in Rome with his
brother Henry, who was to serve as a decoy, on the pretence of a hunting trip, but made off to the north, leaving Henry to send off to Rome
presents of wild geese supposedly from Charles. Disguised as a
courier, Charles made his way through a winter-gripped Europe to
Savona, on the Gulf of Genoa, and thence, with fewer disasters than his
father had encountered 30 years before, to Antibes in the south of
France. On 20 January 1744 he reached Paris, and moved on to Gravelines near Dunkirk, where he lived in strict privacy under the name of
the Chevalier Douglas.

As usual, British intelligence had easily penetrated the Jacobites'
security. The principal cipher clerk in the Vatican was on the Hanover-

[*] Leadam, p. 380, 10,000; Aronson, p. 131, 'over seven thousand'; Selby, p. 11, 6000.
Hozier, I, p. 468, however, puts the number at 15,000.

ian pay-roll, as was a senior clerk in the French Foreign Office, and the latter, in February 1744, supplied details of the French invasion plans, which were sufficiently convincing for George II, on 15 February 1744, to send a warning message to Parliament. Reinforcements were now poured into Kent, Sussex and Hampshire while of the 10,000 soldiers immediately available in England 7000 were earmarked to defend London and the south-east.

Marshal Saxe had never been happy about the operation he was to command; nor was Louis XV, who had been talked into supporting the attempt by his ministers. But, as so often, no one was prepared to halt the machine once set in motion and on Friday 26 January 1744 Admiral Jacques de Roquefeuil sailed out of Brest with a fleet of 22 ships, with instructions to cover the embarkation of the army at Dunkirk and then to lure the English fleet away towards the Isle of Wight.

By the time de Roquefeuil had reached the island Admiral Sir John Norris, a first-class sailor, had assembled his force in the Downs off Dover. On Saturday 17 February 1744 de Roquefeuil, having found the seas off the Isle of Wight apparently free of English warships, sent a despatch-boat to Dunkirk advising de Saxe to embark his men. He then sailed on to Dungeness where Sir John Norris's fleet now appeared in strength. It delayed attacking till the following morning, and a calm during the night enabled the French ships, showing no lights, to make their escape and simply drift down Channel, only to be overtaken around midnight by a ferocious north-east gale. This not merely scattered them but wreaked havoc on the transports which had got out of harbour; 12 were sunk of which seven went down with all on board. The remaining transports crept back into Dunkirk, while de Roquefeuil's warships, driven far to the west, only managed several days later and badly battered to re-enter Brest, the nearest friendly port for vessels of their size. The English ships, though separated, escaped with only trivial damage. The 1744 invasion attempt was abandoned and Marshal Saxe, with great relief, led his surviving troops to attack Flanders instead.*

* The sources differ as to whether the main confrontation was off Dungeness or Dunkirk and even as to the date and duration of the gale. I have given what seems the likeliest account.

13

GOING TO SCOTLAND

I am determined to go to Scotland, though unaccompanied even by a single company of soldiers.

Prince Charles Edward, May 1745

The failure of the 1744 invasion left Prince Charles Edward with no occupation except to hang about in Paris, getting into debt and bad company, whom he described, in his distinctive spelling, as 'very preety yong men'. He took what comfort he could from France's declaration of war on England on 4 March, followed by George II's counter-declaration on the 29th, which gave the attempted invasion of his kingdom, not unreasonably, as a *casus belli*.

Prince Charles spent the next few months planning a new invasion, to be financed by the sale of his late mother's jewels. 'I have,' the young man told his father, 'taken a firm resolution to conquer or dye, and [to] stand my ground as long as I have a man remaining with me.' To another correspondent he wrote, in a letter clearly corrected since, 'I am determined to go to Scotland, though unaccompanied even by a single company of soldiers.'

The prince's enthusiasm and persistence were such that French scepticism, following so many previous failures, was overcome and King Louis's government finally put at his disposal 60 volunteer officers and cadets to help man the 64-gun *Elisabeth*, captured from the Royal Navy, and the 18-gun light frigate the *Du Teillay*. On 5 July they set sail with a fair wind, but the adventure ended almost before it had begun for, 120 miles [192 km] off the coast of Brittany, the little task-force was challenged by the 60-gun *Lion*. Much to the prince's disgust the captain of the *Du Teillay* refused to join in the action for fear of endangering his passenger's life, but the *Elisabeth* suffered 57 killed and 176 wounded and such serious damage that she had to be sent back to Brest, taking with her her precious cargo of arms and French volunteers. The *Du Teillay*, against the advice of the prince's officers, went on alone. 'You'll see. It will be all right,' he replied to all objections, and on 25 July 1745, he landed at Borrodale, on the Scottish mainland, about 27 miles [43 km] west of Fort William.

The government in London proved remarkably complacent about the re-appearance of a Stuart claimant on British soil. George II was, very typically, in Hanover and there was a disposition to postpone doing anything decisive till he got back. The government did offer a reward of £30,000 for the Pretender's capture, to which he cheekily replied with an offer of the same sum for 'The Elector of Hanover', but the authorities in Scotland reacted feebly and reluctantly to the news. The Commander-in-Chief in Scotland was Lieutenant-General Sir John Cope, later the subject of a derisory song 'Hey, Johnny Cope', and unkindly described at the time as 'a little, dressy, finical [i.e. fussy] man'. An officer for nearly 40 years, he should have been more than a match for a 24-year-old civilian but the first brush between the two sides, though neither commander was present in person, suggested otherwise. Early on the morning of Friday 16 August the governor of Fort Augustus, in the middle of the 'Great Glen' line, sent two companies of foot soldiers south-westwards to reinforce Fort William, along General Wade's new military road. Eight miles [13 km] short of their destination they had to cross a narrow, single-arch bridge over the River Spean, which gave its name, High Bridge, to the locality. A sergeant and soldier whom the officer in charge, Captain Scott, had sent forward to reconnoitre were seized by Highlanders hidden behind the parapet, and, uncertain of the enemy's strength, Scott decided to retreat. When, after five or six miles [8-10 km], his men reached another defile, between Loch Lochy and a steeply sloping mountain to the east, they found the Highlanders had arrived before them, and after a brisk action, in which he eventually found himself hemmed in on three sides, Scott, himself wounded, and with two men dead, accepted terms of surrender.

The action at High Bridge, a trivial engagement in military terms, was of great psychological importance. The Jacobites had drawn first blood and totally defeated a regular force sent against them. News of the victory spread as the clans began to muster at the appointed time at Glenfinnan, which, with the mountains rising all around the tranquil waters of the loch, provided an intensely dramatic setting for the formal beginning of the campaign. At first, Charles found only 150 clansmen, all of them Macdonalds, waiting to greet him but then the distant skirl of bagpipes was heard and the Camerons, 700 or 800 strong, came down the hillside in orderly columns, escorting the prisoners captured at High Bridge. The veteran Jacobite who had arrived with Charles on the *Du Teillay*, the Marquis of Tullibardine, climbed a small knoll and hoisted Charles's white, blue and red silk flag before reading James's proclamation, quoted earlier, appointing Charles as his regent. It was Monday 19 August, 1745.

Soon after the ceremony more men came in, and the remaining arms were distributed, each 'stand' consisting of a musket, bayonet and brass-hilted infantryman's sword, though some of the Highlanders preferred their own basket-hilted broadswords. Charles also had around 24 light guns of 1-2 lb [0.5-1 kg] calibre, on field carriages, but, draught horses being scarce, they proved more of an embarrassment than a help. By the end of that first day, however, Charles already had under his command 1200 men and one horse, his troops' first equine prisoner, the charger captured from Captain Scott.

While Charles had been summoning the clans to Glenfillan Sir John Cope, 100 miles [160 km] away, as the crow flew, in Edinburgh – though far further even by Wade's splendid new roads – had been making his counter-preparations. His first, probably sound, instinct had been to keep most of his available troops to shield Edinburgh, while reinforcing Fort Augustus, the central point in 'the Chain' of three forts linked by the military road along the Great Glen. On 13 August Sir John issued orders for his various detachments to assemble at Stirling, the key strategic point controlling the approach to Edinburgh and the road into England, and on the 19th, the very day that Charles was hoisting his standard, Cope himself moved up to Stirling, 80 miles [127 km] from Glenfinnan, where he organised his column for the coming march. He had under his command about 2000 men[*] with four light field pieces, four heavier guns and a cumbersome wagon-train, carrying three weeks' provisions.

On 21 August the expedition reached Crieff, 18 miles [29 km] from Stirling, and on the evening of Thursday 22 August, moving along Wade's military road, the royal army camped at Dalnacardoch, near Dalwhinnie. Here he learned from one of the officers captured in the High Bridge action and since released that Prince Charles was preparing to block the passage of the royal army at the Corrieyairack Pass, through which it would have to pass to reach Fort Augustus.

This famous pass, about seven miles [11 km] south-east of Fort Augustus, was, as mentioned earlier, Wade's most masterly feat of engineering. To reach its summit anyone approaching from the Dalwhinnie direction would have to negotiate 17 sharp zig-zag bends, exposed on every stretch to small-arms or artillery fire. Once over the peak, during the long decline towards Fort Augustus, the troops would also have been highly vulnerable to bombardment, before reaching an even more dangerous point, a ravine crossed by a bridge. Cope decided the risks were too great and, rather than attempt to fight his way through to Fort Augustus, led his men instead down the other military road, from Dalwhinnie to Inverness, a distance of 58 miles [93 km]. On 29 August, after hurrying away from the sound of gunfire,

---

[*] See Jarvis, Vol. I, pp. 25-47, for a most thorough examination of the size of Cope's army, especially p. 43. Other sources estimate the size of the column at no more than 1500.

the royal army marched into Inverness.★

Charles now faced his own crucial decision, whether to pursue Cope or continue south, leaving an undefeated and hostile army in his rear. Boldness triumphed and they moved on towards Perth after sending a detachment of the Camerons to try to capture the fortified barracks at Ruthven, where it was left to stalwart Sergeant Molloy of Guise's Regiment to give them their first rebuff. The Highlanders surrounded Ruthven, offering Molloy and his dozen men the choice of moving out unharmed or being overrun and hanged, but he refused, and beat off an attack by 150 Highlanders. 'I expect another visit this night,' he reported to General Cope, 'but I shall give them the warmest reception my weak party can afford.' The main Jacobite army now moved on from Dalwhinnie to Perth, and from there to Edinburgh. On the morning of Monday 16 September the mere approach of a small reconnaissance party firing pistols was enough to send the defenders fleeing in terror. On Tuesday 17 September 1745 King James VIII was proclaimed at the Market Cross and his chosen regent, Prince Charles, rode into the city wearing Highland dress, crowned by a blue velvet bonnet and the now ubiquitous Jacobite badge, a white cockade.

While Prince Charles had been capturing Perth and advancing on Edinburgh Castle Cope had led his main army east from Inverness to Aberdeen and then, making use of his superiority in seapower, had it shipped to Dunbar on the East Lothian coast, about 34 miles [54 km] due east of Edinburgh. Both sides were now eager to come face to face, and as General Cope moved forward from Dunbar towards Edinburgh the Jacobite army moved out to meet him. The government forces took up a position near Tranent, ten miles [16 km] east of Edinburgh, just inland from the village of Prestonpans on the Firth of Forth. Determined not to be taken unawares by an attack under cover of darkness, Cope's men, on his orders, 'stood all night under arms' only to find, as dawn broke through the morning mist, that the Jacobites were attacking from a totally unexpected direction, the east, to his rear, instead of the west, to his front.

Cope commanded about 2300 men, with the main body of infantry in the centre, a detachment of dragoons on either flank and three more behind. On his right were six small, one-and-a-half pounder [0.73-kg] guns and six Coehorn mortars protected by a 100-strong guard. Prince Charles had about 2500 inexperienced men, no horse and no guns.

Cope's monopoly of artillery ought to have been decisive but the Highlanders were only 400 yards [365 m] away when with a 'hideous shout' they burst out of the mist, with the sun behind them, and charged towards the inexperienced gunners, broadswords in hand, with a bloodcurdling yell. The mere sight and sound, accompanied by

★ The choices available to Cope and the arguments for and against each are admirably and exhaustively examined by Jarvis, Vol. I, pp. 3-24.

a few shots, was enough to send these unblooded troops fleeing in terror, carrying with them most of the powder horns needed to prime the guns. The infantry detailed to guard them let off only a couple of volleys before also taking to their heels. As the dragoons beside the cannon prepared to advance, the Highlanders dashed forward and slashed at the horses' noses, which sent the unfortunate animals, maddened with pain, into headlong retreat, scattering the supporting line behind them. The whole of Cope's foot, after firing three volleys, found themselves within five minutes of the start of the battle fighting hand to hand, bayonet against broadsword, and a mass slaughter, mainly by claymore, followed. Cope's army ultimately lost around 300 men dead and 400 wounded, with another 80 officers and 1000 men captured. The Jacobite losses were about 40 dead and 90 wounded. In almost a quarter of an hour, an incredibly short time for an encounter battle, it was all over, and, to round off a crushing defeat Cope's baggage train, including his money chest containing £4000, was captured without a fight. He eventually managed to assemble about 170 of his foot, all that had survived, and some 450 horsemen, and led them southwards towards Coldstream, by what was long remembered as 'Johnny Cope's road', and thence next day to Berwick. Here he was coldly received by an elderly general who, according to later legend, greeted him with the remark: 'Good God! I have seen some battles, heard of many, but never of the first news of a defeat being brought by the General Officers before!'

Charles's decisive victory at Prestonpans transformed his prospects. Already he was well enough off to pay his army, with 6d [2.5p] a day for the rank and file and 1s 0d [5p] for the gentry, and soon after Prestonpans a ship bringing money, arms and a French ambassador-cum-political-adviser arrived at Montrose, 62 miles [99 km] from Edinburgh, followed by two others carrying six field guns and a number of Irish officers.

Even without French intervention, the situation in Scotland was serious enough. The initial tendency, on the part of both government and public, to assume that the Jacobite adventure would soon peter out, was replaced, as the news of the fall of Edinburgh and Cope's defeat at Prestonpans sank in, by feelings of outrage and alarm, which were soon expressed in a fervent outburst of patriotism. The anniversary of King George's coronation, on 11 October, provided the occasion for great patriotic demonstrations, with at Newcastle, which might soon be in the front line, 'bonfires in several parts of the streets and beer given to the common people'. The king's birthday, on 30 October [English style] brought another outburst of anti-Scottish and anti-papist sentiment. Versions of the recently introduced song *God Save Great George Our King* were now heard on all sides; a little later the text was finalised and it became the national anthem.

Devotion to the throne also manifested itself in a popular demand for the king's third son, William Augustus, Duke of Cumberland, to be made Commander-in-Chief of the anti-invasion forces. Cumberland was four months younger than Prince Charles, though, like him, he had seen action at the age of 13. Still only 24, he was currently campaigning in the Low Countries, but once the allied army on the Continent had gone into winter quarters he was brought home and his arrival in England, on 19 October, caused morale to soar.

While Charles remained, apparently inactive, at Edinburgh, the British government was making vigorous preparations to give him a warm reception when, as expected, he advanced into England. During the next few weeks three armies were assembled, forming a pattern of defence in depth. The former road-builder, now Field Marshal, Wade, with 6000 men, was despatched to Newcastle, prompting a notable pun by a local woman: 'Since we could not COPE with out present difficulties, we must WADE through them.' Command of the main army was entrusted for the moment to a veteran Huguenot general, Sir John [later first Earl of] Ligonier, aged 65, who had also been called back from the Continent, though it was understood he would become subordinate to Cumberland as soon as the latter was ready to take over. This army numbered ultimately around 10,000 and was assembled in the Midlands around Coventry, the artillery, cavalry and main force of infantry being billeted on Meriden Common, six miles [10 km] away. A third force, of about 4000 regulars, was collected around Finchley, on the northern approaches to London. To bring the regular regiments up to strength handsome bounties were offered. Anyone who joined the Guards between 6 and 24 September was promised £6, or, between then and the end of the month, £4.

With, as always, the important exception of the London trained bands, who formed a reserve several thousand strong for the troops at Finchley, no one felt much faith in the militia. When on 5 September the Lords Lieutenant of the four most northerly counties were ordered to make their respective militias ready for immediate service, it emerged that neither Northumberland nor Durham had been reimbursed by central government for the money they had previously spent in keeping the force mustered, while the authorities in Cumberland admitted candidly: 'Tis so long since the militia was raised that we are apprehensive the arms are either lost or in bad order.'

If the Young Pretender had marched into England directly after Prestonpans, which had been fought on 21 September, he would have found a country ill-prepared to resist him, but many of his followers were reluctant to cross the Border. Since Charles's father claimed the throne of England as well as Scotland, however, he was virtually obliged to take the initiative and eventually, on Friday 1 November 1745, the 5-6000 men of the Jacobite army, of whom 300-500 were cavalry,* marched out of Edinburgh heading south and at Dalkeith split into two columns, one led by the Duke of Perth, going via Peebles, Moffat, Lockerbie and Ecclefechan, the other, led by Charles on foot, through Kelso, Jedburgh and Hawick. On 9 November they crossed the English border and were re-united at Longtown, nine miles [14 km] north of Carlisle.

The Whigs had contemptuously dismissed the invaders as 'bare-arsed banditti', an ill-judged description, for many of their officers had served in the English army and the force had been organised in an orthodox fashion, into divisions and regiments, often based on individual clans. Charles's best general, Lord George Murray, had persuaded him to take the south-west route into England, to keep the Pennines between himself and Field Marshal Wade, and the Jacobites therefore advanced on Carlisle, while the deputy-mayor and clergy observed their approach apprehensively through 'a very large spying glass' from the cathedral tower. Their untrained but nervous eyes, and rumour, vastly exaggerated both the ferocity and size of the advancing army. The Highlanders were said to live on a diet of children, while the prince's quartermaster put in a well-timed but no doubt inflated demand for the town to provide billets for 13,000 foot and, a more accurate figure, 300 horse. Colonel Durand, in command of the defences, who had only a few militia and the usual garrison 'invalids' under him, sent a desperate appeal for assistance to Field Marshal Wade, while the sudden departure of people returning to the surrounding countryside – Saturday 9 November 1745 was a market day in Carlisle – added to his difficulties, as an eye-witness recorded:

> It was impossible for the garrison to fire upon them for some time without risk of injuring their neighbours along with their enemies. But in less than half an hour, the country people dispersed themselves, when the garrison of the castle fired a ten-gun battery upon them, which it is believed killed several.

On 13 November Colonel Durand learned from Wade that he was not coming to the relief of Carlisle since the roads through Yorkshire were inadequate for his artillery. The militia lost heart at this news; they had already been on duty for a month, and had been treated with extraordinary meanness by the citizens they were defending, who, they complained, 'would not even allow straw for the poor men to lay upon' while 'some were eight, some seven, and all six nights and days under arms upon the walls'. At a meeting with the Lords Lieutenant, it was recorded, 'many of them being so sick by this great fatigue, and out of all hopes of relief from His Majesty's forces, absolutely refused

---

* The secondary sources disagree, as usual, both as to the precise date and the size of the Jacobite army and over such details as whether the prince was on horseback or on foot.

to hold out any longer', whereupon the city corporation, conscious that already some of the militia had disappeared over the walls and fearing further desertions, voted by 24 to 15 to capitulate. The white flag was thereupon hoisted on the city walls and Durand led 400 still loyal militia into the castle and prepared to hold out there until help arrived. The Jacobites now threatened to bombard Carlisle if the castle did not surrender, causing the remaining militia, on 15 November, to desert, leaving Durand with only the 'invalids' to form the garrison, while the civil authorities, horrified at the threat to the town, seem to have encouraged him to capitulate. At all events a Council of War, called by Durand, decided that 'the castle being not tenable, it is for His Majesty's service that it be abandoned'.

Wade himself described the surrender of Carlisle as 'very scandalous and shameful, if not treacherous', but it would have held out if he had been more encouraging. The sad truth was that, at 72, he was past his prime. 'The marshal,' complained one of his officers even before they set out on the futile march to Carlisle, 'is infirm and peevish . . . both in body and mind, forgetful, irresolute and perplext.' 'Many of the soldiers,' it was recorded, 'were obliged to lye on the ground tho' [it was] covered with snow,' and 'could get nothing to eat after marching thirteen hours.'

Another general consoled himself with the thought that 'as the rebels are flesh and blood as well as us . . . they must, while this bad season lasts, suspend all operations', but was rapidly proved wrong. After leaving a small garrison in Carlisle, and richer by a number of cannon, 1000 stand of arms and 200 horses, Prince Charles, on Wednesday 20 November 1745, resumed his march south.

By the 24th the invaders were in Kendal and town after town now capitulated without resistance. Lancaster, Preston, where the Old Pretender's advance had foundered, and which his son reached on 26 November, and Wigan all fell at the mere approach of the all-conquering young prince. But still the expected flood of recruits failed to come pouring in, though 200 unemployed, given the proud title of the Manchester Regiment, were enrolled in that city when, on 28 November, it was, as legend had it, captured by 'a drummer and a whore', the latter being the lady companion of the recruiting sergeant.

The English armies could hardly be said to have been outfought since they had not yet fought at all. Now their generals were to be out-manoeuvred. Like Charles himself, the government had seriously over-estimated the likely degree of Jacobite sympathy he would encounter and they were particularly apprehensive about the security of Chester, which barred the way into North Wales. Cumberland's initial appreciation was that Charles would attempt to cross the Mersey either at Warrington or Crossford and he ordered the Lord Lieutenant of Cheshire, who was also official governor of Chester Castle, to make

both bridges impassable, though they were not destroyed. The Jacobites in fact opted for Crossford, where they repaired the bridge, and
on 1 December marched on to Macclesfield. Prince Charles managed
to keep his opponent guessing as to his real intentions, for he now
divided his forces. The bulk of them he himself led south-east towards
Leek and Derby, and beyond that, perhaps, London, while Lord
George Murray took the remainder south-west towards Congleton,
apparently en route to Chester.

Cumberland decided that Wales was the more likely objective,
though he tried to cover himself by arranging for the road between
Buxton and Derby to be broken up by the Derbyshire militia to slow
Charles down should he take it instead. If no great tactician, the Duke
was already justifying his popularity with his men by showing concern
for their health, insisting that they should be housed in billets. Without
this precaution 'half the battalions,' he believed, 'would have been at
the hospital already'. To find sufficient shelter, however, meant
spreading his forces over a wide area, the cavalry between Stone and
Stoke on Trent, a distance of eight miles [13 km], the infantry over
more than 40 miles [64 km] between Stafford and Warwick.

On 1 December Cumberland moved some of his cavalry forward to
Congleton, from which they withdrew after confirming the presence
of Lord George Murray's troops, but this intelligence left the Duke
more undecided than ever about the Jacobites' real objective, as his
private secretary admitted in a letter, dated 2 December 1745, to
London:

> To this hour we can't judge with any certainty whether they really
> intend to slip by us into Derbyshire or to march to Wales through
> Cheshire . . . If by staying at Lichfield His Royal Highness had re-
> solved to provide against their reaching Derby, he must have left
> them at liberty to have got into Wales without any difficulty . . . If
> the motion was a feint, then indeed we shall by our advancing be less
> in reach of keeping them out of Derbyshire.

Lord George Murray's march had indeed been a feint. From Congleton he turned south-east for Leek instead of going westwards into
Wales and on 3 December rejoined the main Jacobite army at Leek.
From there, unimpeded by the militia's earlier road-breaking, they
pressed on to Derby, which was reached on Wednesday 4 December.
Prince Charles Edward had now, against vastly superior forces,
advanced 500 miles [800 km] in 19 weeks from a remote corner of the
Outer Hebrides to the very heart of England, a mere 125 miles [200
km] from the capital; his advance guard, at Swarkestone Bridge, six

miles [10 km] beyond Derby, was even closer.*

That evening he devoted to discussing the agreeable question of what he should wear for his triumphant entry into London.

Victory, perhaps to their own surprise, now seemed almost within the invaders' grasp but at a Council of War, held at the prince's headquarters in Exeter House, Derby, on the morning of Thursday 5 December, Lord George Murray, whose tactics so far had been masterly, astounded his fellow-commanders by remarking that 'the first thing to be spoken of was how far it was prudent to advance further'. They could not, he pointed out, avoid a battle indefinitely and even if they defeated Cumberland's army, estimated at 12,000, the remnants would still bar their way to London, while Wade's 9000 men would be undefeated in their rear. It would be better to withdraw while the going was good.

To this unheroic proposal Charles retorted passionately that 'rather than go back, I would wish to be dead and buried 20 feet underground', but Murray's reputation was by now such, and his arguments so well mustered, that he won over his colleagues. The decision leaked out among the officers, one of whom burst in on a later meeting to protest passionately against it: 'What is this?' he demanded. 'You are going to fly without seeing the enemy? . . . It would be far better to take the risk and push on.' 'Never were our Highlanders in higher spirits notwithstanding their long and fatiguing march . . .' commented another. 'We judged we were able to fight double our number of any troops that could oppose us.'

To prevent an outcry by the troops, or even a mutiny, against the decision, they were told they were turning back only to dispose of General Wade. Thus deceived, lied to by the leaders they had trusted, in the chill, grey dawn on Friday 6 December 1745 the unbeaten Jacobite army turned its back on its objective and the long and pointless retreat – pointless because they could never hope for a better opportunity than this – began.

The news of the Young Pretender's invasion of England had initially been received in London with complacency, which gave way to concern and then serious alarm. 'Coffee houses in town are now like Quakers' meeting houses,' observed one Londoner at this time. 'Hope and fear may be read in every man's face.' False atrocity stories, misguidedly spread to encourage a spirit of resistance, and well-founded rumours that the French were waiting on the far side of the Channel to

---

* At Traquair House, near Peebles, a traditional centre of Jacobitism which still contains the unused gates which the then owner vowed would never again be opened until the Stuarts were restored, is a map which shows Prince Charles as having reached Coventry, with another force occupying Derby. As the map-maker, Finlayson, was arrested in 1751 for alleged Jacobitism, I assume this reflects his sympathies rather than the military facts.

launch a second invasion added to the prevailing gloom and when, on what the diarist Horace Walpole described as 'Black Friday', people in London learned that the Jacobites were already at Derby something approaching panic swept the capital. But the panic soon subsided, helped by the news that the Scots had already turned tail. A contemporary cartoon by William Hogarth, now at the height of his reputation, showed the soldiers sent to Finchley being plied with drink and welcomed by grateful young women and a positive passion for raising funds to provide clothes and other comforts for the troops now swept the capital.

The Scots were meanwhile retreating along the same route by which they had advanced, but to a very different reception. The *Derby Mercury* published on 12 December a description it would not have dared print a week earlier: 'They were dressed in dirty plaids and as dirty shirts, without breeches and some without shoes. They really commanded our pity rather than our fear.' At Manchester Charles's advance guard, instead of being welcomed by bonfires, was greeted by an angry mob and was lucky to get away unharmed.

Hating the enemy as he did – it was, after all, their aim to deprive his father of the throne – Cumberland was incensed at seeing them get away. As soon as he learned of the rebels' withdrawal from Derby, he sent orders to Field Marshal Wade to intercept them from the west while his own army set off in pursuit from the south. Without prompt action, Cumberland warned Wade, 'these villians may escape back unpunished, to our eternal shame'.

Wade was with his cavalry at Doncaster when he received Cumberland's orders on 8 December, his infantry being 12 miles [19 km] further north at Ferrybridge [or Ferry Bridge] near Castleford. By 10 December he had reached Wakefield, but Bonnie Prince Charlie was still 37 miles [59 km] south-west of him, at Manchester. He therefore decided to send the bulk of the army back to its base at Newcastle, while 500 cavalry, commanded by General James Oglethorpe, set off across the Pennines to try to harass the enemy flanks and rear.

An army in retreat was very different from one advancing. Apart from rifling the chests of the Excise offices in the towns they had occupied, the Scots had while in England behaved with remarkable correctness, but now they were increasingly described as thieves and ruffians, an attitude epitomised by the verses written about a group of Yorkshire sportsmen who formed themselves into a unit of amateur warriors known as 'The Royal Hunters':

Let us unite
And put to flight
These monsters of our isle.
The fox and hare

Awhile we'll spare
To seek a worthier prey . . .

Cumberland now sent orders to the Lords Lieutenant of Lancashire, Westmorland and Cumberland to break up the roads, tear down the bridges and block possible escape routes by felling trees but by the time he reached Preston, on 13 December 1745, when he was joined by the cavalry sent by General Wade from Newcastle, Prince Charles's troops had reached Lancaster, 20 miles [32 km] further north, though General Oglethorpe's detachment was a mere three miles [5 km] behind and almost in contact with the enemy rearguard.

Just when Cumberland seemed to be well placed to achieve his aim of fighting a full-scale battle against the Jacobites the government in London intervened. It had been watching apprehensively the activities of Prince Charles's brother Henry, who, his father, the Old Pretender, had written to Louis XV a few weeks earlier, 'cannot bear to remain in Rome while his brother is in Scotland'. On 29 August 1745 the younger Stuart, still only 20, had slipped secretly away and on 24 October 1745, while he was on the road, a Treaty of Alliance was drawn up at Fontainebleau, under which the French king promised 'James III', as he was styled, to help him against their 'common enemy', described, for diplomatic reasons, not as king of England but as Elector of Hanover.

In fulfilment of this agreement a huge force, variously put at 15,000 and 30,000 men, had been assembled between Dunkirk and Boulogne, to follow up any initial success in a landing on the south or east coast, though the final choice of destination was to be left to the last moment, being largely dependent on the wind. Although Prince Henry was nominally in command the real leader of the expedition was the Duc de Richelieu, a wordly, loose-living sophisticate, who found Henry's piety irritating. 'You may perhaps gain the kingdom of heaven by your prayers,' he told him in an unkind moment, 'but never the kingdom of Great Britain.'

The British government placed most of its faith in dealing with a second invasion on the navy, under the overall command of Rear Admiral George Anson [later Admiral Lord Anson], who reinforced the home fleet by 17 major warships, brought back from the Mediterranean or released from convoying duties. Rear-Admiral John Byng was sent to patrol off the east coast of Scotland to intercept reinforcements arriving from France and though, as already mentioned, two ships did get through, at least three others were captured. Responsibility for the defence of the coast rested on 'Old Grogram-breeches' or 'Old Grog', Vice-Admiral [later Admiral] Edward Vernon, a popular hero, but disliked by the Admiralty because of his brusque manners. The dispositions Vernon made were to become a model on similar occasions in the future and are best summed up in his own words:

> It was always my opinion that a strong squadron kept at sea to the westward and a squadron of smaller ships in the North Seas were the only secure guardians to these His Majesty's kingdoms against invasions.

A strong force of 26 heavy line-of-battle ships was based on Plymouth to protect the western approaches and patrol up-Channel towards the Nore, while Vernon himself took command of a smaller fleet, of rather weaker vessels, in the Downs, which could either sail west down the Channel or north-east to intercept an enemy making for the Thames estuary. A light squadron was also posted off East Anglia, to move north to support Byng or south to assist Vernon, as the situation demanded. Vernon's most valuable innovation, however, was to establish an intelligence service and early warning system using the sloops, cutters and small yachts which regularly plied the Channel, all manned by volunteers. Even the sceptical Horace Walpole was impressed at the result, as his diary for mid-September testifies:

> The best of our strength is at sea. The Channel is well guarded . . . Vernon, that simple, noisy creature, has hit upon a scheme that is of great service; he has laid Folkestone cutters all round the coast, which are continually relieved and bring constant notice of everything that stirs.

The seaborne invasion danger only really became acute when, in November, Prince Henry finally reached Paris, masquerading, not very convincingly, as the Duke of Albany. A meeting between him and Louis XIV was not a great success, but the young man made a generally good impression and though they had missed the ideal moment, when Prince Charles was threatening London from Derby, the French do seem to have been in earnest, as a letter to Prince Charles from the French Minister of Marine, the Comte de Maurepas, dated December 1745, confirms:

> Here we are at last on the eve of the mighty event. We have completed at Dunkirk and neighbouring ports all the necessary preparations for the embarkation of 12,000 men commanded by the Duc de Richelieu . . . If all goes well . . . the disembarkation could take place before this month is out.

In England, false alarms, as so often at such times, added to the prevailing tension. On 11 December the rumour spread that the French were landing in Pevensey Bay, like William the Conqueror 700 years earlier. Although the truth was soon established the fright was sufficient to cause orders to be sent to Cumberland and Sir John Ligonier to bring the army back from the north.

Even before the order recalling Cumberland had reached him, on 15 December 1745, the government had regained its nerve and a second order, cancelling the first, was despatched the following day. Cumberland, an eye-witness recorded, 'jumped around the room with joy' on learning he could resume his pursuit of the rebels, 'and declared that he would follow them to the further part of Scotland.' But the delay was sufficient to postpone the encounter which both the Duke and Prince Charles – though not the latter's generals – were seeking, though hostility to the retreating invaders was visibly growing. In Kendal the Duke of Perth's horsemen were stoned and attacked by a mob armed with clubs, and as they approached Clifton on the outskirts of Penrith they came under fire from militiamen hidden behind the hedgerows. Charles had done all he could to slow down the retreat, issuing orders that 'not so much as a cannonball' was to be left behind – an instruction literally, and profitably, followed by the Glengarry clan who, when the carts transporting ammunition up Shap Fell, between Kendal and Penrith, broke down, carried it up in their plaids, at sixpence [2.5p] per cannonball.

The first real brush between the two sides came on 17 December when Cumberland's horsemen approached the rear of the baggage train between Shap and Penrith, but it was not till next day that a more serious encounter occurred. Lord George Murray who had, as he had promised, skilfully directed the withdrawal, having got his cannon and ammunition safely over the River Lowther bridge into Penrith, found his rearguard about to be overwhelmed by Cumberland's advance cavalry at Clifton, six miles [10 km] to the south. He therefore took up a defensive position behind a series of hedges, but it was 5 pm and almost dark by the time the two sides came into contact. The fighting which followed took place spasmodically as the moon emerged from behind a cloud or one side fired at the other's musket flashes and the Battle of Clifton turned out to be little more than a skirmish. The attempt to disrupt the retreat was, however, beaten off, with around 40 casualties, dead and wounded, on the Hanoverian side and a dozen on the Jacobite, and Charles was able to get the rest of his army safely back into Penrith.

On the morning of Tuesday 19 December the rebels re-entered Carlisle, where Charles left a garrison of 400 men, drawn largely from the 'Manchester Regiment' who had no wish to cross the Border, and all his guns, except the light Swedish cannon recently sent from France. On 20 December the whole of the rest of the Scottish army assembled at Longtown, on the English side of the River Esk. The icy river was at least 4 ft [1.2 m] deep and no boats could be found, but cavalry were stationed below the ford to catch any unfortunates who were swept away, and the infantry then crossed in lines abreast, holding on to each other. Once on the far side the pipers played while the men danced reels until they were dry. Thus, damply and noisily, ended the invasion of England by the Young Pretender; the whole campaign south of the Border had lasted less than six weeks.

As 1745, a year of defeat and near disaster, came to an end the government in London was far more concerned about the enemy presence just across the Channel than the more distant one beyond the Scottish border. The county in most immediate danger was Kent, but the death of the Lord Lieutenant had left the local defence arrangements in disarray and one of his deputies could only promise 'If the French come in March we shall be ready with our militia,' which was not, in late December, very reassuring. An appeal for volunteers in the local newspaper produced, however, an impressive response with 8000 armed men, including 4000 on horseback, parading on Barham Downs, near Canterbury, a traditional assembly point, on 22, 23 and 31 December. 'What may not be expected,' wrote the enthusiastic deputy-lieutenant previously quoted, to the Duke of Newcastle, 'now that the spirit is lighted up, and the hearts of the country people inflamed with a desire to defend their country and particularly against the French?'

The Jacobites still had a toehold in England at Carlisle, which Cumberland reached on 21 December, the day after the rest of the rebels re-crossed the Border into Scotland. Clearly the town could not hold out without the castle, which the Duke contemptuously dismissed as 'an old hen-coop which he would speedily bring down about their ears'. Six heavy 18-pounder siege guns were brought from Whitehaven, a cumbrous, three-day, process, but on 28 December the siege began and on the morning of the 30th, after Cumberland had hanged four prisoners outside the walls 'as a specimen of what the rest may expect', a white flag was hoisted. The garrison finally capitulated at 4 pm, enabling the Duke to write complacently: 'Now we may have the happiness to say that this part of the kingdom is clear of all the rebels.'

Cumberland was for the moment needed in England and after, to everyone's relief, the discredited Field Marshal Wade had turned down the post of Commander-in-Chief in Scotland it was, on 24 December, accepted by Lieut.-General Henry Hawley, known from his record as a disciplinarian as 'Hangman Hawley'.

After crossing the Border Charles's army had split up, but the two sections were reunited at Abington, between Moffat and Douglas, after which, with a short interval between them, both went on to Glasgow, which was reached on 26 December. The numbers under his command had grown since he had re-crossed the Border, with the accession of some additional clans and the arrival of 800 men, Scots and Irish formerly in the French service, including two squadrons of horse, who had landed at Montrose on 22 November. The same ship had brought two 16-pounder, two 12-pounder and two eight-pounder

[7.3, 5.5 and 3.6-kg] guns, which were now to prove their value. With these new reinforcements about 4000 men were, by early January 1746, assembled at Perth and on the 3rd Charles left Glasgow to besiege Stirling. The town, protected only by a dry-stone wall, surrendered within a few days, on 8 January 1746. The castle, a very different proposition, still held out. General Hawley had only reached Edinburgh on 6 January, and having built up his strength, wrote optimistically of 'driving the rascally scum out of Stirling'. His complacency remained unshaken when, on Thursday 17 January 1746, having advanced from Edinburgh towards Stirling he found that the rebels, far from fleeing, had moved forward to meet him at Falkirk, a small town about ten miles [16 km] to the south-east.

Hawley decided on an immediate attack by his dragoons on the enemy right wing before his own weary infantry had got into line, convinced that the Highlanders would break and run at the mere sight of the royal cavalry charging sword in hand. The reality proved very different. The rebels held their fire till the dragoons were within ten yards [9 m] of them, then replied with 'a very sharp, popping kind' of volley which did such execution that one bystander 'saw daylight through them in several places'. Eighty of 400 dragoons were brought down and the rest fled. As the rebels, sword in hand, ran after the retreating cavalry, some of the royal infantry stood their ground and tried to take them in the flank but the heavy rain had left most of their cartridges too damp to fire and the frustrated musketeers thereupon also took to their heels. It was the weather which really decided the issue for, one observer wrote, 'It blew a great storm and rained and hailed so hard that the water came out of the soldiers' shoes.' Eventually, as dusk fell, both sides, 'being sick of one the other' abandoned the battlefield, the rebels retiring to Stirling, the royal troops to Linlithgow, en route for a humiliating return to Edinburgh. The Battle of Falkirk had been another Jacobite victory, Prince Charles having lost 50 dead and 80 wounded, while Hawley's casualties, suffered in a mere 20 minutes, amounted to 350 killed and another 300 taken prisoner.

On Hawley's recommendation five officers were court-martialled for cowardice or neglect of duty but he himself survived, though in effect superseded by Cumberland, who, with the French not having stirred from Dunkirk, left London on 25 January 1746, taking over in Edinburgh on the 30th. On the very morning after his arrival in the Scottish capital the Duke left for Stirling, where the castle was proving too hard a nut for the Jacobites to crack, and, several hundred men having been lost to no purpose, the siege was finally, soon after the Battle of Falkirk, abandoned, Lord George Murray and other senior commanders having persuaded the prince, much against his will – 'Good God! Have I lived to see this?' he cried, on receiving their joint letter – that it might take months to starve Stirling Castle into surrender. They therefore favoured withdrawal beyond the River Forth, hoping to raise a new army of 10,000 men to resume the offensive in the spring.

The retreat began on 1 February 1746, the Jacobites splitting, for reasons of private convenience and internal politics rather than on sound military grounds, into three columns, all making for Inverness. Prince Charles's stopped, on 7 February, at the fortified barracks at Ruthven, whose garrison and commander, now promoted to Lieutenant Molloy, had beaten off the Jacobites five months before. This time, however, his dozen men engulfed by thousands of Highlanders, Molloy was forced to surrender, on favourable terms, the victorious Jacobites eagerly seizing his stock of food and then using its own gunpowder to demolish the barracks; the resulting ruins remain to this day. An even easier victory followed, at Moy, nine miles [14 km] short of Inverness, where the prince was staying the night of 16-17 February at the local big house, Moy Hall. Word of his presence had reached the army commander at Inverness and 1500 men were secretly sent off to capture him, but his hostess got wind of the plan and sent the prince to shelter in the woods, having posted four servants with a local blacksmith to watch for the approaching column. When, at a dip in the road and in the faint light of dawn, they opened fire, while the stentorian-lunged blacksmith shouted orders to the imaginary battalions behind him, the advancing 1500 troops were seized with panic and fled, defeated by five civilians.

On 18 February, following 'The Rout of Moy', Inverness was occupied by the Jacobites without resistance, and three days later Fort George, the eastern pivot of Wade's Highland line, capitulated after only a few shots had been fired. Next it was the turn of Fort Augustus, in the centre of the Great Glen. The main barracks fell to the rebels on 28 February and the remainder of the buildings on 5 March, after a lucky shot had blown up the magazine.

The real prize, the main surviving government stronghold north of Stirling, was Fort William on the west coast, which Cumberland was not prepared to lose. King George's command of the sea, which had already prevented French assistance reaching Prince Charles's headquarters at Inverness, proved valuable once again, for food was now sent to Fort William from Liverpool, arms from Dublin and troops from Glasgow. The siege began on 7 March 1746. The garrison consisted of 200 regulars, plus some Argyllshire militia, and was vastly outnumbered by the Jacobites, but the defenders enjoyed naval support, for several vessels lay alongside the fort and assisted its guns in some effective counter-battery fire.

Cumberland also felt some anxiety about the security of Blair Castle, situated about eight miles [13 km] north-west of Pitlochry, the ancestral home of Lord George Murray, who obtained permission from Prince Charles to try and regain it from the government forces occupying it, but his light guns proved ineffective against the castle's 7-ft [2.1-m] thick walls. On 2 April 1746 he gave up the attempt and headed hastily north 'in a great hurry and confusion'. On the following day Brigadier Stapleton, in charge of the investment of Fort William, also withdrew. What had caused the sieges to be abandoned was the news that Cumberland was at last making his great move forward.

While Charles had been withdrawing northward the sloop *Prince Charles*, formerly, until taken as a prize, His Majesty's Ship *Hazard*, had been on its way to him from France with some Irish troops, arms and, most important of all, £13,600 in gold. She had hardly set out when the unwelcome attentions of a British privateer forced her back to Ostend and, at her second attempt, she was intercepted again, off Banff, but for a second time escaped. Third time, however, was to prove unlucky. The *Prince Charles* was just about to anchor in Tongue Bay, midway along the northern coast of Scotland, on 25 March 1746 when the 24-gun *Sheerness*, which far outclassed her, appeared and opened fire. After a heroic action, the Franco-Irish captain of the *Prince Charles* reluctantly gave the order to abandon ship and set off bravely to lead the survivors across country, carrying their precious cargo, to Inverness, 70 miles [113 km] away. He proved unfortunate again, being stopped and, after a brisk battle, captured, by pro-government Highlanders. The Royal Navy had meanwhile managed to refloat the battered *Prince Charles*, which once more changed hands, and again became H.M.S. *Hazard*.

During February Cumberland at last led his army forward from Perth, and on 27 February he entered Aberdeen, 70 miles [113 km] north-east of Perth, and 80 miles [128 km] due south of Inverness. Between the two lay the formidable barrier of the River Spey, which, as late as 17 March, was said to be 'so swelled with snow melting down from the hills that it will not be fordable without going a great way up the country'. The duke had already sent forward a large detachment under General Humphrey Bland to the Strathbogie district, the principal town of which was Keith, seven miles [11 km] east of the Spey, but they were surprised by a far smaller fighting patrol of 200 rebel foot and 40 horse, who had crossed the Spey under cover of darkness. Now, in a classic delaying action, they forced the royalists to surrender after a mere seven of them had been killed. If not quite another 'Rout of Moy' it was not much better, but the only real consequence was to harden the hearts of the royalist commanders. By 23 March General Bland was pleading to be ordered to advance and 'drive this Highland banditti to . . . the Devil'.

At last the moment to silence all the doubters with a decisive victory arrived. On 4 April two officers reported the River Spey to be 'low and fordable in . . . many places' and by 12 April, after being joined by the forces from Strathbogie, Cumberland's army reached the river, where the water level had dropped significantly in the preceding few days. The subsequent crossing 'in the finest weather that could be wished' was reminiscent of Prince Charles's negotiation of the River Esk four months before; the troops 'with great cheerfulness' waded through water that 'came up to their middles', to be rewarded on the far bank with rum and a biscuit.

Tuesday 15 April 1746 was Cumberland's twenty-fifth birthday and he used the occasion to give his troops a rest. Brandy, meat and bread and cheese were distributed and he rode round the encampment raising his hat in response to the men's cheers and delivering an admirably concise address: 'My brave boys, we have one march more and then all our labour is at an end; sit down at your tent doors and be alert to take up your arms.'

With both sides eager for action the stage was set for a full-scale encounter battle. It was Charles who, by barring Cumberland's way forward, really dictated the site, a stretch of open moorland about 500 feet [150 m] above sea level, between the Moray Firth and the River Nairn, five miles [8 km] east of Inverness, known to the Scots as Drummossie Moor. The English called it Culloden, after the adjacent house and park.

It was Cumberland who dictated the time of the coming battle. Between four and five o'clock his army was already marching in four columns towards Inverness, the cavalry, on the left, across open country, while the artillery and baggage on the right clattered and rumbled along the road. A sharp easterly wind hurled hail on the troops' backs as they marched. 'It was a very cold rainy morning,' wrote one private later to his wife, recalling that pre-dawn march on Wednesday 16 April 1746, 'and nothing to buy to comfort us . . . not a dram of brandy or spirits . . . nothing but a loaf and water.' Many of the rebels, after a planned night attack had been called off at the last minute, had gone off into Inverness in search of food or were sleeping exhausted, unwilling to be roused, when news arrived of Cumberland's approach. Charles refused, however, to fall back on Inverness to give the foragers time to come in. He even rejected an emotional plea for delay which the senior French envoy made on his knees, after which the thwarted ambassador hurried back to Inverness and began to burn his official papers.

Around 11.30 am Cumberland deployed his four marching columns into three lines abreast and the troops moved forward in their battle formation until, 500 yards [460 m] ahead, they found themselves facing the rebel lines, stretching from Culloden park on the rebel left to the walled Culwiniac farm enclosure on their right. As it was by now one o'clock Cumberland's staff suggested the men might halt to have their dinner but he replied, according to tradition, 'No, they'll fight all the better on empty bellies. Remember what a dessert they got to their dinner at Falkirk.'

Cumberland had around 9000 men under his command, consisting of 15 regular battalions, about 900 horsemen, and some 6000 locally raised Highlanders and militia. His artillery, standard three-pounder [1.4-kg] guns, was arranged in five pairs between the various front-line regiments, with some additional guns and Coehorn mortars set on high ground to the rear and to the left.

The Jacobite army, thanks to the numerous absentees who had gone foraging, numbered no more than 5000, arranged in two ranks, with most of the Highlanders in front and the Irish and French in the rear. The rebel cavalry were on the left of the second line. The prince's artillery, a mixed bag of 13 pieces, varying from one-and-a-half- to five-pounders, was placed in three batteries in the centre of the front line and on the flanks, but was ill-served by inexperienced gun crews.

Although the royalists later alleged that the rebels had that morning received 'a double portion of oatmeal and whisky for incouragement' and that a 'graite many . . . that we took prisoners were drunk', these must have been a fortunate minority, but everyone agrees that the prospect of action had had a reviving effect on even the hungriest and weariest. 'The highlanders,' testified one Jacobite present, 'though faint with hunger and ready to drop down with fatigue and want of sleep, seemed to forget all their hardships at the approach of the enemy.'

Cumberland was on record as believing that a battle without a cannonade was like a dance without music and Culloden began as a gunners' battle. The Jacobite front ranks had earlier been faced by a wind hurling sleet and rain in their faces, but, according to one royalist eye-witness, 'about one o'clock . . . the weather grew fair' and the royal guns, firing at will, were soon causing great destruction in the enemy lines, first with round shot, then with anti-personnel grape and case. 'Their lines were formed so thick and deep,' observed one eye-witness in Cumberland's army, 'that the grapeshot made open lanes quite through them, the men dropping down by wholesale.'

Prince Charles had intended to wait for Cumberland to attack, but after his troops had endured this merciless fire for 20 minutes or more one commander warned Lord George Murray that his men 'were turned so impatient that they were like to break their ranks' and the Pretender agreed to an immediate attack. So eager were the Highlanders to be in action that they charged forward prematurely, to be swept by further fire from the hated artillery as well as by musket shots from the opposing infantry and from a detachment under the 18-year-old [later Major-General] James Wolfe, posted on the royal left flank, which took them in enfilade.*

One supply officer, watching from the rear, described the carnage which followed: 'Nothing could be more desperate than their attack and more properly received. Those in front were spitted with the bayonets; those in flank were torn in pieces by the musquetry and grape shot.'

The walls of Culwiniac Farm provided no real protection, being easily breached by the Argyll militia, after which 'Hangman' Hawley's dragoons poured through the gaps and round behind the rebel right. Charles's cavalry rallied to hold off the 500 enemy horse which broke through into the rear of his lines and formed a protective corridor down which he, and those of his men still able to fight, slowly withdrew, fiercely resisting. As the royal troops moved forward to take possession of the battlefield, littered with discarded weapons and the dead and wounded, Cumberland despatched a messenger to HMS *Gibraltar*, in the Moray Firth, for biscuits and cheese, rum and brandy for his victorious but hungry troops. Then he rode among them, thanking each regiment by name, with such cries as, 'Wolfe's boys, I thank you! You have done the business,' while his weary, blood-stained warriors hoisted their caps on their bayonet points and shouted 'Billy! Billy!' It had been a classic victory, won by well-trained troops, skilfully handled. Cumberland had lost only 50 men killed and 260 wounded, the Jacobites at least 1200 dead. Prisoners and wounded were few, most of those who had fallen or been disarmed being killed as they tried to surrender or lay helpless on the battlefield.

The news that the nation was safe reached London on 23 April, when a special celebration edition of the *London Gazette* was hastily issued. Next day the guns of the Tower fired a victory salute and Sir John Ligonier wrote to Cumberland on the 25th: 'This town has been in a blaze these two days. Return as soon as you please. No lady that prides to the name of an English woman will refuse you.'

Two weeks after the great victory at Culloden the last battle of 'The Forty-five' was fought at sea in Loch nan Uamh, a sea inlet on the coast of Inverness-shire about 30 miles [48 km] west of Fort William. Here, on 30 April 1746, two 36-gun French ships, the *Mars* and the *Bellone*, arrived bringing, too late, weapons, ammunition, brandy and gold and carrying soldiers for their protection. The French had hardly anchored and landed their cargo of arms, powder and money when, on 3 May 1746, Commodore [later Admiral] Thomas Smith sailed into the loch, in HMS *Greyhound*, mounting 24 guns, accompanied by two smaller vessels, the *Terror* and the *Baltimore*. The resulting battle continued for six hours and both sides suffered severely, though the *Mars* and *Bellone* managed to get away unchallenged next morning carrying

---

* Wolfe was a brevet-major, i.e. he held the acting, unpaid rank of major while officially still a captain.

various prominent fugitives. The trip home must have been hazardous for *Mars* alone had suffered 72 hits, leaving 29 of her complement dead and 85 wounded, and she now had three feet [0.9 m] of water in her hold.

Prince Charles Edward was not among the runaways although to rescue him had been the task force's real objective. The most romantic period of the whole adventure now followed as, often resembling a ragged beggar more than a would-be king, the young prince moved across to the west coast, hiding in caves and foresters' huts, until at the end of June he made his most famous journey, 'over the sea to Skye', posing as an Irish sewing maid. His former general, Lord George Murray, after a final reproachful letter to the Prince, had long since fled to Holland to end his days in exile, and most of Charles's other leading supporters had by now either escaped abroad or been rounded up.

While 'Bonnie Prince Charlie' was continuing his wanderings Cumberland was inflicting a fearful vengeance on all who had supported him. The Duke, like many Englishmen of his time, seems to have regarded the whole of Scotland with almost pathological aversion. 'I tremble for fear,' he wrote, 'that this vile spot may still be the ruin of this island and our family.' General Sir John Ligonier described the post-Culloden operations in Scotland as 'the disagreeable hunting of those wild beasts', and one civilian address of thanks to Cumberland referred to his vanquished foes as 'wolves and tygers . . . mountain savages'. When, on 25 July 1746, he re-entered London it was like the day when the news of Culloden had arrived, with ringing bells and blazing bonfires, plus a thanksgiving service in St Paul's, at which Handel's specially composed anthem, 'The Conquering Hero', was sung for the first time. Already, however, reports of the atrocities in the Highlands were causing revulsion in London and when that month Cumberland was made a freeman of a City livery company it was suggested that the most appropriate would be the butchers', giving Cumberland his enduring nickname.

The government's official vengeance was less severe than Cumberland's private campaign. Only 120 of the 3400 rebels taken prisoner were executed and at least 40 of these were deserters from the royal army. Nearly 1300 prisoners were ultimately released. There was, however, a general attack on distinctively Scottish institutions. On 12 August 1746 the Disarming Act became law, making it illegal for anyone in the Highlands to own or carry specified types of weapon, including broadswords, or to wear Highland costume.

But the real prize eluded George II's government. On 6 September 1746 two new French privateers, *L'Heureux* and *Le Prince de Conti*, reached Loch nam Uamh and on 19 September the Prince was summoned from his impromptu shelter on the slopes of Ben Alder in Inverness-shire, a mere 25 miles [40 km] from Fort William. Before dawn next morning he was on his way back to France.

14

GOD AND LORD ANSON

They are certainly making such preparations as have never been made to invade this island since the Spanish Armada; but I trust in God and Lord Anson.

Lord Lyttelton in London, Summer 1759

The defeat of Prince Charles at Culloden lifted the danger of invasion from France. By the time Charles landed, at Roscoff in Brittany, on 29 September 1746, his brother Henry had returned to Paris and the French had realised that the Stuarts could be of no further use to them. The prospect of a Stuart restoration receded still further when, in May 1747, Henry, Duke of York, still only 22, was appointed a cardinal by the pope; becoming known as Cardinal York, he took priest's orders a year later. 'Cardinal Stuart,' wrote the British minister in Florence to Horace Walpole, 'by putting on the cowle [i.e. cardinal's hat] has done more to extinguish his party than would have been effected by putting to death many thousand of deluded followers.' Charles was horrified, conscious that his brother was now disqualified as a man of God from leading an invasion, and, as a celibate, from having a legitimate heir. The news, wrote the Young Pretender, very typically, was 'a dager throw my heart'.

Even sadder times followed. Under the Treaty of Aix-la-Chapelle, provisionally signed on 30 April 1748, and finally concluded on 18 October, which ended the War of the Austrian Succession (and of Jenkins's Ear), the French agreed – as they had in relation to the Old Pretender under the Treaty of Utrecht in 1713 – to recognise the Hanoverian succession and to refuse shelter to those who challenged it.

Charles was reluctant to acknowledge that his cause was lost. On his return from Scotland he had asked the French government to provide him with 18,000 men for a fresh attempt and had then visited Spain to seek help from Ferdinand VI, but, like Louis XV, the Spanish king was non-committal. The Stuarts had had their chance and failed to seize it. Henceforward they were a minor annoyance on the very fringes of European politics rather than a serious menace to British security. When, on 1 January 1766, the Old Pretender died in Rome, aged 77, his elder son assumed the title of Charles III and six years later he at last married, but his wife bore no children. The former Young Pretender himself lived to be 67, and on his death, in Rome on 31 January 1788, his brother Henry began to call himself Henry IX. By the time he died, childless, at Frascati on 31 July 1807, aged 82, England had more pressing concerns to trouble her than a Stuart restoration and, by an agreeable turn of fate, the last of the line was kept alive by a pension from the real King of England.

Immediately after Culloden the British government resumed the policy of trying to tame the Highlands with brick and rubble. Major [later Lieut.-Colonel] William Caulfeild resumed his former duties as Inspector of Roads, until his death in 1767. Scotland was now divided into four military districts, containing 15,000 men, with new military posts scattered across them, and work on extending the road network in Argyllshire to link Dumbarton and the Western Isles began in September 1746. All told, by 1767 Caulfeild had added nearly another 900 miles [1440 km] to Wade's original network at a cost – about which the government grumbled though they paid up – of £130,000.

Along with the new roads new forts were erected, the most important being a new Fort George [or Fort St George], built at Ardersier in Inverness-shire, several miles to the east of its predecessor, on a promontory projecting into the Moray Firth. Long before it was finished, in 1769, at a cost of £175,000, Scotland was once more tranquil.

By 1755 serious friction had developed between England and France over their respective Far Eastern and North American colonies, and it was rapidly learned in London that the French had, though reluctantly, decided that only a major invasion of England itself could force the English to keep ships at home or bring them back from overseas. The driving force was Charles Louis Fouquet Belleisle, Duc de Belleisle and Marshal of France, a soldier of vast experience who, reported one British agent on 26 January 1756, 'told a friend of mine that it must be attempted, though [i.e. even if] they were sure to lose all the troops and vessels of the expedition.'

What was novel about the invasion plan of 1756 was the proposal to deliver the attack by three simultaneous thrusts, towards Scotland, Ireland and – the real attack – on England itself. The French believed that as smugglers in rowing boats constantly managed to get ashore on the English coast, an invasion fleet, given a favourable southerly wind and a calm, dark night, should be able to do the same, and hoped to use some of these clandestine sailors as pilots.

The war was in fact fought largely in the Mediterranean and is best remembered for the execution of Admiral Byng, in March 1757, for his failure to protect British-held Minorca. But the enemy success there was not followed by an invasion of England. The warships based at Brest and Rochefort, at the mouth of the River Charente, were never able to sail up-Channel to escort the transports being assembled be-

tween Dunkirk and Cherbourg, thanks to the effective watch kept by
the Royal Navy, employing the dispositions which Admiral Vernon
had pioneered in 1745. The feint attacks towards Scotland and Ireland,
designed to draw off the British warships from the Channel, were also
frustrated by the patrolling frigates, ready to summon heavier support
from Portsmouth and Plymouth.

The invasion danger, and the loss of Minorca, tapped a wave of
fierce patriotism which carried into office an outstanding politician,
detested by George II but destined to become one of Britain's greatest
war leaders. William Pitt the Elder [later Earl of Chatham] had been
educated at Eton and Oxford before briefly serving in the cavalry and
entering Parliament, for the 'rotten borough' of Old Sarum. He now
formed a highly effective partnership with the Duke of Newcastle, a
superb party manager who as First Lord of the Treasury was nominally head of the government. Pitt, however, as principal Secretary of
State, was the real prime minister, directing foreign affairs and conducting the war.

Pitt realised that the defence of the British Isles could not be conducted in isolation and that the defence of the homeland must form
part of a worldwide strategy. He had such success that, late in 1758, the
new chief minister of France, Lieut-General Etienne François Choi-
seul-Amboise, Duc de Choiseul, Louis XV's answer to George II's
Pitt, decided to revive his predecessor Belleisle's plan for the invasion
of England. De Choiseul planned to enlist the help of Russia and
Sweden and, less probably, to persuade the Dutch to use their navy to
attack their former ally. The year 1759 was the *annus mirabilis*, the year
of marvels, in which British arms were triumphant throughout the
world, but each fresh victory made the French more eager to strike at
their enemy's heart and homeland.

Pitt had refused to hold back a single soldier intended for service
overseas or to recall any vessels serving on distant stations, but he
ordered a further 34 sail of the line to be commissioned and, during that
dangerous summer, increased the number of seamen serving in home
waters from 18,000 to 35,000. In Admiral [later Admiral of the Fleet],
George Lord Anson, Pitt had a First Lord of the Admiralty after his
own heart, a resolute professional who had been a captain at 27. Anson
well knew that if control of the Channel was lost all was lost and on 5
April he assured the king that his fleet, with 30 ships of the line, would
by the following month outnumber the French, with their 27 warships
between Brest and Rochefort.

Anson was well served in his turn by Rear-Admiral Sir Edward
[later Lord] Hawke, who after replacing the disgraced Byng in the
Mediterranean, had been brought home to command the Channel
fleet. He first hoisted his flag at Spithead, but on 13 May was at Plymouth, a location entirely in line with Anson's thinking. 'The best

defence for our colonies, as well as for our coasts,' he had argued the
previous year, 'is to have a squadron always to the westward . . .
[which] may in all probability either keep the French in port, or give
them battle with advantage if they come out.' Hawke, taking the strategy a stage further, now moved his ships from Torbay to enemy
waters off Brest, maintaining from his arrival there on 24 May 1759 a
close blockade of the port.

In spite of Hawke's presence the number of enemy ships at Brest
rose, within ten days, from 11 to 17, as the French began the build-up to
invasion. The plan was essentially that first worked out in 1756 but it
had now been elaborated and refined. Thanks to the cooperation of the
Austrians in Flanders, the French had been able to extend the embarkation area and the main assault would now be delivered second, not
first. The new intention was for an escort of 35 to 40 ships of the line,
assembled from Toulon and Brest, to sail first to Brittany, to convoy
the 20,000 men assembled there to somewhere near Glasgow, from
where they were to march on Edinburgh.

While the British army was, the French hoped, hurrying north to
cope with this initial attack, the same warships – here lay the originality
of the plan – would sail north-about round Scotland and down through
the North Sea to Ostend. Here a second fleet of transports would be
waiting with another 20,000 men, who would assemble and embark at
the last moment to secure the maximum surprise. While the escorts
would hold off the Royal Navy the transports would make a short,
100-mile [160-km] crossing, to around Maldon on the River Blackwater in Essex, a mere 40 miles [64 km] from London. As intended in
1756, there would also be a second diversion. A French cruiser squadron, led by a famous privateer captain, would sail from Dunkirk to Ireland, to discourage the Irish army from coming to the rescue of the
English.

The British public was well aware that an invasion was threatened.
In May 1759 the *Annual Register* revealed the scale of the proposed
attempt:

> Ten thousand workmen are employed at Havre de Grace in building
> 150 flat-bottomed boats, 100 feet [30 m] long, 24 [7 m] broad and 10
> [3 m] deep. 100,000 livres are paid to them weekly. These boats are
> to have a deck, and to carry two pieces of cannon each, and to use
> either sails or oars, as occasion may require. Some will carry 300
> men, with the baggage, and others 150 horse with their riders; 150
> more are building at Brest, St Malo, Nantes, Port L'Orient, Mor-
> laix and other ports of Brittany.

Although the army now had its largest-ever establishment of 85,000

men the great majority were serving overseas,* but Pitt tried to offset
the shortage of troops by increasing their mobility.

Many of the regulars left in the country were stationed, as a central
reserve, in the Isle of Wight, ready to be carried round the coast by
transports anchored at the Nore – the same craft that made the French
fearful of sudden landings on their own coastline. On 30 May the king
announced that the militia was to be mobilised and might – an important innovation – be required to serve where 'occasion shall require', i.e.
if necessary outside their own counties.

Few could have been less suited for the military life than the historian
Edward Gibbon who, as he admitted in his *Autobiography*, 'never
handled a gun . . . seldom mounted a horse' but, living with his father,
a country gentleman, at Buriton, near Petersfield, he felt obliged to
apply for a commission as a captain in the South battalion of the Hampshire militia, 476 strong, of which his father became major and a local
nobleman, 'after a prolix and passionate contest' with the Lord Lieutenant, lieut.-colonel. He was duly commissioned, despite his total lack
of training or aptitude, on 12 June 1759 and, after his unit had been
called out in 1760, served in various parts of the country, though he
soon regretted his patriotic impulse and did not enjoy what he called
'my bloodless and inglorious campaigns'.†

Though Pitt was always sceptical about the likelihood of an invasion
he clearly thought the extra half a million a year it cost to keep the militia under arms was money well spent. The public, unlike Pitt, expected the enemy at least to make the attempt and, with nerves at full
stretch, there were the inevitable false alarms. 'This day,' recorded one
diary-keeper in Sussex on 7 July 1759, with, in the circumstances,
admirable *sangfroid*, 'received by post the disagreeable news of the
French being landed at Dover' – a complete fiction, as it soon appeared.
Pitt, however, set a splendid example of calmness, placing his faith in
the navy, and sober-minded citizens followed his lead. 'We talk of
nothing here but the French invasion,' wrote one London-based peer,
Lord Lyttelton, that summer. 'They are certainly making such preparations as have never been made to invade this island since the
Spanish Armada; but I trust in God and Lord Anson.'

As always, England's first line of naval defence ran along the
enemy's coast. One group of ships kept watch on Dunkirk and the
Flemish ports; a second, ready to protect the Thames estuary, lay in the
Downs just north of Dover; a third was at Spithead, covering Portsmouth and watching Le Havre; a fourth was in the Mediterranean, off

---

* Fortescue, II, p. 476: 'The regular troops left in England were but few'. The dispositions listed in Marcus, Vol. I, p. 305, add up only to 46,000 men overseas, which leaves
a large number unaccounted for.
† As Gibbon's *Autobiography* is readily available, I have not quoted extensively from it
here, but it gives an excellent picture of the militia at this period.

Toulon; and the fifth, and most important, was Admiral Hawke's squadron, whose close blockade of Brest, from his base at Plymouth, was to become a model for the future.

Hawke's standing patrol along the French coast was maintained by three groups of ships, as closely in touch as sea and weather allowed. Frigates patrolled close inshore along the two main passages leading into the Brest road and its splendid harbour. An advance force, in two sections, situated near the Black Rocks and St Mathieu Point, at one end of the adjoining bay, provided a second line of defence. Hawke himself and his remaining ships were a little further out, in a sea area 15 leagues [45 miles or 72 km] off Ushant, ready to hasten to wherever they were needed.

A purely defensive strategy made little appeal to Pitt and he now eagerly supported a plan devised by Anson to carry the war into enemy waters. On the night of Wednesday 4 July 1759 Rear-Admiral George [later Admiral Lord] Rodney in the 60-gun *Achilles*, led four 50-gun ships of the line, five frigates and six bomb-ketches, described earlier, into Le Havre and, impudently anchoring in the main channel, began next morning a heavy bombardment of the docks, the warehouses storing timber, the construction yards, and, most important of all, the completed flat-boats intended for the coming invasion. A neutral eye-witness reported that the building holding the stores of planks, pitch and cordage was entirely destroyed, while of the 600 shells which had fallen in the town 100 had landed on the basin and harbour.

Although the loss of the transports assembled or under construction at Le Havre delivered a serious blow to the French plans, others were still being built or collected at ports all along the Bay of Biscay, from Lorient [or L'Orient] to Bayonne, including Nantes, La Rochelle and Bordeaux, and the plan, as the English government knew, was for them to assemble at Brest, where the Commander-in-Chief of the naval side of the invasion, Admiral Conflans [Hubert de Brienne, Comte de Conflans] had arrived in early July. The intention was for them to be escorted by the combined fleets from Brest and Toulon and the combination of the two, to outnumber any force likely to be brought against them, was a vital part of the French plan. While, however, Admiral Hawke had been keeping a vigilant eye on Brest, Admiral Edward Boscawen had been busily patrolling off Toulon. Boscawen was another of Anson's fire-eaters, a robust forthright sea-dog known to his men as 'Old Dreadnought', from the name of the ship he had captained during one famous engagement, and he had used his 15 large ships and dozen smaller 'cruisers' to cause endless annoyance to the French and to tie up ten battalions of French infantry, waiting to repel an anticipated but imaginary landing. Even Boscawen, however, had to withdraw to refit and revictual and thanks to Byng's blundering, which had robbed England of Minorca, that meant going all the way to Gibraltar, which he reached on 3 August.

At eight o'clock in the evening of 17 August 1759 the single frigate which Boscawen had left to watch the Straits arrived in Gibraltar harbour with the alarming news that the enemy was about to escape them after all. Some of Boscawen's ships lacked sails, none was immediately ready for sea, and many of the crews and officers were ashore, including Boscawen himself, but the moment the message arrived the admiral leapt from his chair, leaving his dinner unfinished, and within an unprecedented two hours the first ships were weighing anchor. Before breakfast on Saturday 18 August 1759 Boscawen was in sight of his quarry, or part of it, for eight of the Frenchmen had broken away to make for Cadiz. That left seven, easily outnumbered by Boscawen's 15, plus frigates, and he used his superiority to crushing effect in an action which began around 1.30 pm and continued next day, when the last four French ships were driven into Lagos Bay, about 19 miles [30 km] east of Cape St Vincent, on the coast of Portugal, where Boscawen pursued them into Portuguese waters. Two of the enemy ships, including the French flagship, were run on the rocks under full sail to escape capture, three more were burnt and two captured. When the news of his victory in the Battle of Lagos, as it is known, reached London on 6 September even the perpetually anxious Duke of Newcastle gave way to optimism. 'I own,' he admitted unnecessarily to his colleagues, 'I was afraid of invasion till now.'

Newcastle's natural nervousness soon reasserted itself for the French had clearly not abandoned their plan and had even managed to bring the transports at Nantes, on the River Loire, to join those further up the coast at Vannes in the Gulf of Morbihan, about midway between St Nazaire and Lorient. But the main force of transports, along with the fleet intended to escort it, was still hemmed in by Hawkes's blockade. On 14 October Louis XV himself signed orders instructing Admiral Conflans to set the whole invasion scheme in motion by clearing the way across the Channel. 'I leave it to your experience and courage to profit by any circumstance you may think favourable,' he wrote, 'to go out and attack the squadrons and vessels blockading at Ushant and at Belle Île [or Belle Isle or Belleisle, in Quiberon Bay]. Then . . . I give you full authority to . . . escort the Morbihan flotilla as soon as it is ready to sail.'

Fortune for the moment seemed to be favouring the French. A second attempt by Admiral Rodney to attack the transports at Le Havre had found the defences there too strong for his bomb-vessels to get within range, while a storm off Dunkirk had enabled a French squadron shut up in the port to make its escape. The very night that this news reached London, however, 16 October, a far more sensational despatch arrived from Canada, reporting General Wolfe's capture (during which he was fatally wounded) of Quebec, the decisive event in the loss by the French of their North American colonies.

Defeat in Canada merely sharpened France's desire for revenge in Europe and as October gave way to November conditions in the Channel and Bay of Biscay worsened, making it ever harder for the British squadrons to hold their stations. Finally, on 10 November, Hawke warned the Admiralty that he had been forced by a gale and the resulting damage back into Torbay and two days later, when he tried to return to Brest, he was driven back again. Before the British fleet was back in position Admiral Conflans was able, on 14 November, to get out to sea with 21 ships of the line and five smaller warships. His intention was to pick up the 18,000 troops assembled in the area behind Quiberon known as the Morbihan and transport them to Scotland, as the first stage of the great invasion plan.

By fortunate chance, often a major factor in war, Hawke, on the afternoon of 16 November, learned from a victualling ship which was returning empty from taking supplies to the blockading force that it had sighted the French fleet the previous day. Although he could only guess at the enemy's destination Hawke did not hesitate, as his despatch to the Admiralty next day confirms: 'I have carried a press of sail all night, with a hard gale at south-south-east, in pursuit of the enemy, and make no doubt of coming up with them at sea or in Quiberon Bay.'

It was in fact off Belle Île just south of the entrance to the Bay, which then curves east towards Vannes, where the invasion force from the Morbihan was waiting to embark, that soon after dawn on the morning of Tuesday 20 November 1759 Hawke was able to make the classic signal 'French fleet in sight'.

The southern entrance to the Bay was protected by a fearsome group of rocks, Les Cardinals, to port and a treacherous shoal, Le Four, to starboard and, with the weather worsening, Admiral Conflans was confident Hawke would not dare to pursue him through this hazardous gap without the benefit of local pilots, but he had underrated both his adversary's daring and his seamanship. So, too, had Hawke's own navigating officer, who having warned him of the dangers was firmly told: 'You have done your duty in this remonstrance; you are now to obey my orders. Lay me alongside the French admiral!'

Hawke's squadron, 28 strong, now bore down upon the French from windward at top speed, all sails set, and around 2.30 in the afternoon the eight warships in the van opened fire on the French rear division, the start of a fierce engagement which caused its most powerful unit, the 80-gun *Formidable*, to surrender, and three 74-gun warships, the *Héros*, the *Superbe* and the *Thesée* to founder.[*] Hawke himself

---

[*] As usual, accounts of the action, and even the names of the ships given in the secondary sources, do not agree. I have mainly followed Sanderson pp. 147-8, with additional details taken from Hozier, II, pp. 192-193 and Corbett, *Seven Years War*, II, pp. 65-70.

achieved his wish, fighting a private duel in his flagship, the *Royal George*, with Conflans in the *Soleil Royal*, the largest vessel in the French navy, which, for the moment, escaped.

Darkness fell around 5 pm and the ships that had survived the battle faced heavy seas and a fierce gale. Three French ships, having jettisoned their guns, managed to get over the bar into the Vilaine [or Villaine] River and some others successfully stood out to sea. Next morning the gale frustrated attempts to use fireships against those which had got into the Vilaine but, in attempting to evade its pursuers, the *Soleil Royal* was forced on to an offshore shoal and burned by her own crew. The final French losses were seven ships of the line, with about 2500 men killed in action or drowned, and another four vessels, trapped in the Vilaine, unfit for action for a long time. Hawke's own losses amounted to two ships, a 74 and a 64, and 300-400 men. There could be no question now of the French fleet overwhelming the British and escorting an invading army to Scotland and Essex. 'Thus we wind up this wonderful year,' wrote Horace Walpole on 30 November as the news of Quiberon arrived, the phrase heard on all lips and picked up that Christmas by David Garrick in the aptly named pantomime, *Harlequin's Invasion*:

> Come cheer up my lads, 'tis to glory we steer,
> To add something new to this wonderful year;
> To honour we call you, not press you like slaves,
> For who are so free as the sons of the waves? . . .

> They swear they'll invade us, these terrible foes;
> They frighten our women, our children, and beaus;
> But should their flat-bottoms in darkness get o'er,
> Still Britons they'll find, to receive them on shore.

For centuries to come English schoolchildren were to learn the rousing chorus which followed:[*]

> Hearts of oak are our ships,
> Hearts of oak are our men,
> We always are ready,
> Steady, boys, steady,
> We'll fight and we'll conquer again and again.

Hardly had Admiral Hawke received, on 28 January 1760, the thanks of the House of Commons and a £2000 a year pension, when the sole surviving fragment of Choiseul's giant invasion plan was at last implemented. The same storm which had swept Hawke's blockading

---

[*] Only while writing the present book did I realise that *Hearts of Oak*, which I learned at a Berkshire junior school around 1935, was part of a longer song. Few schools, I suspect, still teach it.

1 The Dutch attacking the British fleet in the Medway, 1667

2 Harwich and Landguard Fort (on right), c. 1700

3   The Citadel, Plymouth, 1737

4   Tilbury Fort today

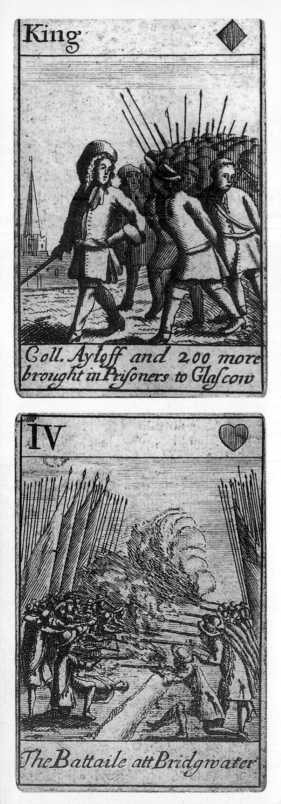

King ◆

Coll. Ayloff and 200 more brought in Prisoners to Glascow

Qveen ◆

the godly Maids of Taunton presenting their Colours upon their knees to ye D. of M.

IV ♥

The Battaile att Bridgwater

5, 6, 7 Contemporary playing cards commemorating Monmouth's rebellion. They show the collapse of Argyll's simultaneous rising in Scotland, Monmouth's triumphant entry into Taunton and his defeat at Sedgemoor, near Bridgewater

8 The landing of William of Orange in Torbay, 1688

9 William III's victory at the Battle of the Boyne, 1690

10   The Duke of Cumberland, c. 1758   11   Field Marshal George Wade, with road-builders in background

12   The Battle of Culloden, 1746

13 *(Right)* John Paul Jones (a contemporary portrait), c. 1779

14 *(Below)* The battle of Flamborough Head, 1779

15 *(Foot)* The surrender of the French at Fishguard, 1797

16 *(Below)* The defence of Dover Castle, 1803.
(Illustration to a contemporary song, 'Britons to Arms!!!')

17 *(Right)* William Pitt as Commander of the Cinque
Port Volunteers

18 The barracks at Weedon in the Midlands to which the Royal Family would have retreated in the
event of a successful French invasion, pictured 50 years later, in 1859

19   The flotilla at the Hope near Gravesend in line of battle, 1804

20   Martello Tower at Bexhill, drawn in 1817

21   The Metropolitan Volunteers, being reviewed by George III in Hyde Park, 1799

cruisers away from Ushant and enabled Conflans to get out of Brest had made it possible for the privateer captain, François Thurot [or Thourot] to take his little five-ship fleet, carrying some 1270 soldiers and 700 seamen, out of Dunkirk. They faced, in that notoriously stormy winter, a long and arduous voyage, and via Sweden and Norway, the most roundabout invasion route ever adopted. Thurot's first attempt to land in Ireland, near Londonderry, was a failure and one of his ships became separated and never rejoined him, leaving four to turn up next on the Isle of Islay off the coast of Argyll in western Scotland, where, with a courtesy rare among invaders, he paid for the provisions he needed. With his supplies he received news of Conflans' defeat at Quiberon Bay, which meant that his small-scale diversion had now become the main, indeed only, invasion, but he bravely pressed on to Ireland and, by now having lost another ship, finally landed a force variously put at from 600 to 1000 men at Carrickfergus, on the north side of Belfast Lough, on Friday 21 February 1760.*

Belfast itself was a mere eight miles [13 km] away but Thurot's military commander, General de Flobert, who was already at odds with his naval colleague, refused to attack it. Carrickfergus itself, lacking walls and protected only by a ruined castle, rapidly surrendered when the garrison's ammunition ran out and the Belfast authorities were sufficiently intimidated to send the French provisions when they demanded them. Then, to their relief, on 26 February, Thurot sailed off, having heard that a force of several thousand regulars and volunteers was being got together to attack him.

News of the attack on Ireland reached the Admiralty the day after the French had re-embarked. Orders were sent to no fewer than four squadrons to try to engage him in the Irish Sea or, as a last resort, to intercept him off Brest on his way home; but in the event none of them was needed for he was caught, almost by chance, near Kinsale on the southern coast of Ireland at daybreak on 29 February 1760, by three frigates which had taken refuge there during the recent storm. In 90 minutes, the battle was over. Thurot fell on the deck of his flagship, the *Maréchal de Belleisle*, and all three French ships, having suffered 300 casualties – the English total was 40 – surrendered. It was a fitting postscript to the year of victories and the real end of the invasion danger.

During 1760 the long run of British success continued, culminating, on 8 September, with the surrender of all Canada to the British crown. But the war had not finally been won when, on 25 October 1760, George II died suddenly, a venerable 76, of a heart attack, 'in the greatest period,' as Horace Walpole wrote, 'of the glory of his country and of his reign'.

* Corbett, *Seven Years War*, II, p. 89 and Leadam, p. 469. Hozier, II, p. 196 fn 1, points out that this is the date favoured by the French authorities, but at least one English source prefers the 28th.

The new king, 22* when he ascended the throne, had studied fortification in the schoolroom, but he was not, by either temperament or
training, a soldier. An amiable, approachable individual of wide interests, he rapidly became known to his subjects as 'Farmer George'.
To his first speech to Parliament, on 18 November 1760, the king
added in his own hand the robust declaration: 'Born and educated in
this country, I glory in the name of Britain.'

This was all very fine, but glory came expensive. The war, which
cost £15,500,000 in 1760, required supplies of £19,600,000 to be voted
for 1761, to support a huge army of 110,000 men, mainly serving overseas. The navy consisted of nearly 81,000 men, serving in 378 vessels,
though only 285 of these were of any size, qualifying as first to sixth
rates, and what really counted in any major action were the 121 ships of
the line, manned by 70,000 sailors. For home defence on land the
government looked largely to the militia, which was brigaded with
regular formations to improve its training and hurried about the
country to each area that seemed in danger.

New recruits to keep the militia up to establishment, and to allow
longer-serving members to go home, were selected by ballot. Edward
Gibbon's battalion of the Hampshire militia had finally been mustered
at Winchester on 4 June, 1760. Recalling his comfortable officers'
quarters in the south, he commented that 'the ballot of the ensuing
summer renewed our vigour and youth', but the working-men of the
north resisted having their lives interrupted and at Hexham in Northumberland a serious anti-ballot riot occurred in which 42 men were
killed and another 48 wounded. The war, seemingly interminable, was
by now unpopular, and in October 1761, having failed to persuade his
colleagues to declare war on Spain before she entered into an open
alliance with France, Pitt the Elder resigned. He was rapidly proved
right; Spain pledged herself in December to a Family Compact with
France, forcing England, on 2 January 1762, to declare war on her and
reviving the old nightmare of a joint Franco-Spanish fleet sweeping up
the Channel to land a papist army on English soil.

The French invasion plan of 1762 was very different from all those
that had preceded it. The Duc de Choiseul did not expect to occupy
England, much less incorporate it in Louis XV's empire, but merely to
distract his enemy from further conquests overseas and encourage an
early peace. A copy of his plan was sent to Spain on the very day, 14
April 1762, that he replied encouragingly to a British approach about
opening negotiations to end the war. Although the Spanish fleet numbered around 49 ships of the line, including those inadequately manned
for sea, and its army perhaps 70,000 men, their part in his plan was

* Like everyone else of his generation, George III had two birthdays, having been born
on 24 May (1738) under the old calendar. This became 4 June under the new one,
adopted in 1751. Like his subjects, he celebrated the later date as his birthday.

purely diversionary, to invade Portugal, a traditional ally of England. The Spaniards themselves were keen to attack Gibraltar, make yet another descent on Ireland, or pay off old scores in the West Indies, but de Choiseul discouraged all these ventures.

All previous invasion attempts had been betrayed by the massive concentration of troops and ships begun long in advance. De Choiseul planned to collect only eight small vessels between Dunkirk and Calais, too few to attract any agent's notice but sufficient to carry a small force to secure the initial beachhead, which would then be rapidly reinforced. The main, second and third wave, army, consisting of 100 battalions, or about 50,000 men, would be held in reserve until the last moment between the Lower Rhine and the River Meuse, apparently intended for Westphalia. Only at the last minute, by forced marches, would it suddenly make for the Channel coast.

The British fleet in September 1761 consisted of 54 ships of the line on home stations or within easy recall, plus 58 frigates, but was seriously undermanned by more than 15,000 seamen. France should, de Choiseul hoped, be able to assemble a striking force of 22 large vessels from Brest, Ferrol, 13 miles [21 km] north-east of Corunna, and Cadiz, sufficient to obtain local superiority at the decisive point, provided Spain contributed eight ships. De Choiseul acknowledged that the invasion depended on securing 'the command of the Channel and a superiority in that sea for at least five weeks'. Before, however, the plan could be put to the test preliminary peace terms had been agreed and England's victory in the Seven Years War was confirmed by the Treaty of Paris on 10 February 1763.

Although George III's government behaved generously to their recent enemies, the French felt hard done by. The cry, as so often and so disastrously in European history, was for revenge and preparations for a new invasion began immediately. The driving force was again provided by the king's chief minister, the Duc de Choiseul, author of the never-implemented plan of 1762, and by Louis XV's principal private adviser, Count Charles-François de Broglie, who shared de Choiseul's implacable hostility towards Great Britain. He attributed earlier failures to inadequate intelligence and sent a number of agents to England, including an engineer skilled in map-making, Captain Louis de la Rozière, who was installed, supposedly as a diplomat, in London. De La Rozière was instructed to collect information about arsenals, shipyards and the location of British troops as well as to survey the coast between the Thames estuary and Cornwall. He had managed to reconnoitre the area between the South Foreland and Beachy Head and to study the roads between there and London when he was given away by the careless talk, prompted by malice, of the ambassador's homosexual secretary, a subsequently notorious transvestite, the Chevalier d'Éon, who later lived as a woman. La Rozière had to leave in a hurry, but he brought back much useful information and, promoted to lieut.-colonel, was employed to survey the facilities available on the French coast for embarking the invading army.

By 1765, when de Broglie submitted his plan to King Louis XV, the French government already had in their archives detailed invasion schemes going back for at least a century.*. Profiting by the lessons of earlier failures, de Broglie identified the principal problem as forcing the British fleet to disperse by mounting, with Spanish help, simultaneous threats to Jamaica, Minorca, Gibraltar, Ireland and Scotland. The way would thus be opened for the real attack, by 60,000 men landed simultaneously at Rye, Winchelsea, Hastings and Pevensey, who would march on London. Louis XV was not, however, enthusiastic about the scheme and, after trying for a year to interest him, de Broglie, a soldier, decided to pool his information and ideas with de Choiseul, who, controlling the Ministries of Marine, War and Foreign Affairs, had been making independent plans of his own. De Choiseul recognised, even more acutely than de Broglie, that no invasion was possible without defeating the Royal Navy. He therefore concentrated his attention not on the Kent coast but on the Isle of Wight, where the French had actually landed in the past† and which, once occupied, could serve as a base to paralyse and capture Portsmouth.

De Choiseul, not to be outdone by de Broglie, sent a spy of his own, Colonel de Béville, to England in September and October 1768. De Béville's proposal was for a landing in west Sussex between Littlehampton and Chichester harbour. Part of the army would then advance inland, to Guildford and Dorking, while the remainder marched, via Chichester, to Portsdown Hill, just behind Portsmouth and the main dockyard on Portsea Island. This was protected on the landward side by the Portsea Lines but the garrison would be harassed by small boats taking them in the rear via the channel between Portsea and Hayling Island. Other troops would meanwhile attack Southsea Castle, gain control of the Spithead anchorage beyond it, and be landed at Gosport, the peninsula stretching into the Solent on the other side of Portsmouth. Once Gosport and the Portsea Lines had fallen the Portsmouth dockyard would become unusable, and – reversing the usual proposed sequence – the invaders would then capture the Isle of Wight. Some troops would be left to besiege Portsmouth, while the rest of this force, forming the left wing of the invading army, would turn inland, through Petersfield to Farnham, to come into line with the right wing, already expected to be well established in Surrey. The whole army was then to advance on London, crossing the Thames to the west at Hampton Court, Kingston, Kew and Putney and moving round to occupy

* Patterson, p. 2 fn 3, writing in 1960, states that the oldest plan still extant dated from 1666.
† See *Defending the Island*, pp. 394-5.

the northern heights of Hampstead and Highgate, to cut off London from relief from that direction.

Every invasion attempt so far had foundered on France's naval weakness, but after the end of the Seven Years War in 1763 de Choiseul had put in hand a whole series of reforms. The total number of large vessels, a mere 40 in 1763, was raised by 1771, when he left office, to 64 ships of the line and 50 frigates; stocks of stores were built up and a fourth arsenal, at Marseilles, added to those at Brest, Rochefort and Toulon; improved training and signalling methods were introduced, along with a more scientific study of tactics. Above all, the French managed, where the English had failed, to devise a satisfactory system of lower-deck recruitment, so that eventually 67,000 first-class seamen were enrolled.

After the end of the Seven Years War, in 1763, the Royal Navy suffered its customary peacetime fate of neglect and decay. Within a few years most of its nominal 100 ships of the line were unfit for sea, although by 1770 a new conflict with Spain over the Falkland Islands seemed likely.[*]

That year the great Earl of Chatham, formerly the elder Pitt, laid down the basic principles of British naval policy:

> The first great and acknowledged object of naval defence . . . is to maintain such a superior naval force at home, that even the united fleets of France and Spain may never be masters of the Channel . . . The second naval object with an English minister should be to maintain at all times a powerful western squadron . . . Without it, the colonies, the commerce, the navigation of Great Britain lie at the mercy of the House of Bourbon. The third object . . . is to maintain such a force in the Bay of Gibraltar as may be sufficient to cover that garrison, [and] to watch the motions of the Spaniards.

In France invasion was in the air at court and anyone who put forward a promising scheme was sure of an audience. This receptiveness increased with the succession of Louis XVI in 1774, for he was interested in the navy and his chief minister, the Count de Maurepas, was a former Minister of Marine. De Broglie now revived and expanded his original plan into a so-called 'grand design', the most elaborate yet compiled. The moment was propitious, for on 19 April 1775 the first shots were fired, at Lexington in Massachusetts, in the rebellion of the American colonists, which rapidly developed into a full-scale war and led, on 4 July 1776, to the new United States of America formally proclaiming their independence of Great Britain. This was a serious threat to the homeland's security as well as to its prestige, for England's

---

[*] During 1770 the Spaniards forced a small British force on the Islands to surrender, but in the following year allowed the British post to be restored, leaving the question of sovereignty unsettled.

North American possessions were of great importance to the Royal
Navy. Chatham described them, in November 1777, as 'the nursery
and basis of our naval power', for they had been not merely a dependable source of tar and timber, especially for masts, but of seamen; the
outbreak of hostilities meant that 18,000 American sailors were lost
overnight to the British crown.

The turning point in what had become the War of American Independence came in October 1777, when a British army under General
Burgoyne suffered a spectacular defeat at Saratoga, 180 miles [288 km]
north of New York. France now came out openly on the American
side and began actively to prepare a new invasion to take advantage of
England's difficulties overseas. At the end of 1777 de Broglie submitted to King Louis XVI an improved version of the proposals he had
drafted 12 years before while at about the same time a new figure
appeared on the scene, the 39-year-old Edward Dumouriez, an able
army officer who had caught the eye of the king and been appointed
Commandant of Cherbourg.

Dumouriez was, like so many Frenchmen, fascinated by the idea of
humbling the hitherto unvanquished islanders, and he now undertook
a thorough study of the reasons why past attempts had invariably
failed. His thinking is reflected in his later autobiography, which in-
corporates his *Historical Note on the Various Projects of Descent on
England*.

> A descent upon England was long looked upon as an impracticable
> chimera in face of the countless and invincible naval forces that en-
> circle this island-empire with a line of floating citadels, collected or
> dispersed at will at any threatened points around the coast . . .
>
> Seeing the shortness of the crossing, the frequency of fog in the
> Channel, the length of the October and November nights, and the
> species of calm that characterizes this narrow sea for more than six
> weeks of December and January, I deemed the obstacles by no
> means insuperable, especially for partial 'diversions' and in the
> winter of 1777-8 I laid before the ministry the plans of an expedition
> against the Isle of Wight which were but the preliminary of a great
> project of descent.

Dumouriez made out a powerful case for this initial effort:

> In 1778 England had 50,000 men in America and not 10,000 regulars
> at home that could be collected at any one given spot. The militia
> were not embodied . . . There were in Portsmouth only one batta-
> lion of foot, 600 pensioners, a few marines doing duty in the port, or
> ready for drafting on to the ships or frigates then fitting out . . . The
> Isle of Wight contained a large number of sick men in Newport hos-
> pital, the corn and foodstuffs for the Portsmouth squadrons at Brad-
> ing and St Helen's, and stacked timber and shipyards in full work for

the frigates, corvettes, and cutters of the Portsmouth division at
Cowes. All the defence of the island consisted of a little artillery in
Shanklin Fort, with 150 pensioners . . .

The island would have been a most excellent stronghold, beyond
all danger of starvation if communications with France were cut off.
The soil is very fruitful; there are corn, cattle and horseflesh in abun-
dance; and by sending away to Hampshire all the inhabitants not required in the fields one could have held out there several months.

The little matter of the actual crossing Dumouriez dismissed with the
usual landsman's casualness:

The distance from cape to cape is eighteen leagues [62 land miles; 100
km] or at most twenty to twenty-two [69-76 miles; 111-122 km]
with the bends of the island coastline. A time was to be fixed for the
expedition in the month of November, and by leaving in the evening on the ebb tide we could expect to reach the shores of Wight
with the full morning flood. English and French smugglers would
have provided us with enough of pilots and we had indeed already a
few . . . The embarkation was to take place in the harbour and roads
of Cherbourg in 200 oyster ketches known as *chasse-marées*. These
craft are decked, sometimes sternless and double-prowed, of shallow draught, and excellent sailers. Thirty were to be converted into
gun-sloops, by shoring up the bows to accommodate a 24-pounder
[11-kg gun] . . . These 30 gunboats were to sail in three divisions, at
the head and on the flanks of the flotilla, which in addition would
have enjoyed the escort of the eight gun-sloops of the [French] royal
navy stationed between Havre and St Malo and a few privateers
from there and Cherbourg.

The essence of the plan was surprise.

All these warlike preparations could be made quickly and unosten-
tatiously . . . We were to wait for the oyster-fishing season in the
Bay of Cancale without giving the boats notice and stop them as
they sailed past Barfleur Head . . . The dragoons would take with
them saddle, bridle and pistols. Horses would not have been lacking
in the Isle of Wight. Two hours would have sufficed to embark the
men in Cherbourg Harbour, after a previous rehearsal. Every *chasse-
marée* would have easily held 60 men and the landing would have
taken about the same space of time . . . The landing was to be executed from east to west and embrace the whole southern coast of the
island, from Sandown Bay, where the main body would land, to
Chale, Brixton and Freshwater Bays . . . The longest march for any
of the four columns was about ten miles, which the French foot
soldiers could have done in four hours . . . At Newport the troops
would have taken an hour's rest and then made in several extended

columns for the northern shore of the island, to occupy it in its entirety.

Dumouriez was equally optimistic about the operation's longer-term aim 'to deprive England for ever of her finest port and greatest naval establishment':

> There were to accompany the army corps a number of shipwrights, caulkers, sailmakers and six hundred seamen, who [would] have settled at Cowes and Yarmouth for the winter, and built with the timber in the local yards a large quantity of gun-sloops . . . Some would have been formed into bomb-ketches and armed with mortars and howitzers. This flotilla might have made Spithead untenable and certainly uncomfortable for the home guardships.

At the same time the fleet's normal exit from Portsmouth harbour would have been blocked, forcing it to use instead the more dangerous, shoal-encumbered, Needles passage:

> Last, all the vessels found in the island or fetched from Cherbourg were to be brought into Brading harbour laden with stones and sunk the 800-fathom [4800-ft; 1460-m] fairway that lies between . . . the outer road of St Helen's and the inner one of Spithead.

All this sounded remarkably easy to accomplish, as invasion plans invariably did on paper. Nothing, however, had been done to implement the proposals when, in March 1778, the French signed a treaty of friendship with the Americans. England's oldest enemy was now united with her newest, with results that were soon to become apparent.

15

HERE COMES PAUL JONES

Here comes Paul Jones, such a nice fellow!

Contemporary Dutch song commemorating the exploits of John Paul Jones off the English coast, 1778-79

The new spirit of cooperation between France and the United States was soon being displayed in the operations of an American privateer sailing from French ports. The full story of his operations against the British Isles may conveniently be given here, though this began before and continued after the main French invasion effort. John Paul Jones, though the 'Jones' was added later to conceal his real identity, was the son of an estate gardener from near Dumfries in Galloway. At 13 he sailed as apprentice to a ship-owner operating out of Whitehaven in Cumberland, 36 miles [58 km] south-west of Carlisle, and from ship's boy rose to be third mate on a 'black-birder' or slave ship. The outbreak of war with England gave him his great chance and on 7 December 1775 he was commissioned lieutenant in what was soon to become the US Navy. On 1 November 1777 he sailed from Portsmouth, New Hampshire, in command of the 318-ton USS *Ranger*, a sloop with a crew of 150, armed with 18 nine-pounder [4-kg] guns, to carry news of General Burgoyne's defeat at Saratoga to Benjamin Franklin, the US ambassador in Paris. On his arrival Jones received new, and even more congenial orders to use the *Ranger* 'In the manner you shall judge best for distressing the enemies of the United States'.

Jones, still only 30, already had a reputation as an experienced seaman and he began his new career by capturing several British ships in the Irish Sea, but his announcement that he intended to raid Whitehaven in Cumberland and burn the vessels moored there nearly provoked a mutiny, for his crew, already disgruntled that so many ships had been sunk instead of seized, saw their prospect of prize money once again going up in smoke. Jones dealt with the dissidents characteristically, by holding a pistol at the ringleader's head, but his call for volunteers to go ashore produced such a poor response that he had to lead one boat himself, while a marine officer commanded the other.

Jones's acknowledged aim was to seize some important person as a

hostage to exchange for the American sailors taken prisoner by the
Royal Navy, who were imprisoned indefinitely as pirates, and in his
own words, 'to put an end of burnings in America by making a good
fire in England'. He selected Whitehaven as the scene of his demonstration merely because he already knew its waters, though a reconnaissance revealed not a single large ship, much less any naval vessel, in
the port, the 250 craft there being mainly small colliers or fishing boats.

The port consisted, in April 1778, of two harbours, the North and
the South, divided by a stone pier, at the end of which there was a small
fort. The South Harbour was also covered by a 'lunette' or 'half-moon'
battery, so called from its shape, on the beach, 200 yards [183m] away,
the fort and lunette mounting, in theory, 36 cannon between them.
Jones was not deterred. His plan was based on the marine lieutenant
landing at the Old Quay slipway in the North Harbour and creating a
diversion there, while Jones himself landed, undetected it was hoped,
on the south foreshore, put the battery there out of action and then,
passing round the town, knocked out the North Battery, before joining up with the other party to burn the shipping in both harbours.
They would then regain their boats, with the *Ranger*, no longer in
danger from shore-based guns, coming close inshore to re-embark the
raiders.

The night of Wednesday 22 April 1778 was misty and cold; snow
was visible on the Solway Firth, to the north, and the Isle of Man, to
the west. The two small boats, containing between them about 40
men, had no option but to row towards the shore and duly grounded
around 3.30 am on the morning of Thursday 23 April. By 5 am the
guns of both batteries had been spiked as planned, by having iron
wedges driven into their touch-holes, and the two groups had met as
agreed and set about their work of destruction.

At this point an Irishman among the raiders unaccountably chose to
dash off through the still sleeping streets to raise the alarm. After setting fire to a collier and a house by the harbour, not very effectively,
thanks to a sudden heavy storm, Jones successfully withdrew, despite
the fire of a party of militia, and, when he had re-embarked, of cannon
shot from some guns in the batteries which had escaped being spiked.
The *Ranger* got safely out to sea, with three prisoners aboard, some
others who had been taken having been released, and by 6 am was
making course for Kirkcudbright Bay in the Solway Firth. He left
behind him a town in uproar and the foundations of his fame, for he
had been recognised while in Whitehaven and his identity had been
confirmed by the Irish deserter. Not much damage had been done. No
one had been killed and only 20 or so people, all on shore, even slightly
injured. But the shock to the local population, and indeed to the whole
nation, defied on its own doorstep by a rebellious colonist, was enormous. 'What was done . . .', Jones himself wrote later, 'is sufficient to

show that not all their boasted navy can protect their own coasts,' a disagreeable lesson for any Briton to digest.

The *Cumberland Packet Extraordinary*, faced with the biggest story in its history, made the most of it.

> Late last night or early this morning a number of armed men (to the amount of 30) landed at this place, by two boats from an American privateer, as appears from one of the people now in custody . . . A little after 3 o'clock this morning he rapped at several doors in Marlborough Street (adjoining one of the piers) and informed them that fire had been set to one of the ships in the harbour [and] matches were laid in several others; the whole world would soon be in a blaze, and the town also destroyed . . .
>
> An alarm was immediately spread, and his account proved too true. The *Thomson*, Captain Richard Johnson, a new vessel and one of the finest ever built here, was in a flame. It was low water, consequently all the shipping in port was in the most imminent danger and . . . there was the greatest reason to fear that the flames would, from it, soon be communicated to the town . . . By an uncommon exertion, the fire was extinguished . . . and thus, in a providential manner, prevented all the dreadful consequences which might have ensued.

John Paul Jones's second landing on British soil within a single morning is notable as the most courteous invasion it ever suffered. His aim was to kidnap the Earl of Selkirk from his house on St Mary's Isle, a promontory stretching out into Kirkcudbright Bay. It is highly unlikely that the British government would have agreed to exchange this nobleman, an amiable figure of no political importance, for its American prisoners but at around 11 am on 23 April 1778, John Paul led his little force of a dozen armed sailors through the garden of the mansion. When challenged by the head gardener the Americans pretended to be a press gang, which was sufficient to set 'all the stout young fellows' on the estate running off to the town for safety, but he also informed them that their intended victim was taking the waters at Buxton, and Jones set off back to his boat, until the two officers with him pointed out that, having left Whitehaven empty-handed, the crew should at least be allowed to loot the house.

Faced with his second mutiny in barely a day Jones agreed, though insisting his men must not search or damage the house but merely demand the family silver. The Countess of Selkirk, finding her house surrounded by 'horrid-looking wretches', sensibly agreed and when the butler tried to hide the coffee pot and teapot, still damp from breakfast, she ordered that these, too, be handed over. The members of the household, once they realised that their watches and jewellery were safe, 'asked them a thousand questions' about America, and, as the children's governess later wrote 'they behaved with great civility'. After 20 minutes the officers accepted a glass of wine from their enforced hostess and one, until restrained by the other, even began to write out a receipt for what had been taken. Then they left and, following a three-mile [4.8-km] row, rejoined the *Ranger*.

Half an hour after the intruders had gone, a horde of volunteers arrived – since 'the Forty-five' Scotland had had no militia – and a cannon, dragged from the town on to the Point of St Mary's Isle, fiercely engaged a supposed ship which turned out to be a rock.

This somewhat absurd episode was a mere interlude in a fiercely fought campaign. After leaving the Solway Firth the *Ranger* returned to Belfast Lough to attack the nearest British warship, the 273-ton *Drake*, armed with 20 six-pounder [2.7-kg] guns; the *Ranger* (316 tons) with her 18 nine-pounders [4-kg guns] somewhat outclassed her. During the battle between the two, which began an hour before sunset on 24 April 1778 off Kilroot Point near Carrickfergus, Jones kept his distance, disabling his opponent by cannon fire and pistol shots aimed at the crew until, resistance having ceased, a boarding party was sent across, to find the decks running with blood and rum – a keg, brought out prematurely to celebrate the expected victory, had been breached by a cannon ball – and the *Drake* was taken in tow.

John Paul Jones's activities had strikingly demonstrated the vulnerability of the coastline and the *Morning Chronicle and London Advertiser* accompanied its report of the raid on St Mary's Isle with some distinctly sharp observations:

> The audacious conduct of the crew of the American privateer at Whitehaven, and on the coast of Scotland, will have this good effect; it will teach our men of war on the coast station, and our cruisers in St George's Channel, to keep a more sharp look out.
>
> The ruinous state of the fortifications of many of our seaport towns, so likewise the open and defenceless posture of many others, at present seems to suggest some very alarming reflections. In all places like Whitehaven, the want of a necessary range of fortifications seems almost inexcusable, especially as the materials are in great plenty at or near the spot, labour cheap, etc.

On his way home to Brest, sailing north-about round Ireland, Jones confirmed his reputation as a maritime Robin Hood by releasing, with a new sail and money in their pockets, some Irish fishermen he had captured, but his arrival back in port, on 8 May 1778, proved a disappointment, for the French failed to give him the hero's welcome he had expected. Nor, since he lacked the four generations of noble blood required for a commission in the French navy, was he offered the command of a French ship. When France declared war on England, on 17 June 1778, Jones remained unemployed and he also managed to fall out with his own crew who, in a petition, called 'his temper and treatment [of them] insufferable'. The new democratic notions of his country-men clearly made the traditionally harsh maritime discipline difficult to enforce. His own officers, he complained, instead of setting an example 'of dutiful subordination . . . introduce the mistaken and baneful idea of licentiousness and free agency under the specious name of "liberty"'.

While the famous privateer was waiting impatiently 'on the beach' in Paris he filled in his time producing ambitious schemes to harass the common enemy, including a large-scale raid up the River Clyde to attack Glasgow, and a major amphibious assault on Liverpool. This last had the support of the man who had come to symbolise the Franco-American alliance, Marie Joseph de Motier, Marquis de Lafayette, who having gone to America to fight for the rebel colonists, in May 1779 returned to France a major-general in the US army. Benjamin Franklin, the official US representative in France, talented inventor as well as an effective diplomatist, considered that Lafayette himself should be in nominal command, with John Paul Jones leading the actual assault. 'There is,' Franklin assured him, 'honor enough to be got for both of you.'

The French, it soon appeared, were preparing a new invasion, of which more will be said later. Jones had been cast for the minor but useful role of leading a small diversionary force of ships to the north of England and Scotland, but his attempts to make his ships ready for sea involved him in constant arguments with the French authorities, and his reputation as a tyrannical captain made it hard to find a crew. It was not till 14 August 1779 that the little five-ship force led by the self-styled 'Commander-in-Chief of the American squadron now in Europe' finally left Brest, but by the 21st it had taken its first prize and others rapidly followed. The Royal Navy had had ample warning that Jones was putting to sea again but, guarding the door of the already raided stable, was patrolling the Cumberland coast, while he made his way round the far side of Ireland and soon reports were reaching London of his activities in Irish waters on the early stages of his voyage, though they took several weeks to arrive.

From Ireland he moved on to the Outer Hebrides, which he reached on 30 August, and then to his most northerly landfall, Foula off the Shetlands, on 3 September. On 16 September, with extraordinary effrontery, Jones sailed up the Firth of Forth towards Leith, the port of Edinburgh, intending to demand a huge ransom of £200,000 – though he was prepared to settle for £50,000 – for not laying the town 'in ashes', the first instalment of the indemnity 'which,' Jones explained, 'Britain owes to the much injured citizens of America.' A change of wind and tide forced the abandonment of this plan, and the marauders had no more luck at their next port of call, Kirkcaldy, for again the wind changed, thanks, it was asserted, to the prayers of the towns-people, gathered on the beach under their minister. Jones now sailed on through the North Sea, towards England, his progress marked by a trail of prizes which were sent back to France, his own ships, as he later wrote to Louis XVI, being 'weakened and embarrassed with prison-ers', whom he still hoped to exchange for Americans.

Meanwhile another 'insult to the coast', to use a long popular term, had occurred. On Wednesday 15 September 1779 the cutter, *Black Prince*, sailing under French colours but with an American com-mander, and crewed by a mixture of Englishmen and Irishmen, sud-denly appeared off Fishguard on the west coast of Wales. A boatload of men came ashore to demand a ransom of 2000 guineas [£2100], or the surrender of the local vicar as a hostage, for not attacking the town. When the townsfolk refused the *Black Prince* began to bombard Fish-guard with its six-pounder [2.7-kg] guns.

The American, or English, renegade in command, Stephen Man-hant, got more than he bargained for. A Fishguard smuggler whose ship happened to be at anchor there opened fire with his single cannon, and another gun was dragged to the edge of the cliff and joined in. By the time the local defence force, the Dewsland Gentlemen Volunteers, had been mobilised and reached the scene Manhant had withdrawn.

John Paul Jones was less easily discouraged, and much more feared, as he began to seem uncatchable. On 20 September he appeared off Newcastle, but decided against attacking it, as his fellow-captains were eager to move on before the Royal Navy, fully aroused since his in-trusion into the Firth of Forth, caught up with them. 'I have had the mortification of *seeing* him . . . this afternoon with three prizes . . .' wrote one irate resident to the Admiralty, '*and nothing in the world to oppose him.*'

Thwarted in his attempts to cause a shortage of coal in London by attacking Newcastle, as the Dutch had done in 1667 when they con-trolled the Thames estuary, Jones did what he could to disrupt the coastal trade. Early on 22 September he captured a Scarborough collier and another vessel and, later that morning, with typical effrontery, signalled for a pilot off Spurn Head, at the mouth of the Humber, and then captured the two boats sent out in response. Finally, to his delight, he came upon a 41-ship convoy from the Baltic, escorted only by a 20-gun sloop, the *Countess of Scarborough*, and a 44-gun frigate, the *Serapis*.

The action that followed was to become a classic of naval warfare. Captain Richard Pearson, of the *Serapis*, on first sighting his opponent, remarked, 'It is probably Paul Jones. If so, there is work ahead!' and his challenge was duly answered by a broadside. Thus, on a smooth sea, under a clear sky and later a full moon, about seven miles [11 km] off the Yorkshire coast, the Battle of Flamborough Head began, around 7 pm on Thursday 23 September 1779. The *Countess of Scarborough* was rapidly captured by one of Jones's squadrons and a two-ship duel developed between his own flagship, the *Bonhomme Richard* and the *Serapis*. Jones, challenged early on in the action to surrender, made the subsequently famous reply: 'I have not yet begun to fight!', refusing to lower his equally famous flag, made for the *Ranger* by the admiring young women of Portsmouth, New Hampshire, who had cut the 'stripes' from their silk dresses and the 'stars' from the wedding gown of a naval wife. The captain of the *Serapis* had meanwhile nailed his Red Ensign to its staff, so that it had to be torn down, when, around 10.30 pm, the English vessel, with five feet [1.5 m] of water in its hold, its holed topsides open to the moonlight, and its rigging and sails almost cut away by gunfire, was forced to surrender. (Jones, as everyone would have expected, welcomed his vanquished opponent on board with great courtesy, and invited him to his own wrecked cabin for a glass of wine.)

Although the *Bonhomme Richard* sank two days later, the Battle of Flamborough Head was an American victory, for the *Serapis* and the *Countess of Scarborough* were sailed back to France as prizes, and 504 prisoners were taken, including, a bitter blow for the Royal Navy, 26 officers. The inevitable 'butcher's bill' was evenly balanced. The *Bonhomme Richard* suffered 150 killed and wounded, almost half its complement of 322, while the *Serapis* acknowledged 49 killed and 68 wounded.

'That Celebrated Seaman', as a sixpenny biography described him, continued to embarrass the British government even after he was on his way back to France. On 24 September 1779, the day after the Battle of Flamborough Head, a member of the government, Lord Carlisle, wrote from his Cumberland estate: 'We have alarms here on our coast. One Paul Jones flings us all into consternation and terror and will hinder Lady Carlisle's sea bathing.' In the last week of September the newspapers were full of reports of the recent battle and rumours of his current whereabouts, but none of the patrols sent in search of him managed to find him until, on 1 October 1779, the *Morning Post* commented despairingly: 'Paul Jones resembles a Jack o' Lantern, to mislead our mariners and terrify our coasts. He is no sooner seen than lost.'

By 3 October Jones's squadron, now consisting, with its prizes, of five large ships, was safe at anchor in the Texel, the roadstead lying behind the island of the same name which shelters the Ijsselmeer [formerly the Zuider Zee] and forms the harbour for Amsterdam, 75 miles [120 km] away. The Dutch were still officially neutral but the public made no secret of their sympathies, as a new song confirmed:

Here comes Paul Jones, such a nice fellow!
A born American, no Englishman at all . . .

He does many bold deeds for the good of his friends.

On the 12th one Englishman resident in Amsterdam wrote angrily to a London newspaper about the Dutch reaction to Jones's presence.

> This desperado parades the streets and appears upon'Change with the effrontery of a man of the first condition. No sooner was it known in France that he was in the Texel, than a courier was dispatched with orders for him to go overland to Paris, where he says he is to have the grant of a fresh commission and a larger squadron, sufficient to make a descent on any part of Great Britain or Ireland . . . The Dutch look upon him to be a brave officer. Nay, they even go so far as to lay odds that before Christmas he lands a force in England or Ireland.

On 27 December 1779 John Paul sailed from Holland. 'For God's sake, get to sea instantly . . . ,' the First Lord of the Admiralty signalled the captain in command of the squadron assigned to blockade the Texel. 'If you can take Paul Jones, you will be as high in the estimation of the public as if you had beat the Combined [i.e. French and Spanish] Fleets.' But, in spite of the Royal Navy, Jones, after a voyage to be described later, sailed safely back to France, where his reception more than made up for the much cooler one he had received after his 'Whitehaven' cruise 18 months before. 'The cry of Versailles and the clamour of Paris became as loud in favour of Monsieur Jones as of Monsieur Franklin,' wrote Franklin himself, 'and the inclination of the ladies to embrace him almost as fashionable and as strong.' 'He is the most agreeable seawolf one could wish to meet with,' wrote one enraptured Parisienne to a friend.

For all his achievements and popularity, Jones was again refused a commission in the French navy and instead sent back to the United States with despatches. On 20 December 1780, soon after his departure, Great Britain declared war on the United Provinces of the Netherlands, giving as its first reason 'That, in violation of treaty, they suffered an American pirate (one Paul Jones, a rebel and a state criminal) to remain several weeks in one of their ports'. Even in his adopted country Jones failed to receive the command for which he had hoped, but, returning to Europe, did succeed in becoming Kontradmiral Pavel Ivanovich Jones, in the Russian navy. He eventually settled in Paris and died at the early age of 45, in 1792. His last appearance in England was in 1786, when he was entertained by the City of London. It was, said one speaker forgivingly, 'better to have him at Lloyds seeking to insure his own cargoes, than at sea seeking cargoes insured by others'.

16

A CHANNEL PROMENADE

We do not wish to commit Spain to entering the war merely in order to frighten England into . . . making peace by a naval promenade in the Channel.

Spanish minister Count Florida Blanca to the French ambassador,
February 1779

While John Paul Jones had been captivating the ladies of Paris the French government had been preparing for the most serious attack on England since the Dutch incursion into the Medway. Aptly known as 'the grand design' its basis was the plan, already described, on which the Count de Broglie had first worked in 1777, which was expanded into a far more ambitious document in December 1778. Some useful intelligence was provided by a renegade Scot, Robert Hamilton, a former lieutenant in the Royal Navy, who became a captain in the French fleet and was employed in reporting on likely landing places. Having considered Plymouth, Dartmouth, Torbay and Harwich he finally, in a memorandum dated 20 March 1779, delivered almost simultaneously with Dumouriez's, recommended, like Dumouriez, Portsmouth and the Isle of Wight. Portsmouth and Gosport between them, he estimated, were protected by only 1000 men and under the right conditions, perhaps after a gale, when few ships were at anchor there, Hamilton believed it might be possible to gain control of Spithead and get men ashore both on the Isle of Wight and at Stokes Bay, on the seaward side of Gosport, and Spit Bank. This latter force would then seize Gosport and bombard Portsmouth Harbour and town from their exposed, western, side.

The British public had not so far been inclined to take the latest invasion threat very seriously and its chief effect had been to encourage feminism. 'I was sorry to see them striding along the walks at Tunbridge Wells with their arms akimbo, dressed in martial uniform,' wrote the authoress Elizabeth Montagu that spring of some fellow members of her sex. 'As many of our modern dames want the modesty of women, I hope they will have the courage of men and . . . drive the French back again if they invade us.'

The nation's real defenders were meanwhile still suffering from those perpetual enemies, neglect and corruption. When war again broke out with France in June 1778 it proved difficult to scrape together 21 ships of the line ready for sea, in spite of a nominal strength of 199 first, second or third rates. That month saw a new invasion alarm, as a French fleet cruised up and down the Channel under Admiral D'Orvilliers and a large French army under Marshal de Broglie was assembled at Vaussieux in Normandy, though this was in fact only a routine 'camp of exercise'. On Monday 27 July 1778 the first major action of the new war was fought some 70 miles [112 km] west of Ushant, and proved indecisive, but convinced Louis XIV's chief minister, the Comte de Vergennes, that he needed Spanish help to clear the way for a successful invasion.

Charles III of Spain was well aware that his country, unlike France, could not support a long, full-scale war; a sudden, successful invasion was another matter, and, in August 1778, the Spaniards suggested an immediate attack by their joint fleets, as a preliminary to a major landing. Vergennes's assessment was more realistic:

> It could not be attempted before next year. A fleet of 60 French and Spanish ships could not easily be concentrated, and it would have to fight in the Channel against an English fleet of 45 of the line . . . A storm or violent gale might disperse the combined fleets; France has no port in the Channel; in fact, innumerable mischances might ruin the enterprise.*

Vergennes next toyed with the idea of an attack on Ireland, but the Spaniards proved unenthusiastic about anything short of an invasion as the Spanish minister, the Count of Florida Blanca, made clear to the French ambassador in February 1779:

> We do not wish to commit Spain to entering the war merely in order to frighten England into a peace from which nothing but the independence of the Americans would be obtained . . . You must . . . convince us that you do not want us to declare war simply in order to terrify the English into making peace by a naval promenade in the Channel.

Vergennes bowed to the inevitable. On 8 March 1779 he wrote to his ambassador, 'We can provide plans which will be sufficiently to the taste of M. de Florida Blanca', and a small planning group, which included the French Minister of War, the Prince de Montbarey, and of Marine, Gabriel de Sartine, was set up. The target date for the operation was fixed at 15 May 1779, at latest, when 30 French ships of the line, plus frigates and corvettes, would join up, off Corunna, from which the Spanish Armada had set sail in 1588, with the 20 battleships promised by Spain. Two weeks of manoeuvres, in which the two

* Patterson, *The Other Armada*, p. 41. Much of the present chapter is based on this invaluable book, including many of the quotations.

navies practised working together, would follow and they would then set sail for Portsmouth, defeating the British fleet, correctly estimated at around 35 major warships, en route. The lighter ships would then be sent to escort the transports previously collected at Cherbourg and in the mouth of the River Orne. The 'army of England' would consist of 20,000 infantry, brought together from Picardy and Artois as well as from the main camps in Normandy and Brittany, and another 12,000 men would be assembled around Dunkirk to divert British attention from the real threat. The task force from Normandy was first to seize the Isle of Wight, then land at Gosport, from which Portsmouth and its dockyard would be bombarded and neutralised, while, as a further distraction, a minor attack would be made on Bristol, with others on Liverpool and Cork, to destroy supplies collected there for transport to America. A fall-back plan, if the opening attack failed to take the Isle of Wight, called for the combined fleet to anchor in Torbay, from which raids might be made on the Channel Islands and Plymouth.

The French and Spanish negotiators now spent some happy weeks agreeing how to divide up England's overseas possessions once she was defeated, the agreement between them being formally signed on 12 April 1779. The French used this period of waiting to obtain up-to-the-minute intelligence about Portsmouth. A French engineer officer, Major Berthois de la Rousselière, and a companion disguised themselves as British seamen and during April 'made several tours of the fortifications on the outside, and of a great part on the inside' of the town. They also studied Gosport, Spithead and the Portsea Lines, finally crossing to the Isle of Wight before, on 7 May, returning to Paris with a highly encouraging report. The fortifications of Portsmouth, they had discovered, were in excellent shape but inadequately manned, by a single militia battalion and some 'invalid' companies. The Portsea Lines also looked formidable, but were ungarrisoned. Gosport was found to be 'virtually without defence, protected on the landward side only by an ill-maintained entrenchment . . . which would fall at the first assault', while the Isle of Wight contained so few troops, so thinly scattered, that it was bound to succumb to a determined attack.

De La Rousselière, newly promoted lieut.-colonel, was set to drawing up a plan of attack. A force of 4000 men, landing on either side of the Cowes river and marching on Newport should, he estimated, be sufficient to secure the Isle of Wight in a single day. Another 6000 to 8000 troops should be sent simultaneously against Gosport, which should be secured with equal ease and from there 24 mortars would make the dockyard and lower town of Portsmouth untenable. To capture and occupy Portsmouth would, however, be a much more difficult matter, requiring not less than 30,000 men. After the capture of the Isle of Wight 20,000 would be collected there and 5-6000 of them would be ferried across the Solent in small boats and landed along the creek separating Hayling Island from Portsea to take the Portsea Lines in the rear, which would only be possible if the guns of Fort Cumberland, on the eastern tip of Portsea Island, were knocked out beforehand by a bombardment by French battleships and bomb-ketches. A simultaneous assault would be made by 4000 of the army which had taken Gosport, while the boats landing on Portsea Island would return to the Isle of Wight to bring the total force up to 20,000 men, and eventually, for the siege of Portsmouth, to 30,000, an operation de la Rousselière predicted would be completed in a week.

Early on the morning of Friday 4 June 1779 the bulk of the French fleet, having stood out from Brest on the previous day, set off for its rendezvous with the Spaniards. Conditions were perfect and not a British vessel was to be seen as the 28 line-of-battle ships, nine frigates, four fireships and eight lesser craft formed into three columns to sail south, while on shore a courier mounted his horse and set off for Spain. On Wednesday 16 June 1779 the Spanish ambassador in London delivered his country's declaration of war.*

Earlier that day, news that the French had left Brest having arrived, Vice-Admiral Sir Charles Hardy, in command of the Channel fleet, had sailed from Portsmouth with 30 ships of the line to prevent the junction of the French and Spanish fleets which, together, would vastly outnumber his own. Morale was high and, one observer reported, 'he never saw more universal good humour in a fleet', but materially the navy was in a poor state. The previous year the House of Commons had learned that one 74-gun warship still lay rotting and empty at Portsmouth though over the previous four years £37,000 had been voted for its repair. In March 1779 the major warships in home waters were 5600 short of their establishment of 24,800 and Hardy had only made up his numbers by transferring men from ships not yet ready for sea. The government's response to the outbreak of war with Spain was, in the early hours of 24 June, to bring forward a retrospective Bill to remove all exemptions from liability to impressment, when the Attorney-General admitted that six to eight ships of the line fit in other respects for sea lay idle at Portsmouth for lack of seamen.

With the issuing, on 9 July 1779, of a royal proclamation ordering the civilian authorities in the maritime counties to be ready to 'drive' the countryside, and move all horses, cattle and food inland if an enemy landed, the familiar routine of an invasion scare was once again launched. As usual, the nation, while most unwilling to be compelled, was very ready to make voluntary contributions to its defence. Many rich men offered to raise new regiments, but George III was unen-

---

* Patterson, p. 76. Hunt, p. 196 and Hozier, II, p. 202. However, Marcus, Vol. I, p. 426, dates the declaration as occurring on 19 June and Cook and Stevenson, p. 206, place it on the 21st.

thusiastic, since such donors commonly expected to command the new units themselves, or at least nominate their officers, and by offering higher bounties tended to attract potential rank-and-file recruits away from the established regiments. The government did, however, agree to the formation of a number of companies of Volunteers, serving part-time and at their own expense. The artisans and workmen of the Board of Works, the back-stage staff of Sheridan's and Harris's theatres, and the American loyalist refugees in London all set up their own units and, by the end of 1779, more than 150, each containing at least 50 men, had been set up in London and in such threatened areas as Dover, Sussex and Devon.

Great Britain had seldom been so isolated as it was that summer. 'We have,' wrote the First Lord of the Admiralty, John Montagu, Earl of Sandwich, whose name has been immortalised by the gaming-snack he invented, 'no one friend or ally to assist us . . . All those who ought to be our allies, except Portugal, act against us in supplying our enemies with the means of equipping their fleet.' The British ambassador at The Hague sent, on 13 July, an equally melancholy report. 'The idea . . . prevails at large through Europe that we are proud, full of our own importance and that it will not be amiss if we are brought a little more upon a level with our neighbours.' King George III, a vigorous 41-year-old, as yet untroubled by illness, declared his intention to put himself, sword in hand, at the head of his subjects if the French dared to land. This resolute lead was followed by the ordinary citizen. Horace Walpole observed in a letter from his home near Twickenham on 24 July, that 'every man [is] . . . confident of success and, when other arguments fail, cry [sic] "Providence has always saved us!"', which argument, I suppose, is built on this simple hypothesis, that God made Great Britain and the Devil all the rest of the world.'

With an army estimated at 40-50,000 strong massed on a 120-mile [190-km] front from St Malo to Le Havre a massive blow was clearly about to be delivered somewhere and by 23 May, even before Spain had declared war, the government had concluded it was destined 'for an insult on our coast or that of Ireland'. The latter, because of its residents' uncertain loyalty was almost a more alarming prospect than the former, but to ordinary Englishmen seemed an attractive alternative. 'I have,' noted Horace Walpole candidly, 'no ill will to poor Ireland, but . . . [it] is at least one door further off than one's own.' By early July, however, Lord North, on the basis of intelligence just arrived from Paris, had correctly appreciated that the main objectives would be Portsmouth and Plymouth, with a possible diversion towards Ireland.

Although no reason existed to expect a landing in East Anglia the customary precaution was taken of establishing one of the major defensive camps north of the Thames, at Warley, near Billericay in Essex, where 6300 men, drawn from four regular and ten militia regiments, were assembled. The other, and principal, concentration of troops was at Coxheath, near Maidstone in Kent, which soon contained five regiments of regulars and 15 of militia, a total of 10,000 soldiers. Advanced positions were also occupied at Pleydon Heights near Rye and behind Hastings. Chatham, Dover, Southampton and Bristol were each protected by one or two militia corps, with reserve forces at Salisbury and Winchester, mainly militia.

The most vulnerable spots in the defensive pattern were the two places in most danger. Portsmouth possessed a first-class governor, Lieut.-General Robert Monckton, who had been Wolfe's second-in-command at Quebec, and he was as conscious of the area's weakness as the French spies who had visited it that April. He recognised, just as they had done, that the Isle of Wight could easily be occupied as a base – Sandown Fort, he warned, urgently needed repair, Carisbrooke Castle reflected 'the ancient way of fortifying before the use of gunpowder' – and that Gosport might be stormed via Stokes Bay, to render the dockyard untenable, and the Portsea Lines might be taken from the rear. He also identified the defects in Fort Cumberland, Lumps Fort and Southsea Castle and warned, in a justly alarmist report to Lord Amherst on 20 July, that 'a very material defect in our situation' was a shortage of artillerymen. Monckton was not the man merely to complain. On 1 August 1779 every available soldier and labourer was hard at work on the most urgent tasks, clearing the ditches around the batteries, repairing drawbridges, strengthening the fortifications at Priddy's Hard, on the Gosport side of the harbour, to accommodate eight 18-pounder [8-kg] guns, and building fieldworks on Southsea Common to provide protection on Portsea Island itself. *Chevaux de frise*, barricades of metal spikes particularly effective against cavalry, were being manufactured for use wherever needed. As for the Isle of Wight, he thought its able-bodied male inhabitants, estimated at 3000 aged from 17 to 50, well able to protect themselves if armed with muskets and light cannon and assisted by army engineers 'to point out and improve the defensive advantages which nature has formed'.

Plymouth, as their secondary objective, had received less attention from the French than Portsmouth, but a study prepared for Vergennes in 1778 suggested that it might be vulnerable to the same type of attack. A direct attack up the Sound towards 'Fort Drake' [i.e. St Nicholas's, later Drake's, Island] and the inner mooring known as the Catwater [or Cattewater] at the mouth of the River Plym, was ruled out as too dangerous, but a fleet, it was suggested, could anchor at the entrance to the Sound, between Penlee Point, to the west of Cawsand Bay, and then disembark its troops either on the right flank, by way of the River Yealm [or Yalm] three miles [5 km] to the west, or on the left near Cawsand and Kingsand. Since the nearest bridge over the River Tamar, separating Devon from Cornwall, which entered the sea via the Sound, was 12 miles [19 km] inland, at Tavistock, the defenders could not reinforce one landing area from the other and would have to divide their forces. A landing party, disembarked at Cawsand, could seize the Maker Heights behind the village and site its guns there, or on Mount Edgcumbe, facing directly across the Sound at the magazines and shipyards on the far side. 'If bomb-batteries or guns firing red-hot shot were established there,' wrote the Count de la Luzerne enthusiastically, 'not a shot could miss'.

The defenders of Plymouth, as of Portsmouth, were well aware of the dangers to which it was exposed. A realistic report on its defences had been prepared back in 1777 by Lieut.-General George Parker, who had briefly commanded the garrison before returning in 1778 to take charge of the field army at Warley Camp. Before leaving Plymouth he had repeated his warning that the dockyard was in danger from an enemy established on Mount Edgcumbe, that the earthworks supposed to defend it from an infantry attack were 'ill-constructed' and 'capable of very little defence', and that the Citadel, at the western end of the Hoe, was 'a place of little strength', due to its openness to bombardment.

By the time Parker's much less able successor, Lieut.-General Sir David Lindsay, arrived in June 1779, much had been done to make good the worst weaknesses in the fortifications, but Lindsay's pleas for further assistance became so alarmist that eventually, on 4 July 1779, the Commander-in-Chief, Jeffery, Lord Amherst arrived in Plymouth to study the situation for himself. He shared Lindsay's concern about Cawsand and Mount Edgcumbe and two regular battalions were now encamped on Maker Heights and at Kingston, on Cawsand Bay, but the redeployment revealed the bad relations existing between the two services; the dockyard officers at first refused to provide boats for the purpose and the dockyard commissioner would not allow former naval gunners now working there to serve as artillerymen, or give other members of his workforce time off for military training. Both sides now invoked the aid of their superiors, and eventually the First Lord of the Admiralty wrote to Lord Amherst pointing out that the needs of the navy must come first and that once men left their ordinary duties, for whatever purpose, 'the whole business of refitting our ships must be stopped'. But in spite of the inter-service friction a good deal was done. Two naval storeships were converted into hulks to narrow the channel leading into the Hamoaze and, as at Portsmouth, a boom was laid across the main harbour entrance. By early July the total garrison of Plymouth was trebled, to 4800 men, including two regular battalions and eight regiments of militia, while 460 men of the Herefordshire militia were stationed at Falmouth.

The nation's mood was much more sombre than in the previous year. 'Even this little quiet village is grown a camp,' observed Horace

Walpole in peaceful Strawberry Hill in Middlesex in September. 'Servants are learning to fire all day long.' The government was inundated with requests for guns and troops, though artillerymen were more welcome than infantry who so often caused trouble that some places petitioned to have them removed or kept at a distance. The Durham militia were withdrawn from Scarborough after brawling with another unit and sent to Whitehaven, which was understandably nervous after being raided the previous year. Its neighbour, Workington, raised the money for a battery position from public subscriptions and borrowed some ships' six-pounders [2.7-kg guns], but also asked the government to supply ten 18-pounders [8-kg guns] of longer range. The principle that local defence should be financed by local efforts remained strong, though clearly hard on working-class towns, with no money to spare to buy cannon, like Sunderland. Here, guns and shot had been supplied in 1778 on the understanding that, as at Whitehaven, the town itself would build the gun platforms and pay for gunpowder, but when it failed to do so the artillery was taken away. The chief property owner in Swansea complained that 14 vessels from the port had been lost to 'piratical vessels' in a week 'almost at our doors' and that there was not a musket or bayonet, much less a cannon, in the town to repel a landing party, but his plea for government protection went unanswered.

After Admiral D'Orvilliers' departure from Brest on 4 June, and Admiral Hardy's from Portsmouth 12 days later, a lull occurred. The Spaniards had now become more enthusiastic about the whole enterprise. On 11 June their ambassador to France laid before Vergennes a paper urging that the invading army should be strengthened, especially in cavalry, and the next day it was agreed that Portsmouth, as well as the Isle of Wight, should be captured. If it appeared too strong, it was agreed on 21 June, Plymouth, followed by Falmouth, might be the target or – an old dream – the whole of Cornwall might be isolated and occupied. To the 16,500 men, plus siege guns and 60 field guns, assembled around Le Havre and on the other side of the Seine estuary, at Honfleur, were added another 15,400 troops with 4.6 guns at St Malo. The commander-in-chief, Noël Jourda, Count de Vaux, was renowned as the conqueror of the island of Corsica 20 years before, but at 74 was past his prime and suffering from a hernia, which prompted tasteless jokes about '*la descente de M.de Vaux*', '*descente*' meaning both 'hernia' and 'invasion'.

The preparations were on a vast scale. Normandy was alive with the sound of rattling artillery trains and wagon-loads of munitions; at Rouen alone two million cartridges were turned out in factories working round the clock. Five hundred ships were moored at Brest and St Malo and in the lower reaches of the adjoining rivers while the troops practised embarkation procedures. Elaborate instructions were drawn up for the occupation of England, once defeated, and orders were drafted to be issued on behalf of the French by mayors and magistrates, who it was assumed would readily cooperate. 'The Englishman is puffed up when he is prosperous, but easily depressed by adversity,' explained the Duke d'Harcourt, commanding the Normandy Division, to his officers. 'His character and the fact that he is accustomed to liberty predispose him against forced requisitions, but he will obey very passively the orders of his justices of the peace, mayors and tax-collectors. It is through them that we must prevail on the people to furnish horses, conveyances and so forth.'

At the end of June the British government stopped the sailing of the regular packet-boats between Dover and Calais to prevent news of its preparations from reaching the enemy, but reports of them lost nothing in the telling. 'Their efforts are incredible . . . ,' wrote the Comte de Vergennes on 2 July to the French ambassador in Madrid. 'We cannot refuse to admire the energy displayed by this nation in perhaps the most critical situation in which it has been placed for a long time.' By 23 July 1779, when the two fleets had at last come together off Corunna, Vergennes, in distant Versailles, was feeling ever more despondent:

> I do not know what the weather is like at sea, but it is terrible here – gale after gale with violent rainstorms . . . Even if the fleets have joined, I doubt if they would dare to operate in the Channel. Yet if we cannot establish ourselves in England before the end of August there will be no time left for an operation of any importance . . . Blackness overwhelms me . . . What a wonderful opportunity is slipping from our grasp . . . England, without resources or allies, was on the point of being taught a lesson . . . but the elements are arming themselves against us and staying the stroke of our vengeance.

The British traitor, Captain Hamilton, who knew the Channel better than his masters, urged D'Orvilliers to get his ships further north while he could, and by 2 August the French admiral was 51 leagues [176 land miles; 282 km] south-west of Ushant, talking confidently of reaching the Isle of Wight within a week. The poor performance of the Spanish sailors, however, upset this optimistic timetable, the winds changed again, and by 6 August he was back almost where he had started, 10 leagues [35 land miles, 56 km] west-south-west of Ushant. He still commanded, however, a formidable armada of 66 ships of the line, organised in joint Franco–Spanish squadrons, of which 16 ships, all of them Spanish, under the elderly Don Luis de Cordova, formed the reserve. At last the wind changed. On 15 August 1779 the combined fleet came in sight of the Lizard; on Monday 16 August 1779 the largest hostile force to penetrate English waters for nearly 200 years was approaching Plymouth, running before the wind on a calm sea.

When Admiral Sir Charles Hardy had sailed from Portsmouth on 16 June D'Orvilliers was already at sea and he failed to prevent the junction of the French with the Spaniards. Hardy's fleet, 30 ships of the line, eight frigates and 20 or so smaller ships, with its 3260 guns and 26,544 men, was actually stronger than D'Orvilliers', with his 28 major warships, nine frigates, 12 smaller vessels, and a fire-power of 3014 guns, supported by 17,891 men. The Admiralty, however, wanted a greater margin of safety, and Hardy himself soon proved reluctant to come to grips with his adversary. He had barely reached his patrolling station, off Ushant, on 22 June when, misled by a deliberately false report from an American schooner captain, he decided to withdraw to the Lizard, reaching it on 2 July, and a strong westerly wind then forced him to Torbay. Under pressure from the king Lord Sandwich urged the admiral to get to sea again, but only on 14 July, while D'Orvilliers was still dithering off Ushant, did he manage to do so. The wind which at last enabled D'Orvilliers to get away from Ushant now forced Hardy back up the Channel, and, having learned that the Spanish fleet had left harbour, he put into Plymouth, from whence he wrote to the Admiralty suggesting he base himself there, or at Portsmouth, to cover them against an enemy attack.

Hardy's reappearance on their doorstep caused dismay to the Admiralty and on George III's instructions he was sent new and unequivocal orders:

> You are . . . to proceed as far to the westward as you may judge necessary, and to use all possible means, with the force under your command, to prevent the enemy from carrying their designs into execution; and not to leave your station while your provisions and water will allow you to keep the sea, unless driven off by stress of weather.

On 15 August 1779, 14 leagues[48 miles, 77 km] south-east of Scilly, HMS *Marlborough* and three other ships on their way to reinforce Hardy narrowly escaped capture when they stumbled on the enemy fleet, spread out 'like a wood on the water'. The sloop *Cormorant* was sent back to Plymouth with the first lieutenant of the *Marlborough* on board and around 4 am on Monday 16 August 1779 he set out for London on the first of a series of hired horses earmarked for just such an emergency. Soon after midnight he was pounding on the door of Lord Sandwich in Blackheath. The First Lord immediately sent a messenger to carry the news to the Admiralty, from which it was passed on to the prime minister and Lord Amherst, though, a hostile commentator noted, most ministers, this being August, 'had fled to their country seats and delivered over the management [of their departments] to clerks in office'.

During Monday 16 August, as the news of the enemy's approach spread, the West Country prepared for an immediate battle. By 11 am 2000 Cornish tin-miners had already poured into Falmouth to reinforce the tiny garrison; at 1 pm the troops occupied their pre-selected battle positions at Cawsand and below Maker Heights, while arms were served out to the dockyard workers, 300 of whom, plus 200 seamen, were sent to man the guns. Militia units from as far away as Hampshire manned the fortifications, while two ships were sent to warn Hardy that the enemy was now behind him. It was a glorious, sunny day, which saw the combined fleet, which had made its landfall off the Lizard the previous day, within sight of Plymouth. D'Orvilliers and Cordova had got into the Channel unchallenged, and the following day, 17 August 1779, they achieved their first victory when the 64-gun line-of-battle ship *Ardent* mistook the enemy fleet for Hardy's and was captured. The noise of the battle, and the surrender of a barely damaged British warship, caused a panic on shore. Shops were shut up while their owners 'made every possible exertion to move off with their families to Truro, Tiverton' and other safer towns. The arrival of a letter from Plymouth, in which the writer claimed to have seen from his window enemy troops already on shore, caused a similar panic in Portsmouth. 'It is supposed that by this time [Plymouth],' reported the *Hampshire Chronicle* on 23 August 1779, 'is reduced to ashes.' D'Orvilliers, however, failed to attack. Instead the combined fleet remained six leagues [21 miles; 34 km] offshore and on 17 August the wind, so often Great Britain's ally, backed to the east and rose to half a gale, forcing D'Orvilliers to weigh anchor and driving both him and Hardy out into the Atlantic. By 31 August the British ships were back almost where they had started, 30 leagues [100 miles; 160 km] from the Isles of Scilly. Next day Hardy anchored off Plymouth. His tactics were still to try to lure the enemy further from their bases. 'I shall do my utmost,' he reported to London, 'to draw them up-Channel.'

The combined fleet was also badly led. On Monday 16 August 1779, with the enemy coast in sight and the Royal Navy nowhere to be seen, D'Orvilliers had sent a despondent despatch home complaining that sickness had weakened his fleet and that the weather might make it hard to reach the Isle of Wight. Later that day new orders arrived from Versailles. The original plan, to seize Portsmouth, was abandoned and D'Orvilliers was ordered instead, once he had beaten the enemy fleet, to send the troops under General De Vaux to capture Falmouth, as a preliminary to occupying the whole of Cornwall. His ships, D'Orvilliers was promised, would be revictualled at sea, enabling them to remain on station throughout September and October.

D'Orvilliers' response, characteristically, was to suggest postponing further action to the following year, but in any case when, on 31 August, he did at last sight Hardy's fleet he was unable to overtake it, being handicapped by the Spanish ships, 'which,' as one French officer complained, 'could overtake nothing and run away from nothing'. The truth was that D'Orvilliers had lost his nerve, demoralised by the death on board of his only son, one of the victims of the fearsome combination of smallpox, scurvy and typhus which now ravaged his ships.

Fortunately for the Combined Fleet, Admiral Hardy was made of similar stuff to the unhappy D'Orvilliers. On 17 August he had, while stationed off Plymouth, learned that the enemy had got past him in the Channel and soon afterwards he received a despatch from the Admiralty urging him to attack if they tried to withdraw. The two fleets now blundered about in unseasonable fog, neither knowing the location of the other, until on 29 August the British sighted the French and Spanish in a sudden clear interval and a cheer ran round the fleet as Hardy issued orders for line of battle ahead. The fog then descended again and it was not until 31 August that the two fleets again made visual contact, about nine leagues [31 miles; 50 km] south-west of Land's End. Hardy, however, refused to attack, deciding instead to draw the enemy further up the Channel. By 11 am next morning he was off Plymouth, from which he informed the Admiralty that he planned to withdraw to St Helen's Roads off the Isle of Wight to obtain fresh water and land 'a great number' of sick sailors; by 3 September he was at Spithead.

This fresh retreat, whatever the reasons – and the total of 824 men sent to hospitals on shore was considered exceptionally small for the time – caused dismay to ministers and disgust to the public. His immediate subordinates were horrified. One of them wrote to the First Lord of the Admiralty, urging him to intervene:

> We are to my astonishment arrived at Spithead . . . Should the French push up to St Helen's we shall be blocked up, or go out at the greatest disadvantage . . . The spirit of our people, the honour of our fleet, and perhaps the safety of our country depend on our not remaining here more than is inevitably necessary. I wish to God you would come down.

Even Lord North was critical of Hardy's actions though George III eagerly welcomed Lord Sandwich's offer to visit Portsmouth to spur Hardy into action. The politicians were well aware of the public disquiet; the *Hampshire Chronicle* had already, on 9 August, dubbed Hardy 'Tardy' and reported that he was acquiring a new coat of arms displaying 'an anchor and hope'. In spite of Sandwich's exhortations the laggard admiral continued to linger in port, while the enemy fleet remained unseen somewhere between the Scilly Isles and Land's End.

The French government was meanwhile experiencing just the same difficulties with D'Orvilliers and the long list of objections with which he responded to every suggestion finally convinced the authorities at

Versailles that all they could hope for was to retrieve their fleet while it was still intact. The Spaniards, their original reluctance to serve under a French admiral now amply justified, were ready to go home and on 3 September 1779 Louis XVI's Minister of Marine accepted the inevitable and ordered D'Orvilliers to return. By 10 September the first arrivals were entering Brest, though the last of the 100 ships, including supporting craft, did not drop anchor for another five days.

Like the French attempt on Portsmouth of 1545* the invasion of 1779 had been defeated more by disease than by English seamanship. D'Orvilliers' flagship alone had lost 61 dead and 560 others ill out of a complement of 1100. All told the French ships, excluding the Spanish, disembarked more than 8000 sick men, while so many others had died and been buried at sea that for the next month the people of Cornwall and Devon refused, it was said, to eat fish.

D'Orvilliers was allowed to resign his command and to retire into private life; he died, in bed, aged 82. Some stories say he entered a monastery and his strong religious faith provoked mocking songs in the Paris streets:

> You always listen to mass,
> But never to reason.
> You are seen going to confession,
> When you should be firing cannon . . .
> Today we name you
> Vice-Admiral of the Capucins.

The fleet D'Orvilliers had commanded was barely home, safely if ignominiously, when planning for a new invasion began, and at a council of war held on 3 October 1779 General De Vaux added a whole new list of possible landing areas – Weymouth, Portland, Torbay, Dartmouth, Start Point, Fowey and the Lizard – to such old favourites as Plymouth, Falmouth and Helford River. The soldiers were ready to try to get ashore almost anywhere, but the naval commanders demurred, and although De Vaux was ready to risk a November invasion, the French government, on 17 October, ordered him to disperse his troops. On 9 November the Spanish admiral Cordova sailed thankfully for home, leaving a subordinate in command of the 20 Spanish sail of the line still at Brest.

The realisation that the present danger had been lifted dawned only slowly on the British government and when Parliament met on 25 November 1779 ministers found themselves vigorously criticised for the pusillanimous performance of its chosen admiral. As one opposition peer observed: 'Did not a British fleet, in sight of their own coast, fly before an insulting and triumphing enemy, and were there not circumstances of humiliation and disgrace attending that flight?

* See *Defending the Island*, p. 396.

. . . a spectacle never before recorded to have happened in the English annals.' The army Commander-in-Chief, Lord Amherst, was also criticised over the 'weak and defenceless' state of Plymouth. Amherst was able to announce the resignation of the governor, Sir David Lindsay, who proved a useful scapegoat; a subsequent attempt to secure a parliamentary committee of enquiry was defeated.

In France the 1779 *tentative* also left a legacy of dissatisfaction. Even the royal family were blamed for the fiasco and the cost of the abortive expedition, and the poor showing of the French navy and its aristocratic officers added to the mounting discontent with Louis XVI's regime. Nevertheless on 9 December 1779 De Vaux's former Chief of Staff submitted the first of five memoranda proposing a new invasion attempt during 1780. This time he favoured occupying some unspecified point somewhere between the Isle of Wight and Cornwall as a base for 25,000 troops, who would then attack London, Portsmouth or Plymouth. The renegade Captain Hamilton also produced his latest scheme, involving Dartmouth, Plymouth and – a new candidate – Exeter, but nothing came of any of these proposals, though in December 1780 the Dutch entered the war against England, extending the hostile coast now facing the British Isles. In January 1781 the French did invade Jersey, perhaps as a first step towards south-west England, but though St Helier was captured a small force of regular troops and militia saved the Channel Islands, and 800 French invaders were killed or taken prisoner.

In July 1781 the Combined Fleet of France and Spain, 49 strong, again entered the Channel. The English Channel Fleet, of 30 ships of the line, retreated to Torbay but, in spite of their overwhelming superiority in numbers, the Spaniards opposed the French commander's desire to attack. In September the enemy withdrew and the plan for a new invasion attempt was abandoned.

Across the Atlantic it was different. With the surrender of the main British army at Yorktown on 19 October 1781, the American War of Independence was really over. On 27 September 1782 George III's government accepted the inevitable and recognised the United States, though a general peace was not established until the Treaty of Versailles on 3 September 1783. Under its terms Britain retained Gibraltar, now recognised, just as the Earl of Chatham's classic statement of strategy had suggested back in 1770, as an outer bastion of the island's own defences.

17

RIPE FOR INSURRECTION

It is a question, Citizen General, of rendering to a country generous and ripe for insurrection, the independence and liberty which it calls for.

Orders from the Directory in Paris to General Hoche, 19 June 1796

News of the outbreak of the French Revolution during the summer of 1789 was received with widespread satisfaction in England. Radicals hoped that the libertarian ideas now current in Paris might spread to London, Tory patriots anticipated that the French would now be too busy at home to menace their neighbours. Both expectations were rapidly confounded. In April 1792 the French government declared war on Austria, and, in effect, on her ally, Prussia. In September 1792 the first great massacre of the inmates of the Paris prisons disgusted people in England and on 22 September France was officially declared a republic, soon afterwards pledging support to any people attempting to throw off its government. On 27 November 1792 the French sent their warships to Antwerp, having a few days earlier proclaimed that the Scheldt was open to the ships of all nations, a clear infringement of the sovereignty of Holland. The English government still hoped to remain neutral and acknowledged the French people's right to choose their own form of government, provided France conducted its affairs 'without insulting other governments, without disturbing their tranquillity, without violating their rights', which seemed increasingly unlikely. In January 1793 the execution of King Louis XVI caused a shock of horror to spread through Europe. Outside its borders, the new republic, it became clear, was but old monarchy writ large; French troops, wherever they appeared, came not as liberators but as conquerors. When George III drove through the streets he was greeted with cries of 'War with France!' On 1 February 1793 France declared war on both England and Holland, and the struggle which during the next 20 years was to dominate Europe and spread over much of the globe had begun.

The French Revolutionary War was even more dangerous to Great Britain than those which had preceded it. The French armies were larger than anything so far seen, for in August 1793 a levy was laid upon the whole male population considered capable of bearing arms. Even more novel, they were not animated by mere patriotism. England, as its prime minister said, was opposing 'armed opinions'.

The war was also unique in other ways. For much of it, King George III was incapacitated by madness, now thought to be due to the physical disease of porphyria, while the nation possessed an outstanding prime minister, William Pitt the Younger, son of another great war minister, Lord Chatham. Pitt's appointment as the king's first minister in December 1783, when he was only 24, was greeted with derisive laughter by the House of Commons but he confounded the critics and effectively directed the nation's affairs until March 1801, and was to return to office later.

Even before France declared war, plans were being discussed for an invasion of the British Isles, many of them drawn up on private initiative. One amateur strategist proposed that 30,000 men should be landed on the banks of the Thames near London, to carry off the royal family and the members of both Houses of Parliament and thus end the war by a knock-out blow. More serious was the scheme prepared by Lazare Hoche, one of the talented men of humble birth to whom the Revolution had given his great chance. The son of a royal groom, he was still a sergeant in 1789 but by 1793 had risen to the rank of general, besieged in Dunkirk but conscious that the British coast was only 40 miles [64 km] away. From here, on 1 October, he despatched to the Committee of Public Safety in Paris a letter which clearly revealed his loathing for England, and dedication to the revolutionary cause:

> Since the beginning of the campaign [in the Low Countries] I have always believed that the English must be fought in their own country. Fifty seasoned battalions, together with fifty newly-raised battalions, twelve to fifteen squadrons of cavalry, three companies of light artillery, and forty siege pieces would suffice. Dash and love of liberty is all that is necessary to overthrow Pitt . . . But, one asks, where are the means of transport? Oh, pusillanimous people, for how long shall we doubt our forces? Let us cover the sea with merchant shipping; let them be equipped for war; let them form a bridge from the coast of France to proud Albion . . . I do not ask for position or rank. I wish to be the first to set foot on the land of these political brigands.

For a time French thinking turned to establishing *Chouannerie* in England, a guerrilla movement made up of small but dedicated armed groups, like the pro-royalist *Chouans* of Brittany, and to deliver a reprisal in kind for the British government's support of similar troublemakers, largely returned émigrés, on French soil. Such plans, however, all rested on two assumptions, that the ordinary people of Britain were waiting eagerly to welcome their liberators and that the Royal

Navy could somehow be evaded or defeated. In fact, although there *was* much discontent in the country, an invasion would have seen all but a tiny minority rallying behind the government and the French became steadily more unpopular with all classes, especially following the Terror, which really began in October 1793, when Marie Antoinette was beheaded, and the official abolition of religious worship in November 1793. As for the navy, the French were painfully reminded that it could not be ignored on 'The Glorious First of June', a major battle fought over five days around that date in 1794, during which eight French ships of the line were sunk or captured in a fleet of 26, while escorting a grain convoy from America into Brest.

The government was already also trying to strengthen England's fixed defences. In 1794 radical alterations to Dover Castle had been put in hand, under the direction of an exceptionally able military engineer, Lieut.-Colonel William Twiss, of whom more will be heard later. Among his later assistants was a young RE lieutenant, John Fox Burgoyne, a future field marshal and Inspector General of Fortifications. The changes represented the most substantial modifications to this key site, the heart of the coastal defence system, since the introduction of gunpowder. The basic principles were the use of earth, rather than masonry, to absorb cannon fire, the provision of firing galleries to protect the ditches, and the building of detached enclosures, often polygonal with projecting bastions, to keep enemy cannon at a distance. Some of the most spectacular work, its remains still visible today, was on the cliff face, where casemates were created by digging tunnels in the easily workable chalk. Dover Castle, when all these improvements had been completed, was intended to bristle with 231 guns, including 13-in [33-cm] mortars, and 68-pounder [31-kg] cannonades.

Such activity cannot have escaped the French government's notice and may have encouraged it to look instead towards a 'softer' target, Ireland. At the same time Irishmen on both sides of the religious divide, but overwhelmingly on the Roman Catholic one, began to see in France their best hope of independence. While in England a French landing was likely to rally all but a tiny handful of citizens behind the government, in Ireland the reverse seemed far more probable. As the regular troops were withdrawn the defence of Ireland was increasingly entrusted to volunteer corps of yeomanry and infantry which might change sides if the enemy landed. One estimate reaching Paris was that 17,000 of the 20,000 members in one nationalistic, and partly Protestant, organisation, the United Irishmen, would fight against, not for, the English authorities, and they were known to be collecting firearms, manufacturing pike-heads and taking delivery of supplies from France.

After so many earlier failures the French might still have hesitated but for the activities of two colourful and persuasive Irishmen. One was a renegade aristocrat, Lord Edward Fitzgerald, born in London in 1763 as the fifth son of a duke, who married a Frenchwoman. In 1792 he arrived in Paris, moving on in 1796 to Hamburg, another centre of Irish intrigue. Here he enlisted the support of the resident French minister, predicting that 150,000 men would rise to support the French once they landed in Ireland, including – a most important consideration – the Irish priests.

Also active in trying to secure French intervention in Ireland was the Dublin-born son of a coachbuilder, Theobald Wolfe Tone, who, having found the Bar not to his liking, had become an active politician and pamphleteer. 'To break the connection with England, the never-failing source of all our political evils,' he wrote in his autobiography, 'and to assert the independence of my country – those were my objects.'

After a visit to America, Tone, now aged 32, landed in February 1796 in Le Havre and rapidly made his way to Paris. Here he assured the authorities that a proclamation by an Irish National Convention, formed on the French model, calling on all Irishmen serving under the British flag to seize their ships and sail them to Irish ports, would cripple British sea power, claming, though the figure was almost certainly false, that two-thirds of all the navy's seamen were Irish.

Tone's plan for the invasion involved 15,000 French troops being landed near Dublin, with another 5000 in the north, plus 100,000 stand of arms and money sufficient to pay 40,000 men for three months. The summer passed, however, while, as one observer commented, Tone was 'sent spinning like a shuttlecock from one government department to another'.

In December 1795 General Hoche, newly appointed Commander-in-Chief of the *Armée des Côtes de l'Océan*, formed from three previous armies, was assigned the task of launching the long-planned *Chouannerie* in England, the actual direction of the operation being entrusted to General Jean Joseph Humbert, who had served with success against the *Chouans* in the Vendée. Humbert was to command 1600 regulars who were to be landed in Cornwall, where, it was hoped the tin-miners might rise in revolt, and to protect his flank he was to destroy the bridges across the Tamar. A force of equal size, but made up of ex-convicts and deserters, kept in order by an ex-criminal called Mascheret, was to be landed simultaneously in Wales. The shipping for both expeditions was assembled at St Malo and departure was scheduled for 29 June 1796. Hoche was to have a fast corvette as his command vessel, and six transports, plus a vessel *armée en flûte*, i.e. a frigate adapted to carry troops and equipment, the whole force being escorted by two brigs and a cutter. At the very last minute, however, a courier arrived with new orders, dated 19 June 1796, which substituted a totally new plan, the fruits of the lobbying in which Fitzgerald, Wolfe Tone and other Irishmen had been engaging in Paris:

It is a question, Citizen General, of rendering to a country generous and ripe for insurrection the independence and liberty which it calls for. Ireland has trembled for several centuries under the odious stranglehold of England. The numerous Defenders which she contains are already secretly armed to free themselves from it . . . To detach Ireland from England is to reduce the latter to be nothing more than a second-rate power; it is to take away from her the greater part of her preponderance at sea.

The expedition to Ireland was even, it now appeared, to take precedence over that other recurring French dream, an attack on India:

The flotilla designed for India will bring . . . 5000 men at least of good troops, whom it will disembark on the Irish coast, in the province of Connaught, and, if it is possible, to Galway Bay. These 5000 men shall be taken from the Armée des Côtes de l'Océan and you will give them the artillery necessary to maintain themselves in Ireland until the arrival of new reinforcements. They should be able to take the whole of Connaught, with the exception of the county of Leitrim. They will occupy also the county of Clare up to the mouth of the River Shannon. They will carry at least 10,000 arms with them.

This large-scale landing, however, was to be only the first of a series:

A second expedition will be prepared at Brest by you, and the Minister of Marine . . . It should be ready before September 1st next. The flotilla allotted to it will take at least 6000 men, drawn also from the Armée des Côtes d l'Océan . . . One part of the troops should be destined to form a cavalry troop who will provide themselves with horses at the moment of their arrival in Ireland . . .

The third expedition will leave from Holland at the same time as the second . . . It will be of 5000 men, the greater part foreign deserters, commanded by French officers . . . This third expedition is also for Galway Bay . . .

The attempts at *Chouannerie* in Wales and Cornwall ought to be considered as useful diversions, capable of contributing strongly to the success of the great Irish expedition.

Preparing such plans, as generations of would-be invaders could have warned all concerned, was a good deal easier than implementing them. France was suffering a severe economic crisis, with the government being forced to issue paper *assignats* and *mandats*, though everyone preferred the gold coins of the old regime. To obtain such essentials as rye and rice officials had to resort to barter, and the workmen in the dockyards, paid in useless paper which the shopkeepers would not accept, frequently went on strike. Never had a proposed invasion been prepared under greater difficulties but, during the summer, the Minister of Marine, Admiral Laurent Truguet, an able officer and future Mar-shal of France, became enthusiastic for a small-boat offensive designed to put landing parties ashore all round the coast of England. The boats, flat-bottomed or with a very shallow draught, made to designs brought from Sweden, would have been able to land wherever there was a sloping beach with a reasonable depth of water. The largest gun-boat, known as a *chaloupe cannonière*, carrying 100 soldiers and armed with four guns, drew no more than seven to eight feet [2.1-2.4 m] of water. A smaller version possessed two guns and space for two horses, while another type, a pinnace, could transport a howitzer and 60 soldiers, who would propel it.

On 17 September 1796 Admiral Truguet issued from the Ministry of Marine instructions for a landing by the new small-boat flotilla to 'Citizen Muskeyn, Capitaine de frégate'. Muskeyn was the energetic officer who had been directing the manufacture of the new craft all along the French coast, from Dunkirk to as far west as Granville, about 60 miles [96 km] south of Cherbourg, on the Gulf of St Malo:

The Executive Directory, wishing to put an end to the audacity and perfidy of the cruellest enemies of the Republic, has decided that the ravages of war shall be carried on to their territory . . . To achieve this end, the Minister of Marine has assembled at Dunkirk a flotilla of gunboats intended to convoy a number of ships sufficient to transport 5000 infantrymen under the orders of General Quantin . . .

As soon as the citizen Muskeyn is assured that the troops to be embarked have arrived at Dunkirk . . . he will cooperate with . . . the citizen Quantin to get them on board. He will do his utmost to hasten this embarkation in order to frustrate the vigilance of the enemy; and, to deceive them as to the true objective, he will give out that he has orders to attack the Îles Marcouf or those of Jersey and Guernsey . . . He will proceed along and hug the coast of France and Holland as far as possible, up to the point where he will judge it best to cross the Channel. But he will steer such a course that he will make a landfall on the east coast of England, above Yarmouth, to avoid the warships which may be based on that port. Having arrived abreast [of] Yarmouth, he will still proceed northwards as far as the mouth of the River Tyne. There, profiting by the surprise and terror which the sudden appearance of the republican forces must inspire, he will, in conjunction with General Quantin, disembark the troops . . . If necessary he will go up the river with his craft to ensure the progress of the troops to Newcastle . . . If circumstances do not allow the citizen Muskeyn to lead his ships as far as the Tyne, he could disembark either in the harbour of Boston, or in the River Humber, but this action . . . should not be taken unless it is im-possible to act otherwise.

The principal difficulty in mounting this invasion of the north-east proved to be assembling the men. The Minister of War, Petiet, seems to have seen it as a golden opportunity to get rid of the riff-raff of his armies; one unit alone, the *Légion Franche* (not to be confused with the perfectly respectable *Légion des Francs*), consisted of men drawn from a dozen different nations, including the English, united by being criminals, deserters or, at best, reluctant warriors. Although nominally all volunteers, half the first contingent refused to embark and those who agreed to go were poorly equipped, sometimes in rags, while even the officers were unenthusiastic. However by mid-October the embarkation was in progress, with one battalion boarding 12 gunboats at Dunkirk, another 12 at Boulogne, the rest of the men, and the *Légion Franche*, being distributed between eight conventional transports.

In August Spain had changed sides and on 5 October 1796 declared war on her former ally, Great Britain. Pitt, however, speaking on 18 October, exuded confidence. 'Our navy,' he reminded the House of Commons, 'is the national defence of this kingdom in case of invasion. In this department, however, little remains to be done, our fleet at this moment being more formidable than at any former period of our history.' He proposed to keep the navy up to strength by 'a levy of 15,000 men from the different parishes for the sea service', in effect conscription, with each parish submitting its quota of unemployed or ne'er-do-wells. The militia was to be expanded by 'raising a supplementary body . . . to be grafted on the present establishment', providing up to 60,000 additional men 'not to be immediately called out, but to be enrolled, officered and gradually trained so as to be fit for service at a time of danger.' The recently imposed tax on 'horses kept for pleasure in England and Wales', Pitt told the House, had revealed a total of 200,000. 'It certainly would not be a very severe regulation . . . ,' he suggested, 'to require one-tenth of those horses for the public service,' a force which 'an invading enemy . . . can have no means to meet . . . upon equal terms'. The tax returns had also disclosed that 'The licences to shoot game taken out by gamekeepers are no fewer than 7000'. Here was another valuable ready-armed reserve: 'Men who, from their dexterity in using fire-arms, might be highly useful in harassing the operations of the enemy'.

If news of this new, velveteen-clad army reached the would-be invaders now massed on the Channel coast it did not deter them. On 9 November 1796, under pressure from Admiral Truguet, Citizen Muskeyn at last set out from Dunkirk to rendezvous with an escorting force waiting at Flushing, but after only two days, and a voyage of only a few miles along the coast, it was back again, Muskeyn himself being lucky to regain dry land, soaked to the skin; some of his men were drowned. The *Légion Franche*, disliking their first experience of the Channel, forced the captain of their transport to return to harbour, and by the 18th the whole force was scattered at five ports from Ostend to Boulogne, its members damp and disillusioned. On 22 November the Directory, the five-man committee which formed the French government, abandoned the project.

The main expedition to Ireland, and the diversionary attack on Wales, remained to be launched, and General Hoche was keener than ever, his reputation now being overshadowed by the brilliant successes of a new general, Napoleon Bonaparte, commander of the army of Italy. As the preparations in Brest intensified the British redoubled their vigilance. In mid-November the rear part of the Channel fleet, 15 sail of the line, was stationed at Spithead, while a squadron of equal size maintained the forward patrol west of Ushant, 210 miles [336 km] away. The waters around Brest were unsuitable for an all-weather patrol by capital ships, but an inshore watch was kept by a force of frigates under Captain [later Admiral] Sir Edward Pellew [later Lord Exmouth]. Nearly 300 miles [480 km] away, in Cork harbour, lay Ireland's last naval line of defence, one 64-gun ship of the line and six frigates.

All really depended on Pellew and on 11 December he sent an urgent despatch to Falmouth via HMS *Amazon*, as well as to Vice-Admiral Sir John Colboys, in command of the main blockading fleet about 40 miles [64 km] west-south-west of Ushant:

> There is now in Brest 21 sail of the line appearing ready for sea, 2 of them three-deckers, and 2 other three-deckers with yards and top-masts down . . . We were so near in as to be fired at from both sides of the Goulette [the main approach channel] and could most distinctly see everything in the port. The ships appear all clean painted as if newly fitted.

Pellew's sharp eye had not detected 'any transports or troops more than common' but, as he complained a few days later, he was 'chased off every day by a squadron of six ships which made it very difficult to reconnoitre the port' and on Thursday 15 December 1796, the day his original message reached England, the French fleet at last weighed anchor and began to assemble outside Brest.

After all the months of planning, the Directory finally decided, on 17 December, it needed General Hoche nearer home, and Admiral Laurent Truguet, the Minister of Marine, set off in person to announce that the expedition had been cancelled. Unknown to him, it had already sailed, and by the time he reached Brest, after a wheel had come off his coach, it was too late to send a fast despatch boat to recall it.

The force which had sailed from Brest on 15 December 1796 under the command of Admiral Morard de Galles, flying his flag in the frigate *Fraternité*, which also carried General Hoche, was a powerful one. It consisted of 45 vessels, of which eight, including an ammunition ship, were transports, 18 were sail of the line, 23 were frigates or corvettes and the rest smaller craft such as brigs and luggers. Five hundred to six hundred men were carried in each of the larger warships and about half that number in the smaller. Hoche put the total at 14,750, Wolfe Tone, who sailed with the expedition as 'Adjutant-General Smith', at 15,100. The moment of departure, after they had been seen off by a French general, was, for him at least, a happy one:

> The cabin was ceiled [i.e. piled high] with the firelocks intended for the expedition, the candle sticks were bayonets, stuck in the table, the officers were in their jackets and *bonnets de police*, some playing cards, others singing to the music; others conversing, and all in the highest spirits . . . At length [General] Warrin and his band went off, and, as it was a beautiful moonlight night, the effect of the music on the water, diminishing as they receded from our vessel, was delicious.*

The French government had originally intended that the expedition should make for Galway Bay, halfway up the west coast of Ireland, but late in September the French Minister of War had been warned, via a spy in England, that 'they have got wind of our project' and Bantry Bay, 270 miles [432 km] from Brest in a direct line, some 36 hours sailing with a favourable wind, was selected instead. This time secrecy was maintained so effectively that even Wolfe Tone did not know their precise destination and most of the ships' captains only learned it when they opened their sealed orders off the Irish coast. The chosen anchorage had been selected on the recommendation of a Dublin solicitor's clerk, E.J. Lewins, who in November had written to the Directory reporting 'the coastline . . . devoid of troops', except for 'Kinsale, at the entrance to the harbour of Cork':

> Slightly further to the south is situated Bantry Bay. I do not know a place in the whole island which is more favourable for making a landing; there one finds not a gun, not a fort, no military force . . . It is but two days from there to the city of Cork . . . Masters of this town, you will have the whole southern part of the island at your feet.

What finally seems to have tipped the scale in favour of Bantry Bay was its attraction as a harbour, for it was a seaman's dream, offering an 18-mile [29-km] long and three- to four-mile [4.8-6.4-km] wide stretch of water, sheltered from winds from any direction and with water 14 to 35 fathoms [84-210 feet; 26-64 m] deep. With the right, westerly, wind the fleet could sail up to the head of the bay and disembark close to

---

* I am indebted for this quotation, and several others in this chapter, as well as for much of the factual information it contains, to E.H. Stuart Jones, *An Invasion That Failed*. See Note on Sources.

the road to Cork, which, apart from the advantages Lewins had listed, was also the major victualling base for the Royal Navy, both in Irish waters and the colonies.

That same wind which had enabled the French fleet to get out of Brest now meant that it could only enter Bantry Bay by a painfully slow process of short tacks, which left Wolfe Tone devoured by frustration, as he made clear in his journal on Wednesday 21 December 1796:

> There cannot be imagined a situation more provokingly tantalizing than mine at this time, within view, almost within reach of my native land, and uncertain whether I shall ever set foot on it. We . . . stood in for the coast till 12, when we were near enough to toss a biscuit ashore; at 12 tacked and stood out again . . . In all my life, rage never entered so deeply into my heart as when we turned our backs on the coast.

Wolfe Tone would have felt even more unhappy had he known that there were at this time a mere 2000 men between Bantry and Cork, with only two pieces of artillery. General Sir Hew Dalrymple, Commander-in-Chief in southern Ireland, believed that the best he could achieve in the event of a major landing was a holding action. 'Our numbers,' he wrote soon afterwards to the Secretary of State responsible for Irish affairs, 'will probably fall so far short of those of the enemy, that a diversion is all to be expected.' A formal appreciation later put the minimum number of troops needed to protect Cork from an attack from the Bantry direction at 15,000.

The first news of the presence of the French reached Richard White, the chief landowner in the Bantry area, on 21 December, after three local sailors, mistaking the incoming ships for British vessels, had been taken prisoner and released, to bear ashore the misleading information that the invading force numbered 80,000. The following day the customs officer at the nearest small port, Berehaven [or Bearhaven], dashed off to Richard White an admirably concise, if somewhat hysterical, confirmatory report:

> The French fleet consisting of some 28 ships of the line and some small vessels are this moment of [sic] this harbour all beating up for Bantry what we are to do or what is to become of us God only knows.

White passed both reports on to General Dalrymple at Cork; the first, carried on a borrowed horse, reached him within four hours, after a breakneck ride of 42 Irish miles [51 English miles; 81 km] over snow-covered roads. Dalrymple's first thought was apparently to abandon Cork to the enemy, and it was left to Richard White, the civilian on the spot, to muster resistance. He called out the yeomanry, organised and

armed his tenants, drove the cattle inland to deny the French food* and
set up a line of observation posts to report the enemy's movements.

So far, however, not a Frenchman had set foot on Irish soil. Thanks
to adverse winds, by 24 December only ten battleships, three frigates
or corvettes and four smaller vessels had managed to claw their way inside the anchorage. The rest, well over half the total, were still tossing
unhappily about outside, unable to risk the entrance, or scattered out
of sight, while one frigate, badly damaged in a collision during a night
of fierce squalls and falling snow, had already had to limp back to
France. During the day, however, the weather eased up a little and a reconnaissance revealed suitable shingle beaches on the south shore of
the Bay, sheltered from an easterly wind. Though involving a long and
difficult pull of three to five miles in ships' boats, all 6000 soldiers now
within Bantry Bay could have been landed within hours.

Unfortunately for the invaders, the *Fraternité*, carrying both the
military commander, General Hoche, and the naval commander,
Admiral Morard de Galles, had become separated from the rest of the
fleet during the voyage from Brest. The decision therefore rested on
their seconds-in-command Admiral François Bouvet and General
Emmanuel de Grouchy [later Marquis de Grouchy, Marshal of
France]. Here was the chance for the understudy to become the star and
on Tone's insistence a Council of War was held on board Bouvet's frigate, the *Immortalité*, on Christmas Eve, at which de Grouchy, somewhat reluctantly, agreed to land the 6400 men and four guns already in
the Bay, and gave formal orders in writing to this effect to Admiral
Bouvet, though with little enthusiasm on either side. The wretched
weather and resulting delays had, however, lowered everyone's
morale; the Irish landscape, perpetually shrouded in mist, rain or
snow, looked miserably unwelcoming; de Grouchy foresaw his men
being abandoned, once the fleet had left, on a hostile shore with no
hope of relief; while Admiral Bouvet feared that if, as was all too possible, the Royal Navy appeared outside, he might go down in history
as the commander who lost a whole fleet. Only Wolfe Tone was in
high spirits that day, though he persuaded himself his companions
shared them:

> At last I believe we are about to disembark . . . Huzza! I apprehend
> we are tonight 6000 of the most careless fellows in Europe, for
> everybody is in the most extravagant spirits . . . I never liked the
> French half so well as tonight, and I can scarcely persuade myself
> that the loungers of the boulevards, and the soldiers I see about me,

* The assumed availability of fresh meat had been a factor in the French planning. When
General Hoche had expressed anxiety about the bread supply in Ireland he had been told
by Lazare Carnot, the Directory member known as 'the organiser of victory': 'Let them
eat beef!'

are of the same hemisphere. To judge the French rightly . . . you must see them not in Paris, but in the camp. It is in the armies that the Republic exists. My enemy, the wind, seems just now, at eight o'clock, to relent a little, so we may reach Bantry tomorrow . . . We propose to make a race for Cork, as if the devil were in our bodies, and when we are fairly there, we will stop for a day or two to take breath.

There was to be no landing on Sunday 25 December. A fierce gale ruled out any thought of launching small boats and soon had the great warships dragging dangerously at their anchors, while the troops and sailors, hungry, shivering and seasick, spent the most miserable Christmas Day anyone could remember. Admiral Bouvet himself, after being forced towards Bere Island, at the western side of the entrance to the Bay, and with one of his anchors dragging, finally cut it free and made for the open sea, signalling, by gunfire and megaphone, to the rest of the fleet to do the same. His orders were not, in the stormy darkness, understood, but when, four days later, the wind changed, Bouvet, with provisions failing and no other ship of his command in sight, after an angry scene between himself and the army commander, flatly refused to return. He decided instead to make for France, and duly anchored in the Cameret Roads off Brest on New Year's Day 1797, back where he had started.

Yet a third naval officer had meanwhile found himself forced to take charge in Bantry Bay, Commodore Bedout, and he too decided, on 26 December, that withdrawal was the only prudent course. More surprisingly, he persuaded Wolfe Tone to agree with him, the Irishman displaying in adversity a commendable resignation:

Certainly we have been persecuted by a strange fatality, from the very night of our departure, to this hour . . . All our hopes are now reduced to get back in safety to Brest, and I believe we will set sail for that port the instant the weather will permit . . . England has not had such an escape since the Spanish Armada, and that expedition, like ours, was defeated by the weather; the elements fight against us, and courage here is of no avail. Well, let me think no more about it; it is lost, and let it go!

Wolfe Tone had remarked, at the end of the futile excursion to southwest Ireland, 'I am utterly astonished that we did not see a single English ship of war, going nor coming back,' and the Royal Navy emerged with little more credit from the Bantry Bay affair than the French. The first firm news that the enemy had arrived off Ireland had reached Vice-Admiral Robert [later Sir Robert] Kingsmill, in command at Cork, on 23 December 1796 and the Admiralty in London on the 31st. Kingsmill had, as already mentioned, only one ship of the line and six frigates at his disposal and by the time they reached Bantry on 7

January 1797 the main enemy fleet had already left, though his ships did capture a frigate and a transport. The main Channel fleet, under its Commander-in-Chief, Lord Bridport [formerly Alexander Hood], did not arrive there until 8 January 1797, accompanied by Kingsmill's squadron, after the last enemy had gone, and though he then set course for Ushant, and actually sighted two French ships still 50 miles [80 km] from safety, both got away. By 4 February the seaman principally responsible for protecting the British Isles from invasion was back at Spithead without having fired a shot.

Sir Edward Pellew was more fortunate. While returning from his wild-goose chase to Portugal he fell in, by chance, with the 74-gun battleship *Les Droits de l'Homme*, on its way back from Ireland. On 13 January 1797, after a fierce fight, she was driven ashore on the Brittany coast, with the loss of 1000 of the 1350 men aboard. All told the expedition to Bantry Bay cost the French around 4000 lives and ten of the 45 ships involved, mainly forced aground, scuttled or captured. Many other vessels required months of costly repair and the rumour that another landing in Ireland was being planned was sufficient to cause mass desertions, which robbed the fleet at Brest of one-third of its 24,000 men. The French government were inclined, however, to attribute the recent failure, as Wolfe Tone had done, to sheer bad luck, though Admiral Bouvet, whose sudden departure had really doomed the whole venture, was demoted. The military commander, Grouchy, though General Hoche thought his 'proceedings ... peculiar', survived to become years later Commander-in-Chief of the French army. No one blamed Hoche, but he died later that year, after assuring Wolfe Tone that the invasion of Ireland 'was a business the Republic would never give up ... If three expeditions failed, they would try a fourth ... until they succeeded.'

In Great Britain a contemporary ballad voiced a more optimistic view:

In Bantry's deep and rocky bay,
The hostile navy rode;
And now arrived the festal hour
When earth beheld her God ...
For thirteen nights and thirteen days
Their scattered navy strove;
And some were wrecked, and some despaired,
Before the tempest drove.
Now ever praised be our God
Who saved us from their hand.
And never more may foe presume
To dare this Christian land.

18

THE FRENCH IN FISHGUARD

I have this instant received certain information of three two-deckers and a lugger having anchored in Fishguard Bay this evening.

Message from Captain E. Longcroft at Haverfordwest to Vice-Admiral Kingsmill, 22 February 1797

After Ireland, Wales. The failure of the Bantry Bay expedition seems, if anything, to have encouraged the French to persist in plans for a landing elsewhere in the British Isles. In Wales some hostility to the government undoubtedly existed among the more extreme nonconformists, who identified both ministers and monarchy with their real enemy, the established Church, but it fell a long way short of potential treason and a landing there made no military sense once the campaign against Ireland, from which it was supposed to be a diversion, had visibly failed.

None the less, plans for it went ahead, the venture having gained a momentum of its own as well as a leader, an elderly American, probably of Irish descent, Colonel William Tate. Tate, now aged about 70, had had a somewhat dubious career. While serving in the American forces in the War of Independence, he had been court-martialled over making some false returns and had later had to leave the country. In June 1795 he had set up house in Paris and in the following year got to know Wolfe Tone. Soon, like Tone, Tate was plaguing the Directory with ambitious schemes to harass the hated British, and, also like Tone, impressed General Hoche, who was looking for someone to lead the secondary attack on the British mainland designed to accompany his major assault on Ireland.

Plans for the two expeditions went ahead simultaneously, with Wolfe Tone, now fluent in French, being employed to render Hoche's orders into English for Tate's benefit. The objectives at this stage were Bristol and Liverpool, the intention being to terrorise the latter city, and perhaps others, into paying a heavy ransom, by destroying the former. The plan of campaign, nothing if not ambitious, called for Tate's force to sail up the Avon at dusk and land five miles [8 km] short of Bristol, where the docks and shipping were to be set on fire. The troops would then re-embark and cross the Bristol Channel, to land on the right bank of the River Taff, and, skirting Cardiff, move on through the border counties to Chester and thence to Liverpool. They were to be given provisions for only four days, being expected to live off the country, but a double ration of brandy, and – none too much in the circumstances – 100 rounds of ammunition apiece. The aims of the operation were set out with admirable clarity:

> The expedition under the command of Col. Tate has in view three principal objects; the first is, if possible, to raise an insurrection in the country; the second is to interrupt and embarrass the commerce of the enemy; and the third is to prepare and facilitate the way for a descent, by distracting the attention of the English government.

Dire warnings followed about the fate of those who failed to welcome their liberators:

> The success of the expedition will likewise be materially forwarded . . . by the terror which the success of the legion and the progress of the insurrection will carry into the bosoms of the unwarlike citizens . . . Subsistence is to be seized wherever it can be found; if any town or village refuse to supply it in the moment [i.e. immediately] it is to be given up to immediate pillage . . . the inhabitants must be obliged to serve as guides, and any who refuse are to be punished on the spot . . . All denunciations against those who join the legion are to be punished by death.

Before he left for Ireland Wolfe Tone was kept busy with these and similar papers as, on 25 November 1796, he recorded in his journal:

> I have been hard at work this day translating orders and instructions for a Colonel Tate . . . to whom the general has given the rank of Chef de Brigade, and 1050 men of the *Légion Noire*, in order to go on a buccaneering party into England . . . The instructions are incomparably well drawn; they are done, or at least corrected, by the general himself, and if Tate be a dashing fellow, with military talents, he may play the devil in England before he is caught.

On 10 December Hoche, shortly before leaving for Ireland, sent an account of the proposed expedition to the Directory:

> I have confided to a man of ability, an ex-soldier, the command of the second legion of irregulars, which I have raised as secretly as possible. It is composed of 600 men from all the prisons in my district, and they are collected in two forts or islands to obviate the possibility of their escape. I associate with them 600 picked convicts from the galleys, still wearing their irons. They are well armed and dressed in their Quiberon jackets. This legion, which has cost next to nothing, has intrepid leaders. It must embark in two frigates and a corvette, and land as near as possible to Bristol, upon which I am

anxious to make a surprise attack.

The 'Quiberon jackets' to which Hoche referred were British uniform issue, captured during an expedition to that area in the previous year. Dyed dark brown, they gave to their wearers the name of the *Légion Noire* or Black Legion. It seemed likely to be all too apt. Wolfe Tone, when he first saw these troops during November, was shocked at their appearance. 'They are', he noted, 'the banditti intended for England and sad blackguards they are. They put me strongly in mind of the Green-boys of Dublin,' i.e. the worst inmates of its toughest prison. A royalist spy a little later, writing to the émigré headquarters in Jersey, described Tate's army as 1400 of 'the most abandoned rogues' from the prisons of Rochefort, Nantes and Lorient, commanded by fanatical Jacobins. 'It is,' he commented, 'difficult to determine which of this atrocious band, the officers or the soldiers, are the most dangerous.'

On 19 January 1797 Wolfe Tone, now back in Paris but again masquerading as Citizen Smith, sent a final goodwill message to Tate offering to do all he could to help through his connection with Hoche, and on 21 January 1797 Tate's commission as a Chef de Brigade in the French army was formally confirmed. His second-in-command was a Frenchman, Chef de Bataillon Le Brun, previously the Baron de Rochemure, and his officers included an Irish-American lieutenant who had only just got back from Bantry Bay, and two Irish-born captains. The rank and file included a number of Welsh-speaking prisoners-of-war, freed from the prison hulks in return for agreeing to serve as interpreters, but no doubt intending, like the conscript émigrés, to desert at the earliest opportunity.

Though Tate was given but poor material for his troops the naval authorities assigned to the expedition a first-class commanding officer, Jean Castagnier, who having served successfully as a privateer captain during the American War, had risen from ensign in the French navy to commodore in four years. Castagnier had also been allocated a number of new, or almost new, ships: the *Vengeance* and the *Résistance*, frigates carrying 345 men and a formidable armament of 28 18-pounder [8-kg] and 12 eight-pounder [3.5-kg] guns; a 24-gun 189-man corvette, the *Constance*, and a little 14-gun lugger, the *Vatour*, just back from Bantry Bay. (It had been the unreadiness of the two frigates for sea in December which had prevented Tate's expedition setting off, as intended, at the same time as Hoche's.)

The return of the unsuccessful expedition from Bantry Bay during January 1797 had provided one unhappy omen for the new venture. Another now followed. On 14 February 1797, in the Battle of Cape St Vincent or St Valentine's Day Battle, Admiral John Jervis [later Earl of St Vincent], Commander-in-Chief of the Mediterranean fleet, ably supported by Commodore Horatio [later Admiral Lord] Nelson, inflicted such massive damage on the Spanish fleet, though outnumbered 27 to 14, as it left the Straits of Gibraltar, that Spain ceased henceforward to be a major maritime power. Nelson's dazzlingly successful tactics, by which he captured two much larger ships, were admirably described as 'Nelson's Patent Bridge for boarding First-Rates' and led to his promotion to Rear-Admiral. For the moment, that old French dream of sweeping the Channel clear of English ships in combination with the Spanish navy was once more dispelled, but news of this overwhelming defeat had probably not reached Brest when, on Thursday 16 February 1797, the four ships of Castagnier's invasion squadron made their way out of the port with the help of a brisk east wind.

Less fortunate than its predecessor, Castagnier's little squadron was rapidly spotted. During the 19th they escaped embarrassing questions from a small Dublin-bound convoy by hoisting Russian colours but were later obliged to sink an over-inquisitive cutter, and during Tuesday 21 February were sighted in turn by a customs cutter from St Ives and a sloop from that port, and named after it, making for Swansea. It was probably from here that the first alarm was sent to London, by the Customs Collector, who stated that the intruders had been seen 'about two leagues [6 miles; 9.6 km] from the north end of the Island [of] Lundy', where they had appeared 'nearly in the same situation' between 10 am and 4 pm at 'four in the afternoon' and 'about ten in the morning'.

The message was correct. The easterly wind which had helped Castagnier to get out of port was now preventing him, even on a flood tide, from sailing up to Bristol and he suggested landing the troops in Swansea Bay. Tate insisted that they should make instead for Cardigan Bay, the alternative destination given to him by General Hoche, and eventually, after a fierce argument, the *Vengeance* and its sister-ship turned west and ran before the prevailing wind along the coast of Wales.

Some uncertainty exists about what now occurred and the sources are contradictory. According to the French version of events two small boats had been sunk off Lundy Island and one of their crew was now forced to act as a pilot to lead the French ships into and round St George's Channel, but this incident does not appear in the Swansea customs' official's account. The French make no reference to an attack on Ilfracombe, about 75 miles [120 km] west of Bristol, mentioned in the despatch which the lieutenant-colonel commanding the North Devon Volunteers sent to the Home Secretary on 23 February:

I yesterday received an express from Ilfracombe mentioning that there were three French frigates off that place; that they had scuttled several merchantmen and were attempting to destroy the shipping in the harbour. They begged that I would immediately order the

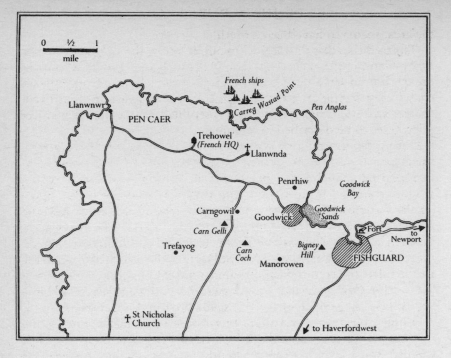

The French at Fishguard

North Devon regiment of Volunteers under my command to march as soon as possible. I have great satisfaction in saying that in four hours I found every officer and man that was ordered to Bideford (15 miles [24 km] from home) ready and willing to march to any place they should be commanded to go. I cannot express the satisfaction I feel on seeing the men so willing to defend their king and country, at the same time as silent, orderly and sober as might be expected at a morning parade of an old regiment. The greatest exertions were made by all descriptions of people to assist and render any service in their power. As I was preparing to march I received an account from Ilfracombe that the French ships were gone from the coast and that tranquillity was restored again to the town.

Although Ilfracombe appeared later on an official map of places which had suffered an enemy landing the gallant colonel himself was dubious about the story. 'How far the report was well founded I cannot possibly say,' he warned, and the attack on the shipping at Ilfracombe, which at least one author* has exaggerated into an actual descent on

* i.e. J.P.F. Miles in *Jemima and the Black Legion, Country Quest,* 1963, Vol. 4, no.1, p. 47: 'A party was landed off Ilfracombe and they set about burning and looting isolated farms.' But Hozier, Vol.II, p. 285 says 'they [the French] anchored at Ilfracombe on the 22nd of February and scuttled several merchant ships, but . . . attempted no further progress in that quarter.'

the area, seems to have been a myth.

The tradition that the local womenfolk, under the stalwartly named Betty Gammon, paraded on War Hill on Rillage Point, which the French would have been obliged to pass, and draped red petticoats round their shoulders to suggest the area was swarming with red-coated soldiers, bears a suspicious resemblance to a similar incident elsewhere, to be described in a moment.

During the morning of Wednesday 22 February 1797 Castagnier's squadron passed Milford Haven, scene of Henry Tudor's successful invasion in 1485, and chased away a revenue cutter from that port, but around 10 am it was positively identified from St David's Head, at the north-west tip of Wales, by a former sea captain turned magistrate, Thomas Williams, out for a morning stroll. He was not deceived by the British colours being flown by the intruders and followed them on shore after sending a messenger to St David's, the principal town of the area, to alert the countryside. Around 4 pm they anchored off Carreg Wastad [or Carregwastad] Point, two miles [3.2 km] west of Fishguard Bay, after which one vessel sailed on into the Bay itself.

Fishguard in 1797 was a minor but prosperous port, at which some 50 vessels a week regularly called, and with its population of 1500 it was the third-largest town in Pembrokeshire. It had already, as described earlier, beaten off one attack by a French privateer, in 1779, and subsequent local pressure on the Board of Ordnance had led to the building of a small fort, the remains of which can still be seen, on Castle Point, a rocky headland a mile [1.6 km] north of the town, close to the Newport road. The Board was far from generous, giving permission for the work, and professional advice on the choice of site, only on condition 'that the inhabitants . . . at their own expense construct platforms for the guns, and provide storehouses for the safe-keeping of the stores . . . and that the inhabitants shall furnish powder.' The guns were only installed in 1785 and not properly manned until 1794, when three gunners from an 'invalid' battalion were sent down to operate them and give instruction to the Volunteers expected to assist them.

This, however, proved to be their finest hour and as the French ship, flying British colours, entered Fishguard Bay and made towards the shore it was greeted by a roar of cannon fire, and, having run up the tri-colour, retreated, to report to Castagnier that the harbour was defended. The guns were in fact mere nine-pounders [4.1-kg guns], easily outclassed by the armament of the French vessels, and they had been firing blanks – in salute to the supposed British visitor, according to the cynics, to alert the local Volunteers according to more generous-minded observers.

It was a perfect day for an invasion. The sea was calm, the weather spring-like, conditions described as 'the finest ever remembered at such a season, when all nature, earth and ocean wore an air of unusual serenity'. Around 5 pm, with sunset approaching, the French began to disembark, in 17 crowded small boats, the soldiers clambering on to the low rocks and then up a low cliff to a flat area of grass at the top, still unchanged today,* and having set fire to the gorse on the clifftop to light their comrades' passage up the steep slope, the whole expedition got ashore without opposition.

An upset boat, however, cost eight men drowned and, more serious, the expedition's guns and artillery supplies, but, Tate being as yet unaware of this, 47 barrels of gunpowder were trundled up the cliff, along with 2000 stand of arms for the expected rebels. By 2 am on Thursday 23 February 1797 the French had established a bridgehead of about 1400 men on the shore of Pembrokeshire without a shot fired against them.

The first warning of the sighting of the French off Lundy Island had been sent to the Home Secretary that morning, with the arrival of the *St Ives* at Swansea, and, via the naval captain there, to the officer in charge at Plymouth and the Admiralty in London. The senior officer, the 'Regulating Captain', at Haverfordwest was equally quick off the mark, contacting the nearest naval authority with ships at his immediate disposal, Vice-Admiral Robert Kingsmill on the other side of the Irish Sea at Cork. Rumour had, however, already enlarged the French frigates and corvette into ships of the line:

> Haverfordwest February 22 1797
> I have this instant received certain information of three two-deckers and a lugger having anchored in Fishguard Bay this evening, and have [i.e. they had] several boats manned alongside to land when the express was sent to me. We are doing everything we can to oppose them but have not one man of war in the harbour. I have sent an express off to the Admiralty. It is but 15 miles [24 km] from Fishguard to Haverfordwest.

About the reaction among the land forces at Fishguard to the arrival of the French there is some uncertainty, since everyone was later anxious to paint his own actions in the best possible light. Away from the fort, the area was totally dependent on part-time soldiers. The Royal Pembrokeshire Militia, formed to cope with such an emergency, were far away, guarding Landguard Fort at Harwich. On the spot were the Pembroke Fencibles, the Fishguard Fencibles and a troop of mounted Yeomanry, a total of 500 men, of whom the four companies of the Fishguard Fencibles, two drawn from the town itself and two from

---

* i.e. in July 1985 when I explored the area and visited the main locations mentioned in this chapter. A monument to the landing, erected much later, stands on a nearby headland.

Newport, six miles [10 km] away, accounted for 280.*

The Fishguard Fencibles had been raised by a leading local resident, and were commanded by his son Thomas, a lieutenant-colonel at 28 but with no military experience. He was attending a dance at a house four miles [6.4 km] from his home and just sitting down to dinner when he received the news of the French ships' arrival. The whole party immediately broke up as the guests hurried home to send off their valuables, while Thomas Knox, very properly, conducted a reconnaissance. The disembarkation had not yet started and he did not at first take the threat seriously, but soon afterwards he learned that men were actually coming ashore. Some of his own men whom he met, with a retired officer, were eager to engage the enemy, but 'not without some murmuring' Knox persuaded them to wait, being still uncertain of the vessels' identity.

The opportunity to attack the invaders while they were at their most vulnerable had been lost and Knox now compounded his mistake by leading his men, keyed up for action, back to Fishguard Fort. Here he learned that a message had already gone to the Lord Lieutenant of the county, and at 8.20 pm was finally convinced that the French were landing by the arrival of a man who had been taken prisoner but had managed to escape. Knox at once sent fresh orders to his subordinate at Newport – 'You must now march your division to Fishguard with all expedition to join me' – posted sentries and settled down to make up for his interrupted earlier meal with bread and cheese.

Knox was still content to leave the initiative to the enemy, whose presence on shore was growing stronger by the minute. Not so Lieut.-Colonel Colby, in command of the Pembrokeshire Militia, whose men, as mentioned earlier, were absent at Landguard, but who happened to be in Haverfordwest when, at 6 pm that Wednesday evening, the first news arrived of events at Fishguard. Colby immediately called out the second-line, supplementary, militia, to take over from the first-line Cardiganshire Militia, who were guarding prisoners-of-war at Pembroke, and summoned the Pembroke Fencibles from the other side of the Milford Haven estuary, and the Yeomanry from Castlemartin. He also arranged with the naval 'Regulating Captain' at Haverfordwest to scrape together as many seamen as they could and collected eight nine-pounders [4.1-kg guns] from the revenue cutters in the harbour, two of which were despatched on carts towards Fishguard and the rest mounted in Haverfordwest Castle to give the French 'a warm reception' if they marched inland. Colby himself rode off to Fishguard to let Knox know that help was on its way, but by dawn he was back at Haverfordwest, from where around noon, the scratch

---

* 'Fencibles' were, strictly speaking, units of men who had volunteered for full-time service at home for 'the duration', but the term was commonly applied, as here, to unpaid part-timers.

force he had assembled set off along the Fishguard road, fortified by
bread, cheese and beer from the Castle Inn. His little army consisted of
about 400 men, 50 of them cavalry, 150 seamen, and the rest fencibles
or militia.

So far the French had caused more alarm than trouble. Colonel Tate
spent his first night ashore sitting on a stone, surrounded by casks of
powder and brandy, while his men slept on the ground around bonfires of furze. So far only one boatload, of 25 grenadiers, had been sent
away from Carreg Wastad, to seek out a suitable headquarters, and
perhaps led by the former servant there, they made their way to Trehowel, a pleasant, solid, two-storey stone farmhouse, three-quarters of a
mile [1.2 km] to the south-west, which still stands, externally little
changed, today. The occupants had already fled, one conscientious
maidservant, it is said, having removed the silver spoons, and another
carrying a mug of beer a mile [1.6 km] away to Llanwnwr rather than
leave it for the enemy to drink.

During the morning of Thursday 23 February 1797 small detachments of the Black Legion were sent inland to find food and transport.
Most of the wagons and horses had been removed by now, but the
men seized livestock wholesale – they featured prominently in the later
claims for compensation – and, such was their hunger, ate some freshly
killed sheep and poultry 'little more than warmed'. An agreeable surprise was that most houses contained large quantities of wine, for a
ship carrying it had been wrecked on the Pembroke coast a few days
before and its cargo had been appropriated by the villagers.

If news of these depredations a mere two to three miles [3.2-4.8 km]
away from his temporary command post at Fishguard Fort reached
Thomas Knox, they failed to stir him into action. He had about 150
men with him, and eight officers, but 30 soldiers, trained in gunnery,
he earmarked to man the Fort – though, lacking ammunition for its
cannon, they could have accomplished little – while he waited for
another 180 men to join him. Meanwhile his scouts were coming in
with alarmist stories of the numbers of Frenchmen they had seen, one
reporting 400 round a single thicket, though the smoke from their
bonfires had made accurate counting impossible. A French prisoner
brought in by some civilians put the total size of the expedition, correctly enough, at between 1200 and 1400. This seems to have made up
Knox's mind. He was, he decided, outnumbered ten to one; no senior
officer was on hand to consult – the nearest regular general, Lieut.-
General James Rooke, head of Severn Command, was 150 miles [240
km] away in Bristol; even the stalwart Lieut.-Colonel Colby was back
in Haverfordwest. The commander of all the non-regular forces in
Pembrokeshire was in theory Lord Milford, the Lord Lieutenant,
though, unknown to Knox, he had just delegated his authority to the
commander of the Yeomanry Cavalry, Lord Cawdor, an energetic

and courageous individual 15 years his junior. They too were at or near Haverfordwest. It was a difficult situation for the inexperienced young commander, and perhaps in deciding to retreat he showed true courage. At all events, instead of attacking the visibly disorganised French, or even posting his men in a strong defensive position beside the road on the hill leading from Goodwick, midway between the village of Llanwnda and the port of Fishguard, he decided to abandon the town and fall back due south on Haverfordwest.

Knox's decision left the one strongpoint in the area, Fishguard Fort, unprotected. He therefore ordered the Volunteer ensign in charge there to destroy such ammunition as it possessed and to spike the guns, but this the three 'invalid' artillerymen refused to do and stayed behind when their supposed defenders marched off, declaring that they 'never saw nor ever heard of such cowardly conduct in their lives'.

According to later evidence the self-appointed Invasion Committee at Haverfordwest, which included the mayor of the town and Lord Milford, had independently decided, as they informed Knox, 'that they thought it most advisable for you to retreat towards Haverfordwest' while Colby and Cawdor got their men together, but the messenger sent to Fishguard with this message met Knox already on his way there, leading his men at such a breakneck pace that he eventually had to call a halt to give the troops from the Fort a chance to catch up. About 1.30 pm Lord Cawdor and his force joined them and there was an altercation over who was in command, which ended with Knox, very sensibly, submitting to the authority of the slightly older – Cawdor was in his early forties – and far abler man, as Lieut.-Colonel Colby advised. This settled, and now with Lord Cawdor and his cavalry at its head, the retreating Fishguard Fencibles turned about face and at last set off back towards the enemy.

At just about this time Colonel Tate and his chief officers were in conference with the naval commanders who had delivered them to Wales. In Castagnier's cabin on the *Vengeance* Tate and the rest signed a statement that he was leaving them with their agreement, and a code of signals, of lights, rockets and smoke from the shore, was agreed for use should the ships return. A somewhat elaborate password, *Deuxième Légion des Francs et République française*, was laid down and around 5 pm Castagnier, with the *Résistance* and the *Constance*, set off towards the north-west, making for Dublin Roads in accordance with his now outdated orders, while the *Vatour* made passage for Brest, bearing a distinctly rosy account of the expedition's achievements. (Already, it was claimed, the whole district was in a state of terror.) William Tate, a tall, thin, aged figure in a blue uniform coat, stood on the clifftop of the Pen Caer [or Pencaer] promontory where they had landed, waving his hat as the white sails disappeared into the gathering February twilight. Now he was on his own.

Despite his earlier show of anglophobia, Tate's heart does not seem to have been in the enterprise he was leading. 'He had been often in battle over his shoes in blood,' Tate later wrote of himself, 'but he had never felt such a sensation as when he put his foot on British soil – that his heart had altogether failed him.' This is perhaps the real reason why, with Fishguard at his mercy and the road towards Newport and Cardigan undefended, he made no attempt to seize his opportunity. Time after time, most recently at Bantry Bay, it had been shown that if an amphibious expedition did not press on inland the moment it got ashore it would fail, but Tate did nothing, while his men showed a desire only to eat and to plunder.

After years of prison rations, and five days at sea, it was eating that came first and contemporary accounts express astonishment at the invaders' appetites. Such looting as occurred was, considering the troops' background, on a remarkably small scale and conducted in an almost gentlemanly fashion. The intruders in one house containing a woman with a newborn child left politely when she pleaded with them; a farmer who had stayed to drink with the enemy lost his savings of 80 guineas [£84] only after foolishly giving away their hiding place. Undoubtedly a good deal of looting did take place, and, no doubt, some wanton damage, though the most famous such incident was due to ignorance. A soldier in one clergyman's house fired at the face of a grandfather clock, convinced that its ticking meant that a man was hidden inside, and the resulting hole can still be seen. *The Monthly Magazine and British Register*, in its account, datelined Haverfordwest 11 March, by 'a gentleman on whose veracity we can rely', gave the invaders a remarkably good character:

> From those houses in which they found inhabitants they took but few things; but entirely ransacked, and gutted, those that were abandoned . . . All things considered the damage is infinitely less than might have been expected. They committed no wanton murders, nor any deeds of great cruelty.

The French did not indulge in wholesale rape, but two sexual assaults were mentioned by Lord Cawdor that August to the Duke of Rutland, which the Duke recorded in his journal:

> During Thursday their marauding parties had committed many depredations . . . They met three women on the road, one of whom . . . who was two months gone with child, they shot in the leg, and afterwards ravished her in the presence of her husband.
>
> One of their officers also, a man of the name of St Leger (an Irishman) went into a farmhouse and ravished a virgin 60 years old. This man afterwards informed Lord Cawdor that he only came over for that amusement and intended no harm to anyone.

Even though the Volunteers had withdrawn the invaders were not left in undisputed possession of Pen Caer and Fishguard that day. Everywhere little groups of Welshmen, or even solitary individuals, fought for their possessions or harassed the French at every opportunity. Two civilians were killed in these informal, unorganised scuffles, though the correspondent of the *Monthly Magazine* commented unsympathetically that 'these by their foolish rashness, provoked their fate'; they had apparently attacked a party of Frenchmen near Carnwnda, who may have been willing to surrender, and killed one of them. Three other Frenchmen, in addition to those lost during the landing, are also known to have died. One was killed in the only real skirmish of the day, with a group of armed seamen from Solva, 13 miles [21 km] away on the coast of St Bride's Bay, near St David's. These had been organised by an engineer from Liverpool who was directing the building of a lighthouse in the area and who led his men with such determination against the enemy holding Carngowil Farm that the French were routed, leaving two men severely wounded and one dead. Tate, who witnessed the little battle, is said to have been deeply impressed and to have remarked that if this was how undisciplined English civilians behaved under fire he dared not contemplate what his men could expect from real British soldiers. In St David's, according to Lord Cawdor's account as recorded by the Duke of Rutland, 'the inhabitants were particularly staunch; they were arming themselves but had not lead enough for balls. A blacksmith who was amongst them cried out suddenly, "Here is a hatchet and there is the cathedral," pointing to the leaden pipes that were on the top of it,' and within minutes these were being shaped into bullets.

Two alleged events that day were to pass into legend. A 47-year-old shoemaker, Jemima Nicholas, is said to have left her shop in Fishguard armed with a pitchfork and unaided brought back 12 Frenchmen as prisoners, earning her the local nickname of 'Jemima Vawr', i.e. 'Jemima the Great'. The tombstone, still plainly legible in St Mary's churchyard, which records this exploit was not erected till a century later, but the vicar who buried her, who had known Jemima all his life, recalled her as 'being of such personal powers as to be able to overcome most men in a fight'.

Even more famous is the tradition that the women of Fishguard formed, almost literally, a stage army, which discouraged the French from attacking. What might be called the definitive version comes from a local man who had heard it from 'old Fishguardians':

Campbell [i.e. Lord Cawdor] ordered all the women of the countryside . . . to be wrapped in the long red cloaks then universally worn by Welshwomen, and supplying [them] as he could with real muskets and bayonets, and others with stakes, pokers, and the old-fashioned roasting spits, lined the stone walls from the Bryn-y-Mor

to Manorowen, with those brave lasses in their tall, steeple-
crowned hats to make the French . . . believe they were in face of
overwhelming force.

A variant on this tale has the women being marched down Bigney Hill
and then, under cover of side-roads, back to the top, to multiply their
numbers, though Lord Cawdor, the best source for the invasion as a
whole, makes no mention of the incident. A letter from a customs official, sent from Haverfordwest on 27 February, expressly states, however, that it was 'above all, about 400 poor women with red flannel
over their shoulders', that 'intimidated the French soldiers' and the
legend, to which tall hats were added later, seems therefore to be
founded on fact.

Cawdor's real, wholly male, army was by 5 pm on 23 February
within a mile [1.6 km] of Fishguard on the road from Haverfordwest.
Although it consisted of only 600 men, with two ships' guns, Cawdor
planned an immediate attack, but this proved too difficult in the dark
and he decided to rest his weary troops until the morning. Conditions
in the French camp had meanwhile deteriorated. The men had been
badly shaken by Castagnier's departure as well as by the universal resistance they had encountered and consoled themselves with eating
and drinking. Tate and his officers meanwhile, though barely a shot
had been fired on either side, met to discuss the possibility of surrender, and to prepare an elaborate written justification for the decision.
The reasons included the lack of food, the indiscipline of the men, who
had been prepared to fire on their own officers, and the 'troops of the
line to the number of several thousand' said to be facing them, a gro-
tesque over-estimate. At around 9 pm Tate's second-in-command and
an English-speaking ADC arrived at a house in Fishguard Square, now
the Royal Oak inn, to negotiate terms with Thomas Knox. Tate's letter, which Knox immediately passed on to Lord Cawdor, was short
but dignified:

> Sir,
> The circumstances under which the body of the French troops under
> my command were landed at this place renders it unnecessary to
> attempt any military operations, as they would tend only to
> bloodshed and pillage. The officers of the whole corps have there-
> fore intimated their desire of entering into a negotiation upon prin-
> ciples of humanity for a surrender.

Cawdor's reply, drafted in the upper room of the future public house,
was uncompromising:

> Sir,
> The superiority of the force under my command, which is hourly
> increasing, must prevent my treating upon any terms short of your

surrendering your whole force prisoners of war. I enter fully into your wish of preventing an unnecessary effusion of blood, which your speedy surrender can alone prevent . . . My major will deliver you this letter and I shall expect your determination by ten o'clock.

At nine next morning Tate's reply arrived, in which he agreed to surrender and, according to an inscription on a table in the Royal Oak, the articles of capitulation were signed there, though this document no longer exists.

A plaque on Goodwick Sands records the final act in the drama which had turned out to possess more of the elements of farce than tragedy. At 2 pm the supposed liberators of the oppressed Welsh marched down from Llanwnda to the beach, with drums beating, and then piled up their arms, though they made a poor advertisement for the Revolution, for some, perhaps conscripted royalist émigrés, tore the cockade from their helmets and shouted 'Au diable la République!' – 'To the devil with the Republic!' Then, after a meal of bread and cheese, the invading army marched off towards Haverfordwest, singing and laughing, vastly relieved to be safely in captivity. They left behind, to be transported by cart later, a few intrepid warriors still too drunk, or too sick from the after-effects of over-eating, to walk.

The officers were disarmed separately, at Trehowel, for fear their devoted followers might fire their first, and last, salvo at them, which perhaps explains why, according to the Duke of Rutland, 'Tate himself was very much confused and frightened when he gave up his sword to Lord Cawdor.'

Thomas Knox was left in charge of cleaning-up operations and eventually delivered 14 cartloads of captured stores to Haverfordwest, including 47 barrels of gunpowder and 12 boxes of hand grenades, sufficient for a respectable battle. This was as near as he ever got to fighting and for him the sequel to the almost bloodless victory at Fishguard was unhappy. Widely accused of cowardice, he eventually challenged Lord Cawdor to a duel, though it was never fought, and that May was forced to resign his command.

Upon his men, and the people of the whole affected area, public praise and thanks were now heaped and the government, with unprecedented speed and generosity, had by August paid out no less than £882 11s 7½d [£882.56] to compensate those who claimed to have suffered loss at the hands of the French. The unfortunate Mary Williams, shot in the foot and perhaps raped, was given the handsome annual pension of £40, which she lived to draw for 56 years.

The French rank and file, after varying spells in jail as prisoners-of-war, were eventually repatriated in exchange for captured Britons, though they were received with dismay rather than enthusiasm, the French government having hoped it had seen the last of them, and

there were public complaints in Cherbourg when a contingent was delivered back there in October. Colonel Tate was repatriated late in
1798, fell in love with a much younger woman and, under her influence, ran up such debts that the French were glad to ship him off,
now in his eighties, back to the United States.

Neither Tate nor Castagnier seems to have been blamed for the
failure of the Fishguard expedition, though it ultimately cost the
French dear. Castagnier, having pointlessly dallied off the south-west
coast of Ireland, ran into bad weather and then, so one of his fellow-
captains complained, abandoned his subordinates and made for Brest
alone. He and his *Vengeance*, as well as the little *Vatour*, got home safely
but the frigate *Résistance* and corvette *Constance* were both caught on 9
March 1797 as they approached the port and captured, without a single
British casualty; the French lost 33 killed or wounded and another 50 as
prisoners. The Fishguard expedition had thus cost the French nearly
2000 men, two valuable ships, a large quantity of supplies – and much
prestige.

The British government, by contrast, benefited enormously from
it. The invasion had provided a massive test, under realistic conditions,
of Pitt's home defence measures and the results were highly reassuring.
There had been an effective 'closing up' of forces from as far away as
Hereford and Gloucester, and some impressive performances by individual units. The New Romney Fencible Cavalry covered 61 miles
[97 km] from Worcester to Brecon in 5 hours, the Brecon Volunteers
marched 20 miles [32 km] to Llandovery in four, double the official
rate of three miles [5 km] in an hour and a quarter. The speed of communications, too, exceeded expectation. The cathedral organist from
St David's Cathedral, carrying the news of a supposed landing near
there on the night of 28 February, one of the many false alarms of the
period, was said to have reached Haverfordwest in 45 minutes, in spite
of the 16 miles [26 km] and 17 hills between them.

The landing of the enemy on British soil also produced a great outburst of patriotic fervour. Recruits poured in to the Volunteer forces,
so often mocked in the past. 'The liveliest zeal pervades every rank of
persons without distinction,' reported the mayor of Bristol to the
Home Secretary on 2 March 1797. A hat passed round on College
Green to buy comforts for the troops as the City Volunteers, formed
only ten days earlier, marched off to guard French prisoners while the
regulars prepared to counter the imaginary landing at St David's Head,
yielded 90 guineas [£94.50] in a few minutes.

Nowhere was more eager to demonstrate its loyalty than Wales and
especially the dissenting community. Some ministers, when the alarm
– it was hardly a panic – was at its height, had offered to lead their flocks
into action against the French, and though a dozen people were eventually arrested on suspicion of having 'aided and comforted the invaders'

the case against the only two actually charged, both Baptists, collapsed. Soon the events of those dangerous days were being remembered 'with advantages'. 'Not one of these men,' commented the *Annual Register* on the Pembrokeshire Militia in its review of the year, 'had ever fired a musket, except for amusement, yet they proceeded against the enemy with the most cheerful alacrity.' 'We did fight famous,' a local tailor who had helped to man a gun at Fishguard Fort was fond of boasting in old age, 'and the French did run away and we did fire after them.'

The nation's relief, as after Bantry Bay, found expression in a patriotic ballad.

Ho, Britons, give attention
To what I have to say,
How Providence did favour us
And mercy did display;
How we were saved in Pembrokeshire
From danger of the Gaul
When they attempted to land here
With musket, sword and ball . . .
God bless our king and country
With plenty, joy and peace,
And may all French and Spanish
From Britain ever cease.

19

A PROUD AND POWERFUL NATION

While other countries are falling to wreck, we stand a proud and powerful nation.

Secretary of War, Henry Dundas, in the House of Commons,
27 March 1798

After two invasion attempts in eight weeks no one in Great Britain could, in the spring of 1797, be unaware of the danger, but the opposition in Parliament did its best to make party capital out of recent events. The overwhelming victory in Wales was ignored and instead there were demands in the House of Commons for the Board of Admiralty to be impeached for not intercepting the French at Bantry Bay. In mid-April the government faced a new and unprecedented difficulty, a mutiny in the fleet anchored at Spithead, and this had hardly been settled when there was a far more serious outbreak, on 12 May, at the Nore, which spread to the ships at Yarmouth and was only put down, in mid-June, with the hanging of the 20 ringleaders and a timely grant of improved pay.

During the summer the French and Dutch pressed on with preparations for yet another attempt on Ireland. The real driving force behind this and other invasion plans was General Hoche, who summoned Wolfe Tone to join him at The Hague. The whole Dutch army, 15,000 strong, was to be employed, with 80 pieces of artillery, and 3000 stand of arms would be supplied for use by Irish sympathisers. Sixteen sail of the line and ten frigates were to carry or escort the troops, while the French planned to mount a separate expedition of their own from Brest, under the command of Hoche himself.

While Hoche was kept employed, for the moment, with another army, Wolfe Tone was left to chafe in the Texel, already on board ship and waiting for a favourable wind, with the expedition's naval commander:

> July 19. Wind still foul. Horrible, horrible! Admiral de Winter and I endeavour to pass away the time playing the flute, which he does very well; we have some good duets.

When tired of his musical soirées with Admiral de Winter, Wolfe Tone walked on the shore with General Daendels, who had been assigned to lead the expedition, counting the increasing number of English sails to be seen waiting outside. The two Dutchmen were meanwhile at odds over the most promising destination for their forces. Perhaps, it was suggested, they should try an easier passsage, to King's Lynn or Harwich, in frigates and fast transports, to evade the blockading cruisers. Daendels, early in September 1797, produced a new scheme, designed to catch the English off guard by ostentatiously disembarking the troops, only to re-embark them in deep secrecy and make for Scotland. A second wave, of 15,000 French troops in Dutch pay, would act as a follow-up force and once the whole 30,000 men were ashore 25,000 would cross the border into England and 5000 sail over the Irish Sea to Ireland. This grandiose plan had no more success than its predecessors. The troops, having eaten up all the provisions intended to sustain them at sea, were put ashore while, on 3 September, Wolfe Tone set off to try and enlist General Hoche's support for their latest plan. But he faced only bitter disappointment, for on 19 September 1797 Lazare Hoche died, of bronchial troubles probably brought on by his futile voyage to Bantry Bay the previous December. His death removed the chief advocate, and obvious leader, of an immediate invasion of England, but there was no slackening of French hostility to its old enemy for two weeks earlier the army had carried out a *coup d'état* in Paris, which had installed two new Directors in power and left the war party in France in the ascendant. On 14 September the British ambassador was presented with totally unacceptable terms for making peace and was then ordered to leave France.

A month later, on Thursday 11 October 1797, the threat of an invasion by the Dutch fleet was, for the moment at least, lifted by Admiral [Adam, later first Viscount] Duncan's great victory off Camperdown, on the Dutch coast. A bitterly fought battle between forces of roughly equal strength ended after four hours with the surrender of his flagship by Admiral de Winter, the only man left unwounded on its deck. All told nine Dutch battleships, plus two frigates, were captured, in a victory with far-reaching consequences, for it restored the reputation of the navy, sadly shaken by the recent mutinies, and showed that its fighting spirit was unimpaired. Camperdown also, as Pitt's Secretary of State for Foreign Affairs observed on 16 October, broke the right wing of the intended invasion, but bad news followed. On the very next day, 17 October, France and the German emperor signed the Treaty of Campo Formio, which put the seal on the recent French victories in Italy and left the general responsible, Napoleon Bonaparte, with an enhanced reputation as a brilliantly successful commander.

Bonaparte recognised that England was now the infant republic's most dangerous enemy. 'Our government,' he wrote to the Directory, 'must destroy the English monarchy, or expect itself to be destroyed

by these intriguing and enterprising islanders. The present moment
offers a capital opportunity. Let us concentrate all our efforts on the
navy and annihilate England. That done, Europe is at our feet.'

He was soon on his way back to Paris, fuming impatiently even at
the brief delay while the horses drawing his carriage were changed, and
on 26 October 1797 his appointment to a new post was announced:

> The Executive Directory decrees . . .
> 1. There shall be assembled without delay, on the coasts of the
> ocean, an army which shall be called the Army of England.
> 2. Citizen General Bonaparte is named Commander-in-Chief of
> that army.

Until the new commander could get back from Italy a 'caretaker' was
put in charge, General Louis Desaix, of whom Bonaparte had a high
opinion. On 12 November he told the Directory that he had 'given all
the necessary orders for moving our columns to the ocean', where
56,000 men were already assembled, and the next day he sent an aide to
Paris to order artillery 'of the same calibre as the English field-pieces,
so that, once in the country, we may be able to use their cannon-balls'.

During 1797 the British government had intensified its preparations
to resist an invasion. A comprehensive analysis of the whole subject
was provided by a 146-page book, *Plans for the Defence of Great Britain
and Ireland*, published that year and written by the Deputy Quarter-
Master-General for North Britain, Lieut.-Colonel [later General]
Alexander Dirom. Although a fortifications specialist Dirom was
notably open-minded about the general value of fixed defences and
even questioned the value of fortified ports, a basic principle of English
defence strategy since medieval times:

> It will appear to be particularly dangerous, in the defence of an
> island, to have a fortress contiguous to the coast, because the enemy
> can bring his cannon and whole force against it, and supply his army
> during the siege without the assistance of land carriage . . . The for-
> tifications . . . for the defence of the dockyards in England can there-
> fore be justified only by necessity, and ought to be kept within the
> least possible bounds, else a considerable part of the army may be
> made prisoners in defending them.

Dirom was also doubtful about that other almost automatic anti-
invasion measure, the siting of guns to cover potential landing areas:

> It is impossible to line the coast of an extensive country in such a
> manner with batteries as to protect it from an invading enemy, for
> they can be placed in few situations in which they may not be
> avoided . . . [or] approached and stormed without much danger to
> the assailants. Batteries ought thus to be erected with great caution,
> and perhaps only in situations strong by nature where they may not

be easily surprised or attacked on the land side. They ought all to have a furnace for heating shot, which is so formidable to shipping.

'Hot shot', or 'red shot', as it was commonly known, was at this time much in vogue, especially among those who did not have to handle it. What the enthusiasts rarely mentioned was that it was highly trouble-some, and even dangerous, to employ, since, apart from the risk of a heated round setting off the charge in the barrel, keeping a furnace or oven alight close to the guns provided a perpetual source of danger. Two recommended designs for furnaces, intended to reduce the risk and facilitate the transfer of the red-hot cannon ball into the muzzle of the cannon, were issued at this time, but the smaller forts probably built their own. Only an occasional hot round could be fired, with per-haps four 32-pounder [14.5-kg] or five 14-pounder [11-kg] balls being heated at a time, for use against ships already battered and broken open by conventional missiles.*

Dirom's final conclusion was a familiar one:

We ought ever to have it in view that a vigilant fleet at sea, and a numerous active army on shore, with a distribution of field artillery always in readiness near the coasts, are the best and only certain means of defence.

A similar conclusion was reached in the same year by a far senior officer, Lieut.-General Sir David Dundas, in command in the threatened south-east. His report 'on the possibility of a general inva-sion of Great Britain' stressed that there were three areas from which an invasion might come, The Netherlands, the French Channel ports, and Brest and the Bay of Biscay, which meant that the defences had to be spread too thinly for safety. Nowhere, concluded Dundas, could be considered really safe. Yorkshire and Lincolnshire were ill-placed to receive help from outside. 'Very little force could be collected or oppo-sition made to a sudden descent on any point of the Dorset coast . . . No considerable opposition could be made to a descent near Exeter and a march to that city.' The defences of Falmouth, which 'would be advantageous to an enemy as a place of rendezvous', were 'very mod-erate'. The whole of southern England was full of small bays into which, with a favourable tide and wind, small craft could safely pene-trate. Dundas was an able man with a high reputation, but the govern-ment may well have felt inclined, after reading his general *Observations* and the accompanying *Memorandum of [sic] the Coasts and Bays of Great Britain and Ireland and their General Defence*, to be grateful for the navy, which never made difficulties and always professed its fear that the enemy might not come rather than anxiety that he might.

* For further details on this intriguing, but little-studied, subject see *Aldis*, No. 41, Sep-tember 1988, p.6 and No. 43, April 1989, p.29. The last furnaces were not declared obsolete and recalled to Woolwich till 1872.

Fixed fortifications, even if most professionals considered them of uncertain value, were at least a visible sign that the government took the invasion danger seriously and from 1793 onwards a good deal of such work had already been begun, especially in East Kent. A variety of additional defences were now constructed, which eventually included eleven forts between Deal and Eastbourne of a simple triangular design, big enough to accommodate four or five 24-pounder [11-kg] guns, with a loopholed brick wall for local defence, plus the usual ditch and rampart. Four batteries were sited 2000 yards [1800 m] apart on the tip of the Dungeness peninsula, which, projecting five miles [8 km] out into deep water, was identified as the area at greatest risk. The hope was to break up an enemy landing attempt before the troops actually got ashore, but to deal with any invaders who reached dry land a series of earthworks, designed to be manned by infantrymen armed with muskets, was built along the nine miles [15 km] of flat countryside between Dungeness and Hythe. A larger, octagonal, earthen redoubt was also constructed about 500 yards [460 m] inland from Dungeness Point to act as a base for the soldiers protecting the other batteries in the area. On the seafront at Hythe three solid artillery forts were erected about 1100 yards [1 km] apart, named after engineer officers, among them Colonel [subsequently Brigadier-General] William Twiss, Commanding Engineer of the Southern District, of whom more will be heard later.

On 5 December 1797 the ablest general in Europe and the most fanatical and anti-English government were united, with Bonaparte's arrival in Paris, where he was installed not only in his newly announced command, but as a counsellor of the Directory and as generalissimo, or supreme commander, with authority even over the Minister of War. On 10 February 1798 Bonaparte left Paris for a ten-day tour of the invasion ports, which took in Flushing, Ostend, Dunkirk, Calais, Boulogne, Ambleteuse and Étaples. With his customary energy and persistence, and indifference to class, he interrogated ordinary sailors, fishermen and smugglers, often until midnight, and everywhere he enthused those he spoke to with his own determination. One member of the *Commission des Côtes de La Manche*, responsible for issuing contracts for building the shipping he needed, vividly described the impact he made:

General Bonaparte reached Dunkirk on February 11th. He spent the 12th there and on the 13th left for Belgium. During his short stay he investigated all our preparations and works and drew up a plan of armaments to be executed by March 21st. He ordered the construction of fifty large pinnaces and I was enjoined to move heaven and earth to get shipping accommodation for four to five thousand horses, 50,000 men and guns and all necessary supplies; to provide large and small gunboats to the greatest possible number; and so direct these operations that in 15 to 20 days everything should be ready to move off.

The effects of this intervention were rapidly apparent, as an English spy, following close behind, who on 13 February 1798 'met General Bonaparte between Furnes and Dunkirk, going to inspect the port, and make contracts for building flat-bottomed boats', reported to London. Twenty-one such craft, he stated, 'made to row a number of oars, and [with] a mast to strike or lay down as needful' were under construction at Bergues, 'a small town on the side of the canal from Dunkirk to St Omer', eleven at Rouen, 60 at Honfleur, 15 at Calais and at Le Havre 'flat-bottomed boats without number'. The same informant advised that military preparations were equally far advanced. Douai, Cambrai and Peronne were 'all full of troops, horse and foot'. Near Le Havre were 21,000 men 'ready to embark at short notice'.

Already, unknown to this informant, the Army of England, encamped between Flanders in the north and the Morbihan in Quiberon Bay in the south, numbered 70,000.

Naval headquarters for the expedition were at Brest and early on Bonaparte met the Minister of Marine there, when the main outlines of the naval plan were laid down. A sizeable part of the French navy was bottled up by a blockading British squadron in Cadiz, but it was hoped to get together 57 sail of the line, 46 frigates and 72 smaller ships from those already in commission, while another 14 major ships and 16 frigates were already under construction. Small vessels which could cross the Channel and then be used to ferry troops to the beaches were also in demand. The harbour authorities at St Malo, Brest, Nantes and Bordeaux were ordered to hire enough commercial vessels to carry 30,000 men. Holland, since 1796 renamed the Batavian Republic, was to build and supply 170 flat-bottomed boats, and hundreds more were commissioned from ship-builders at Calais, Boulogne, Dieppe, Le Havre, Rouen and Honfleur. It was a scene which had been witnessed on many occasions over the centuries, usually with little result, but this time the Commander-in-Chief clearly meant business. Work began to enlarge the harbour at Boulogne, and privateers, with engineers on board, were sent to reconnoitre the English coast between Folkestone and Rye to identify the batteries which might threaten a landing.

In spite of all his exertions, Bonaparte soon concluded that an invasion in 1798 would be premature. 'It is too doubtful a chance; I will not risk it,' he is said to have remarked and on 23 February he gave formal expression to his doubts in a letter to the Directory:

Make what efforts we may, we shall not for many years achieve the command of the sea. To make a descent on England without having command of the sea is the most dangerous and difficult operation which can be made.

In spite of the doubts of its chosen Commander-in-Chief about the whole venture, the French government, perhaps deliberately to deceive its enemies, encouraged the publication of newspaper articles on the fate in store for England. A number of enormous rafts, 700 yards [640 m] long, 350 yards [320 m] wide and eight storeys high, were said to be under construction, a report taken seriously enough in England for an émigré colonel to be brought out to deny the feasibility of such craft. 'One of them,' he pointed out, 'would require . . . 216,000 trees . . . and the whole would require 618,000 horses, or 108,000 carriages, and as many carters to bring them from the forest to the sea,' numbers beyond even France's resources.

One discreditable feature of the patriotic fervour which now swept the country was violent personal abuse of the man still known to his countrymen as 'General' or 'Citizen' Bonaparte, for whom the English now adopted the derisory nickname 'Boney'. The 'Corsican monster', as he was labelled, recalling his origins on that obscure island, was described as brutal, ugly and debauched, a devil in human form. One particularly absurd story, that he ate children, was immortalised in the verses used to frighten refractory infants into silence:

> Baby, baby, naughty baby,
> Hush, you squalling thing, I say;
> Hush your squalling, or it may be,
> Bonaparte will pass this way . . .

> Baby, baby, he will hear you,
> As he passes by the house,
> And he limb from limb will tear you
> Just as pussy tears a mouse.

During March 1798 it came to seem increasingly likely that the enemy, cannibalistic or not, would soon 'pass this way'. On the 8th the spy already quoted set out from Paris for Calais, noting 'on the road, troops and wagons with arms, without number, moving in all directions'. Next day he observed 91 pieces of artillery in the churchyard at Douai 'getting ready to set out next day for the coast'. His estimate of the total force available for the invasion, was 275,000 men, 'all to be within twenty-four hours march of the coast'.

With Volunteer units springing up on local initiative in every part of the country, the government decided to give its formal blessing to the movement and on 27 March 1798 the Secretary of State for War, Henry Dundas, introduced a Bill 'to enable His Majesty more effectually to provide for the defence and security of the realm, and for indemnifying persons who may suffer in their property by such measures'. The aim, he explained, was that 'every man desirous of coming forward . . . might distinctly know the part he was called on to act', and the Lords Lieutenant were given power 'to embody those who may be prompted to come forward'.

At the same time as it gave a legal basis to the Volunteer movement the government took powers to identify men 'competent to act in the shape of pioneers [and] drivers of wagons' and 'to erect covers for batteries and to raise works in critical situations' and if necessary 'pieces of ground appropriated' for the purpose. The government also pledged that compensation would be paid both to those 'who shall suffer by the attempts of the enemy and the measures taken to resist them', including those whose property was 'destroyed in order to prevent it from falling into the hands of the enemy'.

The Bill was passed unopposed and Dundas in his peroration clearly voiced the sentiments of both sides of the House:

> While other countries are falling to wreck, we stand a proud and powerful nation, in the middle of the ocean, and [the Bill] will also proclaim that there still exists one spot in the world determined to repel the attacks of those who would enslave it.

In the months that followed every section of society was affected by the prevailing patriotism, which found its chief expression in the expansion of the Volunteers, who soon numbered 150,000. Clerics chafing at the bit to play a suitably militant role in the nation's defence were told by the two archbishops, following a meeting on 28 April, that 'it would not conduce in any considerable degree to the defence and safety of the kingdom . . . if the clergy were to . . . be enrolled in any military corps, or be trained to the use of arms'. For the moment all that the combative curates could do was to stir up the martial temper of their flocks and denounce the enemy from the pulpit. Pitt himself was present at St Nicholas Church, Deptford, in May, to hear a sermon on 'Great Britain's insular situation, naval strength, and commercial opulence as a source of gratitude to God', while the Fawley Fencibles were suitably uplifted by an address in St Thomas's, Winchester, on a highly apposite text: 'Remember the Lord, which is great and terrible, and fight for your brethren, your sons, and your daughters, your wives, and your houses.'

A notable part in making everyone invasion-minded was played by specially written patriotic songs, of which the most popular, *The Snug Little Island*, first heard at Sadler's Wells on Easter Monday, 17 April 1797, shortly after the Fishguard fiasco, had by a year later become almost a second national anthem:

> Daddy Neptune one day to Freedom did say,
> If ever I live upon dry land,
> The spot I should hit on would be little Britain,
> Says Freedom, 'Why that's my own island!'
> Oh, it's a snug little island!
> A right little, tight little island,

> Search the globe round, none can be found
> So happy as this little island.

Pictorial propaganda perhaps reached even more people than poetic.
The pavement outside the print-seller's shop in St James's Street became impassable for the crowds struggling to see the anti-French
prints by James Gillray displayed in the window from the beginning of
February 1798. For the moment none of these eager patriots was, however, to have the opportunity to show his mettle in action. On 5 March
1798 the Directory took the formal decision that France's next target
should be Egypt, as a first step towards driving the English out of
India, accepting their general's argument that these operations, by
drawing ships away from the Channel, would also facilitate the invasion of England. Egypt having been occupied during the summer, he
asserted in a long explanation of his strategy on 13 April 1798, England
could then comfortably be disposed of before Christmas:

> We should have in September 400 gunboats at Boulogne and 35
> ships of war at Brest . . . After the return of the expedition which the
> government is projecting in the Mediterranean . . . in the course of
> October or November we should have at Brest 50 men-of-war and
> nearly as many frigates.
>
> It would then be possible to transport to any desired spot in
> England 40,000 men, without even fighting a naval action if the
> enemy should be in stronger force; for while 40,000 men would
> threaten to cross in the 400 gunboats and in as many Boulogne fish-
> ing-boats, the Dutch squadron, with 10,000 men on board, would
> threaten to land in Scotland. An invasion of England, carried out in
> that way, and in the month of November or December, would be
> almost certainly successful.

The British government was unaware that the danger of invasion was,
at least for the moment, to be lifted, and on 14 May 1798 a force of 1400
men, mainly drawn from the Guards, sailed from Margate to attack
the new 14-mile [22-km] long canal, linking Bruges to Ostend, along
which transports and gunboats could reach the coast. The lock gates at
Saas, a mile [1.6 km] from Ostend, were on 19 May successfully blown
up but the following day, unable to re-embark because of the high surf,
the whole force was compelled to surrender, after suffering 163 casualties. The operation had ultimately, it was agreed, been a failure, but it
had also, unknown to those who planned it, been irrelevant. On that
same 19 May the French fleet had sailed from Toulon not for England
but Egypt, in pursuance of the strange new strategy of invading Kent
via Cairo.

20

WIND OF FREEDOM

Oh may the wind of freedom
Soon send young Boney o'er,
And we'll plant the tree of liberty
Upon our Irish shore.

Song of the United Irishmen, 1798

Ireland had always been the Achilles heel in the defences of the British Isles. During 1797 Ulster, though mainly Protestant, had been in almost open revolt and following Bonaparte's arrival back in Paris in early December Wolfe Tone and other nationalists had four meetings with him, the last on 15 January 1798, to urge him to exploit the situation. He showed, however, little knowledge of Irish affairs and the long-expected rebellion finally began in earnest – four days after Bonaparte's departure for Egypt in County Kildare – not far from Dublin, on Wednesday 23 May 1798. A more serious outbreak followed in County Wexford, in the south-east corner of the country, Wexford itself being captured by an army now numbering 15,000, at first led by a Protestant. Eventually 30,000 men were assembled on Vinegar Hill, 13 miles [21 km] north of Wexford and one of the generals commanding the government forces, John [later Sir John] Moore, noted in his diary that if the rebellion continued to spread, or the French arrived, Ireland would be lost. Instead, on 21 June 1798, after Moore had regained Wexford, his fellow commander, General Gerard [later Lord] Lake, stormed Vinegar Hill and dispersed the rebel army for the cost of one man killed and four wounded, but the outbreak and its aftermath left the island seething with discontent and hatred.

The French now planned a fresh invasion of Ireland, in response to intense pressure from the Irish exiles in France, prominent among whom was General Charles Kilmaine, who had originally been intended to command the 1796 expedition later entrusted to the now dead Hoche. Kilmaine's first efforts with the French minister produced, however, little response, as Wolfe Tone sadly recorded:

He was sorry to tell me that he was much afraid that the French government would do nothing; and he read me a letter from the Minister of Marine which he had received that very morning, men-

tioning that, in consequence of the great superiority of the naval
force of the enemy, the Directory were determined to adjourn the
measure until a more favourable occasion. I lost my temper at this,
and told him that . . . the present crisis must be seized or it would be
too late.

Tone was soon afterwards summoned to Paris, where he was able to
put his case to the Directory personally, and his insistence that 5000
men now would do more good than 50,000 once the rising had been
suppressed made obvious sense. General Kilmaine, whom the Directory had made Commander-in-Chief of the invasion army, though no
invasion was yet in prospect, produced two plans during June, one for
sending 17,500 men to Ireland and another, more modest, involving
only 9000. Perhaps the decisive argument was that deployed by the
Dublin solicitor's clerk, E.J. Lewins, who having, as mentioned
earlier, persuaded the Directory back in November 1796 to attempt a
landing in Bantry Bay, had now turned up in Paris as the official representative there of the United Irishmen, and had accompanied Wolfe
Tone on his visits to Bonaparte. Lewins pointed out that the rebels
were already in possession of two major ports, Waterford and Wexford, with the surrounding counties, and of large tracts of other districts, including Dublin. He put their total strength at 50,000, a very
fair estimate, and suggested that a French force of 5000, provided they
took with them enough arms to equip 30,000 Irishmen, would be sufficient to free Ireland for good from English rule. All this may well
have been true when put on paper, but by the time the Directory made
up its mind, during July, the situation had changed; the rebellion was
almost over. As a result the new invasion was prepared in response to a
false prospectus.

The new plan called for 3000 men, under General Hardy, to sail
from Brest, while a secondary force, of 1000, commanded by General
Humbert, simultaneously left Rochefort. If these two combined
achieved a successful lodgement a consolidating army of 9000, under
the Commander-in-Chief, General Kilmaine, might follow. When,
however, on 2 August, a courier from Paris reached Brest with orders
to leave at once, Humbert found he had to depart alone.

French intervention was also eagerly anticipated by all those Irishmen hostile to the English authorities, whose views were made clear
by a currently popular verse:

Oh may the wind of freedom
Soon send young Boney o'er,
And we'll plant the tree of liberty
Upon our Irish shore.

If not 'young Boney' then at least one of his generals was soon on his
way. On Monday 6 August 1798 Commodore Savary led his little

squadron, consisting of the frigates *Concorde*, *Medée* and *Franchise* out of La Rochelle Roads and, by a highly roundabout route which took it far to the west, set course for Ireland. On board were General Humbert, an Irish priest serving as his interpreter, various Irishmen, including Wolfe Tone's brother, Matthew – Wolfe Tone himself was with the main expedition which had not yet sailed – 1036 men, three four-pounder [1.8-kg] guns and, for the benefit of the expected Irish recruits, 5500 stand of arms, 1000 French uniforms and several hundred barrels of gunpowder.

Escaping detection by Lord Bridport's patrolling frigates the French ships made an uneventful voyage to the north-west coast of Ireland, and on the afternoon of Wednesday 22 August 1798, anchored off Kilmunnin Head at the entrance to Killala Bay, some 140 miles [225 km] from Dublin and on the far side of the island. The well-worn ruse of flying an English flag was tried once again, with the usual success and, in marked contrast to what had happened at Bantry Bay, the disembarkation went according to plan. By 7 pm all the troops were on shore.

Meanwhile the advance party, numbering 300, were already pressing inland to Killala, three miles [5 km] away, led by Humbert's second-in-command, General Sarrazin, Matthew Tone, and the expedition's official interpreter, Captain (or Father) Henry O'Kane, who was dressed in an 'Irish green' hunting coat and impressed the watching locals by addressing them in their native tongue. The French, unfamiliar with Irish poverty, were deeply impressed by the evidence of it they now found all round them, as one French captain recorded:

> Never did a country present a more mournful appearance. The men, women and children were almost naked and have no other shelter than a small wretched cabin, which gives no protection against the severity of the weather and which they share with poultry. When we passed by the miserable cabins . . . those inside prostrated themselves at our feet, and with their faces against the ground, chanted long prayers for our success.

The invaders reached a hill outside Killala just as the sun was setting and found their way barred by a force of 80 regular soldiers and yeomanry, who evacuated the position as the French approached and re-formed in a side street. From here they opened fire on Father O'Kane as he galloped into the town and shot dead one of the yeomanry, drawing the first blood of the campaign. Sarrazin now ordered an advance with the bayonet, before which the defenders fled along the road to Ballina or into the grounds of Killala Castle, residence of Bishop James Stock, which was rapidly captured. The Castle made a fine headquarters and the green flag symbolising Irish independence, which Humbert had brought with him, was run up on the episcopal flagpole, while, back at the harbour with the willing help of the locals, the unloading of stores and guns went on throughout the night.

Humbert had no intention of idling away his first few precious hours ashore. Early in the morning of Friday 25 August 1798 he sent General Sarrazin with a reconnaissance patrol of 150 men towards the town of Ballina, eight miles [13 km] due south of Killala, and that evening 500 of his men set out to capture it by a night attack. The English were holding their own until a sudden attack by the Irish from their flank caused them to fall back and before morning the whole force had evacuated Ballina and withdrawn a further ten miles [16 km] to the south.

Soon after their arrival the French had put up well-drafted posters which eloquently advanced the case for a Franco-Irish alliance:

IRISHMEN
You have not forgot Bantry Bay. You know what efforts France has made to assist you.

Her affection for you, her desire of avenging your wrongs and assuring your independence, can never be impaired.

After several unsuccessful attempts, behold at last Frenchmen arrived amongst you . . .

Brave Irishmen, our cause is common. Like you we abhor the avaricious and bloodthirsty policy of an oppressive government. Like you we hold as indefeasible the right of all nations to liberty . . .

Let us unite then and march to glory.

Within 24 hours 1000 men had flocked to the French colours and new contingents arrived in Killala every hour, sometimes led by their parish priests. While the imprisoned bishop watched disapprovingly the recruits were issued with French uniforms and muskets and at once set to drill and weapon-training.

Saturday 24 August was spent in planning the advance on Castlebar, 16 miles [26 km] south of Ballina, but longer by the two connecting roads, one excellent and much used, the other little more than a mountain track in places. At four o'clock on the afternoon of Sunday 26 August 1798 Humbert set out eastwards, amid the cheers of the population, with 800 French soldiers and 1500 Irish auxiliaries led by 100 mounted French dragoons, as if making for the obvious route to Castlebar, through Foxford. Only when darkness had fallen did he swing west towards Crossmolina and take his little army along the rough, narrow road leading up into the mountains, their way soon lit by brilliant flashes of lightning, accompanied however by a blinding deluge of rain. The road proved too difficult for the horses pulling the guns and the animals were left behind, willing volunteers heaving the unwieldy cannon by hand for the rest of the journey.

The English commander in Castlebar, Major General John [later Lord] Hely-Hutchinson, commonly known as General Hutchinson, had, after arriving there on Saturday, prepared a strong defensive position at Sion

Hill, a mile outside the town. He had, he was confident, an overwhelming superiority in numbers, with 500 infantry and 1500 cavalry under his command, plus those who had just arrived from Dublin under General Lake, and, he believed, up-to-the-minute intelligence about his enemy's movements. Not until 5 am on the morning of Monday 27 August 1798 did a breathless farmer stumble into his headquarters with the news that the invaders were coming by the mountain road through Barnageeha. Humbert's feint had succeeded brilliantly, but the English reacted rapidly and within an hour most of the garrison, and 12 pieces of artillery, were safely deployed on Sion Hill, commanding the ground for 1000 yards [900 m] ahead.

All seemed set for a classic set-piece battle between a small, untrained, exhausted, under-gunned force, and a far larger, comfortably entrenched, professional army with ample artillery, but after a preliminary action during the first half hour Humbert realised that the conventional formations, in close column, he had so far employed could never succeed against such concentrated cannon fire. He now changed his tactics, the French units being redeployed in open ranks which stretched beyond both enemy flanks and began to move forward by stages, sheltering wherever they could. The sight of their remorselessly advancing bayonets finally unnerved the English gunners, and that most potent of emotions, panic, seized the English forces, until, as one disgusted English resident recorded, 'like a dam bursting its banks, a mixture of soldiers of all kinds rushed in at every avenue'. By noon it was all over. In all, 186 Frenchmen had been killed or wounded; an unknown number of Irish; and 400 English, or Irish loyalists, with another 200 taken prisoner. The French had captured 12 pieces of artillery and vast numbers of muskets and other stores, sufficient to equip a whole new army. Above all, 'the races of Castlebar', as the disorderly flight was rapidly nicknamed, had inflicted a devastating blow on English military prestige, for most of the fugitives did not stop till they reached Tuam, 30 miles [48 km] away, and some even pressed on a further 30 miles to Athlone, beyond the River Shannon.

French and Irish flags were now hoisted in Castlebar, and a Tree of Liberty planted in the public square. Here on 31 August Humbert formally proclaimed the formation of a provisional republican government, with a local man, assisted by 12 nominated members, as its president.

The recently appointed viceroy and English Commander-in-Chief in Ireland, Lord (Charles) Cornwallis, was at Kilbeggan, 60 miles [100 km] from Dublin, when on 29 August 1798 a message arrived recounting the disaster at Castlebar the previous day. Cornwallis was under no illusions about the need to stamp out the rebellion before it could spread and on 3 September the movements designed to encircle the French forces began. General Lake, with 14,000 men, and General Taylor, with 2500, were sent to bar their way eastward and posted at Frenchpark, 32 miles [51 km] from Castlebar. General Nugent, with 1000 troops, started to move south to Sligo, to the north-east of County Mayo, and Cornwallis himself advanced with another 15,000 to Hollymount, 13 miles [21 km] due south of the French headquarters.

Humbert, on 3 September, abandoned Castlebar for fear of being trapped there and set off north towards Sligo, having ordered the garrisons he had left at Killala and Ballina to join him on the way. His strategy depended on several thousand Irish assembling to join him in the area of Longford, in the centre of Ireland, after which he planned to advance on Dublin. Morale among his men, previously very high, now began to sag as the hoped-for reinforcements failed to arrive from France and the population as a whole, though sympathetic, failed to rise in their support. The summer weather now gave way to cold and persistent rain and though Humbert's advance guard successfully beat off an attack by General Nugent's reconnoitring cavalry, at Tubbercurry, 26 miles [42 km] north-east of Castlebar, the Franco-Irish alliance was already showing signs of strain. Humbert's own second-in-command, General Sarrazin, recorded in his later *Memoirs* the two aides' mutual disillusionment. 'During our stay at Castlebar,' he wrote, 'we were enabled to realise the uselessness of expecting any really effective cooperation from the inhabitants, who appeared to be much disappointed at the small number of our expeditionary force.'

Another, minor, French victory followed, at Carrignagat, half a mile [800 m] from Collooney, seven miles [11 km] due south of Sligo. This battle, too, ended in a disorderly rout, from which Humbert emerged richer by 100 English prisoners and further guns and muskets at a cost on each side of about 60 killed and wounded.

But nemesis was approaching. Humbert the victorious was becoming Humbert the hunted, as the dumping of seven captured cannon, which were impeding his movements, demonstrated. His only real hope now lay in the disaffected areas of County Longford and its neighbour, Westmeath, but risings in both areas, around 4 September, had already been put down, and Humbert's army, consisting now of about 800 French soldiers and 1500 Irish, had no real objective when, on Saturday 8 September 1798, it set out southwards from Cloone in County Leitrim, about 14 miles [22 km] north of Longford. Their strength had been sapped by a curious mischance, the man responsible for guarding the wagon chains having forgotten where he had hidden them, so that eventually much of the ammunition was abandoned, and morale was low, as one of Humbert's own captains observed:

Our soldiers, extremely fatigued and much depressed by the news of the enormous enemy force dogging and surrounding them, had now so neglected order in their march that the army formed a queue more than a league [3 miles; 5 km] long.

A thoroughly confused situation now developed, for, with Cornwallis's forces gathering for the kill, Humbert, on Sunday 9 September 1798, began digging in on a hill called Shanmullagh, overlooking the village of Ballinamuck, eight miles [13 km] north-east of Longford. While he was doing so a party of English dragoons arrived shouting, 'Do not fire, my friends, everything is settled!' They had, it later appeared, overtaken the French rearguard under General Sarrazin, who had surrendered on behalf of the troops he commanded, leaving the dragoons under the impression that the whole army had capitulated. This unhappy misunderstanding ended in ill-feeling and bloodshed as the dragoons were taken prisoner and a brisk battle developed on the hillside. General Humbert, after bravely charging the enemy, was dragged from his horse and captured, but most of the French, regarding this as essentially an Anglo-Irish battle, surrendered after striking hardly a blow. Once they had thrown down their arms they found themselves treated honourably, even generously, as respected brothers-in-arms.

For the Irish it was different. Their allies seemed to have abandoned them, their enemies despised them as rebels, unprotected by the laws of war, and, with everything to lose, they fought heroically on, subjected to a withering fire of grape and canister shot from the English artillery on both their flanks as well as to a storm of musketry. A contemporary English newspaper admitted: 'The courage of the rebels was prodigious; they made a stubborn and desperate resistance.' Late in the battle, as the cavalry swept down over the slopes of Shanmullagh to cut down all those still able to stand, and spearing the wounded who lay on the ground, the cry went up, 'Long pikes to the front or Ireland is lost!' and lost the battle was. Its final stages lasted a mere half hour; the whole action, begun around 9 am, was over by noon.

The pursuit followed. One large group of fugitives, an eye-witness recorded, 'fled into a bog, the whole of which was soon surrounded by horse and foot, who never ceased [firing] while one was alive'. 'We pursued the rebels through the bog,' recorded one soldier in a letter, 'and the country was covered for miles around with their slain.' The main slaughter however was at Ballinamuck itself, as a visitor to the battlefield described:

There lay dead about 500; I went next day with many others to see them. How awful to see that heathy mountain covered with dead bodies, resembling at a distance flocks of sheep, for hundreds were naked and swelled with the weather.

The number of French casualties in the battle of Ballinamuck was negligible, though 844 were taken prisoner. Observers remarked on 'the nonchalance and merriment' of these captives and, after being transported in comfort by canal barges to Dublin, and welcomed by an English military band, they were repatriated. About 500 Irish were killed, another 100 taken prisoner on the spot and 1000 who escaped were rounded up later; about a fifth were ultimately sentenced to death, most of the rest being transported.

The last news to reach France from Ireland had been of Humbert's initial success. The main expedition intended to reinforce him was still bottled up in Brest but on 4 September a single small ship, the brig *Anacreon*, managed to slip out of Dunkirk, and on 16 September, those on board knowing nothing of the capitulation at Ballinamuck, 80 miles [130 km] away in County Longford a week before, it anchored off Iron Island, on the coast of Donegal, some 60 miles [144 km] as the crow flies, though much further by both sea or land, north-east of Killala. On board was another of the brave, romantic but ill-starred figures who abound in the story of Ireland, Napper Tandy, a former Dublin tradesman, aged around 50, who had convinced the French that 30,000 people would rise once he landed to lead them. When 'General' Tandy disembarked, however, he found himself largely ignored and, having learned of Humbert's defeat, defied the government, not very impressively, by hoisting a green flag and getting so drunk that he had to be carried back on board ship; the *Anacreon* then set off for Norway.

While the *Anacreon* was on passage from Dunkirk to Donegal news reached the few French officers and the larger number of Irish rebels still garrisoning Killala and Ballina of Humbert's defeat on 9 September. They bravely resolved to fight on, though Ballina was evacuated and they fell back on Killala to await Lord Portarlington's avenging army, now advancing from Sligo. Its progress was marked, as Bishop Stock, still a prisoner in his own palace, recorded by 'a train of fire . . . flaming up from the houses of unfortunate peasants', but the French refused to desert their allies and, as one of the bishop's household observed, 'rallied the Irish troops and headed them to meet our army' when the final advance from Ballina began. Knowing what had happened after Ballinamuck the Irish fought desperately, their line of retreat back towards Killala being known ever after as 'the pathway of slaughter'. But by three o'clock in the afternoon of Sunday 23 September 1798 the town, defended by around 800 men, was encircled by at least 3000, and before long the attackers had forced their way into the streets and begun what soon became a massacre. A series of trials and hangings followed, along with celebrations by the victors. 'The week that followed the battle,' the bishop himself admitted, 'was employed in courts martial in the morning and most crowded dinners at the castle in the evening.'

After his defeat at Ballinamuck on 8 September General Humbert had been able to send a brief despatch to the Directory in Paris: 'After having made the arms of the French republic triumph during my stay in Ireland, I have been obliged to submit to a superior force of 30,000 troops.' This admirably concise message was still on its way when, on Sunday 16 September 1798, General Hardy, thanks to the temporary absence of Admiral Lord Bridport in Torbay, was at last able to leave Brest, though his squadron was rapidly sighted by an English warship and on 23 September three ships of the line and three frigates set out in pursuit from Cawsand Bay near Plymouth. The French force, under Commodore Bompard, had 3000 troops on board, and consisted of a 74-gun ship of the line, recently renamed *Hoche*, seven frigates and a schooner.[*]

It was soon picked up, and thereafter shadowed, by Lord Bridport's frigates and Bompard was finally brought to battle near Tory Island off the coast of Donegal around 7 am on Friday 12 October 1798, in what became known as Warren's Action, after Rear-Admiral [later Admiral] Sir John Warren, in command on the British side. The English ships outclassed the French, and at 11 am, with 200 men already killed or wounded, the *Hoche* struck its colours; three of the French frigates were captured that afternoon.

Next day one which had escaped managed to send a boat ashore with 60 men but the local yeomanry prevented their landing; this was as close to an invasion as the expedition achieved. During the next three days three more frigates were captured, leaving only two vessels to return to France. The prisoners were put ashore in Ireland, among them Wolfe Tone, who on 19 November cut his throat in Dublin gaol while awaiting execution.

Not knowing that General Hardy's expedition, like Humbert's before it, had already failed, Commodore Savary, who had delivered Humbert's expedition to Killala, now sailed back there with reinforcements, amounting to 1090 troops, carried in three frigates and a corvette. Having left La Rochelle on 12 October 1798, the very day of Commodore Bompard's defeat, he appeared off Killala on the 27th to learn the bitter truth, but again displayed his ability by getting away, at the price of throwing guns, stores and ammunition overboard when chased by some British vessels.

The extent of popular support for the French invaders convinced the government in London that Ireland should be more closely linked to England. On 1 January 1801 the new United Kingdom of Great Britain and Ireland came into being. The Irish parliament was dissolved and the country henceforward, like Scotland, had its own Members at Westminster. A more fundamental, and potentially more valuable change, granting religious and civil equality to the Roman Catholics who formed three-quarters of the population, foundered on the opposition of George III, which led in turn to the resignation, on 5 February 1801, of the great prime minister who had kept Bonaparte at bay. A year later, a colleague, inaugurating a club in Pitt's honour, aptly described him as 'The pilot that weathered the storm'.

[*] Jones, *Failed*, p. 222. Marcus, Vol. II, p. 51, refers to 'eight frigates' and Sanderson, p.64, to nine.

21

A DITCH TO BE LEAPED

It is a ditch that shall be leaped when one is daring enough to try.

Napoleon Bonaparte on the English Channel, 16 November 1803

Fortunately for England, while Ireland had been in turmoil its most dangerous enemy had been preoccupied elsewhere. After sailing from Toulon in May 1798, Napoleon Bonaparte had suffered his first great defeat at the hands of England's rising hero, Nelson, at the Battle of the Nile in Aboukir Bay on Wednesday 1 August 1798, when the French lost eleven ships of the line and two frigates, Nelson's unremitting aim 'to take, sink, burn or destroy' the enemy wherever encountered, being brilliantly fulfilled. But the nation's relief proved short-lived. During April 1799 a new invasion alarm swept southern England as it was learned that a powerful new French fleet was assembling at Brest, though when it sailed its destination proved in fact to be the Mediterranean.

The king's sixty-second birthday, on 4 June, was made the occasion for parades of Volunteers all over the country, and George III himself took the salute at a great march-past in Hyde Park, genially suggesting when the Bloomsbury and Inns of Court Volunteers, composed mainly of lawyers, marched before him that they should be known as 'The Devil's Own.'[*]

On 9 October the Corsican ogre himself arrived back in France and a month later, on 9 November, a coup d'état on his behalf overthrew both the Directory and the French legislative assembly. On 18 December a new constitution entrusted the government of France to three Consuls; Napoleon became First Consul for ten years, with almost unlimited powers. In November 1800 Nelson, now Baron [later Viscount] Nelson of the Nile, arrived back in England and on 2 April 1801 scored another famous victory, over the Danish fleet, in the Battle of Copenhagen, the occasion when on receiving the order 'Discontinue the engagement', he put his telescope to his blind eye. The French still

[*] Wheeler and Broadley, Vol. I, p. 244. Hozier, II, p. 327, attributes this incident to a similar parade on 24 October 1803.

cherished hopes, however, of managing to evade, if they could not defeat, the Royal Navy and around the same date began to assemble a flotilla of transports, organised into 12 divisions between Flushing in Flanders and the Morbihan in Brittany, to land 30,000 troops on the south coast for an advance on London.

Nelson's response was to initiate an inshore blockade of the French coast, interspersed where possible with actual spoiling operations. One against Boulogne on 15 August had little success but reassured Nelson. 'The craft which I have seen,' he summed up, 'I do not think it possible to row to England; and sail they cannot . . . This boat business may be part of a great plan of invasion, but it can never be the only one.'

The danger could not, however, be ignored. 'Great preparations at Ostend,' he next reported. '[General] Augereau commands that part of the army. I hope to let him feel the bottom of the Goodwin Sands.' Nelson's next reconnaissance, with 30 sail, was of the approaches to Flushing, which he thought the most likely port of departure. The enemy vessels were visible across the low-lying maze of offshore shoals and hazardous narrow channels which protected the port, but Nelson, daring not foolhardy, refused to attempt an attack, to the disappointment of the officer blockading the area. 'I cannot but admire Captain Owen's zeal in his anxious desire to get at the enemy,' the admiral noted, 'but I am afraid it has made him [in his mind] overleap sandbanks and tides.' Nelson recommended that the gallant captain should withdraw to Margate Roads if forced by adverse weather, leaving only a few small cutters to keep watch. Nelson himself remained in the Downs, off Deal, suffering, as he always did, from seasickness, and pleading to be allowed to go ashore. St Vincent, however, refused permission. 'The public mind is so much tranquillized by your being at your post,' the First Lord told the great admiral, '[that] it is extremely desirable that you should continue there.'

In October preliminary terms for ending the war with France were agreed, followed on 27 March 1802 by the Treaty of Amiens, under which fighting ceased, with a general restoration of captured territories to their former owners. Few people in England really believed, however, that Bonaparte would remain content with such a settlement and soon French preparations for war were obvious, with a large shipbuilding programme which, during 1804, would raise the French total of ships of the line from 43 to 66. On 8 March 1803 King George III formally drew Parliament's attention to the threatening developments now in progress in the French and Dutch ports and mobilised the militia. On the 13th, during a public audience at the Tuileries the French leader rudely accosted the British ambassador. 'So,' he remarked, 'you are determined to go to war.' 'The English,' he then informed nearby guests, 'are bent on war, but they are the first to draw the sword, I shall be the last to put it back into the scabbard.'

England did indeed draw the sword first, declaring war on 17 May 1803, and the two and a half years that followed marked the climax of the confrontation between England and France which had so often dominated her diplomatic and defence policy. France now possessed an even more formidable, and hardly less absolutist, leader than Louis XIV. Bonaparte, after becoming First Consul for life in August 1802, was declared emperor by the French senate on 18 May 1804, subsequently being crowned by the pope. To his subjects he was now 'Napoleon' or 'The Emperor'. On the same day William Pitt, who had been re-appointed prime minister on 10 May, took his seat, after re-election, in Parliament. Britain versus France was henceforward to be Pitt, as well as Nelson, versus Napoleon.

The whole effort of the French state was now directed towards the planned invasion. A final French victory required a successful invasion and Napoleon put his faith in a short sea crossing, rather than in diversionary feints or landings in more distant parts of the British Isles. He favoured an immensely strong first wave, landing simultaneously, and having once got his 150,000 men ashore believed that he could be in London within five days. The indispensable preliminary was to evade the Royal Navy. 'Let us be masters of the Channel for six hours and we are masters of the world,' he wrote on 2 July 1804, and on 20 July he arrived at the headquarters of the proudly-named Grand Army at Boulogne to direct the invasion, now scheduled for August, in person.

Napoleon's original plan, in 1803 and 1804, was for those of his transports which were oar-powered to cross the Channel while a sudden calm left the sails of the British warships flapping uselessly on their yards or perhaps after a storm had driven the blockading British warships from their station. By this means he could, he believed, in his own phrase 'leap the ditch' fast enough to escape interception and the massed firepower of the British fleet. 'Celerity,' he observed, in a memorable epigram, 'is better than artillery.'

Although he was counting on favourable weather conditions and speed to enable his armada of small landing craft to evade the Royal Navy, Napoleon also intended that many of them should be self-defending and all four main types which he now ordered were expected to carry some form of armament. The largest were the 'prams', or *prames*, resembling large sailing barges, 100 ft [30 m] in length and 25 [7.6 m] in the beam, and requiring a crew of 38. They were able to carry 120 soldiers and were armed with twelve 14-pounder [6.4-kg] guns. Their cost was put at 70,000 frances, ie. £2,800. Next in size were the armed longboats (*chaloupe cannonière*), priced at half this amount, rigged like the conventional brig, 70 to 80 ft [21-24 m] in length, manned by 22 sailors, and able to carry 130 men, plus three 24-pounders [11-kg] and a six- to eight-inch [15-20-cm] howitzer. Then, primarily for horse and artillery transport and the men attending them, came the gunboats or *bateaux cannonières*, three-masted and resembling a lugger or fishing smack. A 24-pounder [11-kg] gun protected the bow and a howitzer or field gun the stern; they could carry, for a cost of 18,000 to 23,000 francs [£720–£920], around 100 personnel, and a crew of six, plus horses which would be hoisted in or out through a movable roof.

Most of the troops were to be transported in pinnaces (*pinasses*), relatively cheap at 8–9000 francs (£320–£360), 60 ft [18 m] by ten [3 m], and with a crew of five sailors. They would be propelled either by lug-sails, small square sails set obliquely to the mast, or by oars, manned by the 55 soldiers on board. Each pinnace also carried two small howitzers or an eight-inch [20-cm] howitzer.

Although the vessels described above were all of sufficently shallow draught to get close inshore or even run aground on the beach, many smaller boats were needed to maintain contact between the larger craft and the shore. These brought Napoleon's total requirement up to more than 3000 vessels, able between them to carry 100,000 men, 3000 horses and 125 guns.

The first order setting the construction programme in motion was issued on 11 March 1803, three days before George III's warning to Parliament. A stream of instructions followed, as the original scheme was expanded and altered, and the original objective of August 1803 was rapidly amended to late September 1803 and then to 23 September 1804, followed by a further postponement till the end of January 1805. It emerged early on that few of the craft built for the earlier invasions, never launched, of 1798 and 1801, remained fit for sea, Only 27 of 193 gunboats which had survived at Dunkirk, Cherbourg and St Malo were considered still usable, though another 60 sloops, without guns and mainly in a very poor state, were tracked down at these ports and at Le Havre, Brest, Lorient and Rochefort. A wholesale requisitioning of small fishing vessels of from one to eight tons displacement was put in hand at Le Havre, Dieppe, Fécamp and Honfleur, which added another 650 bottoms to the total, and a major purchasing programme was undertaken.

To stir up anti-English feeling, and prove that an invasion *could* succeed, the Bayeux Tapestry was taken on tour and official dinners were held at which toasts were drunk, like that given by the Commissary, or port-superintendent of Calais, as reported in a London newspaper in July 1803:

To the men who shall execute the vast project of placing the French and English in their due and respective positions. To the barrack-master who shall issue the first billets at Dover. To the first review of the French troops in St James's Park.

Nothing was more calculated to evoke patriotic outbursts than the First Consul's own presence. Napoleon's tour of the invasion ports, which began at the end of June 1803, was, as it had been five years before, devoted to inspiring his subordinates with his own enthusiasm and weeding out the inefficient. At Antwerp he was furious to find that no new vessels had yet been laid down and that the harbour batteries were in a poor state. He personally fired a gun and had the shot weighed when it failed to reach the intended range; sure enough, it proved to be faulty. At Calais there was worse to come when a British frigate – previously captured from the French, which rubbed salt in the wound – sailed close inshore and drove two of the seven vessels moored there aground, before withdrawing safely. An Englishwoman living nearby learned of the resulting inquest, conducted by Napoleon himself:

> He . . . examined the pointing and elevation of the guns; but upon further enquiry, finding that the cartridges were only filled with the quantity of powder used in saluting, his rage and indignation became uncontrollable. He flew towards the unhappy subaltern, upbraided him with his ignorance and neglect, and, with his own hands tearing the epaulettes from his shoulders, told him he was no longer an officer in the French army.

The presence, in spite of the war, of English residents in France, as well as many silent but observant French enemies of the new regime, ensured that the government in London was kept well informed of what was happening in France and the Low Countries, and the preparations were soon far too extensive to be concealed. They affected not only more than 20 ports on the Channel coast but shipyards far up the Rhine and even the Seine, for Napoleon's fertile brain evolved a scheme for using Paris's two modest shipbuilding yards, where 60 vessels were laid down following orders given in June 1803, to be ready by 23 September. The whole vast effort was directed by the young engineer, Forfait, whom he had first employed in 1798, now elevated to the rank of Inspector-General of the fleet. Under him six committees, one for each of the naval districts, or *arrondissements maritimes*, consisting of a naval officer, an engineer and an *administrateur*, handled the day-to-day details of purchasing ships and placing orders for building new ones with private firms, their operations financed by a 20 million franc [£80,000] loan from the French banks, by gifts from individuals, companies, towns and *départements* which ultimately amounted to 30 million francs, and by donations from the occupied countries; the Italian Republic alone gave no less than 5 million francs to pay for two ships, one bearing its name.

A heavy charge on the budget was the improvement of existing harbours. Napoleon hoped to launch his whole force to sea simultaneously on a single tide and this made it essential to deepen and extend the principal ports involved. The most lasting results were seen at Antwerp, which became thereafter a continuing source of anxiety to England, for £2 million was spent on building a dockyard able to hold an enormous fleet, including 25 large warships. A comparable, if cheaper, effort was needed at Boulogne, where the tide ran sluggishly and even shallow-draught boats might be stranded on the mud at low tide. When not on the parade ground soldiers were employed as navvies, labouring up to their waists in mud to dig out a new artificial basin.

Apart from the difficulties imposed by nature there was always the risk of enemy interference. An essential part of the French plan was to assemble the ships to launch the attack in only a few ports, especially Boulogne. Two stone forts were built, one on either side of the main entrance to Boulogne, and two brigades of horse artillery patrolled the coast between Calais and Dunkirk, and between Dunkirk and the Scheldt, to protect any vessels which ran aground and engage any British ships coming within range. Finally 60,000 men were employed in coastal patrols, but as they made for the nearest harbour at the first sign of trouble, the progress of the various detachments towards their respective rendezvous was painfully slow; one group of seven boats took more than a fortnight to make the 80-mile [130-km] voyage from Cherbourg to Le Havre.

Napoleon was far more at home with the military side of the invasion than with the naval preparations. 'Recruiting is the first great business of the state,' Napoleon told his Chief of Staff, General Alexandre Berthier, a future Marshal of France, and general conscription was now introduced, rendering all French males liable to military service on attaining the age of 20, so that the French army was rapidly expanded to 480,000 men.

The organisational structure which Napoleon adopted was subsequently to be copied by other nations. The expeditionary force was divided into six corps, each commanded by a general of proven ability and the highest rank, that of Marshal of France. The corps were subdivided into divisions of infantry, but attached to them were field and heavy artillery, and two or three regiments of light cavalry, used for reconnaissance or flank protection. The 'medium weight' cavalry, i.e. the dragoons, and the heavy cavalry formed a separate striking force, under their own commander. The men chosen to head the new corps included several names soon to be famous, among them St Cyr, Soult and Ney, while the Commander-in-Chief under the First Consul himself was General Pierre Augereau, still only 46 in 1803, who had begun life as a common soldier before catching Napoleon's eye during the Italian campaign. Napoleon himself was even younger, celebrating his thirty-fourth birthday on 15 August 1803.

Each of the six corps was at first assigned its own camp, 150,000 men finally being spread in a vast arc from the Texel, in northern Holland, to the Pyrenees. There were camps at Utrecht, Ghent, St Omer, Compiègne, which contained the reserve, St Malo and Bayonne. The men's huts were well built and proper beds and blankets were provided. When not drilling, the troops were kept busy digging gardens to improve their own environment, and draining marshland for the benefit of the local population. Morale was high and health, even when summer had given way to winter, remarkably good. When the weather permitted there were swimming lessons, 'So that,' sceptical onlookers observed, 'some of them will be able to get back.'

The encampment at Boulogne, to which units were moved as they became ready for action, soon resembled a small city with its streets of temporary buildings, named after famous battles or successful generals, and additional property was purchased to serve as storehouses and to accommodate the huge number of officials and clerks required to manage its administration. A correspondent to the *Moniteur* reported later in the year the 'happy omen that in digging the ground for the First Consul's camp, a battle axe was found, which belonged to the Roman army, which invaded England', and that 'In pitching the First Consul's tent, also at Ambleteuse, medals of William the Conqueror were found'.

Even while in Paris on other business, as he was most of the time, Napoleon dashed off a stream of orders and instructions of all kinds, sometimes as many as six to the same recipient in a single day. He was constantly seeking information and issuing guidance on even the smallest details, as well as despatching trusted officers with extensive powers to report on the stage of preparation reached in the various areas. 'General Sebastiani . . . ,' ran one typical minute on 30 September 1803, to the Minister of War about the officer investigating the defensive artillery guarding Boulogne, 'must direct the practice of the four batteries every day, selecting some spot on the sea and there placing a white mark or other signal . . . He should take care that there are infantry cartridges for all the batteries and that the hussars are always supplied with these so as to be able to protect with their carbines any forts that are disabled.' The well-being of the ordinary soldier, especially as regards rations, was another constant preoccupation. It was probably Napoleon who later coined the famous *bon mot*, 'An army marches on its stomach.' Already in 1803 he was writing to Marshal Soult that, 'We shall have quite enough cold weather and other inconveniences to combat, without making things worse by bad food.'

To keep everyone around Boulogne on their toes he set up his advanced headquarters in a small chateau in the village of Pont-de-Bricques, then just outside Boulogne, which is 157 miles [251 km] from Paris. From here he made frequent forays into the port to keep everyone on their toes. A wooden hut was erected nearby from which he literally kept an eye on what was happening both around Boulogne and further afield. 'From the heights of Ambleteuse,' he wrote to the Second Consul on 16 November 1803, 'I have seen the coast of England . . . One could distinguish the houses and the bustle. It is a ditch that shall be leaped when one is daring enough to try.'

Information about the English defences had long since been compiled with the help of agents, posing as diplomatic attachés or businessmen, who had taken soundings in the English ports as well as collecting information about the armed forces. To help the French, in the main little better linguists than the English, to occupy and administer the country, a unit of 177 *Guides-Interprètes*, many of them Irishmen or former residents of England, was formed. The landing tables for each type of ship were constantly revised and perfected, and the embarkation of the troops practised so frequently that it was found that 100,000 men could be embarked within half an hour. The boats proved in practice able to hold more men than had been expected and the final size of the invasion army, according to the tables drawn up by Napoleon on 10 September 1803, amounted to 114,554, of whom 76,798 were infantry, 11,640 were cavalry, 3780 manned the artillery, 3780 the transport, and 17,467 were non-combatants, concerned with the medical, supply and similar services. 1760 women were to accompany the invasion, officially at least to serve in the canteens. The load for each type of vessel was also worked out in great detail. One category, for example, was expected to carry 100 fighting men and their equipment, three staff officers, eight surgeons, 27 extra muskets and pioneers' tools, 12,000 cartridges, 1200 rations of biscuit, 150 pints of brandy and four sheep.

Invasions traditionally provided a field-day for inventors and in 1803 two ideas were already in the air which seemed to offer the chance of challenging British supremacy at sea. Steam power had been used successfully to drive a tug on the Forth and Clyde canal in 1802, when it had towed two loaded vessels 19 miles [30 km] in six hours against a strong wind, but neither nation yet thought it worth developing for military purposes.

More immediately serious was the underwater boat devised by an American, Robert Fulton. As early as 1798 Admiral Bruix, then Minister of Marine, had ordered a commission to study this 'machine for the destruction of the enemy's marine forces', but Bruix had not taken up the idea. Napoleon's engineer protégé, Forfait, was more farsighted and provided Fulton with facilities for further experiments with his 'plunging boat', with encouragement, by September 1803, from Napoleon himself. One of the supervising officers reported enthusiastically that, 'M. Fulton . . . remained a whole hour under water with three of his companions . . . and . . . the boat made way at the rate of half a league [1.6 miles; 2.5 km] an hour by means contrived for that purpose.' The idea was too far ahead of its time to have as yet any practical value even though Fulton had also evolved what was ultimately to prove, in conjunction with the submarine, a lethally destructive combination, an underwater torpedo, of which more will be said later. The French government did not take up his offer to sell his underwater vessel outright for 40,000 francs [£1600] plus a fixed sum for every ship his torpedoes destroyed, and he ultimately offered the latter to the British Admiralty instead.

Thanks to the building programme and other reforms of the First Lord of the Admiralty, Lord St Vincent, England entered the second war with revolutionary France, in May 1803, with a fleet far more powerful than ten years before and the early months of the year saw a speeding up of activity. 'Every movement from the Admiralty . . . ,' *The Times* reported on 11 March, 'gives note of dreadful preparations . . . Ten additional sail of the line are ordered to be immediately commissioned.' Next day brought further encouraging news. 'Six line-of-battle ships, in addition to those we mentioned in yesterday's paper, have been ordered into commission . . . In every department of government the utmost alacrity continues to manifest itself.'

The blacker side of the picture was the resumed activity of the press-gang, particularly at Portsmouth. 'It is with the utmost difficulty that people living on the Point can get a boat to take them to Gosport,' acknowledged the *Naval Chronicle* in March, 'the terror of a press gang having made such an impression on the minds of the watermen that ply the passage.' Even civilians who had barely set foot on a boat were rounded up. 'They also pressed landmen of all descriptions; and the town looked as if in a state of siege . . . One gang entered the Dock theatre and cleared the whole gallery except for women.'

The press-gang system was brutal and unfair, but it worked. The 32 ships of the line in commission early in 1803 had by 1 May been raised to 52 and by June to 60, and the familiar routines of blockade began the moment war was declared. That day, 18 May, Admiral Lord Nelson joined the *Victory* at Portsmouth and two days later set sail to take up his war station off Toulon. Admiral Lord Cornwallis had, the day before, 19 May, established himself with five ships of the line and supporting frigates outside Brest, and simultaneously Admiral Lord Keith had assumed command at the Nore of the Channel fleet, which was to watch the enemy coastline between Brest and the North Sea. One squadron, based at Leith or in the Humber, protected the left flank from a landing in Scotland or northern England. Another, based on Dungeness, Yarmouth and the Downs itself, kept a vigilant eye on the area between the Texel and Boulogne. The Admiralty now found an ideal appointment for its most notorious captain, William Bligh, formerly of the *Bounty*, on which he had provoked a mutiny in 1789. A brilliant navigator, he was now sent to prepare charts of the sandbanks off Flushing where the squadron sealing off the mouth of the Scheldt was to be based.

The navy, quietly confident in its professionalism, was always dubious of Bonaparte's ability to get within striking distance of England. 'I do not say the French cannot come,' the First Lord of the Admiralty, the Earl of St Vincent, told his colleagues in the Cabinet that summer in a famous statement, 'I only say they cannot come by sea.'*

Laymen remained apprehensive about the shallow-draught vessels Bonaparte was known to have assembled in vast numbers, a threat to which the government responded by arranging for a substantial fleet of luggers based on Deal to be equipped with 12- and 18-pounder guns, manned by 'hovellers', local small-boat men who worked as unofficial pilots. The professionals, however, remained dubious of the need for such vessels, believing the navy would intercept the enemy long before the invaders got anywhere near the shore, and St Vincent refused to divert resources to building what one admiral in the House of Commons contemptuously dismissed as a 'mosquito fleet'.

The threat of invasion led to a remarkable improvement in communications between London and the coast. Many inventors had suggested sending messages by displaying letters of the alphabet on sites in visual contact with each other, but the first practical system, using shutters within a wooden frame, was introduced by a Frenchman, Claude Chappe, whose *télégraphe* was enabling the French Ministry of Marine in Paris to keep in touch with various ports by 1793.†

Important orders, however, like the abortive attempt to prevent Hoche's expedition to Ireland sailing in December 1797, still went by road. The French system used a single horizontal arm, pivoted at the centre, with shorter arms at right angles to it and could, it was claimed in a descriptive leaflet published in London, 'convey a whole sentence 100 miles [160 km] in five minutes'. The outbreak of war with France in 1793 led to a revival of interest in the idea in England and in 1794 a series of signal stations was set up in Sussex, consisting of a wooden hut and ship's mast, 50 ft [15 m] high. Each was manned by a team of four, and two dragoons were attached to the station to carry messages to the local troop commanders. The system was, however, inferior to the French one, which could send a much wider range of messages far

* Alan and Veronica Palmer (eds), *A Dictionary of Historical Quotations* (Paladin, 1985) p. 232. Kightly, p. 189, attributes the remark to 'Admiral Lord Keith, speaking in Parliament'. Marcus, II, p. 229, correctly credits St Vincent but places it 'in the upper chamber'. Bryant, *Victory*, p. 85, does not say where it was made but amends it to 'by water'. I have failed to find any contribution by St Vincent to the Lords' debates in 1803.
† For an admirably detailed but concise history of the whole subject, see Geoffrey Wilson, *The Old Telegraph*, pp. 4-8, on which I have drawn heavily.

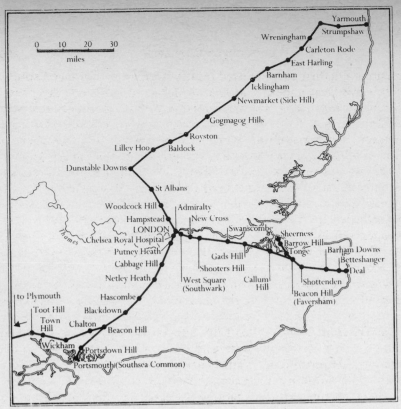

The Admiralty Shutter Telegraph

more quickly, and the Admiralty now began a series of experiments, on Wimbledon Common and Portsdown Hill, overlooking Portsmouth, which resulted in the production of a telegraph both more elaborate and more robust than its French predecessor. The Admiralty telegraph consisted of a network of stations, each of which possessed two tall frames erected side by side on top of a wooden cabin, each frame containing three shutters. Whole words were spelled out in abbreviated form and single letters or numbers stood for commonly used place names like 'Sheerness' and 'Nore' or essential words like 'Fog', 'Frigate' or 'French'. Eventually 64 stations were built at distances varying according to the contours, which dictated the line of sight, from four to ten miles [6-16 km] apart. Each was manned by a lieutenant, often past active duty, a midshipman and two 'foremastmen', or ordinary seamen, who undertook the heavy manual work of hauling the shutters up and down. The posting, though preferable to sea duty for those who did not enjoy being afloat, was no sinecure, for living conditions were cramped, with half the supporting hut earmarked as the operating room, leaving the rest to serve as living quarters and kitchen, and the 'glassmen' had to peer through their telescopes at five-minute intervals at the next station in the chain.

As the stations, which cost around £230 each to build and equip, were not movable, two were needed to send a signal in more than one direction. The first to be erected on the Admiralty roof faced south-east towards Deal, and the line, from which a spur ran off to Sheerness, was finished in January 1796. Another frame faced south-west towards Chelsea, the first in a line leading to Portsmouth Hill and Southsea Common, for Portsmouth, which was completed by December. A third, which split off from the Portsmouth line at Beacon Hill, above South Harting in Sussex, reached Plymouth around May 1806, though a plan to carry it on to Falmouth came to nothing. The final line ran in-land via Hampstead and St Albans to Dunstable Downs, before turning north-east for Yarmouth [i.e. Great Yarmouth] in Norfolk. This was opened in August 1808, enabling the Admiralty to keep in touch with all three main danger areas, the south-east, the south-west and East Anglia.

The speeding-up in communication, at least under satisfactory conditions of visibility, was remarkable. Instead of it taking several hours to bring news to London from Portsmouth, and two days or more for it to arrive from Plymouth to Falmouth, an average-length message could be passed between London and Portsmouth in 15 minutes, and, thanks to the junction at South Harting, the commanders at Portsmouth and Plymouth could keep in touch direct. One such signal, repeated by 20 intermediate stations, received an answer within 20 minutes.

Urban stations suffered from the universal smoke, but the real enemy everywhere was the English climate. In windy, or very cold, weather the shutters might stick, while the whole system was useless after dark or when fog, rain or cloud rendered visibility poor. A study made in 1817 found that on about 100 days a year very few stations were visible to their neighbours, on another 60 they could pass messages for part of the day and that for around 200 they could operate normally. 'The French are landing at Hythe' could reach London in eleven minutes.

Had the signal 'The French are landing' ever been sent in earnest the duty of responding would have fallen on the 40-year-old Field Marshal Frederick Augustus, 'the brave old Duke of York', still remembered for a famous campaign in which:

He had ten thousand men,
He marched them up to the top of the hill,
Then marched them down again.

On 25 August 1803 the Duke signed an official report in which he set out the number of troops he considered necessary to protect different parts of the country. Ireland, always a special case, was excluded; Scotland, he estimated, needed 13,000 men. He went on to list the number of men he considered necessary for the defence of each part of England: The Southern district: 55,000 men; the Eastern district: 30,000; the

Western district: 12,000; London and the Midlands: 10,000; the North-west district: 10,000; the South-west district: 8,000; Yorkshire: 6,000; the Northern district: 6,000; the Severn district: 2,000.

The Duke's scheme required 139,000 men; the army's official strength in 1803-4, according to the Army Estimates presented on 9 December 1803, was 129,000 regulars, plus 110,000 'embodied militia and fencible infantry', i.e. part-timers now called out for full-time service, and 310,000 Volunteers, to be mobilised when needed, excluding another 70,000 in Ireland. The Secretary of War, Charles Yorke, revealed what a bargain the Volunteers provided, costing no more than £730,000, little more than £2 a head. In response to Opposition criticism he conceded, however, that the Volunteers 'may not at the outset be capable of meeting a regular army in line of battle', though still 'eminently useful, by acting on the flanks and rear of the enemy; by making demonstrations, [and] by contributing, with their numbers, to increase to the eye of the enemy the magnitude of our regular forces.' How valuable the Volunteers would prove in action was much debated. At a meeting in Leicester on 1 August 1803, General the Earl of Moira [later Marquis of Hastings], Commander-in-Chief in Scotland, set out its members' role with all the authority of someone who had fought against just such an amateur army, of American colonists:

> It is not probable that it would ever be thought requisite to lead you in battalions against the enemy . . . I should imagine that the general under whom you serve would wish to detach you in small bodies, to hang upon the flanks and rear of the enemy, bidding you avail yourselves of every little bank or inequality of ground behind which you would cover yourselves, whilst your shot would do execution at its utmost range in the columns of the enemy . . . instructing you to retire whensover the enemy should advance in considerable strength against you . . . You must not think this is unworthy of your courage.

The best of the younger generation of commanders, Major-General John [from 1804 Sir John] Moore, preached a similar doctrine from his headquarters at Shorncliffe, favouring the use of harassing tactics even by regular troops. If the French were to live off the country, as they would be forced to do, they must, he pointed out, inevitably abandon their massed battlefield formations and thereby expose themselves to guerrilla-style attack. Moore rapidly became renowned as the advocate of light infantry, with tactics to match, and as the most famous trainer of troops the British army had ever possessed.

The army, if not the navy, believed, in General Moira's words, that it would be 'very feasible for the French to throw ashore five or six thousand men, upon some part of the coast not remote from London', and in trying to decide where this might be the government was fortunate to have the services of a French general, Charles Dumouriez, the only senior officer ever to plan the invasion and the defence of the same country. Dumouriez, born in Cambrai in 1739, had, as mentioned earlier, been commandant of Cherbourg under Louis XVI in 1778, and after the Revolution held a series of important posts before changing sides and, with the warm support of Nelson, being brought to England, probably in 1803. 'He is,' wrote Nelson to Lady Hamilton on 26 August 1803, 'a very clever man; and beats our generals out and out . . . Advise him not to make enemies, by showing he knows more than some of us.' The English military establishment in fact gave Dumouriez a warm welcome, and he was soon at work on a massive report on the defence of England against invasion. When completed, probably in 1805, it ran to 397 pages of manuscript, but Dumouriez was in close touch with the Commander-in-Chief and other generals and his opinions influenced their thinking from soon after his arrival.

Dumouriez was notably less overawed by Napoleon, whom he knew well and detested, than his contemporaries and highly sceptical of his invasion plan:

> It is absurd that a flotilla of from 1200 to 1500 small boats could cross the Channel in perfect order even in calm weather and never break its formation; but even if it did, then on the English coast it would have to fight another flotilla of rowing boats, backed up by blockships, land batteries and troops. Disorder would ensue and the vessels and frigates would catch the invading flotilla in the rear and smash it between two fires against the coast it was seeking to land on.

But, if the French should get ashore, Dumouriez rejected the 'fearful and ruinous measure' of 'driving' the country. The civilians must stay where they were while the army first held and then expelled the French:

> The whole defence should be divided in first and second lines, or in *stationary* divisions intended to dispute foot by foot the different points on the coast and *mobile* divisions meant to afford them immediate support . . .
>
> It would be found advisable to divide the whole army in divisions of 12,000 men, whereof at most an eighth should be cavalry, one half heavy infantry fighting stoutly in battalions and the remainder rangers, sharp-shooters and light infantry fighting irregularly in the French way . . . Each division must have eight field-guns, four howitzers, four mortars and two pieces of cannon per infantry battalion and two companies of mounted artillery to form the vanguards with the light infantry and the light cavalry . . . In a country so destitute of open plains and cut up by countless hedges . . . one must parcel out each of the five arms in small portions and amalga-

mate these.

The most valuable part of Dumouriez's analysis, valid whatever changes in tactics and technology occurred, was his almost mile-by-mile study of the coast, identifying potential landing areas. 'It does not appear,' he commented, 'that the French ever invade Scotland,' and he ruled it out, then dividing England into six 'military districts' and examining each in turn. About the most threatened area Dumouriez had no doubt:

> The most important military district is the sixth, comprising the counties of Oxford, Bucks, Herts, Essex, Berks, Middlesex, Hants, Surrey, Sussex and Kent . . . Here it is that the great defensive must come into play, for presumably it is here that the principal attack will be made: the capture of London is no doubt the chief object of the dreams of Bonaparte, as the sack of the metropolis which he has promised to his army is the great desire of the soldiers and the generals whom he has turned into brigands.

'The real danger,' summed up the renegade general, 'begins at the Humber (1) between the Trent and the Thames; (2) between the Thames and Beachy Head . . . The most suitable places for landing will be found on the east or south-east of England on the sandy and shingly beaches.'

Dumouriez's study looked at every beach and hill with a fresh, invader's eye, but he refused even to contemplate the loss of the capital:

> I will not speak of the particular defence of London, for I refuse to believe that an enemy could ever get near enough to the metropolis when the whole of England was up in arms; when patriotism was firing one of the bravest nations in Europe; and when that nation was fighting for all it held most dear and most sacred.

The British generals perhaps expressed themselves less flamboyantly but were equally confident. If Napoleon's legions landed in Kent General Moore's Light Brigade would struggle to contain him and if unsuccessful, would fall back, leaving the main forces in south-east England, under General Dundas, to take up the struggle. Dundas's tactics were later described by one of his then staff:

> It was his intention, if he should be beaten on the shore, to withdraw his troops, not in the direction of London, but throwing back his right and centre to retreat upon the intrenched camp at Dover. In that strong position he could have brought the enemy to bay, and gained time for the gathering of the strength of Britain around the metropolis. Or, if the general had found that Napoleon disregarded him, and was marching straight upon London, then Dundas would have sallied forth and pressed close upon the rear and right flank of

the enemy's columns. The direct road from Canterbury and the passage of the lower Medway were barred by the intrenched camp at Chatham. The French must have taken their routes by Maidstone, etc. through a more difficult country where their columns would have been delayed by the breaking up of the roads.

Meanwhile it was intended that the army in Sussex would have manned the line of the Downs – 'the great chain of chalk hills' – and that in Essex would have crossed, via Tilbury, to support Dundas 'or have hastened directly to London'. It was here, this authority believed, that the issue would finally be decided:

It was in London itself, or rather along the skirts of Greenwich, Southwark and Lambeth, that it was our business to fight the great battle to the uttermost, day after day, and night after night . . . What mattered the burning of some hundreds of houses when compared with the mighty stake which was at issue. Our best reliance was upon the numbers and the daring courage of Englishmen.

Napoleon had always stressed the importance of the moral factor in war and contemporaries were unanimous that a French invasion would have called forth an upsurge of patriotism and readiness for self-sacrifice which would have gone far to redress the superior quality of the enemy army. 'When I consider the number of men that we have in arms and that they are all Britons, I cannot be afraid,' declared that veteran of defeat, General Cornwallis. Charles James Fox, the Whig politician now turned Volunteer, who had recently visited France and admired Napoleon's libertarian ideas, was equally resolute. 'I believe,' he declared in the House. 'Bonaparte will not try . . . If he does he will be destroyed or at least [be] driven back into the sea.' The patriotic poets, also taking up the sword as well as the pen, had a field day. 'It will be a bloody tussle,' acknowledged the poet Volunteer Thomas Campbell, when reporting that his unit was ready to march at an hour's notice, 'but let us never think of outliving our liberty.' That least martial of Volunteers, William Wordsworth, produced a whole series of poems that autumn which, if of little literary merit, breathed the same spirit of defiance. *To the Men of Kent*, composed in October 1803, was typical:

No parleying now. In Britain is one breath;
We are all with you now from shore to shore:
Ye men of Kent, 'tis victory or death.

22

EXCELLENT AND EXTENSIVE LANDING

The landing on this part of the coast is extensive and everywhere excellent.

Lieut.-Colonel John Brown reporting on south Kent,

10 September 1804

Like most senior officers, neither Dumouriez nor the Commander-in-Chief, the Duke of York, had much faith in fixed defences of a permanent kind but the south-east, because of its special vulnerability, had always been regarded as a special case, and the Duke in his report of 1803 had mentioned a plan recently drawn up for strengthening the area by the use of what became known as Martello towers. Their name, and reputation, had originated back in February 1794, when HMS *Fortitude*, mounting 74 guns, and HMS *Juno*, mounting 32, had attacked a small square fortress on Mortella Point, Corsica.[*]

It had proved an extraordinarily difficult nut to crack, the two ships being beaten off with 60 casualties, and the little isolated tower had only been captured by a landing party after two days of heavy fighting and bombardment by four guns from almost point-blank range. The British officers concerned, who included the future General Sir John Moore and General Sir David Dundas, and the future Admiral Sir John Jervis, had been astonished at the extraordinary resistance the 38-man garrison, with their four guns, had been able to put up. On their return to England a hinged wooden model of the tower was prepared and Jervis, now naval Commander-in-Chief, declared: 'I hope to see such works erected . . . on every part of the coast likely for an enemy to make a descent on.'

It was not until the summer of 1803 that a young Royal Engineers officer, Captain W.H. Ford, was able to gain support from his superior, Brigadier-General William Twiss, Commanding Engineer of the Southern District, for the scheme he had put forward for a chain of low, square towers along the Kent and Sussex coast, close enough together to provide mutual supporting fire, quick to build, and costing

---

[*] The alternative derivation of the name is from 'Torre da Martello', a watch-tower against pirates where the alarm was given by striking a bell with a hammer. Conceivably this is how Mortella Point acquired its name.

less, he estimated, than £3000 each. The towers would, he pointed out, require only a small garrison and in peacetime the guns could be stored inside the building which, once sealed up, would require little maintenance.

The Martello tower was just the type of concept intelligible and attractive to the layman and in a speech on 9 December 1803 the Opposition spokesman, William Windham, made a fervent plea for a full-scale building programme 'from the northernmost point of the coast of Suffolk . . . to a part of the coast of Essex, where a naval defence . . . might be supposed to begin'. The towers might not, he conceded, 'stop the disembarkation of infantry' but 'with artillery and horses . . . would not the slaughter be immense . . . ?'

In spite of the imminent danger of invasion the governmental and military machine remained slow-moving, until on 10 May 1804 William Pitt replaced the feeble Addington as prime minister. Pitt, though only 44, was in poor health, plagued by gout and suffering, in a friend's words, from 'excessive weakness and a total debility of disgestion', but his spirit was unimpaired. Soon after his return to Downing Street he scrapped the modest plan prepared under his predecessor, for the construction of a mere ten to thirteen coastal defence works, at a total cost of £57,000, and ordered a fresh survey to be undertaken. This was carried out by General Twiss, who on 3 September 1804 wrote to the Inspector-General of Fortifications setting out his conclusions and recommending the construction of 58 towers of the kind advocated by Captain Ford, 'placing them [sic] within five or six hundred yards [410-550 m] of each other, in the most advantageous landing places'.

Pitt, most unusually for a politician, thought the army was still understating its requirements, and asked the engineer to consider the whole matter afresh. 'Expense out of the question,' [i.e. no object] noted Twiss on 7 September 1804. 'Revise my earlier report . . . Double expense . . . Thirty million bricks.'

Here was an engineer officer's dream, to be given *carte blanche* in drawing up a scheme for fortifications, and Twiss, an able and imaginative officer, though, at 59, a martyr to rheumatism – 'old age creeps fast upon me', he wrote to a colleague from Dover – took to his horse again and, he reported, 're-examined the coast between Beachy Head and Dover, distant by the nearest road about 66 miles [106 km], but having a shore of greater length by the point of Dungeness projecting so far into the sea'. He now recommended new works at 88 sites, plus the rebuilding of existing defences at Sandgate; the total cost had now risen to £221,000. On 4 October his committee of engineers produced the first outline design and drawings for 'A Bomb Proof Tower, for the defence of the coast', with a summary of the specification:

The interior circle of the tower has a diameter of 26 feet [7.9 m] and the area at the top is calculated to receive one 24-pounder [11-kg] gun, and two carronades of the same calibre, all mounted on traversing platforms, to fire over a high parapet, the crest of which is about 33 feet [10 m] above the foundation. The ground floor to contain a powder magazine and cistern with room for provisions, fuel and other stores. The middle floor to lodge a garrison of one officer and 24 men, having an entrance placed ten feet [3 m] above the exterior ground.

On Sunday 21 October 1804 an important conference was held at Rochester, attended by the Prime Minister himself, the Duke of York, General Sir David Dundas, General Officer Commanding Southern District, the Quarter-Master-General, General Twiss, and some other officers. One of the latter opposed the scheme, apparently fearing it might jeopardise his own pet project for a defensive canal, to be described in a moment, but the meeting was otherwise unanimously in favour of the tower-building scheme, accepting the proposed design and fixing the number of towers at 81, at an estimated total cost of £244,000. It was agreed that they should be circular, not square, not to make them stronger but to save money, and the armament was, it was decided, to consist of one 18-pounder [8.2 kg] gun and two short-barrelled, large-bore pieces known as carronades. It was also planned to build some other new fortifications, to be described later.

The Martello tower scheme was by far the biggest fortifications building programme the Board of Ordnance had ever undertaken and the largest seen in Great Britain since Henry VIII had created his great chain of coastal fortresses in the 1540s.[*]

In spite of the Prime Minister's personal support, however, the pace of construction proved leisurely and General Twiss, in his weekly progress report to the Board of Ordnance, on 9 November 1804 confessed: 'I can only state that they are not begun and from the lateness of the season, and the few materials collected, my opinion is that it will not be proper to begin them until the spring.' About the areas where the towers were required no disagreement existed, the new works being primarily designed to cover vulnerable beaches rather than harbours, for, a few short stretches apart, the south-east coast offered almost everywhere 'rock-free shallow water', ideal for the shallow-draught boats Bonaparte was known to be building in vast numbers.

The first priority was clearly to protect the coastline, approximately 55 miles [88 km] long, between Folkestone and Eastbourne, but instead of requisitioning the necessary sites the Board of Ordnance preferred to take long leases; that at Bulverthythe, between Hastings and Bexhill for example, was acquired for 99 years at a rent of £7 a year. The amount of land required, to allow for associated buildings, could

---

[*] See *Defending the Island*, pp. 380-1.

be considerable, in at least one case amounting to almost four acres [1.6 hectares]. At least 500,000 bricks were required for each south-coast tower, for the larger version later built on the east coast 700,000. An initial order for two and a half million had been placed even before the conference of 21 October and accounts still exist for 13,450,000, which cost the Board of Ordnance £37,450. This was, of course, only the start of the expense, for the bricks were placed in 'hot lime mortar', a mixture of lime, ash and hot tallow which set as hard as iron, and the outer walls were clad in stucco, tests being conducted at Woolwich by the Royal Engineers until the perfect combination, which caused cannon balls to bounce off the walls, was achieved. The walls were also extremely thick. The towers were slightly elliptical in plan, with the thicker shell towards the seaward side, so that it tapered from about 13 ft [4 m] at the base, to about six ft [1.8 m] at the top on the side nearest the sea and five ft [1.5 m] towards the land. The interior diameter at ground level was around 48 ft [14.6 m], narrowing to 45 ft [13.7 m] at first floor level, and 40 ft [12.2 m] on the roof. The overall height from ground to the edge of the parapet was 33 ft [10 m]. The flat roof, forming the gun platform, was covered with lead and surrounded by a parapet six feet [1.8m] high and equally thick. Everything about the Martello towers was solid and built to last, which helps to explain why so many have survived.

The real test was how effective they would have proved in action and here, too, the evidence suggests they would have acquitted themselves very well. On the seaward side each tower presented an unbroken surface and even on the other side no access existed at ground level, the towers being entered by a single door on the landward side 20 ft [6 m] from the ground, reached by a removable wooden ladder. Martello towers in particularly exposed positions were further strengthened by the provision of a dry ditch, crossed only by a drawbridge, the ditch being 40 ft [12 m] wide, and 15 or 20 feet [4.6-6.1 m] deep.

Outside, distributed along flat beaches at 600-yard [550-m] intervals, the Martello towers had the appearance of a row of sand-pies turned out of a child's toy bucket, or of upturned flower-pots, but such homely comparisons faded once inside, where, like Henry VIII's castles, they had the feel of a stationary warship. At ground level, or below it, were the magazine, the fuel and other stores and the water supply, either in a large cistern or from a specially dug well. On the first floor were a further store and the living quarters, with a separate room for the officer in charge, about half the total floor space being used for the 24 men who cooked, ate, lived and slept here. The gun on the roof could be worked by only two while the rest stayed under cover, hoisting up the ammunition and only moving to the roof to fight off a land assault. The towers, though intended to provide mutual support, were equipped to withstand a long siege, and each contained

100 round shot, 20 case and grape shot, 280 miscellaneous types of shell, half a ton of powder and 1 lb [0.45 kg] of slow match.

Building the Martello towers was an enormous undertaking, carried out by contractors. (The principal one, William Hobson, who had built St Luke's Hospital, was a Quaker, but did not let his pacifist views interfere with business.) Orders for bricks were placed all over the southern counties via an Old Bond Street firm of builders' merchants. 'Five hundred men are now employed at Grays in Essex making bricks for the purpose,' reported one newspaper in June 1808. The final cost was around £7000 per tower, double the estimate, but in return the nation had gained a tremendous increase in its security. An enemy ship entering Pevensey Bay would now be exposed to the simultaneous fire of 15 24-pounder [11-kg] guns from their respective towers, this weapon having replaced the three lighter cannon previously proposed. Their round shot could hole an enemy ship a long way offshore, while as the troops disembarked they would meet a hail of case and grapeshot or, the sole real innovation of the period, a storm of shrapnel, named after its inventor, Major Henry Shrapnel. (While previous anti-personnel shells had been exploded at a fixed distance, the bursting point of shrapnel shells was fixed by one of four fuses set for different intervals of time.) The artilleryman's 'Bible', The *Bombardier and Pocket Gunner*, re-issued in 1804, exhorted him to make every round tell. 'Your last discharges are the most destructive,' it counselled. 'They may perhaps be your salvation and crown you with glory.'

Work on the south-coast chain of towers began in the spring of 1805. By the summer of 1806 only six were finished, but the whole line was completed during 1808. By then, so sound had the basic design proved, it had been decided to protect the east coast in the same way, a proposal not implemented until 1809. This second line, extending from near Clacton, at the mouth of the Thames estuary, to Slaghden near Aldeburgh on the coast of mid-Suffolk, where it culminated in a 'one-off' fort of quatrefoil shape, rather resembling Walmer Castle, added 29 to the south-coast total of 74, though the east-coast group were slightly larger and more strongly armed than the original series. By the time the programme was completed, in 1812, some 40 Martello towers were also to be found in Ireland, protecting Belfast, Dublin, Cork, Bantry Bay and other vulnerable points.

The place most likely to attract an invader was still Dover, where the harbour gave on to a valley leading straight inland. Dover was protected to the east by Dover Castle, where a series of major improvements had been undertaken since 1794, but hitherto relatively little attention had been given to the Western Heights, where batteries, protected by earthworks, had first been erected during the invasion scare of 1779. General Twiss had recommended the construction there of 'a respectable fortress' and the Board of Ordnance had acquired two sites, totalling 33 acres [13.4 hectares], in the area as long ago as 1781. Work did not actually begin, however, until 1804.

Three separate but associated projects were involved. The first was the Drop Redoubt, a detached fort close to a sharp descent from the cliffs, which was built between 1804 and 1808. It was primarily designed to serve as a base from which troops could sally out and attack enemy infantry, though some traversing guns, on metal runners, which could fire in various directions, were also installed. The Drop Redoubt was linked by a deep ditch both with the cliff edge, which an enemy might conceivably have scaled, and the second, and much larger, fort now begun, the Citadel, which was still unfinished when the war with France ended. Like the Drop Redoubt the Citadel was surrounded by deep ditches lined with flint and brick, protected in turn by caponniers. The third part of the Western Heights scheme was the building of the Grand Shaft barracks, housing around 60 officers and 1300 NCOs and men, to engage in local defence. The barracks took their name from what General Twiss, who first proposed it in 1804, described as 'a shaft with triple staircase . . . useful in sending reinforcements to troops employed in the defence of the beach and town or in affording them a secure retreat'. Hitherto troops hurrying down towards the beaches and harbour, or climbing wearily up to man the new defences on the Western Heights, had been obliged to use chalk tracks, which in bad weather could be dangerously slippery. Twiss's idea was to build a staircase to the beach from the top of the cliff above. Begun in 1806, it took three years to complete, but was finished for £700 less than the £4000 estimate and proved spacious enough for a man to ride up on horseback for a bet, and so solidly built that it can still be climbed today.*

Like so much nineteenth-century military architecture the Grand Shaft was aesthetically pleasing and beautifully built, as well as highly functional. The three staircases, built of Purbeck limestone, wind clockwise round the single central light and ventilation well, as the 26-ft [8-m] shaft plunges 140 ft [42 m] through the Kentish chalk and clay. Several thousand men, using all three staircases simultaneously, could have clattered down their 200 steps to pour out into what is now Snargate Street within a very few minutes.

The most substantial single project of all those undertaken during the Napoleonic wars was built with the least discussion and delay. Its chief originator was another of the exceptionally able officers specialising in defence engineering whom the invasion danger had brought to eminence, Lieut.-Colonel John Brown, who at 48 had, as his brother later testified, 'made himself by his merit, without any other funds or

* i.e. in September 1989 when I visited it and all the other Dover sites mentioned in this chapter, except the Citadel, which is now a prison.

interest'. A 'thin, slender man, most sober in living both in eating and drinking,' according to his brother, Brown, a dedicated soldier and, reluctantly, a life-long bachelor, had in August 1804 toured the north-eastern approaches to London with the Duke of York and on his suggestion dams had been built in the Lea Valley to flood it against an advancing enemy. On 10 September 1804, after a survey of the south Kent coast, he produced an even more alarming assessment of the danger there and especially of the exposed Dungeness peninsula, much of which was occupied by Romney Marsh:

> The landing on this part of the coast is extensive and everywhere excellent. And . . . the present batteries are placed at a considerable distance from each other and could make little or no resistance after the enemy had gained the beach.

Brown's solution to this old problem was a novel one, the building of a canal as a 'wet ditch' to cut off the most vulnerable end of the peninsula. The waterway should, he suggested, run initially from Shorncliffe battery behind Sandgate, about two miles [3.2 km] west of Folkestone harbour, along the edge of Romney Marsh to Hythe and West Hythe, where it would be commanded by the high ground at Lympne, now well inland though the Romans had once had a harbour there. From here it could easily be lengthened to protect the whole dangerous Dungeness 'triangle':

> This canal or cut should be sixty feet [18 m] wide at top, forty [12 m] at bottom and nine feet [2.7 m] deep, which would always ensure seven to eight feet [2.1-2.4 m] of water and, being everywhere within musket shot of the [Lympne] Heights, under such circumstances it might be deemed impregnable. This would only form part of a greater plan which might be advantageously extended on the same side along the rear of Romney Marsh by Appledore to join the Rother above Boonsbridge.

The proposal instantly gained powerful support. The Commander-in-Chief of the Southern District, General Sir David Dundas, immediately endorsed it, the Commander-in-Chief agreed, and obtained the prime minister's enthusiastic backing for the scheme even before it had been seen and approved, on 27 September, by his political chief, the Earl of Camden [formerly Sir John Pratt], Secretary of State for War. Cost was not even mentioned but Dundas was positively encouraged to spend money on an even more massive scale than the original proposal had required:

> The great work proposed of cutting a canal between the Rother and the beach in Hithe [sic] Bay for the purpose of separating an enemy landed upon the coast of Romney Marsh from the interior of the country is approved by H.M. Government, and I am now to sanc-

tion its being immediately undertaken under your authority, and, further, to desire that this canal in its whole length from the Rother to Hithe may be the greatest dimensions proposed, namely sixty feet [18 m] top breadth and forty feet [12 m] at bottom, nine feet [2.7 m], deep, and should it appear to you that any particular advantage would rise to the defence or convenience to the inhabitants of the country the proposed continuation of the same line of the water defence from Hithe to Shorncliffe may be done upon the same scale . . . The military road proposed to pass in the rear of this canal will, of course, only commence from beyond Hithe where the present great road along the coast goes in front of its line.

The military road was the second part of Brown's scheme, designed to enable troops to be moved more quickly than by slow-moving barge and had the further advantage, as Pitt himself wrote on 3 October 1804, 'of being the most essential benefit to the country in its neighbourhood'. Pitt himself, in his capacity of Lord Warden of the Cinque Ports, took the lead in meeting the objections of local landowners, presiding to such purpose over a meeting held at Dymchurch on 24 October that, as the *Kentish Gazette* reported, those present 'unanimously agreed to give the ground for the work and to leave the valuation . . . to [be decided by] a jury.'

By then work had already begun. The Royal Military Canal, as it became known, suffered none of the delays which fortification schemes usually encountered and, though conceived after the Martello towers, was to be begun, and finished, long before them. Pitt's authority and the enthusiasm of the army removed all obstacles. The leading canal expert of the day, John Rennie, now aged 53, was appointed Chief Engineer. Rennie was, like Lieut.-Colonel Brown, a Scot, and on Sunday 14 October 1804 the two men left London together, staying overnight at Maidstone; on the 15th they met the contractors, with whom they drove a hard bargain, on the 16th began to study the intended line of the first section of the canal from Shorncliffe to Hythe, on the 17th dined at Sandgate with the general responsible for the defence of Kent, Sir John Moore, and on the following day rode with him over the proposed route. On 30 October Brown proudly recorded in his diary that 'a few of the contractors' people began to break ground near Shorncliffe.' By 15 November the cost of the canal, excluding the military road and the solitary lock, at Iden, from the cliffs at Sandgate to the River Rother, was put at £200,000, with a completion date for the first stretch of 1 March 1805, and the rest by 1 June. No problem was encountered in finding the money for the canal was classified as a 'field work', which could be financed by the army with no need for the usual cumbrous procedures beforehand, though the Treasury still demanded meticulous accounts afterwards.

The plan finally agreed by Rennie and the Royal Engineers, under the ultimate supervision of the Quarter-Master-General, General Robert [later Sir Robert] Brownrigg, called for the excavation of 22½ miles [36 km] of new canal, but for a military road 28 miles [45 km] long, since for 5½ miles [8.8 km] between Iden and Winchelsea the channels of the existing Rivers Rother, Tillingham and Brede, suitably strengthened, would form the defence line. In front of the canal would be a towing path and front drain, behind it a parapet, the military road, and back drain, the excavated earth forming a parapet between the canal and military road where the troops would make their stand. Apart from Hythe, where a permanent bridge was required, the canal would be crossed by swivel bridges, or drawbridges, built of wood.

The more he considered the scheme the more reassuring the Commander-in-Chief found it, as an appreciation he wrote on 31 October 1804, when work was just starting, confirms:

> [The canal] when completed may be considered as an almost insurmountable barrier against an enemy's penetrating into the country. From the difficulty of approach across the marsh, the time that will be afforded for assembly from every quarter, and the numbers that may thus oppose him; it ought to operate as [a] great discouragement from making any effort by this, the shortest line of passage.

The building of the Royal Military Canal produced a boom in the construction industry, with contractors competing for labour and advertisements offering jobs in Kent appearing in many parts of the country. The *Kentish Gazette* reported on 6 November how a firm in Bristol had reacted by promising a shilling [5p] a day more 'for good hands . . . be the price there what it may'. By 8 January 1805 the *Kentish Gazette* was describing 'unexampled activity at various places along the whole line . . . Great numbers of labourers, lately employed at the docks and public works of the metropolis are arrived to assist in effecting it.' On 5 February it added that 'such is the ardour with which it [the work] is prosecuted, that the workmen are employed even on Sundays.'

Rennie, being pressed for results by the army, certainly earned his fee, although the Quarter-Master-General considered it excessive. 'Seven guineas [£7.35] a day!', General Brownrigg remarked to the engineer. 'Why it is equal to the pay of a field marshal,' to which, very properly, Rennie replied, 'Well, I am a field marshal in my profession and if a field marshal in your line had answered your purpose I suppose you would not have sent for me.'*

Thereafter, however, much of the work was done by military

---

* Rennie's fee was none the less rather steep. His nearest professional rival, Thomas Telford, had received only three guineas [£3.15] a day as Chief Engineer of the Caledonian Canal, begun in 1803.

labour, including the militia, who pitched working camps in Kent during the summer, with contractors being used for small specialist tasks or labourers engaged as direct labour by the day. Lieut.-Colonel Brown was in charge, and by mid-July, when the work was at its peak, reported that he had 960 men currently at work, of whom 700 were cutting the canal, 200 building the rear rampart and 60 working the hand pumps, plus troops from the Royal Staff Corps formed in 1800, doing the more skilled construction work, and the Royal Waggon Train, established in 1799, forerunner of the Army Service Corps, transporting materials, notably vast loads of shingle from the beach at Hythe, to cover the new road to a depth of ten inches [25 cm]. By the winter of 1806 the canal itself was finished, though most of the military road was not usable until the spring of 1808 and the rest not until April 1809, when the canal was completed both for navigation and as a defence work. The total cost, excluding the pay of the troops involved, amounted to £234,000, remarkably close to the original estimate, and this included a handsome new barracks at Hythe, first occupied in 1810. In addition guardhouses, to protect the canal against smugglers as well as the French, were built to cover the various bridges, and intermediate way-stations between them to house little nine-man detachments of alternating cavalry and infantry. Emplacements for cannon were also built at each crossing point, designed to house 180 12- or 18-pounders [5.8 and 8.2-kg guns], though none were installed until 1812. By that time the Royal Military Canal was well established as a local amenity, well stocked, from 1806 onwards, with 'large carp, tench, perch, pike, eels and every other species of freshwater fish', and providing, by both road and water, a vastly improved transport system, which in turn brought in, through tolls on the canal traffic, a useful income towards it maintenance. Its prompt and efficient completion consolidated John Brown's reputation. In 1809 he was given a handsome honorarium of £3000 on top of his basic lieut.-colonel's £826 in pay and allowances and by 1813 he was a major-general. He kept up his house in Hythe as a seaside retreat and inspected the whole canal for the last time in 1815, a year before his sudden death. He had, he recorded, found it in perfect order.

23

ENGLAND EXPECTS

England expects that every man this day will do his duty.

Admiral Lord Nelson to the fleet off Cape Trafalgar, 21 October 1805

During the summer of 1803 the nation was swept by what Addington described as 'an insurrection of loyalty'. The size of the regular army was increased, though most of it was assigned to service overseas, the militia was mobilised and the government created an entirely new force, the Reserve Army, by an Act passed in July, though, like most such legislation, it was barely on the statute book before it was being amended. The Army of Reserve was a compromise between the voluntary principle and what was seldom acknowledged to be, but was in fact, conscription. Anyone volunteering to join it qualified for a ten-guinea [£10.50] bounty, less two guineas [£2.10] 'for necessaries', and was required to undertake to serve for five years, or the duration of the war plus six months, but could not be sent overseas unless he offered himself for 'general service'. Any parish which failed to produce its quota of volunteers would be required to hold a ballot to make up the shortfall in which the names of all men aged 18 to 40, with various exemptions, would be entered, the unlucky ones being forcibly enlisted. It was, however, as for the militia, legitimate to hire a substitute or, a concession clearly unfair to the poor, pay the government a £20 fine to be let off, though one's name could then be re-entered in the next ballot.

The intention was to raise 40,000 men to serve in home defence in England, Wales and Scotland, but in the end the Army of Reserve made only a small contribution to the anti-invasion forces since nearly 20,000 of its members agreed to be transferred to 'general service' and were thus lost to home defence.

The nation's patriotic impulse, as at other times of danger, found its fullest expression in the passion for part-time soldiering which now seized all classes, but especially those too comfortably off to risk being conscripted into either the militia or the Reserve Army. A new Defence Act, similar to that of 1794, was passed, which empowered the king 'to accept the voluntary services of His Majesty's loyal subjects for the defence of the United Kingdom', but it included a hint of compulsion, for a census was ordered of all able-bodied males aged from 15 to 60, amended by another Act a month later to 17 to 55. Everyone registered was to be assigned to one of four categories, from unmarried men aged 17 to 29 to married men aged over 49. Any, or if the government so ordered, all of these groups might have their names entered in a ballot and, if drawn, be enrolled in a military force and sent to any part of Great Britain, the widow and children of any dying while on active service qualifying for the same scale of public relief as the dependants of members of the militia. At the same time parishes could be ordered to provide arms for the male inhabitants, to be kept under suitable supervision, probably in the parish church, and to see that the men were to be 'trained and exercised two hours at least every Sunday, either before or after divine service', or 'on any other additional day or days in the week, so as to interfere as little as may be with their occupation' up to a maximum of 20 extra days a year.

The Act provided an incentive to turn out regularly, since anyone considered adequately trained could, at the end of 12 months, qualify for a proficiency certificate exempting him from further parades, unless called out in an emergency. Failure to attend training could be punished by a fine of 10s [50p] a day, and bad behaviour on parade by a 5s [25p] fine or imprisonment for a week. In fact, however, the threat of invasion caused so many men to come forward that those regiments of Volunteers formed during the last great alarm in 1797 were soon being engulfed in a flood of newly created rivals. A fair proportion of those enrolled were, strictly speaking, hardly volunteers at all, though not necessarily unwilling to serve; the Prince of Wales's servants, for example, were simply ordered to join the St James's unit to set a good example. Other noblemen offered inducements, like the Duke of Northumberland, who provided free uniforms and equipment for any of his cottagers or labourers who agreed to enlist in the regiment he had set up and commanded, and paid them a shilling [5p] a day while they trained. Many 'institutional' corps were formed, notably by the Bank of England, which raised eight companies to defend its premises, among them one of grenadiers. The Phoenix Fire Office formed its firemen into an artillery unit, which it financed, and one Bath bootmaker marched his 16 workmen down to 'St Margaret's Buildings' to enrol as a body, 'each man determined . . . ,' the Bath Herald reported with a flourish of puns on 23 July 1803, 'to stand up to the last in support of his country and wishing from his soul for a speedy opportunity to leather the French and well strap their quarters.'

Within a few weeks 280,000 men had come forward, a far larger number than the government could hope to equip, and on 18 August 1803 a circular was sent out from Downing Street discouraging the formation of further units, or additional recruitment to existing ones, 'in any county where the effective members of those corps, including the yeomanry, shall exceed the amount of six times the militia'. But it was too late to halt the tide of would-be Volunteers. 'The offers of service already given to me . . . far exceed the number allowed for the county of Aberdeen,' explained its Lord Lieutenant, the Duke of Gordon, in a letter of 24 August 1803. By 8 September he was reporting that he had 'thought it proper to confine his force chiefly to the coast . . . declining the acceptance of numerous offers of service from the internal parts of the county'. Already he had 'very near 12,000' men to fill an establishment of 3840. The government's decision also produced an anguished protest from 'The magistrates and Deputy Lieutenants acting for the County of Anglesey' who, conscious that it could hardly be considered in the front line, pointed out to the prime minister that, 'If, as is commonly supposed, it be the design of the Corsican tyrant to cause diversions . . . by landing in many places at the same time there is no part of His Majesty's dominions, however remote from the enemy, secure.' Indeed his evil eye might already be fixed on this 'island on the Irish Channel possessing an extent of sea coast 60 miles [96 km] in circumference, vulnerable at all points . . . there not being (as they believe) a single regiment within six days march of this place.'

By the first week of September 1803 350,000 recruits had come forward and the movement was proving an administrator's nightmare. Two very different types of regiment existed, the 'Old Volunteers' with their colourful, individual uniforms and self-chosen officers, and the 'New Volunteers', supposed to wear standard military red and to conform to more orthodox military rules. One man who failed to turn up on parade might merely be reprimanded or privately fined, while another could be taken to court for breaking the law. To add to the confusion, in its haste to enlarge the movement the government had ended up by paying two different scales of allowances to the 'Old' and 'New' Volunteers respectively, the former receiving payment for up to 85 days a year, the latter for only 20 days. The rules over the provision of 'necessaries', i.e. equipment, and of the payment of old soldiers to train both, were also at first inconsistent.

What finally converted the Volunteer movement from a source of support for Addington's government into a political disaster was the shortage of muskets, which left at least half those who came forward in the summer and autumn of 1803 without a personal weapon, and after some frustrating weeks many Volunteers flatly refused to turn out again until they were properly equipped. Often they had the support of their commanders, who refused to sign their proficiency certificates, which meant that they were, in theory, liable to be included in the ballot for the militia or Reserve Army, exemption from the ballot being one of the major inducements to join the Volunteers.

The government tried in desperation to persuade the Volunteers to accept pikes, but these were received with derision. In the debate in the House of Commons on 9 December 1803, already mentioned, the Opposition spokesman, William Windham, was particularly scornful:

What would be the situation of these pikemen, at Aldborough [i.e. Aldeburgh] for instance, one of the places where there was a corps of that sort . . . Here was a straight shore with deep water and a beach on which in moderate weather vessels might run with confidence without even shortening sail; and in these circumstances it was supposed that when vessels should thus arrive, containing each a hundred soldiers, and carrying a four- and twenty-pounder on its bow, men were to stand on the shore with their pikes, and push them off . . . You might as well suppose that the enemy was to be kept off by bodkins or knitting-needles.

The government view, however, was that pikes were better than nothing and, as the summer of 1803 was a particularly fine one, the long sunshine-filled days provided ample opportunity for outdoor training.

'You never saw so military a country,' commented one somewhat sceptical minister in a letter. 'Nothing but fighting is talked of. From the highest to the lowest the zeal is wonderful, and I am convinced that should an invasion be tried, you would see all the ladies letting their nails grow that they might scratch at the invader.' Men hoped to do more than scratch. The young Walter [later Sir Walter] Scott, quartermaster of a Border regiment of yeomanry, found mastering sword movements by slashing at turnips stuck on poles on the beach at Musselburgh 'a very poignant and pleasing sensation', providing an agreeable change from his legal duties.

Members of every occupation, however unmartial, answered the call. Charles James Fox, more at home in the House of Commons than on the parade ground, marched modestly as a private within the ranks of the Chertsey, Surrey, Assocation. One evening the performance of a play at the Drury Lane theatre had to be cancelled; the actors were all away drilling. The poet Thomas Campbell, still remembered for *Ye Mariners of England*, turned out to practise arms-drill alongside market gardeners and brewery workers, though showing little aptitude for this new profession. 'Oh what a fagging work this volunteering is!' he protested. 'Eight hours under a musket!' An even more improbable recuit was William Wordsworth, who exercised for two Sundays with the men of Grasmere in Westmorland, though his sister Dorothy confessed to a close friend, 'I have no other hope than that they will not be called out of these quiet far-off places except in the case of the French being *successful* after their landing, and in that case what matter? We may all go together.'

On 12 August 1803 the Speaker, in his address to the king at the end of the parliamentary session, declared, 'The whole nation has risen up in arms,' and this was hardly an exaggeration. On Wednesday 19 October 1803 special church parades were held all over the country. St Paul's Cathedral in London was crowded by the Honourable Artillery Company, and there was a drumhead service in Westminster Hall. On Wednesday 26 October 1803 a crowd of 200,000 cheered the king and the 12,000 Volunteers from Central London he had come to review in Hyde Park.

The French, alas, were less easily impressed. When 30 French soldiers, captured during one of the navy's forays along the French coast, were brought into Deal during November, they showed lamentably little respect for the Volunteers guarding them, one undersized 16-year-old being rudely told by his prisoners to go home and eat more pudding. Pitt's niece, who rode over from Walmer Castle to stare at them, reported that they were confident of being liberated by a victorious Bonaparte by Christmas.

About the loyalty of the English mainland in 1803 no doubt ever existed. Ireland was a different matter. During the period of peace between the signing of the Treaty of Amiens in March 1802 and the resumption of the war in May 1803 the new champion of the United Irishmen, Robert Emmet, the 34-year-old son of a Dublin physician, had visited Paris and pressed the claims of Irish republicans upon Talleyrand and Napoleon. During 1803, with Britain and France again at war, Emmet returned to Paris to buy £3000 worth of pikes and muskets and Bonaparte offered the United Irish delegation 25,000 men and 40,000 muskets, with artillery and ammunition, on condition that 20,000 Irishmen joined the French when their expedition landed. On 23 June 1803, Emmet, with a mere 80 followers, led a march on Dublin, designed to seize the Castle and the arsenals and kidnap the Viceroy, but, in spite of simultaneous outbreaks in Belfast and Kildare, it was a calamitous failure. Emmet, romantically returning from hiding to visit his sweetheart, was caught and, in September, hanged.

'The No-Rising of 1803', as it was nicknamed, confirmed French scepticism about the United Irishmen who, Bonaparte himself commented, 'were divided in opinion and constantly quarrelled amongst themselves'. Nevertheless anything that might divert England's forces, especially her navy, away from the Channel was worth encouraging and orders were issued for a small force of 20 ships to be made ready at Brest for an expedition to Ireland; the initial target date of 22 November 1803 was, at the end of October, extended to 22 January 1804. 'The general in command of the expedition,' Bonaparte stated, 'will be furnished with sealed orders, by which I shall declare that I shall not make peace with England until the independence of Ireland be recognised.' The Irish Legion in France, supposed to provide the backbone of the force, consisted of no more than 49 officers and 13 soldiers, but on 2 December 1803 the First Consul ordered that 16 sail of the line and six frigates should be ready to sail from Toulon by mid-January 1804, presumably to join up with those already at Rochefort and Brest; in the event they never did.

When Parliament met, on 22 November 1803, both government and Opposition benches were filled with Volunteer officers, disgruntled that the movement had not been better treated, while many of the regular and ex-regular officers in the House were doubtful if it should exist at all, but in spite of all discouragement, morale among the Volunteers stayed high. Formal parades and services, subscription dinners and shooting competitions, all kept interest alive as the months passed. For men of any social standing being commissioned in the Volunteers became almost a test of patriotism. Robert Peel, Member for Tamworth in Staffordshire, father of the future prime minister, had taken the initiative in founding the Lancashire Fencibles and the Tamworth Armed Association in 1797 and in the following year raised and commanded the six companies of the Bury Loyal Volunteers, mainly recruited from the employees of his calico-printing works, which earned him a baronetcy. The former, and future, prime minister, William Pitt, as Lord Warden of the Cinque Ports, raised a force of 3000 Volunteers near to his official residence, Walmer Castle, on the Kent coast. Here, a contemporary noted, he endured 'the fatigue of a *drill sergeant* . . . parade after parade, at 15 or 20 miles [24-32 km] distant from each other'. Major-General John Moore, whose headquarters were close by, at Shorncliffe, became a frequent visitor and friend. 'On the very first alarm I shall march to aid you, with my Cinque Port regiments,' Pitt told his guest proudly in October 1803, 'and you have never told me where you will place us.' Moore's reply was discouraging. 'Do you see that hill?' he asked his host. 'You and yours shall be drawn up on it, where you will make a most formidable appearance to the enemy, while I, with the soldiers, shall be fighting on the beach.' Even more distressing was the reception given to the current prime minister, Henry Addington, when he attended the House of Commons on 23 May 1803 in all his sartorial glory as commanding officer of the Woodley Cavalry. Always regarded as something of a figure of fun, he was now greeted with mocking laughter.

By 1803 a wealth of useful material already existed on how each locality should respond to an invasion. Although the authorities in London and the principal ports would now, if conditions were favourable, be alerted by the new telegraph, the ordinary citizen would still look to what one authority, Colonel Dirom, had described in 1797 as 'an ancient and prompt method of giving general warning of approaching danger', namely the time-honoured bonfire. Even where it was not known locally as Beacon Hill, the site was well established through local tradition; an official list of the 16 such places in Kent included Barham near Canterbury, where King John's troops had once mustered. The 14 in Sussex took in Fairlight Down, near Hastings, a famous vantage point, and Chanctonbury Ring. Dorset's eleven ran from Orchard Hill, behind Golden Cap near Bridport, through Black Down, between Abbotsbury and Dorchester, to Puddletown Heath and thence inland to Melbury Hill near Shaftesbury.

Elaborate instructions for building the beacons were issued, like those which Lord Dorchester addressed to a leading resident of Kingston Lacy near Wimborne on 12 October:

> I beg of you that you will give directions for an assemblage of faggots, furze and other fuel, also of straw, to be stacked and piled on the summit of Badbury Rings, so as the whole may take fire instantly and the fire may be maintained for two hours. It is to be fired whenever the beacon of St Catherine's is fired to the eastward, or whenever the Lytchett or Woodbury Hill beacons are fired to the westward.

Other orders specified 'at least eight waggon-loads' of combustible materials, 'with three or four tar barrels, sufficient to yield a light unmistakable at a distance of two or three miles [3.2-4.8 km] to be used by night. By day, a large quantity of hay was to be wetted and set alight, in order to produce a smoke'.

False alarms were a regular feature of invasion scares and 1803 produced some notable ones. Many wealthy residents left Eastbourne in August after a rumour that the French planned to land there; in Pevensey Bay a report rapidly spread that the French were actually coming ashore. In October George Crabbe was woken in Aldeburgh in Suffolk by his son with the words: 'Do not be alarmed, but the French are landing,' to which the poet, very sensibly, replied, 'Well, you and I can do no good . . . We must wait the event,' and went back to sleep. As autumn succeeded summer horses and wagons were earmarked at Hastings to carry the women and children inland and officers at Dover were forbidden to sleep out of camp. The middle of any month always seemed to be an especially anxious time. 'This is the day of the spring tides . . . ' noted one woman on 15 October 1803, 'on which the French are expected to land.'

As autumn gave way to winter, however, scepticism increased. 'What!' wrote Nelson derisively from his post off Toulon. 'He begins to find excuses. I thought he would invade England in the face of the sun! Now he wants a three days' fog that never yet happened.'

Among those who professed regret that the French had not yet made the attempt was that stout-hearted monarch, George III. On 30 November 1803, now aged 65, he wrote in stirring terms to the Bishop of Worcester from Windsor:

We are here in daily expectation that Bonaparte will attempt his threatened invasion; the chances against his success seem so many that it is wonderful he persists in it. I own I place that thorough dependence on divine providence that I cannot help thinking the usurper is [to be] encouraged to make the trial that the ill-success may put an end to his wicked purposes. Should his troops effect a landing, I shall certainly put myself at the head of my troops . . . to repel them . . . Should the enemy approach too near to Windsor, I shall think it right the queen and my daughters should cross the Severn and [shall] send them to your episcopal palace at Worcester.

The king's safety was one of the government's recurrent concerns, for almost every summer from 1789 to 1805 he spent from four to six weeks at Weymouth on the Dorset coast. George III himself was convinced the county was a likely target. 'I cannot deny,' he wrote to his son, the Commander-in-Chief, on 15 June 1804, 'that I am rather hurt that there is any objection made to forming so large an Army of Reserve in Dorsetshire where, or in Cornwall, I think an attack more likely than in Essex, Kent or Sussex.' Dorset was in fact well protected, with a Hanoverian regiment in Radipole barracks on the outskirts of Weymouth, and a brigade of guards and a brigade of militia encamped on the adjoining Radipole Common, while the Dorset Volunteer Infantry and Yeomanry Cavalry were several times reviewed by the king himself. It was probably a happy day for both the king and these loyal subjects when, in May 1804, George III already being in residence there, news reached Weymouth that the French were landing at Portland, fog having blinded the signal stations at Verne, on Portland Bill, and at Abbotsbury and Golden Cap along the coast. Drums hastily called the Volunteers to arms, but, as visibility improved, only peaceful fishing boats were revealed.

During the alarm at Weymouth a carriage stood outside the king's house, Gloucester Lodge, ready to whisk him away to London or Windsor, or, if these seemed threatened, to the Midlands. During 1803 Parliament had voted £100,000 'for erecting buildings for the service of His Majesty's Ordnance' at Weedon, north of Towcester in Northamptonshire. This was a location as far from the sea as it was possible to find but it stood on what had once been the main Roman road north, Watling Street (now the A5), and close to the Grand Junction Canal, ideal for transporting heavy stores to any part of the country. Here, on a 53-acre [21.5-hectare] site, were erected eight large two-storey red brick storehouses, each the size of a small barracks, a large separate enclosure containing magazines built on either side of the canal and surrounded by a high wall with bastions at the corners, and, between them, a handsome central building with two detached wings, containing the residences of the governor and principal officers. This was known as the Royal Pavilion, since in an emergency it would have housed the sovereign and royal family. The Royal Military Depot (later known as the Royal Ordnance Depot) was not expected to face attack by the French; if they had penetrated as far inland as Weedon the country would already have been lost. It was, however, intended to provide a last-ditch Buckingham Palace and to hold a vast reserve of munitions of all kinds: small arms for 200,000 men, field ordnance, ammunition and later, 1000 tons of gunpowder. Admirably laid out, architecturally attractive, and soundly built, Weedon only began to issue stores in 1809 and was never occupied by the royal family.[*]

The traditional first measure of passive defence was to 'drive' the countryside and the Defence Act of 1798, still in force in 1803, gave the local authorities powers 'for removing the inhabitants, with the cattle, corn, grain and fodder from such parts as may be necessary on the approach of the enemy, and likewise to appoint proper places in which such inhabitants, cattle, grain and fodder so removed shall be lodged.'

As time passed, however, these draconian policies came increasingly to be questioned. On 28 October 1803 the Duke of York wrote that everyone engaged since 1801 in anti-invasion planning felt increasing 'distrust of the possibility and expediency of this measure' and in a letter from the Duke to the Lord Lieutenant of Essex in November 1803, a new policy was substituted. Henceforward only horses and draught cattle were to be driven off, and the roads were to be broken up as the army withdrew, suitable sections being identified in advance. It was recognised, however, that individual areas might still have to be evacuated and elaborate preparations were made both for removing the population if necessary and for ensuring it could be fed if left behind. A remarkably thorough survey of resources, both human and material, was now undertaken, more detailed than the first-ever national census of three years before. Nowhere took its anti-invasion planning more seriously than Dorset, and the authorities in Dorchester set out their thinking in an optimistic note to accompany the survey forms:

> If an enemy should land on our shores every possible exertion should be made to deprive him of the means of subsistence. The navy will cut off his course [i.e. source of supplies] and the army will confine him on shore in such a way as to make it impossible for him to draw any supplies from the adjacent country. In this situation he will be forced to lay down his arms or give battle on disadvantageous terms.

Dorset was subdivided for defence purposes into ten divisions and on 1 August 1804 each of these was required to prepare a return indicating how many Volunteers it contained, how many other fit men between

* The 'Royal Pavilion' was demolished in 1972, but most of the site, including numerous 'listed' buildings, was not disposed of until 1984.

the ages of 17 and 55, and how many residents would need help if they had to leave their homes. The assembly point for such refugees, and for transport, was to be determined, and drivers and 'conductors', on the basis of one such escort for every ten wagons, identified. The number of oxen, riding and draught horses to be removed were all noted, along with the available carts. The divisions were also called on to count the numbers of cows, sheep and pigs within their boundaries, and the estimated amounts of wheat, oats, barley, beans, peas, potatoes and hay, down to the nearest quarter [28 lb or 12 kg]. Watermills and windmills were also to be listed along with their capacity for producing flour, and ovens graded according to how many 3-lb [1.4-kg] loaves they could bake per 24 hours.

The government's main anxiety concerned London; the Dutch had been able back in 1667 to set the capital shivering and to threaten its bread supply by depriving the bakers of fuel, after interrupting the coal trade from Newcastle. A store of 30,000 sacks of flour was now held on the Upper Thames to be brought down-river if needed, perhaps on the ten barges which the Basingstoke Canal Company offered to make available 'in the event of invasion', while another transport firm, Pickfords, undertook to supply 400 horses, 50 wagons, and 28 boats if called on.

In contrast to earlier invasion alarms Roman Catholics were no longer regarded as potential traitors, though the Dorset survey did call on the authorities in each division to record the number of aliens and Quakers. Each area was also asked to note how many doctors, teachers and constables it contained, these being regarded as natural leaders if the ordinary administration broke down. The clergy were also to be listed and it was their role which everywhere occasioned the keenest debate. That role, the Bishop of Chester ruled in his diocese, was to stay behind when their parishioners marched off to fight and then 'be most actively and suitably occupied in the general superintendence of the property and female parishioners and children left behind'. In the diocese of Llandaff, however, the vicars and curates were encouraged by their Father in God to stir up their flock into hatred of the enemy:

You will not, I think, be guilty of a breach of Christian charity in the use of even harsh language, when you explain to your congregations the cruelties which the French have used in every country they have invaded . . . They everywhere promise protection to the poorer sort, and they everywhere strip the poorest of everything they possess; they plunder their cottages, and they set them on fire when the plunder is exhausted; they torture the owners to discover their wealth, and they put them to death when they have none to discover; they violate females of all ages; they insult the hoary head, and trample on all the decencies of life.

Just as in France, those unable to serve gave their money. The Bank of England had opened a Patriotic Fund back in 1794 and gave a good start with a donation of £200,000. Meetings at the Mansion House and Royal Exchange raised large sums; the king gave £20,000 and other members of the royal family suitably lesser amounts, down to the five princesses' promises of £100 each a year. Most cities raised at least £500, while private contributions ranged from the Duke of Marlborough's £5000 to the ten shillings [50p] a head of the seamen of HMS *Argonaut*, who promised 'to drive before us into the sea all French scoundrels and other blackguards'. Often, as with Lenten abstinence, moral improvement went hand in hand with generosity. Many corporations, notorious for their lavish dinners, abandoned them 'for the duration' and metaphorically beating knives and forks into swords, gave the money saved to the Patriotic Fund, while the boys of Merchant Taylors School, in an act of heroic self-sacrifice, raised £105 destined otherwise for the tuckshop.

Little place was found for women in all this activity. That the war was not even mentioned in any of Jane Austen's novels, written between 1796 and 1814, has often been remarked on. In August 1803 a 'Female Association for preserving Liberty and Property' was formed in the City of London, it being promised that 'the names of the subscribers . . . will be ranged in their respective columns as maids, wives and widows', but no more was heard of it.

The invasion alarm created a great demand for patriotic plays and songs. The unquestioned masters of the genre were the Dibdin family, to whom the danger from France brought prosperity. In 1796 Charles Dibdin was able to open his own theatre in Leicester Square and the following year saw the phenomenal success of the song 'Snug Little Island', previously quoted, written by his 25-year-old son, Thomas John, after the Fishguard fiasco. On 13 December 1803 a new play by Charles Dibdin, *The English Fleet in 1342*, opened in Covent Garden – it began, somewhat anachronistically, with an overture based on 'Rule Britannia' and ended with the French being suitably routed – and one of his songs also gave general currency to the rumour that Bonaparte was planning a novel way to evade the Royal Navy:

> The French are all coming, so they declare,
> Of their floats and balloons all the papers advise us.
> They're to swim through the ocean and ride on the air,
> In some foggy evening to land and surprise us.

The origin of the balloon story lay in France, where it had been encouraged to maintain interest in the coming invasion, but the idea was by no means wholly fanciful; a large aerial armada was impossible, but a small nuisance force might conceivably have been delivered in this fashion. The Channel had already been crossed by balloon, though from England to France, in January 1785, and in 1804 another French-man was to travel as far as Rome. Napoleon, fortunately perhaps, showed little interest in this particular novelty and refused, unlike other generals of the time, even to use observation balloons but the French press often returned to the theme. A cartoon in a French news-paper, in June 1803, showed a two-man balloon crossing from Calais to Dover, above the caption 'Nouvelle Machine Aerostatique construite . . . per Ordre du Gouvernment, destinée à faire le passage de France en Angle-terre'. Another published in Paris the same month, showing three much larger balloons, was boldly entitled Déscente en Angleterre. Each balloon could, it was claimed absurdly, lift 3000 men.

Another French illustration that same year depicted not only a sky full of balloons and a sea jammed with ships but a large subterranean army, including cavalry and artillery, making its way beneath the sea through a Channel tunnel. This, too, was no mere flight of fancy; an experienced French mining engineer did actually propose such an undertaking, though it never seems to have been started. In England it was also stated that Bonaparte planned to build a bridge from Calais to Dover. This, however, was mere invention, like the attractive tale that he had been seen on board a British fishing-smack, masquerading as a British seaman while he spied out the south-coast defences.

All really depended, as always, on the navy, and the navy's greatest enemy was the weather. The winter of 1803 was bad even by Channel standards, but the three blockading squadrons, off the Texel, off Brest and off Toulon, hung grimly on. In the classic words of an American admiral later in the century, 'Those far distant, storm-beaten ships, upon which the Grand Army never looked, stood between it and the dominion of the world.'* Once, the watching force off Brest was re-duced to a mere four sail and it continued to suffer from adverse winds in the early months of 1804. 'God preserve all our ships!' remarked stal-wart Admiral Lord Keith that February.

The English had more to fear from good weather, for Bonaparte's flat-bottomed transports and almost keel-less gunboats could only have faced the Channel under perfect conditions. Fog accompanied by a flat calm posed a perpetual danger, though a well-informed reader of the London Courier tried to reassure his fellow-citizens in a letter published on 16 February 1804 that even this combination might prove ineffective:

A fog is a very good cloak to the approach of from six to 60 rowing boats, which may be sent to perform some coup de main at no great distance, by surprise . . . but to say that in an enterprise in which probably 200,000 men may be employed, on an extent of coast of

* A.T. Mahan, The Influence of Sea Power upon the French Revolution and Empire 1793-1812, 1892, Vol. II, p. 118. This observation is so pertinent that I have made an exception to my rule of only quoting from contemporary sources.

more than 200 miles [320 km], from Flushing to Cherbourg, . . . fog
is favourable . . . is the height of folly; as well might it be averred
that a man can see better to read in the pitchy darkness of the night
than in the noontide glare of the day. Fogs are favourable to some
enterprises; to this they must be fatal.

Napoleon perhaps reached a similar conclusion, but successive post-
ponements had not yet weakened his commitment to the invasion. 'In
the present position of Europe all my thoughts are directed towards
England,' he wrote to the French ambassador at Constantinople, on 14
March 1804, claiming to have assembled 'nearly 120,000 men and 3000
boats, which only await a favourable wind in order to plant the imperial eagle on the Tower of London.' Two days later the French
accused the English of engaging in germ warfare. A notice issued from
Boulogne warned 'all the ports along the coast' that 'The English,
unable to conquer us by force, are employing their last resource: *the
Plague*. Five bales of cotton have just been thrown upon our coast . . .
All are hereby forbidden to approach any boats or objects that may be
cast on shore.' An investigation yielded, however, only one old hammock washed up on the beach.

On Wednesday 15 August 1804, Napoleon's thirty-ninth birthday,
all 80,000 men encamped near Boulogne were assembled to witness
the distribution of the crosses of the recently instituted Legion of
Honour, in a superbly stage-managed ceremony. The only jarring
note was struck by the British warships patrolling unchallenged offshore, which spoiled the intended high spot of the day, the arrival of a
fleet of new landing craft at Boulogne. The leading flotilla, forced to
keep close to the land, ran aground. 'It threw the emperor into a violent
rage,' one observer recorded, and 'about six o'clock, just as dinner was
served for the soldiers . . . a heavy fall of rain . . . augmented the
emperor's ill-humour.'

It was not in William Pitt's nature to wait to be attacked and he had
ready to hand what seemed the perfect weapon against landing craft
moored in shallow waters, the catamaran, forerunner of the torpedo.
This had been devised by the fertile mind of Robert Fulton, who
having failed to arouse French interest in the device, had offered it to
England. The veteran admiral, Lord St Vincent, whom Pitt had
dropped from the Admiralty, was dead against it. The prime minister,
he declared, was 'the greatest fool that ever existed to encourage a
mode of war which those who commanded the seas did not want, and
which, if successful, would deprive them of it'. Fulton's catamaran
was not a true torpedo for it had to be towed into position and then carried against its target by the tide, but, as a near-contemporary account
shows, it had the potential to do a great deal of damage:

It consisted of a coffer of about 21 feet [6.4 m] long and 3¼ [1 m] broad, resembling in appearance a log of mahogany . . . Its extremity was of thick plank, lined with lead, caulked and tarred. Outside this was a coat of canvas, laid over with hot pitch . . . The contents consisted . . . of as much ballast as would just keep the upper surface of the deck of the coffer even with the water's edge. Amidst a quantity of powder (about 40 barrels) and other inflammable matter was a piece of clockwork, the mainspring of which, on the withdrawal of a peg placed on the outside, would at a given time (from six to ten minutes) . . . explode the vessel.

Fulton's invention was given a very fair, large-scale test under the direction of the highly able Lord Keith on 2 October 1804. For seven hours of an exceptionally dark night a stream of catamarans was launched against a double line of 150 landing craft moored outside Boulogne harbour, but they achieved nothing, and one officer involved professed himself only too ready to 'return the remainder of the machines into store, from which . . . I heartily wish we had never taken them'. Keith, very open-mindedly, advised the Admiralty that the torpedoes deserved another test, which they duly received at Boulogne in December. This time they damaged some civilian property, causing Napoleon to comment that the Admiralty was 'breaking the windows of the good citizens of Boulogne with English guineas'. An experiment under non-operational conditions, in October 1805, when an old brig was sunk in the Downs in sight of Pitt, watching from Walmer Castle, was a complete success, but by then the most urgent need had passed and the idea was allowed to lapse.

Such excitements apart, the winter of 1804 was for the Royal Navy much like that of 1803, but morale remained high, as Nelson, who had himself been continuously at sea in the Mediterranean for months, reported to the Admiralty in December:

> The fleet is in perfect health and good humour, unequalled by anything which has ever come within my knowledge, and equal to the most active service which the times may call for, or the country expect of them . . . Our men's minds are always kept up with the daily hopes of meeting the enemy.

It was the same in the Channel. Vice-Admiral [later Sir William] Cornwallis, in overall command there, was constantly forced off his station off Ushant, and three times in the autumn of 1804 had been driven all the way back to Torbay, with heavy damage to his ships, but always beat his way back to his patrol area. Life was no easier for Rear-Admiral Cuthbert [later Vice-Admiral Lord] Collingwood, off Rochefort, further south, in the centre of the Bay of Biscay. 'I have,' he confessed, 'hardly known what a night of rest is these two months. This incessant cruising seems to me beyond the powers of human nature.' When in command of the inshore squadron off Ushant, where several ships were lost on uncharted rocks, the strain was even greater. 'It was a station of great anxiety,' he admitted, 'and required so constant a care and look-out that I have been often a week without having my clothes off and was sometimes upon deck the whole night.'

In December 1804 Spain declared war on Britain, but in exchange for an avowed enemy the country had gained two far more powerful friends, for in April 1805 Russia concluded an alliance with Britain which was ratified in July, and on 9 August Austria, followed soon afterwards by Sweden, joined it. Pitt had his anti-French coalition at last.

Napoleon meanwhile had changed his strategy. Realising that he could not hope to defeat the Royal Navy in open combat he devised a plan to lure it away by a feint attack on the West Indies. At first all went well. Under cover of a storm Admiral Missiessy escaped from Rochefort in January and, having attacked several British islands in the Caribbean got safely back to his home port in April. On 30 March, Admiral Pierre Villeneuve, one of Napoleon's most favoured subordinates, left Toulon and, in mid-May, anchored at Martinique, before also returning to Europe, in June. But Nelson, learning of Villeneuve's break-out, pursued him across the Atlantic and, by brilliant seamanship, completed the two-way crossing in ten days less than his French rival. By 19 June the British fleet was back at Gibraltar.

On 22 July 1805 an indecisive battle was fought off Cape Finisterre, known as 'Calder's Action', after the British Vice-Admiral Sir Robert Calder, who was blamed for allowing Villeneuve to escape destruction and lead his ships into Vigo Bay to join up, on 2 August 1805, with the Spanish vessels in Ferrol. The Combined Fleet, the formation of which Britain had always tried to prevent, had thus become a reality.

At Ferrol Villeneuve found orders from Napoleon to sail to Brest to raise the blockade of that port and join forces with the ships of Vice-Admiral Ganteaume, who had long been shut up there. Ganteaume was warned to be ready to force his way out the moment Villeneuve appeared, while from Boulogne Napoleon wrote to Villeneuve, on 22 August 1805, 'Get to sea, lose no time, not a moment, and enter the Channel with my united squadrons. England is ours!'

Napoleon realised that it was now or never. He had already decided to embark on a new land campaign, which would mean abandoning the invasion of England. 'My mind is made up,' he had written to his foreign minister, Talleyrand, on 13 August. 'I desire to attack Austria and to be at Vienna before the end of November.' All now depended on Admiral Villeneuve.

Day by day the emperor's staff officers strode the cliffs of Boulogne, telescopes at the ready, to search the horizon for the first glimpse of their fleet's arrival. Meanwhile expectations in England mounted to a new peak. 'There is such an universal bustle and cry about invasion,' complained one peer, 'that no other subject will be listened to by those in power.' With the start of the spring tides all leave was stopped, the Volunteers were warned that they must stay on duty even during harvest, and wagons were earmarked to carry away the treasure in the Bank of England. Nelson's absence – he was out of contact with land on his way past Ushant – caused general concern and when he did appear, at Spithead on 18 August and soon afterwards in London, he was cheered all the way. 'There is but one Nelson,' his former superior, Lord St Vincent, had observed and one duchess now remarked how 'The very children learn to bless him as he passes and sometimes a poor woman asks to touch his coat,' as though he were a king.

Villeneuve, having made his way out of Ferrol with 29 ships of the line and ten frigates, had failed to rendezvous off Finisterre with some expected reinforcements, and instead of making as ordered for Brest and Boulogne had turned feebly back towards Cadiz, where he was promptly blockaded again by Collingwood and Calder. The news roused Napoleon to fury. 'What a navy! . . . What an admiral!' he exclaimed. 'Villeneuve, instead of entering the Channel, has taken refuge in Cadiz! . . . He will be blockaded there . . . It is all over!' On 29 August the great camp at Boulogne was broken up. Instead of embarking for Kent the Army of England set off on foot towards the Danube.

The British government did not yet realise the danger was over and sent Sir John Moore to study the Boulogne area to see if an amphibious landing might destroy the invasion fleet. He reported, on 29 September, that it would be too risky an operation. Two weeks earlier, on 15 September HMS *Victory*, with Admiral Lord Nelson on board, had sailed from Portsmouth and on 28 September had rejoined the main fleet off Cadiz, his arrival, one officer reported, producing 'a sort of general joy'.

While Nelson was on his way towards Cadiz Villeneuve had already left it, having been ordered to take his ships into the Mediterranean. Before they could reach the Straits of Gibraltar he discovered his enemy's presence and turned back to seek safety in the port he had recently left, but he was too late. Nelson now barred his way, and off Cape Trafalgar, roughly midway between there and the Straits, the Royal Navy at last achieved its great aim, to bring the main enemy fleet to battle, even though the Combined Fleet outnumbered the English ships of the line by 33 to 27. On his last visit to the Admiralty Nelson had, it was later recalled, been 'anxiously enquiring . . . about a code of signals, just then improved and enlarged', and it was this which, at 11.45 am on Monday 21 October 1805, carried to the British fleet the soon immortal message: 'England expects that every man this day will do his duty.'

The greatest of all his victories followed: 18 French or Spanish ships were taken or destroyed, and 6000 of the Combined Fleet's men killed or wounded. The English lost no ships, though some were badly damaged, but paid a high price for their success. The message which a breathless lieutenant announced to the Secretary of the Admiralty in the early hours of 6 November 1805, in fog far too thick for the telegraph to function, summed up the universal reaction: 'Sir, we have gained a great victory, but we have lost Lord Nelson!'

As the news spread and the bells pealed this ambivalent response was universal, but of the significance of Trafalgar there could be no doubt. 'The battle of Cadiz,' commented the *Morning Post*, 'cannot fail to impress on our enemies a deep and indelible sense of the invincible title by which we hold the sovereignty of the seas.' The invasion, everyone knew, was off for good, as Pitt made clear in a classic speech at Guildhall on 9 December. 'England,' the prime minister declared, 'has saved herself by her exertions and will, I trust, save Europe by her example.'

For Pitt it was almost the end of the road. He died, exhausted by illness and overwork, on 23 January 1806, aged only 46. Nor did poor Admiral Villeneuve long outlive his capture at Trafalgar. In April 1806, though repatriated, he died by his own hand rather than face his emperor.

Napoleon had, it soon appeared, not yet given up all thoughts of invasion. In 1807 he ordered a survey of the boats assembled two years before, but this revealed that no more than 300 were still serviceable; in 1811, before setting out on his disastrous campaign in Russia, he planned to spend two million francs on a new invasion fleet, but the idea was dropped.

On 23 June 1814, with Napoleon defeated and apparently safe on Elba, the Volunteers were disbanded, but not until 18 June 1815, at Waterloo, was Napoleon finally beaten by England's new hero, Arthur Wellesley, first Duke of Wellington. The defeated emperor was shipped off to St Helena in the South Atlantic, where he died in 1821, still only 51. He had never set foot in the country that had finally encompassed his downfall.

BOOK 3
THE VICTORIANS VERSUS INVASION
1815–1900

24

A BRIDGE OF STEAM

The Channel is no longer a barrier. Steam navigation has rendered that which was before impassable by a military force nothing more than a river passable by a steam bridge.

Viscount Palmerston in the House of Commons, 30 July 1845

For a quarter of a century after Waterloo England was in no real danger of invasion. In 1829 most of the restrictions on Roman Catholics were at last lifted and in 1832 Parliament successfully reformed itself, encouraged by nothing worse than some major riots. All the nation's kings died peacefully in their beds, the sad, demented George III, aged 81, on 29 January 1830, his sane but despised successor, George IV, formerly Prince Regent, a mere 57, on 27 June 1830, and his younger brother, William IV, 'The Sailor King' at, 71, on 20 June 1837, his wish 'to see another anniversary of the Battle of Waterloo' duly fulfilled. The accession of his 18-year-old niece, Victoria, marked a major breach with the past, breaking the connection with Hanover, since under the Salic Law no woman could occupy the Hanoverian throne, and, after an opening decade of hardship and dissension, was to usher in an era of unprecedented national prosperity and expansion.

After the Napoleonic Wars had ended in 1815 massive reductions in spending on the armed forces followed, especially in home defence. By 1841, of 103 battalions each roughly 1000 strong, 78 were overseas, 6 in transit and only 19 in the British Isles. Wherever he was stationed the soldier's lot was a miserable one. With the war won, he was once again regarded as a social outcast; in London, under a regulation dating from Charles II's reign, he was even supposed to be excluded from the parks. The billeting of troops in inns and ordinary houses had, as described earlier, long been unpopular but the widespread building of barracks from around 1820 – the total throughout the country was put at about 140 but of these 106 could hold fewer than 500 men – was also criticised and they were very unhealthy; in Knightsbridge Barracks the annual death rate even in the 1850s was five times that for the rest of the parish of Kensington. The constant cry was that expenditure should be cut back to the level of 1792, before the Napoleonic Wars began, as though since then nothing had changed.

Although the commissioned ranks had a much pleasanter life than their men, entry was virtually confined to those with a private income; in the elite Tenth Hussars the uniform alone, in 1829, cost almost £400. With net pay after essential expenses calculated in 1846 at from £73 for an ensign to £114 for a lieutenant-colonel it was surprising that so many officers were truly dedicated to their profession, as the proliferation of specialist periodicals between 1815 and 1852 confirms. The *Naval and Military Magazine*, launched in 1827 – and later renamed the *United Service Journal* and then the *United Service Magazine* – the *Naval and Military Gazette*, and *United Service Gazette*, both first published in 1833, with a combined circulation of around 1300 copies, were followed by publications like the *Professional Papers of the Royal Engineers*, which appeared annually from 1837, and the *Proceedings* of the Royal Artillery Institution of gunnery officers, from 1848. The Duke of Wellington strongly disapproved of military journals, believing they could only encourage dissension, but every copy reaching a club or mess was seen by up to 100 readers and one colonel declared in the *United Service Magazine* that, 'The best friend the army ever had has been the military press . . . With very rare exceptions all the improvements . . . in the moral and physical condition of our military force have had their origin here.'

Improvement was certainly needed. Wellington, only 46 at the time of Waterloo, was thereafter constantly in high office, as Master-General of the Ordnance from 1818-1827, as Commander-in-Chief of the army, from 1827-1828 and again from 1842 to 1852, and as prime minister from 1828 to 1830 and, more briefly, in 1834. The caustic comment which the *Naval and Military Gazette* made in its review of the events of 1844 was well merited:

In no year . . . have we had fewer changes to remark on . . . The Duke of Wellington has ever been in the army disposed to a con-servative system . . . Whenever his Grace issues orders to the army, we observe that they are generally to enforce the existing regula-tions or to restore a lapsed discipline . . . We somewhat regret that his Grace is not a military reformer – for there is much to reform.

The militia was also in eclipse during these year. In 1817 it had still been, at least on paper, 80,000 strong, but the ballot supposed to take place each October to keep it up to strength ceased in many places to be held and in 1829 Parliament voted to suspend it, a motion annually renewed until 1852. The yeomanry, an all-volunteer, mounted force, numbering in 1817 around 35,000, survived, but by 1851 its strength was down to under 14,000.

The year 1829 also saw the foundation of the Metropolitan Police, to be followed by the creation of similar forces throughout the country, thereby at last relieving the troops of irksome, essentially civilian, duties which kept units dispersed in small scattered detachments, almost impossible to train. But the new opportunity for larger-scale manoeuvres was not seized. As the *Naval and Military Gazette* complained in July 1847: 'We seldom fight regimentally and we seldom drill except regimentally.'

The factor which finally transformed the nation's defence policy in the generation after Waterloo was the development of steam power. Its effects were felt first on land. The railway reached Southampton from London in 1840, Brighton in 1841, Folkestone in 1843, and Dover in 1844. Portsmouth was joined to London, via Chichester, in 1847, and Plymouth in 1849, though the 'iron horse' did not reach Falmouth until 1859. Wellington's natural resistance to change was overcome by his recurrent fear of invasion, to be mentioned in a moment, and by Prince Albert, Prince Consort since 1840, a fervent advocate of technological progress. Once convinced, the Duke displayed all his old mastery of military logistics, ordering that his headquarters at the Horse Guards should establish the facilities needed to transport 10,000 men, 1000 horses and 12 guns from Dublin, Edinburgh and London to the south coast. The result was reassuring. The South Eastern Railway calculated that, even while maintaining half its existing civilian passenger service, it could convey 30,000 men 40 miles [64 km] in three days.

The effect of steam power on the navy was ultimately to be even more traumatic, and in 1815 a steam tug, in passage from Greenock to London, caused a sensation at Portsmouth by 'almost daily steaming up and about the Hamoaze to draw the attention of the population'. One young officer, a future admiral, who watched it, considered its 'ever being put into competition with line-of-battle ships' inconceivable, 'as one broadside would annihilate such presumption', and it was indeed true that the steamship paddle-wheels could easily be knocked out by a single shot. The navy therefore restricted its earliest use of steam to tugs, kept far from the scene of the battle. Undoubtedly, too, senior officers, conscious of the glories achieved in the age of sail, were unwilling to accept that its day was passing, and it was only with the invention of the screw-propeller that steam began to be taken seriously by the Royal Navy. In May 1845 the argument between the advocates of paddle-wheels and screws was settled in a thoroughly sporting manner by a tug of war between the screw-driven *Rattler* and the paddle-equipped *Alecto*, lashed stern to stern.[*] The *Rattler* proved an easy winner, but for the next ten years screws were used in warships only as an auxiliary source of power. There were good reasons for this: the boilers required vast quantities of coal and fresh water, which took up valuable space and limited a ship's range; the

[*] A good account of this famous trial can be found in Lewis, p. 121. Callender, p. 239, dates it, wrongly, in 1842. Hargreaves, p. 421, mentions it but, characteristically, does not date it at all.

winds, by contrast, needed no room, cost nothing and were ever available. In one respect, however, the navy *had* changed, and for the better. Though the press gang was not abolished it was rarely needed, while the demand for crews dropped dramatically, until by 1835 the navy contained a mere 26,000 men and cost, at £4,400,000, only one-third of what it had done 20 years before.

Developments in military and naval communications at first lagged behind those in transport. *The Times* on 9 May 1816 informed its readers that, 'The telegraph frames at the top of the Admiralty are to be removed and the improved semaphore, consisting of a hollow mast from whence two arms project in various directions, will be erected in their stead.' The new system, more flexible in the messages it sent, and far easier to read than the old-style shutters, was rapidly extended from Whitehall to Portsmouth, Chatham, Sheerness, Deal and Dover, and eventually reached Plymouth, but suffered from the same disadvantage of being unusable after dark and during fog. It was the railways, not the services, that saw the electric telegraph's potential; the first short line, from Paddington to Slough, was only opened in 1844, but within a year 500 route miles were in use, and by 1852 almost every place of importance on or near the coast, as far afield as Plymouth, was, in one commentator's words, 'in direct communication with the metropolis', the few exceptions, notably Chatham and Bristol, being likely to be joined up 'in a short time'.

Curiously, for reasons to be explored later, the new telegraph, like steam power, was regarded as making the British Isles more vulnerable to invasion, and the alarmists found a ready audience among a public already excited by the changes occurring all round them. Against these fears the arguments of the 'peace' party in Parliament could make little headway, even when the able and respected Richard Cobden*, who entered Parliament in 1841, became its leader and the persistent advocate of a policy of 'Peace, retrenchment and reform'.

Fixed fortifications, because they were both costly and conspicuous, were a particular source of dissension. The radical writer William Cobbett had noted during one of his famous *Rural Rides* as early as August 1823 that already 'some of the walls and buildings' of the Martello towers on the Kent coast were 'falling down' or had been left unfinished 'as if a spell had been, all of a sudden, set upon the workmen', and that one in Sussex had been sold off for £200. Some others soon afterwards suffered the same fate and in those euphoric, post-Waterloo years the fortifications of East Anglia were also allowed to decay. In 1826 a War Office survey found only Landguard Fort still in full commission; at Hollesley Bay, by contrast, the 'actual presence' was one man, responsible for four Martellos with a garrison in theory of 48,

* For a detailed account of Cobden's career and of his most famous and successful campaign, against the Corn Laws, see my book *The Breadstealers* (Temple Smith, 1984).

while another solitary stalwart manned the two batteries and five Martellos in Felixstowe.

Such weakness could be accepted so long as the one potential enemy, France, was enfeebled by the aftermath of defeat and by popular hostility to the restored Bourbons, but in 1830 Charles X, who had succeeded his more moderate brother Louis XVIII in 1824, was driven out by his subjects, who chose instead the so-called 'citizen king', Louis-Philippe, to rule them.

Louis-Philippe had served in the republican army before being forced to flee from France along with the renegade General Dumouriez, and his rise to power, and France's returning self-confidence, coincided with the increasing domination of British foreign policy by Henry Temple, Viscount Palmerston. (Palmerston's peerage being Irish he sat in the House of Commons.) Educated at Harrow and Cambridge, Palmerston had entered the House of Commons at the age of 22, in 1807, and after holding numerous ministerial posts, in November 1830, still only 46, found his true metier as Foreign Secretary. He remained at the Foreign Office, with only one brief interlude, for eleven years until 1841, and returned to it from 1846 to 1851. Subsequently he twice became prime minister, and only death, while still in office, ended his career.

Palmerston realised that French hostility to England persisted whether she was ruled by emperor, king or senate. 'The policy of France,' he commented in 1831, 'is like an infection clinging to the walls of the dwelling and breaking out in every successive occupant who comes within their influence.' In October 1840, with Louis-Phillipe securely established on the French throne, Palmerston reaffirmed his suspicion of England's nearest neighbour to the British ambassador:

> All Frenchmen want to encroach and extend their territorial possessions at the expense of other nations. Their vanity prompts them to be the first nation in the world . . . It is a misfortune to Europe that the national character of a great and powerful people, placed in the centre of Europe, should be such as it is.

The French had shown themselves notably more open-minded about the implications of steam-power than the British: The British public remained unconcerned by them until, in May 1844, Louis-Philippe's third son, François, Prince de Joinville, a professional sailor, published a pamphlet modestly entitled *Notes sur l'État des Forces Navales de la France*, which was rapidly translated and circulated in England under the distinctly more alarming title *On the State of the Naval Strength of France in Comparison with that of England*.

De Joinville's intention had been to stress the weakness of the French navy in relation to that of England. Now, he argued, steam had made it possible to redress the balance, an opportunity France must seize for, 'In a few hours, an army embarked on board a steam fleet at Portsmouth, or in the Thames, could present itself on our coast, could soon penetrate into our rivers, disembark and destroy our cities, arsenals and commercial riches, with shell or bomb.'

The English press and public as a whole, recalling that de Joinville was Louis-Philippe's son, chose to regard his perfectly reasonable plea for a stronger French navy as almost a declaration of war. His description of France's naval weakness was dismissed as a deliberate ruse to make Britain relax her guard and the efforts of Louis-Philippe and his prime minister, François Guizot, to calm matters down were met with similar scepticism.

The Duke of Wellington was of all men the least likely to be influenced by public opinion, much less the press, but gradually he, too, succumbed to the prevailing atmosphere of anxiety. He became reluctant to leave his desk and, according to a close friend, 'night and day he was preoccupied with . . . the danger of war and the defenceless state of our coasts'. Deaf, rarely speaking and notoriously ill-tempered – he was now in his mid-seventies – the great Duke was still articulate on paper and on 20 December 1844 prepared for the Cabinet a *Memorandum on the Works of Defence of the Naval Arsenals and Dockyards* which made all the more impression because it recognised that the navy was more important for home defence than the army. 'Steamers,' argued the Duke, 'are not prepared and fitted out for defensive, but especially for offensive purposes.' The Duke saw little reason to use steam against steam – 'I feel,' he confessed, 'a great preference for the use of sails wherever they can be used, being sensible to the superiority as seamen of the officers and sailors of the British navy' – though reluctantly conceding there might be a case for it 'in tideways and in narrow channels'.

The re-armers' cause received massive encouragement when on Wednesday 30 July 1845 Lord Palmerston, currently in Opposition, devoted a long speech in the House of Commons to 'the great imperfection of the present state of our national means of defence':

> The Channel is no longer a barrier. Steam navigation has rendered that which was before impassable by a military force nothing more than a river passable by a steam bridge. France has steamers capable of transporting 30,000 men, and she has harbours, inaccessible to any attack, in which these steamers may collect . . . directly opposite to our coast and within a few hours' voyage of the different landing-places on the coast of England.

Peel made a predictable response, declaring Palmerston's conclusions to be 'altogether erroneous', but the Duke of Wellington meanwhile was becoming obsessed by the threat created by steampower. During the late summer and early autumn of 1845, a wet and windy season, the Duke toured the south-east coast, often driven by the elements to retreat to his carriage, but collecting the information to enable him, on 10 September, to submit to the prime minister a long memorandum on the naval defences of the country:

> Circumstances are very different from those that existed in 1779 and in the end of the last, and the first years of the present, century . . . Under existing circumstances, the military possession of the Channel by the enemy is not necessary in order to enable him to make a very formidable invasion of this country . . . In a bay between Sandgate Castle, Folkestone and Dymchurch . . . infantry might be landed at any time of tide and whatever might be the nature of the wind . . . Horses might be put into the sea at half tide . . . Infantry might be landed on a fine beach which extends from Dungeness to Rye Harbour . . . Cavalry and artillery must be taken into Rye leaving Rye Harbour itself for the disembarkation of horses and carriages . . . Near Beachy Head there is a fine beach upon which troops could be landed . . . There are roads leading from Beachy Head upon London, by East Grinstead, and likewise upon Brighton. The small harbour of Newhaven is at no great distance and might be used for landing horses. From Beachy Head to Selsey Bill to the coast of Chichester the shore is rocky, but with wind from the east, troops might be landed at any point.

In June 1846, for reasons unconnected with defence, the government fell. That summer relations between France and Great Britain deteriorated still further over the 'Spanish marriages', whereby, in October, a close link was established between the royal houses of France and Spain. Queen Victoria wrote what Palmerston genially described as 'a tickler' to Louis-Philippe, while Palmerston himself, back in the Foreign Office in the new government of Lord John Russell, set about, in his own words, 'getting the affairs of Europe into trim'. He was, he made clear in a note on 17 December 1846, under no illusion about where England's immediate danger lay:

> Our neighbours are kind, civil and hospitable to us individually, but the French nation remembers the Nile, Trafalgar, the Peninsula, Waterloo and St Helena; and would gladly find an opportunity of taking revenge.

Palmerston went on to review the fortification works already in progress and to warn that it was 'a matter of indispensible [sic] necessity' to build new 'detached works' to protect the dockyards. During the winter of 1846-7 all dockyard employees aged 18 to 55 were invited to volunteer for training in gunnery and the use of small arms and by March 1848 more than 9000 out of a total of 12,000 were receiving training, which involved drilling for two hours two or three nights a week between May and August.

Although the sudden capture of one of the navy's vital bases was now remote, the Duke of Wellington, no longer a minister but still Commander-in-Chief, remained deeply troubled by what he believed to be his country's imminent danger. As he walked below the walls of Walmer Castle, from which on a clear day the French coast was plainly visible, he pictured that famous force of 30,000 men, a number now firmly enshrined in all the alarmists' minds, being ferried across by steamships to land unchallenged on the coast of Kent and, within half an hour, be well inland. 'I am as certain of it,' wrote the aging hero to another equally ancient field marshal on 3 April 1847, 'as if it was passing under my view!'

Other old soldiers shared the same anguished vision, among them the Inspector-General of Fortifications, Major-General [later Field Marshal] Sir John Burgoyne, who had served under Wellington and was still a vigorous 64. On 7 November 1846 Sir John completed his subsequently famous *Observations re the Probable Results of a War with France under Our Present System of Military Preparation* and submitted it to the Duke for his information and comments. As old soldiers tended to do, Sir John took a highly pessimistic view, assuming like Wellington that 'the application of steam power' would benefit the attack rather than the defence, and multiplying by a factor of four the numbers who might safely be got ashore.

Burgoyne's assessment remained unpublished until many years later. Not so Wellington's response. On 9 January 1847 he replied in warm and approving terms to this dismal appreciation, ending with a conclusion destined to be much quoted:

> I am bordering on 77 years of age, passed in honour. I hope that the Almighty may protect me from being the witness of the tragedy which I cannot persuade my contemporaries to take measures to avert.

The Duke had meant his letter to be private and was infuriated when it was mentioned in *The Times* of 1 December 1847 and extensively quoted in the *Morning Chronicle* early in January 1848, thanks to what he angrily described as 'the meddling gossip of the ladies of modern times'. Burgoyne had entrusted the copying of the letter to his wife, who had shown it to a female neighbour and she, believing the Duke would like to see it published, had leaked it to the press. The offender's husband, somewhat unchivalrously, was said to have remarked to the Duke, by way of apology, 'The cackling of geese once saved Rome . . . Perhaps the cackling of my old goose may yet save England!'

Russell himself had by now become convinced of the danger and, on 10 January 1848, circulated to his colleagues a memorandum which neither Palmerston nor the Duke himself could have bettered:

> It can hardly be doubted that the French have for a long time made preparations for a naval war . . . against . . . England; and that the preparations of England have been . . . slackened by the security which the great victories of the end of the last war have inspired.
>
> There are three modes by which the French may injure and assail England on the breaking out of a war:
>
> 1. By sending steamers to alarm our coasts and interrupt our trade as proposed by the Prince de Joinville.
>
> 2. By landing a force to bombard and destroy our naval and military arsenals.
>
> 3. By invading England with an army of 30,000 or 40,000 men and marching at once to London.

Russell's apprehension was shared by the First Lord of the Admiralty, and a rare unanimity soon existed within the government on the need for increased expenditure on defence, if only to satisfy the public demand for action. 'People have got into the habit of talking of the landing of the French on the Sussex coast,' the Chancellor of the Exchequer, Sir Charles Wood [later Lord Halifax] had written to Lord John Russell on 5 January, 'as a circumstance to be expected, almost as a matter of course.' What Richard Cobden later dismissed in his book *The Three Panics* as 'the first panic' about invasion now had the nation in its grip:

> It was the first occasion on which the attempt had been made to terrify the public with the idea of a sudden invasion from France in a time of peace, without a declaration of war, and without the hope of conquest, or even the glory of honourable warfare. The theory degraded our civilised and polite neighbours to the level of pirates.

Even the liberal press refused to support Cobden's campaign against rearmament, and the sober *Spectator* carried that January a solemn warning that, in a surprise attack, '500 [men] might insult British blood at Herne Bay, or even inflict indelible shame on the empire at Osborne House!', the queen's recently acquired retreat on the Isle of Wight. Public enthusiasm for increased defence spending began, however, to decline after, on 18 February, Lord John Russell had announced that it would mean raising income tax to 1s [5p], and less than a week later the international situation was suddenly transformed by the first of the great upheavals of 'The Year of Revolutions'. Instead of entering London at the head of a conquering army the elderly King Louis-Philippe arrived in England to claim asylum as a fugitive, under the uninspired alias of 'Mr Smith', a transformation which Queen Victoria described as 'worthy only of a dreadful romance'. By the end of the month the budget had been withdrawn and the proposed increase in income tax cancelled.

During 1849 James Fergusson, a successful business man who had abandoned commerce to study architecture, published his *Proposed New System of Fortification*, which advocated the use of economical earth, rather than expensive stone, to protect vulnerable points, and May 1850 saw the publication by Sir John Burgoyne, this time apparently without female help, of his *Remarks on the Military Condition of Great Britain*, which repeated all his dire predictions about the effects of steam: 'Every vessel, down to their large fishing-boats, would make a transport, each steamer could carry and tow some thousands of troops . . . In any case of angry discussion or a quarrel . . . *we are at their mercy.*' The same theme of a surprise attack was the basis of Sir Francis Head's *The Defenceless State of Great Britain*, a 410-page book crammed with factual information and almost hysterical comment. Head* had been present at Waterloo as an army engineer, and his book was dedicated 'to that half of our community . . . who . . . have, as yet only read of war'.

Head compared Britain's military position to that of Austria, Prussia, Russia and even Belgium, which could actually muster a larger army for home defence than Great Britain. But it was France which was the real enemy, with its regular military training for all males aged from 20 to 60, its large-scale annual camps and protracted manoeuvres and its vigorous young generals, with an average age of 43: their English counterparts, claimed Head, were aged from 68 to 88 and he held a low opinion of their competence: 'I don't believe,' he quoted, 'the highest authority', as having said, 'there are five general officers in our service who, if you put 70,000 men into Hyde Park, could get them out again.'

Much of his book was so exaggerated and overwritten that even other alarmists criticised it but it breathed a stalwart patriotism which even extended to the English climate and 'The continual irrigations with which we are blessed . . . The British nation . . . ' declared this stalwart baronet, 'as long as our moist soft atmosphere lasts, ever will be more robust in body, in heart and in mind, than the inhabitants of gayer, gaudier and dustier climates.' With Head's central argument, that the coming of steam had created a new strategic situation, it also seemed difficult to quarrrel:

The power of steam . . . has converted what Napoleon . . . called 'The ditch of England' to an esplanade from eight to twelve leagues broad . . . which, with a few exceptions, can almost with the regularity of a railway time-table, be crossed by steamers by day or by night throughout the year . . . Combinations . . . such as

---

* See my book *The Workhouse* (Temple Smith, 1974), p. 63, for an account of his colourful career and character.

Napoleon devised for the invasion of England . . . could now be as securely calculated upon as . . . the arrival at 10.30 pm of the Edinburgh express train at Euston station.

During 1851, despite the Great Exhibition, which Queen Victoria described as 'the greatest triumph of peace which the world has ever seen', the French again came to the aid of the alarmists. Following Louis-Philippe's downfall in 1848 they had elected Charles Louis Napoleon Bonaparte, nephew of the famous emperor, as president of the new republic and on 2 December 1851 the new Napoleon forcibly overthrew the constitution, an action immediately endorsed by a popular plebiscite. Although the 40-year-old Bonaparte was well disposed towards the country which had so recently sheltered him – 'L'Angleterre,' he remarked a year or two later, 'c'est admirable' – his mere name was enough to arouse the worst suspicions of most Englishmen, as Cobden recorded:

> The coup d'état of December 2nd 1845 and re-election of Louis Napoleon as President of the Republic . . . furnished the occasion for the outburst of the second invasion panic. From that day to the meeting of parliament, on the 3rd of February, a large portion of the metropolitan journals teemed with letters and articles of the most exciting character . . . They commenced by assailing personally with unmeasured invective, the author of the coup d'état and heaping contemptuous epithets on the French people . . . and then forthwith they raised the cry of invasion and proclaimed our defenceless condition.

The nation's anxiety now soared to a new peak. 'All the world talks of invasion,' noted one nobleman in his diary on 30 January 1852. 'The alarm seems daily to increase.' 'Grave people talk of invasion as an affair of five minutes,' commented the First Lord of the Admiralty. 'The government will require the support of public opinion and that can only be obtained by convincing our countrymen . . . that we have now a dangerous and faithless neighbour,' wrote the editor of The Times, the chief offender, when the new Foreign Secretary, the Earl of Granville, urged him to change his policy. Granville, to silence the agitation, asked all the British consuls at ports in northern France to report on signs of martial preparations. The answer from Britain's man in Le Havre was typical. There had not been, he assured the Foreign Secretary, 'the slightest symptom . . . in any part of this consular district of any preparations of an offensive or defensive character'. On 26 February 1852 a Foreign Office memorandum to the Admiralty, based on the recent survey, confirmed that the French could muster only nine steamers in commission or readily available in the Atlantic and Channel ports, with another 25 in the Mediterranean; the Royal Navy had 30 in her home ports and another 13 within easy steaming distance.

But, somewhat ironically, the Whig government's attempts to

demonstrate that it was taking action against the alleged danger had
already brought about its fall. Two months before, Lord Palmerston
had been dismissed for prematurely approving of Louis Napoleon's
seizure of power. Now, in his own words, he had his 'tit for tat with
John Russell', when, on 19 February 1852, he defeated the government
on its proposal to re-create a county-based rather than, as he favoured,
a more centralised militia.

The following month the new government, under the fourteenth
Earl of Derby [formerly Edward Lord Stanley] introduced a new Militia Bill, to create a force 80,000 strong, formed of volunteers aged 18 to
35; the unpopular ballot would only be used if too few volunteers came
forward. Those recruited would serve for five years, with 21 to 56 days
training each year, but could be embodied for full-time duty in an
emergency. Wellington made what was to prove his last major speech
in the House of Lords in support of the Bill, which in July 1852 became
law.

Throughout 1852 the flood of alarmist publications continued, with
titles like *The Invasion of England*, 'by an Englishman and a Civilian',
Thoughts on National Defence, by a rear-admiral, and, somewhat less
impressive, *Notes on the Defensive Resources of Great Britain*, by a 'half-
pay Royal Artillery' captain. Richard Cobden identified at least 14 such
works of which the most influential was probably *On National Defence
in England*, by a Swiss officer, Captain Maurice de Sellon, writing
under the name of Baron Maurice. Maurice argued that it was to her
soldiers that island Britain must look for security:

> Whatever the system of defence, the effective strength of the army
> must be augmented and the sooner the better, because the fleet will
> never alone, and of itself, preserve the coast of England from a hos-
> tile descent. England may trust to her fortunate star, and to . . . [her]
> maritime supremacy . . . but would it be wise to conclude hence that
> she is invulnerable? Steam navigation, railroads and electric tele-
> graphs . . . smooth the path leading to her shores.

In spite of the indifference, if not hostility, of the public towards the
army, the recognition was growing that the land forces, as well as the
navy, needed to be strengthened. The last significant step forward had
been around 1839 when the percussion cap, known as a 'detonator', replaced the old style flintlock, and thus ruled out the need for pouring
priming powder into the pan of the weapon. Wellington distrusted all
such changes. 'I have . . .,' be boasted, 'taken the course of leaving inventions and inventors to themselves.' He had even unsuccessfully
opposed the introduction of the new Minié rifle, perfected in 1849 by
the French captain who had invented it. In effective range, which rose
from 150 to 800 yards (137 to 731 m), speed of loading and accuracy,
which was quadrupled, the new weapon was vastly superior to the old.

From February 1852, when the first officers and NCOs arrived at Woolwich to be trained as instructors in the use of the Minié the British army began, at least in small arms fire-power, to be able to meet the French on equal terms.

On 14 September 1852 the Duke of Wellington died. His funeral, delayed until 18 November, caused a great upsurge of patriotism and a sudden re-awakening of pride in the army. Alfred [later Lord] Tennyson, who was so often to encapsulate the national mood over the next few years, now justified his recent appointment as Poet Laureate with a resounding *Ode on the Death of the Duke of Wellington*[*], which recalled the famous letter of five years before:

> Remember him who led your hosts;
> He bade you guard the sacred coasts.
> Your cannon moulder on the seaward wall;
> His voice is silent in your council-hall.

In fact the great Duke's voice was anything but silent. His warning of the nation's vulnerability now took on all the force of a death-bed exhortation, and the earth-fortifications enthusiast, James Fergusson, dedicated *The Peril of Portsmouth*, published later that year, 'to the memory of England's greatest military commander, whose last earnest appeal to his fellow countrymen was a prayer that they would arm to resist an invader'. The famous Lines of Torres Vedras built by Wellington during the Peninsular War in Portugal, had, Fergusson pointed out in his detailed 80-page essay, been made not of stone but earth. 'While all works built *selon les règles* [according to the rules] fall like card-houses,' he went on, 'field-works constructed in haste according to no system at all, may resist even those who never failed before.' The lesson ought not be forgotten in planning the defence of the places on which Great Britain's survival depended:

> If Portsmouth were in possession of an enemy, nearly half of the defensive power of England by her fleet is gone at once; and if, in addition to this, the enemy were able to destroy Plymouth and the Medway dockyards then the French fleet would *ipso facto* be superior to the English and they could then maintain the supremacy in the Channel . . . In possession of Portsmouth they could organise their means of attack at leisure and . . . advance securely on the capital, and, even if eventually defeated, retreat as securely along that line and return in safety with their plunder to their own country.

About such a warning there was nothing new, but already, warned Fergusson, the danger from steam-powered paddle-boats which had

[*] The poem contains the much-quoted:

Not once or twice in our rough island-story,
The path of duty was the way to glory.

so exercised Wellington had been overtaken by a new threat:

> Portsmouth may be attacked by screw line-of-battle ships . . . with every prospect of success. The French now possess four such ships . . . and are understood to be building others. These vessels carry from ninety to a hundred guns of the heaviest calibre and . . . are all equal to at least ten knots per hour in smooth water . . . At this rate of speed about ten minutes would elapse from the time when they first came within effective reach of the guns of Southsea Castle till they were safely past all danger and anchored inside the harbour.

These ten minutes, Fergusson predicted, could be fatal for England for 'one broadside will probably finish the defences of Southsea Castle for ever'. He therefore proposed a new line of guns on earthen ramparts, with 'a parapet six feet [1.8 m] high over which the guns would fire', far harder to knock out and far more cost-effective than strengthening the existing stone defences. As for the danger of an attack from the land, a six-and-a-half-mile [10.5-km] military canal on the east side of Portsea Island, to prevent an enemy assembling on the west beach of Hayling Island and around Chichester Harbour, might be excavated at a cost of no more than 4d [1½p] a yard [0.91 m] and the spoil used to construct a solid rampart. The total bill, excluding additional guns and barracks, Ferguson put at no more than £250,000.

The Peril of Portsmouth, persuasively argued and showing a proper Victorian regard for saving money, made a deep impression and Louis Napoleon now lent fuel to the fire of every patriot's fears. In defiance of the declaration made after Waterloo that no Bonaparte could ever sit on the throne of France, a plebiscite was held on Louis Napoleon's intention to do precisely that and on 2 December 1852 he was proclaimed Emperor with the title of Napoleon III. On the same day, 6 December 1852, that the news of Napoleon's new title was formally reported to Parliament, the government announced that the navy would be increased by 50,000 men, since, 'It was absolutely necessary that we should put our Channel defences in a new position and man the Channel with a large force.'

25

A BLOW TO THE HEART

Any blow that may be launched from Cherbourg will . . . be . . . aimed at England's very heart.

The Times, *13 July 1858*

'We have done more in two years than during the last century.' These words, written by the new Commander-in-Chief, General Sir Henry [later Field Marshal Viscount] Hardinge in November 1854 to Lord Palmerston, who in the following February became prime minister, summed up the vast military changes which followed Wellington's death. Hardinge was already 67 when he succeeded the Duke, but rapidly justified the *United Service Magazine*'s description of him as 'a friend to improvement'. In May 1853 a school of musketry was opened at Hythe. Its range, 1400 yards [1280 m] long, at last enabled effective training to take place and everywhere the training allowance was raised from 30 to 90 cartridges a man. Finding adequate practice grounds for artillery was more difficult. Firing at Plumstead marches, close to Woolwich, the Royal Artillery's base, had constantly to be suspended when there was traffic on the River Thames behind it, but Hardinge in his earlier post as Master-General of the Ordnance had already begun to develop a new, experimental site on the sands at Shoeburyness in Essex and here too the annual training allowance, formerly a mere 30 rounds a gun, was now, in 1853, increased to 140.

At the time of Hardinge's appointment, most of the army was still dispersed about the country in small detachments, partly as a legacy of its 'police-force' role, but also because, as one general warned, 'It is only by keeping the troops scattered and out of sight that we are enabled to keep up any army at all in this country.' Hardinge realised, however, that the upsurge of pro-army feeling following Wellington's death had produced a new situation and in January 1853 the new Secretary at War agreed that funds would be found for a camp for 7000 men during the coming summer. The choice finally fell on a site near Chobham in Surrey, where the rough heathland, with a mixture of dry turf and bog, free of trees, provided ideal terrain for exercising the infantry. The cavalry had, for once, to take second place. Hardinge also saw the camp as providing an opportunity for the troops to learn how to make themselves comfortable under active service conditions. One unit at least arrived unable to build a camp kitchen, but, as an observer remarked, 'The men showed considerable skill and alacrity in hutting themselves . . . out of the brushwood and earth available, and on the whole imparted a confidence to the country that they would not be found wanting when their services might be needed in the field.'*

The camp at Chobham proved a watershed in the history of the British army. 'We have treated, tried and found defective, much that we fancied perfect in the organisation, training, clothing, equipping, and arming of all branches of the service,' acknowledged the *Naval and Military Gazette*. 'We have seen, too, how easily mistakes can be made through ignorance of first principles of manoeuvre.' Almost as valuable was the way in which Chobham consolidated the army's new-found prestige. 'The camp is keeping alive a martial spirit,' Hardinge considered, 'and the good effect will not be limited to the training of the troops; it is pervading the whole population.' He encouraged visitors, especially MPs, for whose benefit the most spectacular exercises took place on Saturdays, and the general public should, Hardinge urged, be given 'the most liberal freedom of the camp, to make it as popular as the [Great] Exhibition'.

In spite of Hardinge's efforts Parliament, with scant regard for the army's needs, agreed in late August 1853, just as the camp was being dispersed, that the site at Chobham should be enclosed and sold, but already he had become convinced that a large, permanent site of 8-10,000 acres [3240-4050 hectares] was needed, on which whole regular divisions, and perhaps even militia battalions, could be camped, or housed in huts, for the five summer months of the year. At Aldershot, then a mere village in mid-Hampshire, he found what he was seeking. Halfway between London and Portsmouth, it was also close to railway lines serving Chatham and Dover. 'This tract of land,' the Commander-in-Chief advised, 'is . . . suited for a permanent camp of instruction in peace and of concentration in war.' £100,000 was immediately found to acquire almost 6500 acres [2633 hectares] but further land continued to be bought for the next six years. It was eventually decided to build permanent barracks, with tents being added in summer, to enable a total of up to three divisions of 10,000 men each to be exercised simultaneously. The recent outbreak of war with Russia, of which more will be said later, had created a favourable climate for such expenditure. 'The state of popular feeling engendered by the war is such,' the Prince Consort observed, 'that you can now ask Parliament for anything you want.' As for the barracks, 'Put permanent buildings on the land and the country will never be allowed to

* Strachan p.167. Most of the quotations in this and the previous chapter come from the same author, to whom I acknowledge a heavy debt.

sell it.' By September 1854 work was already under way and by January 1855 the expenditure of £250,000 had been approved to create what those familiar with the Prussian army's base near Berlin described as an 'improved Potsdam'.

The years which saw Aldershot, soon a large and prosperous town, established as 'the home of the British army' were also a golden age for the re-formed militia. Wellington's funeral generated such a rush to volunteer that by January 1854 66,280 men had enrolled of the 80,000 required and it was decided that no ballot was necessary. Most militiamen were trained as light infantry, or to man fortifications, but by September 1853 no fewer than 3500 were being taught to become gunners.

In the House of Commons Benjamin Disraeli, a future prime minister, complained of the French government being 'painted as corsairs and banditti, watching to attack our coasts without the slightest warning', and when, on 28 March 1854, England and France declared war, it was not on each other but on Russia, in a dispute over the control of the Holy Places in Jerusalem, prompted by fear of Russian ambitions towards Turkey. The Crimean War brought no risk of invasion, and led to a wholly untypical degree of friendship with France. When – that recurrent nightmare of so many generations – the French emperor, in the blue tunic and red trousers of a French general, stepped ashore at Dover he was greeted by a cheering crowd, and Victoria herself paid the new Napoleon the highest accolade in her power: 'The emperor is an *unlike a Frenchman* as possible, being much more *German* than French in character.' That August the Queen and Prince Consort went to Paris and received an equally rapturous reception. Victoria even stood in homage before Napoleon I's tomb, while Edward, Prince of Wales, on her instructions, actually knelt as if at a shrine. 'It seems,' wrote the queen in her diary, 'as if in this tribute of respect to a departed and great foe, old enmities and rivalries were wiped out', and the visit did indeed have important international consequences for it marked the start of Prince Edward's deep and lifelong attachment to all things French.

For the army the results of the Crimean War were traumatic. The catastrophic failure of the medical services and of the supply organisation, which meant that most of the casualties were not lost in action but caused by cold and hunger, provided a lasting lesson for its senior officers and, thanks to the war correspondents and photographers serving with it, to the nation. The resulting shock carried Palmerston into office as prime minister in February 1855, and about the same time, a then novel idea, regular meetings began to be held each week of the Commander-in-Chief, the Lieut.-General of the Ordnance, and their political chief, the Secretary of State for War, with whose post that of Secretary at War was now merged. Thus for the first time a central council existed to direct military affairs and in the same year, not before time, responsibility for the militia was transferred from the Home Office to the War Office.

The Royal Navy had suffered less than the army during the long years of peace, but its elderly commanders had shown a similar reluctance to accept that times had changed. A few years earlier the First Sea Lord himself had complained that 'since the introduction of steamers he had never seen a clean deck, or a captain who . . . did not look like a sweep', but of ten line-of-battle ships assembled in an operational squadron in 1853 only three lacked auxiliary steam power, while of the 13 steam frigates and corvettes collected only five still had the outmoded paddles. The navy in the Crimea learned some salutary lessons, notably that its own solid-shot firing cannon were hopelessly outclassed by the new 'shell guns' which discharged explosive missiles. The Russian fortifications at Cronstadt and Sebastopol proved almost impervious to the allied bombardment, while the French, by draping some of their ships with metal plates – though it was the British who coined the name 'ironclads' for such vessels – proved better able to engage shore-based batteries than the Royal Navy.

The coming of steam, with coal and machinery having to be accommodated as well as the crew, made life for the sailor no easier, but in 1853 a significant improvement had been made in his lot with the introduction of a continuous 20-year engagement which entitled him, like the soldier, to a pension; previously he had been paid off at the end of every commission and had to start his service afresh. The press gang was never formally abolished but, with a proper professional career now available, ceased to be necessary, and simply disappeared.

The Treaty of Paris, imposed on the Russians by the victorious allies in March 1856, marked the end of the honeymoon period of Anglo-French relations. That Napoleon III himself was well-disposed towards England was probably true, but the fear that he might be pushed by public opinion and by anglophobe officers into a more militant policy was far from fanciful.

In January 1858, a new outburst of anti-British feeling occurred in Paris following the Orsini affair, an attempt by an Italian to assassinate Napoleon III with bombs made in England, when some French regiments passed resolutions urging the emperor to allow them to 'seek out and chastise the protectors of these assassins in their own country'. But it was the development of Cherbourg, and especially the opening of a new rail link between there and Paris, that caused most ill-feeling in England, for the great port was a mere 70 miles [112 km] from the coast of Devon. The public was unimpressed by the French, and Cobdenite, argument that by making trade easier the new works would further the cause of peace. 'It is against England alone that it is constructed,' warned The Times bluntly on 13 July 1858. 'Any blow that may be launched from Cherbourg will . . . be short, it will be straight, deadly and decisive, aimed at England's very heart.'

This unspoken fear underlay the week-long festivities at Cherbourg to mark the opening of the enlarged port in August 1858. Although the emperor and his wife entertained Victoria and Albert on their imperial yacht, and the customary speeches were made about the two countries' continuing friendship, there were alarming undertones, not lost on the 30 Members of Parliament and the owners of the 140 privately owned English yachts which attended the celebrations. A statue was unveiled to Napoleon I, hundreds of gold eagles were to be seen on the lamp-posts and the queen was taken to inspect the new and supposedly im-pregnable fort of La Roule. 'Cherbourg protects the emperor against all the world,' commented *The Times* on 9 August 1858, and its cor-respondent's report struck a distinctly un-*cordiale* note:

> Cannons, cannons, cannons, wherever you turned. They poured upon you from every corner, they commanded every turning . . . One could not help wondering what in the name of wonder they were meant to attack or defend.

The queen once back at home expressed her concern that Great Britain seemed about to lose her traditional naval superiority to France. 'It will,' wrote Victoria, 'be the first time in her history that she will find herself in an absolute minority of ships on the sea.' Widespread anxiety also existed that the French navy was also being re-equipped with iron-clads, impervious to British cannon, and furnished with the new rifled artillery with a range of 8000 yards [7300 m], twice that of existing guns, and able to wreak havoc on Britain's 'wooden walls' and on the forts protecting their bases. A committee set up to study rifled gun de-sign reported in November 1858 that Sir William Armstrong's rifled breech-loader, under development and trial since 1854, was superior to its rivals, but this brought no reassurance, for all experience showed that one country rapidly adopted improvements pioneered by another.

In December 1858 the government set up an internal committee of four civil servants to investigate the relative strengths of the British and French navies. On 3 April its report was published. This revealed that Great Britain's steam navy – no one now considered that ships with sails alone really counted – amounted to 464 vessels against France's 264, but most of the Royal Navy's lead consisted of small gunboats and the like; in capital ships France was already equal to the Royal Navy, while in the dreaded ironclads, of which she had four under con-struction, notably the powerful *La Gloire*, she was actually ahead. A new alarmist pamphlet, *Our Naval Position and Policy, by a Naval Peer*, now added to the prevailing excitement. 'Obtaining command of the Channel,' an unidentified French naval officer was quoted as saying, 'France could do . . . at any time, or rather she *has* command of the

Channel at the present moment.'

The spring and summer of 1859 were dominated by questions of defence. On 12 May, as will be described later, the Conservative government formally approved the re-creation of the Volunteer movement, but the work was actually undertaken by Lord Palmerston's Liberal government, which took office on 12 June. The following month the new government announced its intention to appoint a Royal Commission on national defence, which was formally established on 20 August; meanwhile, on 13 August, two important measures initiated by the Conservatives had become law. One set up an Army Reserve, up to 20,000 strong, of ex-servicemen willing to train for 12 days a year and to be recalled to the colours in an emergency. The other created the Royal Naval Volunteer Reserve, of up to 30,000 seamen who agreed to undertake an annual 28 days training.

With a few exceptions, like Cobden, the leading figures in both parties were now committed to a policy of expanding the nation's defences; and back-benchers in both Houses vied with each other in warning of the dire preparations in progress on the far side of the Channel. According to one Conservative MP, Sir Charles Napier, who was, Cobden believed, 'possessed by a morbid apprehension amounting almost to monomania, respecting the threatening attitude of France . . . 30 sail-of-the-line could lie alongside' the new wharves at Cherbourg, 'the troops could walk on board . . . cavalry mounted on their horses could ride on board' and the whole force could set sail confident that its 'modern shell guns would tear holes in the sides of our wooden ships through which it would be easy to drive a wheelbarrow.' A debate on the Navy Estimates on 8 July gave the alarmists their cue for a new spate of warnings and, assured in advance of parliamentary and public support for heavier taxation, the government announced during July that it would be appointing a committee 'to decide,' as Palmerston reminded the House in his reply to the debate of 29 July, 'which were the works best calculated to secure our naval establishments'.

During the debate, a relatively obscure former minister, Edward Horsman, made in the House of Commons what Cobden described as 'the great panic speech of the session':

He apprehended war because he saw the emperor of the French preparing for it; and he anticipated invasion because an attempted invasion must be a necessary accompaniment of the war . . . Those who were not wilfully blind must see the most unmistakable proofs of preparation for invasion . . . The extension of the navy, the fortification of the [French] coast, the enlargement and increase in the number of transports . . . all indicated preparation for a gigantic enterprise . . . Not a moment must be lost . . . Every public or private yard should be put into full work; every artificer and extra hand should work extra hours as if the war were to begin next week . . . Night and day the process of constructing, arming, drilling should go on till the country was made safe.

It was precisely such speeches, Cobden told the House, that might bring about the disaster they were supposed to prevent. 'We are in very great danger of a war with France . . . I have heard persons say, "We had better fight it out and destroy the French navy".' The remedy, he insisted, was to reduce armaments instead of increasing them, but such views were unfashionable.

A week later, on 5 August, Parliament returned to the subject and Palmerston stated confidently that if war broke out, 'we could put into the field something little short of 200,000 fighting men', composed of 60,000 regulars, 100,000 militia, 14,000 yeomanry and another 14,000 pensioners, marines and members of dockyard defence battalions. It might therefore have been wondered why vast new fortifications were needed at all, but the country was in no mood to have its fears allayed and in the grip of something close to hysteria. When, soon afterwards, Cobden set out for France a friend he stayed with en route explained that he would not be visiting the Continent that year for fear of being interned when the war broke out. Meanwhile the country was alive that summer with newly joined Volunteers drilling, and public meetings to form new units, but it was not only these that were taken over by the alarmists, as Cobden complained:

Especially was it so at the Agricultural Societies' meetings, whose orators, instead of descanting on the rival breeds of cattle, or the various kinds of tillage, discussed the prospects of an invasion . . .

'How much will you charge the French for your corn when they land?' cried one of his audience to a sturdy Somersetshire yeoman who was on his legs addressing them; and his reply, 'They shall pay for it with their blood', elicited rounds of applause.

26

RIFLEMEN FORM!

Form! Form! Riflemen form!
Ready, be ready to meet the storm!

'The War', *by the Poet Laureate, published in* The Times, *9 May 1859.*

The summer of 1859 can be seen in retrospect as the turning point after which the nation ceased to look back to the last war against France and began to prepare for the next. This change of attitude was epitomised by the re-formation of the Volunteers, who had officially been disbanded in 1814. The campaign for a Volunteer force only began to achieve results during January and February 1852, when the government did reluctantly approve the formation of one or two units. The first was the South Devon Volunteer Rifle Association, recruited in and around Exeter, the medical superintendent of the local lunatic asylum providing the driving force, though as each man's equipment and uniform cost twelve guineas [£12.60] membership must have been confined to the better-off. The ambiguous official attitude to what appeared to be a wholly patriotic impulse merely encouraged the campaign. The Poet Laureate, Alfred [later Lord] Tennyson in 1852 donated five guineas [£5.25] to the cause and weighed in with a pertinent poem 'Britons, guard your own'. A far lesser figure who ultimately became a national joke, Martin Tupper, was meanwhile firing off a whole series of works on the same theme, often, like his 'Bugle Call from a Volunteer Rifleman', in April 1852, lending themselves to parody:

> Much as ever, more than ever,
> Is the duty high and deep,
> Dozing England to endeavour
> Not to let you go to sleep.

Both in leading articles and in the correspondence columns the press was by now almost unanimously in favour of a national organisation being launched with government support. The politicians might well have been ready to comply, but the soldiers remained hostile, the case being vigorously put by the Duke of Cambridge, who in September

1856 had succeeded the reforming Lord Hardinge as Commander-in-Chief, in a letter to the Secretary of State for War, Lord Panmure [formerly Fox Maule, later Earl of Dalhousie]:

I dismiss at once from my mind all the ideas in the public prints about volunteer corps. If such a system were to be adopted, the spirit of the regular army would be destroyed . . . Volunteers would do as much or as little duty as they liked and in fact they would be an armed and very dangerous rabble.

During 1857 public pressure on the government continued. Martin Tupper returned to the charge in August with 'Hurrah for the Rifle. A Song for Rifle Clubs', which predicted 'That the crack of the rifle shall hint to the foe How terrible once was the twang of the bow', and that month wrote to the *Daily News* complaining that 'our rulers are now bagging grouse upon the moors' instead of tackling the Volunteer question.

In September *The Times*, always the alarmists' chief spokesman, urged that, 'We must popularise the army and martialise the population', and no less active than *The Times* was its younger rival, the *Daily Telegraph*, founded in 1855. Martin Tupper thought that its first editor, A.B. (Alfred) Richards, a former barrister like himself, had more claim than anyone to be the real founder of the mid-Victorian Volunteers. Another claimant for the title of 'father of the Volunteers' is yet another ex-lawyer, Hans Busk, high sheriff of Radnorshire, who was said to have addressed 147 public meetings on the subject between 1858 and 1861, and another constant campaigner was a Liverpool businessman, Nathaniel Bousfield, who tried for four years to obtain government support for a local Rifle Club.

From January 1859 public meetings calling for a single recognised force instead of the existing variety of Rifle Clubs, with their confusing diversity of weapons and uniforms, were being held everywhere. Ministers were also under pressure from another powerful quarter nearer at hand, the Prince Consort. In a memorandum of 6 May 1859, Albert conceded the inherent instability of units founded 'on temporary enthusiasm', and acknowledged 'the danger . . . that their irregular efforts would produce confusion', but nevertheless, as he wrote a few days later, he considered, 'the country's feeling . . . and its instincts sound' in wishing 'to form a Volunteer Corps'. In late April 1859 the French invaded Italy, provoking a conflict with Austria, which in turn, on Monday 9 May 1859, prompted *The Times* to publish a subsequently famous poem, 'The War':

There is a sound of thunder afar,
Storm in the South that darkens the day,
Storm of battle and thunder of war,
Well, if it does not roll our way . . .

Form! Form! Riflemen form!
Ready, be ready to meet the storm!
Riflemen, riflemen, riflemen form!

'Riflemen form!', the title under which 'The War' was later reissued, provided the alarmists with a splendid slogan, and Martin Tupper now achieved a brief moment of undeserved glory for in Paris, where copies of *The Globe* reprinting the poem were seized, it was assumed he was the author, who was identified by the initial 'T'. No Poet Laureate, the French considered, revealing their ignorance of British institutions, would have been allowed to compose a work so offensive to a foreign power. In fact the poem had all Tennyson's hallmarks and may finally have tipped the scale for only three days after its appearance, the Secretary of State for War on 12 May 1859 sent a circular to the Lords Lieutenant formally authorising them to approve, at their discretion, the formation of Volunteer Corps in their counties, under the Act of 1804. This laid down that those coming forward were 'liable to be called out in case of actual invasion or the appearance of an enemy in force', and to qualify as an 'effective' each member would have to do at least 24 days' drill a year, but, except when on actual service, could resign by giving 14 days' notice. Each unit remained a voluntary society, whose members were not, except when on active service, subject to military law, its property being for legal purposes vested in the commanding officer. The CO and his officers were to be nominated by the Lord Lieutenant, their commissions being issued by the crown, but all ranks would have 'to provide their own arms and equipment and to defray all expenses attending the corps except in the event of its being assembled for active service'.

The Prince Consort personally drafted a series of *Instructions to Lord Lieutenants* which he sent to General Peel on 20 May 1859, and they were 'adopted and ordered to be issued forthwith'. This document, issued on 24 May, formed the basis of the 'organisation and working' of the whole Volunteer movement. Albert stressed that these new part-time warriors were not expected to compete with the professionals and challenge the enemy in vast encounter battles but to serve as skirmishers:

> The nature of our country, with its numerous enclosures . . . gives peculiar importance to the service of Volunteer riflemen, in which bodies each man, deriving confidence from his own skill in the use of his arm and from his reliance on the support of his comrades – men whom he has known . . . from his youth up . . . would hang with the most telling effect upon the flanks and communications of a hostile army.

On 24 May, while the prince's circular was awaiting distribution, *The Times* reprinted the advice to Volunteer officers written several years earlier by the now deceased Sir Charles Napier. This, too, urged them to concentrate on essentials:

> Let your practice at a target be constant. Also habituate your corps to long marches of from 15 to 20 miles [24 to 32 km], with arms and ammunition, and also to running, or 'double quick time'.

Napier also tackled the thorny problem of working-class recruits:

> Do not be exclusive in forming your corps. Take your gamekeepers as your comrades and any of your labourers that will enrol themselves. A gentleman will find no braver or better comrades than amongst his own immediate neighbours and tenants. Should you require to throw up a breastwork, they will be more handy with the spades and pickaxes than yourselves.

The new Secretary of State for War, Sidney Herbert, in the government formed by Palmerston in June in succession to Lord Derby's, made no bones about *his* view. 'What we want now,' he said in a debate in the House of Commons on 5 July 1859, 'is to get the middle classes imbued with an interest in our means of defence and I think the Volunteer corps will be useful in doing that.'

The first commission given to a Volunteer officer, on 11 June 1859, went to Nathaniel Bousfield of Liverpool and four days later he marched at the head of 180 men to a civic reception at the Liverpool Exchange. (By 1860 he was a colonel, in command of 2200 men, forming the 1st Lancashire Brigade of Volunteers.) The editor of the *Daily Telegraph* was transformed into Colonel Richards, CO of the 3rd City of London Rifle Corps, while Hans Busk became a captain. As might have been anticipated, only Martin Tupper failed to acquire any military honours. A mere twenty people turned up at a meeting on Wednesday 20 July 1859 at the Town Hall in Guildford, to found a unit based on his home village of Aldbury, and it was not till November that Tupper managed to found 'The Blackheath Rifles' – a name taken from the same locality – with himself as secretary. In this capacity he issued somewhat high-handed warnings to the locals to keep away from the Club's unofficial range – 'Let no-one be gathering sticks in the Heath-field wood on Wednesday afternoon' – and laid down a revealing scale of punishments for various misdemeanours: 'For wilfully pointing a loaded rifle at any bystander: expulsion; For discharging the rifle accidentally: half a crown'. In most places Volunteer units were founded by influential local people asking the mayor to hold a public meeting; sometimes a vicar, the local MP or the Lord Lieutenant took the chair. Occasionally active opposition was encountered, especially in working-class areas, where the slogan 'No vote! No rifle' made a powerful appeal. In December 1859 in Rochdale, home of Cobden's pacifist ally John Bright, the motion to found a corps was heavily defeated, many of the audience, the *Rochdale Observer* explained, regarding the proposal as a 'a Tory device to keep them out of their political rights'. There was similar opposition at Huddersfield, led by its future mayor and MP. Occasionally such critics tried to take over a meeting, but Napoleon III's aggression had split the so-called 'Peace Party' and by 1868 of 90 Volunteer officers in the House of Commons the majority were Liberals.

The Secretary of State for War, Sidney Herbert, directly responsible for the Volunteers, had little faith in them. 'My view . . . ,' he acknowledged in private, 'is to keep up a fair standing army, with a disembodied [i.e. not permanently mobilised] militia behind it, and an auxiliary force of Volunteers, composed of men who will do the work for the liking of it and maintain themselves. But the two first . . . are the really dependable force.' It was Herbert, however, who gave the Volunteers their first real assistance when on 13 July 1859 he sent out another circular which, having reaffirmed the principle that 'the very essence of a Volunteer force consists in their undertaking themselves to bear . . . the whole charges of their training and practice', immediately breached it. The government would, he announced, provide sufficient rifles to equip 25 per cent of the men in each unit classed as 'effectives'; from January 1860 rifles were supplied for the whole strength, and from February a paid adjutant to administer each corps, followed in August 1861 by a sergeant-instructor.

In spite of this modest infusion of public money the Volunteers were initially drawn overwhelmingly from the middle classes, just as Sidney Herbert had intended. Few shared the robust readiness of the Lord Lieutenant of Warwickshire 'to shoulder his rifle by the side of a sweep' if necessary; more typical was the blanket ban on working-class recruitment imposed by the Lord Lieutenant of Cambridgeshire on the grounds 'that if a weapon was given to a man who had no real property, his natural tendency would be to acquire it.'

At this period, when manual workers were enrolled it was often as a kind of private army, and 'Volunteer' was a misnomer, though no evidence exists of any reluctance to serve; the average footman or stable-hand probably found dressing up in military uniform to engage in rifle practice an agreeable change from his normal duties. The queen set an example by providing uniforms and training for her servants at Osborne and Windsor, though anxiety was expressed that if the game-keepers went off to fight the French, the royal pheasants and hares would be at the mercy of the local poachers. More typical were the units formed by one peer at his two family seats in the North Riding of Yorkshire, where, it was noted in December 1859, 'the whole of the male members of the household are daily turned out for drill'. The printers of Edinburgh, however, protested at 'the very old-fashioned notion that if the thing is patronised by the "maister" the men will of course "fall in"', and in Monmouthshire in South Wales the Tredegar Ironworks Rifle Corps remained, it was emphasised, 'entirely independent of the works'.

The real problem arose, however, over the appointment of officers. In August 1859 the Lord Lieutenant of Kent, Lord Sydney, stoutly declared that, 'We ignore all clubs and election of officers.' His refusal to recommend for a commission anyone he considered of inadequate social standing led him to turn down a solicitor, at Sheerness, and, more understandably, the keeper of the garrison canteen at Chatham. The captain of a Southampton company refused to promote a sergeant to become an ensign since, as a draper's son, he was unfit socially to sit at his table, and a similar situation developed at Lyncombe in Somerset, in spite of a widely signed petition in support of the rejected NCO. The poet and schools inspector Matthew Arnold, a Volunteer himself, protested against 'the hideous English toadyism with which lords and great people are invested with the commands in the corps they join, quite without respect of . . . their efficiency'; but probably more people would have agreed with the Surrey Volunteer captain who argued that, 'Society . . . cannot assimilate the social rank of an officer in Her Majesty's service with one who serves beer over a public-house counter, or measures you for a suit of clothes in his shirt sleeves'.*

In democratically minded Tower Hamlets, in East London, the members of one working men's unit declared that 'they would not submit to it' if officers nominated by the Lord Lieutenant were forced upon them, but of 605 Volunteer officers who served in London between 1860 and 1872, 174 were classed as professional men, including doctors, architects, surveyors, civil engineers, civil servants, writers and students; another 73 were described as merchants, 71 as manufacturers, and 51 identified as 'financial', including stockbrokers, bankers and accountants. Only 41 were described as 'gentlemen', i.e. of independent means; in the country the proportion would probably have been higher.

As for the rank and file, these always included many men in what would now be called white collar occupations, but an official study in 1862 suggested that more than half earned their living by their hands, although most of these were classified as 'mechanics and artisans' from the skilled end of the working-class spectrum. The gulf between craftsman and labourer was as wide as that between duke and baronet. Even in industrial Glasgow 'mere labourers' were not accepted as Volunteers and one Manchester unit contained 347 artisans, many of them skilled foundry workers, but only 21 labourers. Often the first company formed remained relatively exclusive, and men from humbler backgrounds were directed towards new units. In Birkenhead five

* This quotation, like most in this chapter, comes from Hugh Cunningham, *The Volunteer Force*, an excellent study to which I am greatly indebted.

companies accepted farm servants and labourers, while four others drew only on the upper echelons of working men. In Edinburgh there were five specifically 'artisan' corps and in the 19th Middlesex Rifle Volunteers in London the most typical occupations were those of clerk, warehouseman or shop worker. Working-class recruits, at first admitted reluctantly, often came to outnumber the original members. At Sydenham, the 8th Kent Volunteers, formed in June 1859, had already shrunk a year later to a mere 62 'efficient' members and were reduced to inviting '53 respectable artisans whose references had been enquired into'. These recruits were allowed to buy their uniforms at the rate of 6d [2½p] a week, though by January 1861 there were complaints of 'some two or three even working at the bench in their [uniform] trousers'.

The desire to enrol working men was not due solely to a wish to maximise the numbers under training. Like the temperance movement,* the Volunteers were seen as a way of exposing the working men to civilising influences and a step in that 'self-help' so attractive to many Victorians. Membership, claimed a colour sergeant in one working-class corps, in 1862, had made men recruited from a part of London once notorious for Chartist sympathies, 'more attached to the government in every way, and less likely ever to promote political agitation'. That same year a captain in the same, admittedly model, unit, told a government enquiry that Volunteering had produced men 'less idle and dissipated, and more respectful to authority' than formerly. 'Casinos, dancing saloons, skittle alleys, billiard rooms and similar places have been closed by the absence of . . . men who once frequented them.' Employers who ran works-based units had even more cause for satisfaction. 'Every man,' in the 24th Middlesex (Post Office) Volunteers, the same enquiry was told, 'knew that unless he behaved well in camp, his PO chief would come to know of his conduct.'

One subject on which all other ranks agreed was that they did not want to be mistaken for regular soldiers – not, their cynical fellow citizens might have observed, that there was much danger of this happening. 'There seems to be strong objection on the part of Volunteers to be dressed in scarlet,' acknowledged an official Inspector of Volunteers in southern England in 1862. One MP in a letter in *The Times* made a thoroughly practical, but distinctly unpopular, suggestion:

> The best uniform for a rifle corps composed chiefly of inhabitants of country towns and villages is a common round frock, such as is worn by labourers . . . the colour of stubble, decayed fern, leaves, sticks etc . . . with a brown soft leather belt . . . to hold the car-

---

* See my book *The Waterdrinkers* (1968) for a detailed history of the temperance movement. Its supporters, largely drawn from the 'peace' wing of the Liberal Party, tended to be hostile to the Volunteers, and also suspicious of the drinking associated with Volunteer parades.

tridges, and a black or green wideawake hat.

The government discouraged dark blue, initially favoured by many Volunteer units, as too conspicuous in the field and recommended a simple outfit of blouse, trousers, greatcoat and cap in light grey, but any regiment remained free to adopt and retain whatever uniform it could afford to pay for.

The campaigners who had claimed that a large reservoir existed of men eager to receive part-time military training were soon proved right. Around 60,000 men were believed, in February 1859, to belong to rifle and other quasi-military clubs, and following the May 1859 circular the recruits began to flow in. The overall strength of the movement was estimated, in January 1860, at between 73,800 and 100,000.*

That month the Queen's Speech at the opening of Parliament referred to the movement as having added 'an important element to our system of national defence' and the Queen and Prince Albert presided at a great review of 18,450 Volunteers in Hyde Park on the afternoon of Saturday 23 June 1860 as splendid as any that Henry VIII or George III had ever witnessed. 'The troops kept the best of time,' *The Times* reported. 'Had the operation been rehearsed several times instead of the 50 corps never having seen one another till that hour, it could not have been better executed.'

In November 1859 the Scottish MP Lord Elcho, who had been the great champion of the working-man Volunteer and had founded the kilted London Scottish unit, set up the National Rifle Association, open to other civilians as well as Volunteers, to promote the sport, and on 2 July 1860 the Queen, discreetly guided by Lord Elcho himself, personally opened the new 1000-yard [914-m] range on Wimbledon Common, scoring a bullseye with a pre-sighted rifle at 400 yards [366 m]. The event actually made a profit, for £2000 was taken in gate-money from the crowds of onlookers, and field-days in which Volunteer units staged mock battles against each other soon became a popular Victorian entertainment.

The Volunteers had by now their own independent, and sometimes critical, periodical, the *Volunteer Service Gazette*, and had inspired a growing number of other publications and articles. *A Volunteer's Scrap-Book*, published in 1861, illustrated the annoyances of the Volunteer life, notably that of a line of small boys marching derisively behind a uniformed Volunteer on his way to or from parade. The 29th Middlesex grew so weary of such attentions that they eventually paraded at 7 am but 'even at that early hour, many young street gamins were to be found bellowing and shouting around the battalion.' The

* Cunningham, p. 15. Cousins, p. 103, says, 'By the end of May [1859] the total had swollen to 134,000', but as he quotes no source and it is not clear if all these joined officially approved units I have followed Cunningham.

whole movement suffered when one trigger-happy novice, early in 1860, fired on a dog, which was annoying him, in Wandsworth Park. All over the country the ritual cry of, 'Who shot the dog?' was raised whenever Volunteers appeared and twelve years later, so reluctant were the simple-minded to let a good joke die, two Southwark Volunteers were charged with assault on a passer-by who sought to give it a new twist by shouting after them, 'Who shot the cat?'

In spite of such incidents the Volunteer movement had clearly come to stay and on 16 May 1862 the government set up a Royal Commission, consisting of six Volunteer and two regular officers, two civilians and an independent chairman, to report on it. This provided the first accurate assessment of its strength, at just under 163,000, of whom 134,000 were riflemen, 24,000 artillerymen, 3000 engineers, and the rest light horse or mounted infantry. The commissioners gave this formidable array a glowing report:

> The present condition of the Volunteer force is, generally speaking, satisfactory, and we believe that, by steady perseverance in the course hitherto pursued, and by due discipline, it will be a valuable auxiliary to the British army as a means of defence.

The Royal Commission recommended a capitation grant of £1 for every man classed as 'efficient' on the basis of his attendances at drill parades – thirty in his first year and nine annually once trained – plus 10s [50p] for specified amounts of rifle practice. In the following year the government embodied these proposals in the Volunteer Act and by 1867 the overall numbers had risen to around 200,000 and in 1870 still stood at around 190,000.

The Volunteer movement was launched just as factories, as well as offices and some shops, began to close by 2 pm on Saturday. 'Those closed shutters,' commented *Punch*, somewhat fancifully, in September 1860, 'are an addition to the Wooden Walls of England.' A strong social element underpinned its activities from the start, with the officers giving dinners to the men; the fortunate Volunteers entertained by their commanding officer at Grimston Park near Tadcaster in West Yorkshire in 1864 were treated to 'a 600-gallon butt of potent Grimston ale . . . flanked by a pipe of port wine and a pipe of sherry'. Sometimes a unit had its own Volunteer Club or reading room, for use after parades, and at least one formed its own Sick and Funeral Society, with a 9d [4p] a fortnight subscription. The government's rule of paying its capitation fee only for 'efficients' gave commanding officers a strong incentive to encourage men to attend regularly and some offered a variety of attractions from chess and billiards to football and cricket, amateur dramatics and a choir, which might give public concerts for unit funds. The big event of the Volunteer year was the annual review held until 1872 – after which the tradition was continued elsewhere – at Brighton, the railways offering cheap excursion tickets, so that many participants brought their families to enjoy a day out.

The first proposal for an annual camp, early in 1861, provoked an outraged response from the Commander-in-Chief:

> I object in the strongest manner to the formation of a Volunteer camp . . . The army [provides] . . . the natural and legitimate force for the defence of the empire. The Volunteer force is merely an *auxiliary* body in the event of invasion . . . and the members comprising it cannot, and ought not, to have time to devote to their duties away from their homes.

It was to be several years before this attitude changed but many units organised camps on a weekend, or overnight, basis, with the members going off to their normal work and returning to spend their night under canvas. Camps also provided useful publicity and even a source of income, for a charge might be made to members of the public wishing to come in to inspect the lines.

For women, in the 1860s and much later, no real role existed in any part of the national defence system, but many realised that they needed at least to simulate an interest in their menfolk's new activity. The *Volunteer Service Gazette* was able to record, on 25 February 1860, how, at the first inspection of the Edinburgh Volunteers 'It was an encouraging sight to witness so many elegantly dressed ladies on the ground, who, in spite of mud and strong easterly wind, bravely stood out the inspection to the end.'

Inevitably, the demands which Volunteering made on husbands' and admirers' time caused some domestic ill-feeling and the *Volunteer Service Gazette* urged its readers, on 6 December 1862, to remember why they were learning to fight:

> Let our chivalry be exhibited in the heartiness of our union with those of the weaker sex . . . It is to preserve this blessed union that we shoulder our rifles and practise at the butts; and we accept the encouragement of lady prize-givers, not only for being the willing slaves of their beauty, but as the protectors and champions of their rights and liberties. If the Volunteer ponders well on these relations, with a pure heart, as he trudges in parade, we believe that . . . he will find some poetry in drill and something as noble as knight-errantry in advancing in line and file-firing from the right of companies.

27

SAFETY OR DESTRUCTION

The use of fortifications . . . would just make the difference between safety and destruction.

Letter from Lord Palmerston to W.E. Gladstone, 15 December 1859

On 20 August 1859 Lord Palmerston's Liberal government formally appointed a Royal Commission 'to consider the Defences of the United Kingdom'. It was required to investigate 'the state, sufficiency and condition of the fortifications' already existing or under construction and to advance 'such suggestion as may seem to you meet as . . . will render our United Kingdom in a complete state of defence'.

The Commission's Secretary, of whom more will be heard later, was a 38-year-old major, William Jervois, a dedicated Royal Engineer. It was said of him that, during his service abroad, he had been 'determined to erect on any barren rock or parcel of land on which the Union Flag had been raised a lasting memento to his gifted skills wherein expense seemed a secondary consideration.' James Fergusson, author of *The Peril of Portsmouth*, was the only civilian member. So hard did the Commission work that its conclusions were laid before Parliament, i.e. published to the world, on 7 February 1860.

The *Report of the Commissioners Appointed to Consider the Defences of the United Kingdom* (Cmnd 2682) was a massive volume of 111 large pages. Recent developments, the Commissioners advised, had created a new situation:

> Since the peace of 1815 the state of naval warfare has been revolutionized. The introduction of steam may operate to our disadvantage in diminishing to some extent the value of superior seamanship; the efficient blockade of an enemy's ports has become well-nigh impossible; the practice of firing shells horizontally, and the enormous extent to which the power and accuracy of aim of artillery have been increased, lead to the conclusion that after an action even a victorious fleet would be . . . seriously crippled.

Equally alarming was the Commissioners' conclusion that it might be impossible to stop an invasion occurring:

The object of the enemy would be in the first instance to land a sufficient force on some unprotected part of the coast, to enable him to
seize and hold a position under cover of which the invading army
might be disembarked. With the power of concentration which
steam now affords, such a force might be assembled before daylight
upon any point selected for the attempt, and thrown on shore in two
or three hours.

After a detailed study the Commissioners had, they reported, decided
that a determined enemy would be able to get ashore somewhere on
the 300 miles [480 km] of coastline, out of a total of 750 miles [1200 km]
between the Humber and Penzance, where a landing was physically
possible. It would, they accepted, be impractical to defend the whole
300 miles, and they therefore reached a predictable conclusion:

Having carefully weighed the foregoing considerations, we are led
to the opinion that neither our fleet, our standing army, nor our
Volunteer forces, nor even the three combined, can be relied on as
sufficient in themselves for the security of the kingdom against
foreign invasion . . . It must never be overlooked, that our very
existence as a nation may depend on the safety of our dockyards . . .
The choice lies only between defence by a small body of men, with
the aid of fortification, or defence by a large body without that aid.

Ingeniously, the Royal Commission now demonstrated that in proposing to spend large sums on stone and mortar it would actually save
the country money. 'To double the number of regular troops now at
home,' the minimum needed to provide real security would, it calculated, 'cost . . . about eight millions at the outset and nearly four
millions annually afterwards'.

The same eight millions expended in fortifications would be far
more effectual for the defence of the dockyards than any such increase of the regular army, would incidentally provide barrack
accommodation for some thousands of men, and would entail no
future annual charge, beyond a small sum for maintenance.

Here was an argument calculated to appeal to every politician and the
Commissioners made the 'fixed defences' option even more attractive
by suggesting that the expenditure could be spread over four years,
with the amount in the most expensive year, the second, no more than
£4,381,000, a once-for-all capital sum, to be compared with the £4
million *annually* which the 'doubled army' alternative would cost. A
further £1,460,000 for works already 'in the pipeline', i.e. authorised
but not yet begun, brought the overall cost of the whole programme to
£11,850,000.

Although the pacifist John Bright denounced the authors of the recent *Report* as an 'aggregate of lunatics' and more patriotic critics

alleged that fixed fortifications were 'un-English', the Defence Committee, consisting of the Commander-in-Chief, the queen's cousin the Duke of Cambridge, the First Sea Lord and other experienced officers, to which the government referred it, found its arguments, not surprisingly, 'convincing and conclusive'. Palmerston's chief difficulty came with his own Chancellor, who had set his heart on reducing taxation and, above all, on abolishing income-tax, and on him the prime minister now exerted all his considerable powers of persuasion, in a private letter dated 15 December 1859:

> My dear Gladstone,
> Sidney Herbert [Secretary of State for War] has asked me to summon a Cabinet for tomorrow, that we may come to a decision . . .
>
> The main question is whether our naval arsenals and some other important points should be defended by fortifications or not; and I can hardly imagine two opinions on that question. It is quite clear that if, by a sudden attack by an army landed in strength, our dockyards were to be destroyed, our maritime power would for more than half a century be paralysed . . . One night is enough for the passage to our coast, and twenty thousand men might be landed at any point before our fleet knew that the enemy was out of harbour. There could be no security against the simultaneous landing of twenty thousand for Portsmouth, twenty thousand for Plymouth and twenty thousand for Ireland.
>
> Now the use of fortifications is to establish for a certain number of days (twenty-one to thirty) an equation between a smaller force inside, and a larger force outside, and thus to give time for a relieving force to arrive. This in our case would just make the difference between safety and destruction.

The recipient of this powerful piece of special pleading was still not wholly convinced and contemplated resignation but Palmerston, for once on the same side as the queen, observed to her that it would be better to lose Gladstone than Portsmouth and in the end he stayed. The total cost of the fortifications was scaled down by £3,930,000, leaving only a total of £7,920,000 'new money' to be found, though work already authorised brought the total cost to £9 million, and, after a surprisingly good-natured debate in the House of Commons, the Fortifications Bill, authorising the raising of a loan for this purpose, and the compulsory acquisition where necessary of land for the new defences, rapidly became law. The decision to go ahead did not end public discussion about the most effective way to protect Portsmouth. Several critics argued that the great line of forts planned for Portsdown Hill was unnecessary, as no enemy could land near enough to Portsmouth to attack it from the rear, and some powerful advocates emerged for more floating batteries, i.e. guns mounted on armoured rafts, as quicker to build than the proposed land- and shoal-based forts at Spithead, and, since they could be towed into a new position, more versatile. Thanks largely to the persistent efforts of Captain Cowper Coles, a naval architect who had taken part in the seaborne bombardment of Sebastopol and was eventually to lose his life when a ship he had designed capsized,* before work could begin the Defences Commission was reassembled in 1861 to consider the results of tests carried out at the artillery testing ground at Shoeburyness, which seemed to show that armour had the edge over even the most modern rifled guns, and the evidence provided by the American Civil War, which broke out in April 1861. This was conflicting, but what did emerge was that the day of the wooden-hulled warship was over. On 8 March 1862 the Confederate ironclad *Merrimac* routed a whole squadron of Northern 'wooden walls', only to meet her match next day in the shallow-draught armoured and turreted *Monitor*, graphically described as a mere 'cheese-box on a raft'. Work on the forts was again postponed while the Commission was reconvened, but it stuck to its guns and reported that the works at Spithead should go forward as planned. These delays, however, and numerous technical changes made for reasons to be described later, resulted in the sea-forts proving by far the most troublesome and expensive part of the whole programme. The dearest, No Man's Land, ultimately cost £462,000 even before its guns had been installed and the last, Horse Sand, was not finished until 1880.

Although Cobden asserted in Parliament that there was no danger from the French navy, last-ditch attempts to frustrate Palmerston's great scheme were defeated by large majorities, though during the debate one MP quoted a couplet about the use of convict labour to build earlier fortifications which was to give the new forts their enduring name of 'Palmerston's follies'.†

The Palmerstonian programme was far larger than Henry VIII's and even outclassed the building of the Martello towers. The preliminary surveying at Portsdown began during 1860 and by March 1861 notices to quit had been issued to all the tenants of the affected premises, including two harmless maiden ladies who had run a tea-garden much patronised by residents of the area. The owner of Portsdown Hill, already rich, became wealthier still after a public enquiry in September 1862 had agreed he should be paid £95,200 for the 900 acres [365 ha] to be bought outright and the rights he had surrendered over another 1000 acres [405 ha] to improve the field of fire from the forts. In 1863 the parliamentary opponents of the scheme made a final attempt to prevent either the Spithead or the Portsdown forts being built. It was defeated

* See Chapter 30, p. 361
† i.e. To raise this fortress of enormous price
      The head of Folly used the hand of Vice. Attributed to Gibbon.
                                    See Patterson, *Palmerston's Folly*, p. 13.

by 132 votes to 61 despite a speech by Cobden, who stressed the environmental damage inflicted on the area. 'Great precipitous ditches,' he complained, had been 'dug in the chalk hills . . . enormous gashes in the sides of these beautiful downs . . . The good citizens of Portsmouth say that when they go out by train in the direction of Havant they sit with their backs to the engine or cover their faces, they are so greatly ashamed of the fortifications.'

The Portsdown site was the most conspicuous and, being within easy reach of London, the most visited, but everywhere on the Royal Commission's list experienced an influx, first of surveyors and contractors, then of building workers. Bricklayers, stonemasons and, above all, labourers, many of them recently employed as itinerant 'navvies' to build the railway network, now largely completed, descended on Chatham, Portsmouth, Portland, Plymouth and Milford Haven. Some unforeseen hold-ups occurred, as at Fort Wallington, at the western end of the Portsdown line, where the clay proved too slippery to support the walls and parapet and both had to be rebuilt.

Similar, but far more acute, problems were encountered during the construction of the shoreline and shoal-based forts designed to protect Spithead. Erecting forts off the north-eastern face of the Isle of Wight to guard the seaward approach to Portsmouth between Ryde and Bembridge proved particularly troublesome. These forts, necessarily smaller and weaker than the massive works on Portsdown Hill and along the Gomer to Elson line protecting Gosport, were originally to have been constructed of granite, but a test in 1865 showed a similar wall crumbling after a mere three shots from a 300-pounder [136-kg] Armstrong gun and layers of iron plating were now added to the original stone, greatly increasing the cost. The most difficult of all to build were the four sea-forts. Horse Sand and No Man's Land, right in the middle of the Solent, 2000 yards [1830 m] apart, and roughly double that distance from the other sea-forts, Spitbank [or Spit Bank] off Southsea, and St Helen's, near Bembridge Point, which formed like them, small, circular islands, resting on sunken foundations, and were accessible only by boat. With their metal ladders and gangways, the whole structure often wreathed in mist or swept by spray, the sea-forts had more of the character of a small warship than of a land fortress. The plans for Horse Shoal and No Man's Land forts showed a circular structure about 200 ft [61 m] across, at high water, and a little more at low water, with two gun decks visible in an apparently impregnable ring all round the sides, above an unbroken, windowless base which contained storerooms and magazines. In peacetime each small room was occupied by a dozen men whose beds, with overhead racks for kit and rifles, were squeezed in wherever there was space. In wartime, to accommodate the enlarged garrison, the troops slept in hammocks slung in the small barrack-rooms behind the gun galleries.

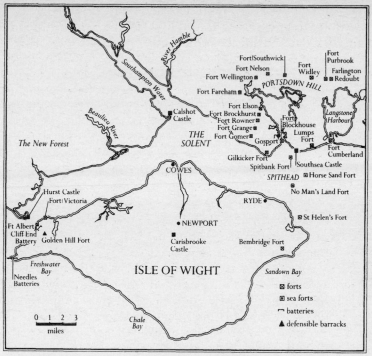

Protecting Portsmouth

At Horse Sand and No Man's Land, for example, beds were provided in peacetime for 90 men, but 'hammock hooks' were installed for around 200, for use under active service conditions.

Although the armament of the four sea-forts varied, in all of them, while construction was in progress the size of the artillery installed was increased. Horse Sand, for example, ultimately carried 25 ten-inch [25-cm] guns on its upper deck and 24 12.5-inch [32-cm] on the lower.*

The principal inspiration behind the land forts erected at this time, though not their sole architect, was the former Secretary of the Royal Commission who in 1862 became Lieut.-Colonel Jervois [later Lieut.-General Sir William Jervois, FRS]. His *Memorandum relative to the Defences of Portsmouth proposed with reference to the Long Range and Accurate Aim of Armstrong's Rifled Gun*, written in January 1859, set out the problem that faced him:

When the works were designed, it was universally admitted that if an enemy could be kept at a distance of 4000 yards [2.3 miles; 3.7 km] from the place to be protected, that place would be safe from bombardment. Now, 9170 yards [5.2 miles; 8.4 km] had been

---

* Spitbank fort has been admirably restored and is an easy boat trip from Portsmouth. In 1986 Fort Nelson and Fort Widley on Portsdown Hill, and Fort Brockhurst, part of the landward defences to the west begun before 1859, could also be visited.

achieved with a 32-pounder and one might be able to direct guns
with the aid of a map.

In spite of his reputation for devising extravagant schemes, Jervois was
concerned to put forward plans for works that were relatively simple
and required a garrison of minimum size. He preferred detached fortresses, sited to give each other mutual support, rather than the costly
continuous lines favoured by foreign engineers and advocated by some
English experts, who had contemplated a single vast ditch encom-
passing the whole of Portsdown Hill or even extending as far as Langstone Harbour. Provided the ground gave a good field of fire the forts,
he argued, could safely be at least a mile [1.6 km] apart, coverage of
musketry or grapeshot being reasonably accurate up to 700 yards
[640 m]. In fact Wallington, at the western end of the Portsdown line,
was nearly 2000 yards [1828 m] from its eastern neighbour, Fort
Nelson, and 2840 [2596 m] from Fort Fareham, which bridged the gap
between Portsdown and the 'Gosport Advanced Line' of five forts,
from Fort Elson, on the western shore of Portsmouth harbour, to Fort
Gomer, overlooking the Solent.

Within the forts themselves Jervois favoured straight lines rather
than the conventional, rounded bastion. 'It will,' he wrote in 1860, 'be
found in almost all cases that a fort with straight faces . . . will adapt
itself much better, and that it will be much more applicable in every
other respect, than one of a bastioned trace.' If, however, the Palmerstonian forts, with their polygonal shape and low profile, bore little
obvious resemblance to most of their predecessors they still possessed,
on closer examination, many of the characteristics of a medieval castle.
Anyone walking through the long underground passages at, say, Fort
Nelson, might well imagine himself, apart from the impeccably neat
Victorian brickwork, below Dover Castle, and above ground the deep
surrounding ditch, crossed by a drawbridge, would also have seemed
familiar.

The new works were designed to keep the new rifled guns out of
range of the dockyards. The main danger was considered to be from
the sea and the walls were thickest on the seaward side – 14 ft 6in
[4.54 m]. To provide 'bomb-proof cover', from shells descending
from above, roofs of up to 20 ft [6 m] thick, of stone, brick and concrete, were provided. An enemy was not expected to get close enough
to storm the forts, but provision for local defence was still included, including ramparts, to be manned by riflemen, a deep ditch, sometimes –
not always by design – water-filled, and caponiers, one- or two-storey
galleries thrown forward into the ditch, usually at right angles to the
inner defences, from which both musketry and artillery fire could be
brought to bear.

The forts presented an impressive example of defence in depth. At

Fort Wallington, the best documented, though since demolished, the attackers as they approached would have had to survive the fire of 17 guns mounted on the ramparts, six heavy mortars mounted in protected casements, and other artillery on the flanks and 'in the gorge', i.e. at the rear. As they stormed the ditch, 33 to 40 ft [12-12 m] wide, and the wall, 29 ft [8.8 m] high, behind it, they would have been exposed to cannon as well as small-arms fire from the two-storey caponiers, and if they did break through into the 'parade', or open space where the garrison drilled, they would have found themselves enclosed by a traverse, or earthwork, built across it for this purpose. A little later, when its armament had been increased and modernised, Fort Wallington had a garrison of eight officers, 171 Other Ranks and 37 horses – a modest enough establishment for a key fortress occupying an area roughly 950 ft by 650 [274 by 198 m]. Despite its splendid workmanship, which can be judged from its surviving neighbours, Fort Wallington cost only just over £100,000, £3000 *less* than estimated.

The Portsdown forts, built on 'green field' sites, hitherto unspoiled – Fort Wallington's guns covered the peaceful expanses of Fareham Common and three miles of open country stretching to the woodlands at the edge of the village of Wickham – were the most impressive and talked-about of the new defence works, but others almost equally spectacular could soon be seen elsewhere. The approaches to Portsmouth were protected by Hurst Castle, on the spit of land reaching out from the Hampshire shore towards the Isle of Wight, where a row of 37 brick and masonry casemates was thrown out to the west of Henry VIII's original fortress, with another 24 to the east. The large number of guns, which required a garrison of four officers and 127 Other Ranks, was explained by the time it took to load and aim the heavy rifled muzzle-loaders now coming into use, a full two minutes per shot. An enemy fleet steaming rapidly up the Solent had a good chance of getting past unscathed unless engaged by a whole series of batteries.

To expose an intruder to simultaneous bombardment from both sides of the water, a new battery of six 7-in [17.8-cm] guns was installed on the chalk ridge above the Needles Rocks, and to accommodate the gunners manning these and the other batteries in the area a 'defensible barracks', Golden Hill Fort, was built near Freshwater, about three miles [5 km] away. South Hook and Golden Hill, with their two-storey brick buildings and iron balconies surrounding an open courtyard, seem built to resist a few lightly-armed tribesmen rather than a powerful European army, but their appeal to a War Department under pressure to economise was apparent. Golden Hill was designed to house, in peacetime, the gunners who manned the coastal batteries along the north-west edge of the Isle of Wight, and in wartime to protect them from a sudden landward attack from the rear.

It was surrounded by an earth embankment and dry ditch and the narrow barrack-room windows were supposed to double as musketry firing slits when required. 'Bomb-proofing' was at first provided by a layer of earth on the roof, but this proved an embarrassment, for it let in the damp and finally slid to the ground. The roof continued, however, to provide a gun platform for six guns, though not the 18 originally intended.

The 'defensible barracks' concept, offering 'two for the price of one', was most enthusiastically applied in the Milford Haven area, which was a long way from any major garrison and, if attacked, would have to wait some days for reinforcements. As well as Pembroke dockyard and its protective batteries, considered vulnerable to attack from the landward side, numerous beaches outside the Haven offered easy landing to an invader. This explains why, between 1841 and 1865, no fewer than four defensible barracks were built outside the dockyard lines. Three were primarily intended to provide accommodation for gunners manning the local batteries, expected, if required, to use their barracks as strongpoints to keep attackers away from their guns, but the 'Old Defensible' on Barrack Hill at Pembroke Dock, finished in 1846, was specifically built to house an infantry unit, though two of the three others, built after 1859, later took on this role.

Another port of particular anxiety – like Milford Haven it had actually experienced a landing in the fifteenth century – was Plymouth. Architecturally the most striking of all these new military buildings was Fort Picklecombe, one of a group of three forts, the others being the sea-fort, Fort Breakwater, and Fort Bovisand, on the eastern shore, designed to command the entrance to Plymouth Sound. A curved, two-tier structure, right on the water's edge at the north-east corner of Cawsand Bay, Picklecombe, designed to house 21 nine-inch or ten-inch [22.9-22.4-cm] guns on each storey, was as attractive as its grim purpose allowed, and, like South Hook and Golden Hill, it is still in use, though for more peaceful purposes, today.*

Strengthening the defences of London rated third in the scale of expenditure recommended by the 1859 Commission, after Portsmouth and Plymouth, but just ahead of Milford Haven. Various works were suggested, including a 'powerful casemated work' at Garrison Point on the northern tip of the Isle of Sheppey, opposite Shoeburyness, where ultimately 36 nine- and ten-inch [22.9-25.4 cm] guns in iron-

---

* Golden Hill, in 1985, housed an excellent museum illustrating life in the Victorian army, as well as a number of craft workshops. 'The Old Defensible' at Pembroke Dock is still in existence, but plans to turn it into a hotel have not so far matured. No Man's Land in the Solent, having been privately occupied, was on offer at £5.75 million in 1990 but now seems likely to be used for corporate entertainment. Fort Picklecombe was in 1976 converted into seaside flats, but still looks impressive from the seaward side, e.g. from the Cawsand to Plymouth ferry.

shielded casemates were installed.

A prominent part in the construction of the Thames defences was played by Charles 'Chinese' Gordon, RE. Commissioned in 1852, Gordon had first worked on the harbour defences at Pembroke before, after service in the Crimea, going to China, from which he returned with a great reputation, to be promoted lieut.-colonel at the early age of 32 and put in charge as CRE [Commander, Royal Engineers], Sheerness, of the rebuilding of the fort at Tilbury, and other fortifications on both sides of the river.

Gordon later declared that these years had been the happiest of his life. He rose early, snatched hasty and simple meals – invariably salt beef and stale bread soaked in lukewarm tea – at his desk and dashed about his district so incessantly that his staff were reduced to following his progress through telescopes. He would urge on the watermen who ferried him from site to site with cries of, 'A little faster, boys, a little faster!' and accompanying officers who fell behind as he darted about the sites on land were upbraided with such remarks as, 'Another two minutes gone. We shall never have those minutes again.' Gordon's progress about his territory was marked by the trail of printed texts and sermons which he left on stiles and scattered from train windows, and his imposing official residence, Fort House, was converted into dormitories for his 'little scrubs', destitute small boys he had rescued from the streets. By the time he left the area, in 1871, Tilbury had incorporated various improvements, particularly extra earthworks he had suggested, and had been largely rearmed with heavy rifled guns along the river face. His ambition to be transported to 'a very bright and happy land' was finally achieved at Khartoum in 1885, making his name immortal.*

In November 1864, while the whole programme was still in its early stages, the two main sites, Plymouth and Portsmouth, received an important visitor, General Franz Eduard Ivanovic, Count Todleben, the Russian whose masterly defence of Sebastopol had greatly influenced British thinking. 'His observations on the details of the several works were generally complimentary,' reported his official host, General Burgoyne, on 3 January 1865. 'Many of the arrangements appeared new to him and to be approved. Others were mentioned with satisfaction and precisely what "he had himself adopted in Russia".'

Later that year, on 18 October 1865, shortly after having his defence policy decisively endorsed in a general election, Lord Palmerston himself died in office, still vigorous at almost 81. In the fortification field (and perhaps, if rumours were to be trusted, in the sexual one as well) Palmerston had indeed accomplished more even than Henry VIII; by 1867 no fewer than 76 forts or batteries had already been finished or

* Gordon's home at Gravesend, Fort House, was destroyed by a German V-2 in 1945. See my *Hitler's Rockets* (Hutchinson, 1985), p. 253.

were in course of construction, though inevitably, with military technology changing so rapidly, many of these took far longer to complete than expected. Fort Brockhurst, on the Gosport line, for example, begun in September 1861, was not finished until December 1874.

The fortifications to which Palmerston had given his name were to be the last to be built on such a scale in Great Britain, though their value remains uncertain. In the spring of 1868 some of them were put to a test of a kind, in elaborate manoeuvres round Portsmouth based on the assumption that the Channel fleet had been lured away, leaving an enemy to land in Sussex and occupy Portsdown Hill, an unrealistic scenario designed to avoid having to pay compensation for damage to the adjoining land. The main 'battle' occurred lower down the slopes, near the Hilsea lines, with pontoon bridges thrown across the Hilsea Channel, a powerful sortie, supported by gunboats and steam launches, up Porchester creek, and a fierce bout of street fighting in the village of Cosham, the 'enemy' being eventually forced to retreat up the road to Fareham and back to their ships.

In 1869 a parliamentary committee reported reassuringly on the new fortifications. The new forts, it concluded, were well sited and built and likely to prove of great value, but the decade following 1859 had seen unprecedented improvements in artillery, both land-based and on board ship, and these inevitably forced up costs. The 1859 Committee had calculated that the works it proposed would require 'not less than 2500 pieces of artillery', which 'at an average of £200 each' mounted to a total of £500,000. By 1874, however, the Director of Artillery was recommending the installation of guns costing £8000 each.

The great strides forward made during the late 1850s and early 1860s in coastal, and indeed all, artillery, concealed a step backwards, a reversion to muzzle-loading, in use since the Middle Ages. The rifled Armstrong gun of 1859 was breech-loading, but the mechanism proved unable to stand up to the heavy charge of gunpowder now required and in 1866 the decision was taken to revert to the older method. The basic armament of the new forts and batteries was therefore the RML, or rifled muzzle-loader, and large numbers of the seven-inch [18-cm] version, weighing 7 tons, and the nine-inch [23-cm], weighing 12 tons, were installed, the shot from the former being able to penetrate seven-inch plate at 1400 yards [1280 m], and from the latter nine-inch plate at 2400 yards [2194 m] so that the new forts should be able to inflict serious, and perhaps fatal, damage on an armoured enemy ship still up to a mile and a half [2.4 km] offshore.

The heavier the gun the more expensive it was to protect, while the smoke when it was fired tended temporarily to blind the crew. An ingenious answer was found by an officer of the Edinburgh Militia Artillery, Captain [later Colonel] Moncrieff, who, in spite of official discouragement, persevered with his Disappearing Carriage, which eventually began to come into use in December 1871. The Moncrieff Carriage operated from a pit, from which it was hoisted up to fire, then lowered on angled arms for reloading, while the crew stayed safely below ground. After various improvements, the introduction of more powerful guns, too heavy for the principle to be applicable, caused the idea to go out of use.

The artillery and engineers were always the ablest corps in the army, free of the incubus of the system of purchase of commissions which prevailed in the infantry and cavalry. A Commission of Enquiry in 1857 had described it as 'vicious in principle, repugnant to the public sentiment of the present day and . . . inconsistent with the honour of the military profession', but the government encountered such fierce opposition in the House of Lords that abolition in 1871 was only achieved by the use of the royal prerogative. 'You may buy your commissions in the army up to the 31st day of October next,' *Punch* warned the 'gallant but stupid' young gentlemen among its readers. 'After that you will be driven to the cruel necessity of deserving them.' Around the same time a determined effort was made to improve the quality of military education for officers, with the development of the Royal Military College at Sandhurst, though attendance there was not yet compulsory. Training for more senior posts was also improved and from 1864 the letters 'p.s.c.', for 'passed Staff College', began to appear after officers' names in the Army List, although there was a lot of leeway to make up if Great Britain was to meet foreign armies in the field on equal terms. 'In foreign armies at the present time the officers have very superior advantages,' one officer told the Committee on Military Education in 1870. 'A Prussian officer,' commented another witness, 'knows perfectly well the whole of the art of war, whereas an English officer may be for years and years in our service and only see one regiment or one battalion.' Manoeuvres, however, now began to become more realistic and even the cavalry began to modernise their methods. The 'fork seat' or 'tongs across a wall' posture, introduced by the Prince Regent, which required the unfortunate rider to perch above the saddle with legs outstretched, was replaced by the more natural 'normal hunting seat', making the cavalryman a far more effective soldier.

By a curious irony the peace-loving, economy-minded Gladstone had, as Chancellor of the Exchequer, raised the money for 'Palmerston's follies'. Now, as prime minister from 1868 to 1874, he presided over the most far-reaching reform of the army of the century, undertaken by his imaginative and outstandingly able Secretary of State for War Edward [later Viscount] Cardwell. Numerous measures were now taken to render the serviceman's lot less burdensome and unhealthy, among them abolishing flogging in peacetime, increasing the allotment of space in barrack-rooms, providing three meals a day and improving educational facilities, so that illiteracy within the army disappeared earlier than among the civilian working population. Henceforward a recruit need not enlist for life but for as little as three years, and during 1870 and 1871 20,000 men were brought back from abroad to join the home establishment, and the 'linked battalion' system already in existence, whereby that part of a regiment serving overseas was rotated with its units at home, was extended.

On 28 June 1870 it was at last established, by royal order, that the Commander-in-Chief was subordinate to the government of the day, not a rival authority answerable only to the sovereign, and he and his staff were now removed from their traditional home in the Horse Guards to the army's administrative headquarters, the War Office, in Pall Mall. A major step was also taken towards integrating into a single coordinated force the regular army, the militia and the Volunteers, the officers of the militia henceforward being appointed by the War Office, not the Lords Lieutenant. Cardwell set up 66 new military districts, covering part or all of the area of a county, each of which contained a depot for the local regiment and served as a base for local units of the militia and Volunteers. This was the real start of the 'territorial' system, with county names beginning to replace the old regimental numbers, and the new depots, though unfortified, provided obvious rallying points for resistance in the event of invasion.

By 1874, when the government fell, the army was in much better shape to meet an invader than it had been a few years before and a further *Report on the Progress in Building Fortifications for the Defence of the Dockyards and Naval Arsenals* painted a highly encouraging picture:

After 14 years of experience, it is now universally acknowledged that the principles of defence recommended by the Commission were sound. Other nations of Europe have constructed, or are now engaged in constructing . . . advanced land forts . . . of the same character, and in some cases resembling in design, some of the forts at Portsmouth and Plymouth . . . Our coast defences are, in fact, acknowledged by engineers of other nations to be superior to anything of the kind attempted elsewhere. Formerly, English engineers studied instruction in foreign treatises and works of defence abroad; now foreign engineers resort to England to learn the . . . modern practice in the art of fortification.

28

THE BATTLEFIELDS OF SURREY

Happy those whose bones whitened the fields of Surrey.

The Battle of Dorking, *1871*

For centuries France had been the enemy. When the Emperor Napoleon III had sent teams of French officers to England to study the landing places and invasion routes used by the Romans, nominally to provide material for his *Life of Julius Caesar*, published in French in 1865, it was not only alarmists who suspected that he planned to succeed where earlier both Caesar and his own great namesake had failed. But suddenly the whole balance of power in Europe was changed by another, even more powerful, individual, Otto [later Count and later still Prince] von Bismarck, prime minister of Prussia, who first welded together the numerous small German states into a confederation, then into a powerful nation. 'The great questions of the day,' Bismarck declared in 1862, 'will not be settled by means of speeches and majority decision . . . but by iron and blood,' and the new-found unity of Germany was duly baptised in blood, in Denmark in 1864, in Austria in 1866 and, most spectacularly of all, in France in 1870. On 15 July Napoleon III declared war on Prussia; on 2 September he surrendered with 83,000 men after a calamitous defeat at Sedan, to become a prisoner. On 18 January 1871 Wilhelm I was proclaimed emperor of a new, united Germany at Versailles, with Bismarck as his chancellor. On 1 March 1871 German troops marched in triumph through Paris, and later that month, humiliated and discredited, Napoleon III landed in England, not as a victorious invader but as a refugee.

Just before Sedan, in August 1870, the journalist A.B. Richards, former campaigner for the Volunteers and now editor of the *Morning Advertiser*, had privately circulated a pamphlet, *The Invasion of England (A possible tale of future times)*, which made use of the fictional form, then a novelty, to warn of the nation's danger. In Richards's story both the Volunteers, fighting heroically, and regular troops, led incompetently, are routed, in identifiable English surroundings, by an unidentified enemy. Neither its style nor its content, however, made it

347

compelling reading and when ultimately published in the *Morning Advertiser*, on 20 February 1871, it attracted little attention.

The initial enthusiasm which had led to the formation of the Volunteers back in 1859 had inevitably dwindled in the subsequent 12 years. Even *The Times*, which had helped to bring the Volunteers into being, had become critical. The traditional Volunteer review on Easter Monday, 10 April 1871, usually an occasion for uplifting references to the members' efficiency and patriotism, prompted this year only a distinctly sour comment:

> If England were about to be invaded, no wise man would think of putting the Volunteers in the first line of the defending army. Still less could they be trusted to work independently in loose order. To attempt it would be ruin.

As it happened, one widely read periodical, *Blackwood's Magazine*, already had awaiting publication a long short story on just such an event, and this it now published in its May 1871 issue under the title of 'The Battle of Dorking, Reminiscences of a Volunteer.' From his opening sentence the author firmly captured the reader's attention:

> You ask me to tell you, my grandchildren, something about my own share in the great events that happened fifty years ago. 'Tis sad work turning back to that bitter page in our history . . . We English have only ourselves to blame for the humiliation which has been brought on our land . . . Even now, though fifty years have passed, I can hardly look a young man in the face when I think I am one of those in whose youth happened this degradation of Old England.

The sensitive patriot is not, however, deterred from continuing his tale to the extent of some 64 printed pages, totalling around 24,000 words. After sketching in the great prosperity of that distant time when 'the streets reached down to Croydon and Wimbledon', he describes how an unspecified foreign power annexes Holland and Denmark and public indignation forces the government into declaring war. Two weeks later, on Tuesday 10 August 1871, the ships still in home waters sail from the Downs to challenge the invader, only to fall victim to 'fatal engines', i.e. mines left behind by the enemy who ignobly refuses battle, and England is at the invaders' mercy.

Such is the urgency of the times that even government offices open the following Sunday and the author, a Civil Servant in an unspecified department, is having lunch at his club when he learns that 'the enemy had landed in force near Harwich and the metropolitan regiments were ordered down there'. Turning a deaf ear to orders to help evacuate the office records, our hero makes for Waterloo to join his Volunteer unit in his home town of Surbiton. Happily he had taken his rifle with him to the office but has no time to go home to collect his remaining equipment 'and,' he records, 'I began the campaign with a kit consisting of a mackintosh and a small pouch of tobacco.'

Eventually, after learning that the reported landing in East Anglia had apparently been a feint, and that the real attack has come at Worthing and Brighton, the narrator's regiment entrains for Surrey and, learning that 'Horsham was already occupied by the enemy's advanced guard', is deployed around 10 am 'a few miles short of it . . . to take up a position threatening his flank, should he advance either to Guildford or Dorking'. Next morning they take up their position near Box Hill:

> From where we stood there was a commanding view of one of the most beautiful scenes in England. Our regiment was drawn up on the extremity of the ridge which runs from Guildford to Dorking . . . There is a gap in the ridge just here where the little stream that runs past Dorking turns suddenly to the north, to find its way to the Thames . . . The main part of the town of Dorking was on our right front, but the suburbs stretched away eastward . . . culminating in a small railway station . . . Round this railway station was a cluster of villas . . . of whose gardens we thus had a bird's eye view, their little ornamental ponds glistening like looking-glasses in the morning sun . . . The natural strength of our position was manifested at a glance; a high grassy ridge steep to the south, with a stream in front, and but little cover up the sides . . . The weak point was the gap; the ground at the junction of the railways and the roads immediately at the entrance of the gap formed a little valley . . . the key of the position; for although it would not be tenable while we held the ridge commanding it, the enemy by carrying this point and advancing through the gap would cut our line in two.

The Surrey Volunteers are soon reinforced with regular cavalry, infantry and artillery, who spread out over the slopes behind the Dorking Gap, while the sunshine and heat haze give way to more typical English summer weather:

> Now a tremendous thunderstorm, which had been gathering all day, burst on us, and a torrent of almost blinding rain came down, which obscured the view even more than the [gun] smoke, while the crashing of thunder and the glare of the lightning could be heard and seen even above the roar and flashing of the artillery. Once the mist lifted, and I saw for a minute an attack on Box Hill on the other side of the gap on our left. It was like the scene at a theatre – a curtain of smoke all round and a clear gap in the centre, with a sudden gleam of evening sunshine lighting it up. The steep smooth slope of the hill was crowded with the dark-blue figures of the enemy, whom I now saw for the first time – an irregular outline in front, but very solid in rear; the whole body was moving forward by fits and starts, the men firing and advancing, the officers waving their swords . . . Our

people were almost concealed by the bushes at the top . . . presently from these bushes on the crest came out a red line, and dashed down the brow of the hill, a flame of fire belching out from the front as it advanced. The enemy hesitated, gave way, and finally ran back in a confused crowd down the hill.

Meanwhile, however, on the road below the hill, it is a different story and, for all the heroism of the Volunteers, here the day is lost:

'We are taken in flank!' called out someone; and, looking along the left, sure enough there were dark figures jumping over the bank into the lane and firing up along our line . . . How the next move came about I cannot recollect, or whether it was without orders, but in short time we found ourselves out of the lane, and drawn up in a struggling line about thirty yards in rear of it . . . the other flank had fallen back a good deal more. Beyond our left a confused mass were retreating, firing as they went, followed by the advancing line of the enemy.

By now it is growing dark and a regular regiment, sent forward to retrieve the situation, finds its way blocked by the fleeing Volunteers, whom the enemy artillery is now engaging at point-blank range; the decisive Battle of Dorking has been lost. Eventually the survivors are back almost where they started, at Surbiton station. Here in 'a goods shed a little in advance of it down the line, a strong brick building', the little knot of Surrey Volunteers make their last stand, but before it is over the narrator has drifted away, weakened by a bayonet cut and a bullet-wound to the house of a friend to find him dying from wounds suffered earlier in the battle. Downstairs he finds his friend's dining room crammed with enemy soldiers, sleeping or eating, the latter 'occasionally grunting out an observation between the mouthfuls', their nationality revealed only by their language:

'*Sind wackere Soldaten, diese Englischen Freiwilligen,*' said a broad-shouldered brute, stuffing a great haunch of beef into his mouth with a silver fork, an implement I should think he must have been using for the first time in his life.

'*Ja, ja,*' replied a comrade, who was lolling back in his chair with a pair of very dirty legs on the table, and one of poor Travers's best cigars in his mouth. '*Sie so gut laufen können.*'[*]

Only at the very end of his tale does the supposed septuagenarian betray his bitterness:

After the first stand in line, and when once they had got us on the

---

[*] 'These English Volunteers are real soldiers.'
'Yes, they can run very well.'
The German in the original is left untranslated and is not italicised.

march, the enemy laughed at us. Our handful of regular troops was sacrificed almost to a man in a vain conflict with numbers; our Volunteers and militia, with officers who did not know their work, without ammunition or equipment, or staff to superintend . . . had soon become a helpless mob . . . Happy those whose bones whitened the fields of Surrey; they at least were spared the disgrace we lived to endure.

The Battle of Dorking caused a sensation. It was soon an open secret that the author was Lieut.-Colonel George [later General Sir George] Chesney RE, who had served in India and who had been a contributor to *Blackwood's* for several years before. That May men reading *Blackwood's* in the London clubs found themselves interrupted every five minutes by other members asking if they had finished with it. In the following month a reprint, in the form of a sixpenny [2½p] pamphlet, sold 80,000 copies, and in four weeks it ran through seven more editions. A flood of publications hoping to cash in on the topic of the hour followed. Sir Baldwyn Leighton, Bart., contributed a 15-page pamphlet, *The Lull Before Dorking*, which advocated the bringing in of 50,000 Sikh troops to close the Dorking Gap till a better trained force was ready and, an idea which was to bear fruit later, urged the planning of large-scale earthworks between London and the coast. *Mrs Brown on the Battle of Dorking*, part of a popular series of the time, had a Cockney woman observing that Chesney, 'tho' a werry foolish old party to rite such a book . . . may 'ave done good . . . The best thing we can do is set to work and mend our ways, harmy, navy and all, so as to be ready for anythink as may 'appen.' Lieut.-Colonel William Hunter decided that what the nation needed to restore its shaken morale was a few words from a public school man, and issued an *Army Speech by an Old Harrovian dedicated to those who have been frightened by* The Battle of Dorking. Serious newspapers like *The Times* and *St James's Gazette* carried weighty articles by experts which challenged Chesney's thesis on professional grounds, but there was no doubt that the country as a whole enjoyed having its flesh made to creep and one publisher cashed in with *Our Hero: Or, Who Wrote 'The Battle of Dorking'*. This attempted some heavy-handed humour at the expense of Chesney's unnamed narrator. 'Judging from his own narrative,' the authors commented, 'he appears to have been of a careful disposition, as he never went to his office without his rifle and mackintosh', while it was also evident that 'he was a frequenter of public-houses' and constantly had 'one eye on the provisions and the other on the "pretty" Mrs T.', the friend's wife widowed by the battle. The joke is kept up for nearly 50 pages and ends agreeably. A German officer, Count Swivelswipes, confronted by the stalwart Sergeant Blower as he attempts to land at Brighton exclaims, in distinctly dubious German, '*Tausend teifels! Das is nicht go. Blower ist hier!'* and mistakenly hits the Crown Prince, who is coming ashore behind him. 'His admirably disciplined troops' immediately fall back and the invasion fails.

More sophisticated, if little more plausible, is *The Other Side at the Battle of Dorking or Reminiscences of an Invader*, again supposedly written in 1921, this time allegedly by M. Moltruhn, a German soldier who is involved in the same battle as Chesney's hero, but in the opposing army. The ending of the story is, also, very different for the parties sink their differences to form a coalition, and – even more improbably – John Bright subscribes £10,000 to the National Rifle Fund. In the end the Germans are glad to have their 'warbroken remnants', shipped home and the two nations become 'true brethren . . . in blood and spirit'. There is a similarly happy ending to *The Second Armada* by A. (probably Abraham) Hayward, supposedly set in 1874, though published in 1871. Hayward perceptively identified Germany as the future enemy: 'The love of military glory, the lust of conquest, supposed to be confined to the Junker class of Prussia, had proved catching and become the ruling passion of the German nation. Their weaker neighbours were subjugated or annexed.'

The Battle of Dorking was soon in demand overseas as well as at home, not only in the British Empire but, in translation, in European countries. (The French version showed on the cover, with evident satisfaction, a German eagle attacking a prostrate British lion and invading hordes storming ashore undeterred by a coastal fort.) Chesney was hardly overpaid for his work – his final cheque, in February 1872, only amounted to £278 8s 10d [£278.44] – but his name was made; later he became an MP and was awarded the KCB. He had pioneered a new literary genre which was to exert vast influence in many countries. The British government was not, however, grateful for having the alleged deficiencies of the nation's defences exposed and on 2 September 1871 Chesney was publicly attacked in a speech by the prime minister, Mr Gladstone:

> I should not mind this 'Battle of Dorking' if we could keep it to ourselves . . . but unfortunately these things go abroad and they make us ridiculous in the eyes of the whole world. I do not say that the writers of them are not sincere . . . but I do say that the result of these things is practically the spending of more and more of your money. Be on your guard against alarmism.

The public, however, had had a fright which it would be slow to forget, and *Punch*, in a caption to a cartoon about the manoeuvres held that month, summed up the prevailing feeling. Modifying the traditional watchman's cry, it read: 'All's (Pretty) Well!'

29

THE OBJECTIONABLE TUNNEL

*She [i.e. Her Majesty] hopes that the government will do nothing to
encourage the proposed tunnel under the Channel, which she thinks very
objectionable.*

Queen·Victoria to the prime minister, Benjamin Disraeli, February 1875

With the Channel a mere twenty-one and a half miles [35 km] wide and
only 216 ft [58 m] deep at its narrowest point, it was natural that the
idea of a permanent link between the two coasts should often have been
considered. By around 1870 the idea already had a long history.*

To many Victorians it seemed a natural sequel to the great railway
boom, while to the Cobdenites a tunnel below the sea bed, always the
most favoured solution, offered a vast expansion in trade, which was
naively assumed to promote international peace and understanding.
The primary motivation for most people, however, was more mun-
dane. The Straits of Dover were notorious for offering a rough sea
crossing; only on about 60 days a year could a whole day's calm be
counted on, and on at least three days in every eight uncomfortably
heavy seas could be expected.

The first conceivably practical plan for a Channel tunnel had been in
fact put forward by a French mining engineer in 1802 to Napoleon I,
but it was not until 1833 that a young French civil engineer, Thomé de
Gamond, began serious underwater surveying of the possible route.
While exploring at a depth of 108 ft [33 m], 'I was,' he complained,
'attacked by voracious fish, which seized me by the legs and arms,' and
already he was encountering 'the obstinate resistance of mariners' to
the whole project, though Napoleon III, in 1856, proved sympathetic,
as did such famous English engineers as Robert Stephenson and Isam-
bard Kingdom Brunel. De Gamond was now favoured with a meeting
with Prince Albert, who passed on a message from the queen, a regular
victim of *mal-de-mer*. 'You may tell the French engineer,' she instructed
her husband, 'that if he can accomplish it, I will give him my blessing
in my own name and in the name of all the ladies of England.' The only
sour note was struck by Palmerston, who was present, and remarked

* For the later history of the project in relation to defence see Chapter 35, p. 427 and
Chapter 38, p. 533-4.

unhelpfully: 'What! You . . . ask us to contribute to a work the object of which is to shorten a distance which we find already too short!' To the Prince Consort's protests the prime minister replied firmly: 'You would think quite differently if you had been born on this island.'

De Gamond's scheme foreshadowed most later ones in its essentials. It involved a stone passage excavated by subterranean mining between Cap Gris Nez and Eastwear Point, accommodating a double set of railway tracks, with nine-mile [14.4-km] sloping access tunnels at either end. Fear of Napoleon III, however, as described in an earlier chapter, prevented further progress. In 1865 the scheme's most powerful English opponent, Lord Palmerston, died and enthusiasm for international engineering projects mounted with the Suez Canal, scheduled to open in 1869, and the nine-mile [14.4-km] St Gotthard Tunnel through the Alps, due to be started in 1872.

A commission of scientific experts appointed by Napoleon III reported that a Channel tunnel was technically feasible, but Napoleon III's ministers had hardly approached the British government for its reaction, in 1870, when the Franco-Prussian war altered the whole situation. The great opponent of spending on armaments, Mr Gladstone, was prime minister, and he was now to coin the phrase which henceforward became the watchword of the anti-tunnellers, in a review of the European situation in the *Edinburgh Review*:

> Happy England! Happy . . . that the wise dispensation of providence has cut her off, by that streak of silver sea which passengers so often and so justly execrate . . . from the dangers . . . which attend upon the local neighbourhood of the continental nations.

Gladstone was not at this stage personally hostile to the idea of a tunnel and in 1872 the Foreign Office informed the French that Her Majesty's Government 'would', in the words of a subsequent official paper, 'be well satisfied to hear that the British and French railway systems were likely to be connected by means of a tunnel.' It was, however, a true Gladstonian touch, unwilling to put up any money; the project was to be left strictly to private enterprise. That year the Channel Tunnel Company was set up in London, backed by the London, Chatham and Dover Railway, and three years later – raising the necessary capital and undertaking the preliminary research was a slow business – Parliament granted the company powers to acquire privately owned land at St Margaret's Bay and begin experimental tunnelling.

In February 1874 Gladstone was succeeded by the more imaginative Disraeli and that December the French ambassador was assured that the British government had no objection to the French scheme. Opposition to the tunnel was meanwhile mounting and the queen was among those who had changed her mind. In February 1875 she wrote to her new prime minister in uncompromising terms: 'She [i.e. Her

Majesty] hopes that the government will do nothing to encourage the proposed tunnel under the Channel, which she thinks very objectionable.'

That year, however, Bills to enable the preliminary work to go ahead were passed by both the British and French legislatures, and the tunnel had by now a powerful new advocate, Sir Edward Watkin, a successful businessman who had deserted the family cotton business to become a railway promoter and Member of Parliament. He was the true successor to Thomé de Gamond who had died, a disappointed man, in 1875. Watkin's engineers successfully sank the first shaft between Folkestone and Dover in 1880 and began to dig out an experimental tunnel, which soon extended half a mile [800 m] underground, and the Submarine Continental Railway Company, controlled by the South-Eastern Railway, was formed to take over all the existing workings.

For the first time the building of the Channel Tunnel began to seem a real possibility and widespread opposition now began to be voiced to the whole idea. A large standing army and conscription, both financed by higher taxation, would, it was argued, become necessary if the great moat provided by nature were abandoned. *The Times*, in June 1881, was among the first newspapers to strike a note of warning:

> As an improvement in locomotion, and as a relief to the tender stomachs of passengers who dread seasickness, the design is excellent . . . From a national point of view it must not the less be received with caution . . . Shall we be as well off and as safe with it as we are now without it? Will it be possible for us so to guard the English end of the passage that it can never fall into any other hands? . . . Nature is on our side at present . . . The silver streak is our safety.

Nor was it only France that now had to be feared. 'A design for the invasion of England and a general plan of the campaign,' warned *The Times*, 'will be subjects on which every cadet in a German military school will be invited to display his powers.' Eventually the government resorted to the reassuring device of an inter-departmental committee, on which the Admiralty, the War Office and the Board of Trade were all represented. This was set up late in 1881, but only made matters worse, for it provided a platform for the man who became the tunnel's most influential and unrelenting opponent. This was the Adjutant-General, Lieut.-General Sir Garnet [later Field-Marshal Viscount] Wolseley, a popular figure, immortalised by the phrase 'all Sir Garnet' to indicate that everything was in perfect order and famous as the original 'modern major-general' of *The Pirates of Penzance*, first performed two years before.

Wolseley's hostility to the tunnel, expressed in a long memorandum

in 1882 and in oral evidence before the successive committees which
now considered the matter, verged on the paranoiac. His basic argument was that a tunnel would throw away the natural advantage provided by that 'great wet ditch', the Channel, and provide 'a constant
inducement to the unscrupulous foreigner to make war upon us':

> A couple of thousand armed men might easily come through the
> tunnel in a train at night, avoiding all suspicion by being dressed as
> ordinary passengers, and the first thing we should know of it would
> be by finding the fort at our end of the tunnel, together with its tele-
> graph and all the electrical arrangements, wires, batteries, etc, in-
> tended for the destruction of the tunnel, in the hands of an enemy
> . . . Trains could be safely sent through the tunnel every five
> minutes, and do the entire distance from the station at Calais to that
> at Dover in less than half an hour. 20,000 infantry could thus be
> easily despatched in 20 trains and allowing . . . 12 minutes interval
> between each train, that force could be poured into Dover in four
> hours.

Earlier alarmists had considered 40,000 men as the minimum needed to
effect a serious landing, but Wolseley dramatically scaled down this
figure to 2500:

> That number, ably led by a daring, young commander, might, I
> feel, some dark night, easily make themselves masters of the works
> at our end of the tunnel, and then England would be at the mercy of
> the invader.

The original inter-departmental committee was followed by a specifically War Office one, set up on 23 February 1882 to consider how the
tunnel could be closed in the event of war. The issue had thus almost
been pre-judged, but Sir Edward Watkin and his Submarine Continental Railway Company did not give up without a struggle. He dismissed the alarmists as 'men who would prefer to see England remain
an island for ever, forgetting that steam had abolished islands' and
derided the risk of invasion, quoting an even more eminent strategist
than Sir Garnet, Count von Moltke, who had declared an attack on
England via the tunnel impossible. The tunnel company also redoubled its efforts to secure the support of opinion-formers for the
tunnel. Parties of up to 80 influential and established people, artists,
clergy, army and naval officers, businessmen and members of the aristocracy, as well as politicians and editors, were taken down by special
train to Dover, lowered six at a time, in a skip, to a spot 163 ft [50 m]
below the ground and then given a tour of inspection, as later described
in a magazine article:

> The visitors were conducted 20 at a time to the end on a sort of trol-
> ley or benches on wheels drawn by a couple of men. In the centre of

the tunnel a kind of saloon, decorated with flowers and evergreens, was arranged, and, on a large table, glasses and biscuits, etc. were spread for the inevitable luncheon. There was no infiltration of water in any part. There they were as in a drawing room and the ladies having descended in all the glories of silks and lace were astonished to find themselves as immaculate on their return as at the beginning of their trip.

Among those provided with subterranean entertainment by the spring of 1882 were the Prince and Princess of Wales, the prime minister, Mr Gladstone, back in office from 1880 to 1885, the Archbishop of Canterbury and at least 60 of Sir Edward's fellow MPs. One journalist in a popular periodical, *All the Year Round*, put out, perhaps, at not himself being invited, commented sourly on eminent people being

> perpetually whisked down to Dover by special trains, conducted into vaults in the chalk, made amiable with lunch and sparkling wines and whisked back in return specials to dilate to their friends (and, incidentally, to the public) on the peculiar charm of Pommery . . . consumed in a chamber excavated under the sea.

His own principles, he insisted, were less easily to be bought, indeed, he demanded, what true Englishman could rest safe in his bed knowing 'that French troops might checkmate our fleet by simply walking underneath it.'

The French found the outcry in England hard to understand. Commentators in Paris pointed out that the French had not invaded England since 1066 while there had been several English landings in France. A British diplomat in Dresden enterprisingly solicited the professional opinion of General von Holleben, Chief of Staff of the 12th (Saxon) Corps, which he duly reported to the Foreign Office:

> General von Holleben . . . remarked that the idea of moving an Army Corps 25 miles [40 km] beneath the sea was one which he did not quite take in. The distance was a heavy day's march; halts must be made; and the column of troops would be from eight to ten miles [12.8-16 km] long . . . We were talking of a chimera.

Reaction in England was less rational. The populist *John Bull* predicted that, 'Perpetual panics and increased military expenditure are the natural result of such a change as that which will convert us from an island into a peninsula.' The *Spectator* foresaw a fatal 'rush on the tunnel being made by Irish Republicans in league with the French, while the wires of the telegraph were cut'. The weighty *Nineteenth Century* published in April a petition against the project circulated during the previous month, which had attracted the support of such influential figures as the Poet Laureate, Lord Tennyson, Robert Browning, the philosopher Herbert Spencer, Professor Thomas Huxley, Cardinal

Newman and Cardinal Manning and the Archbishop of York.

Anti-tunnel meetings, and allegedly open debates which tended to turn into the same thing, were held throughout the country. There was, it was reported, 'some warmth of feeling . . . on both sides' even at a discussion among members of the supposedly progressive Balloon Society in Westminster. A flood of anti-tunnel pamphlets adopting the successful *Battle of Dorking* formula were published, of which the 126-page *How John Bull Lost London: or The Battle of the Channel Tunnel* by 'Grip' is a fair sample. This begins in true *Dorking* style in 1900, with a party of French soldiers lolling at ease in the home of a small grocer near the Strand. The NCO is addressing their unwilling host with typical Gallic courtesy: 'Now den, you von sacré Inglishman, you be kvick and make ze dinner here . . . or you make von tomble out of ze window.' As he scurries to obey, the wretched shopkeeper reflects how he 'had taken shares in the Anglo-French Channel Tunnel'. Eventually, however, the French army having been routed in various overseas battles, the invaders are anxious to get away. The last has hardly reached the far end when 'With a crash that resounded for miles, a huge mass of dynamite was exploded in its interior, the sea rushed down into the avenue which human art had created and the tunnel was no more!'

The tunnel company now faced obstruction from another quarter. On 6 March 1882 the Board of Trade warned it that its exploration rights did not extend between high-water mark and the three-mile [4.8-km] limit, the traditional boundary of British territorial waters – originally fixed as the maximum range of a cannon shot – and on 1 April, a black day for Sir Edward Watkin, he was instructed to cease boring operations forthwith until the War Office committee set up in February, as described earlier, had reported. On 17 May 1882 the Channel Tunnel Defence Committee duly announced its findings. It had exhaustively explored every possibility and the appropriate response. The Committee, on the 'better safe than sorry' principle, opted for every possible precaution. The proposed measures included 'a portcullis or other defensible barrier', a drawbridge, a device for 'discharging irrespirable gases . . . into the tunnel', arrangements for pouring loads of shingle into it, sluices to let in the sea, mines capable of being fired not merely from Dover but from more distant control points inland, and as a last-ditch defence, a truck loaded with explosives on a time fuse which would be sent careering down the track. The members thought the tunnel, as a final precaution, should emerge 'in the immediate vicinity of a first-class fortress', so that it could be commanded by its guns, but still added a final note of warning: 'It would be presumptuous to place absolute reliance upon even the most comprehensive and complete arrangements, in every imaginable contingency.'

The Committee's findings delighted the alarmists and the anti-tunnellers also benefited from the powerful support of the queen's cousin, the Duke of Cambridge, Commander-in-Chief. A little unfairly, he argued that the comprehensive arrangements proposed to protect the tunnel proved the risk inherent in the project: 'If this danger was small, as some would have the country believe,' he asked, 'why should all these complicated precautions be necessary?' The Duke's intelligence department, rarely heard from, had mustered an impressive list of 107 instances over the previous 200 years in which a war had started undeclared or unexpectedly. Sir Garnet Wolseley meanwhile prepared a 20,000-word memorandum warning dramatically: 'Danger of surprise of our fortifications without warning! Fatal result!!' Wolseley was surely a fiction-writer manqué, for his paper had far more in common with *The Battle of Dorking* than the usual military appreciation. It described how on, of course, a foggy night, a French raiding party easily captures Dover, after 'a dashing partisan leader', posing as an English officer returning late to barracks, has talked his way into a fort past a sleepy sentry. By morning Dover is 'in possession of 20,000 of the enemy', who have arrived through the tunnel, and before long 130,000 more have followed and peace terms are being dictated in London.

The tunnel on the English side when, as described earlier, the Board of Trade stopped further progress in April 1882, extended 2100 yards [1920 m] towards France; the French had, by March 1883, when they also stopped digging, built 2009 yards [1836 m] of a pilot tunnel towards England. In October 1882 the government published a Blue Book containing all the principal documents about the tunnel and the anti-tunnellers seized its appearance as the occasion for another attack on the hated scheme. The following year, 1883, saw the publication of C. Forth's *The Surprise of the Channel Tunnel*, the normal work of imaginative fiction, notable only for its ending. After the invader has finally been driven out an Act is passed making it high treason even to propose building a tunnel again. The alarmists had by now clearly won and some overwrought patriots even, in a fashion more Gallic than English, broke the windows of the tunnel company's offices in Westminster. On 17 April 1883 a Select Committee of both Houses of Parliament under Lord Lansdowne was set up to review the whole subject. It did so with great thoroughness, meeting 14 times and asking 40 witnesses some 5396 questions. The Committee, predictably, decided by a majority that Parliament should refuse permission for the tunnel to be built but Sir Edward Watkin did not give up. He revived his famous parties at Dover, holding one specifically for army officers. A humorous cartoon in the *Graphic* recorded the event. 'I say, dear Chappie,' one guest is shown remarking to another, 'if we invade France through the tunnel, I hope I shan't be told off to lead the Advanced

Guard.'

The tunnel had clearly deteriorated since work had stopped on it, as the dismal picture painted by one journalist confirms:

> Onward to no sound, save the splashing made by the tall workmen tramping through the mud, and the drip, drip, drip of the water upon the hood above our heads, we are dragged and pushed . . . under the bed of the Channel . . . Sometimes, in the fitful flashes of light, the eye rests on falling red rivulets, like streams of blood, flowing down the damp walls. So we go on till the electric lamps cease altogether, and the long awful cave is enveloped in a darkness that would be impenetrable but for the glimmer of a few tallow candles stuck into the bare walls of the cutting.

That year Sir Edward re-introduced his Channel Tunnel Bill into the House of Commons, infuriating his opponents by arguing that far from the Almighty having intended France and England to be separate they had until comparatively recently been joined by land. 'Everything that we possess and are . . .,' replied *The Times*, 'we owe to the encircling sea,' and the pro-tunnel motion was rejected by 222 votes to 84. Watkin tried again the following year and his Bill thereafter became (with only one exception) an annual parliamentary event. In 1887 it was defeated by a mere 76 votes, the nearest it was ever to come to success. The following year he gained an important ally, Mr Gladstone, who told the House in June 1888 that he had changed his mind and believed a tunnel could be built 'without altering in any way our insular character or insular security'.

There were other signs that the cause might not be wholly lost. In January 1889 Captain H.M. Hozier read a paper to the Royal Society of Arts, later re-issued as a pamphlet entitled *The Channel Tunnel, A Defence*. Hozier was a soldier turned amateur historian, author of *The Invasions of England*, published in 1876, the most comprehensive study of its subject until the present book. He argued convincingly that it reflected little credit on the English to be fearful of a tunnel below the Channel when even the Italians were content for one to be built through the Alps, and summed up: 'So long as the British navy can sweep the seas, an invasion is impossible, and it does not in the least matter whether the Channel tunnel exists or not.' Parliament continued, however, to reject the Channel Tunnel Bill until 1894, when even Watkin decided he had had enough; he died in 1901. The reason for his failure lay less in the military arguments than in an instinctive distaste for the whole idea. As Lord Randolph Churchill had happily put it during the 1889 debate: 'The reputation of England has hitherto depended on her being, as it were, *virgo intacta*.'

30

THE SILVER STREAK

'The silver streak of sea' is a phrase that . . . soothes the public ear.

Lord Dunsany, The Nineteenth Century, *May 1881*

The debate on the Channel Tunnel helped to remind the nation, if re-minder were needed, of the supreme importance of the Royal Navy. For the rest of the century members of the 'Blue Water' school were in the ascendant, arguing that the country's destiny lay in distant waters. The army was relegated to the humbler role of policing colonial frontiers and conducting minor foreign wars. Against such doctrines the 'Little Englanders', who questioned the value of an empire, and the alarmists of the 'Bolt from the Blue' party made little headway.

The founding charter of the 'Blue Water' school was a pamphlet un-inspiringly entitled *The Protection of our Commerce and the Distribution of our Naval Forces Considered*, published in 1867 by Captain John (later Sir John) Colomb of the Royal Marine Artillery who later became an MP and a constant spokesman for the navy in Parliament. So long, he con-tended, as the Royal Navy kept ahead of its rivals, in size and fighting strength, the country and empire were secure. This was easier said than done. The 20 years following 1860 which saw the launching, as already mentioned, of HMS *Warrior*, then the most powerful ship at sea, were to be a time of unprecedented innovation afloat and the naval architects had to contend simultaneously with changes in materials, motive power, gunnery and armour.

At first a policy of 'backing it both ways' was adopted. HMS *War-rior*, although an all-iron ship, was powered by both steam-driven screw and sail, and with guns mounted in the conventional broadside position, though the new and heavier guns now coming into use really required deck-mounting in turrets, with the capacity for all-round fire. An attempt to mount turrets on a ship still carrying sails, as well as a steam engine, HMS *Captain*, proved a disastrous failure; in 1870 she capsized in a storm with the loss of most of her crew. The real way for-ward, long resisted by traditionalists, was to scrap sails altogether and design an armoured iron ship around its new, turreted armament.

HMS *Devastation*, in service by 1873, showed the shape of things to come. Her low profile, broken only by the funnels and a short mast used for observation and signalling, with her main guns mounted in three turrets, protected, like her hull, by armour, became the characteristic warship silhouette, which was subsequently to alter little. Already by 1874, as the *Report*, previously cited, of the committee investigating *The Progress in Building Fortifications* pointed out, a shell fired at the *Warrior* from a distance of 3000 yards [2740 m] would be able to go clean through one of its armoured sides and out the other. The answer to more powerful guns, at sea as on land, was even heavier ones, to keep the enemy at a distance, and yet weightier armour, but new anxieties now emerged concerning the danger to ships below the waterline. The threat now was from the explosive mine, often at first confusingly known as a 'torpedo', as used by the North in the American Civil War in 1864. Being regarded as part of the land rather than the sea defences, responsibility for submarine mining was given to the Royal Engineers, who set up the first specialist company for the purpose in 1871.

The first submarine mines, weighing 5000 lbs [2273 kg] were laid on the sea bed, usually at a depth of no more than 60 ft [18 km], and wired up in groups, it being reckoned that any ship within a 30-ft [9-m] radius of the explosion should be disabled or sunk. At first the mines were exploded by electrical means by an operator watching from the shore from a so-called 'test room'. Later he merely activated them, leaving the enemy vessel to explode the mines on impact.[*]

The 'controlled minefield', which had been perfected for one-man operation by 1877, provided a new role for long-established forts like Landguard in Suffolk, where a blockhouse and control room were built from which the mines installed in the adjoining river approaches to Harwich could be exploded. The Palmerstonian sea forts off Portsmouth were also used for the same purpose, Horse Sand, finished in 1880, serving as control station for the mines laid to protect the entrance to Spithead. It was not until 1904 that the Royal Navy took over responsibility for all sea mining operations from the Engineers. By then the 'controlled minefield' was going out of fashion, with the development of a superior form of detonator, the 'Hertz horn', invented by the Germans in 1902, and the mine had assumed its lasting form and method of use, suspended from a 'sinker' on the sea bed, independent of the shore and exploded on contact by its target.

In 1882 the British government began to install a totally new form of shore-to-ship defence, the Brennan Dirigeable Torpedo, whose inventor, an Irishman, was paid the handsome sum of £130,000 for his patents. The Brennan was an ingenious weapon, perhaps ahead of its

[*] A replica of a 'test room' with an admirably lucid explanation of the system can be seen in the Royal Engineers Museum at Brompton, near Gillingham in Kent.

time. It had a range of one and a half miles [2.4 km] at a speed of 30 knots [34.5 mph; 55 km per hour] and ran at a depth of eight to ten feet [2.4-3 m], pre-set by adjusting the diaphragm, sensitive to water pressure, in the nose. It ultimately carried a charge of 200 lbs [91 kg] of gun-cotton. Its great novelty lay in its motive power, provided through two contra-rotating propellers driven by 0.05-in [1.3-mm] steel wire of the kind found in every Victorian piano. The wires were linked to large drums on shore, turned by a steam engine, and also enabled the missile to be steered; at night the torpedo emitted a wake of flame, from a phosphorus-type chemical installed at the stern. The missile was said to be so accurate that it could hit a floating fruit-basket at 2000 yards [1828 m]. During one test the torpedo was guided right below its target and then turned round to attack its blind side. From 1887 Brennan Torpedo Stations began to be built throughout the empire. Little is known about them but one, of a total of about ten, was at Fort Albert on the Isle of Wight, where the launching rails, aligned on the light-house on Hurst Castle on the Hampshire mainland, existed until recently.* Others were allocated to the defence of the Medway area and the Thames, at Cliffe Fort, below Gravesend, and at Garrison Point Fort, Sheerness. While most developments affecting defence received extensive coverage in the press the government seems to have regarded the Brennan Torpedo as a powerful secret weapon which would take an invader by surprise, but by 1906 it was being phased out and by 1914 had disappeared from the scene.

Darkness was always likely to prove the invader's friend, and in 1879 systematic tests began of powerful lights covering the Needles Passage. The current was provided by dynamos, but the boilers driving them took two to three hours to get steam up and – as if on board ship – the unfortunate stokers had to work in underground stokeholds in temperatures of up to 115°F [45° C]. Eventually the use of paraffin-powered generators made it possible to bring them into action in 20 minutes, and automatic control equipment was installed. A regular operational procedure was now worked out; the main light picked up the target and a number of 'fighting lights' then followed it, or four to six lights were switched on simultaneously to create an illuminated area. The main enemy was fog, which during the annual exercises in 1895 blacked out the lights during a mock attack on the Thames by torpedo boats. This remained an insurmountable obstacle, but by around 1914 other difficulties had been ironed out. The searchlight installation had become standardised, in the form of a two-storey blockhouse, with the crew safe at, or below, ground level, and the light on the upper floor protected by a sliding iron shutter when not in use.

It was the large, big-gun battleships and cruisers on which public

---

* This unusual military relic was, sadly, destroyed when the site was redeveloped.

pride, or, when possessed by foreign navies, alarm centred. The great change was to breech-loading, tried earlier only to be abandoned, but essential if guns were to achieve greater range and accuracy, with longer barrels. The *Conqueror*, of 1882, was armed with the first heavy breech-loaders, and only two years later, the *Rodney* was given four 13.5-in [34-cm] guns weighing 67 tons. Soon 14 of the Royal Navy's first-line battleships were similarly equipped. There was, too, a great improvement in the destructive power of naval shells with the replacement of gunpowder with dynamite, first produced by Alfred Nobel in 1868 in the naive belief that it would prove 'the agent of peace, helping the miner . . . [and] the railway engineer'. Even more important was the provision of a more efficient and smokeless propellant, cordite, in place of the old black powder, which had left British gunners temporarily blinded as late as the bombardment of Alexandria in 1881.

Even before the torpedo had been perfected alarm was being expressed about the torpedo-boat, a small, fast ship, presenting a poor target. The torpedo-boat rapidly became to late Victorian invasionists what small, shallow-draught vessels had been in Napoleonic times and steam tugs during the 1850s. The Royal Navy had by 1877 produced one of its own, the *Lightning*, also known as T.B. No. 1, a mere 84 ft [25.5 m] long and eleven feet [3.3 m] wide, with a maximum speed of 19 knots [29 mph; 47 km per hour] and carrying a single Whitehead torpedo. The real answer to the torpedo-boat was found in the 'torpedo-boat-destroyer', or later simply 'destroyer', the first, HMS *Havock*, being built in 1893. Its main armament was another novelty, the quick-firing gun. A test at Fort Picklecombe in Plymouth Sound in 1872 had revealed that to fire a 10-in [25-cm] round from one of the rifled muzzleloaders installed there took on average one minute and forty-five seconds, so that a target 4000 yards [3656 m] away, moving at 12 knots [13.8 mph; 22 km per hour] would only be in range for four shots. The Quick-Firing (QF) gun, designed and made abroad, which began to appear in British ships from 1884 and in shore-based establishments from around 1888, could by contrast discharge from 25 to 30 aimed shots a minute. The new guns proved particularly useful for giving some protection to minor ports, providing a weapon able to knock out a torpedo-boat or landing craft even if unlikely to do much damage to a battleship.

The speed of development in the last two decades of the nineteenth century meant a rapid and steady increase in the naval estimates, from £9.26 million in 1870 to almost £13 million in 1886, £21.8 million in 1896 and £27.5 million in 1900. Fortunately the navy was riding high in public esteem and the 'Blue Water' school made the most of the successive scares for which foreign, as well as British, writers were responsible. In April 1881 the *Nineteenth Century* devoted 33 pages to a well-informed article by a foreign expert, Alexander Kirchhammer, impressively described as 'Captain in the General Staff Imperial, Royal Austrian Army'. Its mere title, *The Military Impotence of Great Britain*, was sufficient to cause alarm and the author, displaying an impressive mastery of his subject, took that most effective of stances, that of candid friend. It was true, he conceded, that since 1870 'England has taken the opportunity to resume her natural position as first naval power', but of 203 ships, including 27 ironclads, in commission on 2 October 1880, only 71, 12 of them ironclads, were in the Channel or in home ports. France, by contrast, could concentrate her navy in Europe and 'in a few days collect strong masses of troops on the coast and ship them over to England in a few hours'. Kirchhammer's reference to invasion and the 22 pages he devoted to exposing the weakness of Britain's land forces ensured his article a warm welcome from the 'Bolt from the Blue' party as well as the 'Blue Water' school and both were delighted with a follow-up article the following month, *The 'Silver Streak'* by Lord Dunsany:

> The 'silver streak of sea' is a phrase that has grown familiar to us, and often repeated by our statesmen it soothes the public ear . . .
>
> But what if the supposed immunity be a delusion and the 'Silver Streak' one of those fatal phrases which, like the 'invincible army' of France, lull a nation to such sleep as preluded the catastrophe of 1870 and the infinite humiliation of Sedan?
>
> Invasion by sea *in these days* is less difficult than invasion by land . . . A large army invading by land advances from ten to fifteen miles [17-24 km] a day. The same army embarked advances 240 miles [384 km] a day upwards . . . A large army when marching, being confined to roads, can only move in columns . . . The army embarked can move in close order . . . so as to form at once for attack or defence.

Dunsany's conclusion, in words he quoted from an unidentified source, was 'the paramount necesssity for our fleet being superior not only to any other but to any probable combination of other fleets'. This widely held, but hitherto undefined, belief now became a basic dogma of British defence policy, usually known – since even the Royal Navy did not expect to take on the whole world simultaneously – as 'the two power standard'.

During 1888 there was yet another invasion scare, and an article appeared in the *Daily Telegraph*, in fact inspired by Field Marshal von Moltke, suggesting that the French could, apparently without difficulty, land 20,000-30,000 men between Dover and Portsmouth, for a sudden strike against London. In March 1889 the 'Bolt from the Blue' party scored a notable success when the Secretary of State for War announced the building of a new series of fortifications, of which more will be said later, to protect the capital. This encouraged the alarmists to raise the familiar Gallic bogeyman yet again and in June 1889 the War Office infuriated the Admiralty by asking for their estimate of how many men might be disembarked on the south coast within three days. Their Lordships' reply was crushing:

> Such a contingency as the landing of an enemy on these shores, without interference on the part of our navy, is one which in their opinion could not arise without the annihilation of the Channel fleet, our coast defence vessels, torpedo boats, and armed merchant cruisers, a contingency so remote that it would hardly appear to come within the range of speculation.

The soldiers were not deterred. In April 1890 the two War Office representatives at an inter-service conference, after arguing that 'invasion – though its great improbability is allowed for – is a possibility', asked for the navy's comments on a possible landing between the Thames and Portsmouth:

> (1) On what section(s) of the above coast is the attempt most likely to be made?
> (2) Supposing the enemy had six weeks time for preparation, what troops could be landed on any of these sections . . . ?
> (3) What would be the minimum time in which a division could be landed?

The naval members of the conference reported back to their masters, the Lords of the Admiralty, that in the event of war 'the assumption on which the questions are based . . . might cause . . . a clamour for our fleets to remain in home waters' and the First Sea Lord was infuriated, considering the basic assumption 'so absurd that it would be a sheer waste of time to discuss what might happen'. His irritation was reflected in the official reply sent to the War Office:

> In . . . your June 27 letter it is assumed that the landing of 'the enemy would not be interfered with by the navy, which must be considered as absent from the scene of operations.' Their Lordships can scarcely conceive such an event occurring . . . My Lords have no hesitation in asserting that an invasion of England with 100,000 men would require weeks, if not months, of very careful preparation and the very magnitude of the operation would increase the chance of failure. The accidents of weather must also be borne in mind, as . . . a strong wind from S.E. to S.W. would seriously hamper a landing if it did not stop it for a time.

This majestic snub, which showed, incidentally, that steam had *not* 'bridged the Channel' and that the wind had still to be reckoned with, failed to silence the generals and their supporters, who continued to talk as though a major landing might be made almost overnight whenever the French chose. They continued to press for plans for new coastal defences on the grounds of protecting the navy, much to the Admiralty's annoyance. 'The fact is . . . ,' wrote the First Sea Lord to the First Lord of the Admiralty on 20 September 1892, 'that they are got up by the War Office under the pressure of the Royal Engineers, who have lavished [money] upon them ignorantly but wastefully . . . We want,' conceded Admiral Sir Anthony Hoskins, 'protection to certain places under the new means of attack provided by torpedo boats. But such protection is not to be found in massive forts and heavy guns.' The financial cost of the new forts approved in 1889 was in fact trivial in comparison with the demands made by the Naval Defence Act of 1889. This authorised the laying down of what was almost a brand-new navy, including eight new heavily armed battleships with 13.5-in [34-cm] guns, 38 cruisers and a large number of fast torpedo-boats.

A decisive contribution to the argument about naval spending was made by *The Influence of Sea Power Upon History* by Commander [later Rear Admiral] Alfred Mahan of the US Navy, a three-volume work which appeared between 1890 and 1892. It was rapidly translated into all major languages, and became a world-wide best seller. Mahan chose as his text a quotation from Francis Bacon: 'To be master of the sea is an abridgement of monarchy . . . He that commands the sea . . . may take as much and as little of the war as he will.' Nowhere did his theme, that a strong navy was the provider of prosperity in peace and of victory in war, make a greater impact than in Great Britain. *The Influence of Sea Power Upon History* rapidly became the Bible of the 'Blue Water' school and even Gladstone, the enemy of military expenditure, pronounced it 'the book of the age'. When the author visited England he was entertained by the queen and both Oxford and Cambridge awarded him honorary degrees.

Mahan's book was followed by another influential work, *Naval Warfare*, by Rear-Admiral [later Vice-Admiral] Philip Colomb, elder brother of the MP, Colonel John Colomb, mentioned earlier. Philip Colomb's verbosity led a fellow admiral to describe him caustically as 'a column and a half' but his book spelt out in detail for Great Britain the theories for which Mahan had provided the historical background and was followed by a flood of similar titles. The 'Blue Water' school embraced both political parties, and one of its most influential works, *Imperial Defence*, in 1891, was by the radical politician Sir Charles Dilke MP, with, as co-author, a prominent amateur strategist, Spenser Wilkinson, of whom more will be heard later.

An important corollary to the 'Blue Water' theory was the principle of 'the fleet in being', a phrase used by Admiral Colomb in the *United Service Magazine* in July 1898. It came to mean that the mere existence of a powerful, not necessarily superior, fleet could deter an invader, and, in the longer term, led to admirals husbanding their ships as though, merely by keeping them afloat, they had defeated the enemy. The army, in other words, had to fight the enemy to win; the navy could achieve the same result merely by staying safe in harbour.

In spite of its reputation as 'The Silent Service' the navy now displayed a remarkable talent for publicity. It was assisted by the presence in its ranks of some colourful figures, like 'Charlie B', Captain [later Admiral, Lord] Charles Beresford, who after some notable exploits at sea had become Fourth Sea Lord and served for most of this period as an MP. A highly controversial figure, who later split the navy in a famous feud, 'Charlie B' regularly took parties of his fellow MPs to visit the dockyard and be entertained in the wardrooms of the fleet. Ordinary citizens meanwhile flocked in 1891 to the first Royal Naval Exhibition, which attracted two and a half million visitors in five months, while a series of 'showing the flag' voyages around the coast, known in the navy as 'Hurrah trips', was planned to let the average citizen see the costly vessels for which he was being asked to pay.

The stream of publicity became a torrent following a suggestion by Dilke's co-author, Spenser Wilkinson, in the *Pall Mall Gazette* in October 1894, that no one should vote for any candidate for Parliament who did not support a larger navy. This led to the formation on 10 January 1895 of the Navy League, which defined its aims in admirably clear terms:

(1) To spread information, showing the vital importance to the British Empire of the naval supremacy upon which depended its trade, empire, and national existence;

(2) to call attention to the enormous demands which war would make upon the navy and to the fact that the navy is not at present ready to meet them.

The Navy League's first great success was to secure a public celebration of Trafalgar Day; by happy chance its ninetieth anniversary fell that year, on 21 October 1895. A plan to decorate Nelson's Column was designed to attract the attention of the ordinary man, who, the *Navy League Journal* acknowledged, 'is only half convinced of the value of our empire, and but a lukewarm supporter of large naval budgets.' The *Manchester Guardian* warned that the result would be to annoy France and *Le Jour* rose most gratifyingly to the bait. 'We do not care . . .' it commented rudely on the Trafalgar Day festivities, 'They are a nation of shopkeepers with few victories. We French, if we celebrated our victories, should be at work all year round.' Such reactions suited the League well and it proved highly effective as a propagandist organisation at all levels of society; supporters were urged to 'attack the working man in the train or on the omnibus' and branches of the League were soon flourishing at both Oxford and Cambridge. That year anachronistically, the subject for the Latin essay prize at Oxford was 'British Sea Power'. At Harrow, in March 1898, Admiral Beresford delivered such a powerful address that a branch of the League was immediately founded by the boys themselves, and it was also active in the elementary schools, producing leaflets in admirably simple English:

> Think what would happen if we had a war and our Navy was not strong enough for its work. In a few weeks' time . . . bread and meat and all other food would cost so much that . . . EACH NIGHT YOU WOULD BE CRYING BECAUSE YOU HAD NO SUPPER, AND EACH MORNING BECAUSE YOU HAD NO BREAKFAST.

Trafalgar Day, after the success of the initial venture in 1895, was soon being celebrated in schools with special lectures and lessons and suitably patriotic songs, and the League also sponsored school visits to places like Portsmouth, with prizes for the best subsequent essay.*

Women, beginning to agitate for the vote, were another target group and a special ladies' branch was founded in London, though a proposal in the *Morning Post* in 1896 that they should raise the money to buy an extra ironclad seems to have come to nothing. The *Investors' Review* observed in April that it was useless protesting against the increase in spending on the navy since, 'All classes of the nation appear to be bitten by the craze.' By 1898 the League included a vast number of the aristocracy among its members, many religious dignitaries, four generals and six admirals, though only a modest number – 17 – of MPs, mainly Conservative. Everywhere, however, the pro-naval spirit of the time could be observed. A volume of nautical verse, *Admirals All*, by Henry Newbolt, which included *Drake's Drum*, had to be reprinted 20 times in a year after its publication in September 1898. The existence of the League, declared the *Saturday Review* on 31 March 1900, 'has been amply justified in the increased knowledge possessed by the people of this country of . . . the necessity of a powerful navy . . . The man in the street today grasps the situation in a manner that statesmen failed to do thirty years ago.'

* This practice was continuing in the 1930s, when my elder brother won a typical prize, T.C. Bridges' *With Beatty in Jutland*, Collins, 1930, now in my possession.

31

A POWERFUL ARMY

*It is essentially necessary for this country that it should always have a
powerful army, at least sufficiently strong to defend our shores.*

General Lord Wolseley, Commander-in-Chief, 8 December 1896

In the competition for funds, as in public esteem, Jack Tar, so often
absent at sea, had clearly, in the period between 1870 and 1900,
triumphed over Tommy Atkins, who was all too visible on shore.*

Even the army's claim for an increasing share in expenditure on
home defence rested, at least indirectly, on the sea and the nation's
annually rising maritime prosperity. With work at least in progress,
and in some places complete, on the defences of the navy's dockyards,
apprehension remained about the security of other ports, especially as
they expanded. 'Three times within the past twenty years the battery
for the defence of the Liverpool side of the Mersey has been moved
onwards to meet the extension of the docks,' noted the Director of
Works at the War Office in a memorandum dated 8 January 1875. In
1877 the sub-committee of the government's Defence Committee concerned with non-naval ports considered a six-page paper, *The Defence
of Commercial Ports and Anchorages of the United Kingdom*, prepared for it
by Colonel C.H. Nugent of the Royal Engineers. The danger area,
Nugent pointed out, had now shifted north-eastward to the Humber,
the Tyne and, most notably of all, the approaches to Edinburgh:

> [The Firth of Forth is] the only good harbour of refuge that can be
> made in all weathers from the north of Scotland to the estuary of the
> Thames; it occupies a position in the North Sea in relation to the
> great naval arsenal of Wilhelmshaven . . . In its unprotected state,
> the capital of Scotland, with the wealth accumulated in and around
> it, and the prestige attaching to its inviolability are at stake . . .
>
> The preceding generation was wisely apprehensive with respect
> to the military harbours of our southern shores, the present, if it act
> with equal wisdom, will not neglect our eastern ports; the offensive

* 'Jack Tar' had been in use as an affectionate nickname since the 1780s, 'Tommy
Atkins', a fictional name used to show soldiers how to fill in their attestation documents, since the early nineteenth century.

power by sea of France has for the moment passed away, and already the maritime influence of Germany has received considerable developments and looms still larger in the future . . . Steam has so bridged the seas that the Bremen of today is scarcely farther from our eastern ports than was the Seine of William the Conqueror from our southern shores.

Colonel Nugent found himself close to despair, however, as he contemplated the indifference of most of his fellow citizens to their danger:

It must be confessed that invasion has little real significance for the general public; 80 years have passed since the last invader set foot on British soil, and no man living recollects what then took place . . . Yet this country has, by no means, been exempt from invasion . . . From the commencement of the tenth century there have been 44 invasions and descents, on the average about four a century, or one in every 25 years . . .

What a modern invading army can exact we know from the history of the Franco–German war, and Great Britain is far more wealthy now than France was then, while London is far more open to assault than Paris . . . History repeats itself . . . in vain for us if we neglect to read its lesson rightly.

The 1877 Committee in its Report did not underestimate the difficulties:

It is hopelessly impossible to give absolute protection from bombardment to towns lying upon the seaboard. The long range of existing guns will enable a comparatively small ship at a distance of four or five miles [6.4-8 km] to bombard a town. No amount of passive defence can adequately provide against this danger.

The Committee put the cost of fortifying all the commercial ports at £3,900,000, representing, the writer calculated, no more than 'one-tenth of a penny in the pound' of the country's total wealth, but hoped it might escape the financial burden of protecting what was clearly a national asset, indispensable, on the Committee's own reckoning, to its very survival, by relying on local self-help, as it had done since medieval times: several examples, from Greenock in 1814 to Hartlepool in 1860 were cited, and, confounding their town's notorious reputation for meanness, the gift by the Aberdeen magistrates of the land for three local batteries. If land, why not ships and even men? The Committee suggested that where a torpedo-boat would be more appropriate than a fort, funds should be raised locally to help meet the cost both of the vessel and its crew.

Most of the places considered by the committee already had fortifications of some kind, however inadequate and out of date, and following the 1877 study little seems to have been done to improve them in most cases, except in Scotland, where political reasons existed for placating local anxieties. A start was made in 1879, when three forts, designed to mount four ten-inch [25-cm] rifled muzzle-loaders each, were built on Inchkeith Island in the Firth of Forth and an emplacement for a two-gun battery was erected at Kinghorn, due north of it on the shore of Fife. In 1881 a high-powered sub-committee of the inter-service Military Ports Defence Committee was set up 'to inquire into the defence of the more important Mercantile Ports of the United Kingdom', under the Under-Secretary of State for War, Lord Morley, with Colonel Nugent as its secretary. Its recommendations were far-reaching and, for Liverpool alone, it proposed three new batteries, as well as 'gunboats, torpedo-boats, submarine mines'. The gunboats would, the committee considered, also make it easier to keep up the enthusiasm of the Royal Naval Artillery Volunteers, responsible for manning them. 'Last year,' it learned, '100 of the Volunteers went afloat for a week's cruise and this number might be considerably increased if the gunboats were kept permanently at Liverpool.' The Morley Committee was intended to do for the commercial ports what the 1859 Committee had achieved for the navy's bases but produced nothing like the same results, though it did lead to the establishment of Submarine Mining Companies, whose work has already been described, in a variety of locations.

If an enemy did get ashore, it would be the army's duty to eject him and the period from 1870 to 1900 saw a degree of re-equipment and re-organisation of the land forces comparable with the technological revolution currently affecting the navy. The Prussian army, now setting the pace for the whole of Europe, had demonstrated in the Prusso-Danish war of 1864 the superiority of a bolt-action breech-loading rifle over earlier types, and by 1874 the British army had acquired the Martini-Henry, said to be the best general infantry weapon since the longbow. Accurate in a marksman's hands up to 1000 yards [914 m], or in those of the average soldier up to 400 [366 m], its soft lead slug, of 0.45 in [11.4 mm] calibre, had excellent stopping power, and it was in due course replaced, in 1888, by the 0.303-calibre [7.7-mm] Lee-Metford, modified in 1895 into the famous Lee-Enfield, which by around 1900 had a ten-round magazine, containing a long, thin cartridge with a copper-sheathed lead bullet, propelled at 2000 ft [608 m] a second by smokeless cordite instead of the old black powder, which had so often, as with heavy artillery, left its users temporarily blinded.[*]

Similar developments occurred in side arms. Around 1863 the muzzle-loading pistol gave way to the breech-loading revolver, and by 1887 the Webley, which was to remain in use as long as the Lee-

_____

[*] In the Sudan in 1884 the dervishes broke into a British 'square' while the troops were, for half a minute, unable to see to fire. See Featherstone, *Weapons and Equipment of the Victorian Soldier*, on which I have drawn heavily for much of this chapter.

Enfield, became standard, with its 0.45 in [11.4 mm] calibre and the familiar break-open, self-ejecting action.

An even more striking, though shorter-lived, invention was the Gatling gun, which consisted of a number of breech-loading rifled barrels arranged round a central shaft, turned by a crank, which could fire 600 0.45-in [11.4-mm] rounds a minute. 'The Gatling guns have astonished the Zulus,' reported one correspondent in 1879 but it had a short life before being replaced by the Maxim, the real ancestor of subsequent machine-guns, which used the recoil after each shot to load the next. The Maxim proved effective on the North-West Frontier of India, firing 650 rounds a minute up to 1100 yards [1000 m] and was generally adopted by the British Army, in an improved version weighing only 40 lbs [18 kg], from 1891.

In hand-to-hand combat the infantryman still relied on his bayonet. The triangular type, which the troops knew expressively as 'the lunger', was replaced around 1886 by a longer, 18½-in [47-cm] flatter blade, but eventually this was shortened to 12 in [30 cm]. There were also changes in the sword, carried by non-infantrymen like engineers, gunners, bandsmen and pioneers, as well as by cavalrymen and by officers leading their men in a charge, an image deeply implanted in Victorian minds. Much debate took place on whether the weapon should be designed primarily for thrusting, to cause puncture wounds with the point, or slashing, to produce long cuts with the blade. The author of the standard work on the subject, himself a cavalry officer, complained that the regulation sword, rattling in its scabbard, had 'announced the cavalry's approach a mile off', but had proved too blunt even to penetrate a thick coat. A Select Committee, set up in 1884, found that many sword blades broke in action and a new type was introduced, with a 34½-in [88-cm] blade. By around 1899 the cavalry were also being equipped with short-barrelled carbines, midway in size between the revolver and the rifle.

The classic cavalry weapon was the lance, but the cavalry author quoted earlier had no doubt that its day was past. A troop of lancers trotting forward with pennants fluttering was, he warned, merely likely to 'attract the fire of artillery' and, 'It is well known,' he pointed out, 'that in battle lancers generally throw them away and take to their swords.' In 1900, however, the lance was still in use.

The artillery was more open to innovation. By 1881 the Royal Horse Artillery already had breech-loaders, and by 1885 the field artillery were equipped with a breech-loading 12-pounder [5.4-kg], pulled by six horses. Steady advances in range, reliability and explosive power occurred from around 1880 as cast steel began to replace iron for both guns and shells, gunpowder gave way to cordite, which in turn was in 1898 replaced by the new lyddite, elongated shells replaced spherical shot, and a superior type of impact detonator replaced the former time fuse. It was learned, however, that the French were secretly developing, during 1896-7, a 75-mm [3-in] quick-firing gun – the dreaded 'soixante-quinze' – able to discharge 20 to 30 rounds a minute. By 1900 no British-made quick-firer was yet in service, and the 12-pounder was still the basic Horse Artillery weapon, while the 15-pounder [6.8-kg] formed the backbone of the field artillery, though for heavy duty, against a fortified enemy position, the RA could call on the devastating 40-pounder [18-kg] gun and the 6.3-in [29-cm] howitzer. For a time, as improvements in the hand-gun had outstripped those of artillery, the gunners had been in danger from small-arms fire, but they were now safely distanced from their targets again, for the 12-pounder had a range of 3170 yards [2897 m] and the heavy siege pieces one of 1800-2300 [1645-2100 m]. An invader might also have been greeted by fire from Hale rockets, emitting a loud wailing noise and a trail of white, spark-laden smoke, as they carried their six-pound [2.7-kg] charge up to 1500 yards [1370 m] towards its target, though the rocket's inaccuracy, and the danger it presented to its launching crew, remained notorious.

The accepted doctrine among the 'Bolt from the Blue' strategists was that only a highly mobile army could contain an invader free to land where he chose. A determined effort had been made by the then Sir Garnet Wolseley to lighten the soldier's load. 'It is absurd,' he pointed out in his Soldier's Pocketbook in 1869, 'to expect a man to carry a portmanteau full of things on his back,' and Wolseley attempted to reduce the total burden to 43 lb [19.5 kg] including the pack itself, some 14 lb [6.4 kg] of clothing, and the day's rations. A French officer was able to report by 1902 that the British infantryman's kit weighed only 23.6 kg [52 lb], compared with the French poilu's 24.4 kg [53½ lb] and the German privat's 26.7 kg [58½ lb].

Where the army was likely to be at a disadvantage in relation to its opponents was in its command structure and the quality of its officers. No one questioned their courage but, Lord Wolseley complained, many were, apart from parade-ground drill, 'entirely lacking in military knowledge'. In contrast to its potential enemies, the British Army also lacked a general staff. A Royal Commission under Lord Hartington [Spencer Cavendish, later Duke of Devonshire] recommended in 1890 that, when the post of Commander-in-Chief next fell vacant, a small council of senior officers should replace him, 'freed from all executive functions and charged with the responsible duty of preparing plans of military operations, collecting and coordinating information of all kinds, and generally tendering advice upon all matters of organisation and the preparation of the army for war'. The then Secretary of State rejected the idea and an even more revolutionary one, considered by the Hartington Committee in 1889, to bring the two services together, as partners rather than rivals, under a single Minister of

Defence. But with the enforced retirement, in 1895, of the 76-year-old Duke of Cambridge, Lord Wolseley, the most trusted and open-minded senior officer in the army, at last, at 62, became Commander-in-Chief. Colonel William [later Field Marshal Sir William] Robertson, who having in 1877 enlisted as a trooper in the 16th Queen's Lancers, had by 1888 made the almost inconceivable leap into the commissioned ranks, had no doubt that the change was overdue. The Duke of Cambridge, Robertson recorded, was 'extraordinarily conservative in his ideas and . . . believed . . . that the army as he had found it, created by . . . the Duke of Wellington, must be the best for all time.' Wolseley, by contrast, was, 'The best-read soldier of his time. From 1882 he was the moving spirit in the path of progress.' For the officers a whole new life style now began:

> Apathy and idleness began to go out of fashion and hard work became the rule; study was no longer considered to be 'bad form' but a duty and an essential step to advancement; hunting was no longer admitted to be the only training required by a cavalry leader.

But the effects of the bad old days lingered on. When in 1897 Robertson attended the Staff College, he discovered that, 'Some officers had but a hazy notion of how to make or read a map and were not much surer of themselves in regard to the working of the magnetic compass.' A little later, as an umpire during exercises on Salisbury Plain, the first for 26 years, he discovered others 'who were inclined to look upon the manoeuvres as a kind of glorified picnic in which they could share as much or as little as they desired'. But there were signs of improvement, like Robertson's own selection to join the newly formed Intelligence Branch of the War Office, consisting of 16 officers, of whom three or four formed the Mobilisation Section, 'the only semblance of a General Staff then in existence'. [*]

The policy which Robertson and his colleagues were called upon to implement had been laid down by the then Secretary of State for War, Edward Stanhope, in the document known as the Stanhope Memorandum, dated 1 June 1891. The Memorandum set out as the army's first three responsibilities: 'the effective support of the civil power in all parts of the United Kingdom', 'to find . . . men for India', and 'to find garrisons for all our fortresses and coaling stations at home and abroad'. Only then was a field army for use against invasion mentioned.

The years that followed saw the triumph of the 'Blue Water' school but the new Commander-in-Chief, Lord Wolseley, made a speech at Perth on 8 December 1896 which infuriated the 'big navy' enthusiasts:

---

[*] Robertson's autobiography (see Note on Sources) provides an excellent picture, admirably written, of life in the army in the period covered by this and some subsequent chapters.

I know of nothing that is more liable to disaster and danger than anything that floats on the water. We often find in peace and in the calmest weather our best ironclads running into one another. We find great storms dispersing and almost destroying some of the finest fleets that ever sailed. Therefore, it is essentially necessary for this country that it should always have a powerful army, at least sufficiently strong to defend our own shores.

By 1899 the regular army units stationed in the British Isles consisted of 19 cavalry regiments and 71 battalions of infantry, a total of around 80,000 men. Behind them were the militia with an active strength, of those who had recently attended training sessions, of 94,000. A long way behind, in military value, came the Volunteers. They included nearly 50,000 artillerymen, 15,000 engineers, including seven units of submarine miners, stationed in the Tay, the Firth of Forth, the Tyne, Tees, Humber, Clyde, Mersey and Severn, and 197,000 infantrymen, organised in 213 rifle corps, a total of almost 260,000.

Although the first units had actually been formed in 1859 the Volunteers celebrated their 'coming of age' in 1881 with a series of public displays, admiringly described by Captain J.T. Barrington, RA retired, author of a major book, *England on the Defensive or the Problem of Invasion*, published that year:

> The field manoeuvres of Easter Monday [8 April], the splendid march past at Windsor [9 July], and the more recent spectacle at Edinburgh [26 August], where 40,000 Scotch Volunteers, wet to the skin, defiled – with heads erect and dauntless mien, in a drenching, blinding rain – before the sovereign, have made the year 1881 remarkable in the annals of the force.

The Edinburgh review, if it demonstrated the Volunteers' spirit, also exposed the deficiences of their uniform, as one sufferer complained in a letter to *The Times* on 1 September:

> We were not equipped for such weather. Among the hundreds of circulars and orders issued to us during these 22 years the word 'boots' does not occur once. Plenty of orders as to braid and lace and buttons, but the boots are left to the state and circumstances of the wearer. Many a poor apprentice lad who gallantly went through that day, did it at the cost of his only pair of well-worn boots. Then, as your correspondent remarks, we have no great-coats and cannot afford them.

The government was indeed, like its predecessor, guilty of indefensible meanness towards the movement. The Volunteer was required to pay for every round he fired annually above the regulation 90, and a similar parsimony affected other items of equipment: 'In some,' noted Captain Barrington, 'every man carries, when in marching order, a haversack and water-bottle; in others these necessary articles are rare acquisitions.'

How effective the Volunteers might prove in action was constantly debated. The sharp eye of Captain Barrington acknowledged 'the evidence . . . of pluck, endurance and increasing soldierly bearing' displayed during the Easter Monday review but was critical of the commanders' tactical ability:

> The unreality of the annual displays referred to is fraught with danger. Masses are recklessly thrown forward where there should be open order and dispersion . . . The correctness of formation is apt to be more eagerly sought after than cover from the enemy's fire . . . Strong positions held in force are assailed by direct front attack.

A correspondent of the London *Standard*, in a report appearing on 19 April 1881, was equally unimpressed:

> Their advance was magnificent. Regardless of the withering fire they were drawing – for it hurt nobody – they crowded in their supports and reserves and wave after wave of men swept straight to their marks like a human tide. In doing so they wheeled to their left, profoundly indifferent to the fact that in so doing they were exposing these successive lines to something very like direct enfilade.

The mounted arm of the Volunteers, the Yeomanry Cavalry, numbering around 14,000, had always regarded themselves as a cut above their foot-slogging comrades. They certainly resembled the regular cavalry in at least one respect, a casual attitude to their duties, as Walter [later Viscount] Long, a future Conservative minister, discovered, after joining the Yeomanry as an officer while an undergraduate at Christ Church, Oxford, in 1876. His experiences at home at Warminster in Wiltshire, where he rose to the rank of captain, were probably typical:

> There was no discipline and no serious attempt was made by the officers to learn their work; the field days were carefully arranged beforehand and each officer received from the adjutant a card giving the movement of the day, with the various words of command . . . Everything was done in a leisurely and easy-going fashion. Uniform was of all sorts and kinds. Morning parades never took place earlier than ten o'clock and even then half the time on the drill ground was taken up with parade movements preparatory to inspection.

Many of the men, pressed into joining by their landlords, could not even ride; Long observed that one would try to climb on to his horse from the wrong side and found a general reluctance to dismount among riders fearful that, once on the ground, they would never get back into the saddle unaided. The eight days' annual training was a relaxed affair; all ranks lived in comfort in hotels. If ever called to battle, the Warminster troop's trumpet would, quite literally, have given forth an uncertain sound; its owner, Long discovered, 'who looked magnificent in his bandsman's dress with his bugles slung round him . . . couldn't sound a note to save his life'.

For the ordinary family the great liberator of the period was the bicycle, and enthusiasts were eager to see its military potential developed. The bicycle made its debut at the Easter Volunteer Review, held near Dover in April 1888, and the Cyclist Corps, commanded by the Professor of Tactics at Sandhurst, was formally inspected by that stuffiest of diehards, the Duke of Cambridge. The Corps developed into the 26th Middlesex, with a peak strength of around 200, though short-lived attempts were made to form other wheeled units, and *Cycling* magazine proudly described in issue after issue how the new sport was making its contribution to the nation's defence. On 26 May 1894 it estimated that 2700 cyclists were also Volunteers and on 1 September recorded how the Galloway Rifle Volunteers had won the Volunteer Cyclists Long Distance Challenge cup, having 'ploughed through in grand style in 8 hours 31 minutes' the 100-mile course in the Reading and Basingstoke area, though every man had been required to carry a minimum load, including a 20-lb [9-kg] rifle and bayonet. (Less promising, in military terms, was the high proportion of competitors who came to grief from chains breaking or becoming loaded with mud, and from the cyclist's perpetual enemy, punctures.)

Some enthusiasts seem to have dreamed of the bicycle replacing the horse. The major second in command of the 26th Middlesex Volunteers argued in December 1896 that wherever a horseman could ride a cyclist could pedal and that a cycling reconnaissance unit could manage eight miles [13 km] an hour, against the cavalry average of five and a half miles [8.8 km], and cover 50 miles [80 km] a day over good country, day after day, with no need for rests. In June 1897 the 26th Middlesex showed off their prowess at the Royal Military Tournament at the Royal Agricultural Hall in Islington. One 'prisoner' was rescued by a comrade, who fired his rifle over his passenger's shoulder while trundling him off to safety, and an unfortunate 'spy' was literally ridden over by a whole series of cyclists 'much to the amusement,' *Cycling* reported on 12 June 1897, 'of the onlookers'. Two years later the magazine described the folding bicycle devised for use in the French army, but concluded, gratifyingly, that the traditional British model was more useful.

32

FORTIFYING LONDON

To ask the Secretary of State for War what opportunity Parliament will have of considering the policy of the fortification of London?

Question by J.D. Dalziel MP, in the House of Commons, 17 April 1896

All the authors of accounts of imaginary invasions agreed on one point. The enemy's first objective, once ashore, would be London. Captain Barrington's *England on the Defensive*, already quoted, published in 1881, devoted almost half of its 328 pages to a detailed account of how an invader who had landed in mid-August was by Christmas, having drawn an 'iron grip around the great city', dictating terms at Westminster. In *The Siege of London*, by 'Posteritas', in 1885, it was all over even more quickly. In *The Invasion and Defence of England*, published in 1888, Captain Maude of the Royal Engineers argued that, thanks to the railways, the French baggage trains would reach London 'at the latest by the morning of the fifth day'. He calculated that 144 trains could carry a whole army corps and this was well within the capacity of the South-Eastern Railway, which would obligingly ferry the enemy from the coast between Hythe and Brighton direct to Charing Cross and Victoria:

> The most deadly thrust that can be made at us is obviously one directed straight at the capital, the heart of the national organism, and the shortest line to it from the coast is also the most inviting to attack.

The solution, Maude argued, was a series of fortresses between the capital and the coast:

> The mere existence of such a line of works would render us secure against any fear of invasion, because no commander would dare to embark on . . . the siege of such a fortress, with such an extremely insecure line of communication behind him.

Most alarmists tended to favour both such an outer ring of defences and an inner line of fortifications like those built during the Civil War and planned by Pitt around 1800. Captain Maude brushed aside the little matter of cost – the total, he observed airily, 'in all probability would not exceed £5 million' – while his Artillery contemporary, Captain Barrington, offered a cheaper answer:

> Let us not . . . despise the spade; it is the effective shield against the rifle-bullet. As sword parries sword, or the shield the dart, so the field intrenchment parries or absorbs the bullet. The officer who despises cover may gain a character for boldness at the expense of the lives of his men.

Trenches and small redoubts dug by individual units, and larger-scale lines of earthen fortifications, were now in vogue again, thanks largely to the coming of the magazine rifle, which meant that the infantryman did not need to be sheltered by elaborate fortifications while reloading, and by the advent of the machine-gun. Anti-invasion earthworks had been recommended by James Fergusson for the all-round defence of Portsmouth back in the 1850s, and in 1871 a subsequently eminent artilleryman Major [later Sir William] Palliser had published a widely read pamphlet, *The Use of Earthen Fortresses for the Defence of London and as a Preventive against Invasion*. Great Britain lacked recent experience within its own shores of the value of such defences, but at Alexandria, in July 1882, the Royal Navy's heaviest guns had for ten and a half hours poured shells into the batteries on shore, while putting down a near-rebellion by the Arab leader, Arabi Pasha. When, however, the expert observer Captain George Sydenham Clarke, RE – later author of the standard work, *Fortification* still in print today – went ashore, he found neither forts nor guns had suffered much damage, thanks to the sloping parapets of earth and sand protecting them.

Changes in artillery had also made fixed fortifications more vulnerable. Former 'bombproof' roofs no longer merited the name, now they might have to resist shells filled with TNT, based on Nobel's nitroglycerine, used by the German army, and melinite, comparable to the English lyddite, by the French.

The new philosophy was explained by the Inspector-General of Fortifications, Lieut.-General Sir Andrew Clarke (not to be confused with George Sydenham Clarke) in a memorandum of 1886:

> For the future we must rely as much upon concealment as upon resistance, and the use of earth alone admits of a combination of these qualities . . . Fortified posts will not in future be marked by batteries conspicuously frowning, or granite casemated forts with tiers of guns . . . On the contrary, defences if skilfully designed will be indistinguishable from the ground on which they stand, and . . . will offer no mark to the enemy's fire.

In the same year, 1886, Major Elsdale, RE, published a paper advocating the use of fieldworks, to be built at the last minute in previously identified positions, but supplied from magazines constructed in peacetime at five-mile [8-km] intervals behind them. The new doctrine was enthusiastically taken up by one of the most respected military theorists of the period, Lieut.-General [later General], Sir Edward Hamley, a former lecturer in military history and commandant of the Staff College, then at Sandhurst. Hamley combined a passion for hunting – one officer who could not ride was sent home from the Staff College in disgrace – with an endearing weakness for cats; after the Battle of the Alma he had rescued an abandoned black kitten and carried it with him for the rest of the campaign. He combined his military essays with writing novels and translating foreign poetry. A champion of the Volunteers, his election to Parliament, aged 61, in 1885 provided great encouragement to the movement. A famous speech on 'The Defence of London' to the London Chamber of Commerce, in April 1887, was followed by letters to *The Times* and articles in the *Nineteenth Century*. Hamley, a true Victorian eccentric, became a popular hero, thanks to his readiness to criticise the military establishment and even Conservative ministers, and when there was talk of retiring him the press and public rallied to his support.

Hamley was not a fanatical pro-army enthusiast. 'When the national defences are in question,' he said in the House on 22 March 1886, 'I willingly concede the first place to the navy.' But, he always insisted, even the possibility of a surprise attack, however unlikely, must be guarded against.

> In all schemes of defence it is necessary to secure the safety of London by forces independent of armies in the field, so that no hostile corps suddenly cast upon the coast . . . or which should have succeeded in evading for the moment our field armies, should be able to clutch us by the throat . . . [We should] train them specially for its defence by laying down the positions which they must occupy on any side threatened. A line north from the Thames at Barking would bar the approaches from the Essex coast; one by Erith, through Chislehurst to Bromley, would close the approaches from the coast between the mouth of the Thames and Hastings.

Hamley favoured increasing the number of Volunteers in London from 25,000 to 60,000, and argued that they would be well able to man the defences he had suggested if trained beforehand. He proved so persuasive that he was invited by the Conservative Secretary of State for War, Edward Stanhope, to comment on the official scheme for the defence of London drawn up by one of his (Hamley's) own former pupils, Colonel John [later Major-General Sir John] Ardagh, then Assistant Adjutant-General and subsequently Director of Military Intelligence. Hamley's reply, dated 10 May 1888, paid a tribute to the Volunteers, but stressed their limitations:

> The material of the Volunteer force is excellent, and . . . with a suffi-
> cient amount of training it would be capable of encountering the
> regular forces of an enemy. But with its limited opportunities it
> seems to me that . . . it . . . can only attempt this in defensive posi-
> tions, and that its training should be specially devoted to enabling it
> to occupy and fight in them.

Hamley's view was that the 'entrenched camps to be formed at Aldershot, Caterham, Chatham . . . and on the left bank of the Thames in
Essex, at Tilbury, Warley [and] Epping' were adequate as bases for
regular troops but too far forward and too far apart to be manned by
Volunteers, and he therefore recommended that 'positions should be
looked for very much nearer to London'.

Soon afterwards Colonel Ardagh drafted *The Defence of London*, a
15-page document dated 16 July 1888, which became the basis for
future thinking on this subject for the next decade:

> London is the heart and soul of the British Empire; the focus in
> which are concentrated the vital influences which regulate and con-
> trol government, commerce, finance, and society, throughout our
> vast dominions . . . but there is not at this moment a single work of
> defence of a permanent character, or a single gun mounted for the
> protection of London against an invader who had landed on our
> shores . . .
>
> Projects for an expedition to England have been framed by many
> Continental powers and are known to have been worked out in
> detail by the staff of more than one . . . A statement recently
> appeared in the Continental press that if an army of 100,000 men
> were landed in England, it could march to London and take it with-
> out resistance.[*]

Ardagh concluded 'that the most economical way of giving adequate
security to London is to supplement the force of the defenders by permanent works of fortification'.

The rest of the paper was devoted to developing this proposal in
detail. He listed in an appendix 'thirty localities at which it is proposed
that sites should be acquired' but disclaimed any intention to build
'large permanent forts, with barracks, bomb-proofs, magazines and
heavy guns' which would cost £3 million. Instead 'thirty elementary
works' were proposed, at an estimated cost of £480,000 of which
£280,000 was required for arms and stores, the purchase of land and the
construction work accounting for the rest.

While Ardagh's paper was still under consideration within the War
Office, further support for the 'Bolt from the Blue' party – derisively
known by its opponents as the 'Blue Funk' school – came from a naval

---

[*] Ardagh identified the source as *Vaterland* ['Fatherland'], published in Vienna on 10
April 1888.

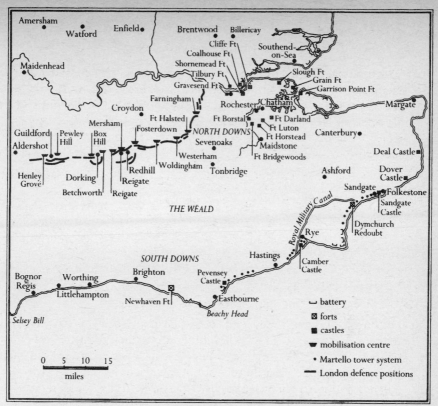

Defending London

exercise held that summer in the Irish Sea, representing the English Channel. To general consternation, in the Admiralty as well as elsewhere, the 'enemy' not only succeeded in breaking out of the ports in which he was supposedly trapped, but was also able to 'bombard' British ports, 'sink' friendly merchantmen and land raiding parties of marines. These events coincided with a new invasion scare, featuring France and Russia acting in concert. The Naval Defence Act of 1889, already mentioned, followed and, on Monday 11 March 1889, the Secretary of State, Edward Stanhope, in introducing the Army Estimates, reaffirmed that 'our uniform policy and practice is to give the preference in every respect to the requirements of the navy . . . Everyone hopes and thinks that our first line of defence should be strong enough to defend this country from the possibility of invasion.' The government had, however, to consider providing 'additional security, necessary only in what may be a remote contingency':

> There are certain strategical positions round London commanding roads and railways which are essential to its defence. These have been carefully examined by our most experienced officers, and places have been marked out, where, upon the occurrence of grave emergency, certain steps, arranged in every way beforehand, could at once be taken . . . These are the positions on which, on London being threatened, the defenders of London would in a few days be

concentrated and intrenched . . . Almost all this work is . . . left to
be rapidly carried out when the emergency arises. There are, however, a few sites of especially urgent importance which would form
the backbone of the defensive line and in which certain articles
which would be required at the shortest notice could be stored, and
where it will be possible hereafter to exercise some of the defenders
in the actual place which they might have to defend. The cost of
these precautions will be inconsiderable.

The announcement of the new programme, in the middle of a long and
wide-ranging speech, attracted no particular attention. The creation of
what became known as the London Defence Positions arounsed
nothing like the controversy the Palmerstonian programme had provoked 30 years before. Although the location of the main works must
have become well-known, little was said about them in the press or
Parliament and the cost appeared in the Army Estimates for the years
1889/90 to 1895/96 under the reassuring heading of 'for purchasing and
utilizing sites for mobilization stations, especially for the Auxiliary
Forces'.

The complete scheme, as worked out by a three-man committee set
up in 1890, which completed its work in March 1892, involved constructing a line of defence works covering a distance of 72 miles [115
km], stretching from North Weald near Epping, 18 miles [29 km]
north-east of Central London, to Vange, near Basildon, and then, on
the other side of the Thames, from Farningham along the crest of the
North Downs to Guildford, 29 miles [46 km] south-west of the
capital. The planners divided the line, the later official *Handbook* on it
explained, 'into ten regularly prepared positions, barring the principal
roads which cross the line between the coast and London', with each
sector responsible for a front of from seven and a half to four and three
quarters miles [12–7.6 km]. Additional entrenchments were proposed
both at the Guildford end, for a further four miles [6.4 km], and at the
Farningham end (three and three quarters miles or 6 km) towards the
bank of the Thames near Dartford, these being 'known as the Shere
and Darenth Valley Extensions'. Similar excavations were proposed
on the north side of the river, westwards from North Weald and south-
westwards beyond Brentwood towards Canvey Island. 'Advanced
positions,' from one half to three miles [0.8–4.8 km] in front of the
main works were also proposed for Guildford, Dorking and Red Hill
[i.e. Redhill], and 'the outlying position of Wrotham . . . forming a
connecting link between the London Defence Positions and the fortress of Chatham', which 'bars the main road from Maidstone to
London, and so hinders a hostile flank movement on Farningham or
Dartford'.

Although the whole line was to be surveyed at once, with sites for trenches and emplacements being selected, only a small part of the work was to be carried out immediately, namely the construction of the Mobilisation Centres, which were to provide assembly points for pre-selected formations of Volunteers. Although referred to by laymen as 'forts' many of the Centres provided little more than a sheltered site where the novice soldiers pouring in could be issued with arms, as the subsequent *Handbook* made clear:

> While some of these works, eg Pewley Hill, Reigate and Halstead, are well sited to command the country to the front and to cooperate in the defence of the main position, others, such as Henley Grove, Boxhill [i.e. Box Hill] and Betchworth, are retired from view and would probably only be of value as reduits [i.e. redoubts], to be held with a view to reoccupying the position should it have been temporarily forced.

The Mobilisation Centres were, in other words, merely the strong points in a chain later to be constructed. The original idea, that the Volunteers themselves would dig out the defences linking them to the next site, was rapidly dropped. The Inspector-General of Fortifications was instead 'to carry out all the necessary work by civil labour' when an emergency developed, a week being considered adequate to complete it. Fort Halstead, midway between Farningham and Westerham, was designed to accommodate field artillery, but most of the forts would only have housed infantry, lining the ramparts or firing through loopholes in the iron gates. Box Hill was typical. The full site, to allow for an adequate field of fire, covered six acres [2.4 hectares] and was acquired from a local family, on 25 March 1891, for £2221. Here was erected a semi-circular fort about 225 ft [68 m] across at its widest and about 120 ft [36 m] from front rampart to rear fence, with a sunken area into which the shell and cartridge stores opened; a caretaker's cottage, outside the main perimeter, completed the installation. A 'military road', in fact little more than a footpath, led up the hillside to the entrance, the stone pillars of which were more reminiscent of a country house than a military installation. Betchworth, commanding the other side of the famous Dorking Gap, was somewhat more impressive, as was Reigate, next in line to the east, a little way behind the town itself. Here the comparison with an ancient British fort, or even a Stone Age one, is hard to avoid, with a large deep ditch surrounding a central, grassed-over area, and stone steps leading up to the fire-step. So well did the Victorian navvies and builders do their work that even today, although the surrounding slopes, then bare, are now heavily wooded, the stone steps leading to the fire-step are still usable, the store room and magazine have their original wooden doors, and the original spike-topped fence, once intended to keep out the French infantry, still stands to discourage English vandals.*

As finally evolved, the 1889 plan for the defence of London called for 200,000 men, mainly Volunteers, and 400 guns, among them 30 batteries of 4.7-in [120-mm] breech-loading field guns, and 70 batteries of 15-pounder [6.8-kg] breech-loaders, plus some obsolete rifled muzzle-loaders. Only a limited amount of ammunition was to be kept in the Mobilisation Centres, ten railway stations being earmarked as advanced depots for additional supplies, with larger, main bases at Woolwich and Nine Elms (Battersea) serving the forces south of the river, and at Bishopsgate those to the north. The strategic thinking behind the plan was that, with the route up the Thames well guarded by conventional forts, erected or strengthened since the 1860s, and the even more recently improved defences of Chatham threatening his flank, an invader would be forced on to a few routes, leading from Sussex and West Kent into Surrey; the danger to Essex was always regarded as much less serious. His way would then be blocked first by the field army, then by the 'Lines of London', on to which the army, if beaten, would fall back, helping to stiffen the Volunteers already manning the Mobilisation Centres and adjoining entrenchments. The planners considered that 2000 men per mile of line should provide security, or delay the enemy long enough to enable the navy to cut off his supplies and the field army to plunge into his flanks from the great camps at Chatham and Aldershot. 'On the south of London,' wrote the defence commentator Spenser Wilkinson in his book, *The Volunteers and the National Defence*, in 1896, '60,000 men and 150 guns are assigned to a front of 34 miles [54 km] from Guildford to Halstead, while on the north-east, a front of 24 miles [38 km] is given to about 30,000 men with 80 guns', the two forces being linked, when the need arose, by a pontoon bridge at Gravesend. By this time all that could be done in advance had been done, as the 'Historical Summary' in the *Handbook for the London Defence Positions* later confirmed:[†]

> Camping grounds were selected for 18 Volunteer brigades and 57 position batteries, and maps of these camps showing water supply &c., were prepared. Advanced depots were selected and maps and reports of railway stations were made, showing the proposed arrangements for detraining, &c.

Like every similar programme the London Defence Positions scheme was scaled down long before it was complete. Three of the forts on the Essex side of the Thames were never started; two, also in Essex, were based on ordnance stores which already existed at Tilbury Fort and at

---

* Neither Box Hill Fort, of which little remains, or Betchworth, where the original design is still clear, is at present open to the public, but an impression of both can be gained from outside. The description above is based on a visit in July 1985.

† The *Handbook* is dated 1903, but is no doubt based on earlier documents containing similar information.

Warley, near Brentwood. But 13 were brand-new constructions on greenfield, or more commonly green-hill, sites, the whole programme costing only £160,671, of which £28,578 was for the land.

During the 'London in danger' agitation the alarmists' previously favoured target, Portsmouth, had taken second place in the public mind, but in June 1895 it was again pushed into the foreground, at least locally, by the up-and-coming magazine and newspaper-owner, Alfred Harmsworth [later Lord Northcliffe] who was in the following year to launch the sensationally successful *Daily Mail*. His motive for playing the invasion card was not patriotic, but circulation-boosting and vote-catching. Harmsworth, a dynamic 29-year-old, had recently, in March 1895, been adopted as Unionist, i.e. Conservative, candidate for Portsmouth, and immediately bought the local Portsmouth *Evening Mail*, which was renamed the *Southern Daily Mail*, though carrying only the name *The Mail* as its masthead.*

It was Harmsworth's own idea to run a serial involving the occupation of his intended constituency by a foreign power and the commission having been turned down by the leading mystery writer of the day, of whom more will be heard, William Le Queux, the young newspaper proprietor commissioned a Canadian freelance author for the purpose, engaging a naval historian to provide specialist advice. The story, promoted by large posters showing waves of foreign soldiers launching bayonet charges against Portsmouth's gallant defenders, and a drawing of the Town Hall under shell-fire, was entitled *The Siege of Portsmouth. A Story of the Great War in the Year 189-*. '189-' soon proved to be 1897, when France and Russia are supposed to fall out with Great Britain in a quarrel over Egypt and Turkey. The second instalment on the following day, Thursday 18 July 1895, saw the British fleet, returning from its annual manoeuvres, overwhelmed by the French and Russians, and by Friday the citizens of Portsmouth were reading of 'The Capture of Lord Wolseley – The Landing of the French on English Soil – The Advance on Havant'. All duly ended disastrously, as the genre demanded, but there was an interesting novelty, for the writer was instructed to include in the story the leading local members of the main political parties, and other well-known citizens. 'Put in old Jack Palin,' Admiral Lord Charles Beresford, whose support Harmsworth had enlisted, told the obliging author. 'He was a boatswain under me and he taught Prince George to swim!'

The Siege of Portsmouth failed in both its aims. *The Mail* attracted no extra readers; Harmsworth was beaten by the Liberal candidate, though elsewhere the Conservatives were more successful and Lord Salisbury, who in June had replaced the Liberal Lord Rosebery, re-

---

* To add to the confusion, the relevant volumes in the British Library are labelled the *Evening Mail*, although the papers within are headed *The Mail* and Pound, p. 181, misleadingly describes it as the *Southern Daily Mail*.

mained prime minister, ushering in ten more years of Conservative rule. During this decade the London Defence Positions programme went ahead, though the Volunteers never seem to have occupied the Mobilisation Centres for even the briefest exercise and they remained unvisited except by troops delivering ammunition and other stores. What had clearly become a great military white elephant was briefly disclosed to public view in the same year when, on 17 April 1896, J.H. Dalziel, a Scottish Radical MP, asked 'What opportunity Parliament will have of considering the policy of the fortification of London by the erection of a fort in the neighbourhood of Guildford . . . ?' He went on to mention 'the erection of two forts in the neighbourhood of Dorking', and 'the suggestion of the erection of forts at Betchworth and elsewhere'. The minister replied, somewhat blandly, that 'the scheme for the defence of London was laid before Parliament on the introduction of the Army Estimates', when, as has been seen, it was mentioned only briefly and in passing, and Dalziel let the matter drop. Ultimately 13 Mobilisation Centres were built, one or more to each of the 'Defence Positions'. To each a specific Volunteer division was assigned, which when mobilisation was announced would assemble at a pre-arranged point and then move forward into it. Every division would then acquire, an official report promised, 'a General Officer with a suitable staff' for whom premises were also pre-selected. The most fortunate division, the 22nd, was to have its headquarters in a hotel, the White Lion in Guildford, but more commonly a country mansion was named, such as Highfield House, Knockholt, for the Westerham sector, and Green Court, Crockenhill, for the Darenth position. The whole operation south of the Thames would be directed from Croydon and, for the district north of the river, from Warley.

By 1903 work on the Mobilisation Centres, except for the one at Westerham, was complete. In that year, the secret *Handbook for the London Defence Positions*, already quoted, provided a comprehensive 47-page guide laying down in great detail the establishment of each Position, along with such information as the number of days' food supplies to be held at the suburban railway stations serving as advanced depots. 'A scheme is being worked out . . . ,' the *Handbook* assured its readers, 'for the establishment of base hospitals for 20,000 sick and wounded in public and other existing buildings in London.' If a battle were ever to be fought at Dorking, at least its casualties would be well cared for.

22 Portsmouth, c. 1836

23 The barracks at Dover, c. 1850

24 The Duke of Wellington 25 Viscount Palmerston, c. 1844 26 Field Marshal Sir John Fox Burgoyne (painted c. 1813)

27 Installation of a gun in the Gilkicker battery, Portsmouth, 1871

28　Garrison Point Fort, Sheerness

29　Fort Widley on Portsdown Hill, Portsmouth

30　Fort Picklecombe, near Plymouth (a recent photograph)

31　Spitbank Fort in the Solent (a recent photograph)

32 The Channel Fleet, 1869

33 Rifled muzzled loader on a Moncrieff disappearing carriage, in the firing position

34 Sir Edward Watkin, MP, champion of the Channel Tunnel

35 *(Far right)* Visitors being lowered into the Tunnel workings, 1882

36 Visitors being entertained underground

37 Watching a boring machine in action

38 Field Marshal Lord Wolseley

39 General Sir Edward Hamley

40 Major-General Sir John Ardagh

41 *(Below)* London Mobilization Centre, Box Hill (photographed in 1980)

42 *(Right)* Damage from shellfire in Scarborough, December 1914 (5 people were killed in this house)

43 *(Left)* Trenches defending Chatham, c. 1918

44 *(Above)* Pillbox for machine guns on the Isle of Sheppey, 1918

50 *(Right)* Shot down bomber in Dorset, August 1940

45 Field Marshal Lord Ironside

46 Air Chief Marshal Lord Dowding

47 Field Marshal Lord Alanbrooke

48 Emergency road block in Kent, 1940

49 A camouflaged coastal strongpoint in Northern Command, 1940

51   Maunsell fort in the Thames Estuary

52   Sea defences under construction at Clacton, 1941

BOOK 4
FROM KAISER TO FÜHRER
1901–1945

33

THE MAIN MEANS OF HOME DEFENCE

These forces will be recognised as the main means of home defence on the outbreak of war.

Memorandum by Richard Haldane, Secretary of State for War, on the
proposed Territorial Army, 23 November 1906

The nineteenth century ended for Great Britain in dismay and near-disaster. In October 1899 a war had broken out, against the independence-seeking Boers in South Africa, rapidly followed by 'Black Week' in December, during which the army suffered a series of humiliating defeats. On 22 January 1901 Queen Victoria died, after a reign of 64 years, long before, in May 1902, the war was finally ended by a peace treaty. The Boer War spectacularly exposed the army's weaknesses. The first British generals in command were totally outclassed; the cavalry proved initially far less effective than their amateur opponents; the infantry in their scarlet coats made easy targets – 'khaki' now speedily replaced the old uniforms; and the artillery were outranged by the Boers' German-made guns. Rudyard Kipling, the poet of the new expansionism, put it succinctly:

> Let us admit it fairly, as a business people should,
> We have had no end of a lesson; it will do us no end of good.

The Royal Commission which investigated the conduct of the war revealed much that was wrong. The man who had ultimately won it, first as Chief of Staff and then as Commander-in-Chief, was Lieut.-General Herbert Lord Kitchener [later Field Marshal Earl Kitchener], whom one member of the Commission, the influential and well-connected Lord Esher [Reginald Brett, Viscount Esher], a friend of the new king, described as 'a man of great penetration, decision and organising power'. Kitchener himself complained of 'a want of serious study of their profession by officers', and there was ample evidence of the weakness of the Intelligence Department of the War Office. Colonel Robertson, in charge of the Foreign Section, later noted that 'on taking over the new duties I found that . . . there was not, with one exception . . . a single up to date statement giving a comprehensive and considered estimate of the military resources of any foreign country', the chief source of information being, 'some small non-confidential handbooks, largely compiled from newspapers'. As for the military attachés serving in British embassies abroad, 'it was not uncommon for an officer to be chosen because he was a society favourite or had an attractive wife.'

In 1904 on the recommendation of a committee presided over by Lord Esher, the government, on 6 February, radically reorganised the War Office, setting up an Army Council, rather on the lines of the Board of Admiralty, and abolishing the post of Commander-in-Chief. The Intelligence Division, now part of Military Operations, was given increased status and more than doubled in size. The most important change that year, however, was the creation by the prime minister Arthur [later first Earl of] Balfour, in a minute dated 4 May 1904, of the Committee of Imperial Defence, to replace earlier bodies, some with a similar name, which had exercised much less authority. The new CID consisted of all the senior ministers with naval and military, or overseas, responsibilities, the chancellor of the exchequer, the ubiquitous Lord Esher, who continued to attend as the king's personal representative even when the government changed, and the professional heads of both services. The prime minister took the chair *ex officio*, but, unlike the Cabinet, the CID had a permanent secretariat which recorded and followed up its decisions and the secretary of the CID became an important figure in his own right.

The traumatic shock administered by the war in South Africa affected every part of the land forces. The report of the Royal Commission on the war had already brought changes in the regular army, and in 1903 the government set up another Royal Commission, on the militia and the Volunteers, under the chairmanship of the Duke of Norfolk, which reported in May 1904. The militia presented no particular problem, but the Volunteers, 242,000 strong, all now enjoying the vote and well represented in Parliament, were a different matter. The Royal Commission's finding that 'The Volunteer Force, in view of the unequal military education of the officers, the limited training of the men and the defects of equipment and organisation is not qualified to take the field against a regular army,' confirmed earlier suspicions, but implementing any radical change was likely to prove both troublesome and unpopular.

Killing off, or taming, this sacred cow which had long outlived its usefulness proved beyond the capacity of Balfour's Secretary of State for War, the Hon. St John Brodrick [later Earl of Midleton] and his attempt to make camp in effect compulsory and to create a smaller but more efficient Volunteer force foundered in the face of widespread opposition in Parliament. His successor from October 1903, Hugh Arnold-Forster, bravely tried to carry out the recommendations of the Royal Commission, but a note from the War Office to commanding officers on 20 June 1905 which pointed out 'that many Volunteers units are reported . . . not to be in an efficient state to take the field' provoked so great an outcry it had to be withdrawn. Whatever showing the Volunteers might have made against an invader, they successfully defeated the government which, when for different reasons it fell in December 1905, left its opponents to solve the problem.

The Yeomanry, the virtually independent mounted force dominated by comfortably-off landowners, posed fewer difficulties. A number of its members had served in South Africa and the officer quoted earlier on his unit's lackadaisical approach to its duties a few years before found that the war led to 'an entirely fresh start. We went into camp on Salisbury Plain in September instead of going into quarters in towns in May.' Even more revolutionary, it was now laid down that 'no officer would be promoted unless he had a thorough knowledge of his duties' and 'no trooper would be raised to non-commissioned rank unless he could pass a reasonable examination. These changes . . . made a wonderful improvement and produced in due course a really efficient military force.'

The government formed in December 1905 by Sir Henry Campbell-Bannerman, a reforming Secretary of State for War under Gladstone back in the 1890s, was far stronger than Balfour's. It won a famous landslide election victory in January 1906, and remained in firm command after Herbert Asquith [later first Earl of Oxford and Asquith], in April 1908, replaced the dying 'C-B'.

Not for the first time, it was now left to the 'peace' party to reform the armed forces and, by a further irony, the chief responsibility fell on a man best known for his passionate admiration for a foreign power. Richard [later Viscount] Haldane, who served as Secretary of State for War until June 1912, was in December 1905 a 49-year-old lawyer, educated in Scotland and Germany; the latter he later incautiously described as his 'spiritual home'. Haldane was a highly intelligent man with, for a barrister, an unusual handicap. 'I have no gift of expression . . . ,' he admitted to a colleague, 'but I seem to see very clearly . . . what needs doing.' His supremely eloquent Cabinet colleague, Lloyd George, described him as 'the most confusing clever man I have ever met', and Haldane's muddled style and 'reedy voice' were made worse by his constant use of literary allusions above his audience's head, especially from German authors. When he rose to present the Army Estimates in 1907, one MP scribbled a note to another suggesting they should leave the Chamber rather than endure 'three hours from Schopenhauer', the nickname Haldane had acquired on publishing a three-volume translation of this pessimistic German philosopher.[*]

It was Haldane's own suggestion that he should become Secretary of

[*] i.e. *The World as Will and Idea*, translated by Haldane in 1883 from the original by Artur Schopenhauer (1788-1860).

State for War, although the prime minister told him that 'Nobody will touch it with a barge pole', and proposed the Home Office, a far more prestigious ministry. But Haldane got his wish and his appointment rapidly proved an inspired choice, revealing him to be outstanding in a ministry of exceptionally able men. The auspices on the Monday he went to Buckingham Palace to kiss hands on taking office, 11 December 1905, hardly seemed promising:

> It was a day of the blackest fog that I remember . . . We stuck in the darkness of the Mall. I got out to see where we were and could not find the carriage again . . . By trudging through the mud and feeling among the horses' heads I at last got to the War Office, then in Pall Mall . . . I was a little exhausted when I arrived . . . handed the seals to the Permanent Under-Secretary to take charge of, and asked the tall ex-Guards soldier in attendance for a glass of water. 'Certainly, sir: Irish or Scotch?'

The problem faced by Haldane in modernising the nation's land defences was threefold. The first was the abysmal state of the regular army:

> We had not in 1906 a single [infantry] division that was a reality. Moreover the [cavalry] brigades, such as they were, wholly lacked accessories without which they could not sustain the strain of war. Their transport was deficient and so were their medical organisations. Only 42 batteries [of field artillery] could be put in the field, a number which a proper General Staff would have pronounced to be ludicrously inadequate.

The regulars' first line of support was the militia whom Haldane dismissed as 'neither organised nor equipped'. As for the Volunteers, Haldane considered that, lacking transport and medical services, they were wholly ineffective, while the Yeomanry, though more efficient, hardly added up to a national cavalry force:

> The Yeomanry were an excellent peace organisation of a separate kind, still largely run by the country gentlemen. But these heterogeneous corps had histories and traditions and people who . . . were devotedly attached to them. To break with tradition . . . was likely to be a serious undertaking.

The third, and most serious, obstacle Haldane was likely to face was the opposition of his own Liberal backbenchers. Pacifist sentiment, masquerading as a concern for peace, was still rampant in their ranks, and a more honourable if sometimes misguided desire to save money for social reform at the expense of the forces; the next six years were to see the foundation of the welfare state in a great programme that stretched from health and unemployment insurance to old age pensions. Haldane recorded in his *Autobiography* this attempt to persuade him to let sleeping dogs lie:

> The argument used by some of the average Liberals . . . was 'Do not attempt great improvements . . . but concentrate . . . on reducing the estimates.' My reply was that economy and efficiency were not incompatible; that I believed we could obtain a finely organised army for less money than at present, but a finer army we must have, even though it cost more.

Haldane's first major speech, in introducing the Army Estimates in the House of Commons on 8 March 1906, came as an agreeable surprise to his colleagues. 'I had no idea,' the prime minister told a friend, 'that Schopenhauer would cut such a figure in the barrack yard.' He delighted his own supporters by announcing a small reduction in the Estimates and by setting his face firmly against conscription and universal military training. He also, as proof of his commitment to fresh thinking, firmly grasped one military nettle, that of the London Defence Positions completed only a few years before:

> Anyone who knows Surrey, and goes down into the neighbourhood of Dorking, will find there certain curious structures . . . large wire fences surrounding seven to nine acres [2.8-3.2 hectares] of land, and a large construction that looks more like a water-tank than anything else . . . I stumbled upon one the other day when taking one of my reflective walks and, going in, found 3300 rounds of ammunition, cordite, lyddite, shrapnel, and the latest pattern of gloves for people working with intrenching tools . . . I estimate . . . that there was no less than £25,000 worth of stores there . . . I asked . . . how many men had been there for work, and the answer was, 'I never saw a unit in the three years I have been here.' I asked when the guns had last been there and was told they had always been at Woolwich. I asked whether there were any more of these constructions and was told that from a neighbouring hillock I could see a dozen more with the naked eye. These constructions had a definite origin, in a time when the navy was not the navy of today . . . Now, with the consent of the government and of the Defence Committee . . . they are going to disappear root and branch.

The demise of the Mobilisation Centres, like their creation, was inserted into the middle of a much longer speech and attracted no particular attention. On the following day the CID formally minuted that, 'in view of the conclusion that a serious invasion of the United Kingdom is impossible, so long as our naval supremacy is maintained, the London defences should be abolished', and on 25 February 1907 it was announced that the sites were to be sold. By December 1909 the first to go, at Farningham, was already disposed of.

The abolition of the 'Lines of London' was a logical step since Haldane already planned to disband the Volunteers who were to have manned them. As early as January 1906 he had submitted to the Army Council the first of six memoranda explaining his intention to create two separate armies, a Striking Force (later re-named an 'Expeditionary Force') of regulars, for which the former militia would provide a ready-trained reserve, and a Territorial Army (later officially known as the 'Territorial Force'), operated by local associations and providing in effect a Reserve Army of part-time soldiers. The Territorials would be mobilised full-time, like the old militia, in an emergency, and then given six months' intensive training, and though their only obligation would be to home defence, it was hoped that most would agree to serve overseas.

Haldane intended that the new force should become 'the grand reserve of the nation' and his memorandum of 25 April 1906 made clear that it would not just be the Volunteers in new uniforms:

> The difference between the Territorial Army and the existing Volunteers will be very marked . . . The Old Volunteer Force . . . existed almost entirely on the basis of . . . home defence . . . The Territorial Army will exist for an entirely different purpose.

Haldane was well aware that in attempting to disband the Volunteer movement, a popular body with powerful friends though not a single member of it had ever fired a shot in anger, he faced a tough fight. 'It required,' he decided, 'a comprehensive statute . . . I employed my old "devils" [i.e. legal assistants] at Lincolns Inn to aid me in constructing a preliminary draft . . . It became the Territorial and Reserve Forces Bill.'

While the legislation was being prepared Haldane, on 12 July 1906, delivered another three-hour speech outlining his plans, in terms designed to appeal to his own economy-minded back-benchers.

> We have applied to the army the same procedure that an accountant would apply in investigating the affairs of a business; we have gone through it bit by bit and asked in what condition that bit is, and what justification there is for the money spent upon it. We have put . . . the determining question, 'What does that officer, that man, that money mean, tested by the standard of efficiency in war?'

Haldane bravely proclaimed that in reducing the regular army by 20,000 not even the hitherto sacred Guards regiments would be spared, and he proclaimed himself firmly a 'Blue Water' adherent: 'The first purpose for which we want an army is for overseas war. The fleet defends our coasts.'

The proposed changes were announced in detail on 30 July and while other MPs set off for the grouse moors Haldane travelled to Germany, in response to a personal invitation from the Kaiser. King Edward, already holidaying in Europe, whom Haldane met en route, was concerned that his Secretary of State for War might cut an unimpressive figure, on foot, among the mounted German generals and wearing his customary frock coat and top hat. (Haldane had warned his hosts that 'not even the imperial command would induce me to get on the back of the peaceablest horse in the whole Mark of Brandenburg.') The French, with whom that January confidential staff conversations had started, were concerned Haldane might attend a parade on Sedan Day, 2 September, when the Germans celebrated their great victory of 1870, but he managed to spend it tactfully out of sight in the German War Office. The visit was, in its way, a success. He met the younger von Moltke, Chief of the German General Staff, who 'spoke with approval of our new organisation of our army', while Wilhelm II also put himself out to be agreeable in his inimitable, Germanic, fashion:

> I went with him to the parade on the Tempelhofer Field and there sat in a carriage from which I watched him reviewing his troops. He galloped up to me . . .
> 'A splendid machine I have in this army, Mr Haldane, isn't it so? And what should I do without it, situated as I am between the Russians and the French? But the French are your allies, so I beg pardon.'

That September Haldane, by a simple executive order, and deeply impressed by his experiences in Germany, at last created a General Staff for the British army, to undertake the planning for future operations; he had already brought home from India one of the few senior officers who had enhanced his reputation in South Africa, Major-General Douglas [later Field Marshal Earl] Haig to join it, believing, as he wrote, that 'Haig had a first-rate General Staff mind'. During the autumn he met the commanding officers of the militia, earmarked for virtual disbandment, at Lord Derby's country house at Knowsley in Lancashire, and in December 1906, as if to symbolise its new outlook, the War Office moved from its ancient premises in Pall Mall to a new building in Whitehall. (Haldane described his new office as 'very gorgeous, but not as comfortable as my old quarters'.)

On 1 January 1907 the Army Council issued the formal orders creating the Expeditionary Force, and on 25 February Haldane introduced the Army Estimates for the coming year, delighting the Liberals by showing a saving of £2 million. But the real test, the Territorial and Reserve Forces Bill, was still to come. The Liberals showed little enthusiasm for it and most of the debates took place with the government benches almost empty, but on 9 April 1907 the crucial second reading was carried by 283 to 63, and in the House of Lords, hostile to most major Liberal measures, it encountered little opposition. The Bill's unexpectedly easy passage was largely due to the behind-the-scenes support of the king. Edward VII had welcomed Haldane's appointment, praising his 'sound common sense and great powers of organising' in contrast to the ineffectiveness of his 'hopeless' predecessor, and he was always unstinting in his encouragement. 'The only thing he criticised,' wrote the Secretary of State after one three-hour conversation with his sovereign, 'was my hat, which he said I must have borrowed from Goethe.' The king invited his minister to meet Arthur Balfour, Leader of the Opposition, at Windsor Castle and encouraged the Conservative leadership in both Houses not to score party points against the Bill. Once it was passed, His Majesty, on 26 October 1907, also used his influence to disarm opposition among the Volunteers, inviting the Lords Lieutenant to Buckingham Palace to obtain their help in launching the new Territorial County Associations; they would, it was hoped, become their respective presidents. 'The king's intervention has produced the requisite steam for the engine and I am working day and night to take full advantage of the moment,' wrote Haldane to his sister – he remained a life-long bachelor – on 1 November. That autumn he spent travelling about the country addressing meetings and trying to persuade the suspicious Volunteer officers to support the proposed Territorials.

Shortly before the new force came into existence a strong attack was launched on it in the House of Lords by the 76-year-old Field Marshal Lord Roberts [Frederick, first Earl Roberts], a national hero, immortalised by Kipling's poem 'Bobs', since he had saved the situation in South Africa. The last Commander-in-Chief before the post was abolished, Lord Roberts, of whom more will be heard later, believed that nothing less than conscription could make the nation safe and on 12 March 1908 he poured scorn on the idea, an essential part of Haldane's plan, that the Territorials should be equipped with artillery. Only a week later, however, Haig, now Director of Military Training, was able to report favourably on the Lancashire Artillery Volunteers' performance during manoeuvres with regular units, and on 1 April 1908 the Volunteers ceased to exist and recruiting for the new Territorial Force officially began.

The Territorials' official establishment, announced on 18 March 1908, was 302,199 men and 11,898 officers, a total of just over 314,000. The regular army contained nearly 167,000, making the total potential peacetime strength of the British land forces 481,000. These now consisted of a self-contained Expeditionary Force of six infantry divisions and four cavalry brigades, with the former militia serving as its Special Reserve and the Territorials, when up to full strength, providing another 14 infantry divisions and 14 brigades of cavalry, with their own transport and medical services.

The overriding question in the spring of 1908 was whether the men

who had known only the undemanding obligations of the departed
Volunteers would accept the far sterner discipline and tougher training
of the Territorials. Within a week Haldane was optimistic. 'The
Volunteers are pouring in and . . . the new army is going to be a real
success,' he wrote on 7 April 1908. By the time of the next Army Estimates, introduced on 4 March 1909, the Territorials numbered
240,000, and the Special Reserve had attracted 70,000 men, only 10,000
short of its establishment. Already the Officers Training Corps, which
had that year replaced the old Volunteer companies in the public
schools and universities, had 17,000 members and, though hostility
from the recently founded Labour Party successfully kept it out of
most local authority schools, it was to become an established part of
the educational scene.*

Edward VII (to whom the Kaiser, on a visit to England, had sung
Haldane's praises) invited Haldane to stay at Windsor to witness the
presentation of colours to 108 Territorial battalions in Windsor Great
Park on 19 June 1909. Haldane described his reactions in a letter to his
mother:

> The ceremony on Saturday was really splendid. The king was
> greatly pleased with his new army. Fortunately it was beautifully
> fine till all was over. It was a curious experience to stand beside the
> king and watch the outcome of three years of strenuous days and
> nights of missionary enterprise . . . I have been fortunate in that the
> things for which I have worked most strenuously . . . took outward
> and visible form, which does not often happen to the work of polit-
> icians.

Already, new inventions were appearing which threatened to trans-
form the nature of twentieth-century warfare as the steam engine and
rifled gun had revolutionised that of the nineteenth. In 1909 the War
Office began experimenting with mechanical transport, and a committee was set up to investigate the military use of aircraft. Haldane
made his first flight the following year, in an airship, immaculate as
ever in his frock coat and top hat, and in 1912 the Royal Flying Corps,
from which in 1914 the Royal Naval Air Service broke away, leaving it
an exclusively army service, was established. Haldane had meanwhile,
somewhat reluctantly, moved to the House of Lords, and in June 1912,
even more unwillingly, left the War Office to become Lord Chancellor. He would have preferred to be First Lord of the Admiralty, but
Winston Churchill had only recently taken up the post, in October
1911, and was not to be dislodged.

* The OTC was still flourishing in the 1930s when I was, at the age of 13, compulsorily
enrolled in the school unit. A little later it changed its name to the less elitist Junior
Training Corps and, later still, after 1945, to the Combined Cadet Force.

34

F IS FOR FLEET

F is for fleet that we keep at Spithead.
It makes every foreigner wish he were dead.

Rhyme in Edwardian alphabet book, c.1907

Between 1900 and 1914 the Royal Navy changed even more drastically than the army. One young Royal Marines lieutenant, Maurice [later Lord] Hankey, recorded the priorities prevailing in the Mediterranean fleet in January 1899:

> Today (Sunday) is sacred in the navy to the great fetish 'brass and paintwork' . . . It is said that if a general engagement was imminent and the future of the Empire was at stake, before clearing for action the brasswork would be polished and the paint touched up.

A commander's efficiency, noted this same observer, was judged solely on 'the brightness of the ship's paintwork, brasswork etc.,' irrespective of his seamanship or tactical skill, but now all this was to alter. 'The new admiral Fisher,' Hankey wrote home on 5 September 1899, 'has joined the fleet. He is said to be a tremendous scoundrel but I like his looks.' This favourable verdict was rapidly confirmed, as another letter, of 26 September, made plain:

> The new admiral has been making a series of experiments in various forms of night attack by torpedo-boats . . . This is the first practical exercise I have seen done out here . . . In every case the captains of the [torpedo] 'boats' and 'destroyers' have shown the most consummate ignorance of the elements of tactics and common sense, [so] that every boat and destroyer must have been destroyed by the guns of the battleships long before getting within range . . . This is only typical of the crass conservatism of the Navy.

Vice-Admiral Sir John [later Admiral of the Fleet Lord] Fisher was 58 when these words were written and already famous throughout the navy as a fierce and fearless innovator. From 'Jackie' Fisher's first appearance in a senior post, as head of the Gunnery School at Portsmouth in 1883, where he rapidly got rid of the ancient smooth-bore guns and introduced modern quick-firers, he had roared through the musty, tradition-bound wardrooms and offices of the navy and Admiralty like a force nine gale, being soon notorious for his restless energy, combative temperament and vigorous schoolboy style – his letters were enlivened with such phrases as 'totus porcus', for 'going the whole hog'. In the process the service became bitterly divided between the 'Fishermen' or occupants of 'the Fishpond' and the rest, especially the supporters of Rear-Admiral [later Admiral] Lord Charles Beresford, MP, 'Charlie B', a dashing figure who, as already mentioned, was idolised by the public.

In spite of such internal opposition the fleet created during the next few years became known as 'the house that Jack built'. Fisher improved every area of the navy that he touched, and there were few which he did not touch. He was totally dedicated to his profession, and immensely hard-working, sometimes up at 4 am and often, to the despair of his staff, at his Admiralty desk even on Sundays. A man of fierce convictions, he was nevertheless ready to be persuaded. 'A silly ass at the War Office wrote a paper to prove me inconsistent,' he once remarked. 'I wouldn't give a d— for a fellow who couldn't change his mind with a change of conditions.'

Warmly admired or bitterly detested, wherever he served, Fisher was, for much of the Edwardian period, far more important in shaping naval policy than the First Lord of the Admiralty. He made his first mark as a reformer in Whitehall as Second Sea Lord, between June 1902 and August 1903, where he established a common training system for officer cadets up to the age of 19, first at Osborne, then at the Royal Naval College at Dartmouth. He failed in his attempt to have fees at these establishments abolished, though with only 3 per cent of families earning enough to support a son there 'we are', he complained, 'drawing our Nelsons from too narrow a class'. He also did his best to reduce the snobbish prejudice against engineering officers, who became increasingly important with every advance in naval technology. Hitherto those few who reached flag rank had been known derisively as 'chauffeur admirals' but Fisher now insisted that, for at least the early years, intending engineers should train alongside other cadets.

From 1903 to 1904 Fisher held an appointment, as Commander-in-Chief, Portsmouth, where he was able to practise as well as preach two of his favourite doctrines. The first was the need for a higher standard of gunnery. In the fleet's firing practice in 1898 only 31 per cent of the shots fired hit their target and in 1901 the First Lord of the Admiralty, the Earl of Selborne [formerly William Palmer], proclaimed as his motto: 'Gunnery, gunnery, gunnery!' Before long, thanks to various technical improvements and more serious attention to the subject, the best captains were achieving 80 per cent. Though a man of orderly habits, lacking any obvious vices, Fisher was on record as saying of one rear-admiral whose ships achieved a high standard of gunnery, 'I don't care if he drinks, gambles and womanizes; *he hits the target!*'

Fisher's other obsession was, very properly, with the navy's readiness for immediate mobilisation. In the late nineteenth century it had taken 14 days to get ships commissioned after the first orders had been issued. By 1901 this had already been cut to five, but Fisher was still not satisfied, and the period was eventually brought down to between 12 and 19 hours. '*Suddenness,*' he insisted, in one of his typically quotable pronouncements, 'is the secret of success at sea . . . A fleet always ready to go to sea at an hour's notice is a splendid national life preserver.'

The spirit of improvement affected every hallowed corner of the navy, and Fisher challenged every custom which diverted funds from essentials. 'There is only so much money available for the Navy,' he pointed out. 'If you put it into chairs that can't fight, you take it away from ships and men who can.' Edward VII called him, only partly in jest, 'a Socialist' and Fisher later wrote that, 'What I am most happy about during my years at the Admiralty is what has been done for the Lower Deck.' This included better pay and promotion prospects, improved living conditions on board ship and, symbolising the breach with the past, the abolition of the 'hard tack', or ship's biscuit, with the provision of ships' bakeries to supply fresh bread. Another change, begun before Fisher's day but completed under him, followed the discovery that German ships, being painted grey, were far harder to detect at a distance than British, which had white upper works, funnels picked out in yellow and masts and fighting tops in orange. From the summer of 1902 a drab but practical grey began to be universally adopted instead.

In 1900 the navy had still contained large ships armed with muzzle-loaders, 'no more entitled,' as one admiral observed, 'to be called line-of-battle ships than a Chinese junk', and in April the Navy League, to the Admiralty's annoyance, organised sandwichmen to march up and down Whitehall with placards naming these outmoded vessels. In July 1901 a *Punch* cartoon showed an 'Admiralty optimist' asleep in a rowing boat, with storm clouds gathering overhead. By September 1903 a specialist naval writer, formerly one of Their Lordships' chief critics, was able to write that, 'In every branch of the British service, a new energetic spirit is apparent and the confident and almost careless attitude handed down from the hard-fought Battle of Trafalgar is being banished.'

The dynamic admiral's greatest opportunity came with his appointment in 1904 as First Sea Lord, the operational and professional head of the Royal Navy. He arrived at his desk on that most sacred of naval anniversaries, Trafalgar Day, 21 October, describing it to a friend as 'a good fighting day to begin work . . . I am,' he wrote, 'ready for the fray. It will be a case of *Athanasius contra mundum*. Very sorry for *mun-*

dum, as Athanasius is going to win.'*

Fisher had already begun as he meant to go on in an earlier meeting with the First Lord, the Earl of Selborne, at which he disclosed his plans for transforming the navy. 'I sat him in an arm-chair in my office,' he told a friend, 'and shook my fist in his face for two and a quarter hours without a check; then he read 120 pages of foolscap and afterwards collapsed.' By 6 December the Admiralty was already announcing a whole series of reforms in a memorandum unassumingly entitled *Distribution and Mobilization of the Fleet* and Fisher's driving energy ensured that the momentum of change was kept up. A typical Fisher exhortation read:

> We must have no tinkering! No pandering to sentiment! . . . No pity for anyone! We must be ruthless, relentless and remorseless! We must . . . have The Scheme! The Whole Scheme!! And Nothing but The Scheme!!! This must be done regardless of everything and everybody – whether Chancellor of the Exchequer, Foreign Office, or Colonial Office.

What 'The Scheme' consisted of was, first, the scrapping of 154 ships from the list of effective units with, to quote Arthur Balfour, 'one courageous stroke of the pen', these vessels being in Fisher's own striking phrase, too weak to fight and too slow to run away. The ships that remained would be reorganised to keep them available, even those in reserve, by means of a 'nucleus crew', of two-fifths of their normal complement. '*Readiness for sudden action*', he stressed, 'has to be the keynote of all we do.' The ships in reserve would be fully manned on mobilisation, and were anchored at their probable war stations of Plymouth, Portsmouth and Sheerness. Fisher was, however, sceptical of the likelihood of an invasion, as he made clear during 1904:

> The Navy is the 1st, 2nd, 3rd, 4th, 5th . . . ad infinitum Line of Defence! If the Navy is not supreme, no Army however large is of the slightest use. It's not *invasion* we have to fear if our Navy is beaten, IT'S STARVATION!†

Fisher believed, like Mahan and all Mahan's 'Blue Water' disciples, that the best protection of any country was to retain command of the sea far from its shores, and he was not much troubled by the thought of coastal raids. 'The old idea that ships can take towns and so influence military operations,' asserted Fisher, 'is exploded. If a squadron . . . were to attempt such a thing, the telegraph wire would bring

---

* i.e. 'Athanasius against the world', a reference to the solitary stand of the Patriarch of Alexandria against opposition within the early Christian church. He died, victorious, in AD373.

† This quotation is reproduced as it appears on p. 65 of Marder, *The Anatomy of Sea Power*, on which I have drawn heavily in this chapter. I have also made extensive use of the same author's *From the Dreadnought to Scapa Flow*.

armoured cruisers on to their necks before they could do any mischief whatever.' For coastal defence Fisher welcomed the great novelty of the time, the submarine, the early history of which has already been mentioned. The first practicable submarine was a French invention and in January 1898 a target battleship steaming at a stately ten knots [11.5 mph; 18 km per hour] was successfully torpedoed by a missile fired by the *Gustave Zédé* while underwater. The submarine began to be a potential menace just when the threat from the motor torpedo-boat seemed to have been met by the development of machine-guns and quick-firing cannon, though the accurate range of a torpedo was increasing; by 1905 it was 3000 yards [2740 m]. No effort was made by the French to conceal their achievement, indeed the performance of their first submarines was probably exaggerated. The Royal Navy was not impressed. Among senior officers there was widespread reluctance to acknowledge the existence of a new weapon that might challenge Britain's supremacy at sea. One admiral confidently predicted that 'before very long, we shall hear no more about them', and another described submarines, in a much quoted phrase, as 'underhand, unfair and damned un-English'. The truth was, however, that if other nations introduced underwater craft the Royal Navy was forced to follow suit and the First Lord of the Admiralty, on 18 March 1901, announced the ordering of five submarines though he added, 'these inventions . . . I confess I desire shall never prosper.'

Fisher from the first grasped the submarine's potential, and it was largely due to him that the post of Inspecting Captain of Submarine Boats was created in 1903, this specialist reporting on 13 May that 'there is no function that the minefield might fulfil' in coastal defence 'that cannot be better performed by a mobile defence such as a submarine'. The Director of Naval Intelligence supported him in a memorandum that October:

> The establishment of submarine stations along the South Coast of England ought to go a long way towards dispelling the ever-recurring fears of invasion so dear to the 'old women of both sexes' mentioned by Lord St Vincent [in Napoleonic times]. To these (a few live in the War Office), it may be pointed out that the French in all their utterances on the subject . . . point out with pride that the existence of their submarines as part of the *Défense Mobile* makes any attempt at invasion of French territory the act of a lunatic. They are quite right and the argument cuts both ways.

That month submarines began to replace minefields as the principal means of defence at Sheerness, Portsmouth, Plymouth and Pembroke, orders being placed for delivery of ten boats a year, the maximum the sole supplier, Vickers Ltd, could turn out.

Later that year, as First Sea Lord, Fisher threw all his weight behind the submarine building programme, causing his arch-enemy, Beresford, to describe the new craft derisively as 'Fisher's toys'. As yet no effective answer to the submarine had been found. Nets, ramming, towed explosive missiles and 'hand charges' dropped from small boats had all been tried, with little success; the development of its real enemy, the depth charge, was to come a little later.

In October 1905 a navy war council was set up under the First Sea Lord, roughly equivalent to the general staff soon to be appointed for the army, and around the same time the Channel fleet, responsible for home defence, was strengthened at the expense of the Mediterranean fleet.

To ensure that an enemy was kept at a respectful distance from Great Britain's shores the navy still looked to its capital ships, a term reintroduced in 1909 to cover both battleships and the more powerful cruisers. Here, too, the Fisher years were a time of dramatic change. Hitherto the Royal Navy's warships had been scattered about the oceans in a pattern that had not greatly changed since the days of sail. Fisher, however, insisted that the guiding principle in selecting locations should be strategic 'and not sentimental' and pointed out that steam power and wireless telegraphy had made possible a speed of concentration previously impossible. He considered that, 'Five strategic keys lock up the world!', the two essential to home defence being Dover and Gibraltar.*

The self-same factors that affected the Royal Navy also applied to its likeliest rival, Germany, and the threat from Germany was significantly increased by the building of the Kiel (originally the Kaiser Wilhelm) Canal, a 61-mile [98-km] channel linking the North Sea with the Baltic, which was opened in 1895. This virtually doubled Germany's naval strength by enabling the Baltic fleet rapidly to reinforce her north-west shores. Hitherto the Germany navy had hardly been taken seriously in Great Britain. When, in the early 1860s, the first stirrings of interest in naval matters had become evident in Germany, a *Punch* cartoon had shown a hardy British tar giving a puny, bespectacled German a toy boat and telling him to 'run away and play with it'. A similarly arrogant attitude was encouraged in British children even in the nursery, by a crudely chauvinistic alphabet teaching book:

F is the fleet that we keep at Spithead.
It makes every foreigner wish he were dead.

As late as 1897 the German navy was still only the sixth largest in the world and it was not till 14 September 1901 that the first serious reference to the need for 'The Home Fleet . . . to be on a par with the formidable German force which is being rapidly developed in the North Sea' was made by the Director of Naval Intelligence in a note to the

* The other three were Singapore, the Cape of Good Hope and Alexandria.

First Sea Lord.

The emergence of Germany as a naval power meant, along with the new emphasis on defending the north-east coast already described, a redistribution of the warships available for home defence. By the end of 1904, though not announced till the following spring, a new Channel Fleet had been formed, based on Dover, consisting of 12, later 17, battleships. It also contained a squadron of the latest cruisers. Its first line of reinforcement was the new Atlantic Fleet, eight modern battleships plus armoured cruisers, based on Gibraltar. Three-quarters of Great Britain's best warships were now readily available to confront the German fleet, and combined manoeuvres were planned twice yearly for the North Sea in accordance with a dictum of Fisher's hero, Nelson, much quoted by him: 'The battle ground should be the drill ground.'

The redistribution of the fleet was achieved gradually and with little publicity but the navy made the most of the other major development forced through by Fisher, the creation of a new class of ships far more powerful than any other afloat. HMS *Dreadnought* was launched by King Edward VII at Portsmouth on Saturday 10 February 1906 amid public celebrations, and with newspaper coverage, appropriate to a great national victory. The *Dreadnought*, displacing 17,900 tons, was two knots faster at 21 knots [24 mph; 39 km per hour] than any warship already under construction or in existence, and mounted a battery of ten 12-in [30-cm] guns, also outclassing any other; eight of these could fire a simultaneous broadside, weighing 6800 lbs [3087 kg]; her nearest rival, the *Lord Nelson*, could achieve a broadside of 5300 lbs [2410 kg].* To accommodate the new guns, the old mixture of smaller calibres was scrapped, the *Dreadnought* relying on 27 quick-firing 12-pounders [i.e. with 5.4-kg shells] to keep torpedo boats at bay.

The *Dreadnought* soon showed her superiority to other battleships. In battle practice in 1907 she proved able to deliver 75 per cent more weight of shell on a target lying 8000 yards [7300 m] away, and scored 25 hits in 40 rounds fired. She had, at a stroke, given Great Britain mastery of the seas and left Germany, in Fisher's exultant word, 'paralysed'; if the Kaiser did build his own dreadnoughts they would be too large to pass through the recently completed Kiel Canal.

Great Britain was not left to enjoy her lead for long. In April 1906, two months after the launching of the *Dreadnought*, the German parliament carried a new Navy Law authorising the widening of the Canal, to be completed in June 1914. In August 1906 the Germans announced plans to build a dreadnought – the name now given to the whole class – even larger than the original, and later that year a further six armoured cruisers were added to the existing programme. Also in August 1906

* In later versions all ten large guns could engage the same target with a single broadside.

King Edward VII and Kaiser Wilhelm II, for once united, agreed at a private meeting that the forthcoming Peace Conference at The Hague, designed to secure arms limitation, was 'a humbug' and so it proved. The liberal journalist, J.L. Garvin, in the *Fortnightly Review* that October, showed equal realism. 'She [i.e. Germany] has challenged the naval supremacy which is the life of our race . . . That is precisely why we have been so urgently moved to settle our outstanding differences with the rest of the world.' That month the next step in redistributing the available ships was taken with the creation of a Home Fleet, based on the Nore, consisting of six battleships, six cruisers and 48 destroyers, shortly afterwards joined by the *Dreadnought* as its flagship.

The navy now had little doubt that a war with Germany was inevitable. The Admiralty, in a memorandum on 'The Home Fleet' in December 1906 had referred to 'our only potential foe now being Germany'. On 4 October 1907 Fisher wrote to King Edward reporting that '[Admiral von Tirpitz] has privately stated in a secret paper that the English Navy is *now* four times stronger than the German Navy! *And we aim to keep the British Navy in that strength* . . . Ten Dreadnoughts built and building and not one German Dreadnought last March!' On 9 November 1907 at the Lord Mayor's banquet the First Sea Lord assured his audience they might 'sleep quiet in their beds', but ten days later the Germans announced an amended Navy Law, duly passed in February 1908, providing for a new programme for building dreadnoughts and battle cruisers and eventually raising the German fleet to a total of 58 such ships. The Anglo-German naval race was now well under way and the mere possibility of Germany getting ahead was sufficient to cause public anxiety. In the winter of 1907-8 the cry was raised of 'two keels for one', i.e. two British dreadnoughts for every one laid down by the Germans. The government, the Liberal and Labour Parties, the press and indeed the whole nation were divided as to whether more should be spent on the navy even at the price of the social reforms to which ministers, with their huge Commons majority, were committed. 'Is Britain going to surrender her maritime supremacy to provide old-age pensions?' asked the *Daily Mail* on 25 February 1908, when the navy estimates were published.

The Kaiser himself now inadvertently took a hand. A private letter from him to the then First Lord of the Admiralty, Lord Tweedmouth, an outstandingly ineffective minister who was dropped shortly afterwards, which declared that England had no reason to fear the German navy, had the reverse effect when its contents appeared in *The Times* on 6 March 1908. British scepticism was justified. Only four months later Wilhelm was minuting on a report from the equally tactless and bellicose German ambassador in London, von Metternich, dated 16 July 1908:

I have no desire for a good relationship with England at the price of the development of Germany's navy. If England will hold out her hand in friendship only on condition that we limit our navy, it is a groundless impertinence and a gross insult to the German people and their emperor . . . The [Navy] Law will be carried out to the last detail; whether the British like it or not does not matter! If they want war, they can begin it, we do not fear it!

The Kaiser again displayed his talent for making bad worse in an interview published in the *Daily Telegraph* of 28 October 1908 which admitted that most of his subjects were hostile to England, though he was personally friendly. The next British naval estimates, in March 1909, produced the predictable outcry that they were (a) inadequate or (b) outrageously excessive, but for the opening of the subsequent debate, on 16 March, the House of Commons was crowded as if for Budget Day. The prime minister, Asquith, claimed that Britain would by April 1912 have 20 dreadnoughts and battle-cruisers to Germany's 17, the leader of the Opposition, Balfour, that Germany's strength would in fact be 21. Even a margin of three, however, seemed to the public perilously slim. A great agitation began for a yet larger programme. 'We want eight, and we won't wait,' a slogan coined by a Conservative MP, George Wyndham, was heard on all sides. The king himself was known to support the soon sacred figure and Lord Esher was said to have declared that the Board of Admiralty should be hanged if they did not order the extra ships. The Navy League, a breakaway anti-Fisher organisation called the Imperial Maritime League, and a new pressure group, the Society of Islanders, all helped to orchestrate the almost hysterical agitation and eventually the government, somewhat half-heartedly, gave way and ordered the extra ships.

Fisher had one other service to render the navy. Since its first appearance as a possible fuel for warships in the 1880s he had been known as an 'oil maniac' but, by around 1910, while oil had been accepted for submarines and destroyers it was still not employed for capital ships. In July 1913, however, it was announced that henceforward oil would replace coal as the navy's source of power and in the following year even the *Royal Sovereign* class dreadnoughts now under construction were altered to use it.

On 25 January 1910, his sixty-ninth birthday, Lord Fisher, as he had become two months earlier, resigned as First Sea Lord, his work largely accomplished. Winston Churchill, who arrived at the Admiralty as First Lord in October 1911, shortly before his thirty-seventh birthday, later wrote, 'There is no doubt whatever that Fisher was right in nine-tenths of what he fought for . . . He gave the Navy the kind of shock which the British Army received at the time of the South African War. After a long period of serene and unchallenged complacency . . . it was Fisher who hoisted the storm-signal and beat all hands to quarters.'

The troublesome Beresford, who had described Fisher as 'our dangerous lunatic' and whom Fisher in turn had labelled a 'blatant, boastful ass', retired from active service in 1911 but continued his mischief-making with dinner parties for influential people at his Mayfair home. 'Beresford,' commented his old enemy, 'says that he can do more with his chef than by talking.' This was probably true. In the House of Commons, where he sat as MP for Portsmouth from 1910, Beresford proved an ineffective performer. 'Before he got up to speak,' commented Winston Churchill, who had to answer him, 'he did not know what he was going to say . . . when he was on his feet he did not know what he was saying and when he sat down he did not know what he had said.' But on at least one matter both men were agreed, the danger from across the North Sea. It now became Beresford's practice to greet those around him: 'Good morning – and another day nearer the German war!'

35

THE ENEMY IS ENGLAND

I cannot now resist the conclusion that every German thinks that 'the enemy is England'.

A.J. Balfour MP to the Sub-Committee on Invasion, 29 May 1908

For nearly a thousand years France had been the traditional enemy. But those not obsessed by the past were now beginning to look not across the Channel but the North Sea. The real turning point, after Germany's emergence as the greatest land power in Europe in 1870, was the accession to the German throne in June 1888 of 29-year-old Wilhelm II, and his dismissal, in March 1890, of Bismarck as his Chancellor. 'Kaiser Bill', as he later became known to the British, was in many respects a modern-minded and progressive ruler, but almost medieval in his obsession with the Hohenzollerns' supposedly divine right to rule Germany and his desire for martial glory, fostered by a typically Germanic education, despite a withered arm, at a brutally strict military academy. Another Germanic trait, a sheep-like tendency to follow blindly an autocratic leader, led to the Kaiser being regarded by many of his countrymen with sycophantic adulation, but he remained popular in England and no outcry followed when, in 1890, the little island of Heligoland, off the coast of Schleswig-Holstein near the mouths of the Weser and the Elbe, was handed over to Germany in exchange for Zanzibar.

Mahan's *Influence of History upon Sea Power*, published that year, was 'devoured' by the Kaiser and in a lecture to the German War Academy in February 1895 he reminded his audience that no nation could become a world power without a strong fleet. An article by a General Staff captain in a German military weekly when published in the *Royal United Services Institution Journal* a year later, in March 1897, caused a sensation. A powerful fleet was essential to Germany, argued Captain Baron von Lüttwitz, to enable her to follow a 'world policy', and this meant either an agreement or a conflict with England. The latter possibility he viewed with resignation, if not enthusiasm:

The unassailableness of England is a legend. Through the introduction of steam and electricity [i.e. the electric telegraph] the situation has much changed since 1805, to the disadvantage of England. The assembling and rapid transport of invading armies has, in consequence, been essentially facilitated.

In April 1898 the Reichstag carried the First Navy Law, which set out a six-year programme for the construction of 12 new battleships and other warships, and two years later, in June 1900, the Second Navy Law doubled the new establishment. But the Kaiser still received a warm welcome at Queen Victoria's funeral. 'The German emperor had a noble reception today from the citizens of London,' reported Lord Esher in a letter on 5 February 1901.

Wilhelm was not personally hostile to Great Britain but a speech at the Elbe regatta that June – 'Our future is on the water. We have fought for our place in the sun and won it' – seemed almost a direct challenge to the British Empire. In Germany it was received with rapture. The Navy League in England had by 1901 15,000 members; its German counterpart that same year could boast of 600,000.

If the general public were as yet barely troubled by Germany's growing strength the professionals were becoming increasingly conscious of it. 'I had not been a year in my new post,' later wrote the then Lieut.-Colonel William Robertson, who became head of the Foreign Section of the Intelligence Division of the War Office on 1 January 1901, 'before I became convinced . . . we ought to look upon her as our most formidable rival.' But no one believed that the German fleet was as yet anywhere near powerful enough to challenge the Royal Navy unaided. A memorandum of 7 February 1903 used a striking metaphor to explain the reason:

> A war between Germany and Great Britain would in some ways resemble a struggle between an elephant and a whale, in which each, though supreme in its own element, would find difficulty in bringing its strength to bear on its antagonist. For this reason it is not very likely, under existing conditions, that either Germany or Great Britain will be eager to enter on a contest.

If war should break out, however, the author of the paper considered, 'The invasion of England will be given a prominent place in the German plan of campaign,' for the Kaiser commanded 'exceptional transport facilities', able to deliver 100,000 men to England in a mere 30 hours.

Germany moved firmly into the foreground so far as the general public was concerned with the publication during 1903 of the best and most successful of all imaginary invasion stories, *The Riddle of the Sands* by Erskine Childers. This full-length, 120,000-word novel begins with a bored young Foreign Office official being invited to join a friend on his small sailing boat at Flensburg in Schleswig-Holstein, and their subsequent exploration of the sheltered channels behind the Frisian Islands south of Heligoland. They eventually discover, after many adventures, a huge fleet of invasion barges, destined for the east coast of England, but the hero gets safely back to England to rouse the authorities and the planned invasion is abandoned.

Childers, aged 33 when his book was published, was a comfortably-off, fiercely patriotic Liberal with a job, a House of Commons clerk-ship, which left him ample leisure for sailing. He had taken his little 30-ft [9-m] cutter, the *Vixen*, single-handed through the North German waters he described, but his publishers considered an attack by Germany so far-fetched that they insisted on heavy cuts and the inclusion of a love interest. 'I was weak enough to "spatchcock" a girl into it and now find her a horrible nuisance,' Childers confessed while writing the book during the summer of 1902.*

With a true author's instinct, however, he refused their plea to alter the title, and *The Riddle of the Sands* was the publishing sensation of the season. Childers was invited everywhere to meet leading politicians, including Winston Churchill, and there was another upsurge in demand for the book seven years later, in 1910, after two British naval officers were imprisoned for alleged spying on Borkum, in the heart of *The Riddle of the Sands* coastline; one admitted in court he owned a copy and had read it three times.

The growing fear of Germany led during 1903 to a hitherto inconceivable rapprochement with France, encouraged by Edward VII's dislike of his German relations. The turning point came during his visit to Paris in May 1903, followed by a return visit to London by the French president that July. In April 1904 the final stages of a new Anglo-French treaty were signed, the start of the famous *Entente Cordiale* between these former enemies. When, in October, the fleet of France's ally, Russia, mistakenly bombarded some fishing vessels from Hull (the 'Battle of the Dogger Bank'), mistaking them for torpedo-boats, the dispute was resolved without war. That year, the usual autumn manoeuvres were based on a supposed 'enemy' landing north of the Thames. The press release that was issued, itself a sign of the changing times, was at pains to explain that 'the invasion of Essex was to be regarded as the invasion of a foreign territory by an English army dependent on a fleet which had definitely secured command of the sea'.

When looking at the coast with an invader's eye, the generals' choice fell on an increasingly popular resort:

> Clacton is one of the places . . . peculiarly well adapted for a descent on our coast by a foreign power. The beach is well suited for pur-

---

* The verb 'spatchcock', meaning 'forcibly insert', was currently in vogue after being used by an unsuccessful general during the Boer War.

poses of disembarkation, the anchorage is protected by the Gun Fleet [i.e. Gunfleet] Shoal, between which and the shore it is possible for warships and transports to form up. Water sufficiently deep to take ships of large tonnage is found close to the shore and the approaches from inland to shore are such as would assist an invader.

A good deal of trouble was taken to hamper the defending, 'Red' commander. His forces were split at the start of the exercise to 'prevent their being concentrated in less than two days' and his horses supposedly struck down by an infectious disease, epizootic lymphangitis, no doubt as unpleasant as it sounded. The use of fixed defences, like those at Harwich, was excluded from the exercise and their garrisons were not allowed to play any part in it.

The attack was under the command of one of the army's accepted stars, Lieut.-General [later Field Marshal] Sir John French, subsequently first Earl of Ypres. French, in the role of invader, sailed from Southampton with 12,000 men, 2700, healthy, horses, and 42 guns in ten transports, escorted by six cruisers. This army duly disembarked, unchallenged, around Clacton on Wednesday 7 September 1904, with Colchester, 12 miles [19 km] inland, as its initial objective, from which it was to swing 15 miles [24 km] south-west to seize the harbour at Maldon, on the River Blackwater.

French's troops found their way barred by those of the defending commander, who acquitted himself well:

> General [Sir Arthur] Wynne made an excellent use of the facilities for delaying action which the numerous ditches and hedgerows of Essex afforded and, although an inferior force, succeeded in delaying his opponent while at the same time evading any decisive combat.

It had been intended that French's force should leave as they had arrived, to simulate an attacker merely delivering a raid in strength, but by Tuesday 13 September, conditions had changed:

> So heavy a sea was running off Clacton that the admiral declared it would be impossible to re-embark any troops. Sir John French . . . was forced to face General Wynne's advance with his back to the sea and with the certainty that his opponent must speedily be strongly and continuously reinforced.

The Chief of Staff in his secret report professed himself 'fully satisfied' with the results of the 1904 exercise and it led to the conclusion that though an enemy might get ashore on the east coast he would have to pay a heavy price if he tried to re-embark his troops and equipment. Less reassuring, however, was the private note that the Secretary of State for War, who had been in Europe during the Clacton manoeuvres, sent to the prime minister on 15 September, four days

before the Chief of Staff's report. 'I have returned from a short visit to
the Continent,' wrote Hugh Arnold-Forster, 'more than ever convinced of the danger of the situation . . . We are simply playing at the
business here, and, in my opinion, nothing but the grace of God and
the navy can save us from a tremendous lesson one of these days.'

Invasion was at the top of the agenda of the newly created Committee of Imperial Defence, which set up a standing Sub-Committee
chaired by the prime minister to keep the subject under review. On 11
May 1905 Balfour reported its findings to the House of Commons. He
began by examining in detail the 'long-standing quarrel' between
soldiers and sailors as to the feasibility of invasion. 'This division of
opinion . . . ,' Balfour reminded the House, 'goes right back to Elizabethan times.' It was the first task of the CID to try and settle the argument. Lord Roberts and other experts had calculated that the minimum number of enemy troops required to attempt an invasion was
70,000, who, even if 'lightly equipped as regards artillery and . . .
cavalry', would, according to Admiralty estimates, require 250,000
tons of shipping to carry them. Collecting so many transports would,
Balfour pointed out, be bound to attract British attention:

> By the time they reached our coasts the alarm would long since have
> been given to every ship between the Faroe Islands and Gibraltar and
> every ship available, every cruiser, torpedo-boat, destroyer . . .
> would be concentrated at the point of danger . . . How is it possible
> that this helpless mass of transports could escape the attack of these
> torpedo-boats and submarines . . . ? Does anybody think that is an
> enterprise which would be undertaken by any sane person? Serious
> invasion of these islands is not an eventuality which we need
> seriously consider.

At last it had been publicly stated that invading England in strength
was not, as the alarmists seemed to suppose, as simple an operation as
making a day trip from Boulogne, but the risk of a hit-and-run attack
remained. A note dated 12 December 1905 and signed by Balfour,
though he had left office two days earlier, *The Possibility of a Raid by a
Hostile Force on the British Coast*, identified the likeliest landing point as
east of Portsmouth, but from the evidence collected at Clacton estimated that it would take 30 hours to disembark a force of even 10,000
men, giving the navy ample time to intervene. The 2800 infantry, 2000
marines, 200 sailors and three field batteries earmarked to protect
Portsmouth on mobilisation should, the note argued, be adequate for
the purpose, supported as they would be by the heavy guns of the
Palmerstonian forts on the Portsdown Hills.

How real *was* the danger of a German invasion at this period? The
first serious study of such an operation seems to have been made in
1897. The enemy, argued Vice-Admiral von Knorr, in presenting the

conclusions of the German Admiralty Planning Section to the Kaiser on 31 May, would be bound to attack the German coast if war broke out, and Germany's best chance would be to strike first, before the Mediterranean fleet had been recalled. The planners recommended a sudden strike against the Thames, to disrupt England's coastal trade and annihilate her reserve fleet, and then hurrying an invasion force across the Channel, since a maximum of 15 days would be available to carry out this attractive programme. It would be essential to make use of the Scheldt estuary, which would mean a prior alliance with Holland or, a detail to any true German, 'we must establish ourselves there by force.'

Nothing came of the von Knorr proposals, for attention turned instead to occupying Denmark, to protect Germany's flank during the alternative operation put forward by the German War Office, the Schlieffen Plan, an attack on France by a 'left hook' through Belgium and Holland.

In 1901 a German pamphlet, *Operation Über See* [*Operation Overseas*], examined the possibility of an invasion of England as part of a maritime war and by 1903 its existence was known in London. Three years later, the new War Minister, Richard Haldane, had reached the conclusion that the best way to prevent an invasion was to adopt the Admiralty strategy of defence at a distance, as he recorded in his subsequent *Autobiography*:

> The continued occupation by a friendly nation like the French of Dunkirk, Calais and Boulogne, the vital northern Channel ports of the Continent, was . . . an objective on which to concentrate. The accomplishment of this implied that we should have an Expeditionary Force sufficient in size and also in rapidity of mobilising power to be able to go to the assistance of the French army in the event of an attack on the northern or north-eastern parts of France.

The alarmists still anticipated a 'Bolt from the Blue' and on 13 March 1906 *The Times* carried a striking full-page advertisement for *The Invasion of 1910* by William Le Queux, the oustanding mystery-writer of the day. It included a large map of the British Isles, showing the remorseless advance of a German army, and described the bombardment and sacking of London. Before the book had even appeared it was – a publisher's dream – denounced in Parliament, on 15 March 1906, and rapidly became the best-seller of the year. Serialised in the *Daily Mail*, *The Invasion of 1910* reached a wide public, including the Kaiser himself. The book was of a kind already familiar, though longer than its predecessors – it runs to 550 pages – and William Le Queux claimed to have travelled 10,000 miles [16,000 km] by car to study on the ground the routes and battle-grounds described, with accompanying maps, in his book, and to have consulted numerous military experts, including

Lord Roberts. While *The Invasion of 1910* was still the sensation of the hour in London Richard Haldane was, in August 1906, in Germany, where he met the Chief of the German General Staff, Helmut von Moltke the younger, nephew of his even more famous namesake.

> He observed that in his building there were no plans for the invasion of England. I looked out . . . at the Admiralty General Staff building . . . and asked him whether what he had said applied to that building also.
>
> 'No,' he replied. 'The German Admiralty has of course thought out the invasion of England, but it would be an uncertain business.'

Late in 1907 the Sub-Committee on Invasion resumed its investigations. On 29 May 1908, A.J. Balfour, who had, he admitted, been shown many 'very valuable documents', though out of office, appeared before it in the pleasant first-floor room where the CID regularly met, with its painted wall panels and carved fireplace, in a terraced house at No. 2 Whitehall Gardens, built when Napoleon was the potential enemy.[*]

Balfour began, in his typical politician's way, by saying that his earlier public statement had been misunderstood. 'My speech of 1905 . . . ,' he complained, 'has been charged with the crime of persuading the country that an army is really an unnecessary part of our national defence, because the fleet by itself is competent to prevent invasion.' But, whatever had been believed then, the situation now was different:

> New conditions *have* arisen which require us to resurvey the situation. In the first place, Germany is substituted for France as the real source from which our greatest danger of invasion is for some time likely to arise . . . The Germany navy has enormously increased, German mercantile marine has enormously increased, and the accommodation in German ports has enormously increased. The Germans have . . . made immense preparations, which would enable them to embark troops far more quickly than they could have embarked them five or six years ago, and incomparably more quickly than the French ever could in any of their Channel or North Atlantic ports . . . They have . . . perfected their railway arrangements, so that there will be no difficulty in concentrating with extreme rapidity the troops they require . . . The Germans have what the French never have had . . . ports in which both ships of war and transports are concentrated naturally in the ordinary course of naval administration and trade . . . The French transports would have had . . . very different rates of sailing, they would have been very numerous, and they would have crossed a sea which, though narrow, is as crowded from end to end with shipping as Piccadilly is

---

[*] The house was demolished in 1938 and the site is now occupied by the Ministry of Defence.

with cabs and motor buses. It is impossible that anything in the nature of secrecy could be maintained while this transit was taking place. But . . . if once we can imagine a German force embarked in relatively few transports – I think the lowest estimate of the transports is about 40, and the highest of them is about 60, is it not? – if once we can imagine these transports concentrated outside the German harbours and away from the immediate attack of shipping . . . a surprise would be possible to a degree which would be quite impossible in the overcrowded waters of the English Channel.

Balfour had no doubt where the nation's real danger now lay:

I was one of those most reluctant ever to believe in the German scare. But I cannot now resist the conclusion that every German thinks that 'the enemy is England' . . . The German Staff and, what is much worse, the German nation, have ever before them the vision of a time when the opportunity will come for displacing the only power which stands between it and the universal domination of Europe.

The report was duly laid before the full CID, at its hundredth meeting on 22 October 1908, a major occasion, with the prime minister in the chair and the Foreign Secretary Sir Edward [later Viscount] Grey, Richard Haldane and Admiral Fisher all present, along with David Lloyd George as Chancellor of the Exchequer. The report's conclusion differed little from those reached by the last full-scale enquiry five years before:

1. That so long as our naval supremacy is assured against any reasonably probable combination of powers, invasion is impracticable.
2. That if we permanently lose command of the sea, whatever may be the strength and organisation of the Home Force, the subjugation of the country to the enemy is inevitable.
3. That our army for home defence ought to be sufficient in numbers and organisation not only to repel small raids, but to compel an enemy who contemplates invasion to come with so substantial a force as will make it impossible for him to evade our fleets.
4. That in order to insure an ample margin of safety such a force may for purposes of calculation be assumed to be 70,000 men.

The CID accepted the report, which was essentially a triumph for the navy and a defeat for the 'Bolt from the Blue' party, in spite of the powerful advocacy of Lord Roberts. Like his famous predecessors Wellington and Wolseley he had become convinced, as an elderly, retired, Commander-in-Chief, of the danger of a massive invasion and, unlike them, he believed the answer lay in the compulsory military training of all adult males, described by his supporters as 'National Service'. Its critics contended that this was a euphemism for conscription, a measure totally alien to the British tradition and anathema to the vast majority of the government's supporters in Parliament.

'Bobs', as he was widely known, even in official circles, was the army's last Commander-in-Chief. He arrived at his office one morning in 1905 to find it taken over by officers working for the new head of the army, the first Chief of the Imperial General Staff, and though he continued to serve on the Committee of Imperial Defence, he eventually resigned from it to become president of the National Service League. Fighting his last campaign with all his traditional commitment and vigour, 'Bobs' (now in his seventies) stumped the country to preach the need for universal military training and warn of the danger from Germany. So violent did his attacks on the Hohenzollerns become that King Edward himself pleaded with him, at the request of the Cabinet, to modify his language, while one Liberal politician suggested, rather ungenerously, that the former C-in-C's army pension should be terminated unless he would mend his ways.

On Wednesday 27 January 1909 the campaign for conscription reached the West End with the first night of *An Englishman's Home*, a full-length three-act play with a cast of 15. The author, identified simply as 'A Patriot', was in fact Major Guy du Maurier, brother of a well-known actor-manager Gerald [later Sir Gerald] du Maurier, who controlled Wyndham's Theatre, where it was staged. *An Englishman's Home* is set at Myrtle Villa at Wickham in Essex, which, when the curtain rises, is shrouded in thick fog on a Boxing Day morning. The villa's owner, Mr Brown, is highly critical of a young Volunteer who calls in on his way to the rifle range, and soon afterwards more alleged Volunteers appear, who turn out to be enemy soldiers under the command of Prince Yoland, 'Captain in the Black Dragoons of Her Imperial Majesty, the Empress of the North'. The house is eventually captured and poor Brown, having taken part in the battle for Myrtle Villa, is made prisoner in his own sitting room and, as a civilian under arms, taken out, despite the screams of his daughter, to be shot, leaving Prince Yoland to occupy his chair. 'Do we stay here?' asks one of his officers and is told, in a striking curtain line: 'Yes, here, in what the late owner called "An Englishman's Home".'

The Times, which over the years had often championed the alarmist cause, dealt gently, if justly, with this latest manifestation of it, in its review on the following day:

> The production of such a play . . . furnishes startling testimony to the hold which the great national defence question has taken of the thoughts and imagination of the English public. The thing itself is crude enough and indeed somewhat amateurishly done; what is sig-

nificant is that the thing should have been done at all . . . Not a good
play in itself, hardly indeed a work of art, but of real importance as
. . . a 'sign of the times'.

Before long the audiences for du Maurier's drama included members
of the royal family and they proved enthusiastic. 'Last night,' noted the
weekly illustrated magazine *Black and White* in its regular 'London's
Plays' feature on 2 February 1909, 'it was received with rousing cheers
. . . May it run for ever.' The magazine had its own reason for welcom-
ing *An Englishman's Home* for in the same issue it drew attention to 'the
opening chapters of our new serial story, *The Great Raid*, which com-
mences on page 352'. This was described as 'an essentially human story
of men and women caught up in a great national catastrophe which
they are powerless to avert', but was yet another trudge over a now
well-trampled route, with 'The Battle of Canterbury' replacing 'The
Battle of Dorking' and 'The City Territorials' doing duty for the now
disbanded Surrey Volunteers.

The oddest example of imaginary invasion literature to appear that
year was *The Swoop*, a long short story written in five weeks for publication as a shilling paperback, by the subsequently famous P.G. [later
Sir Pelham] Wodehouse. Wodehouse was then 28 and still struggling
to establish himself, and *The Swoop, or How Clarence Saved England. A
Tale of the Great Invasion* treats the whole German danger as a joke. In
Chapter One, 'An English Boy's Home', Clarence Chugwater, a 14-
year-old Boy Scout, is shown despairing of his family because 'not a
single member . . . was practising with the rifle, or drilling, or learning
to make bandages'. Soon his distress – ' "England – my England!" he
moaned' – is justified, for he finds in the Stop Press column of the evening paper the news he is half-expecting:

> Fry not out, 104. Surrey 147 for 8. A German army landed in Essex
> this afternoon. Loamshire Handicap: Spring Chicken, 1; Salome, 2;
> Yip-i-addy, 3. Seven ran.

Soon there are, as his less patriotic brother puts it, 'two rummy-
looking chaps coming to the front door, wearing a sort of fancy dress',
who turn out to be German officers, but the visitors are baffled by their
hosts' insistence on treating them as ordinary guests:

> 'Perhaps a cup of tea? Have you come far?'
> 'Well – er – pretty far . . . In fact from Germany.'
> 'I spent my summer holiday last year at Dresden. Capital place.'

Far from striking terror into the citizens, however, when they bombard London, the victorious Germans receive a public vote of thanks
for destroying the Albert Hall and Royal Academy while 'the late
English summer had set in with all its usual severity . . . The coughing
of the Germans at Tottenham could be heard in Oxford Street.' In the

end it is almost a relief to their commander, Prince Otto, to find his force surrounded by Boy Scouts, 'armed with catapults and hockey sticks'. Threatened with 'such a whack over the shin' if he resists, he is taken off into captivity, while the victorious Clarence – ' "I am England", he said with a sublime gesture' – is soon being paid £1000 a week to appear on the music halls as 'the Boy of Destiny'.

The Swoop was a well-sustained joke, which neatly incorporated every cliché of alarmist literature, but was destined not to be reprinted until 1979, four years after its author's death, following a conspicuously unpatriotic life.*

The new 'biographs', showing short, jerky, silent films, were a novel feature of Edwardian life and here, too, the topic of the hour made its appearance. In *The Invaders* hundreds of German spies are seen attempting to take over the country, and some, dressed as women, daringly peel off their ankle-length skirts to reveal the uniforms beneath. No one yet took the cinema seriously, but a notable part in encouraging the gullible to regard every German as an actual or potential spy was played by William Le Queux, whose alarmist tract published in 1906, *The Invasion of 1910*, has already been mentioned. Le Queux's large readership included Winston Churchill, and he had certainly travelled widely in Europe and the Middle East, and served as a war correspondent for the *Daily Mail*, though his claim to have been consulted by the British government on foreign intelligence networks seems more doubtful. The author listed his recreations in *Who's Who* as skiing, revolver practice and experiments in wireless, a suitably spy-like selection, and in 1909, the year which saw the production of *An Englishman's Home*, Le Queux published *Spies of the Kaiser*, a book of 14 chapters each recording a separate adventure on this theme. The Le Queux stories, featuring a barrister as narrator, and his friend, 'a typical athletic young Englishman, aged about 30, clean-shaven, clean-limbed', provide an interesting anthology of alarmist fears at this date. In one story the Forth Bridge is narrowly saved from being blown up by Germans planning to bottle up the British fleet. In another, *The Back-Door of England*, a plot to land near Weybourne on the east coast is foiled after a German maid is spotted listening at the door during a shooting party in Norfolk.

Spies of the Kaiser, although fiction, was, Le Queux insisted in a preface, 'based upon serious facts within my personal knowledge. That German spies are actively at work in Britain is well known to the authorities. The number . . . at this moment . . . working in our midst

---

* Wodehouse spent the First World War in safety in the United States and the Second in comfort in Le Touquet in France and, after a period of internment, in Germany. In 1941 he made a series of propaganda broadcasts for the Nazis, and after the war repudiated his British citizenship and settled in America. Late in life he was, misguidedly in my view, awarded a knighthood.

... are believed to be over 5000.' All this effort, Le Queux warned, was directed to *Der Tag*, the day when the members of this sinister network would emerge to smooth the path of the enemy army. He summed up: 'No sane person can deny that England is in grave danger of invasion by Germany at a date not far distant.'

During 1909 a counter-espionage section was formed at the War Office under an officer, Sir Vernon Kell, convinced that war with Germany was inevitable. But not everyone recognised the approaching danger. 'Willy' Robertson, newly promoted to Brigadier-General and Chief of the General Staff for the Aldershot Command, the most important of the seven in the British Isles, found training areas hard to come by, even for short-term manoeuvres. 'One large landowner ...' Robertson discovered with disgust, 'declined to allow us the use of some "common" land which came under his control as lord of the manor, although he was a prominent member of the National Service League.'

Nevertheless the 'home of the British Army' was, if somewhat uncertainly, preparing for war. Aldershot now offered a school of mechanical transport, and another of ballooning and flying, while even the cavalry had admitted the need for change and accepted 'a new pattern sword' designed for 'lightning-like thrusts'. But the call for economy remained paramount, and instead of practising with the real thing battalions sent men to watch demonstrations of grenades being thrown by sappers; each 'live' grenade cost £1, a non-explosive dummy a mere 2d [1p].

The year 1910 brought a new monarch, for on 6 May King Edward VII had died, aged 68. His son and successor, George V, 44 when he ascended the throne, had been sent to sea as a 14-year-old boy and served as a naval officer until his late twenties. Kaiser Wilhelm was not impressed by him, observing that the new king did 'not possess a military mind'. Relations between the two countries remained superficially friendly until the notorious Agadir incident in July 1911, when Germany, in what seemed a deliberate gesture of provocation, sent the gunboat *Panther* to this Moroccan port. Soon afterwards Lloyd George delivered a public warning that Britain was not 'to be treated, where her interests were vitally affected, as if she were no account', at which the German ambassador, Count Paul Wolff-Metternich zur Gracht, a name of ill-omen in Europe,* insolently told the Foreign Secretary he should see his colleague 'turned out of the government'. Sir Edward Grey retorted icily: 'This conversation must end.'

That December the 'War Book Committee', a standing sub-committee of the CID, began to compile a detailed list of the actions to be

---

* The Austrian statesman Prince Metternich (1773-1859) was considered responsible for the policy of reactionary repression prevailing in Europe after the Napoleonic Wars.

taken by nine major government departments on the outbreak of war. Its directing force, and soon the great coordinator of all such preparations, was an individual, like Lord Esher, almost unknown to the general public but immensely influential behind the scenes, Maurice Hankey, a former Royal Marines Officer who, as mentioned earlier, had served in the Mediterranean under Admiral Fisher. In 1908 Hankey had become Assistant Secretary of the CID, and in March 1912 Secretary, at a salary of £1500 a year, equal to a major-general, at the age of 35. Hankey was a somewhat stuffy and humourless figure: his life was one of total dedication to his duties, from his morning cold bath, via his modest apple and sandwich lunch at his desk, to his belated departure from Whitehall Gardens for his Surrey home and late night family prayers. He was a trusted informant of King George V, a confidant of both generals and admirals and a friend of leading politicians of both parties.

In 1912 the Committee of Imperial Defence set up an Air Sub-Committee, with the indispensable Maurice Hankey as its secretary, and the Royal Flying Corps, as mentioned earlier, was established. Although Louis Blériot's pioneering cross-Channel flight in 1909 had been greeted with the cry – false, as it soon appeared – that Great Britain was no longer an island, the alarmists were a little slow to exploit the new opportunities to frighten their fellow citizens which conquest of the air had provided. The development of the Zeppelin by Germany, not yet recognised as an aeronautical dead-end, was therefore eagerly seized upon by those wishing to rouse their countrymen to its supposedly imminent danger. Their efforts were vigorously countered by a classic anti-alarmist work, *The Six Panics*, published in 1913 by F. W. Hirst. Hirst's book, as he made clear, was inspired by Cobden's *The Three Panics*, designed to serve a similar purpose in 1862. Cobden, as described earlier, had effectively exposed the hollowness of the invasion threat in 1847-8, 1851-3 and 1859-61, to which Hirst now added a fourth panic in 1884-5, 'The Fifth or *Dreadnought* Panic' of 1906-9 and, the latest addition to the list, 'The Sixth or Airship Panic' of the current year.

> Towards the end of February 1913 . . . the panic-mongers decided that the naval situation was too unpromising and fell back upon the air . . . Circumstantial reports suddenly began to appear in the *Daily Mail*, [the] *Standard* and other newspapers of airships hovering at various points along the East Coast . . . In a few days the *Daily Mail* was able to announce: 'It is now established beyond all question that the airships of some foreign power, presumably German, are making regular and systematic flights over this country'.

Some of the reports, from the east coast, which might have been approached by German airships during test flights, may well have been true, but most were clearly imaginary, as the Berlin correspondent of one of the papers not affected, the *Sunday Times*, reported in its issue of 2 March 1913:

> All the week the German press has been laughing at John Bull's panicky nerves. The story of the phantom airship, the 'flying German', as they call it here, flashing red and green lights over the inviolate coasts of Britain, is naturally a source of unmixed joy to the German editor . . . The view to which Germans in general are coming round is that the English fomenters of the fable are not insane, appearances to the contrary notwithstanding, but that the whole scare is a clearly rigged manoeuvre to force the government to come forward with a big air-fleet Bill.

The threat from the air, as yet minimal in fact, featured little in the government's defence plans. Its main anxiety remained the possibility of German naval raids on British ports and seaside towns. During January 1913 Maurice Hankey and the members of the Committee of Imperial Defence visited the Bristol Channel to inspect its fortifications and Hankey also accompanied the prime minister and First Lord of the Admiralty on the Admiralty yacht *Enchantress* on an inspection of the navy's bases in Scotland. 'Winston and I went ashore to look at the local forts,' wrote Hankey to his wife from Dundee, and on 1 February 1913 from Rosyth: 'This morning I gave the prime minister a . . . lecture on the subject of the Forth defences, and completely won him and Winston to my point of view.'

Although no one in government really believed an invasion was possible, the prospect of a major raid, perhaps designed to disrupt mobilisation, remained. During the naval manoeuvres held in the summer of 1912 the commander of the 'enemy' fleet managed, as mentioned earlier, to evade the defending ships and his fleet remained unmolested during four hours of calm weather off Filey, seven miles [11 km] south of Scarborough, long enough, in Churchill's opinion, for them to have disembarked 12,000 men.

In July 1913 a much more realistic exercise was held in the North Sea, beginning with a theoretical declaration of war at 5 pm on Wednesday 23 July 1915, after which the 'Red' (or German) Fleet, under Admiral John [later Admiral of the Fleet Earl] Jellicoe, then endeavoured, successfully, to stay unmolested off the landing place for four hours, time to discharge 6000 men, though, soldiers being scarce, only 1000 were actually landed. It was later considered that 48,000 men could also have been disembarked at Blyth in Northumberland, and at Sunderland, 16 miles [26 km] down the coast, but that an attempt at a third landing in the Humber estuary had failed, when two transports were 'torpedoed'.

The result of the exercise was soon known to the press, who reverted to their favourite theme of the exposed east coast, and Lord

Roberts sent a public message to the National Service League warning of 'the possibility of a raid which might entail a vital blow at the heart of the Empire'. The official inquest into the exercise also caused the government some embarrassment, for the Royal Navy, which had always insisted it could keep the country's shores inviolate, now admitted that this might be beyond its ability. The Umpire-in-Chief, an admiral of the fleet, was particularly alarming:

> [Raids] provided the attack is a surprise, may be partially successful, especially in misty weather. The coastal patrol . . . is not sufficient. It therefore appears necessary to have fixed defences at the principal seaports in the United Kingdom . . . of sufficient strength to be able to check a determined raid for some hours until a battle fleet can be concentrated on the spot.

With neither service prepared alone to keep the invader at bay, a compromise was arrived at. During 1913 the army accepted responsibility for the land defences of Dover, Sheerness, the Tyne and the Forth, while the Admiralty agreed to protect Harwich, the Humber, Hartlepool, the Tees, the Tay, Aberdeen and Cromarty.

That year also saw the appearance of yet another imaginary invasion story. Hector Hugh Munro, better known as 'Saki', a successful short-story writer, was 42 and had a solid reputation when he published *When William Came*, a novel which differed from its many predecessors in that it began with England already under occupation. It ended 160 pages later with the first real sign of mass resistance, after the Germans had organised a procession through London of British Boy Scouts, as a sign of reconciliation between victors and vanquished:

> In thousands of English homes throughout the land there were young hearts that had not forgotten, had not compounded, would not yield . . .
>   In the pleasant May sunshine the Eagle standard floated and flapped, the black and yellow pennons shifted restlessly, Emperor and Princes, generals and guards, sat stiffly in their saddles, and waited.
> And waited . . .

Like Childers before him, Munro had had trouble with his publishers, who insisted on revisions, while the author was desperate to see his book on sale before it was too late. When it did appear, highly priced at 6s [30p], late in the year, it had a warm reception. *The Times Literary Supplement* of 20 November 1913 described *When William Came* as a 'remarkable tour de force worked out with great cleverness' in spite of its unwelcome message that much of the aristocracy and literary establishment would rapidly adapt to living under German rule.

On 13 January 1913, in between the two naval exercises, the CID had, on the prime minister's orders, revived its Sub-Committee on Invasion, with himself as its chairman and Hankey as its secretary. It now studied in detail all the changes, such as the development of the Territorials, the expansion in German port capacity and the introduction of aircraft, which had taken place since the last formal enquiry in 1908, but its conclusions were remarkably similar to those of earlier investigations. It was still thought that the maximum force which might evade the navy was 70,000, and – a new conclusion – that when first mobilised the Territorials alone could not be trusted to deal with them, so that, 'In the earlier stages of war . . . it is undesirable to leave less than the equivalent of two divisions of regular troops in this country.' This was in effect a victory for the Germans, as it meant cutting the size of the proposed British Expeditionary Force from six divisions to four. The report was approved by the full Committee of Imperial Defence on 14 May 1914, its last formal statement of anti-invasion policy. The conclusions were not made public, but the German Naval Attaché, who had been highly encouraged by the 1913 east coast manoeuvres, seems to have guessed at them and Winston Churchill had, on 17 March, given the country a clue when he had told the House of Commons of the homely metaphor used by one naval commander 'who said that for the navy to have to guard this country without any military force . . . would be like playing an international football match without a goalkeeper'.

The decade from 1903, when the navy began to regard Rosyth, on the northern shore of the Firth of Forth just above the Forth Bridge, as a 'Scottish Portsmouth', was marked by a steady development of protection for other ports. In 1905 an *ad hoc* Committee on the Armaments of the Home Ports allocated them all to one of three categories, according to the likely scale of attack, with defences to match, from 9.2-in [23-cm] guns for those which might be attacked by battleships, down to 4.7-in [12-cm] quick-firers where the worst threat was likely to come from torpedo-boats. Class 'A', considered vital, included Portsmouth, Plymouth, the Medway and Pembroke Dock; Class 'B', at risk from, at worst, armoured cruisers, was made up of Portland, Dover and the Firth of Forth. Class 'C', expected to have to deal only with light, unarmoured craft, consisted of the Thames, Harwich – though this was later 'promoted' to the status of a fleet anchorage, requiring heavier defences – the Humber, the Tees, Hartlepool, the Tyne, Sunderland, the Tay and Aberdeen.

Attack from the landward side was still considered the most promising way to capture a port, especially after Port Arthur had been taken by the Japanese in the Russo-Japanese war. After driving off the attacking warships, the defences had finally succumbed, on 1 January 1905, to a land assault by 50,000 men, after a siege lasting five months. During August and September 1907 a major exercise was held which attempted to set what had happened in China* into an English context. A powerful enemy army was assumed to have landed in Kent, but needed to capture Chatham, which threatened its right flank as it advanced on London. The subsequent siege operations involved nearly 3600 men, as well as such comparative novelties as searchlights and a captive balloon. Basically, however, with its mines and counter-mines, the whole affair had an out-of-date feel. The chief lesson, known already, was that the defence lines, a mere one and three-quarter miles [2.8 km] away, were now too close to keep the dock-yards out of range of modern artillery, though some useful experience was gained in constructing machine-gun positions and erecting barbed-wire barricades.

In 1909 a Home Ports Defence Committee was set up as a permanent Sub-Committee of the CID. Already attention was focused on the North Sea coast facing Germany. The decision to develop Rosyth as a base had been taken as long ago as 1903, because apart from a spacious anchorage, it offered uninterrupted passage towards Germany, 375 miles [600 km] away, though it was vulnerable to enemy minelaying and, a point stressed by Admiral Fisher, ships therein were liable to be trapped by the demolition of what he called 'that beastly bridge' across the Forth. His preference was for the Cromarty Firth, around In-vergordon, about 14 miles [22 km] north of Inverness, and also linked to the main railway system. A third possibility, first surveyed as long ago as 1750, though Fisher claimed to have discovered it as a possible fleet anchorage, was Scapa Flow, a great natural harbour nine miles [14 km] across in the Orkney Islands, with ample room, numerous en-trances and a reputation for strong tides and bad weather which would make access difficult for intruding enemy torpedo-boats and sub-marines. It was, however, unsuitable to accommodate floating dock and repair facilities, considered by the Admiralty essential, and in the end the CID in December 1912 accepted the Admiralty's preference for Cromarty, though Scapa Flow was to be kept in reserve as a wartime anchorage for light forces.

In 1911 a Committee on the Land Defences of Portsmouth, Ply-mouth and Chatham had decided that they needed to be protected against an invasion by up to 70,000 men and it was recommended that the Portsdown line, along the hills behind Portsmouth, should be ex-tended to Langstone harbour in the east and to Fontley in the west. At Plymouth there were no great changes, with Crownhill Fort still re-garded as the key to the defences, and at Chatham the line built in the 1880s from Borstal to Darland and thence to Twydall was still regarded as well sited to protect the dockyard. A further Committee, on the Defence of Coast Fortresses and Coast Batteries against Land Attack,

---

* Port Arthur was in 1905 Chinese territory, though leased to Russia.

in 1912, underlined as emphatically as any alarmist could have wished the risk of a sudden and fatal surprise raid. Blockhouses, ditches, walls and barbed wire, with carefully situated searchlights, were recommended to prevent sudden assaults by enemy infantry, though little was done before 1914 to implement this extensive programme.

The change to oil fuel created new installations requiring protection, and far more vulnerable ones than the former coal dumps. A large Admiralty oil storage depot at Immingham Docks, just below Hull on the southern bank of the Humber, was an obvious target for a German raid, and in 1913 two batteries of six-inch [15-cm] guns, with associated searchlights, were set up on either side of the estuary. It was also decided to build 'sea-forts', roughly resembling those in the Solent, on Bull Sand, a mile [1.6 km] off Spurn Point, at the end of the Spurn peninsula, and Haile Sand, near the Lincolnshire shore, but the sites, constantly under water, proved difficult and by 1914 not a pile had been sunk.

During all this activity another old defence problem re-emerged, that of the Channel Tunnel. The past history of the project was reviewed on 19 June 1906 by the Committee of Imperial Defence, which was mildly sympathetic to reviving it:

> The heated controversy of the early eighties has subsided. Our relations with France have been placed on a satisfactory footing, and the idea of French aggression no longer haunts the imagination of the public. Moreover, the plain lesson of the whole of our past history – that the navy is the proper and necessary protection against invasion of an Island State – has been accepted, while the Committee . . . has recently affirmed the principle that, so long as our naval superiority is maintained, invasion is impossible.

In the following year the English Channel Tunnel Company – headed, however, by a French baron, and banker, sought parliamentary support to re-open the long-abandoned workings with, as an added precaution, the proviso that the French end of the tunnel should double back in a horseshoe pattern to expose it to bombardment by the British fleet. The resulting viaduct, it was pointed out, would provide 'a magnificent *point de vue* for tourists'. Parliament remained unconvinced.

On 29 July 1909 the CID again briefly considered the matter, but inconclusively, and in 1913 a deputation of 90 Members urged the prime minister to allow the project to go ahead. They were supported by the Liberal *Daily News*, which argued that the invention of the aeroplane had ended Great Britain's claim to be an island, though *The Times* continued its traditional hostility. When next the proposal came before the Committee of Imperial Defence the moment was hardly propitious: the date was July 1914.

36

THE MAILED FIST

Hotels, boarding houses, churches . . . cottage and mansion – all paid their share of the toll exacted by the might of the Mailed Fist.

The German Raid on Scarborough *1914*

When the long-expected European war finally broke out it took most civilians by surprise. Few could have foreseen the grim process by which the assassination of the heir to the Austrian throne, in Serbia on 28 June 1914, led, it seemed remorselessly, to Germany's declaration of war on Russia on 1 August, and on Russia's ally, France, on 3 August, followed by her invasion of Belgium, causing Britain's own declaration of war on Germany at 11 pm British time on Tuesday 4 August 1914.

Summer had always, since medieval times, been the chosen season for war, and Great Britain's navy and army were both in peak condition when the Serbian crisis broke. It found the army preparing for its annual manoeuvres in September, based on an invasion theme, the forcing of the Severn by a superior army, while many Territorials were already assembled for their summer camp. The navy was even better placed. A test mobilisation of the fleet had begun on 15 July, in place of the usual summer exercises, and on the night of 29-30 July a large part of it steamed silently, lights extinguished, through the Straits of Dover and up the North Sea to Scapa Flow which the Admiralty had, after all, decided to use as a major base. Soon afterwards the Grand Fleet, as it was renamed in September, under Admiral Sir John [later Admiral of the Fleet Earl] Jellicoe, took up new battle stations, the battleships at Scapa Flow and Cromarty and the battle cruisers at Rosyth, while a 'Second Fleet' was assembled at Portland.

The CID had devoted many weary hours, as has been described, to establishing that an invasion was not a practical military operation but now it, and the government it advised, both lost their nerve. 'Willy' Robertson, largely responsible for home defence until that autumn he joined the BEF in France, observed the result. 'For a great part of the war, the standard of 70,000 possible invaders was not only retained but increased; and a considerable number of troops were for long kept back in this country.' The new Secretary of State for War, Field Marshal Herbert Lord Kitchener might have caused the Cabinet to change its mind but he was as apprehensive about invasion as any pre-war alarmist, and soon invasion mania was even infecting the Admiralty. On 23 October Churchill wrote to the First Sea Lord, Vice-Admiral Prince Louis Battenberg, calling for extra precautions to be taken:

> From 1st Nov. begins the maximum danger period for this country, ending during January when new armies and Territorials acquire real military value. During this period [there will be] very likely deadlock on land, enabling Germany to economise troops for an invasion. If ever to be attempted, this is the time.

Admiral Battenberg was soon afterwards, most unjustly, forced to resign because of his alien origins and foreign name, and on 31 October, at Churchill's request, Lord Fisher, now aged 74 but as combative as ever, returned to his old post as First Sea Lord.

He had hardly arrived when an action occurred which, it seemed, might be the prelude to invasion. Around 7 am on Tuesday 3 November 1914 the little armed mine-sweeper *Halcyon*, based on Lowestoft, reported that she was in action against a superior force, later identified by the Germans as consisting of seven cruisers, which had replied to her challenge with a salvo of 11-in [30-cm] shells. Two destroyers two miles [3.2 km] away, *Lively* and *Leopard*, immediately, in the best Nelsonian tradition, steered towards the sound of gunfire and came to her rescue, but by this time, as Fisher and Churchill learned when they were called from their beds to the Admiralty War Room, shells were falling in the sea and on the beach of the minor resort of Gorleston-on-Sea, two miles [3.2 km] from Yarmouth (also known as Great Yarmouth). The attack was soon over and by 7.45 the Germans were making off to the south-east while the other destroyers of the Yarmouth Patrol were hastily putting to sea. Churchill was itching for a fight but the enemy got away. The *Halcyon* received minor damage, with three men wounded; Gorleston-on-Sea, the first British town to face enemy bombardment for more than a century, suffered hardly at all.

The Germans' appearance off the east coast lent fuel to fears of an impending invasion. Lord Fisher thought the attempt would be made on Tuesday 17 November when both tide and moon would be favourable for a night landing. Kitchener agreed, but considered the following Friday, 20 November, a second possibility. New minefields were hastily laid and a central striking force of 120,000 was earmarked for despatch to any threatened area, but the approaching armada failed to appear, and by the end of November even the government had accepted that the Germans were not coming after all.

Early in December 1914 Admiral Franz von Hipper, in command of the German battle-cruiser squadron, prepared to make a second foray against England. Hipper was a dashing natural leader and first-class seaman, an amiable Bavarian contemptuous of Prussian 'correctness'. Von Tirpitz's intention was probably to defy the Royal Navy in its own waters, partly to offset the recent British victory in the Battle of the Falkland Islands and, as a secondary aim, to bring the British Grand Fleet to battle under unfavourable circumstances. Behind the raiding cruisers a formidable group of 14 dreadnoughts and eight older battleships, forming most of their High Seas Fleet, was assembled, to pounce on any weaker British squadrons sent to intercept them.

Thanks to a captured enemy code-book and its highly efficient wireless interception service the Admiralty knew well in advance that another cruiser sortie was planned, and at 7 pm on Monday 14 December 1914 Admiral Sir Arthur Wilson, a former First Sea Lord retained as a special adviser, warned Churchill and Fisher that a cruiser foray was impending. Early on the morning of Tuesday 15 December 1914 Admiral Hipper's five heavy cruisers, with the 2nd Scouting Division of light cruisers and destroyers, left the River Jade, the sheltered area which lay between the port of Wilhelmshaven and the open sea. During the afternoon other squadrons of battleships steamed out of Cuxhaven, the whole force, under the command of Admiral von Ingenohl, making a rendezvous north of Heligoland. Then, with the battleships safely in the rear and a screen of lighter, more expendable, vessels spread out in front, the raiders set off westwards through the darkness for the coast of England.

The British were uncertain where on the 300 miles [480 km] of North Sea coastline the expected attack would fall, but the likely area was limited by the two large minefields the Germans had laid and which the Royal Navy, making the best of a bad job, had added to, off Southwold and Newcastle. A gap roughly 25 miles [40 km] wide existed between the minefields, from south of Scarborough to north of Whitby, through which an enemy might approach the Yorkshire coast.

The first contact came around 4.20 am on Wednesday 16 December when one of the destroyers forming von Ingenohl's advanced screen reported sighting a British destroyer, part of the British forward patrol, and around 5.30 four British destroyers engaged the enemy cruiser *Hamburg*, one of them firing a torpedo at her, which missed. News of the presence of British destroyers – although, as he might have guessed, they were there primarily to report and could not possibly have stood up to his heavier units – alarmed von Ingenohl. He had been specifically reminded before setting out that because of the need to protect the German coast – the Germans, too, feared an invasion that had never been planned – 'The fleet must . . . be held back and avoid action which might lead to heavy losses.' He decided he dare not risk his powerful force being engaged by an even stronger British one and at around 6.10 am ordered the battleships to turn for home.

Meanwhile Admiral Hipper, with no heavy support left to cover his withdrawal, pressed steadily onwards, though sending back the lighter cruisers and destroyers with him because they were making heavy weather of the rough seas. He kept only his five other cruisers and a single minelaying light cruiser. A short distance from the coast the squadron split in two, the *Blücher, Seydlitz* and *Moltke* turning north-west towards Hartlepool, the *Derfflinger* and *Von der Tann* making for Scarborough, with the *Kolberg*, which then turned south towards Filey, seven miles [11 km] away, and began to lay more than a hundred mines off that port to protect his flank.

The war had already hit Scarborough, a town of some 40,000 people who lived largely by the holiday trade, hard. That summer's heatwave carried the temperature on 2 July to a near record 84°F [29°C], and the *Scarborough Evening News* reported encouragingly on 7 July that, 'The weekend at the Spa strengthened expectations of an unusually successful season.' On Thursday 30 July, two days after Austria had declared war on Serbia, the paper assured its readers that 'the piles of advance luggage are as great as in any previous year on the eve of August Bank Holiday', but that Sunday, 2 August, came devastating news. 'The North Eastern Railway Company,' the posters read, 'regret to announce that they have been compelled to cancel all excursions advertised to run from North Eastern stations for Sunday August 2nd, Monday August 3rd and Tuesday August 4th.'

The harbour at Scarborough contained no naval craft or coastal artillery and the town virtually no military installations, though there was a small barracks occupied by new recruits receiving basic training. The only other military objectives in the area were the naval wireless station, at Sandy Bed behind the town, and the War Signal Station, formerly the coastguard post, on Castle Hill, overlooking the harbour and main beaches.

Since the shelling of Great Yarmouth a month before a sense of unease had lain over the east coast. After the headmistress of Queen Margaret's School for Girls had, in mid-November, written to the parents of her 170 boarders offering them the chance to withdraw their daughters no fewer than '130 . . . of us,' one of them later recalled, 'left in 36 hours – amid *anger* and *scorn* and *contempt* for the cowardice of our parents.' This school had made preparations to evacuate the rest, with 'little bags of money and rations . . . stored ready for any emergency', but neither here nor in the other schools in the town had shelter accommodation been provided.

The morning of Wednesday 16 December 1914 was grey and mist patches hung over the sea. It was barely light when, just before 8 am the German warships approached the coast, causing no alarm, for although they knew a raid was likely the Admiralty had given no warning, even to the coastguards. The first notification the warrant officer in charge of the Signal Station on Castle Hill received was when one of his men arrived to tell him, 'There are some strange ships in sight and we cannot make out what they are.' As the two men hurried towards the Signal Station to investigate, shells were landing by the Castle walls. By the time they reached their destination it was a heap of rubble.

The first shells had been fired according to one observer, aptly enough the town's boating inspector, from a distance of 'two and a half miles [4 km] out to sea', but after the opening salvo of 30 shells – directed apparently at the Castle, under fire for the first time since the Civil War – elicited no return fire, the enemy ships shortened the range to a mile [1.6 km], as they steamed round the projecting peninsula of Castle Hill. Directly below it lay the harbour, at the northern end of South Bay, behind which was the town, with the railway station lying a little way inland just behind the centre of the Bay. For, according to one account,* precisely eight minutes, the two ships made their way south.

Then, when about half-way to Filey, they turned round, to bring into action their port broadside guns and, after a lull, resumed the bombardment for another eight minutes before, around 8.30, steaming off up the coast towards Whitby.

During their two trips along the Scarborough waterfront the *Derfflinger* and *Von der Tann* kept up a heavy and continuous bombardment, concentrated at first on property near the sea and then apparently lifting fire to land up to a mile [1.6 km] inland. Contemporary estimates of the number of shells fired vary from 50 upwards, and two later investigators settled for 776, 333 of them of large calibre. Most of the rest must have been small shells from quick-firers or little of Scarborough would have been left standing. The damage was unevenly distributed. 'The East and North Wards suffered but little comparatively,' one contemporary booklet reported. 'The Central, South and West severely . . . Hotels, boarding houses, churches, chapels, private residences, schools, business premises, warehouses, workshops, cottage and mansion – all paid their share of the toll exacted by the might of the Mailed Fist.'

Testifying to the accuracy of the German gunners' aim, several properties were hit repeatedly. The Grand, Scarborough's leading hotel, in a splendid hillside position overlooking South Bay, was struck by what the *Scarborough Pictorial* on 23 December called 'several shells', and up to 36 were said to have fallen all around it, causing damage assessed at £13,000.

* i.e. Anne Walker, p. 22. I have mainly followed this excellent, though unpublished, account, which also gives the number of shells quoted above.

Although damage to well-known buildings attracted most attention, ordinary houses were worst hit. 'There are over 150 homes wrecked . . . ,' wrote one resident of West Street to a friend two days later. 'Three houses within 20 yards [18 m] of this one are now nothing more than a heap of brick.' It was in such places, less substantial than larger buildings, that most of the casualties occurred; in view of the early hour few people were yet about in the streets. Among those killed were 'a postman delivering a letter to a maid at the door when a shell hit the building and blew the postman and the maid and the bag of letters to bits'. Other victims included a 15-year-old Boy Scout, killed by a shell fragment as he ran towards the newsagents to buy a copy of a local paper containing his photograph, and a baby aged 14 months, the youngest fatal casualty, who died with his nurse. In the worst single incident, four of the occupants of an end-of-terrace house in Wykeham Street were killed and two injured by one of the last shells to be fired. Inevitably, too, there were some apparently miraculous escapes, which revealed to British civilians for the first time the capricious behaviour of high explosive. One milkman on his round turned, while calling at a house, to see a shell bursting by his cart, which killed the horse but left every drop of the cart's contents unspilt.

With a few exceptions most people in Scarborough reacted admirably to finding themselves under fire. No official shelters existed, but the son of a man who owned a provision shop in Rothbury Street remembers how, 'Father said, "Open the cellar doors" and people went down there for shelter, and it was soon full.'

> At 8.30 am the gunfire stopped . . . The people in the cellar came out and went home. At 8.45 am our provision hand and the apprentice had arrived, a postman was delivering letters, milkmen were on the move with their churns, a horse-drawn lorry from the . . . coal depot was on its way.

But it was not quite like an ordinary morning:

> The St John Ambulance people started to bring past dead people on their hand carts to go to the mortuary in the Corporation depot in Dean Road. The men looked very pale and nervous. It had been an unpleasant job for them to do.

The injured were also promptly cared for. Existing patients in the hospital, a commemorative booklet claimed, 'left the hospital to make room, though they could scarcely crawl'. The damage to property was also efficiently dealt with, as one local nurse described in a letter to a friend in Canada:

> One of the most wonderful things was the rapid and cool way in which practically a few minutes after the firing ceased the corporation men, plumbers, glaziers, joiners, shop men and women, and

private people were sweeping, brushing and generally clearing away the debris, boarding up or glazing windows, mending roofs, building up chimney stacks, and pulling down, by means of long lengths of rope, loose pieces of masonry from the tops of houses.

Even while the bombardment was still in progress people had begun flocking to the railway station. The driver of the one train claimed to have removed the locomotive from the engine sheds – Scarborough then, as now, was the terminus on a branch line – with shells falling all round him, but to have left for Cloughton only one minute late. Once the guns had fallen silent, 'The station,' *The Times* booklet on the affair reported, 'was crowded with people clamouring to get away.'

The railway company seems to have regarded this unexpected influx of passengers as an opportunity to make up for their lost tourist trade. 'One of the booking clerks,' the *Manchester Guardian* reported next day, 'said he had "had the time of his life" booking passengers to York, Leeds and other inland towns', and the takings that day amounted to a record £600. 'No one,' the *Scarborough Mercury* confirmed that same day, 'was allowed in the station without a ticket . . . Two women and three children were short of 1s 9d [8p] . . . However people in the crowd made up the amount.'

Even more people took to the roads leading out of Scarborough, making for the villages of Scalby and Seamer. Among them were the remaining pupils of Queen Margaret's School, who included the 16-year-old Winifred Holtby, a future best-selling novelist. Her letter to a friend describing the morning's events was published in the *Bridlington Chronicle* and later sold as a 3d [1½p] pamphlet in aid of the Red Cross. The girls had been enjoying their breakfast porridge and the 'end-of-termy feeling in the air' when the bombardment began, but their obviously redoubtable headmistress mustered her charges in the cloakroom and instructed them: 'Put on your long coats, tammies and thick boots; we are going for a walk into the country till it is over.'

We dressed and started . . . Just as we got through the gate another shell burst quite near, and 'Run!' came the order – and we ran. Ran, under the early morning sky, on the muddy, uneven road, with that deafening noise in our ears, the echo ringing even when the actual firing stopped for a moment . . . ran, though our hastily clad feet slipped on the muddy road.

Over the town hung a mantle of heavy smoke, yellow, unreal . . . In an instant's pause I looked round. I heard the roar of a gun and the next instant there was a crash, and a thick cloud of black smoke enveloped one of the houses in Seamer Road; a tiny spurt of red flame shot out . . . We were moving to the level crossing, when a shell struck the ground some 50 yards [46 m] away, throwing up earth and mud in all directions . . .

We crossed the line into the Seamer Valley. Along the road was a stream of refugees; there was every kind of vehicle, filled to over-flowing with women and children; yes, and men, too. I saw one great brute, young and strong, mounted on a cart horse, striking it with a heavy whip, tearing at full gallop down the road, caring nothing for the women and children who scrambled piteously out of his path, with the fear of death on his craven face . . .

There was a young mother with a tiny baby clutched in her arms; an old woman, only partly dressed, with her pitiful little bundle of worldly goods on a rickety perambulator; there were mothers with tiny children clinging to their skirts, crying for fear of this unknown horror. There was one particularly touching old couple, tottering along side by side, perhaps the the last time they would ever walk together . . . then, with a warning honk! honk! a splendid car swept by at a terrific speed with one occupant – a woman wrapped in costly furs, alone in that great car, yet she could not stop to take up one of the poor old women who stagggered on weary to death, yet fleeing for their lives.

The examples of selfishness witnessed by Winifred Holtby were con-fined to the rich. The humbler people helped each other. The nurse previously quoted learned of one such act of kindness: 'One man on Seamer Road was driving with a load of manure; he instantly tipped up his cart and loaded up with children walking out to Seamer.' Villagers in the area around Scarborough offered tea and soup to the frightened families passing their doors and the Queen Margaret's girls, already fortified by 'chocolate, dates and biscuits', were taken in by a local vicar who 'had a fire put in the parish room and turned us in there to give vent to our high spirits in songs and games' before they took the train back to Scarborough to pack and be sent home.

Some 43 miles [69 km] up the coast from Scarborough lay Hartle-pool, or, more correctly, the Hartlepools; the port consisted both of the original town to the north of Hartlepool Bay, and of West Hartle-pool, which had spread along the bay and inland. Hartlepool was very different from Scarborough. Its population of 91,000 worked in the six docks and two tidal harbours, in the shipbuilding yards and marine engineering works and in the great steelworks which spread inland up the River Tees as far as Middlesborough. By December 1914 it also sheltered a sizeable naval force, consisting of two light cruisers, four destroyers and a submarine, though in 1905 it had been classified by the Committee on the Armaments of the Home Ports as 'Category C', likely to be attacked only by light, unarmoured vessels. Hartlepool was in 1914 defended by a Territorial unit, the Durham Royal Garrison Artillery, with an establishment of 320. Its commander, Lieut.-Colonel L. Robson, later wrote a detailed account of the events of 16

December, which provided a unique example of a 'ship to shore' duel on the English coast.

The town was protected by three six-inch [15-cm] guns, with a maximum range of 11,200 yards [10,241 m], all mounted on the promontory which protected the harbour entrance. Two of the guns, mounted in 1899, formed the Heugh* Battery, while 150 yards [137 m] away, on the very tip of the promontory, close to the lighthouse, was the single-gun Lighthouse Battery. The 'Fortress Commander', based at West Hartlepool, had received, at midnight on 15/16 December, a warning from the War Office: 'A special sharp look-out to be kept all along the East Coast at dawn tomorrow, December 16th,' and orders had been issued 'to take post from 7 to 8.30 am. If all quiet at latter hour,' commanders were told, 'troops may return to billets.'

Oddly enough, no special warning seems to have been sent to the Senior Naval Officer at Hartlepool, but at 5 am on Wednesday 16 December his four destroyers, *Doon, Moy, Test* and *Waveney*, left harbour for their regular daily patrol, which was maintained five miles [8 km] out to sea, parallel to the coast. With a speed of 24 knots, but armed only with four 12-pounder [5.4 kg] guns and two 18 in [46-cm] torpedo tubes, the ships were heavily outclassed by the German cruisers now steaming towards the east coast.

The sea was calm, under an overcast sky, when at 8 am the South Gare battery, several miles to the south, reported to the RA commander at Heugh Battery, 'Dreadnoughts steaming north', and almost simultaneously, the observers in the lighthouse, almost on the spot, informed him, 'Three warships coming in at great speed'. To his enquiry, 'What nationality?' the coastguards on duty reported, 'They are our ships . . . flying the White Ensign and have answered our signals.' As it loomed out of the mist from behind the lighthouse, however, one officer in charge of the Heugh Battery instantly recognised the leading ship, the *Seydlitz*, as German, and almost immediately it opened fire.[†]

The time was 8.10 am, 12 minutes after the first shells, unknown to the gunners at Hartlepool, had landed at Scarborough.

The three German warships mounted between them 64 guns, of which the most formidable were the 20 11.2-in [28-cm]. They were supported by eight 8.2-in [20.8-cm], 18 5.9-in [15-cm] and 18 4-in [10-cm]. German naval gunners had a reputation for accuracy, which was soon vindicated. Their first round fell a mere 25 yards [23 m] to the left of the guns, as seen from the sea, and killed an RA sentry and three men of the Durham Light Infantry, a spot later commemorated by a

---

* Colonel Robson refers to this throughout his account as 'Hough', but this seems to be a mistake.
† Murley, p. 346. Robson, p. 428, says the leading ship, which opened fire first, was the 'Van Der Tan', i.e. *Von der Tann*.

bronze plaque:

> This tablet marks the place where the first shell from the leading battle-cruiser struck at 8.10 am on 16th December, 1914, and also records the place where . . . the first soldier was killed on British soil by enemy action in the Great War, 1914-18.

The same shot totally knocked out the two batteries' telephone system, and the second killed two more gunners, who had left shelter to help the infantrymen. A third hit one of the terraced houses immediately behind the Battery, killing two women, the first civilians to die at Hartlepool. The *Seydlitz* and the *Moltke* now settled down to deliver their broadsides against the Heugh Battery, while the *Blücher* concentrated its fire on the single-gun Lighthouse Battery. With the telephone out of action, the Battery Commander posted himself midway between his two guns and passed his orders by megaphone. This, noted a Royal Artillery historian, 'was apparently effective in spite of the noise of our guns and the arrival of enemy projectiles', although 'The rush of air from the 11.2-inch as they passed low over the battery in salvoes fired at 5000 yards [4570 m] was so great that the Section Commander and gun-floor numbers together with any odd personnel that happened to be on the manning parade were knocked flat.'

It was the Heugh Battery that bore the brunt of the battle. Its two guns managed to fire 108 rounds during the action, the single gun of the Lighthouse Battery a mere 15, partly because of the lighthouse obstructing its aim, but also because of a break in the electrical circuit resulting from a detached lead. The three guns between them, it was later calculated, fired at the rate of one round per minute, a good deal slower than was possible in theory, but a creditable achievement for men in action for the first time. At 8.20 am, leaving the *Blücher* to keep up fire on the two batteries, first the *Seydlitz*, then the *Moltke* moved a little to the north, out of the defenders' range, one to near the North Sands, almost opposite the railway station, the other to seaward of the site of the long-defunct Cemetery Battery. Both ships now began to bombard West Hartlepool, firing their shells over Old Hartlepool and the harbour.

What was happening at this same time at Scarborough was now repeated even more destructively, for the area affected was both more densely populated and industrialised, and the scale of attack much heavier: including the bombardment of the British batteries the German ships, according to their own official account, fired 1150 rounds, 'at the rate,' the principal local historian of the bombardment believed, 'of over 30 every minute'. They varied, he believed, from 309 to 706 lb [140-305 kg] in weight, while 'the 11.2-in [28-cm] armour-piercing shell, as fired by the 41½-ton gun of the *Seydlitz*, was capable of piercing 16 inches [41 cm] of armour at 3000 yards [2742 m].'

This observer, Frederick Miller, claimed to have identified four lines of fire, with destruction spread widely to either side of them as the two ships changed position frequently to expose in turn their port and starboard broadsides, and gradually raised the elevation of their guns until the final rounds landed up to 10 miles [16 km] inland in the open country beyond West Hartlepool. In the town itself the damage was spectacular, beginning with the knocking out of the main gas works, followed in the next few minutes by a cement works, a water works, the electric tram station, a large engineering works, a shipyard, the goods station and the main West Hartlepool Railway Station. In the docks six ships suffered varying degrees of damage, three of them with fatal casualties among those on board. A vast amount of civilian property was also damaged, including 600 private houses. Eventually 487 claims for compensation were submitted. 'No area,' wrote an RA officer, 'seemed to have been untouched. It was as if a gigantic rake had been drawn across each spot.'

The bombardment of the forts had lasted 15 minutes. That of the targets on land lasted a further half-hour, till the three warships ceased fire at 8.48 am and headed homewards, pursued by a few final, if ineffective, rounds from the shore, the last fired at 8.52 am at a range of 9200 yards [8400 m].

The German ships did not get away totally unscathed. The *Blücher*, which needed a refit in Kiel when she got home, following three destructive hits, lost eight men killed and three wounded. The *Seydlitz*, also hit three times, had one man wounded; the *Moltke*, hit once, escaped without casualties.[*]

The toll among British servicemen was heavier: seven men killed and 13 wounded on HMS *Patrol* and HMS *Waveney* – roughly half on each ship – and another seven soldiers killed and 13 wounded in the coastal batteries.

Civilian casualties were far more numerous. At Scarborough, it later appeared, 18 people had been killed and 80 seriously injured but because it was well known as a seaside resort its losses at first overshadowed those of Hartlepool, which were also grossly understated: *The Times*, on 17 December 1914, reported them as 29 dead and 64 wounded. The true figures, though still the subject of some dispute, were 119 dead and more than 400 seriously injured.[†]

The events of that day remained fresh in the memory of one boy of

---

[*] For detailed casualty figures, about which there is some disagreement, see the editions of *The Royal Tank Corps Journal* and *The Sapper* cited in my Note on Sources.
[†] On Scarborough see *The German Raid*, no page number. On Hartlepool see Martin, p. 94. *The Royal Tank Corps Journal* mentions 300 wounded; Wood (who puts the dead at 112) 'more than 200'; Murley, p. 351, 112 killed and 'about 200' wounded; Miller, p. 123, 'up to February 18 1915' 118 dead and 'certainly not less than 400' other casualties. The six-year-old quoted is Robert Wood, pp. 207-9.

six, whose father held the key to a municipal mortuary. The first unexpected arrival was a corporation driver with the body of 'a young lad', who told his father, 'You'd better get yourself down there quick and get the place open, because there'll soon be plenty more!' a prediction rapidly fulfilled: '35 bodies were brought into a place built to accommodate four'. Even more harrowing was the arrival of the bereaved:

I can well remember the wails of the distraught relatives who had wandered distractedly from place to place seeking loved ones who had gone out to work as usual that misty morning and had not returned . . .

I can still recapture the eerie atmosphere in which I sat, neglected, in our familiar kitchen, scarcely understanding why so many distressed strangers were coming in and out, with my mother giving them what comfort she could. The gloom was intensified by the feeble rays of the candles, for the gas had been cut off when the gasholders were hit.

As the echoes of the gunfire off Hartlepool died away, a new bombardment was beginning at Whitby, off which the *Derfflinger* and *Von der Tann* appeared shortly after leaving Scarborough, 16 miles [26 km] down the coast. News of what had happened there had not reached its smaller neighbour, an attractive fishing port, when the two ships, as the *Whitby Gazette* reported on 18 December, 'were observed by persons on the Piers passing Saltwick'.

At first they were not thought to be enemy vessels, but at 9.05 they opened fire . . . For seven minutes until 9.12 the bombardment was of a very heavy character, about 200 shells falling in the town and district.*

Some of the first shells burst near the Coastguard Station damaging it and killing one of the men on duty. Other shells fell in the harbour and did no damage. For the most part they burst over residential property beyond the railway station . . . The bombardment ended with the same dramatic suddenness as it commenced and the warships made off seawards.

Whitby was totally undefended, though the Germans later described it as a 'fortified town', and contained only two targets of any conceivable military importance, the Coastguard Station and the Telegraph Station on the East Cliff, near the ruins of Whitby Abbey. Both stations were struck by the Germans' second salvo, and the Abbey was also hit. ('The ruins,' commented *The Times* the following day, 'had escaped the ravages of the gales to fall victim to the vindictive spite of an enemy who boasts of his "Kultur".') A great many private houses were hit, mainly by shells passing over the East Cliff, but only three people were

---

* The official history, i.e. Corbett, Vol. II, p. 34, says 'about 50 rounds' were fired.

killed, a coastguard, a railway 'ralleyman' leading a horse drawing a wagon, and an elderly invalid woman. A number of people suffered minor injuries from shell splinters and one unfortunate Boy Scout, on duty at the Telegraph Station, had to have his leg amputated, but as the *Whitby Gazette* commented, 'It has been remarked how few were the casualties, considering the great amount of damage done to property.'

Everywhere as people emerged from their temporary shelters, one topic of conversation dominated all others. 'After the firing ceased,' observed one eye-witness, then a small boy in Scarborough, 'all the neighbours came out into the street, giving various opinions of what should be done, not only to the Kaiser, but the Commander-in-Chief, Home Fleet, with loud demands of "Where is the navy?"'

Where indeed *was* the navy? According to a local historian[*], the first warning was given by a woman on duty at the Head Post Office in the Hartlepools who, on her own initiative, sent the vital message to London at 8.28 am.

Four minutes later the news reached the First Lord of the Admiralty:

> On the morning of December 16 at about half past eight I was in my bath, when the door opened and an officer came hurrying in from the War Room with a naval signal which I grasped with dripping hands. 'German battle-cruisers bombarding Hartlepool.' I jumped out of the bath with exclamations . . . Pulling on clothes over a damp body, I ran downstairs to the War Room. The First Sea Lord had just arrived from his house next door . . . Telegrams from all naval stations along the coast affected by the attack, and intercepts from our ships in the vicinity speaking to each other, came pouring in two and three to the minute . . . Everything was now sent to sea or set in motion.

Churchill was optimistic:

> The war map showed the German battle-cruisers identified one by one within gunshot of the Yorkshire coast, while 150 miles [240 km] to eastward *between them and Germany*, cutting mathematically their line of retreat, steamed in the exact positions intended, four British battle-cruisers and six of the most powerful battleships in the world . . . Meanwhile telegraph and telephone were pouring the distress of Hartlepool and Scarborough to all parts of the kingdom, and by half-past ten, when the War Committee of the Cabinet met, news magnified by rumour had produced excitement. I was immediately asked how such a thing was possible. 'What was the navy doing and what were they going to do? In reply . . . I explained

---

[*] Bailey, p.27. It seems unlikely, however, that the gallant spinster would accurately have identified battle-cruisers; possibly a naval signal arrived at the Admiralty simultaneously.

that subject to moderate visibility we hoped the collision would take place about noon.

The hoped-for battle never occurred:

> Our fleet . . . were very close to the enemy, groping for him in a mist which allowed vessels to be distinguished only within 2000 yards [1829 m]. At 3 o'clock I went over and told the War Committee what was passing . . . I returned to the Admiralty. The shades of a winter evening had already fallen. Sir Arthur Wilson then said, in his most ordinary manner, 'Well, there you are, they have got away.'

Proud of their victory, the Germans struck a silver medal commemorating 'The bombardment of Scarborough and Hartlepool by German ships, 16 December 1914', and featuring an angel-like figure bearing a laurel wreath with the inscription: 'God blesses the United Armies'. The reference to Scarborough, the most peaceful of resorts, though the Germans claimed that it was defended by a battery of six guns whose crews had run away, produced widespread derision. Souvenir postcards showing the damage done to visibly civilian homes and shops were soon on sale, and the attack joined the invasion of 'gallant little Belgium' as an example of the enemy's true character. The magazine of the Municipal School recorded how 'one of our scholars fell a victim to this exhibition of German frightfulness', a phrase which now came into popular use, while the MP for Hartlepool described its shelling as 'a colossal act of murder by ingrained scoundrels that will stamp them for all time as heinous polecats'. 'Remember Scarborough – Enlist Now' became the theme of a nationwide recruiting campaign; every shell which had hit the town, it was claimed, had produced a thousand new volunteers. The *Daily Express* encouraged its readers to write abusive letters to that former admirer of Germany, Lord Haldane; he received 2600 in a day and on entering a London theatre was loudly booed. The attack on the east coast led everywhere to a new bitterness towards the enemy. Advertisements in the press urged people to buy nothing of enemy origin, not even Christmas tree decorations from Austria, while one corset manufacturer proudly announced that it had 'No German capital, no German partners, no German hands, no German steels, no German trimming, nothing that is German'.

The Royal Navy, once the initial sense of outrage was over, escaped criticism even in Scarborough and on 20 December Winston Churchill wrote to the mayor a typically optimistic letter:

> I send you a message of sympathy, not only on my own account, but on behalf of the navy . . . We admire the dignity and fortitude with which Scarborough, Whitby and the Hartlepools have confronted outrage. We share your disappointment that the miscreants

have escaped unpunished. We await with patience the opportunity that will surely come . . .

Whatever feats of arms the German navy may hereafter perform, the stigmas of the babykillers of Scarborough will brand its officers and men while sailors sail the seas.

After 16 December people all along the east coast became understandably nervous. Two days later a near panic occurred at Hartlepool after a report that, as the then six-year-old schoolboy previously quoted remembers, 'the Germans were once more in the Bay, and . . . had given us two hours grace in which to get out before they renewed their onslaught':

> No one stopped to wonder why the enemy should suddenly become so considerate . . . Workers in the shipyards hurried home with their tools still in their hands. The station was besieged by people anxious to take any train anywhere so long as it was out of town. All the roads to the country were crowded with folks in various stages of undress, pushing perambulators and handcarts laden with their most precious possessions. At least one family sat solemnly down around the kitchen table and ate up the Christmas cake, determined that it should not be left for the Germans.

People in Scarborough were little more relaxed. 'When some mines were shot the other day by mine sweepers . . .' a local woman reported in a letter to a friend on 30 December, 'the people on the foreshore ran out of their houses with large parcels. They have had orders to be ready to leave at a moment's notice.' many people evacuated themselves that when the schools reopened, on 5 January, one had only 319 pupils present of the 450 on its roll and by the end of the month 43 had been removed for good.

The minefield laid by the Germans to cover their withdrawal proved a great nuisance. It had cost the British several vessels by the end of January and tied up a good deal of minesweeping effort. But Churchill's hint of vengeance on the recent raiders was rapidly justified: the armoured cruiser *Blücher* was sunk by Beatty's battlecruisers in the Battle of the Dogger Bank on 24 January 1915. The rest, though the *Seydlitz* and *Moltke* were to be badly battered at Jutland in May 1916, survived till the end of the war.

37
HOLDING THE COAST

We understood we were to hold the coast until the troops in the depots and camps were rushed up.

The Town Clerk of Southwold, Commander of a Special Service Unit of Volunteers, 4 June 1918

For civilians December 1914 was the turning point. After the raid on the east coast no one could feel wholly safe from enemy attack. Fear of invasion revived and the Town Clerk of Southwold in Suffolk noted how during April 1915 'soldiers began to seriously fortify the town', until the low cliff was draped with barbed wire, fencing crowned its edge and a whole system of trenches and firing positions was dug out behind.

The government now found itself, most reluctantly, obliged to re-vive the Volunteers, which the Territorials had been intended to re-place. These proved frustrating times for men like this local govern-ment official who had become adjutant of the Lowestoft Battalion of the Suffolk Corps, which was soon drilling three nights a week:

> The work of organisation was difficult and tedious owing to . . . the government as usual discouraging the affair as much as possible. Their only contribution was a brassard or armlet of red with G.R. [for George Rex] on it which was issued to each member. All the rest of the equipment, rifles, uniforms, ammunition etc. had to be found by the Corps, also instructors and all expenses of formation and working.

In December 1915 General Sir William Robertson returned from serv-ing as Chief of Staff to the BEF to take over as Chief of the Imperial General Staff from the inept Lieut.-General Sir James Wolfe-Murray, whom Churchill had derisively labelled 'Sheep' Murray. He was now, to extend Churchill's gibe, put out to grass. Robertson, who had de-voted much time earlier in his career to studying the invasion problem, was far from happy about the situation he had inherited:

> The number, composition and distribution of the home defence troops bore little relation to the actual situation; the general plan of defence was fundamentally faulty; and with some commendable ex-

ceptions the defences themselves were insufficient and often of unsuitable types.

Almost simultaneously Field Marshal Sir John French was brought
home from France, having failed to defeat the Germans in the field, to
become Commander-in-Chief of all troops in the United Kingdom.
These eventually numbered around one and a half million men, of
whom, for various reasons, only half a million were available as potential drafts for France. Robertson and French now faced the problem of
trying to strengthen the country's defences while at the same time trying to send more men overseas. It was still possible, although unlikely,
that a raid in strength might be directed against the British Isles, either
as a desperate last throw or to divert British troops from the Western
Front, and much effort was devoted to providing additional protection
for London and the principal ports and naval bases.

The Thames and Medway Defence Plan, designed to prevent an
actual landing as distinct from merely naval intrusions, had been
worked out before the war. The basic strategy was one of defence in
depth and of relying on field-works, a policy rapidly vindicated by
events in Belgium and France. The costly fortresses along the German
frontier had failed to halt the enemy's advance; it was the humble
trench, thrown up by a sweating soldier with a spade, that had
wrecked the Schlieffen Plan and brought stalemate to the Western
Front. At Shoeburyness, on the Essex side of the estuary, an extensive
network of trenches and barbed-wire entanglements was constructed,
with individual blockhouses providing strongpoints. On the Isle of
Sheppey, on the Kent side, a similar line covered the approaches to
Sheerness, and there was a third around the batteries on the Isle of
Grain.

Apart from these defences, forming the coastal 'crust', from around
October 1914 a series of 'stop lines' was constructed, made up of separate positions but forming a continuous front when all were manned.
One was built between the River Swale and the high ground north of
Maidstone. The old line of the London Defence Positions, abandoned
by Asquith and Haldane seven years earlier, was brought back into
occupation, some of the sites previously selected now being equipped
with six-inch [15.2-cm] and 9.2-in. [23.3-cm] howitzers.

North of the Thames, during the first winter of the war, no fewer
than 300,000 men were deployed. One defence line ran from north of
Chelmsford to Maldon and Danbury Hill, another, the last main barrier guarding the capital, from Ongar to Epping. Each new development in France tended soon afterwards to be adopted in England. The
first pillboxes, named after their flat circular shape, now appeared on
British soil, copied from the Germans on the Western Front. When, instead of the original concrete blocks, the enemy adopted reinforced

concrete, poured into wooden moulds and strengthened with metal rods, the Royal Engineers in England followed suit, though later a distinctively English, hexagonal style developed. The larger versions, though designed for infantry occupation and intended to mount nothing heavier than a machine-gun, could accommodate artillery and stand up to a direct hit by a six-inch [15.2-cm] or even an eight-inch [20.3-cm] shell.

On the outbreak of war the most important anchorage of all, Scapa Flow, had lacked a single gun on shore. Some three-pounder [1.4-kg] and 12-pounder [5.6-kg] guns were hurriedly removed from ships for use on land, and by 1915 all the main entrances to the great harbour were covered by four-inch [10.2-cm], six-inch [15.2-cm] and 12-pounder guns. Although the most vulnerable entrances were temporarily blocked by booms, blockships and underwater steel trestles, Scapa, as was to become all too apparent later, was difficult to protect, and Admiral Jellicoe at first led his great battleships and cruisers ingloriously out to sea when enemy submarines were believed to be about.

The other main point of danger in Scotland was the Firth of Forth and additional guns were provided after the declaration of war to protect ships anchoring west of the Forth Bridge, followed in the spring of 1916 by the creation of a separate anchorage east of (i.e. below) it, nearer the open sea. By the autumn of 1917 new batteries of from two to four guns of varying calibre, from 4.7-in [12-cm] to six-inch [15.2-cm], plus some batteries of four-inch [10.2-cm] quick-firers, had been installed on the islands scattered about the estuary, surrounded by barbed wire, trenches and pillboxes adequate, it was hoped, to resist a sudden *coup de main*.

On the north-east coast of England, the later famous 'Tyne Turrets' were set up to cover the approaches to Newcastle. Each contained two 12-in [30-cm] guns from the elderly battleship HMS *Illustrious*, but the construction work proved so troublesome that they were not ready to fire before the war was over.

With the whole weight of British naval strength shifting northwards, the Humber also assumed a new importance, and a new anchorage came into use opposite Grimsby. Heavy guns were installed to protect it at Spurn and Kilnsea, at the two ends of the Spurn peninsula, and the two sea-forts planned just before the war, as previously described, were now completed – at Bull Sand, a mile [1.6 km] from Spurn Point, and on Haile Sand, on the opposite, Lincolnshire, shore. Building these massive constructions, with their four storeys of solid stonework and 12 inches [30 cm] of armour, intended to accommodate four six-inch [15.2-cm] guns, proved extremely difficult but the problems were eventually overcome. Further south additional guns were also erected at Felixstowe, Portsmouth, Southampton and Plymouth.

Along the west coast of the island, the most important work was at

Gourock at the mouth of the Clyde, to which, in April 1915, two 9.2-in [23.3-cm] guns were moved from Ireland. Additional emplacements were also built along the Bristol Channel.

In May 1915 the lackadaisical Asquith had been forced to convert his government into an all-party coalition, and the now bitterly unpopular Haldane was dropped from office. So, for different reasons, was Winston Churchill. The new ministry rapidly had to abandon the long-cherished tradition of all-volunteer forces, though 50 Liberal and Labour MPs voted against the first Military Service Bill before it became law on 27 January 1916. Bachelors and childless widowers aged 18 to 51 were now made liable to call-up and in May compulsory enlistment was extended to married men. In June 1916 Lord Kitchener was drowned, being succeeded as Secretary of State for War by David Lloyd George, and on 6 December 1916 Lloyd George became prime minister and head of a small War Cabinet. Henceforward the war was to be waged with a new vigour and determination.

In April 1916 that old nightmare of an Irish rebellion combined with an attack on the mainland seemed about to come true, for simultaneously with news of the Easter Rising in Dublin, on Easter Monday, 24 April, Admiral Jellicoe at Scapa Flow learned that part of the German High Seas Fleet was at sea and the rest raising steam. Once again the Naval Intelligence Department proved far superior to the Operations Branch, and by 11.40 pm had correctly predicted that the enemy was on course for Great Yarmouth and should reach it in two hours. It was a fine, starlit night, with no mist to provide an excuse should the Germans get away. The moon came up around 2 am and around 3.50 am on Tuesday 25 April 1916 the English commodore found himself in sight of the whole enemy attacking fleet, a mere eight miles [13 km] distant. He turned away, hoping to entice the enemy to follow him towards the guns of the heavier ships hurrying southward to join him, but the German admiral rejected the bait. At 4.10 am his battle-cruisers, unchallenged from either sea or shore, opened fire on Great Yarmouth. The first salvoes fell short, in the water, but the next burst on the town. After only ten minutes, however, the whole force ceased fire and made its way ten miles [16 km] south towards Lowestoft, which was shelled from around 4.30 am for only 15 minutes, the bombardment being cut short when the light cruisers from Harwich appeared on the scene. The British submarines deployed to cut off the enemy withdrawal had less success. Only one, the *H5* – submarines were not yet respectable enough to merit names – even sighted the Germans and she and her two sister ships were all bombed by 'friendly' aircraft, perhaps the earliest example of such a misunderstanding in British history. Happily the airmen's aim was poor and the indignant submariners got safely back to port.

The raid was another triumph for the Germans, although the

defending cruisers had saved Great Yarmouth, which was hardly touched, and prevented a major disaster at Lowestoft, where 200 houses were damaged but very few people killed. The strict censorship now in force prevented the same detailed coverage of the attack as in 1914, but it nevertheless came as a shock to public opinion, which was not much reassured by a letter from the First Lord of the Admiralty, Arthur Balfour, to the mayors of Great Yarmouth and Lowestoft, explaining why the fleet had not prevented the Germans getting clean away. Public attention was soon diverted, however, to the reprisal raids made by British ships and seaplanes against the German coast in early May 1916, and by the great Battle of Jutland on 31 May 1916, when the Grand Fleet and the High Seas Fleet at last came to grips in the major action which both had so long sought. Both sides, with some justice, claimed Jutland as a victory; the English losses had been heavier but thereafter the German battleships stayed in harbour.

On the night of Thursday 25 January 1917, during a freezingly cold gale, light German forces made a sudden dash against the east coast at Southwold, about ten miles [16 km] south of their last target, Lowestoft. Southwold's Town Clerk recorded the night's experiences in his diary:

> I . . . had been in bed about ten minutes when there was a double explosion followed almost directly by another very loud and close, like the lifeboat gun. I jumped out of bed, but in a moment came crashes of gunfire, very fast and loud and I told the missis to hurry and get the baby down as the Germans were upon us. I ran down to get a light and make up the bomb-proof table with a terrific and rapid fire going on all the time. Before we got things right the firing ceased just as abruptly as it began and we heard no more. It lasted five minutes from 11.05 to 11.10 and in that little time they put 68 shells and two starshells into and over us.

Southwold had escaped very lightly. Almost all the shells fired exploded in the sea or landed harmlessly inland and the five that hit the town caused no casualties and little damage. The Town Clerk was indignant, however, that its ordeal should be dismissed too lightly:

> Some of the papers called it a comic bombardment and a silly raid just as they did about the early Zeppelin raids, but to those who were in it there was nothing comic or silly . . . To speak as the papers do is to encourage the Germans to come again and make a job of it.

The Germans did come again, though not to Southwold. The same diarist's entry for Monday 14 January 1918 recorded succinctly: 'This night the Huns bombarded Yarmouth again, putting in 50 to 60 shells in 7 minutes, killing 7 and wounding many more.' This was however the last such raid, and by now the real danger, just as Admiral Fisher had predicted, was starvation, not invasion.

The U-boat blockade was defeated by the convoy system, imposed upon a reluctant Admiralty by Lloyd George, and in April 1917 the United States declared war on Germany. On 21 March 1918 General Erich von Ludendorff's great offensive began, which was to carry his armies to within 40 miles [64 km] of Paris. The pressure was now intense to send every fit man, and many who were barely fit, to France, leaving the British Isles to be defended by part-timers. Events had, as mentioned earlier, already forced the government to re-form on a smaller scale a Volunteer movement of the kind disbanded in 1908, though it now consisted solely of men exempt from conscription on grounds of age, occupation or health. 'From what one has heard since I feel sure the Volunteers were on the brink of mobilisation this Easter time,' wrote the Town Clerk of Southwold, previously quoted, now adjutant of the Lowestoft Battalion, on Easter Monday, 1 April 1918. He now launched his own recruiting drive among farm workers, describing 'the very critical state of the Western Front . . . The response was useful but not great.' When, in early June, 'The Scheme came out for Special Service Companies of Volunteers to undertake active service on the coast', he was the first to give in his name.

> England was being denuded of troops to hold up the German offensive and replace our enormous casualties and it was necessary to take men from the East Coast and send them out to France and the Volunteers were asked to find 15,000 men to replace these until the Americans arrived in force. We understood we were to hold the coast until the troops in the depots and camps were rushed up in case of attack but . . . most of the available men from the camps had already gone . . . The position was critical in the extreme.

These Volunteers, like the militia during earlier invasion alarms, now became full-time. On 29 June 1918 this peaceful lawyer-cum-local government official found himself 'in command of a Special Service Company, 84 strong, at Bawdsey Manor near Felixstowe', most of them under canvas, though their CO 'got into an empty room in the stables'. For a month the unit trained and shared 'in the ordinary routine of the coastal defences' until, on 26 August, his company's full-time duty was completed and others came to replace them. By then, as he noted, 'We were turning the tables on the Germans' and others had obviously formed an equally optimistic view for, back at Southwold on 30 August, he 'found the town full of visitors' providing 'the best season since 1914'.

Air power had introduced a whole new element into the problem, and means, of protecting the British Isles. The story began, inappropriately and unimpressively, on Christmas Eve 1914, when a German aeroplane dropped a bomb near Dover which broke some windows.

On Monday 19 January 1915 two or three airships raided Norfolk, two British civilians, the nation's first such victims, being killed at Great Yarmouth at 8.30 pm. The Tyne was raided on 14 April, the east coast several times that month, and on 31 May, another milestone, London was the target for the first time, when a single Zeppelin dropped more than a ton of bombs which killed seven people and injured 35.

In April 1915 responsibility for enforcing restrictions on lighting, hitherto a patchwork of differing regulations according to area, and under a variety of authorities, became centred on the Home Office, and in May a new warning system, under War Office control, was set up. A network of observer posts, at first manned by troops but later the police, was also created.

From January 1916 the raids became steadily more serious, and that month responsibility for air defence was transferred from the Admiralty, airships having been regarded as a form of warship, to the Commander-in-Chief, Home Forces. Soon afterwards a memorable 'first' occurred when the guns at Tilbury managed to hit Zeppelin L15, which came down in the sea off the Kentish Knock, the graveyard of many a would-be invader in earlier times.

The guns near the mouth of the Thames now served a dual purpose, providing local defence to the oil stores and supply jetties which had become a feature of the area, and as the outer line of defences obstructing an aerial approach to London up the line of the Thames. A similarly dual role was found for the fighters, which were already proving far more effective than anti-aircraft fire. The first squadrons protecting London were based at airfields close to the coast at Southend, Dartford, Grain and Woodchurch, near Tenterden in East Kent, but they were also, it was recognised, well placed to engage any landing-craft which might attempt to get ashore in the Thames estuary; ground-strafing had proved itself in France to be highly successful.

By the autumn of 1916 it seemed that the Royal Flying Corps and Royal Naval Air Service, acting together, had mastered the Zeppelin, which was highly vulnerable to attack, but on 28 November, a landmark not recognised as such at the time, a solitary aeroplane dropped six bombs on London. Thereafter, however, the civilian population enjoyed a welcome respite until in May 1917 large twin-engined biplanes, known as *Gothas*, began to appear over southern England. On Wednesday 13 June 1917, around midday, the Germans achieved their most destructive raid of the war, when 162 Londoners were killed and another 426 injured by 118 bombs dropped on the City of London and the East End. On the morning of Saturday 7 July 1917 another attack, though somewhat less successful, caused an even greater public outcry, when a formation of 20 enemy bombers flew unchallenged over London, presenting, as the Press Association reported, 'an unbelievable spectacle as in stately procession it moved slowly . . .

daringly low'. Sir William Robertson, summoned to a Cabinet meeting that afternoon, found that he 'could not get a word in edgeways . . . One would have thought the world was coming to an end', and the *Daily Mail* compared the experience with that useful yardstick of national humiliation, the Dutch intrusion into the Medway in 1667.

Air defence now became a major issue. For the first time the government began to consider the possibility of the use of poison gas against the civilian population – it had made its appearance on the Western Front in May 1915 – of mass raids involving 500 or more bombers and of large fires being started which a local fire brigade could not control. Public shelters now began to be provided and the humble sandbag made its first appearance on the streets of London. After the Germans, beginning on 4 September 1917, turned to raiding at night, warnings became an almost nightly event in moonlit periods, and what was later called 'trekking' began with a mass exodus each night from the East End, which had borne the brunt of the bombing. The underground also became crammed with shelterers.

The last Zeppelin raid on London occurred on 19 October 1917, and on the north-east coast on 13 March 1918. On 1 April 1918, largely as a result of the recent attacks, a third armed service, the Royal Air Force, came into existence, intended both to improve home defence and to undertake reprisals against Germany. These proved ineffective in discouraging further raids on England, but better-organised fighter squadrons, improved anti-aircraft fire, and a balloon barrage, from which 'aprons' of wire cables were suspended, proved more successful. The last major raid on London, in which 44 were killed and 179 injured, occurred on Whitsunday, 19 May 1918, the real end of the German air offensive. It had represented a major success for the enemy, who had compelled the British government to keep at home 600 aircraft desperately needed in France, although the maximum number of German aircraft used in a single raid, and that exceptionally, was 41. The mere presence of German aircraft over the British Isles had , however, disrupted the movement and production of munitions, causing a drop in output of up to 60 per cent on the day after a raid as the workers stayed at home. It was also believed, perhaps falsely, that if the heavy raids of September 1917 could have been kept up for a month a collapse of morale would have occurred in the poorer parts of London, those which, for industrial purposes, really mattered.

The casualties inflicted on civilians were trivial in comparison to those suffered by British troops in France. In three and a half years 1117 civilians and 296 servicemen had been killed in air raids on Great Britain; another 1350 and 100 respectively had been seriously injured.*

All told, 103 separate raids had occurred, 51 by airships and 52 by aeroplanes, which had between them dropped around 300 tons of bombs, giving an overall average of 4.7 deaths and 4.8 serious injuries per ton, though in London (i.e. the Metropolitan Police District, which included the less densely populated outer suburbs) the casualty rate was higher: 75 tons of bombs had caused 670 deaths and 1960 injuries (including minor ones), i.e. 8.9 deaths and 26 injuries per ton.

In individual raids these figures had been exceeded and it was what happened in the few exceptionally destructive incidents that tended to be remembered. One single unlucky hit in particular, early in 1918 on Odham's Printing Works at Long Acre, near Charing Cross in Central London, was to be constantly cited though the casualties there, 38 dead and 85 injured, were wholly untypical. The full effect of the misleading intepretation of all these statistics will be apparent later, but already by November 1918 they were exerting a powerful influence on defence policy, where the belief had taken root that bombing was potentially, if not already, a powerful enough weapon to cause an unacceptable number of casualties and produce a total collapse of civilian morale.

How powerful fear of the bomber had already, if unreasonably, become, was strikingly illustrated when, at 11 am on the morning of Monday 11 November 1918, the maroons sounded to mark the signing of an armistice. Instead of pouring into the streets to celebrate many people in London at first fled into shelters and basements, supposing that this was another air-raid warning and that the enemy was returning.

What happened at Southwold, free at last of the fear of invasion and shelling, was more typical:

> Flags soon came out, the bells began to ring and a few of us adjourned to the mayor's house and cracked some bottles of Fizz. An impromptu meeting was called and the mayor read the official telegram from the Swan balcony, some soldiers came up on a wagon with the Kaiser in effigy, which they tied to the Town Pump and burnt amidst cheers.

And so at last, with 745,000 British dead and nearly 1,700,000 wounded, totals far exceeding the total strength of the British forces at the start of the war and amounting, with men taken prisoner, to nearly half all those who had enlisted, it was over. The homeland itself, in spite of the near panic caused by the air raids, had survived almost untouched. Not a single German soldier had landed on British soil, in-

---

* Cruttwell, p. 498, fn. 2. O'Brien, p. 11, gives a total figure of 4280 casualties, which presumably includes those slightly injured. The distinction between 'serious' and 'minor' injuries later adopted, though in 1918 not yet formalised, was between those required to stay in hospital overnight and out-patients able to go home after treatment.

deed neither seaborne raid nor invasion ever seems to have been contemplated. On Saturday 21 June 1919 most of the German High Seas Fleet which had already surrendered to the Royal Navy was ingloriously scuttled by its crews at Scapa Flow, taking to the bottom most of the surviving ships which had once bombarded the coast of England. A week later, on 28 June 1919, the Treaty of Versailles was signed, whereby Germany undertook to limit her army to a mere 100,000, all Volunteers, to restrict the size of her future fleet, and not to create an air force. But already the Kaiser, the one man responsible above all others for the misery and suffering of the preceding four years, had escaped punishment by fleeing to Holland instead of being hanged, as public opinion demanded. Already the German navy had, as mentioned above, dishonourably deceived its captors. It remained to be seen how seriously the defeated Germans would take these latest promises.

38

A NEW MENACE

In view of . . . the vastly increased air menace to this country the Committee fully realise that the coast defences of the home ports cannot be given a very high degree of priority.

Report of the Home Defence Sub-Committee of the Committee of Imperial
Defence, 29 October 1937

On the afternoon of Armistice Day 1918 Lloyd George, coining what was to prove a constantly quoted phrase, told the House of Commons: 'I hope we may say that . . . this fateful morning came to an end all wars.' This was certainly the fervent hope of all his countrymen. The ghastly slaughter in Flanders had generated an intense revulsion against the very idea of war which was to colour the nation's thinking for years to come. All three parties, for the Labour Party was now a power in Parliament, and soon to replace the Liberals as the main Opposition, eagerly sought to reduce expenditure on defence. No representative of the Service departments was present when the Cabinet Committee on Finance agreed on 11 August 1919 its targets for the future: no more than £75 million each for the army and the RAF, and £60 million for the navy.

Four days later the full Cabinet laid down what became known as the Ten Year Rule:

> It should be assumed, for framing revised Estimates, that the British Empire will not be engaged in any great war during the next ten years and that no Expeditionary Force will be required.

Invasion was for the moment off the agenda and during the year the total of British troops under arms, excluding India, was reduced from 3,500,000 to 800,000. By November 1920 it was down to 370,000, all regulars, for in March 1920 the last conscripts had been demobilised.

In June 1920 the Committee of Imperial Defence, with its civilian members and permanent secretariat, had been revived, and though inter-service rivalry prevented the formation of a single Ministry of Defence, a Chiefs-of-Staff committee consisting of their three professional heads, formed to meet a sudden emergency in 1922, became a permanent instrument of defence planning. The committee was unable to prevent further cuts in defence spending which followed the setting up of a Committee on National Expenditure, under Sir Eric Geddes, which wielded the later notorious 'Geddes Axe'. The army came off worst, the Army Estimates for 1922-3 being cut again, to £55 million. Such reductions now became an annual event, with public approval, as the Chief of the Imperial General Staff, General Sir Frederick [later Field Marshal Lord] Cavan acknowledged in a private letter to Sir William Robertson in September 1924:

> Our great and threatening danger is that the public see the necessity for a strong Air Force because they don't want to be bombed, and a strong Navy to escort food and the necessities of life to their shores, because they don't want to be starved, but they don't realise at all that neither Air Force nor Navy can operate without the protection of the Army.

The CID, and particularly its immensely influential Secretary, Sir Maurice Hankey, scored one notable success, over an old adversary. It had, as mentioned earlier, turned down the idea of a Channel Tunnel in July 1914, though Marshal Foch is later said to have declared that had one existed 'the war would have been shortened by at least two years'. In 1924 an all-party committee of MPs reported in favour of the tunnel, which now attracted the support of 400 Members, a comfortable majority including the prime minister himself, Ramsay MacDonald, head of the first-ever Labour government. MacDonald gave an encouraging response to a pro-tunnel deputation at the end of June 1924, but behind the scenes the service chiefs and, above all, Maurice [now Sir Maurice] Hankey remained unrelentingly hostile. Hankey was also Secretary to the Cabinet and to the Privy Council, and had become regarded as the great authority on all defence questions. An exhaustive Note, dated 21 June 1924, which he circulated, mustered over 21 large pages every possible argument against the tunnel, warning of the awful danger should Northern France ever be 'in the possession of a people like the Russian Bolsheviks, or even the Germans', and recalling the crisis of Ludendorff's offensive of 1918.

To the familiar threat of a sudden raid to seize the tunnel's mouth, Hankey now added what he described as 'many instances of the "bolt from the grey"', i.e. by the German army, during the recent war, while far from it being easy to destroy the tunnel when required, Hankey's diligent research had yielded many recent examples of bridges destroyed prematurely or, alternatively, too late. He cunningly added another reason why MacDonald and his Labour supporters should hesitate: 'The existence of a Channel Tunnel would certainly have given an immense impetus to the demand for compulsory military service'.

To make assurance doubly sure, Hankey had also secured the support of the Chiefs-of-Staff, for once unanimous, and by the time Mac-

Donald had, on 1 July 1924, invited all his living predecessors as prime minister – Balfour, Asquith, Lloyd George and Stanley [later Earl] Baldwin – to a special meeting of the CID the battle against the tunnel had really been won, as MacDonald's diary entry for that day makes plain:

> Presided over meeting of C.I.D. with ex-premiers present on subject of Channel Tunnel. Amazed at military mind. It has got itself and the country in a rut where neither fresh air nor new ideas blow. My burdens are so many and so heavy that I cannot take up the Tunnel at present, but it must be taken up. Meeting most unsatisfactory.

So persistent, however, were the tunnel's advocates that in 1929 they produced a new argument, the need to create work during the current Depression, and elaborate technical feasibility studies were made, but in May 1930 the CID once again, on Hankey's prompting, turned the proposal down. The reason he advanced in the supposedly impartial paper which he wrote and circulated to the committee reflected little credit on the public – 'In the past our people have been peculiarly susceptible to panic, particularly in regard to invasion' – nor on the wartime governments and military commanders:

> During the Great War naval, military and air forces were often diverted from their proper strategical role owing to anxiety regarding home defence, aggravated by the naval raids on Yarmouth, Hartlepool, Scarborough and Lowestoft . . . Whatever the feeling in quiet times, the Tunnel would be a source of anxiety in case of war or threat of war.

Hankey also revealed little faith in the *Entente Cordiale*:

> Nothing can alter the fundamental fact that we are not liked in France and never will be, except for the advantages which the French people may be able to extract from us . . . The more military attitude of the French, when considered in conjunction with the more impulsive tendencies of the Latin character, are factors that ought not to be overlooked when considering the Channel Tunnel . . . Napoleon is credited with the statement that Antwerp is a pistol pointed at the heart of Britain. The Tunnel would give the pistol a useful barrel.

The Members of the House of Commons were less convinced and in the following month a pro-tunnel motion was lost by only seven votes. Thereafter, however, the project disappeared for several years from the realm of practical politics, recalled only by occasional press stories under such headlines as 'The Poor Old Tunnel'.

The 'ten year rule' laid down in 1919 was reaffirmed in 1925, 1926 and 1927 and then, in 1928, made permanent, with the ten years concerned

starting afresh each day. What money the services did receive was
largely ill-spent. The navy managed to maintain its traditional two-
power standard, the French and Italian being the two fleets considered,
but clung to the battleship, little used in the recent war, at the expense
of destroyers and the new aircraft carriers. The RAF, under its wartime
chief, Hugh [later Marshal of the Royal Air Force Lord] Trenchard,
Chief of the Air Staff until 1929, asserted its hard-won independence
by maintaining that bombing alone could win a war. The army, as ever
the poor relation, squandered its resources on that ludicrous anachro-
nism, the cavalry. At the Staff College membership of the Drag Hunt
was compulsory, and the army's equine obsession was even more in
evidence at the Royal Military Academy, Sandhurst. A standard
question for candidates for commissions, designed to establish their
social suitability as well as their professional aptitude, was: 'What pack
do you hunt with?'

Along with the idealisation of the horse went a contempt for its replacement. 'The cavalry will never be scrapped to make room for the
tanks,', confidently predicted one brigadier in the Royal United
Services Institute *Journal*, and a general lecturing at the same Institute
in November 1919 declared bluntly: 'The tank proper was a freak. The
circumstances which called it into existence were exceptional and not
likely to recur.' As late as 1927 the Director of Military Training is said
to have protested, 'If they mechanise anything more, we shall have no
army left.'

The modernisation of the army was not merely delayed by internal
disagreements, but also by political pressure. Labour MPs hostile to
the horse as the epitome of class distinction were counterbalanced by
others to whom the tank seemed the symbol of aggression. The future
Field Marshal Lord Craven, CIGS from 1922 to 1926, found himself
abused in the House of Commons for recommending that £100,000 be
spent on new tanks and forbidden by the Treasury to acquire additional wireless sets even after the meagre Army estimates had been
approved. During the manoeuvres of 1929 anti-tank guns had to be represented by coloured flags. To the critical eye of the best-known
advocate of mobile armoured warfare, Major-General John ('Boney')
Fuller, who as early as 1919 had written a prize essay predicting that
tanks would ultimately replace cavalry, and even infantry, as the most
important arm, the trial mobilisation of the 1st Division at Aldershot in
1931 was reminiscent not only of 1914 but of 1899, with its 5500 horses
and 740 horse-drawn vehicles, including ambulances dating from the
Boer War. All, he observed, would have been sitting targets for enemy
aircraft.[*]

Fear of invasion had in the past often loosened the national purse-

* On the influence of Fuller and his disciple Basil Liddell Hart, and indeed on the inter-
war army generally, see Bond, *Policy*, on which I have drawn heavily for this chapter.

strings, but a CID paper of 7 October 1925 had acknowledged the 'extreme improbability' of any such attack:

> The only country who could conceivably obtain unrestricted use of
> French or Belgian territory is Germany, but as the German navy is
> so restricted by the Treaty of Versailles, which prevents her becoming a first class naval power for some years after the outbreak of war,
> it is not necessary to consider her in this connection.

More anxiety existed over Ireland, which in December 1922 had been legally divided into the Irish Free State, later known as Eire or the Republic of Ireland, consisting of 26 counties, and Ulster, or Northern Ireland, made up of the remaining six. Among the victims of the 'Troubles' accompanying separation was Erskine Childers who, like many republicans, had served heroically in the British forces during the war, but was now executed for bearing arms against the new Irish Free State. After the division of Ireland the government in London retained control over the three 'treaty ports' of Queenstown, Berehaven and Lough Swilly, though in June 1926 it was recommended that their defences be scaled down. Belfast Lough, the other most important site, posed no problem, being safely within Ulster.

On the mainland, meanwhile, some coastal defence sites were sold off and the three principal groups of forts, around Portsmouth, Plymouth and Chatham, survived only as barracks and stores. In 1929, however, the process began of modernising coastal batteries still in use, after tests at Portsmouth had shown that modern warships could often escape being hit by coastal artillery at a range of 18,000 yards [16.5 km]. The 9.2-in [23-cm] guns generally in use were improved, and firing in salvoes, rather than by single rounds, became the rule. The 12-pounder [5.45-kg] quick-firers intended to deal with motor-torpedo-boats were at the same time replaced by twin six-pounders [2.7-kg] guns with a higher rate of fire. The expectation was now less of sinking enemy ships than 'of inflicting on them sufficient damage . . . to place them at a disadvantage in subsequent naval action'.

The Territorial Force had been stood down in 1920 but in 1922 was revived as the Territorial Army. It had become responsible for manning coastal defence batteries, and its members now automatically accepted a liability to serve overseas. Recruitment was slow for patriotism was at a discount. One Labour council refused permission in 1927 for a TA unit to hold Sunday morning drills on one of its housing estates, and many disbanded Officers' Training Corps companies in their schools, as liable to encourage warmongering. The alarmist literature of Edwardian times was now washed away by a flood of anti-war books and plays. Erich Maria Remarque's novel *All Quiet on the Western Front*, published in England in March 1929, was almost as successful there as in his native Germany, where it became the all-time best–seller after the Bible until displaced by Adolf Hitler's *Mein Kampf*. Robert Graves's autobiography about life in the British front line, *Goodbye To All That*, appeared in the same year. The great stage hit of 1929 was R.C. Sherriff's equally disillusioned *Journey's End*.

Mingling with the understandable revulsion against the last war, and exploited by high–minded pacifists and sensation–minded journalists, was a more than rational fear of the next. The danger from the air, because it affected civilians and was still largely unknown, was shamelessly exploited by pacifists and, hardly less dangerous, high–minded internationalists, to create a new 'blue funk' school in favour of peace at almost any price. The official planners were not immune from the prevailing atmosphere, indeed positively encouraged it. As already mentioned, the number of people (including servicemen) killed by bombing in the United Kingdom between 1914 and 1918 had been tiny: based on the estimated population in 1918 a civilian had had approximately a 0.00259 per cent chance of becoming a fatal casualty. The total of those, including servicemen, who had been killed by enemy action within Great Britain and Ireland amounted to 0.19 per cent of those who had died on active service,[*] mainly in France.

No one, however, seems to have performed these calculations. Instead the number of casualties in the few serious raids in the Great War was taken as the norm and the likely total, as the air forces of other powers grew more powerful, was simply scaled up, with no allowance made for the public evacuating itself from the cities or becoming more skilled at taking shelter. Similarly, and with equally misleading results, the disgraceful near–panic in the Midlands and East End in 1916–17 was interpreted to mean that millions of British citizens would cravenly abandon their workplaces and homes at the first real test, plunging into shelter and refusing to emerge. That repeated raids might inure them to such reactions, or even provoke an eagerness to fight back, never seems to have been considered.

In November 1921 the Committee of Imperial Defence called on the three service Chiefs of Staff to report on the likely scale of future air attack. The CID itself, in a paper that month, suggested that France, the only potential enemy, could drop up to 44 tons each 24 hours, 13 of them at night, compared with the 10.5 tons delivered in the worst Zeppelin and aeroplane raids of 1917 and 1918. By 1923 the figures had risen to 168 tons in the first day and night, dropping to a regular nightly load of 84 tons by day three.

In January 1924 the CID decided to appoint an Air Raid Precautions Sub–Committee, known as 'The ARP Committee', the first use of

---

[*] These are my own calculations, based on the casualty figures given in the previous chapter, and an estimated population in 1918, including Ireland, of 43,116,000, which in fact included servicemen stationed overseas. The actual risk was therefore even less than I have suggested.

these subsequently famous initials. The six-man committee, meeting under Home Office auspices and including Sir Maurice Hankey, met for the first time on 15 May 1924, under the chairmanship of Sir John Anderson, with a pacifist-minded Labour government in power. It adopted early on the 'multiplier' of 50 casualties per ton of bombs, one-third of them fatal, from which it deduced that there would be 5000 casualties in the first 24 hours of an attack, 1700 of them fatal; 3750, 1275 of them fatal, in the second 24 hours; and 2500, 850 of them fatal, each 24 hours thereafter. The Air Staff believed that an enemy would concentrate on daylight attacks, which would be three times as heavy as those at night. The ARP Committee's first report, submitted to the CID and then partly considered by the Cabinet in December 1925, covered every aspect of the subject, from 'evasion', later known as evacuation, to anti-gas measures. It was doubtful about the black-out, recording the widely held view that in the recent war 'the darkening of English cities was overdone', and recommended more experiments on the subject.

The ARP Committee was re-formed in April 1929 as the ARP (Organisation) Committee and a Ministerial (or Policy) Committee under the Home Secretary was also set up to give the planning now in progress added authority. The proceedings of both committees remained secret for the government was still bemused by dreams of disarmament, and of an international ban on chemical weapons or even all aerial warfare. At the London Naval Conference in 1930 Ramsay Mac-Donald had actually agreed that Great Britain would build no new capital ships for the next five years and would limit its strength in cruisers to 50, half what the Admiralty considered the minimum for safety.

Both France and Italy had refused to give similar undertakings about their navy, and the latter was now a power to be reckoned with, since in 1922 Benito Mussolini had established himself as its Fascist dictator. In May 1930, the month after the Naval Conference ended, he delivered a speech which summed up the difference between his point of view and that of the British government:

> Words are a very fine thing; but rifles, machine-guns, warships, aeroplanes and cannon are still finer things . . . Right unaccompanied by might is an empty word.

In 1931 Japan invaded Manchuria, the first major act of international aggression since 1914. It was not before time that, in March 1932, the 'ten year rule' was officially abandoned by the British government. It was also becoming concerned that having started to consider air raid precautions before other nations it now seemed to be falling behind them. During 1932 the French Minister of the Interior, Pierre Laval, issued for sale to the public a pamphlet entitled *Practical Instruction on*

Passive Defence against Air Attack, outlining a full-scale scheme for a national organisation. Even more alarming, the confederation of German industry produced a similar scheme for protecting its members' factories against air attack, in cooperation with the German government.

In January 1933 the Nazis came to power in Germany, with Adolf Hitler being appointed Chancellor. He had never made any secret of his immediate aim. As he himself wrote a few years later, 'No human being had declared or recorded what he wanted more often . . . the abolition of the Treaty of Versailles.' In April 1933 the British government appointed the first full-time official concerned with Air Raid Precautions, a former general and RE officer who now became Air Raids Commandant (Designate). His first request, to spend £150,000 on research, the total ARP budget at the time being only £20,000, was turned down, but he was successful in defeating suggestions that the ARP structure should be staffed by troops or form a para-military organisation. His aim, he explained was 'organising the whole civilian population to protect themselves':

> The ARP Service must create and maintain its own honourable status and prestige and not lean upon some other Service. It would be contrary to the principle of this civilian organisation to resist attack upon civilians if it were to be incorporated in the Territorial Army or any other military organisation.

In Germany Hitler was meanwhile establishing himself as dictator and on 19 August 1934 90 per cent of those taking part in a plebiscite endorsed the Nazi take-over of power and Hitler's assumption of the role of national *Führer* or leader. That year the Committee of Imperial Defence recommended that planning should begin for a possible war with Germany, though it was, they thought, unlikely to come before 1939. In March the prime minister at last admitted that the CID had been considering air raid precautions as 'an essential accessory to . . . home defence' for the past ten years; in July 1934 he announced a five-year programme of expansion for the RAF and, a few days later, made an important pronouncement: 'Since the day of the air the old frontiers are gone. When you think of the defence of England, you no longer think of the chalk cliffs of Dover; you think of the Rhine.'

The nation moved, with barely a pause, from disarmament to rearmament. In 1933 the Navy Estimates had sunk to a record low of £50 million and spending on the Army to £38 million; by 1937 the Army alone was receiving £82 million.

On 4 March 1935 the British government announced its rearmament plans, justifying them on the grounds that 'Germany was . . . rearming openly on a large scale.' Great Britain's 'desire to lead the world . . . by our example of unilateral disarmament,' it somewhat naively admitted, 'has not succeeded'. Five days later Germany formally notified the other European powers that she already possessed an air force, a flagrant defiance of the Treaty of Versailles. The Germans announced another blatant breach of the Treaty, the re-introduction of conscription, with the immediate aim of building up a peacetime army of 36 divisions, or 550,000 men, three times the size of Great Britain's. At least one powerful voice had been raised in the House of Commons drawing attention to the danger from Germany. In November 1934 Winston Churchill, currently out of office, had declared that the German Air Force was approaching the RAF in strength. The government spokesman, Stanley Baldwin, immediately described this statement as 'completely wrong', but on 22 May 1935 had to eat his words and told the House that Hitler had recently informed the Foreign Secretary that the *Luftwaffe* had already achieved parity with the RAF.

Both Churchill and Baldwin, who in June 1935 became prime minister, had been deceived, but the results proved beneficial. On 9 July 1935 the first ARP circular to local authorities was issued, requiring them to prepare local schemes in accordance with the national guidelines it laid down, and the public were warned, in a notable understatement, that if war came it would be 'impossible to guarantee immunity from attack' from the air. The Home Office Estimate for 1935-6 included a small allocation for ARP purposes, £92,000, and already an Air Raid Precautions Department, with a total staff of eleven, had been set up in a few rooms in Westminster. Some people still refused to recognise that it took two powers to make peace but only one to fight a war, and that summer the League of Nations Union obtained more than 11,500,000 votes in its pro-disarmament Peace Ballot, though only 2,350,000 opposed military measures as a last resort against an aggressor.

That October, in an overt act of aggression, Italy invaded Abyssinia, and on 7 March 1936 Hitler occupied the Rhineland, another breach of the Treaty of Versailles, and one which removed a protective buffer between Germany and France. 'The 48 hours after the march into the Rhineland,' Hitler himself later confessed, 'were the most nerveracking in my life,' but the democracies did nothing. The policy of what became known as 'appeasement' was under way. The press endorsed the politicians' spinelessness. *The Times* leader described Hitler's action as 'a chance to rebuild'.

In July 1936 the Spanish Civil War began, with Italy and Germany soon giving active support, as well as official recognition, to what was essentially a Fascist rebellion against an elected government, and in November the two dictators entered in an alliance, the Rome-Berlin 'axis', to which during 1937 Japan was added, forming the Anti-Comintern Pact. The Spanish Civil War produced a sharp division of opinion in Great Britain but resulted in the Left becoming notably more sympathetic towards rearmament. 1936 was also the 'year of the three kings', with the death on 20 January of the 71-year-old George V, the abdication on 11 December of his eldest son, Edward VIII, an immature 42, and the accession of Edward's 40-year-old brother. George VI was a former naval officer who had served at the Battle of Jutland, a conscientious sovereign free of the pro-Nazi sympathies of which Edward and his appalling wife were later, probably with good reason, suspected.

A landmark in aerial warfare was the daylight bombing, on 26 April 1937, of the small Basque town of Guernica, by German aircraft assisting the Spanish rebels, or nationalists, according to one's point of view. Enormous damage was done, though the number of casualties, probably involving about 1000 dead, was exaggerated. The bombing of Guernica, on a market day and against an undefended town, was eagerly seized on both by the alarmists and the peacemongers to assist their propaganda, and Spanish experience encouraged the British government in the fear of the 'knock-out blow' which already dominated its thinking. It was particularly apprehensive about poison gas which, though not employed in Spain, had been used in Abyssinia against unprotected tribesmen. A government school for training instructors in anti-gas precautions was opened in April 1936 and on 12 January 1937 the minister responsible announced that civilians in danger areas would be issued with a free respirator, soon known as 'a gas mask', a provision later extended to the whole country. In the same broadcast an appeal was made for ARP volunteers, and on 4 March 1937 the setting up of the Air Raid Warden service, the backbone of the whole ARP system, was announced; training was also being provided in dealing with incendiary bombs. A decision to introduce a universal black-out on the outbreak of war was taken later that year and arrangements were agreed for a public warning system.

The need for evacuation of the cities began to be considered after a special sub-committee of the CID had reported to the Cabinet in June that the likely weight of attack had now been dramatically scaled up. The Air Staff now predicted that a new war might begin with the enemy delivering 3500 tons of bombs in the first 24 hours, to be followed by a regular 600 tons a day. Applying the now standard 'multiplier' of 50 casualties per ton, this meant casualties of around 200,000 a week, of whom 60,000 would be killed. It was little wonder that the government now approved capital expenditure of £37½ million, and planning for an ARP service of nearly 1,400,000 men and women, half of them part-time.

On 4 November the ARP Bill was introduced which imposed on all local authorities the duty of preparing plans 'for the protection of persons and property from injury or damage in the event of hostile attack from the air', the cost being shared between local councils and Whitehall. Although the Opposition spokesman, Herbert Morrison, admitted it was 'a necessary Bill' he moved its rejection, on the grounds that the whole expense should have been borne by central government, and this became the regular Labour line, used by some councils as an excuse for doing little to implement the subsequent Act, when it came into effect on 1 January 1938.

During 1937 the whole question of home defence was considered in detail. On 7 January 1937 a Sub-Committee of the CID examined the prospects of invasion, taking as its starting point the classic study of 1908, previously quoted, and a subsequent enquiry by a Joint Planning Sub-Committee and the Deputy Chiefs of Staff in 1929-30, when France was still the potential enemy. Now, the situation was very different, with 'the possibility of air-borne, in addition to sea-borne, land attack.'

> At one time 150 soldiers with 18 aeroplanes were reported to be practising daily in the Island of Sylt . . . Another report was that a battalion of 'air infantry' (parachutists) had been formed at Berlin . . . These reports do not suggest that Germany has yet either contemplated or trained for so ambitious a project as a parachute raid upon Great Britain . . . The danger that Germany would attempt air-borne land attack on any considerable scale is negligible. On the other hand, small-scale raids landing demolition parties to destroy vulnerable points would be feasible and not improbable.

A list of 27 possible targets 'outside large centres for which guards . . . are to be provided in war for protecting against sabotage' was attached. Naval objectives featured high on the list, but it also included the Forth Bridge, chemical factories at Billingham, Hull, St Helens, Huddersfield and Birmingham, numerous ammunition factories and depots, including Woolwich Arsenal, and, a significant sign of the times, the aero-engine works at Derby. The Committee thought such attacks improbable and it also showed a refreshing degree of faith in the British public:

> Unless the raiders murdered civilians and destroyed non-military targets the alarm they would cause in the few hours at their disposal might be very limited. The moral effect of 'frightfulness' might be to harden resistance rather than to break it down.

Finally, the CID urged, the mistakes of 1914-18 when 'Germany benefited from . . . a threat which never materialised' should nor be repeated: 'In any future war neither this remote threat, not the actual execution of a raid by Germany should be allowed to tie in England more than that minimum of troops necessary to meet real military dangers.'

On 28 May 1937 the arch-apostle of appeasement, Neville Chamberlain, became prime minister, but preparations for war continued.

On 29 October 1937 the Joint Oversea [*sic*] and Home Defence Sub-Committee of the CID produced an exhaustive report on 'Home Ports. Local Naval and Seafront Defences', which updated its last such study, in 1927, 'based on the contingency of war with France'. The Committee recommended a wholesale reclassification of naval bases, with the old Category 'B', with defences to be manned 'as soon as possible after the outbreak of war', being abolished. Henceforward there would be only Category 'A', with defences 'installed in peace time to be fully manned before the outbreak of hostilities', and Category 'C', 'for which defences schemes should be prepared to meet probable war requirements'. Scapa Flow was, not surprisingly, promoted to Category 'A', which now included 20 places, among them all the traditional danger points from the Forth to Plymouth, including the Tyne, Harwich, the Thames, Dover and Portsmouth, and from Swansea and Milford Haven to the Mersey and the Clyde. In every case the 'Proposed Local Naval Defences' were listed in detail, revealing all too clearly the ports' present vulnerability. The Tees and Hartlepool, for instance, which had actually been attacked in 1914, had at present only three of the six 9.2-in [23.4-cm] and six-inch [15-cm] guns required, and one of the four 'concentrated moving lights' it needed. Almost everywhere booms and boom vessels, needed to fend off attack by motor torpedo-boats, the danger from which was thought to have increased, were also lacking. The Sub-Committee, with notable restraint, acknowledged the other, even more urgent, claims on the service departments:

> In view of our heavy defence commitments all over the world, and of the vastly increased air menace to this country in particular, the Committee fully realise that the coast defences of the home ports cannot be given a very high degree of priority . . . At present, however, . . . the War Office have an annual allotment of only £75,000 for the coast defences of the home ports and at this rate the modernisation of these defences will not be completed for some 45 years.

Everyone except the prime minister, who still hoped to buy Hitler off by concessions in Europe, now recognised that a war was coming, and even Chamberlain agreed about the danger from the air. In a memorandum considered by the Cabinet on 22 December 1937 the recently appointed Minister for the Coordination of Defence set out the nation's military priorities as involving 'first, the security of the United Kingdom (particularly from air attack)'. No one, not even the other forces, now disputed the overriding claims of Fighter Command, set up in 1936 and in process of being re-equipped with fast eight-gun monoplanes able to challenge the dreaded *Luftwaffe*. 'The Air Defence of Great Britain is absorbing all the money which was intended for the Field Force,' commented General Sir William [later

Field Marshal Lord] Ironside, soon to become Chief of the Imperial General Staff. 'The Air Ministry dictates what it wants and the Army bears the cost.' But he did not dispute the emphasis being placed even within the army on anti-aircraft guns. 'You must,' he observed in his diary that August, 'make your fortress secure before you think of issuing from it.'

On 13 March 1938 Hitler forcibly incorporated Austria within the German Reich and during the summer began to demand the transfer to Germany of the Sudetenland, the province of Czechoslovakia bordering on Germany which contained Czechoslovakia's border defences and her largest arms factories. At Munich, on Friday 30 September, Chamberlain forced the Czechs to agree and totally capitulated to Hitler's demands. The prime minister's reception in England was one of hysterical approval; few echoed Winston Churchill's protest in the House of Commons: 'We have sustained a defeat without a war.'

The Munich crisis provided an opportunity for a sudden, unscheduled dress rehearsal of the ARP services. On 24 September the Home Office instructed local authorities to begin digging trenches; a rudimentary warning system was set up and experiments in introducing a black-out were made. Plans to deliver to every household an official booklet, *The Protection of Your Home against Air Raids*, and to begin the evacuation of schoolchildren from London were about to be implemented when Chamberlain arrived back from Munich. The 11 (later 12) Regional Commissioners had, without publicity, taken up their posts, each being responsible for overseeing ARP within his Region, and authorised in emergency, such as invasion, to become a virtual dictator within it. Thirty-eight million gas masks were distributed and the crisis produced an influx of recruits into the ARP services so that within a week many districts reached their full complement of wardens, though most were untrained and lacked equipment. A single minister, the Lord Privy Seal, Sir John Anderson [later Lord Waverley], now became what Chamberlain described as 'Minister of Civilian Defence'. Anderson's name was to be immortalised by the steel shelter[*] which, on 21 December 1938, he announced was to be made available free to all who required it, below a certain income level – estimated at ten million people – and other types of protection were to be provided for another ten million.

The defence estimates for 1939 included a figure for Civil Defence of £42 million, much of it accounted for by the cost of shelters, almost a five-fold increase on 1938, but the three services were still far greater spenders. *Their* bill for 1938-9, £388 million, was to rise in the coming year to £523 million.

[*] The public (and a poem by A.P. Herbert) gave Sir John the credit although the name seems originally to have derived from the engineer mainly responsible for the design, Dr David Anderson.

The Munich crisis was unique in providing an opportunity for a post-mortem on the plans to fight a war which had, at the very last minute, been called off. The army's main contribution, since no one expected an invasion, had been to man the 44 anti-aircraft guns defending London; the Territorial Army units responsible had been called out on 26 September. The navy had duly been mobilised on 28 September, though not for long, and a week later, on 6 October, the Admiralty produced, for the CID, a *Review of Precautionary Measures taken during the Czechoslovakian Crisis* which highlighted the weaknesses revealed. Some would take time to remedy, like the general shortage of destroyers and minesweepers; some were more easily dealt with, like providing an aerodrome for local defence, to be manned by the navy-controlled Fleet Air Arm, at Scapa Flow.

The greatest beneficiary of Munich was the RAF. The sole limiting factor on its expansion was now the physical capacity of the factories to turn out more machines. In September 1938 Fighter Command had had six squadrons of modern Spitfires and Hurricanes; by September 1939 under the new plans, it would have 26; by June 1940, 47. Hardly less important, means were at last beginning to exist of providing sufficient early warning to enable the defending fighters to reach the enemy's operational height by the time he crossed the coast. This problem had plagued the authorities ever since the first German raids in 1915; the Observer Corps, also mobilised at the time of Munich, could only report aircraft in visual range. The first attempt at more distant detection, around 1929, had involved what were known as 'acoustic mirrors', long curved walls designed to collect and concentrate the sound of distant engines, but they proved a scientific dead end, and by September 1938 the true answer had been found in RDF, or Radio Direction Finding, later known as radar. Its unseen shield at the time of Munich only covered the Thames estuary but by a year later stretched from the Orkney Islands to beyond Portsmouth, restoring something like equality to the balance between the aerial intruder and the defending fighter.

Whether, as in 1914, a British expeditionary force should be sent to France was much debated, but on 8 March 1939 the Secretary of State for War, Leslie [later Lord] Hore-Belisha announced the intention to prepare a 19-division BEF, 13 of these being drawn from the Territorial Army, of which that month the peacetime establishment was increased from 130,000 to 170,000. The Treasury opposed a planned further expansion to 340,000 but, so serious were the times, it no longer had the final word. Two weeks before, on Wednesday 15 March 1939, Hitler had occupied Czechoslovakia, making it a German protectorate, in defiance of the Munich Agreement, and on 31 March Chamberlain undertook on behalf of his colleagues 'to lend the Polish government all support in their power' if, as seemed inevitable, Poland was next to be attacked. ('A guarantee a day keeps Hitler away,' it was mockingly said, though it manifestly didn't.) On 26 April, under pressure from Hore-Belisha and to please the French, though the army already had all the men it could equip, Chamberlain announced the introduction of peacetime conscription, a final breach with the tradition which had lasted for centuries.

The new conscripts, misleadingly known as militiamen, were to be required on reaching the age of 20 to undergo six months' military training in one of the three services, to be followed by three and a half years in the Reserve, during which they might be recalled for annual training or, in an emergency, for full-time duty. They would not in peacetime be required to go overseas. In fact only one intake, of 35,000, was ever recruited under the 1939 Military Training Act, and its members were destined to serve a good deal longer than six months.

During May *An Englishman's Home* was revived on the London stage but created nothing like the impact it had done 30 years before. 'Today,' commented *The Times*, faithful to appeasement to the last, 'the picture of invasion has lost its power to startle.' In July the military commentator Basil Liddell Hart published, in *The Defence of Britain*, an equally reassuring message. 'There is,' he told his readers, 'sound cause for discounting the danger of invasion.'

Just as the first militiamen, to great publicity, were reporting for training, the first ex-regular reservists were being recalled by the Navy, followed by the other services, and during the summer the country moved steadily towards a war footing. The real turning point came on Tuesday 21 August, with the announcement of an impending non-aggression pact between Germany and Russia, signed two days later. On 24 August Parliament, its members recalled from holiday, passed an Emergency Powers Bill giving the government almost un-limited authority, and about the same time many large companies, national organisations and thousands of private citizens began to evac-uate themselves from the cities, especially London. Friday 1 September 1939 was the decisive day. That morning Hitler invaded Poland, general mobilisation was proclaimed in Great Britain, the Civil Defence services were ordered to report for duty and mass official evacuation, which was to see one and a half million schoolchildren and other 'priority' classes moved in the next three days from 'danger' into 'reception' areas, began; at nightfall the black-out came into effect. The one and a half million people now enrolled in Civil Defence waited for the enemy bombers which, according to the last cheerful estimate, should in the next 14 days be delivering 100,000 tons of bombs, creat-ing general havoc, a breakdown of morale and five million casualties.

39

DUE PRECAUTIONS

He thought . . . that we should treat the possibility seriously and take due precautions.

Minutes of Cabinet meeting on invasion recording the contribution of the
First Lord of the Admiralty, Winston Churchill, 27 October 1939

The Second World War began for Great Britain with, appropriately, a false alarm. A friendly civilian aircraft set the sirens sounding in London directly Neville Chamberlain had announced the declaration of war over the radio, another 'first', at 11.15 am on Sunday 3 September 1939. The 'phoney war' followed, with the RAF dropping nothing more lethal on Germany than leaflets while the men of the British Expeditionary Force, crossing to France from 4 September onwards, merely dug in and trained. For the Royal Navy the war was real from the start, with several ships being torpedoed, among them the battleship *Royal Oak*, sunk with the loss of nearly 800 of her crew on 14 October *inside* Scapa Flow. On Monday 16 October 1939, in the first air attack of the second German war, nine[*] enemy aircraft attacked British cruisers and destroyers in the Firth of Forth, doing slight damage to three of them and killing or wounding 25 of those on board.

Two bombers were shot down by locally based Spitfires. Next day, 17 October, Scapa Flow was raided by an equally small force, of which one bomber, hit by gunfire, crashed on the island of Hoy. One ancient battleship turned depot ship, the *Iron Duke*, which lacked armour and guns, was hit.

These raids, trivial in themselves, caused Winston Churchill, recalled to become once again First Lord of the Admiralty, much anxiety; as he warned his Cabinet colleagues a few days later, 'we were fighting this war with the last war's ships, which were not designed against heavy air attack'. His lively and restless mind was already troubled by the fear of an enemy landing, as he revealed in a note on 21 October to the First Sea Lord:

I should be the last to raise those 'invasion scares' which I combated

[*] Collier, *Defence*, p. 82. Churchill, *Second* World War, Vol. I, p. 442, refers inaccurately to four bombers shot down and gives a notably more cheerful account of this raid than Collier, the official historian.

so constantly during the early days of 1914-15. Still, it might be well for the Chiefs of Staff to consider what would happen, if, for instance, 20,000 men were run across and landed, say, at Harwich, or at Webburn Hook, where there is deep water close inshore . . . The long dark nights would help such designs. Have any arrangements been made by the War Office to provide against this contingency?

'Webburn', its local pronunciation, was in fact Weybourne, a small wind-swept village on the Norfolk coast, two miles [3.2 km] west of Sheringham, in the middle of the broad curve of East Anglia between Great Yarmouth and the Wash. This had been a favoured site of the alarmists for centuries as the traditional, if inaccurate*, rhyme, confirmed:

He that would Old England win
Must at Weybourne Hook begin.

Churchill's remedy, as he proposed to the First Sea Lord two days later, was for 'a certain number of mobile columns or organised forces that can be thrown rapidly against any descent', though he also added, in a notable surrender of the navy's traditional role, that it might be 'that the air service will be able to assume full responsibility'.

For once it was the government, not the public, currently preoccupied with adjusting to the black-out and other unwelcome features of wartime life, which was prone to suffer 'invasion-itis'. At 1.40 am on the morning of Thursday 26 October 1939 a highly detailed report reached the Foreign Office from the British minister in Belgrade of supposed plans for the invasion of Britain, and a special committee of the War Cabinet was called together at 9.30 pm on Friday evening to study the evidence.

The heart of what was supposedly the German plan was a massive air strike by 5200 aircraft, divided into four task forces. One would drop 12,000 parachute troops on the east coast; a second would attack the navy; a third, RAF aerodromes and the railway system; while a fourth would cover the disembarkation of a seaborne army 23,000 strong, including tanks, and the arrival of a follow-up force of a further 45,000 men the next night. To prevent the BEF being summoned home or (even more improbably) the French coming to their ally's aid, a diversionary attack using 'a new type of flamethrower' and armour-piercing aerial torpedoes would be delivered against the Maginot Line, the supposedly impregnable system of underground fortifications built over the past decade along the Franco-German border.

These final details were sufficient by themselves to arouse suspicion about the report's authenticity. Churchill, however, was reluctant to

---

* 'Inaccurate' because no invader, successful or unsuccessful, had ever started at Weybourne, though this rhyme went back to at least the eighteenth century and probably even earlier.

dismiss the danger out of hand, and the committee's minutes reveal his
thinking:

> The Germans were faced with the necessity of undertaking some
> great operation, either against ourselves or against the French. They
> might shrink from sacrificing vast numbers in an attack on the
> Maginot Line, whereas they might well gamble on a hazardous ven-
> ture against Great Britain, which, if it succeeded, would cause us
> great loss and confusion, and, if it failed, would only entail the loss
> of 80,000 men. He thought, therefore, that we should treat the pos-
> sibility seriously, and take due precautions.

The following day the War Cabinet was duly informed of the committee's conclusions, which were given added weight by the opinion
of the Air Ministry, which had not been represented the night before,
that Germany did indeed possess the 5200 aircraft mentioned in the
mysterious report, and a sufficient force of 'trained parachute infantry'
for the operation described. Churchill now announced to his colleagues the Admiralty's proposed anti-invasion dispositions. One submarine would keep forward watch along the Heligoland Bight; ten
more would form a screen 'across the possible route of an expedition';
35 destroyers would be scraped together from escort duties to be in
readiness in the Humber and at Harwich; four cruisers would be
detached to Rosyth, in the Firth of Forth, ready to provide heavy support against the main German troop transports; and the remaining
heavy ships of the Home Fleet would remain in the far north to reduce
the risk of their being knocked out by air attack. When the War Cabinet met at noon next day, Saturday 29 October, Churchill drew attention to a vulnerable site much nearer home. The London parks, he suggested, might provide an attractive landing ground for enemy
parachute troops and that same day he ordered that a 'stand of arms'
sufficient for 50 men 'be placed in some convenient position in the
basement in the Admiralty building' for local defence. The real shield
against invasion, however, remained the navy, and following the tor-
pedoing of the *Royal Oak* and the bombing of the *Iron Duke* a vigorous
debate had been going on about moving the heavy ships of the Home
Fleet from Scapa Flow. Scapa was temporarily demoted to providing
refuelling facilities for destroyers, while reinforced booms and anti-
submarine nets, additional blockships and a controlled minefield were
installed there to protect the main fleet on its return. It was also decided
to increase the number of searchlights and barrage balloons and to
strengthen the anti-aircraft defences to a total of 88 and 40 light guns.
Scapa Flow, as well as receiving RAF cover from the Orkney Islands,
was also to be shielded by aircraft based at Wick, the nearest point on
the mainland, where the airfield was to be enlarged to accommodate

four squadrons.

The real problem was where the fleet should be based while Scapa Flow was being made secure. 'Admiralty opinion,' Churchill noted later, 'favoured the Clyde', this being on the 'safe' side of Scotland, furthest from the enemy, but the Minister for the Coordination of Defence, Lord [formerly Admiral of the Fleet Sir Alfred] Chatfield, was more courageous and urged upon Churchill that it seemed wrong to leave the east coast 'devoid of capital ships'. He found a ready ear in the First Lord. 'It seems to me serious,' Churchill commented, 'for all heavy ships to yield up the North Sea for two and a half days,' the time it would take for the main British forces to sail north-about round Scotland before engaging the enemy off East Anglia. The Firth of Forth, with its 64 guns, was also better protected than the Clyde, with its 24. 'Why then should we choose the Clyde at the cost of uncovering the island?' The C-in-C Home Fleet, too, preferred, unlike Admiral Jellicoe in the First World War, to be nearer the likely battlefield. He favoured Rosyth in the Firth of Forth as, in Churchill's words, 'more suitably placed geographically', even though 'more vulnerable to air attack'. In the end, the ships previously at Scapa Flow were distributed in ports along the west coast of Scotland, while the defences of Rosyth were strengthened to provide a base on the east side, where, as the First Lord observed in a minute of 1 November 1939, 'the strong ships of the fleet can rest in security'.

On Monday 13 November 1939 the first enemy bombs of the war were dropped on British soil – those previously aimed at the fleet had landed in the water – by enemy raiders attacking, for no very obvious reason, the Shetland Isles. No damage was done and the only casualty was a rabbit, which briefly became a national celebrity. Its alleged corpse (some cynics suggested that one dead rabbit looked much like another) was displayed on the stage of the London Palladium, while the audience, somewhat heartlessly, sang 'Run, Rabbit, Run', one of the hit songs of the time.

This was a long way from the knock-out blow which had been expected and by the end of 1939 complacency was widespread. Most of the original evacuees had now returned, but the black-out was still rigorously enforced, petrol had already been rationed and food rationing was due to start, though at first on a small scale, in a few days' time. On the outbreak of war the original militiamen's term of service had been lengthened to 'the duration' and conscription was extended to men aged up to 41. (Ultimately it covered men from 18 to 51, though none over 45 were actually called up, and was also extended to single and childless married women, though the vast majority were permitted to opt, if they wished, for service in essential civilian occupations, especially factory work, rather than the women's forces.) What was lacking was any real sense of direction from the government.

Although the struggle at sea was real enough the American-coined phrase, 'The phoney war', gained general currency, and Churchill himself later described this period as 'The twilight war'. As 1940 began he was already seeking to reduce the numbers tied up in defence of the fleet. On 3 January 1940 he urged the First Sea Lord to consider reducing the number of searchlights, now 108, estimated as necessary for the air defence of Scapa Flow, since 'the Fleet will often be at sea', and the number of troops required to protect the anchorage from ground attack. He put the total needed at 5000, in contrast to the 10,000 to 11,000 now contemplated. Churchill thought the prospect of such a raid extremely remote:

> For a place like Scapa, with all this strong personnel on the spot, parachute landings or raids from U-boats may be considered most unlikely. There is therefore no need to have a battalion [of infantry] in addition to the artillery regiments. The commander should make arrangements to have a sufficient emergency party ready to deal with any such small and improbable contingencies.

As for the risk of a full-scale invasion, since the alarm back in October 1939 a plan, coded-name *Julius Caesar*, had been perfected and this remained in force, with minor changes, until May 1940. *Julius Caesar* was based on the assumption that routine aerial reconnaissance could not be relied upon to detect an invading fleet, and that the British Home Fleet, sheltering on the wrong side of Scotland, could not intervene until a substantial enemy force had got ashore.

The planners estimated, with reasonable accuracy, that the Germans had 1000 transport aircraft available for assault purposes, sufficient to carry 4000 parachutists and another 6000 airborne troops. They could, it was believed, along with simultaneous air attacks on the RAF and Home Fleet, pave the way for a seaborne landing by at least one division, to carry which, it was estimated, 20 transports of 4-5000 tons would be required, plus 25 to 30 escorting destroyers, to cover a crossing lasting 20 hours. The Commander-in-Chief, Home Forces, in January 1940 was General Sir Walter Kirke, a former gunnery officer, now aged 63, an experienced conventionally-minded soldier whose proposals for dealing with airborne troops included using cavalry as well as armoured forces. Kirke believed that if the airborne troops could be defeated the follow-up seaborne assault would be bound to fail, and that to have any chance of success at all the Germans would have to capture a port. The three Commands at risk, Scottish, Northern and Eastern, were therefore ordered to earmark infantry to protect ports in their areas, the numbers required being put at one division each in Scotland and the North, and two in Eastern Command, plus three in reserve. General Kirke's actual forces consisted at this time of nine divisions, one of them armoured, three training divisions and four earmarked for special tasks, like aiding the civil power in the event of massive air raids. The *Julius Caesar* troops were distributed around the coast from near Portsmouth to Invergordon and Scapa Flow, with concentrations behind Harwich, Yarmouth, the Hartlepools and the Firth of Forth, the 2nd Armoured guarding the area behind the Humber estuary. Only training divisions or 'special' divisions were stationed on the western side of the country and south-west of Portsmouth.

By the late spring of 1940 the United Kingdom seemed far more secure than in September 1939. In March the Home Fleet had returned to Scapa Flow and the magnetic mine, which had caused heavy losses since its first appearance in the opening weeks of the war, had been mastered. The number of light anti-aircraft guns in service had more than doubled, that of heavy guns had risen by 20 per cent. The radar chain was complete and 30 German aircraft were already believed to have been shot down – the actual total was 27 – at least one-tenth of those despatched. The Air Officer Commanding, Fighter Command, Air Chief Marshal Sir Hugh [later Lord] Dowding, was already unhappy about the sending of six squadrons of fighters to France, but had 51 available for home defence, not far below the 53 considered necessary.

The overall strategic situation was much less satisfactory. On 4 April 1940 Neville Chamberlain had, disastrously for himself, boasted that Hitler had 'missed the bus'. On 9 April the Germans invaded Norway and occupied Denmark. 'We have been completely outwitted,' Churchill wrote to the First Sea Lord and the nation's indignation increased when a British expeditionary force, which began to land in Norway on 15 April, was decisively defeated. The now discredited Neville Chamberlain was still clinging to office when, in the early hours of Friday 10 May 1940, the Germans launched their long-expected offensive in the West, the classic encircling movement through Belgium towards France being this time accompanied by the invasion of Holland. That morning several members of the Dutch government arrived at the Admiralty, 'haggard and worn, with horror in their eyes', to seek Winston Churchill's help, his ready response being almost his last act as First Lord. At 6 pm that evening he was appointed prime minister and also became Minister of Defence. At 3 am the next morning, Saturday 11 May 1940, he went to bed, to sleep soundly. 'I thought,' he later admitted, 'I knew a good deal about it all, and I was sure that I should not fail.'

40

NO SURRENDER

We shall defend our island whatever the cost may be . . . We shall never surrender.

The prime minister, Winston Churchill, in the House of Commons,
4 June 1940

The nation was brought face to face with the possibility of imminent invasion on Tuesday 14 May 1940. The Germans had that day broken through the French lines at Sedan, and Holland was on the verge of defeat; she formally capitulated next day. Thus when, at 6 pm that evening, the new Secretary of State for War, Sir Anthony Eden [later Lord Avon] broadcast an appeal to men 'not at present engaged in military service' to join a new part-time army it fell on receptive ears:

> We want large numbers of such men in Great Britain, who are British subjects, between the ages of 17 and 65 . . . to come forward now and offer their services . . . The name of the new force which is now to be raised will be 'The Local Defence Volunteers' . . . This name describes its duties in three words . . . You will not be paid, but you will receive a uniform and will be armed.*

The LDV was formed on a false prospectus. Eden had begun his speech by referring to the 'dropping of parachute troops behind the main defensive lines' in Holland and Belgium, but in reality airborne forces had played only a small, if essential, part in the already unfolding pattern of German victory, providing, like the 'fifth column' of traitors supposed to have assisted the enemy advance, a convenient alibi for generals defeated by basically conventional, if brilliantly handled, means. The overwhelming response to Eden's appeal took the War Office by surprise. Would-be recruits had been told to report at their local police stations and eager queues formed at some almost before Eden had finished broadcasting; within 24 hours 250,000 had come forward, by the end of the month about 300,000. The Germans, through their leading English language broadcaster, 'Lord Haw Haw', the renegade Irishman William Joyce, proclaimed the new body illegal:

* For fuller extracts from this speech and a more detailed account of the whole subject see my book, *The Real Dad's Army* (Arrow, 1974).

The preparations which are being made all over England to arm the civilian population for guerilla warfare are contrary to the rules of international law. German official quarters warn the British public and remind them of the fate of the Polish *franc-tireurs* . . . Civilians who take up arms against German soldiers are, under international law, no better than murderers, whether they are priests or bank clerks.

To give the LDV at least the semblance of a uniform its members were issued with armbands, often at first home-made, lettered 'LDV', followed by denim overalls and army-style field-service forage caps. The initial issue largely consisted of the very large or very small sizes the army could most readily spare, and the unflattering result was that the first LDVs could hardly have been a greater contrast in appearance to the resplendent Volunteers of Napoleonic and Victorian times. They were also much worse armed. Some 70,000 rifles were found for those in the most threatened areas, and a public appeal for weapons yielded another 20,000 shotguns, sporting rifles, and such oddities as elephant guns and antique blunderbusses, though for months many LDVs carried nothing more lethal than a pitchfork, a golf club, or a home-made cudgel.

Recruits for the LDV continued to pour in as the news got worse. On 26 May the evacuation of the British army, forced back to Dunkirk, began; on 27 May Belgium surrendered; on 4 June the last of the 200,000 British troops were rescued from the beaches. Most of the army had been saved but at a heavy cost in lost equipment, which included 475 tanks, 38,000 other vehicles, 1000 heavy guns, 400 anti-tank guns, 7000 tons of ammunition, 8000 Bren guns, the main infantry automatic weapon, using standard 0.303-in [7.7-mm] ammunition, and 90,000 rifles. The whole United Kingdom, with invasion an immediate possibility, contained a mere 12,000 Bren guns and fewer than 600,000 rifles. The only essential not lacking was men. Already the army contained 1,650,000 men, the RAF 291,000, the navy 271,000, and the call-up had so far hardly got under way, with only those aged 19 to 27 yet registered for military service. The three services were scheduled to reach a combined strength of 2,600,000 by September and almost 2,900,000 by the end of the year, far outstripping the available arms; during June the factories, working day and night, were expected to add only 2000 Bren guns and 124,000 rifles to the nation's stocks. Supplying the other, heavier or more complicated items, from artillery to wireless sets, would take even longer.

The appearance of un-uniformed, often unarmed, LDVs at home-made roadblocks, or drilling in parks and playgrounds, was only the first of the many signs that summer – the most glorious in living memory, appreciated all the more because of the severe winter – that the country was now visibly preparing for invasion. The great, though groundless, fear at this stage was of treachery within the gates, to pave the way for enemy landings, probably by air, all over the country. As early as 21 May the Dutch Foreign Minister had blamed his country's rapid defeat on parachutists supposed, quite falsely, to have dropped in a variety of disguises: nurses, tramcar conductors, monks and nuns. It was the nuns who caught the popular imagination and soon reports of suspiciously burly figures with army boots and hairy legs beneath their habits were to be heard on all sides. The newly-appointed Commander-in-Chief, Home Forces, of whom more will be said later, gave a lead in credulity, as his diary for 30 May reveals:

> Fifth Column reports coming in from everywhere. A man with an armband on and a swastika pulled up near an important aerodrome in the Southern Command. Important telegraph poles marked, suspicious men moving at night all over the country . . . I put piquets [sic] on all over the place tonight. Perhaps we shall catch some swine.

To frustrate the machinations of such malcontents, on 31 May the removal of all signposts was ordered and the blacking-out of all place names, even on shopfronts, war memorials, station platforms and in telephone kiosks, a measure which did no harm to the Germans but vastly inconvenienced loyal citizens. (A Punch cartoon a few weeks later showed a small boy saying to a clearly lost Army officer, 'I'll tell nobody where anywhere is.') Around the same time Local Invasion Committees were formed to coordinate preparations in each area. As finally formalised, a little later, the Committees were required to plan emergency feeding arrangements, identify disused wells that might be brought back into use to provide a water supply, list the number and location of useful articles like wheelbarrows and stretchers, and, above all, see that the government's proclaimed policy for the civilian population, 'Stay Put', was observed. If evacuation was thought necessary it would be along previously identified routes, of which our supposedly advancing soldiers would stay clear.*

On Tuesday 4 June 1940 the new prime minister formally put the country under notice to prepare for invasion in a speech to the House of Commons:

> We are told that Herr Hitler has a plan for invading the British Isles. This has often been thought of before. There has never been a period in all these long centuries . . . when an absolute guarantee against invasion, still less, against serious raids, could have been given to our people . . . That chance . . . has excited and befooled the imag-

---

* For a fuller account of anti-invasion preparations as they affected the civil population, see the chapter entitled 'Anticipation' in my If Britain Had Fallen (Hutchinson, 1972).

ination of many Continental tyrants . . . We must never forget the solid assurances of sea power and those which belong to air power if it can be properly exercised.

One of the most famous of all his perorations followed:

We shall defend our island whatever the cost may be. We shall fight on the beaches, we shall fight on the landing grounds, we shall fight in the fields and in the streets, we shall fight in the hills; we shall never surrender.

'Rhetoric,' Churchill himself insisted, 'was no guarantee of survival.' But his speeches, whether over the air, though he disliked broadcasting, or in print, were an important factor in sustaining the nation's high morale that summer and unlike its predecessor in Napoleonic times, the government was able to address the citizen directly through both media. In June it began to distribute to every household a leaflet on what to do *If the INVADER comes:**

The Germans threaten to invade Great Britain. If they do so they will be driven out by our Navy, our Army and our Air Force.

Uncompromising, if somewhat unrealistic, advice was given on what to do if nevertheless the enemy did appear on your doorstep:

DO NOT GIVE ANY GERMAN ANYTHING. DO NOT TELL HIM ANYTHING . . . THINK BEFORE YOU ACT. BUT THINK ALWAYS OF YOUR COUNTRY BEFORE YOU THINK OF YOURSELF.

On 8 June the last British troops left Norway and on 10 June Italy declared war on Great Britain and France. On 13 June it was ordered that the church bells should not be rung again except to announce an invasion, a decision described by *Ringing World* as 'a stunning blow to ringing'. On 17 June the last gap in the hostile shore now confronting the British Isles between the Seine and the Pyrenees was filled, when France capitulated. 'Well, now it is England against Germany and I don't envy them their job,' wrote the head of Fighter Command to the prime minister that 'Black Monday'. On the following day, Tuesday, 18 June, the anniversary of Waterloo, Churchill made in the House, and subsequently broadcast, the classic speech which added at least two famous phrases to the language:

The Battle of France is over . . . The Battle of Britain is about to begin . . . The whole fury and might of the enemy must very soon be turned on us. Hitler knows that he will have to break us in this island or lose the war . . . Let us therefore brace ourselves to our duty and so bear ourselves that if the British Empire and its Com-

* The use of capitals, etc is reproduced here as in the original.

monwealth lasts for a thousand years men will still say, 'This was their finest hour.'

On 10 May, a Home Defence Executive had been set up under the chairmanship of the Commander-in-Chief, Home Forces, General Kirke, with representatives from the Ministry of Home Security and the service departments. On 27 May General Kirke was replaced by General Sir Edmund [later Field Marshal Lord] Ironside. He moved that day into his new headquarters, at Kneller Hall, Twickenham, just west of London, which he described as 'the most awful Victorian country house'. Already he took a highly defeatist view of the outcome of the expected battle. On 7 June, three days after Churchill had promised to 'fight on the beaches', the C-in-C Home Forces was issuing instructions for his earlier diaries to be sent to Canada. 'There is,' he confided to the current journal, 'no use their remaining in Hingham [his family home in Norfolk]* to be overrun.'

Good grounds existed for the defending general's pessimism. For the defence of more than 400 miles [640 km] of threatened coastline he could call on only one weak and incompletely equipped armoured division, and 15 inexperienced infantry divisions averaging less than half their establishment of 15,500, giving them a total fighting strength of 116,000. All the units were desperately under-equipped, with only about one-sixth of their entitlement of field-guns, and many of these were obsolete 18-pounders [8-kg guns] or ancient 4.5-in [11.4-cm] howitzers, instead of the modern 25-pounders [11.3-kg guns] left behind by the BEF. A return on 1 June 1940 showed a total of 963 tanks in the country, but many of these were awaiting repair or classed as obsolescent and 160 of them were 'infantry tanks' armed only with machine-guns. Anti-tank rifles were desperately scarce. Only one division, in Eastern Command, had its full establishment of 307. The 1st London Division, manning the south-east corner of Kent between the Isle of Sheppey and Rye, which covered more than 70 miles [112 km] of coastline, had only 23 field guns, no anti-tank guns, no medium machine-guns and only 47 anti-tank rifles of its authorised 307.

The basis of Ironside's defensive strategy was to delay the enemy while he assembled his best units, such as they were, for a counter-attack. The main position to be held at all costs was the 'GHQ line', designed to protect London and the industrial and northern Midlands. The GHQ line covered about 400 miles [640 km], before its later extension northwards via Newcastle to Edinburgh. The route worked out in early June 1940 ran from Middlesbrough inland to just west of Richmond in Yorkshire, and then, via two overlapping sections, to a point midway between Hull and Leeds, and then to the north-east corner of

---

* Not 'Higham' as stated by Wills, p. 9, an important difference. East Anglia might be occupied by an ultimately unsuccessful invader, but the loss of Higham, in Yorkshire, would imply a total defeat.

the Wash. It was resumed at the south-west corner, and then extended through Cambridge to Maidstone, before swinging due west to Aldershot and then north to around Henley, where a spur ran on northwards to near Aylesbury to protect London from the rear, while the main line ran due west to the Bristol Channel and covered Bristol itself.*

The GHQ Line was intended to provide a continuous anti-tank barrier, making extensive use of natural features like rivers and canals, the gaps between them being filled by specially dug anti-tank ditches. The basic design was V-shaped, 5 ft 6 in [1.7 m] deep, and 12 ft [3.6 m] wide at ground level, with a rampart of excavated earth on the 'enemy' side, which doubled the resulting drop.

Where the ground was unsuitable for a ditch, other types of obstacles were erected, and the designs for these, too, rapidly became standardised, though they were built on site, in a variety of shapes: cubes, cylinders, pyramids, elongated blocks five feet [1.5 m] by three feet [0.9 m], with triangular ends tapering to a ridge three feet [0.9 m] high, known as 'coffins', and, equally inappropriately named and also now rare, 'buoys', consisting of two concrete cones about six feet [1.8 m] apart, on bases linked by a steel bar. The commonest type, still to be seen in many places, were cube shaped, with each surface either 3ft 6 in [3.2 m] or 5 ft [1.5 m] long. There were also many stone cylinders, 2ft 6 in [0.76 m] or 3 ft [0.9 m] high and 2 ft [0.6 m] wide, and pyramids, tapering to a slightly flattened point 2 ft [0.6 m] above a base either 4 ft [1.2 m] or 3 ft [0.9 m] square. These last were known ingloriously as 'pimples'; the Germans and French, from whom the British had borrowed the design, described them, more grandiosely, as 'dragons' teeth'.

To supplement the concrete blocks much use was made of rail barriers made of steel, consisting of sharp-angled triangles bolted to a metal base. A common experience that summer was to have to wait while a bus or car negotiated the successive groups of blocks or angle irons erected on alternate sides of the road to slow down an enemy.

To protect the anti-tank barriers, and hold off infantry as well as armoured attack, the GHQ Line incorporated a large number of pillboxes. By 1918, as mentioned earlier, it had been found that a concrete pillbox could survive a direct hit by an eight-inch [20.3-cm] shell and German experience in Poland in 1939, betrayed by a captured report, confirmed that the standard German high explosive shell remained ineffective against reinforced concrete. Even before the new C-in-C Home Forces had worked out his strategy, pillboxes and similar structures were going up along the coast and at threatened points inland. In

* Detailed records of the line have not survived and none of the published maps is wholly satisfactory. The map in my own *If Britain Had Fallen* follows that in the official history (Collier, p. 128), but, as Wills, p. vii, points out, Collier's map is itself inaccurate. The map on p. 487 of the present book mainly follows that on Wills p. 10.

June the Directorate of Fortifications at the War Office issued speci-
fications for 13 different types, though Commands were free to modify
the details to suit their particular needs.

Much the most common form of pillbox was the hexagonal (Type F
W 3/22 in official documents), with walls eight feet [2.4 m] long and 15
in [38 cm] thick, and a solid, reinforced concrete roof. It provided
accommodation for six men, five supposedly armed with a light
machine-gun and one with a rifle. Another version, intended for eight
men, had walls ten feet [3 m] long, a 'Y'-shaped internal wall and external walls up to 3 ft 6 in [1.1 m] thick, to enable it to resist shellfire.
The largest pattern generally built at this time was designed to house
the two-pounder [0.9-kg] anti-tank guns, now too precious to risk, as
intended, in the open field, and it could, by removing its wheels, be
converted into an emplaced weapon. Such buildings (F W 3/28s to the
experts) can still be seen near many coasts and river crossings. Also to
be found, often overlooking beaches, are gun emplacements for the
heavier six-pounder [2.7 kg] field gun, identifiable by the curved, low
front wall, and the solid stone canopy above, to give overhead protection against counter-battery fire. Being roofed in, it was difficult for
the pillbox to be used in an anti-aircraft role, and to overcome this
problem some pillboxes were designed to have a Bren, or the heavier
Lewis, gun mounted on their roof.

The fewer the openings in a pillbox the less vulnerable to attack it
was, but the inevitable result was poor visibility and various types
offering the capacity for all-round fire were devised, often by commercial firms with experience in the concrete business. The simplest was
really a concrete pipe, set in the ground on end, the Norcom, six feet
[1.8 m] across, and four inches [10.2 cm] thick, the concrete being
poured on site. Another version had walls 12-ins [0.3 m] thick and six
inches [15 cms] of concrete to form the roof. Excluding levelling the
site it cost only £30. Sunken pillboxes, since they interfered less than
the conventional types with the landing of aircraft, were often used for
airfield defence. The equivalent of the famous Moncrieff Disappearing
Gun was the five-man Pickett-Hamilton Counterbalance Fort, which
cost around £250 and could, by the use of jacks, be hoisted up from
lying flush with the ground into a firing position within only four
seconds. Later a hydraulic version was designed, raised by compressed
air.

General Ironside hoped to halt the invader long before he reached the
GHQ Line on a series of stop-lines, some parallel to the GHQ Line but
many at right-angles to it, as part of the general strategy of making
enemy movement difficult. Ironside's first line of defence, however,
was what he described as an 'extended crust' along the beaches, with
rows of anti-tank obstacles and pillboxes of the types already
described. The beaches were also heavily mined, with barbed wire

erected on the landward side of the minefields.

For a protracted, serious attempt the Germans would need to acquire a port quickly and though the major ports already had reasonably solid defences the lesser ones were barely protected at all. A series of 'Emergency Coast Batteries' was accordingly equipped with guns from four-inch [10-cm] to six-inch [15-cm] in calibre, scrapped by the navy after being removed from ships after the First World War but happily hoarded for a rainy day, which had now arrived. Since 1918, however, coastal artillery emplacements had become more elaborate. Then the fashion had favoured open mountings, with only a low parapet, but with the advent of the low-flying aeroplane, casemates, with a solid roof and front wall pierced only by the firing aperture, had returned to favour. No fewer than 153 such batteries, each consisting of three guns and manned by around 140 officers and men, were constructed between July and December, another heavy burden for the suddenly hard-pressed construction industry.

Although he was presiding over the greatest programme of fortification building since the days of Palmerston, Ironside was under no illusion that earth and concrete alone could keep out the invader. 'We cannot,' he wrote on 1 June, 'make the whole place a fortress, but we can probably canalise the routes of attack.' He was concerned that this policy should not lead to what was soon known as 'Maginot-mindedness'. 'There must,' he told his senior officers in an Order of the Day on 11 June, 'be no question of cowering behind an obstacle . . . waiting to be attacked. The enemy must be located instantly, isolated and attacked before he can gather strength.' The prime minister was unenthusiastic about the building programme for other reasons. On 25 June he complained to the Secretary of State for War that many troops were being denied training in order to build fortifications. 'I found it extremely difficult to see even a single battalion on parade in East Anglia during my visit,' he commented. 'All the labour necessary should be found from civilian sources.' He considered it 'shocking' that only 57,000 civilians were being employed for this purpose and, when three days later this total was reduced even further to 40,000, demanded, 'Pray let me have a full explanation.'*

The amount of effort involved was prodigious. Around London alone nearly 100 miles [160 km] of anti-tank ditches were being dug and in the far north, where there were no anti-tank guns at all, 'every mechanical digger in Scotland,' to quote the RE Lieut.-Colonel at Command Headquarters, numbering around 170, was 'used to dig the 10-30 miles [32-48 km] continuous anti-tank ditch across the Fife Plain.' In the South, in addition to actual excavation, one section of the GHQ Line protecting Bristol near Glastonbury could only be built by

* Churchill, *Second World War*, Vol. II, p. 151 and p. 565. The true figure seems to have been 150,000. See Mallory and Ottar, p. 135.

drilling and blasting through solid limestone. Near Taunton the swing bridges over the Canal were removed but had to be replaced by easily-demolished baulks of timber to allow farmers access to their land; along the Kent and Avon Canal, near Devizes, barges were used to ferry heavy materials to inaccessible sites.

Building pillboxes to cover the tank stop-lines required even more work, largely civilian. One RE general found himself that May asking a large contractor if he could build 200 pillboxes along 50 miles [80 km] of coast in the next three weeks. In Southern Command, the only one for which details have survived, the GHQ 'Red' Line covering the 68 miles [109 km] from Great Somerford, near Malmesbury in Wiltshire to Tilehurst, near Reading in Berkshire, consisted not merely of 17 miles [27 km] of anti-tank ditches and 11 anti-tank emplacements, but 186 of the more solid, shell-proof type of pillboxes. The 58 miles [93 km] of the 'Blue' sector, running from near Tilehurst to Bradford-on Avon, involved building 5 miles [8 km] of ditch, 15 anti-tank emplace-ments, and 170 shellproof pillboxes. Stopline 'Green', covering the 91 miles [145 km] from Highbridge, on the coast near Burnham-on-Sea, to Freshford, just north of Trowbridge, and thence via Stroud to a point six miles south-west of Gloucester, required 20 miles [32 km] of anti-tank ditches and 319 pillboxes, 271 of them of the more solid shell-proof type. The beach defences which the Command was required to provide included 1052 pillboxes, 247 of them shellproof.

Equal feats of engineering were called for by other Commands, especially Eastern, which contained five forward stop-lines as well as a long stretch of the GHQ Line itself. Everywhere the building trade suffered a sudden demand for labour, both skilled and unskilled. Although the number of unemployed nationally had dropped sharply since the start of the war[*], on the coast evacuation and other factors had disrupted normal life and deprived many people of their usual work.

One man then employed as a joiner in the Hull area witnessed the re-sult:

> The Labour Exchange asked for volunteers to go constructing pill-boxes and tank defences . . . All sorts of riff-raff came. Some who thought a drawing was something you see on a lavatory wall. The 'all-sorts' included trawlermen, fish-bobbers, labourers and various tradesmen. Twenty per cent [of the labourers on the site] . . . were experienced in building and one in placing reinforcing rods and shuttering . . . As for concrete mixing, I think we all took that as a matter that any silly b—— knows how to do.

[*] Fleming, p. 88, fn 1, says that there were 'throughout the summer . . . something like 1 million unemployed', but the official *Statistical Digest of the War*, p. 8, gives the total for June as 645,000, of whom 211,000 were women, not considered suitable for building work.

Each morning that summer a small army of unlikely looking labourers could be seen in many coastal resorts setting off, carrying spades and axes, for their appointed beach, like ninth-century peasants on their way to fortify one of King Alfred's *burhs*:*

This was the daily routine of one man then living in Essex:

I was on the defences of the coast; first on tide-work, erecting long iron spikes set in concrete on the beach at Jaywick [i.e. Jaywick Sands, just down the coast from Clacton]. Being below the high-tide mark, what a race we had to beat the incoming tide. Working all hours of the day and night, by moonlight often enough, to finish our section, with the youngest lads 15 years of age to one glorious old-age pensioner of 82, who inspired us all with his tireless energy, working in his bare feet and legs in the cold sea water . . . trousers rolled above his knees.

My memory of that period was one of long hours, work, poor conditions, lack of warm food in isolated parts of the country or on the beach and the dreadful tiredness we suffered without honour or glory. We were never mentioned.

A seven-day 60-hour week was commonplace at this time and, especially for those not used to manual labour, the work was extremely hard. Machines, apart from the universal portable concrete mixers – a single octagonal pillbox required five tons of cement and 20 cubic yards [15.3 cubic metres] of ballast – were few. Foundations were dug out by pick and shovel, concrete was poured into frames made on the site and metal reinforcing rods added to the walls and roof by hand. At Runswick Bay and Kettleness on the north-east coast, five miles [8 km] beyond Whitby, one builder remembers cement and other materials being loaded into sandbags before being conveyed down the narrow and dangerous paths to the beach by a human chain, while water carts had to be filled at streams inland and then manhandled to the cliff edge to fill hosepipes and buckets.

In the south-east, after the Battle of Britain had started, the work could be dangerous as well as exhausting. The Essex builder quoted earlier recalls seeing three of his workmates lying on the ground, huddled beneath a sheet of corrugated iron from which their feet protruded, as bombs came down nearby, while at least one workman was killed in action, at St Osyth near Clacton, caught by machine-gun bullets as he struggled to finish work on a pillbox top before the concrete set.

So vast was the construction programme now undertaken that the Director of Fortifications and Works distributed a note in early July urging *Economy of Cement in Defence Posts*, which recommended using brick cladding, or earth and rubble backing, to reduce the amount of

* See *Defending the Island*, pp. 106-7.

concrete needed. Shortages also developed in timber, as in the days of sailing ships, though England's 'wooden walls' now consisted of the frames built on site to hold the liquid concrete as it set. Enterprising builders cut up scaffolding planks for the purpose and at Brookwood in Surrey railings collected during the recent 'scrap for salvage' drive were used in place of reinforcing rods. At Middle Wallop, Hants, the 'swords into ploughshares' tradition was even more decisively reversed, as anti-tank obstacles and pillboxes incorporated bed-springs patriotically supplied by the Slumberland Company.

With sunny days and, thanks to double summer-time, long light evenings on their side, some firms achieved a remarkable output. A Farnham firm, assigned 24 pillboxes as part of the 'Blue' sector of the GHQ Line, brought men in each day from up to 20 miles [32 km] away in four gangs, which created a pillbox 'production line'. The first group would excavate a site and instal the concrete base, to be followed by the bricklayers and carpenters who built the shell, then by the gang who filled this with concrete, and finally, once the walls were dry, by the roof construction team.

If the army engineers, who placed the contracts, and the building industry, notorious in peacetime for unreliability, both rose to the challenge of the times the same could hardly be said of Department F W 6 at the War Office. Any contractor wishing to tender for a contract was required to obtain the relevant form, price 5d [2p], and attach a 6d [2½p] stamp to make it valid. While carrying out the resulting work he was likely to be urged to make haste and to include last-minute alterations considered necessary by the army officers on the spot regardless of cost, but once the job was finished it was a different story. One man at Thorney, near Peterborough, had on 21 June 1940 begun to build 21 pillboxes, of three different types, with associated road-blocks, even before the official contract arrived, and had then worked a 12-hour day, seven days a week, for the next five weeks. When he finally presented his bill, for £2852 2s 8d [£2582.13], the War Office attempted to reduce it to £1211, 'remembering that this work had necessarily to be carried out in a time of National Emergency in the defence of our Country'. This argument, however, worked both ways and the contractor concerned, having pointed out that, 'We did not hesitate when called upon,' finally got his money, though not until July 1941.

Henry VIII had dealt with the acquisition of land for his forts by a simple, lordly, Act of Parliament, and under Regulation No. 50 of the Defence Regulations 1939 George VI's government was empowered to enter or build on any privately owned land, providing compensation was paid on a recognised scale. The amounts involved were modest: for having to accommodate a pillbox in a field no more than 5s [25p] per annum, and for the enclosure of two acres [0.81 hectares] by barbed wire £2. Some works, however, provided greater problems.

How, for example, did one value the loss to the owners of a pier in which the army had made a large hole when the only 'trippers' likely to use it were German soldiers? Dredging a river to make it a more effective tank-trap could also have unforeseen consequences. One angler near Warminster claimed that his fishing had thereby been spoiled and sought £50 damages.

In one respect at least the great building programme could not be faulted. Camouflage Officers, often professional artists in civilian life, were at last able to make full use of their hitherto wasted talents. Among them was the leading theatrical designer, Oliver Messel, who went to immense pains to enable the pillboxes of the stop-line near Taunton to blend into the landscape. On the canal a pillbox was, under his directions, transformed into a workman's hut; in a field one became a straw stack; at Ilminster station a third disappeared beneath an apparent heap of coal, with wheelbarrow and shovel to complete the illusion. Messel even obtained from Elstree Studios some 'genuine' imitation stone, consisting of plaster on canvas, and with this created a lodge, apparently gatehouse to a large estate, where a pillbox commanded an important road. Other pillboxes suffered a transformation, once finished, into car park attendants' huts, summer houses, and storage dumps beside railway lines. Advertisement hoardings, which could be of any size one wished and placed anywhere, provided useful cover for a pillbox. (One, at Woodbridge in Suffolk, proclaimed the attractions of the 'Hotel Continental', which promised: 'Warm reception for visiting troops'.) At Folkestone the humorists of the 725 Construction Company, RE, provided several surprisingly solid 'Bathing Cubicles' on the front and an equally misleading 'Public Convenience' on the path leading from the harbour, the two 'shielded' entrances being duly labelled 'Ladies' and 'Gentlemen'.

The great building programme launched during May had, by late July, produced some 8000 finished pillboxes, about one-quarter of them of the more solid, shellproof, type, while another 17,000 were under construction or planned. The number of anti-tank blocks is unknown but must have been even larger. An unknown soldier in the Green Howards inscribed in the wet concrete of one four-foot [1.2-m] cube at Taddiford Gap on Hordle Cliffe in Sussex the no doubt heartfelt sentiment: '6th Bn, Ex-BEF. 31 July 1940. The last block.'

Reminders of the past could be seen everywhere that summer. One pillbox, suitably camouflaged, was built into the Roman walls of Pevensey Castle. The LDV patrolled the walls of Southsea Castle, built by Henry VIII to keep out the French. There were troops stationed at Landguard Fort, which in 1667 had beaten off the Dutch. All round the east and south-east coasts pillboxes were erected within a few yards of Martello towers, built to keep out Napoleon, and others overlooked the Royal Military Canal, now transformed into an anti-tank ditch. Around Portsmouth, Palmerston's great forts along Portsdown Hill, which had never fired a shot in anger, had a new lease of life as barracks and storage depots or as sites for anti-aircraft guns.

The author of *Parachutes over Britain*, one of the paperback booklets on irregular warfare rushed into print that summer, lamented that while 'In Spain almost any villager can tell you the exact street corner where barricades have always been raised in the past . . . our history . . . gives us very little information on the tactics of street fighting.' However, the peace-loving English did their best and, until the troops and builders arrived, roadblocks made of old farm wagons, tar barrels and broken machinery appeared on many a village corner. One of the most effective consisted of an ancient steam-roller, while at Margate disused wheeled bathing machines were trundled into position on a road behind the sea-front. A common form of early road-block was a tree trunk pivoted at one end on a concrete block and fastened to a wheel at the other, which would be left by the roadside till required.

As well as parachutists, the Germans had used troop-carrying aircraft in the Low Countries and glider-borne infantry, and a second wave of building was now directed towards preventing such landings in England. As early as 12 May Professor Frederick Lindemann [later Lord Cherwell], Churchill's trusted Scientific Adviser, had pointed out that parachute troops 'are probably not a great danger unless they are rapidly reinforced by troop-carriers landed in large fields'. He recommended that holes be dug in 'all flat fields more than 400 yards [366 m] long' and Churchill approving the idea – 'Let this be done today' – on 1 July, extended it: 'If they are large enough for a troop carrier to land . . .', he ruled, 'fields under crops should *not* be excepted from this treatment.' He agreed, too, that the area affected should be extended from a radius of five miles [8 km] from vulnerable points to ten [16 km]. Two days later one of Churchill's staff complained that 'The Ministers of Agriculture and Home Security are putting all kinds of obstacles in the way of action, not German aircraft,' but a great deal was nevertheless achieved. Wigwam-like tripods of poles, rows of old cars, and rusty ploughs and harrows were placed on parks, sports grounds and other open spaces. The ideal barrier consisted of rows of heavy posts, sunk 4 ft 6 in [1.4 m] deep in the earth, securely anchored enough to tear off the wing of a glider attempting a landing. 'The work was extremely hard . . . ,' wrote one civilian unused to manual labour who volunteered to help, 'but exerted a powerful fascination. At last we were permitted to do something for the country.'

By early July no one could doubt from the transformation of every town and village in the eastern and southern half of the country, that the government was in earnest about resisting invasion and a new spirit was observable everywhere. It is encapsulated in the notice observed in an unidentified pillbox, signed by its commander, a corporal:

Hitler has taken Poland,
Hitler has taken Denmark and Norway,
Hitler has taken Holland, Belgium and France,
Hitler will not take this pillbox!

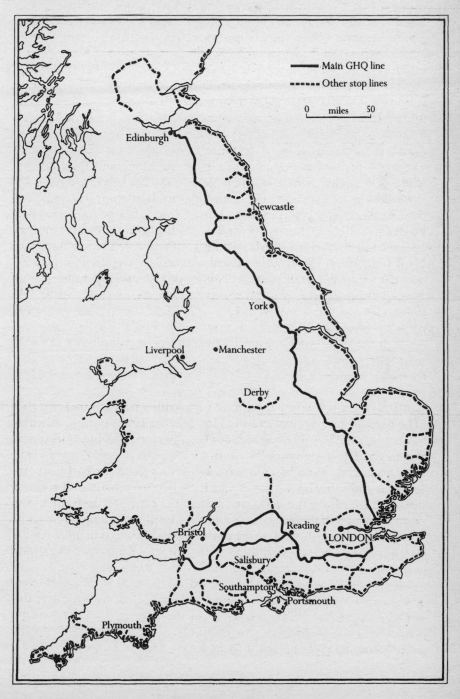

Defence Lines, 1940

41

AN EXCEPTIONALLY DARING UNDERTAKING

The invasion of Britain is an exceptionally daring undertaking.

Adolf Hitler to Admiral Raeder, 21 July 1940

Until July 1940 the Germans had given no serious attention to the problem of invading England. On 23 May 1939, when Hitler had told his generals of his plan to attack Poland, he had already confidently predicted the defeat and occupation of the Low Countries and France. 'Britain,' he told his deferential audience, 'can then be blockaded from western France at close quarters by the *Luftwaffe*, while the navy with their submarines can extend the range of the blockade.'

Nevertheless on 13 December 1939, 'The Commander-in-Chief of the Army . . .', the German navy learned, 'has ordered an examination of the possibility of a landing in England . . . in a study to be called *North-West.*' The resulting plan resembled those so often drafted by pre-war English alarmists, with the east coast between the Wash and the Thames singled out for attack. The main landings, made simultaneously by sea and air, would be at Yarmouth and Lowestoft, and would involve an infantry division, the 7th Parachute Division, to be followed by other airborne units, and – a nice old-fashioned touch – a brigade of cyclists. Another infantry division would land simultaneously at Dunwich and in Hollesley Bay, between Felixstowe and Orford Ness, and two more, as a diversion, north of the Humber, with Leeds as a possible objective. A second wave, of two armoured, one motorised and one infantry division would follow, making a total of eight to be delivered by sea in the first two waves.

This prospect clearly alarmed the Naval Staff, who commented on the proposals on 4 January 1940:

The transport required for the forces specified by the General Staff amounts to about 400 medium-sized steamers, with in addition a large collection of auxiliary vessels of the most varied nature, some of which must first be constructed . . . Assembly of the ships will be difficult . . . The time in which to prepare the transport ships is proposed as about three months . . . but this estimate presupposes that at least one year previously certain measures had been taken in the dockyards.

The *Luftwaffe* General Staff, aware of how easily lumbering troop-carriers and gliders could be shot down, was equally sceptical, as its response to the army's proposals, sent on 30 December 1939, makes clear:

The airborne landing planned will run into the strongest point of the enemy air defence, which it will not be possible to eliminate . . . The planned operation can only be considered therefore under conditions of absolute air superiority . . . The proposed transportation by sea is continually subject to enemy activity . . . A combined operation with a landing in England as its object must be rejected.

On 21 May, the day after the German armies had reached the Channel coast, Admiral Raeder discussed 'in private with the Führer,' the Naval Staff war diary recorded, 'the possibility of a later landing in England.' On 27 May the Chief of the Naval Staff Operations Division, Admiral Fricke, circulated for discussion his *Studie England*, a totally new invasion plan. This favoured the south-east and east coast between Portland and Great Yarmouth and was based on the new situation, which left the Germans able to embark troops along the whole coastline as far south as Cherbourg. Fricke's plan stressed that the RAF must first be rendered powerless. 'The effectiveness of our own small fleet,' he candidly reminded his readers, 'cannot and will not be great.'

With the campaign in France still in progress the navy began, from 31 May, to make active preparations for an operation not yet ordered. Bases already captured were earmarked for use and the collection of suitable craft, including inland tugs and motor-boats, followed the occupation of each fresh district. On 6 June the possible use of heavy coastal artillery to bar the Straits of Dover began to be examined and around the 9th a detailed study of the English coast, especially the area from the Wash to the Isle of Wight, was put in hand. The first preparations, allowing for the replacement of wind by petrol and wood by steel, were not very different from Napoleon's. There was the same demand for small boats, and for novel weapons to take the enemy by surprise. Light 50-mph [80-km per hour] craft, powered by aircraft engines, of which much was hoped, failed to stand up to their sea-trials, but a submersible tank which crawled along the sea-bed, steered through a periscope, and 'breathed' through a chimney-like tube, seemed more promising. This 'war tortoise', later given the more martial name of 'war crocodile', resembled a rectangular sectioned concrete sewer pipe, 90 ft [27.4 m] long, 20 ft [6.1 m] wide, and 12 ft [3.6 m] high. It was supposed to crawl along the sea-bed on caterpillar tracks and then lumber up the shore to discharge 200 fully equipped

men. Though the idea was taken seriously, none ever seems to have
been produced.

Britain had been expected to make peace when France fell but it
rapidly became clear that this was not going to happen. On 20 June,
three days after the French surrender and two days after Churchill's
'finest hour' speech, Raeder discussed the new situation with Hitler.
An immediate invasion was clearly not feasible. The German army,
always dependent on thorough pre-planning and preparation, was not
ready for such an operation and only 45 seaworthy barges suitable for
beach landing had yet been assembled. Hitler and the armed forces,
however, rapidly came to share the view expressed by a senior official
of the German Foreign Office on 30 June that, 'Britain will probably
need one more demonstration of our military strength before she gives
in.' On 2 July the *Führer* authorised that start of formal planning of an
invasion by the three high commands and on 12 July, having consulted
them, his personal military adviser, General Alfred Jodl, set down his
modestly entitled *First Thoughts on a Landing in England*:

> In the Channel we can substitute command of the air for the naval
> supremacy which we do not possess and the sea crossing is short
> there . . . The landing must therefore take place in the form of a river
> crossing in force on a broad front . . . The role of artillery will fall to
> the *Luftwaffe*; the first wave of landing troops must be very strong;
> and, in place of bridging operations, a sea lane completely secure
> from naval attacks must be established in the Dover Straits.

On 13 July Hitler, at his Austrian mountain retreat, the *Berghof*, discussed the proposals with the Army Commander-in-Chief, General
von Brauchitsch and his Chief of Staff, Colonel-General Franz Halder.
Both, perhaps reflecting Hitler's own change of heart, displayed increased enthusiasm for the idea and on Tuesday 16 July 1940 Hitler
issued his *Directive No. 16, Preparations for a Landing Operation against
England*:

> As England, in spite of her hopeless military situation, still shows no
> sign of willingness to come to terms, I have decided to prepare, and
> if necessary to carry out, a landing operation against her. The aim of
> this operation is to eliminate Great Britain as a base from which war
> against Germany can be continued, and, if it should be necessary, to
> occupy the country completely.

Spectacularly successful though he had been, Hitler's heart was never
in *Operation Sealion*, as it was now named. 'On land I am a hero, at sea I
am a coward,' he once told Admiral Raeder, and only three days after
issuing Directive No. 16 he used an appearance in front of the Reichstag to remind the British government of his desire for peace.

Mr Churchill ought perhaps, for once, to believe me when I prophesy that a great Empire will be destroyed – an Empire which it was never my intention to destroy or even to harm . . . In this hour, I feel it to be my duty before my own conscience to appeal once more to reason and common sense in Great Britain . . . I can see no reason why this war must go on.

Hitler's 'Last Appeal to Reason', as it became known, was not so much rejected as ignored. 'I do not propose to say anything in reply to Herr Hitler's speech, not being on speaking terms with him,' Churchill told his staff and Churchill's private secretary, reflecting Downing Street opinion, commented in his diary: 'It looks as if the German military authorities are becoming doubtful about their ability to invade us.' This was true: Hitler, occasionally a maniac but no fool, was well aware of the emerging problems and on 21 July he shared his anxieties with Admiral Raeder:

> The invasion of Britain is an exceptionally daring undertaking, because even if the way is short this is not just a river crossing, but the crossing of a sea which is dominated by the enemy . . . Operational surprise cannot be expected; a defensively prepared and utterly determined enemy face us and dominates the sea area which we must use . . . The prerequisites are complete mastery of the air, the operational use of powerful artillery in the Straits of Dover and protection by minefields. The time of the year is an important factor, too . . . If it is not certain that preparations can be completed by the beginning of September, other plans must be considered.*

The initial target date was 15 August, but on 29 July, the Naval Staff warned that, to satisfy the necessary conditions of moon and tide, the earliest feasible period was around the end of September. At a major conference on 31 July, at which the heads of both the German High Command and the army were present, Admiral Raeder seized the opportunity to instruct them in some of the disagreeable facts of maritime life. To launch the assault at the traditional hour, dawn, meant crossing at night, when aerial reconnaissance to detect the movement of British warships towards the Channel would be impossible. But 'large numbers of slow, unwieldy transport units concentrated in a small space, mixed with motor-boats of the most varied types, and escorted by light units of the Navy . . . make it necessary to have a certain amount of light for navigational reasons.' Then the tides had to be considered. 'A landing at high tide,' though it made disembarkation easier, 'has the disadvantage that craft are grounded and immobile for about twelve hours.' He favoured landing 'about two hours after high tide' and making the crossing as a full moon was giving way to its last

* The text of this important statement is a combination of that given by Bullock, pp. 594-5 and Wheatley, p. 43, which complement each other. The latter book is the outstanding authority on the whole subject and I have drawn heavily on it for this chapter.

quarter. This argued for the period 19-26 September; the earlier alternative, 20-26 August, was now unattainable. But Raeder made no secret of his opinion that, 'The best time for the operation, all things considered, would be May 1941.'

Raeder's hesitation clearly echoed Hitler's own doubts, and the *Führer's* ruling left his options open:

An attempt must be made to prepare the operation for 15 September 1940. The decision as to whether the operation is to take place in September or is to be postponed until May 1941 will be delayed until after the Air Force has made concentrated attacks on southern England for one week.

Orders embodying these decisions were issued on the following day and apart from the *Luftwaffe* offensive, which will be described later, intense preparations by both the other services now began. The original grandiose dreams of landing 40 divisions had now shrunk to a more realistic 13, i.e. about 260,000 men* n the first wave, to be followed by a second once the original landing craft had returned to collect it.

Raeder's staff estimated that they would require 1722 barges, 1161 motor-boats, 471 tugs and 155 transports. By stripping Europe's rivers and canals of most of their craft, a large proportion of these – for example, 386 of the 471 tugs needed – were got together. The river barges had a capacity of 1300 tons, those from canals one of only 500-800 tons but a conveniently shallow 6 feet [1.8 m] draught, and in both types concrete floors were installed and the bows converted into collapsible ramps down which men and vehicles could charge ashore. Few barges were self-propelled, and it was planned that some would be pushed by two small minesweepers attached to their stern, though the resulting hybrid would be unmanoeuvrable and have a maximum speed of a mere four knots [4.6 mph; 7.2 km per hour].

The sea was totally unfamiliar to most German soldiers and even the existence of the tides came as a surprise. The commander of 38 Corps, having gone swimming with his ADC and driver, was astonished when 'the waves suddenly started lapping round our Mercedes on the beach' and they had to obtain 'a tractor to tow it out of the incoming tide'. A Mountain Division, ordered to parade at the same time and place each day for swimming lessons, was equally amazed to find on the second day that the sea was no longer where it had been on the first. The troops also practised going on board their intended transports. Horses as well as men were involved in the rehearsals, for only

* This is the figure given by Fleming, p. 243, and assumes the German divisions (a) had the same establishment on paper as the British and (b) were up to strength, which the British certainly were not. See also Wheatley, p. 40, which refers to 'three divisions' and to '90,000 men . . . increasing . . . to 260,000 men'. Other sources also refer, unhelpfully, to divisions rather than to the number of troops involved.

motorised and armoured divisions were fully mechanised and 4200, it
was calculated, would still be required for the first wave of troops and
another 7000 for the second, follow-up force, more than had sailed
with Duke William of Normandy in 1066.* One division requisitioned
a number of donkeys to act as stand-ins during embarkation exercises
but they had to be driven to the beach in lorries and, once there, proved
uncooperative.

These, however, were all minor difficulties. 'All ranks,' wrote one
corps commander, expecting to land in the first wave, 'showed the
utmost keenness in training for their unaccustomed task . . . We were
convinced that, like everything else, it could be mastered in due
course.' The real difficulty lay higher up, in the continuing disagreement between the navy and army. The army's initial plan, issued on 17
July, but regularly amended until it emerged as described here around
the end of July, envisaged an attack on a wide front covering nearly 200
miles [320 km] from Ramsgate to Lyme Bay. Six divisions, crossing
from the Pas de Calais, were to land between Ramsgate and Bexhill,
four, coming from around Le Havre, between Brighton and the Isle of
Wight, and three, sailing from Cherbourg, between Weymouth and
Lyme Regis. These first 13 divisions would be followed by a second
wave of nine panzer and motorised divisions and a further 19 would
bring the total force committed to 41, two of them airborne. The initial
objective was a line from Gravesend to Southampton, taking in the
North Downs and, incidentally, the Dorking Gap. The second line to
be reached ran from Maldon to the Severn, which would leave London
surrounded and ripe for the plucking. Thereafter armoured columns
would press northwards to seize the industrial areas of the Midlands,
followed by Liverpool and Glasgow on the west coast, Hull, Newcastle and Leith on the east. Then, von Brauchitsch believed, all resistance would collapse, the whole operation being concluded in a
month.

There was one defect in this attractive scenario and Raeder pointed it
out: the German Navy totally lacked the capacity to transport or protect on passage an army of this size. At the conference on 31 July,
already mentioned, he pointed this out to such effect that soon afterwards von Brauchitsch 'very reluctantly' abandoned the left-flank
assault on Lyme Bay altogether. He dug in his heels, however, when
asked to confine the landing to the 45 miles [72 km] between Folkestone and Eastbourne. Here, he protested to Field Marshal Keitel on 10
August, the British could, according to German intelligence, bring
superior forces to bear against him and during the 14 days he would
need to widen his bridgehead, the enemy might build up a strong
defence line between Chatham and Brighton. The chance of a sudden

* See *Defending the Island*, p. 152.

break-through, rapidly exploited, as in France, would therefore be gone. Von Brauchitsch Chief of Staff, General Halder, put it even more strikingly to his naval opposite number, Admiral Schniewind. 'I might just as well,' he told Schniewind on 7 August, 'put the troops . . . straight through a sausage machine.' Von Brauchitsch flatly refused to give up the planned secondary landing near Brighton, and in the end this was retained.

On Friday 30 August the Operations Branch of the Army General Staff issued its *Instruction for the Preparation of Operation Sealion*, which, with some subsequent modifications, represented the final German plan for the invasion of Great Britain. The army's 'Task' was defined as 'to land strong forces in southern England, defeat the British army and seize the capital . . . Preparations are to be made in such a way that the operation can be carried out from 15 September.' The *Proposed Method of Execution* followed:

> The *Luftwaffe* will destroy the British Air Force and . . . achieve *air superiority*. The Navy will provide mine-free corridors and, supported by the *Luftwaffe*, will bar the flanks of the crossing-sector . . . The *Army*'s landing will first win local bridgeheads with the specially equipped forward echelons of the first-wave divisions. Immediately afterwards they will widen these bridgeheads into a connected landing-zone . . . As soon as sufficient forces are available, an offensive will be launched towards the first operational objective, i.e. Thames estuary-heights south of London-Portsmouth . . . After gaining the first operational objective, the further task of the army will be . . . to defeat the enemy forces still holding out in southern England, to occupy London, to mop up the enemy in southern England, and to win the general line Maldon (north-east of London) – Severn estuary.

The reference to 'forward echelons' was significant. On 'S-Tag', equivalent of the later 'D-Day', only elements of the nine first-wave infantry divisions, plus the 7th Airborne Division, were to land, amounting, for the seaborne troops, to no more than 60,300 men. Of these 26,800, sailing from Rotterdam, Antwerp, Ostend, Dunkirk and Calais, were to storm ashore between Folkestone and St Leonards; 13,400, embarking at Boulogne, were destined for the Bexhill to Eastbourne area, and the remaining 20,100 for the third assault, between Beachy Head, just west of Eastbourne, and Brighton. They were to be supported by 250 tanks and parachute troops, who would seize the Downs behind Brighton and the high ground north and north-west of Folkestone, and establish crossing points, for the use of the troops coming off the beach, along the Royal Military Canal, and road-blocks, to hold off British reinforcements, on the Canterbury–Folkestone road. Once these bridgeheads were safe the remainder of the nine assault divisions would follow, along with the senior commanders, who were strictly enjoined in a supplementary *Order No. 1 for the Execution of Sealion*, issued by Army Group A on 14 September, not to arrive on the enemy shore until '*after* forces required for the *fighting* have crossed and *progress* has been made inland'. The Germans were under no illusion about what awaited them. 'The British will resist with every means . . . ,' warned the *Instructions*. 'Bitter fighting is to be expected.'

42

COMMANDING THE CHANNEL

It would not seem unreasonable that the enemy should attempt gradually to ... command the Channel at its narrowest point.

Winston Churchill to the Chiefs of Staff, 27 August 1940

By mid-July, when the Germans began seriously to prepare for an invasion, the British were far better placed to repel it than they had been even six weeks earlier. Everywhere pillboxes, tank-traps, road-blocks and anti-air-landing obstacles had sprung up or were hastily being built, and thanks to prodigious efforts in the factories, and American help, both the regular forces and the LDV were already better armed as well as better organised. On 10 July 250,000 rifles, with 77 million rounds of ammunition, and 300 75-mm [3-in] field guns, with 50,000 shells, had arrived from the United States and been distributed to the army within 48 hours. By 16 July the prime minister informed the War Cabinet of the 'very, very great progress which has been made in the past month in improving the defences of this country against invasion'. By early August 12 divisions were deployed to resist an enemy landing, with three more in reserve.

On 18 June Lieut.-General Sir Henry Pownall, formerly Chief of Staff to the BEF, had been appointed Inspector-General to the LDV and immediately set out to impose some order upon it. 'This party,' he confided to his diary two days later, 'already over half a million strong, was started some five weeks ago ... without, I gather, enough time for previous thought and organisation by the War Office or GHQ Home Forces ... The result ... is a rare "dog's dinner".'

The even more pressing problem of lack of arms was, however, beginning to be overcome. Around the end of July half a million rifles dating from the First World War, of the wrong, i.e. non-standard – 0.3-in [0.76-cm] – calibre, with only a few rounds apiece, but far better than nothing, arrived from the United States. On 23 July, with its numbers now climbing towards the million mark, the LDV was officially renamed the Home Guard, a name suggested by the *Daily Mail* on 14 May, and used by Churchill in a broadcast on 14 July. On 3 August it was re-structured into platoons, companies and battalions, like the regular army, and badges of rank were introduced, though commissions and military titles were still avoided, and on 6 August Army Council Instruction 924 confirmed its new status as part of the armed forces of the crown. It was not to develop, as some of its members with Spanish Civil War experience had hoped, into a 'people's army' of freebooting irregulars.

In fact, unknown to the public, and to most Home Guards, such a guerrilla force did already exist, in the 'Auxiliary Units' of which around 20 were now set up, consisting of regular soldiers selected to form 'stay-behind parties' in an area up to 30 miles [48 km] from the coast if it was occupied by the Germans. They were reinforced, in deep secrecy, by a larger number of Home Guard 'patrols', formed of men with an intimate knowledge of their home area, who dropped out of their ordinary units and trained to go, quite literally, underground when the moment came. Eventually, despite the misgivings of one Regional Commissioner, concerned about the likely fate of any such saboteurs who were captured and the reprisals which might follow, the Home Guard element in the Auxiliary Units consisted of around 3000 men, belonging on paper to three special, but never mentioned, battalions. Kent alone contained 25 hide-outs for local patrols. Most of the operational bases from which the patrols would operate were designed to be occupied by a maximum of 14 men for up to three weeks and they were built by special tunnelling companies of the Royal Engineers. The entrances, as in an adventure story, were elaborately concealed; at Lydden, near Margate, a 'solid' wooden wall could be moved aside, at Wootton, on the Dover/Folkestone road, a cattle manger had a false bottom. So well was the secret kept that one farm-worker member of an Auxiliary Unit near Dover found himself suspected by his wife, thanks to his frequent unexplained absences, of having a highly demanding affair.

The outstanding British military weakness remained a lack of capacity to deal with tanks. Deliveries of British tanks, even of the lighter cruiser and infantry kind, still averaged, between June and August, only 123 a month, while, as Churchill complained on 16 July, an output of 120 anti-tank guns a month did not go far to meet an estimated requirement of 7000. Some curious tank substitutes were devised, like the 'Bison', a rectangular pillbox mounted on a lorry chassis which carried 10 to 20 men behind four inches [10 cm] of concrete and cost a mere £150-175. Some Home Guard units produced home-made armoured fighting vehicles by bolting metal plates to cars and vans. The universal anti-tank remedy was the Molotov cocktail, a bottle filled with petrol or paraffin, ignited by lighting a fuse of twisted cloth in the neck. Ironside, on 30 May, recommended using 'Molotov cocktails to deal with tanks from the windows of houses', and thousands were made that summer, though many bottles proved reluctant to break and, when they did, often produced a meagre blaze. The close range from which it had to be thrown, a mere five to 15 yards [4.6-13.7 m], made the Molotov something of a suicide weapon; so clearly, was a 'flame-thrower', discharging inflammable dry-cleaning fluid through a stirrup pump, which a Durham Home Guard unit invented.

But fire, properly controlled, was a formidable weapon, and its use was encouraged by Lord Hankey, who having retired as Secretary of the Cabinet and CID before the war, had been recalled to Whitehall, as a minister, by Chamberlain in 1939. Hankey's interest in flame warfare dated back to his classical education, in which he had learned of the use of 'Greek fire' in the ancient world, and he now worked with the Petroleum Warfare Department, set up early in June,* to examine its modern possibilities.

Initial hopes of 'burning the invader back into the sea' by the use of perforated pipes which spread petrol over the surface of the water proved over-optimistic, for except under ideal conditions the waves extinguished the flames or even hurled a tidal wave of fire on the beach. In a flat calm, however, on 24 August, the sea was in a widely whispered phrase 'set on fire', on the shore of the Solent, as the head of the Department concerned described:

> Ten pipes were rigged from the top of a 30-foot [9 m] cliff down into the water well below high water mark and ten Scammel tanker wagons connected to them delivered oil at the rate of about 12 tons an hour. Admiralty flares and a system of sodium and petrol pellets were used for ignition and within a few seconds . . . a wall of flames of such intensity raged up from the sea surface that it was impossible to remain on the edge of the cliff and the sea itself began to boil.

This proved an exceptional experience and no Flame Barrage, as it was officially known, would have greeted the Germans in 1940, but if they had got ashore, the invaders *would* have faced an ordeal by fire as they moved inland. 'Flame Fougasses', 40-gallon [182-litre] drums containing a mixture of tar, lime and petrol, usually mounted in a battery of four, were set up in the banks overlooking sunken roads and other narrow points in roads and lanes, awaiting detonation by an explosive charge. They would then project a fierce jet of flaming liquid designed to stick to any vehicle it encountered. Several thousand of these were installed, and in some places, as at Dumpton Gap in Kent, an even simpler device, the Static Flame Trap, was used, with a tank of petrol installed above a dip in the road, which would be flooded with it when an enemy tank appeared and ignited by a Home Guard with a Molotov cocktail.

Neither the British public nor the German army knew of an even

---

* Collier, p. 135. Fleming, p. 208, says the Department 'was officially constituted on 9 July'.

more desperate expedient proposed by the prime minister. On 30 June, Churchill suggested to his Chief Staff Officer, General Hastings [unofficially 'Pug' and later Lord] Ismay:

> Supposing lodgments were effected on our coast, there could be no better points for application of mustard [gas] than these beaches and lodgments. In my view there would be no need to wait for the enemy to adopt such methods. He will certainly adopt them if he thinks it will pay.

Churchill took an equally relaxed attitude to other outlawed weapons. The 'best way of killing Huns', he remarked while practising at a rifle range near Chequers on 11 August, would be to use shortened, snubnosed bullets. The objection that they were against the rules of war he brushed aside on the grounds that the Germans would give him 'very short shrift' if captured.

Although General Ironside's proposals for an 'extended crust' on the likely invasion beaches, with stop-lines and the GHQ Line behind them, 'stood approved', in Churchill's words, when considered by the Chiefs of Staff on 25 June, he was never wholly reconciled to them. On the following day an officer much more to his taste, General Sir Alan Brooke [later Lord Alanbrooke] was appointed General Officer Commanding-in-Chief, Southern Command, an unenviable assignment, for Brooke discovered that the five miles [8 km] of coastland around St Margaret's Bay, north-east of Dover, the nearest point to France, was protected by only three anti-tank guns, with six rounds each. 'Brookie' had made his name in France as had his ablest divisional commander, now stationed in his area, Major-General Bernard [later Field Marshal Lord] Montgomery. 'Monty', as he became universally known, was 52, a combat-hardened commander who exuded confidence. His 3rd Division had hardly begun to take over the Brighton to Bognor sector of the Sussex coast on 17 June when a stream of orders began to issue from his headquarters at Lancing College. Montgomery was concerned at the number of civilians still inside his likely battleground. All ranks were instructed that their families must be sent away from the Divisional area by Monday 1 July, and he also laid down that 'all beaches, esplanades and amusement parks on sea fronts were . . . to be cleared of all civilians by 1700 hrs daily'. Before long Montgomery was himself descending, accompanied by one of his newly appointed subordinates, Brigadier Brian [later Lieut.-General Sir Brian] Horrocks, to issue peremptory instructions on the spot, as their recipient described:

> 'Who lives in that house?' he would say, pointing to some building which partly masked the fire from one of our machine-gun positions. 'Have them out, Horrocks. Blow up the house.'

On 28 June Churchill wrote to the Chiefs of Staff on what was to become a favourite theme, that the expected battle would be decided, 'not on the beaches, but by the mobile brigades and the main reserve':

> The safety of the country depends on having a large number . . . of 'Leopard' brigade groups which can be directed swiftly, i.e. within four hours, to the points of lodgment. Difficulties of landing on the beaches are serious . . . but difficulties of nourishing a lodgment when exposed to heavy attack by land, air, and sea are far greater.

This doctrine accorded well with Montgomery's views and when, on 2 July, he met Churchill for the first time while the prime minister was visiting the south coast, the two warriors reached an immediate understanding, as Montgomery recorded:

> He impressed me enormously . . . and not only because he approved whole-heartedly of my dispositions. I refused to string my divisions out as you spread butter on bread, being weak everywhere and strong nowhere. I deployed a minimum in the front line to break up and disorganise any invasion and kept the maximum in reserve for counter-attack. He was delighted with these mobile reserves and kept referring to them as 'leopards, waiting to pounce on the enemy'.

That day General Ironside moved into new headquarters at St Paul's School in Hammersmith, but to his relief the Chiefs of Staff agreed, as he wrote, 'that I should not try to fight the battle from London . . . I should like to have an armoured car anyway and . . . didn't want even with that to be continually on tap.' Some of his frequent meetings with Churchill were clearly proving a strain, and on Friday 19 July Ironside, as he confided in his diary, was summoned to the War Office and 'told that I was to be replaced by Alan Brooke as C-in-C, Home Forces . . . and made a field marshal'. Ironside, according to Churchill, 'accepted his retirement with . . . soldierly dignity', but the new Commander-in-Chief, on taking over at St Paul's School, found his predecessor had left not a note behind to facilitate the hand-over, only a reminder that the Rolls-Royce he had used as C-in-C was his private property.

Alan Brooke's promotion was followed by Bernard Montgomery's. On 21 June he became a lieut.-general and commander of 5 Corps, so that he was now responsible for the defence of the coast all the way from Bognor to Lyme Regis, including the Isle of Wight and, for operational purposes, Portsmouth. He marked his arrival by a wholesale dismissal of commanding officers, describing several of those he had inherited as 'old and decrepit', 'obviously extremely idle', 'completely and utterly useless'. He now began, to Churchill's warm approval, to withdraw troops from their fixed defences for aggressive training, and his reputation as a trainer soon rivalled that of his famous predecessor who had defended the south-east against Napoleon, Sir

John Moore. A similarly combative attitude was enthused into III Corps by its new commander, General [later Sir] James Marshall-Cornwall, whose two divisions held the northern half of East Anglia. On 26 July he found himself invited to dinner with the prime minister at Chequers:

> As soon as the champagne was served he started to interrogate me about the condition of my Corps. I told him that when I had taken it over I had found all ranks obsessed with defensive tactical ideas, the main object of everyone being to get behind an anti-tank obstacle. I had issued orders that only offensive training exercises were to be practised, and that the III Corps motto was 'Hitting, not Sitting', which prefaced every operation order.
>
> This went down tremendously well with the PM, who chuckled and chortled. 'Splendid! That's the spirit I want to see!'

Although Churchill was always more sceptical about it than his ministers, the government took the invasion danger seriously. From 24 June the gold reserves had begun to be shipped to Canada and plans were made for the royal family to follow if necessary. On 1 August, the Duke of Windsor, a potential Quisling – 'his inclinations,' ran one draft telegram prepared by the Colonial Secretary, 'are well known to be pro-Nazi' – was sent off to become governor of the Bahamas, to keep him out of harm's way. Plans had long existed for the government to move westwards if London became untenable through bombing and the arrangements for this 'Black Move' were now perfected. The 'Higher Control Party', including the prime minister and War Cabinet, were destined to occupy offices at Hindlip Hall near Worcester, while he lived with his immediate staff at a nearby country house. The service departments were to be housed in various buildings in Malvern, Droitwich and Worcester.

Invasion alarms were frequent that summer. The Invasion Warning Sub-Committee, an offshoot of the Joint Intelligence Committee, met for the first time on 31 May. On 3 June, neatly blending two alarmist nightmares, it noted a report that 'German soldiers in civilian clothes are embarking at Naples for Spain, whence they will be sent from Cadiz for an attack on Ireland.' A remarkably accurate forecast of *Operation Sealion*, inadvertently provided by the German Military Attaché in Ankara, reached the Committee on 21 June and, on the following day, a warning from Bucharest of German plans to instal long-range guns to cover their Channel crossing. ULTRA intelligence,[*] obtained by deciphering material enciphered by the 'Enigma' machine, also provided clues to the Germans' intentions.

On 28 June Downing Street learned of *Luftwaffe* anti-aircraft units

[*] I have indicated elsewhere (see *Air Raid*, pp. 258-266) why I am sceptical of the often exaggerated claims made for this source of intelligence.

asking for large numbers of maps of the British Isles and on 29 July another order reminded *Luftwaffe* pilots not to attack quays along the south coast because, British Intelligence concluded, the Germans wanted to leave them intact for their own use.

While Churchill's own staff were noting, on Tuesday 9 July, 'invasion said to be on Thursday', the prime minister remained far more doubtful that an attempt would be made. 'In Britain, whatever our shortcomings,' he later wrote, 'we understood the sea affair very thoroughly,' and here at least the Germans were heavily outnumbered and outclassed. The naval defence of the British Isles at this time was organised into a series of Commands: Orkneys and Shetlands, taking in the far north of Scotland and including Scapa Flow; Rosyth, with the Firth of Forth in its centre, responsible for the area as far south as Flamborough Head; the Nore, from there to the North Foreland, including the Thames estuary; Dover, stretching almost to Beachy Head; Portsmouth, from there to beyond Portland, and then round Land's End in a vast semi-circle, including the whole of Ireland and reaching right up to the mid-Hebrides, Western Approaches, with Plymouth close to its south-west boundary. The Commands were divided into Sub-Commands, often based on major ports like Yarmouth and Milford Haven, and it was recognised that for defence purposes the most important places were the Humber, Harwich, Sheerness, Portsmouth and Plymouth. The ships originally based at Dover were withdrawn when shellfire and air raids made it untenable.

To provide advance warning, the Admiralty looked to the reconnaissance aircraft of Coastal Command and to its own 35 submarines. As it neared the British coast the enemy armada was likely to encounter one of the large fleet of small ships, sloops, Harbour Defence Patrol Craft, Armed Examination Vessels, gunboats and even lighter ships of which 200 to 300 were permanently at sea between the Wash and Sussex, to provide a floating 'trip-wire'. The task of dealing with the escorting warships and scattering and sinking the transports would have fallen to those most useful maids-of-all-work, the destroyers, with the lighter, *Aurora* and *Nigeria* class cruisers lending their support. Their numbers and dispositions varied but the situation on 14 September was fairly typical. On that date one battleship, two cruisers and four destroyers were at Plymouth; one cruiser and 12 destroyers at Portsmouth; two cruisers, 16 destroyers and four corvettes at Harwich; and three cruisers and four destroyers in the Humber. Further north outside the immediate invasion area, three battleships, two cruisers and 12 destroyers were stationed around Rosyth, and an aircraft carrier, a battleship, six cruisers, four of them of the heavier 'county' or 'town' class, and four destroyers at Scapa Flow. Although guarding against a sortie by Raeder's capital ships from Norway or the waters north of Denmark, these last two groups could have arrived in the Channel or off East Anglia in good time to deal with German re-inforcements; one destroyer in May had made the 530 miles [850 km] voyage from Scapa Flow to Dover in a mere 24 hours.

By summoning ships home from Gibraltar or detaching them from escort duties the Royal Navy could have given itself an even greater margin of superiority. As it was, the forces assigned to repel invasion totalled one aircraft-carrier, five battleships, 16 cruisers and 48 des-troyers or corvettes, plus another 700 lighter, but increasingly strongly armed, patrol vessels. The total German fleet consisted of two ancient battleships, two modern battle-cruisers, five or six other cruisers and perhaps ten destroyers, plus an unknown but modest number of smaller vessels.

Thanks to the additional guns now being installed, as already described, and the construction of pillboxes to guard them on the land-ward side, the navy's traditional harbours were also expected to be secure and numerous blockships, eventually covering fifty places, were used to narrow the possible routes of a seaborne attack. Dover, Harwich and Rosyth as well as, following the *Royal Oak* tragedy, Scapa Flow, already had booms designed to deter submarine, as well as surface, attack, and similar barriers were now set up at the entrances to the Thames, the Humber and Plymouth harbour. Open beaches near the major ports were protected by a new form of boom, made up of floating canvas tubes filled with kapok, normally used to stuff cushions, from which wire nets were suspended. About 100 miles [160 km] of coast were protected in this way and another 80 [128 km] by an 'explosive' boom, of mines attached to a wire framework. The Wash, large enough to shelter a whole fleet of transports, had its own boom five miles [8 km] long, plus a defensive minefield. Mines, both floating and land, were laid everywhere on a vast scale, but the most important minefield of all, in the Straits of Dover, had become ineffective as the Germans could avoid it by keeping close to the French coast, now in their hands.

The Germans' growing control of the Channel became disagreeably evident on Thursday 22 August when shore-based guns on Cape Gris Nez opened fire on a convoy, though without scoring any hits, and that evening the gunners turned their attention to a larger, stationary target, the English mainland. For the first time in history, shells from enemy land artillery now landed on British soil, destroying several houses and injuring four civilians. Thenceforward such bombard-ments became a regular feature of life in what its residents ruefully re-named 'Shellfire Corner'.

Churchill had long anticipated such action and had pressed for the installation of long-range guns around Dover to provide counter-battery fire. One 14-in [35-cm] gun was in position by 22 August and duly replied to the German salvoes, but this was not enough for

Churchill, as a sharp note to General Ismay and the Chiefs of Staff five days later, on 27 August, confirmed:

> It would not seem unreasonable that the enemy should attempt gradually to . . . command the Channel at its narrowest point. This would be a natural preliminary to invasion . . . What are we doing in defence of the Dover promontory by heavy artillery? Ten weeks ago I asked for heavy guns. One has been mounted. Two railway guns are expected . . . We ought to have a good many more heavy guns lined up.

By the beginning of September the 'heavy gun strength towards the sea', in Churchill's phrase, consisted of two 9.2-in [23.3-cm] and six six-inch [15-cm] guns, installed for coast defence before the war, plus, as new additions, the one 14-in [35-cm], which had opened fire on 22 August, two 6-in [15-cm] naval guns, and two four-inch [10-cm], also naval. Four 5.5-in [14-cm] from HMS *Hood*, were in process of being installed, and two 13.5-in [34-cm], rescued from the old battleship *Iron Duke* were being mounted on a specially built railway behind St Margaret's Bay. Nicknamed 'Winnie' and 'Pooh', these last two soon became famous. Churchill believed that 'although still inferior in numbers to the enemy we . . . had a powerful fire concentration', while for local defence 'one of the 18-in [46-cm] howitzers I had saved after the first war and twelve 12-in [30-cm] howitzers were installed for engaging enemy landings . . . and would have brought a terrible fire on any landing area'.

In what one local British battery commander described as the 'Conflict across the Strait' the advantage lay with the Germans. Their original *Siegfried* battery – a more martial name, it must be conceded, than 'Winnie' and 'Pooh' – of four 38-cm [15-in] guns, stationed south of Gris Nez, was by mid-September joined by Friedrich-August, Grosser Kurfürst, Prinz Heinrich, Oldenburg and, the Teutonic imagination then flagging a little, batteries M-1 to M-4, the whole array, consisting of no fewer than 29 guns of calibres from 17-38 cm [6.7-15 in], distributed in nine emplacements from east of Calais to north of Boulogne. These proved a constant source of nuisance and danger to the dwindling number of civilians living in and around Dover; the population was now less than half the pre-war figure. During September they came under shellfire six times, each bombardment being signalled by an air raid warning, sounded twice in succession. On one day alone, 9 September, 150 shells were fired and the general opinion was that such bombardments were worse than bombing or machine-gun attacks.

The British gunners, as the battery commander previously quoted later described, kept a close watch on the gun-flashes on the far side of the Channel:

The look-outs, when they observed the flashes, would start a stop-watch and after about 54 seconds, call out for all to duck, a moment or so before the salvoes landed. The shells would splinter, and it was these splinters which caused the major amount of casualties. On occasions, the Germans tried air bursts over the town and defences, and although somewhat frightening, [these] were no more effective . . . The stories in the press at the time, recording 'huge gun duels across the Channel', could only have been put out for propaganda purposes . . . A couple of rounds from 'Winnie' and 'Pooh' could by no stretch of the imagination match the eight-gun salvoes fired from the German long-range guns. The shell line . . . , appeared to be through the centre of the town, through the market square and . . . seemed remarkably good and accurate.

Local civilians took a less professional attitude. They were not perhaps aware of the traditional rhyme, supposedly addressed by a medieval or Tudor gun to its crew:

Polish me well and kept me clean
And I will put a ball on Calais Green.

The trouble about putting balls on Calais Green was that this invari-ably provoked a reponse, probably heavier than the original salvo. Actions initiated by the British gunners became so unpopular – the men were, somewhat unfairly, described locally as 'trigger happy' – that the police were notified in advance, so the 'shellfire' warning could be sounded before the inevitable retaliation began.

43

WHY DOESN'T HE COME?

When people . . . in Great Britain . . . ask 'Yes, but why doesn't he come?'
we reply: 'Calm yourselves! . . . He is coming!'

Adolf Hitler, 4 September 1940

German mastery of the air over and around the British Isles was the essential prelude to a landing, since it alone could redress the Royal Navy's crushing superiority at sea. After its unimpressive debut in the opening months of the war little had been seen of the *Luftwaffe* in British skies. On 16 March 1940 another raid on Scapa Flow had resulted in the death of the first civilian to be killed by enemy bombers, and on 30 April two others died and 160 were injured when a mine-laying Heinkel was shot down on to Clacton. The first deliberate attack on the mainland came on 10 May when, causing no damage or casualties, a single aircraft dropped bombs near the villages of Petham and Chilham, close to Canterbury. Thereafter a handful of enemy planes, or a single aircraft, frequently appeared over various parts of the country, and from 18 June such visits became a nightly event. Nine people were killed at Cambridge on 19 June, and the same night the first bombs fell on the London Region, at Croydon, causing, a local historian noted, 'eight bomb craters in the fields'.

The air war was now clearly hotting up. On the night of 21 June, 50 bombers made raids over many parts of the country and, with the final signing of the French armistice on the following day and French bases now available to the *Luftwaffe*, more serious attacks began, some obviously directed at naval targets. Portland dockyard was bombed on 4 July and on the 10th a sizeable force of 70 bombers attacked Swansea and Falmouth in daylight, killing 30 people.

Heavy attacks on shipping in the Channel and North Sea began on Wednesday 10 July, since considered by the defenders to mark the opening day of what later became known as the Battle of Britain. The most serious result was the loss of destroyers while escorting offshore convoys. Two were damaged on 25 July in a joint attack by Stuka dive-bombers and German motor-torpedo-boats, and two days later, on Saturday 27 July, HMS *Wren* was sunk off Aldeburgh and HMS

Codrington at Dover, leading, as mentioned earlier, to its abandonment as a destroyer base. The following Monday, 29 July, another precious destroyer was sunk by Stukas off Portland. The Germans regarded these attacks, however, as a mere preliminary to their main offensive, which was now switched from naval targets to the RAF.

On 30 July Hitler ordered Göring to prepare 'immediately and with the greatest haste . . . the great battle of the German Air Force against England'. On its result the launching of *Sealion* depended. 'If after eight days of intensive air war the *Luftwaffe* has not achieved considerable destruction of the enemy's Air Force, harbours and naval forces,' Hitler told Admiral Raeder the following day, 'the operation will have to be put off till May 1941.'

The actual numbers of machines available to the two sides varied from day to day, but on 10 August the two German *Luftflotten*, or air fleets, allocated to the offensive, excluding a third based in Norway and Denmark, consisted of 875 long-range bombers, 316 dive-bombers and 929 fighters. The RAF could put into the air 600-700 fighters.[*]

On Monday 12 August the new phase of the Battle really opened with the bombing of several coastal airfields and the destruction, its significance hardly realised by the Germans and not exploited, of the key radar station at Ventnor in the Isle of Wight. Officially Eagle Day, as the Germans labelled it, was Tuesday 13 August, when 1485 sorties were flown, largely against airfields in Hampshire and Kent, and against ports like Portland and Southampton. The intention in this opening phase, which lasted till 18 August, was to bring the RAF up to battle and to destroy it, but on that first day of all-out combat 45 German aircraft were shot down for the loss of 13 British fighters, though both sides overestimated the enemy's losses; the RAF claimed 69 'kills', the Germans 88. Such exaggerations, though unintended on the British side, were to be a feature of the coming Battle, and the jubilant headlines in the press, and announcements like '62 for 8' chalked by newspaper vendors on their boards, as if reporting a cricket match, were to be an important factor in maintaining morale.

Thursday 15 August 1940, a gloriously warm and sunny day, saw the first great climax of the Battle. The Germans made their greatest effort so far and also tried to outflank the defences by a sudden foray by about 150 bombers, escorted by long-range fighters, from bases in Scandinavia against the north-east coast between Tynemouth and Sunderland. They failed to achieve surprise and 23 of the raiders were shot down. All told that day the Germans lost 75 aircraft, the RAF 34,

[*] Wheatley, p. 63. The figures given by Churchill, *Second World War*, Vol. II, p. 285 are slightly different. Keegan, pp. 93-4, puts the Germans' strength at 1000 heavy bombers, 300 dive-bombers and 800 single-seat fighters against 600 RAF fighters 'serviceable daily'.

though – almost more serious – 17 of the pilots were killed, and 16 wounded, leaving only one unhurt. The British public was told, and believed, that 182 German machines had been shot down. The resulting jubilation was all the greater because it was widely believed that Hitler had boasted that he would be in London by this date, just as Napoleon had been expected, as mentioned earlier, on 15 October 1803.

That day, reviewing the situation, Göring told his commanders that more fighters must be allocated to protecting the dive-bombers, and that Messerschmitt 109s, the German equivalent of the Spitfire and Hurricane, should be assigned to escorting their larger brothers, the twin-engined Me 110s, supposedly fighters themselves. The *Reichsmarschall* ordered that the current daylight raids should 'be directed exclusively against the enemy air force', the *Luftwaffe*'s real target. The operations at night were 'essentially dislocation raids, made so that the enemy defences and population shall be allowed no respite'. At the same conference Göring declared that, 'It is doubtful where there is any point in continuing the attacks on radar sites, in view of the fact that not one of those attacked has so far been put out of action,' a serious miscalculation. His staff meanwhile were absurdly over-optimistic in their estimate of Fighter Command's strength. Air Chief Marshal Dowding was believed, at 10 am on 16 August, to have only 300 serviceable aircraft left; the actual figure was more than 700.

Sunday 18 August brought more massed attacks against RAF airfields south and south-east of London, and the operations room at one of them, Kenley, about four miles [6.4 km] south of Croydon, was knocked out, after more than 100 bombs had hit the aerodrome, destroying ten hangars and, even worse, four Hurricanes. Croydon itself was also badly damaged, as was West Malling, five miles [8 km] west of Maidstone, and Biggin Hill, roughly midway between them. The controller at Kenley moved into emergency premises over a shop in the village, but the airfield was temporarily out of action and the interruption of its command facilities was a serious matter.

Fighter Command, at Stanmore, just north-west of London, controlled the defending forces through four Group headquarters. The key Group was No. 11, under Air Vice-Marshal [later Air Chief Marshal Sir] Keith Park, at Uxbridge, which operated through six sector headquarters at Westhampnett, near Portsmouth, Northolt, Kenley, Biggin Hill, and on the far side of the Thames – no barrier to the airmen – Hornchurch and North Weald. These in turn were each responsible for a number of airfields, housing between them 25 squadrons who guarded, in Churchill's words, 'the whole of Essex, Kent, Sussex and Hampshire and all the approaches across them to London'. To the south-west and west of No. 11 Group's area was No. 10 Group, to the north of that No. 12, and, protecting the northern counties beyond the

Humber, No. 13. This was little involved in the Battle, but both No. 10 and No. 12 Groups were often in action, as well as being continually called on to reinforce the hard-pressed and contantly embattled No. 11.

On 19 August Göring re-assembled his fighter commanders at his lavish home, Karinhall, to confirm his current objective. 'Until further notice,' he ordered, 'the main task of *Luftflotten* 2 and 3 will be to inflict the utmost damage possible on the enemy fighter forces.' On the following day the cloud closed in, enforcing something of a lull on both sides for the next five days. To the British this unexpected breathing-space was particularly valuable, enabling the ground crews to get damaged aircraft back into service, and making it possible to fill in craters on those airfields where civilian labourers (contrary to the later myth of universal courage that summer) had taken to the shelters during raids. Above all it enabled the weary pilots to rest. Although between 8 and 18 August 175 Spitfires and Hurricanes had been shot down, 30 more had been destroyed on the ground and 65 damaged in combat beyond repair within their own squadrons, there was no real shortage of machines, but the 94 pilots killed or missing in the same period, and the 60 put out of action by wounds, were harder to replace.

On 19 August, while Göring had been issuing his orders to increase pressure on 11 Group, Keith Park had warned his controllers of the need to husband its most precious resource. 'During the next two or three weeks,' he told them, 'we cannot afford to lose pilots through forced landings in the sea. Avoid sending fighters out over the sea to chase reconnaissance aircraft or small formations of enemy fighters . . . Against mass attacks coming inland despatch a minimum number of squadrons to engage enemy fighters. Our main object is to engage enemy bombers . . . If heavy attacks have crossed the coast and are proceeding towards aerodromes, put a squadron, or even the sector training flight, to patrol under clouds over each sector aerodrome.'

On the following day, Tuesday 20 August, the nation's gratitude to Dowding's pilots was summed up by Churchill in a famous sentence: 'Never in the field of human conflict was so much owed by so many to so few.' Four days later, on Saturday 24 August, the skies cleared and what both sides expected to be the decisive phase of the Battle of Britain began. At 2.15 that afternoon, after a series of attacks which left almost every building in ruins, the airfield at Manston near Ramsgate, on the exposed Kentish coast, found itself cut off from Group headquarters, contact only being restored by a member of the Observer Corps on a bicycle. The airfield was then evacuated, but others near the coast were in not much better straits and after dark, for the first time since 1918, bombs were dropped on various parts of London, especially the working-class boroughs to the north and east, though this was in fact due to bad navigation, not intent. Thirty-eight German aircraft had been shot down that day, at the cost of 22 British fighters, but only one bomber was brought down during the night, a highly significant difference.

This pattern of devastating, but costly, attacks on airfields by day, and of wide-ranging, and apparently invulnerable, raids on industrial targets at night, continued for the next few days. The real threat, however, was to Fighter Command. On 27 August the Combined Intelligence Committee warned that upon the results of the attacks on airfields 'will depend the decision as to invasion' and the prime minister, touring the affected area the next day, was incensed, as he noted in a minute on 29 August, to find that, in spite of the efforts of the RAF personnel on the spot, craters at Manston were still unfilled four days after its last raid. 'I must protest emphatically against this feeble method of repairing damage . . . All craters, should be filled within 24 hours at most.'

The unrelenting, and cumulatively serious, attack on Fighter Command continued with, despite Göring's doubts about such targets, a series of attacks on Friday 30 August on radar stations from Dover to Beachy Head, seven being put temporarily out of action when the main supply cable was cut. Power was rapidly restored but keeping the airfields, and especially the vital Sector Stations, in action, proved more difficult and that day, apart from several less important bases, North Weald, Kenley and Biggin Hill were all attacked again. That Friday Biggin Hill was bombed from a high level at noon, again soon after 1.30 pm, then for a third time later in the afternoon and, most heavily of all, in the early evening around six o'clock, when almost every building above ground was destroyed by 1000-pound [454-kg] bombs dropped from a low level, the power and telephone lines were severed, and 39 airmen and WAAFs were killed and another 26 wounded. Such destruction more than made up for the 36 German planes, not 62 as then believed, shot down, for the loss of 25 RAF fighters. Biggin Hill remained operational, but only just, and next day was singled out for attack again, so that for a time only one squadron could use it. Several other places were in little better plight. By nightfall, on Saturday 31 August, Fighter Command had suffered its heaviest losses of the whole Battle: 39 machines destroyed and 14 of their pilots dead. The margin between the two sides was growing narrower; the *Luftwaffe* had had 41 aircraft shot down.

Signs were now mounting that invasion preparations were nearing their climax. On 3 September two spies, caught within hours of landing at Hythe, revealed their belief that a landing in Kent was imminent, while another pair were rounded up soon after coming ashore at Dungeness – one had given himself away by trying to buy a drink at Lydd outside licensing hours. On 4 September Air Ministry Intelligence drew attention to the preparation of 15 aerodromes between

Dunkirk and the mouth of the Somme to receive dive-bombers and fighter units, and of five more advanced landing-grounds nearer the coast. 'It may,' suggested the report's author, 'indicate their re-employment on a large scale in preparation for an invasion of the South and South-East Coasts.'

Hitler himself encouraged such speculation by the speech which he delivered on Wednesday 4 September to a hysterically cheering, all-female, crowd of nurses and social workers in Berlin:

> When people are very curious in Great Britain and ask, 'Yes, but why doesn't he come?' we reply: 'Calm yourselves! Calm your-selves! He is coming! He is coming!'

The German army now contributed its piece to the jigsaw with, as was learned on 5 September from another deciphered Enigma signal, all leave stopped from Sunday the 8th. But what seemed the decisive clue was 'a striking increase' in the number of barges at Ostend, which, the Joint Intelligence Committee learned on Saturday 7 September, had risen since 31 August from 18 to 270.

England's first line of defence was traditionally the enemy ports, and on 4 July Bomber Command had been ordered by the Air Ministry to direct special attention to them and to German shipping. The Com-mand's own preference, however, was for attacking the enemy home-land, which coincided with Churchill's combative desire to hit back and the British public's desire to hear news of RAF attacks on enemy targets, especially Berlin. During the whole of July and August Bomber Command's effort against barges and shipping outside Ger-many was trivial, a mere 66 tons, while 468 tons were directed at aero-dromes outside Germany, and 1454 tons against what the 'bomber barons' considered their proper destination, German industry. The one significant success, on 12 August, was an attack on the Dortmund-Ems canal in the Rhineland, along which motor-boats were being brought towards the Dutch coast. Two of the five Hampdens involved were shot down, but their sacrifice was richly rewarded: the aqueduct carrying the canal was blocked for ten days. As more barges accum-ulated in the Channel ports attacks on them were intensified, though largely left to the medium bombers, the Blenheims, which on the nights of 5 and 6 September were sent against the French and Belgian harbours.

The prime minister's principal anxiety was about the situation in the air.

> In the fighting between August 24 and September 6 the scales had tilted against Figher Command . . . In the life and death struggle of the two Air Forces this was a decisive phase . . . There was much anxiety at Fighter Headquarters at Stanmore . . . This same period had seriously drained the strength of Fighter Command as a whole

. . . 466 Spitfires and Hurricanes had been destroyed or seriously damaged. Out of a total pilot strength of about a thousand nearly a quarter had been lost.

The expected concentration of landing craft had still not occurred, but if, as the British believed, the main assault would be on the east coast, the barges might still be lurking, just as in *The Riddle of the Sands*, behind Heligoland, and among the sandbanks along the Dutch coast. During the night of 6 September, after 60 vessels had been sighted off Calais, the Admiralty had ordered all cruisers, destroyers and smaller ships to be kept at immediate notice for sea. The army was also anticipating action, with all the units in Home Forces under orders to be ready to fight within eight hours. On the afternoon of Saturday 7 September, a splendidly sunny and warm autumn day, the climax seemed to be approaching, for around 5 pm a large force of German bombers broke through to London and started huge fires on both sides of the river below Tower Bridge. Here at last, it seemed, was the knock-out blow expected twelve months ago. No one in London guessed at the true reasons for the Germans' change of policy, that Göring had failed to realise how effective the attacks on Fighter Command's airfields had been, and that Hitler, infuriated by the recent raids on Berlin, had encouraged him to divert his bombers into undertaking reprisals. 'If they attack our cities, then we will raze theirs to the ground,' the Führer had told his hate-filled female audience on 4 September. Now the razing was beginning.

When the Chiefs of Staff met at 5.30 pm, with smoke from the burning docks pouring skyward in increasing volumes, streams of German aircraft still passing high over the capital, and the fire-bells of appliances dashing eastward echoing through the Saturday afternoon streets of the West End, the Director of Military Intelligence reported that Intelligence thought a landing 'imminent', perhaps on the following day. It was decided to order all defence forces to 'stand by at immediate notice' and at 8.07 pm the code-word *Cromwell*, meaning 'conditions suitable for invasion', was issued.

The result was the most dramatic of all the false alarms which had punctuated British history. The true significance of *Cromwell*, first adopted back in June by General Ironside, had long since been forgotten, and in many places, as excited duty officers contacted their superiors and news of what was happening spread to the Home Guard, it was interpreted to mean 'invasion in progress'. In some areas the church bells were rung, which actually *did* mean this, and as they heard the sound distant places, so far unaffected, in turn joined in with echoing peals, until the sleeping countryside was alive with armed, or all too often unarmed, men.

In East Anglia the enemy assault seemed actually to have begun as over-zealous commanders blew up key bridges and three Guards officers were killed by mines laid prematurely by the roadside. A potentially worse tragedy was avoided when the local railway superintendent refused to blow up the main railway yard at Lincoln, as ordered by two RE officers, without further instructions from higher up.

Apart from providing useful lessons about not over-reacting in an emergency, the night's events also revealed some of the deficiencies which still remained in the nation's defences. At an army workshop near Stockton-on-Tees in County Durham, a long way from the likely firing line, the best the officer in charge could do was arm his men with heavy spanners. A Home Guard at Potters Bar, in Hertfordshire, found himself reporting for duty bearing his wife's broom handle; he had nobly given her the garden fork to defend their home. At Cromer trenches on the beach were manned by young sailors under instruction who at least had rifles, even if they had hardly seen them before. Near Lewes, a farmer manning a pillbox found himself in the possession of rare riches, a whole 50 rounds of ammunition, though he was not greatly cheered by the arrival of an army officer who declared: 'There is to be no retirement!' At Dover the coastal batteries, when the *Cromwell* signal arrived, were ordered to '"Stand to" . . . All the guns of the defences were loaded . . . ,' one commander later recalled. 'Additional trays of ammunition were brought up on the electric hoist . . . and were stacked at the rear of the guns. We also primed all the hand grenades. These were issued to all ranks down to bombardier, but [I] retained half a dozen for myself.'

Here was the true spirit of September 1940, but by around 5.30 am on Sunday 8 September suspicions were beginning to dawn that the Germans were not even at sea, much less landing, and with daylight they were confirmed:

Next morning was a clear, bright day and, in fact, we could see right across the Channel to the French cliffs. Instead of a vast armada of ships approaching our shore, there was not a vessel in sight. It was not long afterwards that we received the signal to 'Stand down'.

44

STANDING FIRM

If we stand as firm as we did in 1940, all will be well.

Diary entry by Lieut.-General Sir Henry Pownall, 31 December 1940

The 7th of September was the watershed. By switching the main weight of their air offensive to night attacks on British cities the Germans had given the RAF the breathing space it needed, though this was not yet realised. The main day raid on Saturday 7 September which had begun what soon became known as 'The Blitz' had undoubtedly been a victory for the *Luftwaffe*, and that night Göring jubilantly telephoned his wife to boast that 'London is in flames' and broadcast to the German people to hail this 'historic hour'. Meanwhile, unmentioned by him, Bomber Command was for the first time sending some of its then 'heavy' bombers, 26 Hampdens, to join the 'light' Battles and 'medium' Blenheims, in bombing the Belgian and French ports. On Sunday morning, while Londoners were beginning the massive, soon to be familiar, task of clearing-up – or leaving the capital in search of safer quarters – German radio announced that the *Reichsmarschall* had now taken personal command of aerial operations.

During the day, although several airfields were attacked yet again, the German effort was relatively small and the real assault, on London, came after dark. That night, however, as German bombers crossed the Channel British warships below them were going in the opposite direction. Five motor-torpedo-boats from Harwich, six destroyers from the Nore and five from Portsmouth, plus two cruisers, were sent against the invasion ports, with surprising results. At Ostend two MTBs sank three, or possibly four, medium-sized steamers; at Dunkirk three other MTBs found nothing; at Calais, visited by three destroyers and a cruiser, there was no threatening armada and the Germans, apparently fast asleep, were left undisturbed; at Boulogne, the other cruiser, with three destroyers, their presence having been discovered, bombarded the inner harbour. The five destroyers from Portsmouth, sweeping the coast between Le Touquet and the Seine, found, like so many mariners before them, the elements more troublesome than the enemy. 'A very violent and sustained thunderstorm broke,' the flotilla's war diary recorded, 'and the low cloud and heavy rain reduced visibility.' Like the other groups, this one got home safely, to confirm that if the Germans *were* planning an invasion from the Channel ports it was as yet nowhere near ready to be launched.

During Monday 9 September 28 German aircraft were shot down for the loss of 19 British fighters, and at six o'clock that evening the German heavy guns between Cape Gris–Nez and Wissant opened up a violent bombardment. In the next five hours nearly 200 shells rained down on Dover, though the official report revealed that, 'Casualties and damage [were] remarkably light; five persons, including one soldier were killed, two houses and a garage demolished and about 20 other buildings damaged.' That night six destroyers each from the Nore and Portsmouth, with four MTBs, paid another visit to the nearest Channel ports and scoured the coast from St Valery, where William I had in 1066 waited for a favourable wind,* to Le Touquet, but apart from brief bombardments at Calais and Boulogne nothing was achieved and little enemy shipping sighted.

These results seemed puzzling, since groups of vessels likely to form part of an invasion fleet were being observed sailing south round Cape Gris–Nez. The explanation, unsuspected by the Admiralty, was that the Germans were keeping these ships out of harm's way, in Le Havre and Cherbourg, until the last possible moment. Poor visibility and rough seas, which had succeeded the recent idyllic conditions, had also hampered operations. 'The weather conditions, which for the time of year are completely abnormal and unstable,' complained the German naval staff in Paris on 10 September, echoing other reluctant invaders from the Duke of Medina Sidonia onwards, 'greatly impair transport movements and mine-sweeping activities for *Sealion*.'

The contradictory evidence made it difficult for the British government to decide whether an invasion was seriously intended or not, and, if intended, where it would fall. A deciphered Enigma signal on Wednesday 11 September referring to the need for *Luftwaffe* units to avoid unnecessary transport operations seemed to indicate, Military Intelligence concluded, the possible 'movement of troops and armaments for invasion purposes' and that day Churchill warned both his colleagues and the country that the danger remained very real. A 'powerful armada', he told the War Cabinet that morning, 'was being deployed along the coasts of France opposite this country.' That evening the prime minister broadcast to the nation:

> No one should blind himself to the fact that a heavy, full-scale invasion of this island is being prepared with all the usual German thoroughness and method, and that it may be launched at any time

* See *Defending the Island*, pp. 150-1.

now . . . Therefore, we must regard the next week or so as a very
important week for us in our history. It ranks with the days when
the Spanish Armada was approaching the Channel and Drake was
finishing his game of bowls, or when Nelson stood between us and
Napoleon's Grand Army at Boulogne . . . Every man and every
woman will therefore prepare himself to do his duty, whatever it
may be, with special pride and care.

The British still remained uncertain where the blow was likely to fall.
Churchill had all along favoured the east coast; on 10 July he had written: 'The main danger is from the Dutch and German harbours, which
bear principally upon the coast from Dover to the Wash. As the nights
lengthen this danger zone will extend northwards.' In fact the reverse
had occurred, and happily the new C-in-C Home Forces showed
better judgement. General Brooke, Churchill wrote later, 'pointed out
about the end of the first week of August that the threat of invasion was
developing on the south coast as much as the east'. German troops
were assembled along the French coast, and there were other in-
dications, too. The two mountain divisions equipped with mules, reported to be training near Boulogne, were more likely to be intended
for the Kentish cliffs (in fact at Folkestone) than the flat and salty shallows of Suffolk or Norfolk. As late as 8 September even Brooke, however, was still contemplating a two-pronged thrust on either side of the
Thames estuary. 'Everything,' he wrote, 'pointing to Kent and East
Anglia as the two main threatened points.' The truth was that the Germans had never had any thought of attacking the east coast, but had
opted all along for the shortest possible sea passage, across the Straits of
Dover, though Churchill in his memoirs claimed robustly that the
British appreciation had been sound:

> This does not mean that in choosing the south coast as their target
> they were thinking rightly and we wrongly. The east coast invasion
> was by far the more formidable if the enemy had had the means to
> attempt it.

The truth was, however, that one had to fight the enemy where he
chose to land and not where, according to correct military principles,
he ought to have landed, and eventually the steady movement of
barges and tugs south-westward provided an unmistakable clue, and
prompted a vigorous British response. On the night of Churchill's
speech and the following one, 12/13 September, destroyers, MTBs and
fast gunboats again stood out from the Nore, Portsmouth and Plymouth to sweep the opposite coast from Holland almost to the Channel Islands, which, abandoned by the British government, had been in
enemy occupation since the end of June. The British intruders carried
out what was almost a tour of inspection, entering the mouth of the
Maas, Flushing and the Scheldt, Ostend, Dunkirk, Calais, Boulogne,

Le Touquet and even heavily fortified Cherbourg, surveying them for signs of invasion preparations and shelling, or attacking with torpe-does the port installations and any vessels, mainly mine-sweepers and trawlers, they encountered. It was an awesome demonstration that, at night at least, the Germans did not yet have command of the Channel, for all the attackers got back to England unharmed.

The Germans now learned that even the feint attack from Scandina-via towards the north-east coast, *Herbstreise* or 'Autumn Journey', was unlikely to be as smooth as its code name implied. In his speech of 11 September Churchill had revealed that the British government were aware of 'preparations . . . to carry an invading force from the Norwe-gian harbours' and the Germans were probably aware of the precau-tionary move two days later, on 13 September, of a 'reception com-mittee' from Scapa Flow to Rosyth. The battleship HMS *Hood* was already stationed there and it was now joined by two more battleships, *Nelson* and *Rodney*, two cruisers and eight destroyers – more than enough to annihilate the heavy cruiser *Hipper*, the three light cruisers and the four unarmed transports, including the famous pre-war liner, *Bremen*, earmarked for this diversion.

On 12 September the German Naval Staff officially accepted that air supremacy in the Channel did not yet exist. 'Considerable German fighter superiority', they judged, mistakenly, had been achieved, but Bomber Command, with its barge-destroying and mine-laying potential, still troubled them. On Friday 13 September Hitler, attend-ing a lunch in Berlin with Göring, the army C-in-C von Brauchitsch and other senior officers, professed himself delighted with the results the *Luftwaffe* was achieving against London, which, he predicted, would defeat Great Britain without an invasion. Admiral Raeder was not present, but had that day informed the *Führer* that the *Luftwaffe* had so far failed to 'provide conditions for carrying out the operation'. His warning was underlined when that night Bomber Command for the first time directed its whole night's effort against the invasion ports, although it amounted only to 91 sorties.

That Friday *Sealion* had seemed to be 'off'. Next day, Saturday 14 September, it appeared to be on again. A 'successful landing followed by an occupation would end the war in a short time,' Hitler told his Service chiefs in Berlin. He now seemed, however, to regard the threat of landing as ancillary to the bombing campaign. 'The attacks up to now,' General Halder, the Army Chief of Staff, quoted him as saying, 'have had an enormous effect, though perhaps chiefly upon nerves. Part of that psychological effect is the fear of invasion, and the idea of its imminence must not cease . . . The English may yet be seized with mass hysteria.' How very far the British were from being either beaten or demoralised was made clear that very night when the RAF doubled its previous night's effort, with results gloomily recorded in the German Naval Staff's War Diary:

> In the night of 14/15 September the enemy continue their bomber attacks, directing their main effort on the coast between Boulogne and Antwerp. In Antwerp . . . considerable casualties are inflicted on transports (five transport steamers in part heavily damaged; one barge sunk; two cranes destroyed; an ammunition train blown up; several sheds burning).

Next day it was Fighter Command's turn to deliver the same un-palatable lesson. That Sunday, 15 September, saw the climax of the Battle of Britain. Winston Churchill, visiting 11 Group headquarters at Uxbridge, gravely asked of Air Vice-Marshal Park much the same question he had put exactly four months before to General Weygand at the height of the Battle of France: 'What other reserves have we?' and received the same answer: 'None.' But Park was no Weygand. That day 56 German aircraft were shot down, at a cost of 14 British pilots and 25 Hurricanes and Spitfires. Public morale soared at the news, false though it was, that 183 German planes had been destroyed and took it, rightly enough, as a turning point.

Two days later, on 17 September, the German Naval Staff War Diary summed up, perhaps with more relief than regret, the admirals' assessment of the worsening prospects for invasion:

> The continuing bad weather has further delayed the assembly of transport; and planned mine-sweeping and mine-clearance activity was prejudiced or prevented by the weather . . . The enemy air forces are still by no means defeated; on the contrary they are show-ing increasing activity in their attacks on the Channel ports and in their mounting interference with the assembly movements.

The diary went on to record the contents of a signal just received from General Jodl, at Hitler's headquarters:

> For these reasons the *Führer* decides to postpone *Operation Sealion* for an indefinite time. The postponement still does not mean the final renunciation of *Sealion* . . . The threat to England of an im-minent invasion is to continue. The *Führer* still wishes to be able to carry out a landing in England even in October, if the air war and the weather conditions develop favourably.

Jodl's message had in fact contained no explanation – the reasons were the Navy's, not Hitler's – and that night the RAF delivered by far their most successful strike yet against the invasion fleet, which was badly battered all the way from Dunkirk to Cherbourg. The most spectacu-lar results were at Dunkirk where 26 barges were sunk or damaged, 500 tons of ammunition blown up, and harbour installations des-troyed, but other vessels, including a steamer, were sunk and casualties inflicted, at Boulogne, Calais and Den Helder. Next day, 18 September, Raeder's Chief of Staff, Admiral Fricke, warned Jodl that it had become imperative to disperse the shipping already assembled in the invasion ports, 'otherwise,' in the words of the Navy's War Diary, 'with energetic enemy action such casualties will occur . . . that the execution of the operation on the scale previously envisaged will in any case be problematic.'

Fricke made his case to such effect that even Hitler was persuaded:

The *Führer* decides the same evening that dispersal of transports may take place in accordance with the Naval Staff's intentions, but without allowing any weakening of the *Sealion* preparations to be outwardly apparent . . . Naval forces may be widely dispersed. The steamers provided for *Herbstreise* can be returned . . . The Wehrmacht High Command promises timely notification of the intention to execute *Sealion*, that is, about fifteen days before the date of execution.

These orders were duly carried out, though Hitler tried to insist that ten days' notice, not fifteen, should be adequate to bring the scattered armada back together, but not all the vessels so painfully assembled got away. During the second half of September Bomber Command's offensive against what its crews called 'Blackpool Front' because of the 'illuminations' provided by German searchlights and anti-aircraft guns reached its peak. One airman described a typical trip: 'It was an amazing sight. Calais docks were on fire. So was the waterfront of Boulogne . . . The whole French coast seemed to be a barrier of flame broken only by intense white flashes of exploding bombs and vari-coloured incendiary tracers soaring and circling skywards.' The Germans later assessed their losses at 21 transports out of 170 and 214 of 1918 barges, i.e. rather more than 10 per cent of the whole force; a few tugs and motor-boats, much smaller targets, were also damaged. The immediate result, noted with relief in London, was a sharp drop in the number of vessels in the five main invasion ports between Flushing and Boulogne, from 1004 on 18 September to 691 by the end of the month. By 20 September six destroyers and a torpedo-boat, spotted at Cherbourg only two days before, had also left, returning in fact to Brest. The missing vessels had mostly not gone so far, those from Flushing being next photographed in a nearby canal, and the absentees from Ostend being detected on the canal between there and Bruges, but reassembling them would obviously take time. On 2 October the German Supreme Command formally acknowledged that, 'The ten-day warning period previously applicable to *Operation Sealion* can no longer be maintained', and next day Army Headquarters assured Army Group 'A' that it would now receive at least 20 days' notice, so that the invasion could not, at earliest, be mounted much before

November.

The army successfully pressed to be released even from this obligation so that it could get on with serious training, and on 12 October
Hitler issued a directive abandoning preparations for *Sealion* for 1940.
'Should a landing in England again be considered in the spring or early
summer of 1941,' Hitler added, 'the required degree of preparedness
will be ordered at the right time.' In this vague double-talk *Sealion*
finally foundered. Orders implementing Hitler's decision were sent
out by the Army and Navy High Commands on 15 October, thereby,
as one admiral put it, committing the operation to its 'winter-sleep', a
hibernation from which few expected it would ever be wakened.

Sealion had been defeated before it sailed by the RAF, assisted by the
Royal Navy. The British army had played no part in this success, but,
by late September, it was not merely in every way equipped and
trained to give a far better account of itself than it would have done in
June or July, but was also at last in the right place. The seven divisions
formerly manning the sector from the Thames to the Wash had now
been reduced to four, plus an armoured brigade. The garrison of the
south coast, from the Thames westward, was simultaneously strengthened, from five divisions to nine, plus two armoured brigades, with,
as a reserve for either front, three infantry divisions and two armoured
divisions; a fourth infantry division was protecting London.

By now, after the grand climacteric of 15 September, the Battle of
Britain was entering its final phase, with the daily raids becoming
steadily fewer and lighter. By later British reckoning it officially ended
on Thursday 31 October 1940, a day of dismal drizzle, the end of that
dangerous, golden summer and the start of the long grey years of unrelenting endeavour. The Battle had been a decisive British victory, in
which the Germans had lost 1733 aircraft (not the 2698 claimed) since
10 July and the RAF 915, not, as the Germans believed, 3058.

To the night bomber there was as yet no answer, and the tailing off
of the daylight offensive overlapped with the opening of the Blitz.
London was to be bombed nearly every night from Saturday 7 September 1940 to Saturday 10 May 1941, with occasional but devastating
diversions to other, smaller targets: Coventry, Birmingham, Manchester, Sheffield and other inland industrial cities. The major ports all
suffered heavily. In Liverpool, victim of the 'Maytime' raids in the
spring of 1941, 1450 people were killed, 76,000 made homeless and 33
ships sunk or damaged; the centre of Plymouth was totally destroyed;
Portsmouth, which had stood sentinel on the Channel throughout
British history, was altered more in a few fearsome nights – particularly that of 10 January 1941, when 930 civilians died, plus many naval
personnel, and the dockyard installations were largely wrecked – than
it had been through all the previous centuries. The Blitz saw more
British citizens, both servicemen and civilians, killed or injured than in

all previous invasions and raids combined, and also incomparably more damage done. By 31 December 1940 more than 22,000 civilians had been killed in Great Britain and more than 28,000 seriously injured since 7 September, compared with fewer than 1700 deaths and 2300 other major casualties between the start of the war a year before and 6 September 1940. In 1941, which saw the ending of the main air attack, almost 20,000 civilians died and more than 21,000 were badly hurt. Millions of families suffered major damage to their home or its total destruction. These figures were bad enough, but fell far short of the pre-war predictions. The last such estimate had envisaged 950 tons of bombs a night causing 16,150 fatal casualties and 31,350 others. The actual figures for the heaviest raid on London, on 10 May 1941, were 711 tons of high explosive, plus many incendiary bombs,* which together caused 1436 deaths and 1800 cases of serious injury.

Instead of 17 deaths and 33 cases of serious injury per ton, the bombing in fact caused two deaths and two and a half other major casualties per ton; the experts, with the famous 'multiplier' which had exerted so powerful an influence on pre-war planning, had got it wrong by a factor of ten.

The Blitz was the worst ordeal to which the civilian had so far been subjected at enemy hands, but it never came remotely near to bringing about the internal collapse that the panic-mongers had predicted, and in which Hitler, against all the evidence, still believed. Throughout that long winter the citizen had more immediate concerns than fear of invasion, and the country was in any case growing stronger by the day. The first of the fifty ancient destroyers which Churchill had persuaded the Americans to hand over was delivered, though on the far side of the Atlantic, in late September. Their arrival, and new building, made it possible, in Churchill's words to the Defence Committee a month later 'to bring up the destroyer strength in the Western Approaches', covering the coast from Plymouth round to Glasgow, 'to 60 by the 15th November'. The Channel no longer had to be stripped of its defending warships to provide convoy escorts. Military Intelligence, on the basis of an Enigma message about *Sealion* units resuming their training, concluded on 27 October 'that the invasion of UK and/or Eire is not imminent', and next day the Combined Intelligence Committee cautiously interpreted the movement of shipping eastwards out of the Channel, as revealed by reconnaissance photographs, as likely, 'if maintained' to 'reduce the risk of invasion'. On 5 November, proclaiming that the danger was considered over, Admiral Forbes led the Home Fleet back from Rosyth to Scapa Flow.

* O'Brien, p. 419, fn. 2. This is the German figure. The British one given by O'Brien is 440 tons, while Argyle, *Chronology of World War II*, p. 63, says 795 tons and Mosley, *London Under Fire*, p. 269, '498 tons of high explosive and incendiary bombs and landmines'.

The previous week, General Pownall, who had been moved from his Home Guard post to become GOC Northern Ireland, had been summoned back to London for a conference on 'invasion forecasts for the winter':*

> In Winston's view, and it was generally supported by all the Service representatives, the threat of invasion to England had largely diminished . . . It is nevertheless still being kept in being, partly because Hitler may wish to have it 'laid on' for us in the future at some date, and partly because it forces us to keep quite a lot of our resources of all kinds at home.

This conference, on 31 October, really laid the invasion ghost to rest for the winter. Reconnaissance flights to detect an approaching invader were now scaled down, and, in December, virtually suspended, though Coastal Command continued its general patrols over the North Sea, the frequency varying from daily to three times a week.

Neither Churchill nor Brooke had ever shared Ironside's enthusiasm for fixed fortifications and after November 1940 no more shellproof pillboxes were built on the beaches. The erection now began of a new type of barrier just below low-water mark, known as the 'Z1', or, more martially, when it was securely anchored to the sea-bed beneath, the 'Wallace Sword'. This consisted of a framework of steel tubes, of the kind used by builders for scaffolding, about nine feet [2.7 m] high, and supposed to be able, since the assaulting vehicle would be forced to crawl slowly up the sand or shingle, to stand up to a tank weighing up to 35 tons. More than 15,000 miles [24,000 km] of tubing were used to form this new ring fence round much of the south and east coasts. Photographs which showed the troops involved apparently paddling in the sea, and giving each other pick-a-back rides, provided a totally misleading impression, as one private who worked on the new barrier between Milford-on-Sea and Highcliffe in Hampshire discovered:

> The scaffoldings were quite large structures, clamped together on the beach and carried bodily out into the sea by 25 of us, when the tide was at its lowest (often 3 or 5 am in November). We used to go blue with the cold on moonlight nights . . . When a long line of obstacles were carried out into the sea, all the tall men had to carry the shorter men out to join the sections together with further clamps and steel scaffolding. Sometimes the waves went right over our heads and it was indeed a very frightening experience to those of us who could not swim.

By early 1941 much of the original scaffolding needed replacement and

---

* Gilbert, *Finest Hour*, pp.879-881, gives details of the discussions at this meeting, which he describes as 'of supreme importance for the future conduct of the war', and lists the 24 ministers and senior officers present.

the opportunity was taken to strengthen the defences further. With the problem of delayed-action bombs in the blitzed cities now coming under control, 725 Bomb Disposal Company, RE, found itself transformed into 725 Construction Company and in February 1941 took over responsibility for maintenance of the beach defences between Folkestone and Hythe, marking its arrival by enlarging the existing modest gap in Folkestone pier to one 50 yards [46 m] wide. By hiring concrete mixers from local builders up to 100 anti-tank 'pimples' a day were added to the 1000 already in position and a pillbox was ingeniously hung on the underside of the pier, to be reached via a manhole in its 'deck'.

Simultaneously with the strengthening of fortifications their whole value was beginning to be questioned; as *Tactical Notes for Platoon Commanders*, drafted in February 1941, pointed out, fixed defences were merely part of a general scheme in which mines, trenches and barbed wire were also important, and should be evacuated once the enemy was within grenade-throwing or flame-thrower range. Home Guard manuals stressed that, when housing an anti-tank gun, pillboxes should be regarded as 'static armour' intended to destroy the enemy, not as shelters; no more men should squeeze inside than could use their weapons effectively from it. The new doctrine called for 'nodal points' and 'anti-tank islands' to break up an attack, even if the invaders managed to bypass them, and some in key positions were now equipped with a reserve of three days' water and rations, as well as ammunition and light signals.

Previously the only full-scale, systematic study of the effectiveness of different types of fortification had been the building, back in 1939, somewhat prematurely it now seemed, of half a mile [800 m] of wall on Salisbury Plain to represent the Siegfried Line defending the German frontier. The Road Research Laboratory now turned its expertise to more martial purposes and by April 1941 was studying the effects on British anti-invasion fortifications of shells fired by the German 88-mm [3.5-in] gun, which combined a rapid rate of fire with remarkable accuracy, so that a small section of wall could be fatally weakened by a whole series of hits; with eight armour-piercing shells it could penetrate 6 ft 6 in [2 m] of concrete. By April 1941 the new specification for anti-tank emplacements was raised to include walls which could stand up to six rounds striking an area six feet [1.8 m] square, fired from a range of 500 yards [457 m], and with roofs which could withstand a 250-lb [114-kg] bomb.

Most pillboxes were meant only to provide cover against small-arms fire, but in May 1941 GHQ, Home Forces, ordered Eastern and Southern Commands to review the effectiveness of their existing pillbox defences and in June the walls of some were strengthened to provide 3 ft 6 in [1.1 m] of protection. That month, following a general review of anti-invasion defences by General Brooke, work on the former stop-lines ceased, though an attempt was made to keep in repair pill-boxes still considered necessary. The main emphasis, however, was on improving anti-tank obstacles. The original simple 'V'-shaped anti-tank ditch was widened to 18 ft [5.5 m] at ground level, and deepened to nine feet [2.7 m], with the excavated earth adding another three feet [0.9 m] in height to each bank. In mid-August 1941 a tank equipped with a two-pounder [0.9-kg] gun was used to test all the obstacles then in use. The results showed that reinforced concrete cylinders stood up best to shellfire, but that anything which slowed up the tank helped the defence, even the impromptu barriers of the kind erected a year earlier.

All solid obstructions were, however, now going out of favour, along with the strategic thinking of the previous June, since they might restrict the movement of the defending forces. The technique now favoured was to use coils of tough Dannert wire to catch in the tracks of the advancing tank, so that it became itself the barrier blocking the way forward. Some of the great concrete cubes so hurriedly con-structed the previous summer were subsequently demolished, or, literally *en bloc*, toppled into the rivers beside which they had been erected.

Training was the keyword everywhere during the winter of 1940/41 and the succeeding months, as from November General Brooke thinned out the first-line troops playing a purely static rôle to two divi-sions near Dover and one in Norfolk. Seven weaker divisions, with, as yet, an establishment only two-thirds of its proper level and little artil-lery or transport, were left in close support. The other first-line infantry and armoured divisions were thus freed to concentrate on training, especially in mobility, on which Brooke placed great stress. They learned to make forced moves of up to 40 miles [64 km] on foot, or 200 miles [320 km] in vehicles, and then go immediately into action. To improve the organisational structure a new South-Eastern Com-mand was carved out of the former Southern Command, covering the vital area between the Thames and Portsmouth, the likeliest objective if Hitler did finally come as he had threatened.

The autumn of 1940 brought for the British Army one unusual, if minor victory. On Friday 27 September the latest mark of Junkers 88, part of a force which had that day caused heavy casualties and damage elsewhere in Kent, ran out of petrol and made a forced landing at Graveney, near Faversham. When men of the London Irish Rifles moved in to take the crew prisoner the Germans opened fire. After a brisk fire fight, in which two of them were wounded, the airmen sur-rendered. A British officer, later awarded the George Medal, there-upon dismantled the time-bombs intended to destroy the bomber, which fell virtually undamaged into British hands, a most satisfactory end to the first engagement between British infantry (as distinct from artillery) and enemy forces to be fought on British soil since Napoleonic times.*

The Home Guard, formed in haste with little in the way of weapons, uniforms or supporting facilities the previous summer, was in November 1940 given a new and enhanced status. It had grown, according to the Under-Secretary of State for War, 'to something like 1200 battalions, 5000 companies, 25,000 platoons'. Now every battalion was given a full-time organiser, with funds 'to cover postage, telephones, clerical assistance and all that sort of thing', and the Home Guard acquired a Director-General of its own at the War Office, responsible to the C-in-C, Home Forces, for its administration; for operational purposes, if the enemy landed, the Home Guard would come under the orders of the local army commander.

Although the minister, in announcing these changes, declared he did not want the organisation to lose its 'free and easy, home-spun, moorland, village-green, workshop or pithead character', normal army ranks were now introduced and selection for commissions provided an opportunity to dislodge some of the virtually self-appointed commanders, highly patriotic but sometimes visibly incompetent or 'past it', who had emerged in the chaotic, early days. The Selection Boards, it was generally felt, did a good job and the issue of proper uniforms and weapons also benefited morale.

As the year ended General Pownall, until recently its first Inspector-General – 'The Home Guard are indeed a peculiar race,' he wrote on moving to Northern Ireland – clearly felt confident about the future, as his diary made clear:

> *31 December.* The year ends quietly enough, here at any rate. There were rumours that Hitler meant to do landings, somewhere, over the Christmas period, but these were probably put about by the Germans themselves . . . I have little doubt that they will go for England, and probably Eire at the same time, sometime in the spring or early summer. That is the one way that Hitler can prevent . . . the war dragging on until 1942 . . . But if we stand as firm as we did in 1940, all will be well.

* Rootes, *Front Line County*, p. 88. I am much indebted to this excellent history of Kent during the war, a model of its kind.

45

THE GREATEST STRUGGLE

Your share in the greatest of all our struggles for freedom was a vitally important one.

Special Army Order issued by King George VI to the Home Guard,
2 December 1944

Nineteen hundred and forty was always to be remembered as uniquely glorious in the history of the British people. 'This,' in Churchill's famous phrase, 'was their finest hour,' and merely for the nation to have survived without being defeated, or at least invaded, was a triumph. As the year ended, amid particularly devastating air raids on London, the danger of invasion remained real. In January 1941 the Advanced Headquarters of GHQ Home Forces moved from St Paul's School closer to the seat of government, occupying part of the large underground suite below Great George Street, behind Whitehall and close to Downing Street, now known as the Cabinet War Rooms.*

General Brooke's Chief of Staff, Lieut.-General Bernard Paget, had long been established there and Brooke was delighted with the spot from which in an invasion he would, as C-in-C, Home Forces, direct the defence of the country. 'The headquarters,' he noted in his memoirs, 'was deep down in the basement and covered over with a thick apron of reinforced concrete . . . All the offices were well fitted out with special ventilators, telephones, message conveyors, map rooms, etc. It was in every way an excellent battle headquarters.'

Hitler had already, in the closing months of 1940, begun to look else-where for his next conquest. On 18 December he set in motion the initial planning for an attack on Russia. On 20 May 1941, German air-borne troops landed in Crete. On 1 June the last British troops were evacuated from the island, beaten solely by parachutists and infantry landed from aircraft. On Sunday 22 June 1941 came the start of Operation Barbarossa, the German campaign against Russia, but the Chiefs of Staff, always more apprehensive than Churchill, thought a German invasion of England was still possible. They estimated, with reasonable accuracy, that Hitler could still spare six armoured, four airborne

---

* The War Rooms have been excellently restored and are open to the public.

and 26 infantry divisions for the purpose, and that he could support it with 2000 bombers and dive-bombers, 1500 fighters and 1000 transports, though these were in fact exaggerations.

The lesson of Crete seemed to be that if Hitler could conquer one island by air power alone, despite the presence of the Royal Navy, he might well be tempted to attack another, and even the prime minister grossly over-estimated the danger of airborne attack. The actual number of men dropped or landed on Crete was barely 30,000, and the Germans did not have the parachutists, the Junkers 52 transports or the gliders, which each carried a mere nine men including the pilot, to deliver a blow of the same kind against England, especially in the face of a still unbeaten RAF. Nevertheless it was perhaps wise to be cautious and Churchill's minute of 29 June 1941 to the Secretary of State for War was, though founded on a false assumption, typically combative in spirit.

> We have to contemplate the descent from the air of perhaps a quarter of a million parachutists, glider-borne or crash-landed aeroplane troops. Everyone in uniform, and anyone else who likes, must fall upon these wherever they find them and attack them with the utmost alacrity –
> Let every one
> Kill a Hun.
> This spirit must be inculcated ceaselessly into all ranks of HM Forces . . . Every man must have a weapon of some kind, be it only a lance or a pike.

In a similar memo sent the same day to the Secretary of State for Air the prime minister urged that, 'Every man in Air Force uniform ought to be armed with something – a rifle, a tommy-gun, a pistol, a pike or a mace and . . . have his place in the defence scheme.' The reference to the mace, last used against invaders at the Battle of Hastings, does not seem to have been followed up, but Churchill's hint about pikes led to their being issued that autumn to Home Guard units throughout the country, in the form of a 3 ft 6-in [1.1-m] length of metal pipe, with a 17-in [43-cm] bayonet fitted into it. Assurances that it would be useful for street fighting failed to overcome the universal contempt for this weapon, which had been rejected as out of date even in Elizabethan times[*] and, after many embarrassing cartoons and tactless cries of 'Gadzooks!' when pike-bearing Home Guards appeared in the streets, it was, by wise commanders, quietly left in store.

That summer of 1941, a new leaflet, signed in facsimile 'Winston S. Churchill', and uncompromisingly entitled *BEATING THE INVADER. A MESSAGE FROM THE PRIME MINISTER* was distributed to every home. A much more polished production than its

---

[*] See *Defending the Island*, p. 428.

predecessor, *If the Invader Comes*, its message could be summed up in two phrases: 'STAND FIRM' and 'CARRY ON'. The vexed question, debated ever since *An Englishman's Home*, as to how far a civilian could go in resisting an armed German, was answered boldly: 'You have the right of every man and woman to do what you can to protect yourself, your family and your home', and the leaflet breathed a spirit of resolute optimism:

> Where the enemy lands, or tries to land, there will be most violent fighting . . . It may easily be some weeks before the invader has been totally destroyed, that is to say, killed or captured to the last man who has landed on our shores. Meanwhile, all work must be continued to the utmost.

By the end of July 1941 Germany was so heavily committed in Russia, the Joint Intelligence Committee reported, that she could not possibly disengage her forces to re-open a front in the west before September, the accepted end of the 'invasion season'. Even the Chiefs of Staff admitted that a landing was unlikely before the spring of 1942. Nevertheless the possibility remained, and on 12 August 1941 GHQ, Home Forces, issued orders to Eastern, South-Eastern and Southern Commands to reconnoitre sites where heavy anti-aircraft guns, 'the only means with which to engage the German 90-ton tank', could be used in a ground defence rôle. GHQ, Home Forces, went on to draw attention to the places identified as particularly vulnerable:

> It is considered that the following are the most likely beaches for the landing of these tanks:

LITTLEHAMPTON	WORTHING
WALMER	DEAL
CLACTON	FRINTON
1½ MILES NORTH & SOUTH	
OF FELIXSTOWE	
ALDEBURGH	SIZEWELL
WEYBOURNE	

In September 1941 further pillbox construction, except in special situations, was stopped, and between 29 September and 3 October 1941 the first full-scale anti-invasion manoeuvres since 1940 were undertaken. *Exercise Bumper* was so-named because it was based on the premise that an 'enemy' force, commanded by the General Officer Commanding Eastern Command, from near Norwich, would bump into the defending army under the GOC, Southern Command, Lieut.-General Harold [later Field-Marshal Lord] Alexander, of whom Churchill had a high opinion. This was hardly justified by what now occurred. During the exercise, in which four armoured divisions and nine infantry divisions were involved, Alexander, complained Brooke in the subsequent post-mortem, set up his headquarters in the wrong place, exposed his left flank to an enemy counter-attack and, worst of all failed 'to press forward ruthlessly'. The real hero of the day was Bernard Montgomery, who had been appointed Chief Umpire of *Bumper* and whose summing-up of its lessons before 270 senior officers at the Staff College on 10 October was described by Brooke himself as 'masterly'. 'Monty' went on to organise *Exercise Greatbinge* covering only his own Corps, in Kent and Sussex, which was a great success, but by the time it took place, on 17 November 1941, he had been promoted again, to become GOC of the new South-Eastern Command, with its headquarters at Reigate, in succession to General Paget, who was shortly to take over command of Home Forces. Montgomery, characteristically, signalled his arrival by re-naming his new command 'South-Eastern Army' and by putting in hand an energetic winter training programme. At the 'Corps Study Week', held in the unmilitary surroundings of the Spa Hotel, Tunbridge Wells, his pamphlet *Lessons learned during the first two Years of War* was a 'set book', which stressed the need for close cooperation with the RAF as well as the need for tanks, artillery and infantry to act together. He even, unusually for a senior officer, found a role for the Home Guard. To defeat a German invasion in 1942, Montgomery told his officers, 'the efficient cooperation of the Home Guard is essential.'

Churchill had not in the past rated the risk of invasion high but Hitler's rapid progress in Russia seems to have changed his mind. On 20 October 1941 he confided in President Roosevelt his belief that once the Russian front had become stabilised Hitler planned to 'gather perhaps 50 or 60 divisions in the West for the invasion of the British Isles'. He anticipated parachute and other airborne landings 'on a yet unmeasured scale' and there were reports of the preparation of 800 transports able to carry 'eight or ten tanks each' across the North Sea but capable of 'landing anywhere upon the beaches'. The country therefore needed to be prepared 'to meet a supreme onslaught from March [1942] onwards'.

Next day, 21 October 1941, Churchill reminded the Defence Committee of 'the importance of continuous photographic reconnaissance of the invasion ports', and on 26 January 1942 the Combined Intelligence Centre duly produced a report showing that the total number of enemy landing craft, completed or under construction, was fewer than a hundred and that there was 'no evidence so far of the intensified effort which would be required to reach by the Spring the figure of 800'. Churchill was delighted. 'I was always sceptical about these 800 vessels,' he wrote gleefully to the new C-in-C, Home Forces, 'and repeatedly questioned the trustworthiness of the rumours . . . The deductions founded upon them as to the scale of invasion are obsolete.'

During 1941, as previously urged by Churchill, additional guns were installed at Dover. At Fan Bay a battery of three six-inch [15-cm] guns, with an extreme range of 25,000 yards [14.2 miles; 23 km] had been added in February. In October four more 9.2-in [23.3-cm] calibre guns, able to hit targets up to 31,000 yards [17.6 miles; 28.3 km] became operational. Two others, even larger, formed the Wanstone battery. These 15-in [38.1-cm] guns had a range of 42,000 or, if supercharged, 50,000 yards [23.9 miles; 28.2 km or 28.4 miles; 45.5 km], and were known, inappropriately as 'Clem' and 'Jane', after the deputy prime minister Clement Attlee, and the popular, and usually half-undressed, strip-cartoon heroine. Three other heavy, railway mounted 13.5-in [34-cm] guns, already in action, had more martial names, Sceneshifter, Gladiator and Piecemaker; a fourth weapon, a massive 18-in [46-cm] howitzer, though promisingly christened Bochebuster, was never fired in anger.

Life as an artilleryman at Dover, the only part of the British Isles now regularly under enemy fire, had been dangerous even before the Germans occupied the French coast. As early as November 1939 one man, his commander recalled, had been 'swept over the Admiralty Pier and drowned' while going on duty, and the elements remained throughout the war a more unrelenting enemy than the Germans:

> The journey along the breakwater could be particularly hazardous . . . There was no protecting rail, and it was a case of choosing a gap between the high waves, which swept right over the breakwater in wintertime, and then making a dash for it . . . It was not unknown for the high seas to sweep the 100-lb [45-kg] shells from the gun platforms and personnel with them . . . The look-outs on each gun, during this weather, were permitted to stand within the gun shields for protection, provided they maintained a look-out through the gun ports . . . Later it became even more dangerous, as by early 1941 German planes were constantly machine-gunning, during a sweep along the mole.

For most places in Great Britain during 1941 the only German presence was overhead. The ending of the main blitz on London in May, was followed by widespread 'hit-and-run' raids, in which many places suffered frequent but relatively light attacks. The total civilian casualty figures for the year, just under 20,000 dead and some 21,000 seriously injured, were not much below those of 1940, but nearly two-thirds were suffered outside London.

The Intelligence estimates prepared in the autumn of 1941 had warned that the Germans might assemble for invasion, in the spring of 1942, no fewer than nine armoured divisions, consisting of 2000–3600 tanks, with another 11 divisions employed to make diversionary landings. The Admiralty had stated that it might require five to seven days to move its forces to disrupt such an operation after it had actually begun, a period during which General Brooke confirmed, 'it would be perfectly possible to lose this country and the war'. He still feared a two-pronged thrust through East Anglia and the south-east simultaneously, though the Inter-Service Committee on Invasion believed a frontal attack through Kent and Sussex – which was what *Sealion* had envisaged – more likely. Everyone agreed on the need for a 'coastal crust' currently manned by 38,000 men, to prevent a sudden landing. Only the prime minister remained stoutly sceptical.

Between these discussions, in the autumn of 1941, and the period they concerned, the spring of 1942, General Brooke's appointment as Chief of the General Staff was announced; he formally took over on 25 December 1941. He was succeeded as Commander-in-Chief, Home Forces, by Lieut.-General Sir Bernard Paget.

The global situation now changed again. On 7 December 1941 Japan attacked both Great Britain and the United States and four days later Germany also declared war on the US. In January 1942 the first American troops arrived in Northern Ireland. By the spring of 1942, about which the British had so recently been apprehensive, even the pessimists agreed that the danger of invasion had declined. At the same time the number of men under arms within the British Isles had risen, to 1,500,000, of whom 850,000 belonged to Home Forces, immediately available to resist an enemy landing.

The Home Guard had also, at least on paper, become a force to be reckoned with, now numbering 1,600,000, though its character had changed. From January 1942 it had become partly a conscript force, into which male civilians aged from 18 to 51 could be directed, being thereafter required to attend for up to 48 hours training or other duty a month, under penalty of a month in jail or a £10 fine. The old 'housemaid's clause' by which members could resign on giving two weeks' notice was, from February, abolished and volunteers were, like 'directed men', obliged to stay in until victory or old age (put at 65) set them free.

The change in status, highly unwelcome to those who had volunteered back in 1940, came just as the Home Guard was beginning to be adequately equipped. Its best arms, like the Vickers gun and the hand grenade, were the same as those issued to the regular army, but some items were specially designed for their use, prompting the cynical observation of one ex-officer turned LDV that, 'A Home Guard weapon was one that was dangerous to the enemy and, to a greater degree, to the operator.' To this category seems to belong the Northover projector, a drainpipe-like object 'designed . . . ,' in the words of one disillusioned user, 'to discharge glass bottles containing a phosphorous mixture which burst into livid flames, giving off quantities of suffocating smoke' but with 'a natural tendency for the shock of discharge to break the glass bottles in the breech'. The Spigot Mortar,

originally known by the medieval-sounding name of the Blacker
Bombard, which could fire a 14-lb [6.4-kg] missile 800 yards [730-m],
was better regarded. More in the true Home Guard tradition was the
Smith Gun, which could project a 10-lb [4.5-kg] shell 1000 yards [914
m], and be towed behind a 'Baby' 7 h.p. Austin, but had to be tipped
on its side to be fired. The Thompson sub-machine gun made a brief
appearance only to be withdrawn, to the relief, it was said, of one
general who declared, 'We do not intend to introduce the methods of
the Chicago gangster into European warfare.' The Home Guard was
consoled with the cruder and lighter Sten, liable if carelessly handled,
the user was warned, to blow one's fingers off.

In 1941, with Anti-Aircraft Command under pressure to release
trained gunners for service overseas, some of the new 'Z' batteries,
firing rockets, began to be manned by Home Guard volunteers, and
during 1942 the practice was extended to the guns. Eventually around
142,000 Home Guards, i.e. about one-tenth of the force's peak strength
of, in March 1943, around 1,793,000, served at some time as artillerymen, either in ordinary batteries or in light anti-aircraft units defending the factories and railway depots where they worked, and they were
credited with a number of 'kills'. Another 7000 helped, from early
1942, to man coastal artillery batteries. Of 260 batteries still in use
when, in the autumn of 1943, the Chiefs of Staff agreed that they were
no longer needed, 75 were Home-Guard manned.

Just as the number of guns on land was being reduced more were
being installed offshore. During 1942 and 1943 a series of 'Maunsell
forts', named after the civil engineer who had proposed and designed
them, were set up in the Thames estuary. Though primarily intended
to carry anti-aircraft guns, the forts also provided a transmission site
for the new low-level radar, which could detect sea-hugging aircraft
making for London, enemy mine-layers, and E-boats attacking coastal
shipping. Two types of Maunsell fort, very different in appearance but
similar in purpose, were developed, both being constructed on shore
and then towed out to be lowered on to the sea-bed. The six army
forts, erected three and a half to six miles [6-9 km] from land, consisted
of a set of seven two-storey steel boxes, supported by thin 'legs',
anchored to a concrete base on the sea bottom, and linked by bridges
made of tubular steel. The central box contained a control tower, and
others housed respectively searchlights, a Bofors gun, and, in four
cases, a 3.7-in [9.4-cm] anti-aircraft gun. Each octagonal 'box', containing stores, ammunition or living quarters for the gun crews, was
about 36 ft [11.5 m] at its widest, and the whole fort covered an area of
about 400 ft [122 m] by 300 [91 m]. The four naval forts, up to nine
miles [15 km] out at sea, consisted of two concrete towers on a solid
submerged base, linked at the top by a single platform carrying guns
and radar aerials. The twin towers were divided into seven levels, of

which five were below the waterline, containing stores and the crew's quarters; each circular room, 22 ft [6.7 m] across, housed 12 men, with their mess tables and two-tier bunks. There was no space for recreational facilities but the general verdict was that it was no worse than being at sea.

Nineteen forty-two and 1943 were a period of much lighter air attack. During 1942 the main German effort was put into the 'Baedeker raids', directed between April and October against historic cities of no strategic importance, but the total bomb load equalled only a single month's at the height of the Blitz, and the death toll for the year dropped to 3200, with 4100 others seriously injured. During 1943 a series of scattered raids, mainly on London and coastal targets but with some 'hit-and-run' attacks elsewhere, saw the number of dead drop still further, to 2400, while the defences, assisted by airborne radar and improved ground defences, brought down a much higher proportion of the attackers. The RAF had now virtually established air superiority over the United Kingdom and the Channel at night as well as by day.

The prospect of an invasion had dwindled to negligible proportions and the island was filling up with armed men preparing not to repel the Germans on 'S Tag' but to re-enter Europe on the allied equivalent, 'D-Day'. The Home Guard's traditional rôle, of fighting local delaying actions in small detachments, was now upgraded to one of combining into substantial formations to challenge the large-scale suicide missions the Germans might, it was suggested, launch to disrupt the allied embarkation.*

Pillboxes were now regarded as more likely to shelter the enemy than protect the defenders. One Home Guard, in a Suffolk battalion, recalls subjecting a pillbox to ten rounds from a Spigot Mortar at a range of 600–700 yards [550–640 m]. 'I doubt if anyone would have survived after the first hit,' he concluded. 'The pillbox, however, would still be usable for a new lot of occupants!'

The war had given a new lease of life to the old dream of a Channel Tunnel. The chairman of the War Cabinet's Scientific and Engineering Advisory Committee was the Tunnel's most unrelenting enemy, Maurice Hankey, and in May 1941 he wrote to the Chiefs of Staff suggesting that if they faced 'a very long war' the Germans might re-open the old workings. The War Office consulted an eminent civil engineer as to whether a tunnel might be built clandestinely, but his advice, a colleague recorded, was that 'provided we kept reasonably alert, the Germans could not dig the tunnel without being detected'. Accordingly periodic reconnaissance flights were made over the original tunnel workings, but the only signs of activity proved to be harmless: the Germans were making use of the earlier excavations to get rid of old

* See my *The Real Dad's Army*, p. 102.

machinery and discarded shell-cases. Even the most fearful eventually accepted that attempts to dig a new tunnel would easily be detected by photographic reconnaissance, whether the spoil formed vast heaps on land or was dumped in the sea, when its high chalk content would discolour large areas of the water. Some anxieties remained, however, even after Hankey was replaced in March 1942 by the less alarmist R.A. [later Lord] Butler. On 1 July 1942 a specialist team was sent to visit the abandoned sites around Dover – they enjoyed, it was reported, 'a good wartime lunch' – but the experiments with naval listening devices which followed proved reassuring. 'Small noises', like a soldier using a pickaxe, could be heard through the chalk up to 150-200 yards [137-183 m] away, and 'large noises', like an express train, up to a mile [1760 yards, 1600 m]. Also in 1942 a brief possibility emerged that the tunnel might be built from the British side to supply the allied armies after D-Day, but it vanished when calculations confirmed that, even on the most optimistic estimate, it would take eight years to complete. The headquarters of the Channel Tunnel Company had meanwhile, justly some felt, been destroyed in the Blitz.

It was in fact in the normal way, by sea, that most American and British troops crossed the Channel on D-Day, Tuesday 6 June 1944. It had taken all the strength of Great Britain and the United States, two years of preparation, and complete mastery of both the sea and the air, to enable the allies to land in the first 24 hours some 130,000 seaborne troops and 22,500 from the air. Here was the final refutation of all the alarmists' fables about a massive invasion of the British Isles being mustered overnight and delivered without warning. D-Day provided another lesson, too. The 'Atlantic Wall' guarding 'Fortress Europe' was far more formidable than anything General Ironside and his successors had constructed, but did not prevent the invaders getting ashore on all the intended beaches and advancing inland.

D-Day was really the end of England's invasion history. The next intruders to arrive were unmanned aircraft, the flying-bombs, the first of which landed in Kent at 4.13 am on Tuesday 13 June 1944. Until the end of August, when the launching sites were evacuated, they proved a destructive menace in London and 'Doodlebug Alley' to the south-east, but by then had been mastered by a combination of fighters over the sea and inland, massed guns, making use of radar-directed fire and proximity fuses, along the coast, and a line of barrage balloons forming a long-stop along the North Downs. The flying-bombs had dwindled to a minor nuisance when, at 6.34 pm on Friday 8 September 1944, the first rocket landed at Chiswick, in West London. Against this new threat no defence existed and the rockets continued to arrive unchecked until 4.37 pm on Tuesday 27 March 1945. By then 1115 had reached the British mainland, or exploded offshore, of a total of 1403 launched, killing 2754 people and seriously injuring 6523. The last flying-bomb was shot down off Orfordness at 12.43 pm on Thursday 29 March 1945, bringing the total of incidents reported on land to 5823, in which 6184 civilians and 2917 servicemen, the latter including rocket casualties, had died within the British Isles, and 17,981 civilians and 1939 servicemen had been seriously injured. The two weapons, aptly named by the Germans V (for *Vergeltung*, i.e. Revenge) -1 and V-2, although pointing the way to a different type of danger to the island in the future, never had the faintest prospect of affecting the course of the war.

Piloted raids virtually ended after June 1944, only to be resumed late in February 1945, and on 3 March nearly a hundred enemy aircraft crossed the coast to attack Bomber Command airfields. The last raid of all, by a handful of aircraft, came on 20 March 1945.

Artillery attack on England had already ceased. The last round fired by the German guns around Cape Gris-Nez, shortly before, like the V-1 launching sites, they were overwhelmed by the allied armies, landed in Castle Street, Dover, at 7.17 pm on Wednesday 26 September 1944. The Germans had by now succeeded in killing, with 2226 shells, some 148 civilians and 69 servicemen in the area, and seriously injuring 403 civilians and 100 members of the Forces; a source of grief and nuisance but no real contribution to a German victory.

The final reckoning showed a total of 60,595 civilians killed by enemy action, including shelling, during the Second World War, and 86,162 seriously injured. An additional 1206 members of the Home Guard were recorded as dying of injury or illness due to their service, from training and other accidents and, in a few cases, from enemy bombs or gunfire while on duty. Two Home Guards had been awarded George Crosses, the civilian equivalent of the VC, and thirteen received George Medals.

The danger of invasion was never declared officially to be over, but in September 1944 conscription for the Home Guard ceased and on Sunday 3 December it was formally stood down in nationwide parades and with royal thanks. 'History will say,' declared George VI in a Special Army Order, 'that your share in the greatest of all our struggles for freedom was a vitally important one.' On Tuesday 8 May 1945 came Victory in Europe Day; the Germans' second attempt to enslave Europe had failed, thanks to their inability to conquer the sea and invade the British Isles. The Japanese finally capitulated on Wednesday 15 August, to end the Second World War.

No-one, even in the euphoria of victory, doubted the continuing need for an army, a navy and an air force, but May 1945 marked the beginning of the end for coastal artillery. That month the Chiefs of Staff considered a paper by the Defence of Bases Committee which made various recommendations for reductions in the batteries still guarding Great Britain's shore, and on 2 December 1946 the same committee issued a report which provides a final picture of these fixed defences. Forty-two batteries were listed, in roughly the same number of locations, of which twenty-eight were recommended for retention. The Director of Military Operations warned, however, that they might ultimately 'be superseded by unorthodox weapons as a result of research at present in progress'. So indeed it proved. In 1956 Coastal Artillery was abolished, the end of Great Britain's traditional invasion history. No one since 1945 has produced an old-style imaginary invasion story but a 'post-alarmist' school of writers has emerged, describing in frightening detail what might have happened had the Germans attempted an invasion in 1940, and inspiring more than one film and television programme. Their work seems to confirm, however, that fear of invasion belongs to the past. The Home Guard, in spite of half-hearted attempts to revive it, is now only a memory, though the Territorial Army, emphatically not confined to home defence, remains. Almost all the ships and guns which kept the enemy at a distance have been broken up or melted down. Only the fortifications, and all too few of them, remain, often engulfed by gorse and bramble, or transformed to serve peaceful purposes. The defence works erected in 1940 can also still be seen in many parts of the country. Along the 'GHQ Line' inland, pillboxes can be found doing peaceful duty as pigsties, garden sheds, builders' stores and, in one case, as a shelter for that most tranquil of species, fishermen. On the coast gun-emplacements have been opened out to serve as seafront shelters, or as 'hides' for bird-watchers. No one would dare to demolish Dover Castle but of the sites of the great guns which once guarded the Channel at Wanstone and the North Foreland only a few concrete fragments and crumbling gun-pits are left to puzzle future archaeologists. 'Winnie' and 'Pooh', which once thundered defiance from what is now Kingsdown Golf Course, have been removed as they got in the way of the players, a final riposte to that famous rhyme about the golfers at Deal whose game was nearly spoiled by the news that the Germans had landed.*

Yet it is not in bricks or concrete that the story of Great Britain's defence against invasion can best be read. Those who see such traces of the past, on promenade or beach or estuary should look beyond them to the sea itself. It is the sea which has served and shielded us, and, century after century, saved us. Linked to Europe by subterranean passage we may now be. But islanders we have always been and will remain.

* See my *How We Lived Then*, p. 465.

A NOTE ON SOURCES

This bibliography is arranged under the following headings:

Reference Books
Individual Subjects
Official Documents Consulted
Guides to Individual Areas
General Bibliography

Cross-references are provided where appropriate, except in the case of Official Documents, which are arranged chronologically. Where a book has proved particularly helpful this is indicated in a footnote in the relevant chapter. Where the edition of a book I have used may differ substantially from the text as originally published I have given both dates. The place of publication is London unless otherwise stated, except for the Clarendon Press and Oxford University Press (OUP), which are at Oxford, the Cambridge University Press, at Cambridge, and David and Charles Ltd, at Newton Abbot, Devon. Where no date of publication was given I have suggested what seems the likeliest date from internal or external evidence. The publisher, where known, is given for books from 1900 onwards. Diaries, letters, etc. are under the name of their author, not their editor, but biographies are under author, not subject, with a cross-reference. Where the identity of an author writing under a pseudonym is known, the main entry is under that name, whatever appeared on the original title page, with a cross-reference to the *nom-de-plume*. The list of reference books is not exhaustive but indicates those I have consulted most frequently. My debt to the Fortress Study Group is acknowledged elsewhere and will be evident to anyone reading this bibliography. The Group's journal, *Fort*, is available in major libraries and anyone seeking further information about membership should contact the Hon. Secretary of the Group listed there.

REFERENCE BOOKS

Chambers Biographical Dictionary, 2 vols, Edinburgh, 1975 (f.p. 1974).

Concise Oxford Dictionary of English Literature, OUP, 1970 (f.p. 1939).

COOK, Chris and STEVENSON, John, *The Longman Handbook of Modern History, 1714-1980*, Longmans, 1983.

Dictionary of National Biography, The, OUP, numerous editions.

Everyman's Dictionary of Literary Biography (ed. D.C. Browning), Pan, 1972 (f.p. Dent, 1958).

FALKUS, Malcolm and GILLINGHAM, John (eds), *Historical Atlas of Britain*, Book Club Associates, 1981.

JAMES, Charles, *A New and Enlarged Dictionary in French and English, in which are Explained the Principal Terms, with Appropriate Illustrations, of all the Sciences that are more or less Necessary for an Officer and Engineer*, 2 vols, 1810.

MITCHELL, B.R., with the collaboration of Phyllis Deane, *Abstract of British Historical Statistics*, Cambridge University Press, 1962.

Oxford Dictionary of Quotations, The, OUP, 2nd edition revised, 1959.

Parliamentary History of England from the Earliest Period to the year 1803 . . . continued downwards in the work entitled 'Hansard's Parliamentary Debates', Hansard, 1820 and continuing.

Penguin Encylopedia of Places, The (ed. W.G. Moore), Penguin, 1971.

SANDERSON, Michael, *Sea Battles. A Reference Guide*, David and Charles, 1975.

SMURTHWAITE, David, *The Ordnance Survey Complete Guide to the Battlefields of Britain*, Book Club Associates, 1984.

Statistical Digest of the War, HMSO and Longmans, 1951.

Statutes at Large, The, from the first year of James I to the 10th Year of the Reign of William III, Vol. III, 1770 and continuing.

Who Was Who, A. & C. Black, various dates and continuing.

INDIVIDUAL SUBJECTS

TEIGNMOUTH 1690

Anon, *Devon and Cornwall Notes and Queries*, Vol. 13, pp. 33-4, Exeter, 1924-5.

Anon, *Great News from Tingmouth, Torbay and Exon, giving an Account of the Several Actions of the French Invaders . . . In a letter from Exon*, 1690, document 244,687 in Devon and Exeter Institute.

CARRINGTON, N.T. et al, *The Teignmouth, Dawlish and Torquay Guide*, 1828.

GRIFFITHS, G.D. and E.G.C., *History of Teignmouth*, Brunswick Press, Teignmouth, 1965.

LUTTRELL, Narcissus, *Luttrell's Diary. A Brief Historical Relation of State Affairs from September 1678-April 1714*, Vol. II, 1 January 1689/90–31 December 1692, pp. 83-4, OUP, 1857.

LYSON, D., *Magna Britannia*, chapter on *Devonshire*, 1822.

MACAULAY, Lord [Thomas B.], *History of England from the Accession of James the Second*, 4 vols, 1849–55, Vol. III, pp. 648–54.

NORTHCOTE, Lady Caroline, *Devon. Its Moorlands, Streams and Coasts*, Chatto, 1908. [Includes, p. 105, *The Teign*, a poem which begins 'Brave Devonshire Boys', of which a fuller text under the latter title is in the Exeter City Library.]

PARRY, Hubert, *Notes on Old Teignmouth*, W.J. Southwood, Exeter, 1914.

TRUMP, H.J., *West Country Harbour*, Brunswick Press, Teignmouth, 1976.

See also FOORD, HARGREAVES, HOZIER, OGG, *James II*, ROBB.

WHITEHAVEN, 1778 and John Paul Jones, 1747–1792

CHANDLER, David, *Whitehaven and John Paul Jones* (pamphlet), Whitehaven and District Lions Club, n.d. but post-1971.

CHAPPELL, Russell E., 'The Gardener's Bold Boy. John Paul Jones at Whitehaven', *Country Life*, 4 April 1985.

CRAWFORD, Mary McDermot, *The Sailor Whom England Feared*, Eveleigh Nash, 1913.

FANCY, Harry, 'The Gardener's Bold Boy', follow-up to article of 4 April, *Country Life*, 30 May 1985.

— — *Whitehaven and its Defences* (leaflet), Friends of Whitehaven Museum, 1985.

JACKSON, Ian R., *The John Paul Jones Cannon* (pamphlet), Beth-waites, Workington, n.d.

John Paul Jones. Reprint from *Lloyd's Evening Post*, Monday 27 April to Wednesday 29 April 1778, Vol. XLII, No. 3252, Friends of Whiteha-ven Museum, 1977.

— — *Battle between the* Bon Homme Richard *and the* Serapis, Old South Leaflet No. 152, Directors of the Old South Work, Boston, n.d.

— — *History of John Paul Jones, The Pirate* (pamphlet), Glasgow, n.d., re-issued by Whitehaven Museum and Art Gallery, n.d.

MORISON, Samuel Eliot, *John Paul Jones. A Sailor's Biography*, Little Brown, Boston, 1959.

PREEDY, George R., *The Life of Rear-Admiral John Paul Jones*, Herbert Jenkins Ltd, 1940.

SEITZ, Don C. (ed.), *Paul Jones. His Exploits in English Seas during 1778–1780. Contemporary Accounts Collected from English Newspapers*, Dutton, New York, 1917.

FISHGUARD 1797

Bibliography of Fishguard (includes other topics beside the 1797 landing), Dyfed County Council Cultural Services Department, Haverford-west.

Bibliography of the Fishguard Invasion, 1797, Notes and Queries, Vol. 158,

1930, pp. 166–7.

The French Invasion of Pembrokeshire, 1797, Carmarthenshire Record Office, Topic List no. 4, n.d.

Anon, *The Building of Fishguard Fort* (pamphlet), n.d.

Anon, *Historic Sites and Scenes of England* (pamphlet), Great Western Railway, 1924.

Anon, Letter from Naberth, 27 February 1797, *National Library of Wales Journal*, Vol. VI, 1949–50, p. 303.

Anon, *Notes and Queries*, 8th Series, Vol. 9, January–June 1986. (This describes the inscription on a cutlass presented to a customs official for 'meritorious conduct' during the 1797 landing.)

Anon, 'The French Invasion of Fishguard in 1797', *Young Wales*, Vol. IV, February 1898, pp. 40–42.

Anon, 'Account of the Late Descent of the French in Wales', *The Monthly Magazine and British Register*, January–June 1797, pp. 172–4.

Anon, *Chambers Journal of Popular Literature*, No. 315, 14 January 1869 (fictional account).

BOWEN, George, Letter from Bath, 26 February 1797, *National Library of Wales Journal*, Vol. VII, 1951–2, p. 271.

DAY, E. Hermitage, *The Last Invasion. An Account of the French Landing at Fishguard*, offprinted from *The Treasury*, pp. 425–31, n.d. or place of publication.

FENTON, Ferrar, Articles reprinted from The Antiquaries Column in the *Pembroke County Guardian* in *Pembrokeshire Antiquities*, Pub. Solva, near Haverfordwest, 1897, pp. 63–70.

FENTON, R., *An Historical Tour through Pembrokeshire*, 1811.

FREEMAN, E.C., 'Last Invader', *Country Quest*, Vol. 6, No. 8, 1966.

HARRIES, John, *Welsh Patriotism on the Landing of the French at Fishguard* (pamphlet), Haverfordwest, 1875.

HARRIES, Joseph, *An Authentic Account of the Invasion by the French Troops on Carrig Gwasted Point near Fishguard* (pamphlet), Haverfordwest, 1842.

HORN, Pamela, *History of the French Invasion of Fishguard 1797* (pamphlet), Presili Printers, Fishguard, 1980.

JONES, Commander E.H. Stuart, *The Last Invasion of Britain*, University of Wales, Cardiff, 1950.

JONES, G.C., 'The French Landing in Pembrokeshire, 1797', *Young Wales*, Vol. III, No. 28, April 1897.

JONES, John A. Rupert, *Notes and Queries*, Vol. CLVIII, February 1930, p. 137. (This recounts what happened to the French ships used in the expedition.)

LAWS, E., 'The French Landing at Fishguard', *Archaeologia Cambriensis, The Journal of the Cambrian Archaeological Association*, Vol. XIV, 4th series, London, 1885, pp. 311–24.

LLANGAN, Rev. David Jones, 'The Year 1797 in the Life of the Rev.

David Jones Llangan', *Transactions of the Calvinistic Methodist Historical Society*, Vol. XXIII, Caernarvon, 1938.

MILBURN, J.S., 'French Muskets Fire Again', *Country Quest*, Vol. 14, No. 5, 1973.

MILES, J.P.F., 'Jemina and the Black Legion', *Country Quest*, Vol.4, No.1, 1963.

PARRY, John, 'Letter from Haverfordwest, 1797', *Bygones Relating to Wales and the Border Counties*, April-June 1902.

PEEL, J.H.B., 'The Last Invasion of Britain', *Sunday Telegraph Magazine*, 31 January 1969.

ROWLANDS, Rev. Dan., *Some passages taken from the diary of the late Rev. Dan. Rowlands, Sometime Vicar of Llanfiangelpenybont*, Fisher Unwin, 1892.

SALMON, David, 'The French Invasion of Pembrokeshire in 1797', *Transactions of the Historical Society of West Wales*, Vol. XIX, Carmarthen, 1929, pp. 129-206. (This compilation includes official documents and contemporary letters and other accounts.)

—— 'A Sequel to the French Invasion of Pembrokeshire', *Y Cymmrodor*, The Magazine of the Honourable Society of Cymmrodorion, Vol. XLIII, London, 1932, pp. 62-90. (This reproduces documents used in the trial of two Welshmen accused of collaborating with the French.)

The Descent of the French on Pembrokeshire, W. Spurrell, Carmarthen, 1930. (Similar to the previous work cited, but with an introductory essay.)

'Histories of the French Invasion of Pembrokeshire', *Journal of the Welsh Bibliographical Society*, Vol. V, 1937-1942, published Carmarthen. (This usefully classifies the material under the headings of 'Original, Derivative and Fictitious'.)

WILLIAMS, T., 'Letter from Fishguard dated 3 March 1797', *Notes and Queries*, Vol. CLI, June-December 1926.

WILLIAMS, W.R. (ed.), Extracts from *The Times* on the Fishguard landing, in *Old Wales, A Monthly Magazine of Antiquities*, Vol. I, No. 1, Talybont, Breconshire, 1905.

'THE BATTLE OF DORKING', 1871

Anon, *The Battle of Dorking, A Myth* (pamphlet), 1871, in *Tales 1869-72*, in British Library, ref. 12331 AA 56.

Anon, *The New Battle of Dorking*, Grant Richards, 1900.

BLOWER, Sergeant, and CHEEKS the Marine (pseudonyms), *Our Hero: or, Who Won the Battle of Dorking? A Military and Naval Review of the Now Celebrated Pamphlet* (fiction), 1871.

BROWN, Mrs, see SKETCHLEY.

CHESNEY, G.T., *The Battle of Dorking. Reminiscences of a Volunteer* (fiction), reprinted from *Blackwood's Magazine*, May 1871.

LEIGHTON, Sir B., Bart, *The Lull Before Dorking* (pamphlet), 1871.

MOLTRUHN, M. (pseudonym), *The Other Side at the Battle of Dorking, or Reminiscences of an Invader* (fiction), attributed on title page to 'August 1921', n.d. but *c.* 1871.

SKETCHLEY, Arthur (under pseudonym 'Mrs Brown'), *What Happened after the Battle of Dorking, or The Victory of Tunbridge Wells* (fiction), n.d. but *c.* 1871.

THE CHANNEL TUNNEL, FROM *c.* 1880

BERNEY, Rev. T., *The Battle of the Channel Tunnel and Dover Castle and Forts*, 1882.

FORTH, C., *The Surprise of the Channel Tunnel*, 1883.

'GRIP'(pseudonym), *How John Bull Lost London; or The Battle of the Channel Tunnel*, 1882.

HOZIER, H.M., *The Channel Tunnel*, paper read at the Society of Arts, 20 January 1889, reprinted 1889.

MARQUAND, David, *Ramsay MacDonald*, Cape, 1977.

WHITESIDE, Thomas, *The Tunnel under the Channel*, Hart-Davis, 1962. (The indispensable source, though it lacks any bibliography, references or index.)

See also BARRINGTON; Official Documents listed below.

LONDON MOBILISATION CENTRES, *c.* 1890

The Centres were sometimes referred to as the 'London Defence Positions', although, strictly speaking, they were merely part of the whole Defence Positions scheme.

Anon, *Box Hill. The Short Walk* (leaflet), National Trust, n.d.

Anon, Report 'Pewley Fort for sale', *Guildford Times*, 28 August 1965.

CHAPMAN, Geoff and YOUNG, Bob, *Box Hill* (pamphlet), 1979.

HAMILTON-BAILLIE, Brigadier J.R.E., Fort Halstead of the London Defence Positions, *Fort*, Vol. 3, 1975.

KING, D.W., 'The London Defence Positions and Mobilisation Centres, 1888-1907', *Journal of the Society for Army Historical Research*, Vol. 55, No. 224, Winter 1977.

– – *A Note on the Surrey Defence Works of the Nineties* (duplicated n.d.). (A shorter version of the above.)

LITTLEDALE, Helen, LOCOCK, L.M. and SANKEY, J.H.P., *Box Hill* (pamphlet), Box Hill Management Committee of the National Trust, 1984 (f.p. 1952).

SMITH, Victor, 'The London Mobilisation Centres', *London Archaeologist*, Vol.2, No. 10, Spring 1975.

See also ARDAGH and *Handbook for the London Defence Positions* in Official Documents bibliography. See also HAMLEY and SHAND in general bibliography.

THE EAST COAST RAIDS, 1914

See Imperial War Museum Booklist No. 1184, 'The Raid on the Hartle-pools', which also includes material relating to Scarborough and Whitby.

Manchester Guardian, 17 and 18 December 1914.

Manchester Guardian History of the War, 1914, Vol. I, pp. 353-60, Hey-wood, 1914.

The Times, 17 and 18 December 1914.

See also CORBETT, *Naval Operations*, in main bibliography.

THE HARTLEPOOLS

Anon, Poem 'An Innocent Victim', recited in 1915, in the collection of the Central Library, Hartlepool.

Anon, *The Batteries and the Bombardment* (leaflet), Borough of Hartle-pool, n.d.

Anon, 'Guns and Ships', *Royal Tank Corps Journal*, Vol. 17, 1936, pp. 238-40.

Anon, 'Bombardment of the Hartlepools', *The Sapper*, Vol. 11, New Series No. 10, March 1965, p. 279.

Anon, Verses on Zeppelin raids beginning 'Way down in "monkey town"', (typescript), in Central Library, Hartlepool, n.d. but *c*.1915.

BAILEY, Brian, *A Town Under Fire*, New Horizon, 1980.

DAVIDSON, John, 'Some Notes made at the time of the Bombard-ment of Hartlepool' (manuscript), in the Central Library, Hartle-pool.

HAMMERTON, Sir John, *The Great War . . . ' I was there'. Undying Memories of 1914-18.* Vol. I (of 3), Amalgamated Press, 1938, pp. 259-63.

MARTIN, Major R., *Historical Notes and Personal Recollections of West Hartlepool*, Robert Martin Ltd, Hartlepool, 1924.

MILLER, Frederick, *Under German Shell-Fire*, Robert Martin, Hartle-pool, 1915.

—— *The Hartlepools in the Great War*, West Hartlepool, 1920.

MURLEY, Captain W.A., 'The Bombardment of the Hartlepools', *Journal of the Royal Artillery*, Vol. LXI No. 3, April 1934-January 1935, pp. 341-59.

ROBSON, Colonel L., 'Bombardment of the Hartlepools', *Journal of the Royal Artillery*, Vol. XLVIII, No. 10, 1922, pp. 427-30.

RUTTER, Jessie, 'Recollections of the Bombardment of the Hartle-pools' (manuscript), in Central Library, Hartlepool.

WOOD, Robert, *West Hartlepool: The Rise and Development of a Victorian New Town*, Hartlepool County Borough, 1969.

YORKE, Major F.A., 'The Bombardment of the Hartlepools', *Journal of the Royal Artillery*, Vol. LVII, April 1930-January 1931, pp. 84-90.

SCARBOROUGH

Useful bibliographies can be found in the account (unpublished) by Anne Walker, cited below, and in another account, which I have not consulted, in the library of the North Riding College of Education, Scarborough.

Anon, *The German Raid on Scarborough Dec. 16th 1914*, E.W.T. Dennis and Sons, Scarborough, *c.* 1915.

Anon, Letter from Scarborough, signed 'Alec', 18 December 1914, in North Yorkshire County Library, Scarborough.

HOLTBY, Winifred (there described as 'A schoolgirl under fire'), letter published in, and subsequently reprinted by, the Bridlington *Chronicle*, 1 January 1915.

MOULD, David, *Remember Scarborough*, Hendon Publishing Co., 1978.

Scarborough Evening News, 17 December 1914.

Scarborough Pictorial, 23 December 1914.

Scarborough Mercury, Souvenir Supplement entitled *The Bombardment of Scarborough*, 15 December 1984.

WALKER, Anne, The Bombardment of Scarborough 16th December 1914 (manuscript thesis), May 1982, in the library of the North Riding College of Education, Scarborough.

WHITBY

Anon, *Whitby. December 16th, 1914*, (Extract in North Yorkshire County Library, Whitby, source and date unknown.)

Whitby Gazette, 18 December and 24 December 1914.

OFFICIAL DOCUMENTS CONSULTED

For a useful map entitled *Tracks of the Invasions of the United Kingdom*, with an accompanying table listing all invasions and landings from 55BC to 1795, originally prepared *c.* 1800 and recirculated by the Defence Committee in 1877, see CAB 7/6 under that year.

1603–1714

Report on *The State of the Navy*, *c.* 1608, in ADM 7/825.

Correspondence relating to the court martial of Admiral Torrington, 1690, in ADM 7/8831.

1714–1815

Estimates for the Repair of Landguard Fort, 1731, and 1733, are in WO 55/2269/2.

A report from Falmouth on Pendennis Castle, 20 March 1744, is in WO 55 2269/3.

Correspondence on works in the Portsmouth area, including Southsea Castle, in 1745, 1748 and 1750 is in WO 55/2272.

Reports on visits to Rye Harbour in 1698, 1718, 1743 and 1756 are in WO 55/2269/8.

The reports from The Hague warning of a possible French invasion, dated 1 February and 10 February 1756, and from Madrid, 13 February 1756, are in WO 30/54.

On the defence of Ireland, see correspondence between the Secretary of State and the Lord Lieutenant, 2 May 1771 and September 1771, in WO 30/54.

A report on the defences of Portsmouth dated 25 February 1771 is in WO 115/B.

A note from General Roy on Portsmouth, of the same date, is in WO 30/54.

General Roy's *General Sketch of a Plan for Depriving an Enemy that Might Attempt to Land on the Coast of Sussex and Kent*, of 29 August 1779, is in WO 30/54.

An undated, unsigned report on the defence of Milford Haven, probably by General Roy and belonging to the 1770s, is in WO 30/54.

General Roy's report on the defence of Plymouth, August 1770, and further *Remarks concerning Plymouth suggested by the emergency of the present moment*, dated 25 August 1779, a detailed study of the Suffolk and Norfolk coasts, dated 12 August 1778, an undated study of landing places between Land's End and Leostaff [i.e. Lowestoft] by Roy, a note on retreat to the interior, also by Roy, both undated but from around the same period, a note by Roy on invasion prospects generally and proposals for the provision of a central magazine to supply London, dated 29 June 1798, and a Report on the Coast of Kent, undated and unsigned, apparently dating from around 1779 and possibly by General Roy but in a different hand, all appear in WO 30/115B.

Correspondence on 'arrangements for depriving an enemy between Hants and Cornwall', 26 June 1779, is in WO 30/115B.

Remarks on the New Defence at Plymouth, 1780, are in WO 30/54.

A report from the Lieut.-Governor of Landguard Fort, 15 February 1793, is in WO 30/54.

A note from General Roy to the Duke of Richmond on 'the present situation', dated 22 April 1793, is in WO 30/54.

On the use of floating batteries and red-hot shot, see note by Sir David Dundas, c.1795, in WO 30/115C.

On the Duke of Richmond's report concerning the Southern District, dated 16 February 1795, see WO 30/115C.

Documents relating to the Needles Passage in 1795 are in WO 55/2249.

On the defences of Dorset see reports from March 1793 and 1796 in WO 30/116.

A note by Sir David Dundas on the possibility of invasion in 1797, listing the likeliest locations, is in WO 30/115C.

A letter recommending the building of Martello towers, dated 7 April 1798, is in WO 30/100.

On General Roy's strategy for the defence of the South see his note, dated 22 April 1793, in WO 30/54.

Details of proposed troop movement routes in Kent, dated 4 August 1798, are in WO 30/56.

A letter to Major-General Brownrigg on the defence of the Tyne and Wear area, 7 August 1804, and other defence reports for the period 1770-1803 are in WO 30/57.

A list of signal stations at 8 August 1803 is in WO 30/56.

A letter from the Commander-in-Chief on fortification policy, with specific reference to Portsmouth, Plymouth, Dover and the London area, dated 25 August 1803, is in WO 55 1563/2.

A letter to the Commander-in-Chief on building fieldworks, dated 3 September 1803, is in WO 30/56.

Plans for the deployment of the Volunteers, dated 11 August 1804, are in WO 30/56.

The use of a floating dam as part of the River Lea Defences, dated 26 August 1803, is in WO 30/56.

Various letters and reports as detailed below can be found in WO 30/56: 9 August 1803, on the beacon signalling system; 3 September 1803, on defence policy generally; 2 March 1804, on the flooding of Pevensey Levels; 15 March 1804, on defence positions in the Dorking area; 27 March 1804, on the provision of a boom at Dover; 6 April 1804, on the defence of the Western Heights at Dover and 16 April 1804, on other works there; 16 September 1804, on the use of Sea Fencibles in the Dungeness area; 4 October 1804, on the design of 'a Bomb Proof Tower' and 9 October 1804, on the design's cost and merits.

Various letters on the defence of Berwick, Liverpool, Lincolnshire, Dover and North Wales for the period 1803-04 are in WO 30/57.

An estimate of the number of French troops at various locations, undated and unsigned, but dating from c.1805, is in WO 30/56.

Reports on Measures of Defence, for the Eastern District, 1795-1805 are in WO 30/100.

1815-1900

A detailed assessment of the coast defences in 1826, with details of the garrisons, both actual and on paper, is in WO 55/1548.

Return of the number of Towers, Batteries, Castles and Coast Defences in the Western District, 1826 is in WO 55/1547/17.

Letter on French artillery to Lieut.-General Sir H. Vivian, Bart, dated 14 January 1841, in in WO 55/1547/17.

The Duke's memoranda to Sir Robert Peel on Naval Defence, 10 September and 9 October 1845 are in WO 55/1548/20.

Various reports of the Committee on Coast Defence, 1852-3, including consideration of the use of 'coast batteries against steamers and ships of war', giving details of recent experiments and the use of hot shot and of shells are in WO 55/1563/7.

The Report of the Commissioners Appointed to Consider the Defences of the United Kingdom, published on 7 February 1860, is in ZHC I/2577 but more easily consulted elsewhere, as Cmnd 2682.

The report on the visit to England in November 1864 of General Todleben is in WO 55/1548/23. (See also HUGHES in main bibliography.)

A report by Brigadier General John Adye on public apprehension about invasion, December 1870, is in WO 33/22. (This includes an account of the distribution of the army and of the military strength of the United Kingdom in relation to other countries.)

A detailed report by Brigadier Adye on recent changes in guns and explosives, dated 1 February 1871, is also in WO 33/22.

A report by Major-General G. Balfour on Army Recruitment, dated 24 December 1870, is in WO 33/22.

The 1870 Report of the Special Committee on Mitrailleurs, i.e. foreign machine-guns, and the relative merits of the Gatling gun, is in WO 33/22.

A note on improving the North Battery at Liverpool, dated 29 March 1855, is in WO 55/1563/7.

A note by General Burgoyne, *Proposed Principles for Works of Defence for Great Britain*, 10 November 1855, is in WO 55/1548/22.

General Todleben's Observations on English Defences, 1864, are in WO 55/1548.

A report by W.F. Drummond Jervois on experiments relating to sea defences at Shoeburyness, with a drawing of the proposed sea forts, 1865, is in WO 33/17A.

Report on Passive Obstructions for the Defence of Harbours and Channels and Memorandum on Army Organisation, 1866, are in WO 33/17A.

A memorandum by J. Peel on Army Organisation, December 1866, is in WO 33/17A.

Discussions relating to the effectiveness of rifled guns against armour plating, and on use of breech-loading rifles by the Volunteers, by the 1868 Committee on Ordnance, 21 September 1868, are reported in WO 33/19.

Conclusions of the *Commission on Active Observations and Submarine Explosive Machines*, 1868, are in WO 33/19.

Report on the Progress in Building Fortifications for the Defence of the Dockyards and Naval Arsenals, 1874, is in WO 33/26.

Memorandum on the expansion of the docks at Liverpool, dated 8 January 1875, is in CAB 7/6.

The Report of the Committee on Commercial Harbour Defences, including the Firth of Forth, the Humber, the Tyne, and Holyhead, April 1877, is in CAB 7/6.

The report of the Sub-Committee on the Defence of Commercial
Ports, which deals with submarine mining and the deployment of
troops, 1881, is in WO 33/37.

General Dumouriez on English Defences, i.e. Dumouriez's book of
around 1805, was re-issued with an accompanying note in June 1880,
and can be found in WO 30/116.

The Report of the Committee on Coast Defences, 1870, an exhaustive 93-
page study, can be found in WO 33/25, and was re-issued on 17
January 1873. This version is in CAB 33/48.

Correspondence and various notes relating to the completion of the
defences agreed in 1860, including details of the deficiencies in guns
at Portsdown Hill and Plymouth, dated 29 April 1878, 16 January
1885 and 20 November 1885 can be found in WO 333/48.

The Report of the Committee on Commercial Harbour Defences, 1887, includes recommendations on Landguard Fort and Harwich, the
Thames, the Medway, Dover, Portland and Plymouth, and the evidence of witnesses on the value of minesweeping and the possibility
of panic in London in the event of a landing in East Anglia, is in CAB
7/6.

The Report by Colonel J.C. Ardagh entitled *The Defence of London*, 16
July 1888, is in WO 33/48.

The *Handbook for the London Defence Positions (Provisional)* 1903, was
consulted in the War Office library but is now in the Public Record
Office.

1900–1918

The Report on a conference between the Admiralty and the War Office
on coast defence, 18 December 1900, is in CAB 3/1.

A note on the possibility of invasion by Germany, dated 7 February
1903, is in CAB 3/1.

War Office comment on Admiralty policy for the use of troops in
coastal defence, dated 14 February 1903, is in CAB 3/1.

A draft report on the possibility of serious invasion, dated 11 November 1903, is in CAB 3/1.

The memorandum by the Secretary of State for War on his recent visit
to the Continent, dated 15 September 1903, and a report by the Chief
of Staff on the army manoeuvres of 1904, dated 19 September 1904,
are in the Balfour Papers in the British Library, BL Add. MS 49722.

A note on the possibility of rifle instruction in schools, dated 30
October 1905, is in CAB 3/1.

A memorandum by the prime minister, *The Possibility of a Raid by a
Hostile Force on the British Coast*, dated 12 December 1905, is in CAB
3/1.

A note on the reasons why Germany is now regarded as the likely
enemy, not France, and a study of the possible landing places on the

East Coast, dated 20 July 1907, is in CAB 3/2.

The *Statement Made by Mr. A.J. Balfour before the Sub-Committee on Invasion*, 29 May 1908, is in CAB 3/2.

The *Report of the Sub-Committee on Invasion*, of the CID, dated 22 October 1908, is in CAB 3/2.

A note on the setting up of the Home Defence Ports Committee, dated 1 July 1909, is in CAB 3/2.

A note on the general principles concerning fixed defences followed by the CID, dated 24 February 1910, is in CAB 3/2.

A study of the defences of Scapa Flow and the Humber, and examination of size and efficiency of the existing auxiliary forces, 1910, is in CAB 3/2.

A memorandum on Home Defence, with the views of the Admiralty on 'local coast defence', dated 23 March 1911, is in CAB 3/2.

A study of reports on the fixed defences at Rosyth and the Firth of Forth, dated 23 March 1911, is in CAB 3/2.

A memorandum on the Defences of the North-East Coast by the Home Ports Defence Committee, April 1912, is in CAB 3/2.

A note on the provision in peacetime of intelligence about hostile raids on the coast and a review of arrangements during the mobilisation period, including the use of cyclist battalions, dated January 1914, is in CAB 3/2.

The *Memorandum by Mr Balfour* on the current risk of invasion, dated 24 October 1914, is in CAB 3/3.

A summary by G.K. Scott Moncrieff of coast fortification policy in the preceding 60 years, March 1918, is in WO 32/5528. (This document provides a comprehensive survey of the subject, since the 'Palmerstonian' report of 1860.)

A note on the defence of the coast, especially in the Dover area, and the possibility of small raids there, February 1914, is in CAB 3/2.

Recommendations on the defence of the Shetland Islands, June 1913, are in CAB 3/2.

1919-1946

A report on the vulnerability of the British Isles to air attack by France, dated 8 November 1921, is in CAB 3/3.

A note on the danger to Rosyth and Pembroke docks, with reference to Germany and France as potential enemies, dated 7 October 1925, is in CAB 3/4.

A note on the need to retain British control over coast defences in the Irish Free State, dated 26 October 1925 and June 1926, is in CAB 3/4.

A note on the Anti-Aircraft Defence of Home Ports, c.1929, is in CAB 3/4.

A note on the Air Defence Intelligence System in Coastal Areas, dated 22 April 1929, is in CAB 3/4. (This includes a reference to acoustic mirrors.)

A note on Coastal Defences, May 1932, is in CAB 3/5. (This includes a reference to the use of aircraft against ships.)

The CID Memorandum on Belfast Coast Defences, 8 April 1936, is in CAB 3/6.

Seaborne and airborne Land Attack on the British Isles: A Review, 7 June 1937, is in CAB 3/6. (This paper examines what size of force might be landed on the English coast and comments on the effects of German rearmament.)

The CID memorandum recording anxiety at lack of defence against air attack, especially in relation to Germany, dated 14 October 1937, is in CAB 3/7.

Home Ports. Local Naval and Seafront Defences, a detailed CID memorandum of 29 October 1937, is in CAB 3/6.

A note arguing that the defence of Plymouth and other ports against air attack must be a priority, June 1938, is in CAB 3/7.

A *Review of Precautionary Measures taken during the Czechoslovakian Crisis*, November 1938, is in CAB 3/8.

A note on Modern Coastal Defences, June 1939, is in CAB 3/8. (This paper details the degree of risk, and proposed scale of defence, for various ports.)

Anti-Aircraft Defence at Scapa Flow, August 1939, is examined in CAB 3/8.

A *Priority List for Location of H.A. [Heavy Anti-Aircraft] Guns*, dated 12 August 1941, is in WO 199/509. (This lists the beaches most likely to be used by enemy tanks.)

Interim Scales of Coast Artillery Defence at Ports and Bases at Home and Abroad, 2 December 1946, reference D.B. (46) 25. (Not in PRO. Privately supplied to the author.)

The Channel Tunnel

For Field Marshal Lord Wolseley's memorandum of 16 June 1881, see file CAB 3/2.

The CID report of 19 June 1906 is in CAB 3/1.

The CID report of 21 June 1924 and the prime minister's subsequent statement to the House of Commons, dated 7 July 1924, are in CAB 63/36.

The CID report of May 1930 is in CAB 3/5.

On developments during the Second World War see Admiralty files M 05978/42 and ADM 1/11924, and War Cabinet files 1910/188/26 and CAB 21/1190.

See also: BERNEY, FORTH, 'GRIP', HOZIER, MARQUAND and WHITESIDE in main bibliography.

GUIDES TO INDIVIDUAL AREAS

BERWICK-UPON-TWEED

MACIVOR, Iain, *The Fortifications of Berwick-upon-Tweed*, HMSO, 1983 (f.p. 1967).

DEVON AND CORNWALL

WOODWARD, Freddy, *The Royal Citadel* [Plymouth] (pamphlet), n.d., c.1988.

DORSET

ANDREWS, E.A., and PINSENT, M.L., 'The Coastal Defences of Portland and Weymouth' in Supplement to *Fort*, Vol.9, 1981.

Anon, *Dorset Coastal Fortifications Portland and Weymouth District*, no publisher indicated, n.d.

DOVER

Anon, *The Grand Shaft and Western Heights* (leaflet), Dover Museum, n.d. but c.1989.

Anon, *The Grand Shaft* (leaflet), Dover District Council, n.d. but c.1989.

Anon, *The Western Heights* (leaflet), Dover District Council, n.d. but c.1989.

BROWN, R. Allen, *Dover Castle* (pamphlet), English Heritage, 1985 (f.p. 1974).

GREAT YARMOUTH

Anon, *Historic Yarmouth* (pamphlet), Great Yarmouth and District Archaeological Society, 1980.

HARWICH

Anon, *The Harwich Redoubt* (pamphlet), The Harwich Society, n.d. but c.1983.

TROLLOPE, Charles, *The Defences of Harwich* (pamphlet), Penpaled Books, n.d. but c.1983.

— — 'The Defences of Harwich', *Fort*, Vol. 11, 1983.

ISLE OF WIGHT AND THE NEEDLES

Anon, *Victoria's Forts* (pamphlet), Isle of Wight County Council, Newport, n.d. but c.1985.

CANTWELL, Anthony, *Fort Victoria. A History* (pamphlet), Isle of Wight County Council, 1985.

— — *Freshwater Redoubt* (leaflet), privately published, 1985.

— — *Golden Hill Fort* (pamphlet), privately published, 1985.

CANTWELL, Anthony and SPRACK, Peter, *The Needles Batteries* (pamphlet), privately published, 1981.

— — *The Needles Defences* (pamphlet), The Redoubt Consultancy, Ryde, Isle of Wight, 1986.

RIGOLD, S.E., *Yarmouth Castle, Isle of Wight* (pamphlet), Historic

Buildings and Monuments Commission, 1978.

LANDGUARD
RAYNER, Doreen, *Landguard Fort, Felixstowe* (pamphlet), Felixstowe History and Museum Society, 1983.
WOOD, D.A., *Landguard Fort, Felixstowe* (pamphlet), privately published, 1982.
See also LESLIE in main bibliography.

LONDON AND THE THAMES ESTUARY
BENNETT, D.A., *A Handbook of Kent's Defences* (pamphlet), Kent Archaeological Society, 1977.
GULVIN, K.R., *Fort Amherst* (pamphlet), Fort Amherst and Lines Trust, Chatham, n.d. but *c.*1986.
SAUNDERS, A.D., *Upnor Castle, Kent*, Historic Buildings and Monuments Commission, 1983 (f.p. 1967).
SMITH, V.T.C., *Defending London's River. The Story of the Thames Forts 1540-1945*, North Kent Books, Rochester, 1985.

MILFORD HAVEN
JOHN, Brian, *Milford Haven Waterway* (pamphlet), Pembrokeshire Coast National Park Authority, Haverfordwest, 1981.
WHEELER, N.J., *The Fortification of Milford Haven and Pembroke Dock* (leaflet), Pembrokeshire Coast National Park Authority, Haverfordwest, n.d., but *c.*1987.

PORTSMOUTH
Anon, *Western Defences of Portsmouth Harbour. Stoke Bay Lines*, Gosport and Fareham Teachers' Local Studies Group, n.d. but *c.*1985.
BROWN, Ron, *The Portsmouth Guidebook*, Milestone Publications, Horndean, n.d. but *c.*1984.
COAD, J.G., *Fort Brockhurst* (leaflet), Department of the Environment, 1981 (f.p. 1979).
CORNEY, Arthur, *Fortifications in Old Portsmouth. A Guide*, Portsmouth City Museums, 1980 (f.p. 1965).
— — *Fort Widley and the Great Forts on Portsdown* (pamphlet), Portsmouth City Museums, 1984.
MITCHELL, G.H. and COBB, P.D., *Spit Bank Fort, Portsmouth, History and Description* (pamphlet), United Kingdom Fortifications Club, Portsmouth, 1983.
PATTERSON, A. Temple, *'Palmerston's Folly'. The Portsdown and Spithead Forts* (pamphlet), No. 3 of *The Portsmouth Papers*, Portsmouth City Council, August 1980.
WILLIAMS, G.H., *The Western Defences of Portsmouth Harbour 1400-1800*, No. 30 of *The Portsmouth Papers*, Portsmouth City Council, December 1979.

SUSSEX

Anon, *The Fortifications of East Sussex* (pamphlet), East Sussex County Council, 1979.

Anon, *Fort Newhaven* (pamphlet), English Life Publications, Derby, 1983.

WEEDON

Anon, *Royal Ordnance Depot – Weedon, Northamptonshire* (duplicated), document 183/83 (M), Property Services Agency, 1983.

Anon, *The Former Royal Ordnance Depot, Weedon, Northampton* (pamphlet, i.e. particulars of sale), Hillier Parker May and Rowden, 1984.

ROGERS, Byron, 'Still Waiting for Napoleon', *Sunday Telegraph Magazine*, 18 December 1983.

MAIN BIBLIOGRAPHY

Anon, *A Chronological History of Great Britain to be Published Every Year*, 1716.

Anon, *A Guide to the Cabinet War Rooms* (pamphlet), no date but *c.*1984.

ALANBROOKE, Viscount. See BRYANT, FRASER.

Allen's Guide to Tenby, 1869. (Useful on local Palmerstonian forts.)

ANGLESEY, Marquess of, *A History of the British Cavalry*, 3 vols, Leo Cooper, 1973–82.

ANNE, Queen. See GREEN, GREGG.

ASHLEY, Evelyn, *The Life and Correspondence of Henry John Temple, Viscount Palmerston*, 2 vols, 1879.

ASHLEY, Maurice, *The Glorious Revolution of 1688*, Hodder and Stoughton, 1966.

— — *Charles II: The Man and the Statesman*, Weidenfeld and Nicolson, 1971.

— — *James II*, Dent, 1977.

— — *Charles I and Oliver Cromwell. A Study in Contrasts*, Methuen, 1987.

ARNOLD, Colonel B.E., *Conflict across the Strait. A Battery Commander's Story of Kent's Defences 1939-45*, Crabwell and Buckland Publications, Dover, 1982.

ARONSON, Theo, *Queen Victoria and the Bonapartes*, Cassell, 1972.

— — *Kings over the Water. The Saga of the Stuart Pretenders*, Cassell, 1988 (f.p. 1979).

ASHTON, Robert, (ed.), *James I by his Contemporaries*, Hutchinson, 1969.

AUBREY, Philip, *The Defeat of James Stuart's Armada 1692*, Leicester University Press, Leicester, 1979.

AYLING, Stanley, *George the Third*, Collins, 1972.

BARNES, David, 'Thoughts on the Brennan Torpedo', *Casemate,*

Newsletter of the Fortress Study Group (credited to the Secretary), No.18, June 1986.

— — 'Searchlights', *ibid.*

BARNETT, Correlli, *Britain and her Army 1509-1970*, Allen Lane, 1970.

BARRINGTON, Captain J.T., *England on the Defensive or The Problem of Invasion*, Kegan Paul, 1881.

BARTLETT, C.J.H., *Great Britain and Sea Power, 1815-1853*, Clarendon Press, 1963.

BAXTER, Stephen B., *William III*, Longmans, 1966.

BERNARDI, F. von, *Germany and the Next War* (trans. A.H. Powles), Edward Arnold, 1914.

BINGHAM, Caroline, *James I of England*, Weidenfeld, 1981.

BLATCHFORD, Robert, *The War that was Foretold*, 1914 (Reprinted from *Daily Mail* articles of 1909, with postscript dated 25 August 1914.)

BOND, Brian, *British Military Policy between the two World Wars*, Clarendon Press, 1980. See also POWNALL.

BOWLE, John, *Charles the First*, Weidenfeld, 1975.

BOXER, C.R., *The Anglo-Dutch Wars of the 17th Century, 1652-1674*, HMSO, 1974.

BOYLE, Andrew, *The Riddle of Erskine Childers*, Hutchinson, 1977.

BOYNTON, Lindsay, *The Elizabethan Militia, 1558-1638*, Routledge and Kegan Paul, 1967.

BRODRICK, George C. and FOTHERINGHAM, J.K., *The History of England from Addington's Administration to the Close of William IV's Reign (1801-1837)*, Longmans, 1919. (Part of the excellent The Longmans Political History Series.)

BROOKE, John, *King George III*, Constable, 1972.

BROWN, Peter Douglas, *William Pitt, Earl of Chatham*, Allen and Unwin, 1978.

BROWNING, Andrew (ed.), *English Historical Documents 1660-1714*, Eyre and Spottiswoode, 1953.

BRYANT, Arthur (ed.), *The Letters, Speeches and Declarations of King Charles II*, Cassell, 1935.

— — *The Years of Endurance, 1793-1802*, Reprint Society, 1944 (f.p. Collins, 1943).

— — *Years of Victory, 1802-1812*, Reprint Society, 1945 (f.p. Collins, 1944).

— — *Samuel Pepys, The Man in the Making*, Reprint Society, 1949 (f.p. Collins, 1933).

— — *Samuel Pepys, The Years of Peril*, Reprint Society, 1953 (f.p. Collins, 1935).

— — *Samuel Pepys, The Saviour of the Navy*, Reprint Society, 1953 (f.p. Collins, 1938).

— — (ed.), *The Turn of the Tide 1939-43. A Study based on the Diaries and*

Autobiographical Notes of Field Marshal the Viscount Alanbrooke, Collins, 1957.

BUCKINGHAM. See LOCKYER.

BULLOCK, Alan, *Hitler, A Study in Tyranny*, Pelican, 1962 (f.p. 1952).

BURGOYNE, General, *The Military Opinions of General Sir John Fox Burgoyne, Bart*, (ed. Captain the Hon. George Wrottesley), 1859.

BUTTERFIELD, Herbert, *George III, Lord North and the People*, Bell, 1949.

CALLENDER, Sir Geoffrey, *The Naval Side of British History, Part I, 1919-1945*, Christophers, 1952. (For Part II see HINSLEY).

CANTWELL, Anthony, 'The Needles Defences', in *Fort*, Vol. 13, 1985. See also *Guides* bibliography.

CAPPER, D.P., *Moat Defensive. A History of the Waters of the Nore Command, 55 BC to 1961*, Arthur Barker, 1963.

CARSWELL, John, *The Descent on England. A Study of the English Revolution of 1688 and its European Background*, Barrie and Rockliff, 1969.

CASSAR, George H., *Kitchener: Architect of Victory*, William Kimber, 1977.

CHANCE, J.F., 'The "Swedish Plot" of 1716-17', *English Historical Review*, Vol. XVIII, No. LXIX, January 1903.

CHANDLER, David, *Sedgemoor 1685. An Account and an Anthology*, Anthony Mott, 1985. See also Whitehaven bibliography.

CHAPMAN, Hester W., *The Tragedy of Charles II in the Years 1630-1660*, Cape, 1964.

CHARLES I, King. See HIBBERT, MORRAH, WATSON.

CHARLES II, King. See BRYANT, CHAPMAN, FALKUS, FRASER.

CHILDERS, Erskine, *The Riddle of the Sands* (fiction), Nelson, 1903. See also BOYLE.

CHILDS, John, *The Army of Charles II*, Routledge, 1976.

— — *The Army, James II and the Glorious Revolution*, Manchester University Press, Manchester, 1980.

CHATHAM, Earl of. See BROWN.

CHURCHILL, Randolph S., *Winston S. Churchill, Vol. II, Young Statesman 1901-1914*, Heinemann, 1967. See also GILBERT.

CHURCHILL, WINSTON S., *The World Crisis 1911-1918*, 2 vols, Odhams Press, n.d. but *c*.1939 (f.p. 4 vols, 1923-29).

— — *The Second World War. Vol. I, The Gathering Storm*, Cassell, 1948; *Vol. II, Their Finest Hour*, Cassell, 1949. See also GILBERT, MORGAN.

CIVILIAN, A. (pseudonym), *Regulars and Volunteers. Who Shall Defend England?*, 1859.

—— *The Invasion of England! How are we Prepared to Meet it?*, 1859

CLARENDON, Edward Earl of, *The History of the Rebellion and Civil Wars in England by Edward, Earl of Clarendon* (ed. W. Dunn Mackay), 6 vols, Clarendon Press, 1889.

—— *Clarendon. Selections from the History of the Rebellion and The Life by Himself* (ed. Gertrude Huehns), OUP, 1978.

CLARK, G.N., 'The Barbary Corsairs in the 17th Century', *Cambridge Historical Journal*, No.1, Cambridge University Press, Cambridge, 1944, pp. 22-35.

—— *The Later Stuarts, 1660-1714*. In the *Oxford History of England* series, Clarendon Press, 1947 (f.p. 1934).

CLARK, Norman H., 'Twentieth Century Coastal Defences of the Firth of Forth', *Fort*, Vol.14, 1986.

CLARKE, Comer, *England Under Hitler* (fiction), New English Library, 1972 (f.p. Consul Books, 1964).

CLARKE, George Sydenham, *Fortification: Its Past Achievements, Recent Developments and Future Progress*, Beaufort Publishing, Liphook, 1989. (Facsimile reprint of original edition, 1890.)

CLARKE, I.F., *Voices Prophesying War 1763-1884*, Panther, 1970 (f.p. OUP, 1966).

CLARKE, John, *The Life and Times of George III*, Weidenfeld, 1972.

CLOWES, William L. *et al.*, *History of the Royal Navy*, 7 vols, Sampson Low, 1897-1903.

COBDEN, Richard, *The Three Panics. An Historical Episode, in Vol. II of The Political Writings of Richard Cobden*, 1867 (f.p. as pamphlet, 1862).

COLLIER, Basil, *The Defence of the United Kingdom*, in *History of the Second World War* series, HMSO, 1957.

—— *A Short History of the Second World War*, Collins, 1967.

COLLIER, Richard, *1940. The World in Flames*, Hamish Hamilton, 1979.

COMPTON, Piers, *The Last Days of General Gordon*, Robert Hale, 1974.

CORBETT, Sir Julian S., *England in the Seven Years War*, 2 vols, Longmans, 1918.

—— *Naval Operations* in *History of the Great War Based on Official Documents*, Vols. I-III, Longmans, 1920-3.

COUSINS, Geoffrey, *The Defenders. A History of the British Volunteer*, Muller, 1968.

COX, Richard, *Sea Lion* (fiction), Futura, 1974.

CREASY, E.S., *The Invasions and the Projected Invasions of England from the Saxon Times. With Remarks on the Present Emergencies*, 1852.

CROWE, Captain J.W., *Yesterday and Tomorrow, or Shadows of the War*, 1856.

CRUTTWELL, C.R.M.F., *A History of the Great War 1914-1918*, Clarendon Press, 1936.

CUNNINGHAM, Hugh, *The Volunteer Force. A Social and Political History 1859-1908*, Croom Helm, 1975.

CURTIS, Gila, *The Life and Times of Queen Anne*, Weidenfeld, 1972.

Cycling. For reports on cycling and the Volunteer Movement see issues of 1 Sept. and 13 Oct. 1894, 9 Feb. and 30 Nov. 1895, 29 Feb. and 5 Dec. 1896, 20 Feb. and 23 June 1897, 28 May 1898, 22 July and 24 Nov. 1899.

DALY, A.A., *History of the Isle of Sheppey*, 1904

DAVIES, J.D. Griffith, *George the Third*, Ivor Nicholson and Watson, 1936.

—— *A King in Toils* [i.e. George II], Lindsay Drummond, 1938.

DAVIS, Godfrey, *The Early Stuarts 1603-1660*, Clarendon Press, 1949 (f.p. 1937).

de JOINVILLE, Prince, *On the State of the Naval Strength of France in Comparison with that of England* (trans. Peake), 1894 (f.p. 1845).

DIROM, Lieut.-Colonel A., *Plans for the Defence of Great Britain and Ireland*, Edinburgh, 1797.

DOUGLAS, David C. (ed.), *English Historical Documents Vol. XI, 1783-1832*, Eyre and Spottiswoode, 1959.

DOUGLAS, Sir Howard, *On the Naval, Littoral and Internal Defence of England*, 1860.

DUFFY, Christopher, *Siege Warfare. The Fortress in the Early Modern World, 1494-1660*, Routledge, 1979.

du MAURIER, Guy. See A PATRIOT.

DUNLOP, J.K., *The Development of the British Army*, Methuen, 1938.

DUNSANY, Lord, 'The "Silver Streak"' *Nineteenth Century*, No. LI, May 1881.

EARLE, Peter, *The Life and Times of James II*, Weidenfeld, 1972.

—— *Monmouth's Rebels. The Road to Sedgemoor 1685*, Weidenfeld, 1977.

EHRMAN, John, *The Younger Pitt*, 3 vols, Constable, 1983-5.

ENSOR, R.C.K., *England 1870-1914*, Clarendon Press, 1946 (f.p. 1936).

ESHER, Lord, *The Journals and Letters of Reginald Viscount Esher, Vol. I, 1870-1903* (ed. Maurice V. Brett), Nicholas and Watson, 1934. See also FRASER.

EVELYN, John, *The Diary of John Evelyn* (ed. E.S. de Beer), OUP, 1959.

FALKUS, Christopher, *The Life and Times of Charles II*, Weidenfeld, 1972.

FARRER, James Anson, *Invasion and Conscription. Some Letters from a Mere Civilian to a Famous General*, Fisher Unwin, 1909.

FEATHERSTONE, Donald, *Weapons and Equipment of the Victorian Soldier*, Blandford Press, Poole, 1978.

FERGUSON, James, *The Peril of Portsmouth; or French Fleets and*

English Forts, John Murray, 1852.

FINCH, Daniel, Mss, Historical Manuscripts Commission 71, Vol. IV 1692, and Addenda 1690-91, HMSO, 1965. (On French invasion plans 1692.)

FIRTH, C.H., *Cromwell's Army*, Methuen, 1962 (f.p. 1902).

— — *Oliver Cromwell*, Putnam, 1947 (f.p. 1907).

FISHGUARD: For French landing at, see separate bibliography.

FLEMING, Peter, *Invasion 1940*, Hart-Davis, 1957.

FOORD, Edward and HOME, Gordon, *The Invasion of England*, A. and C. Black, 1915.

FORTESCUE, Sir John W., *A History of the British Army*, 10 vols, Macmillan, 1899-1920.

FRASER, Antonia, *Cromwell. Our Chief of Men*, Panther, 1975 (f.p. Weidenfeld, 1973).

— — *King Charles II*, Macdonald Futura, 1980 (f.p. Weidenfeld, 1979).

— — *King James VI of Scotland, I of England*, Weidenfeld, 1974.

FRASER, David, *Alanbrooke*, Collins, 1982.

FRASER, Peter, *Lord Esher, A Political Biography*, Hart-Davis, 1973.

FULFORD, Roger, *George the Fourth*, Duckworth, 1949.

GANDER, Terry, *Military Archaeology. A Collector's Guide to 20th Century War Relics*, Patrick Stephens, Cambridge, 1979.

GARDINER, S.R., *History of the Commonwealth and Protectorate, 1649-1660*, 3 vols, Longmans 1897-1901. (Windrush Press reprint in 2 vols, 1989.)

GASH, Norman, *Mr Secretary Peel*, Longmans, 1961.

GENERAL STAFF (pseudonymn), *The Writing on the Wall*, Heinemann, 1906.

GEORGE I, King. See HATTON, IMBERT-TERRY, MELVILLE.

GEORGE II, King. See DAVIES, TRENCH.

GEORGE III, King. See AYLING, BROOKE, DAVIES.

GEORGE IV, King. See HIBBERT.

GEORGE VI, King. See WHEELER-BENNETT.

GIBBON, Edward, *Autobiography*, Everyman's Library, 1948 (f.p. 1796).

GIBSON, John S., *Ships of the '45*, Hutchinson, 1967.

GILBERT, Martin, *Finest Hour. Winston S. Churchill 1939-1941*, Book Club Associates, 1983 (f.p. Heinemann, 1983). See also CHURCHILL.

GLOVER, Richard, *Britain at Bay. Defence against Bonaparte 1803-14*, Allen and Unwin, 1973.

GOOCH, John, *The Plans of War. 'The General Staff and British Military Strategy, c.1900-1916'*, Routledge, 1974.

GOODWIN, John E., 'Fortifications against a French Invasion of the East Kent Coast of England: 1750-1815', *Fort*, Vol.16, 1988.

GORE, M., *National Defence* (pamphlet), 1852.

GRAVES, Charles, *The Home Guard of Britain*, Hutchinson, n.d., but *c*.1943.

GREEN, David, *Queen Anne*, Collins, 1970.

GREEN, Mary Anne Everett (ed.), *The Letters of Queen Henrietta Maria*, 1857.

GREGG, Edward, *Queen Anne*, Routledge, 1980.

GRINNELL-MILNE, Duncan, *The Silent Victory. September 1940*. Bodley Head, 1958.

HALDANE, Richard B., *An Autobiography*, Holder, 1929. See also KOSS, MAURICE.

HAMILTON, Nigel, *Monty: The Making of a General 1887-1942*, Coronet, 1981 (f.p. Hamish Hamilton, 1981).

HAMILTON-BAILLIE, Brigadier J.R.E., 'More Notes on the Siege Exercises at Chatham, 1907', *Fort*, Vol.6, Autumn 1978.

HAMLEY, Lieut.-General Sir Edward, *National Defence. Articles and Speeches*, 1899. See also SHAND.

HANGER, Colonel George, *Reflections on the Menaced Invasion*, E. and W. Books, 1970 (f.p. 1804).

HANKEY. See ROSKILL

HANNA, Colonel H.B., *Can Germany Invade England?*, Methuen, 1912.

HANNAH, W.H., *Bobs. Kipling's General. The Life of Field Marshal Earl Roberts of Kandahar*, Leo Cooper, 1972.

HANNAY, David, *A Short History of the Royal Navy, 1217-1688*, 1898.

HARGREAVES, Reginald, *The Narrow Seas*, Sidgwick and Jackson, 1959.

HATTON, Ragnhild, *George I, Elector and King*, Thames and Hudson, 1978.

HAY, Edward, *History of the Irish Insurrection of 1798*, James Duffy, Dublin, 1847.

HAYES, Richard, *The Last Invasion of Ireland* [i.e. 1798], M.H.Gill, Dublin, 1937.

HAYWARD, A., *The Second Armada, A Chapter of Future History* (fiction), 1871. (Published anonymously.)

HEAD, Sir Francis B., Bart, *The Defenceless State of Great Britain*, 1850.

HENRIETTA MARIA. See GREEN, MACKAY, OMAN, TAYLOR.

HIBBERT, Christopher, *Charles I*, Weidenfeld, 1968.

— — *George IV, Prince of Wales 1762-1811*, Longmans, 1972.

HIGHAM, Robert (ed.) Security and Defence in South-West England before 1800 (pamphlet), University of Exeter, Exeter, 1987.

HINSLEY, F.H., *The Naval Side of British History, Part II, 1919-1945*, Christophers, 1952. (Continuation of earlier work by CALLEN-

DER, cited above.)

HIRST, F.W., *The Six Panics and Other Essays*, Methuen, 1913.

HODGSON, Norman, 'An Introduction to the Defences of Dover', *Fort*, Vol.6, Autumn 1978.

HOGG, Ian V., *Coast Defences of England and Wales 1856-1956*, David and Charles, 1974.

— — 'The Rise and Fall of the Disappearing Carriage', *Fort*, Vol.6, Autumn 1978.

HOGG, R., 'The Tyne Turrets: Coast Defence in the First World War', *Fort*, Vol.12, 1984.

HOLMES, Richard, *The Little Field Marshal. Sir John French*, Cape, 1982.

HORE-BELISHA, Lord [Leslie], *The Private Papers of Hore-Belisha* (ed. R.J. Minney), Collins, 1960.

HORN, D.B. and RANSOME, Mary, *English Historical Documents 1714-1783*, Eyre and Spottiswoode, 1957.

HOULDING, J.A., *Fit for Service. The Training of the British Army 1715-1795*, Clarendon Press, 1981.

HOWELL-EVERSON, Douglas, 'Victorian Fortress Strategy in the United Kingdom', *Fort*, Vol.15, 1987. See also Channel Tunnel bibliography.

HOZIER, H.M., *The Invasions of England*, 2 vols, 1876.

HUDSON, Derek, *Martin Tupper, His Rise and Fall*, Constable, 1949. See also TUPPER.

HUGHES, Quentin, 'Russian Views on the English Defences in 1864', *Fort*, Vol.7, 1979.

— — 'Letters from the Defence Committee in 1861', *Fort*, Vol.8, 1980.

HUGHES, T., 'The Volunteer's Catechism', *Macmillan's Magazine*, July 1860.

HUNT, Ian, 'Plymouth sound? The Defence of the Naval Station', *Fort*, Vol.11, 1983.

HUNT, William, *The History of England from the Accession of George II to the Close of Pitt's First Administration (1760-1801)*, Longmans, 1905.

HUSSEY, Frank, *Suffolk Invasion. The Dutch Attack on Landguard Fort, 1667*, Terence Dalton, Lavenham, 1983.

Illustrated London News, The Report on Easter Volunteer Review and the Cyclist Corps, 7 April 1888.

IMBERT-TERRY, Sir H.M., *A Constitutional King. George the First*, John Murray, 1927.

Invader, The. Short silent film, in the National Film Archive, shown in *Timewatch* by BBC Television, 10 October 1985.

IRONSIDE. *The Ironside Diaries 1937-1940*, ed. Colonel Roderick Macleod and Denis Kelly, Constable, 1962.

ISMAY, General. *The Memoirs of Lord Ismay*, Heinemann, 1960.

JAMES I, King. See ASHTON, BINGHAM, FRASER, STEE-HOLM, WILLSON

JAMES II, King, See ASHLEY, EARLE, TREVOR.

JARVIS, Rupert C. (ed.), *Collected Papers on the Jacobite Risings*, 2 vols, Manchester University Press, Manchester, 1972.

JOHNSON, Franklyn A., *Defence by Committee. The British Committee of Imperial Defence 1885-1959*, OUP, 1960.

JONES, Commander E.H. Stuart, *An Invasion that Failed. The French Expedition to Ireland, 1796*, Blackwell, Oxford, 1950.

JONES, John Paul. See separate bibliography under title 'Whitehaven'.

KEEGAN, John, *The Second World War*, Hutchinson, 1989.

KENNEDY, Paul (ed.), *The War Plans of the Great Powers 1880-1914*, Allen and Unwin, 1979.

KENT, Peter, 'The Militant Trinity: The role of Wellington, Burgoyne, and Palmerston in Fortification Policy, 1830-1860', *Fort*, Vol.14, 1986.

KENYON, John R., 'A Hitherto Unknown Early Seventeenth Century Survey of the Coastal Forts of Southern England', *Fort*, Vol.11, 1983.

KIGHTLY, Charles, *Strongholds of the Realm*, Thames and Hudson, 1979.

KIPLING, Rudyard, *Rudyard Kipling's Verse, Definitive edition*, Hodder, 1982 (f.p. 1940).

KIRCHHAMMER, Captain Alexander, 'The Military Impotence of Great Britain', *Nineteenth Century*, No.L, April 1881.

KNIGHT, Dennis, *Harvest of Messerschmitts*, Frederick Warne, 1981.

KNIGHT, W. Stanley Macbean, *The History of the Great European War*, Vol.1, Caxton Publishing, 1914.

KNOX, Captain C., *The Defensive Position of England*, 1852.

KOSS, Stephen E., *Lord Haldane. Scapegoat for Liberalism*. Columbia University Press, New York and London, 1969.

LAMPE, David, *The Last Ditch*, Cassell, 1968. (Plans for British Resistance to German Occupation, 1940.)

LANGUTH, A.J., *Saki. A Life of Hector Hugh Munro*, Hamish Hamilton, 1981.

LEADAM, I.S., *The History of England from the Accession of Anne to the Death of George II (1702-1760)*, Longmans, 1912.

LENMAN, Bruce, *The Jacobite Risings in Britain 1689-1746*, Eyre Methuen, 1980.

— — *The Jacobite Cause*, Richard Drew, Glasgow, 1986.

LE QUEUX, William, *The Invasion of 1910*, Eveleigh Nash, 1906.

— — *Spies of the Kaiser*, Hurst and Blackett, 1909.

LESLIE, Major John Henry, *The History of Landguard Fort in Suffolk*,

1898. (A uniquely valuable and comprehensive account of one fort's history.)

LEWIS, Michael, *The Navy of Britain*, Allen and Unwin, 1948.

LILLEY, W.E., *The Life and Work of General Gordon at Gravesend*, n.d., but post-1871.

LOCKYER, Roger, *Buckingham. The Life and Political Career of George Villiers, First Duke of Buckingham, 1592-1629*, Longmans, 1981.

LODGE, Richard, *The History of England from the Restoration to the Death of William III (1660-1702)*, Longmans, 1910.

LONG, Viscount [Walter], *Memories*, Hutchinson, 1923. (Includes first-hand account of the late-Victorian and Edwardian yeomanry.)

LONGFORD, Elizabeth, *Victoria R.I.*, Pan, 1966 (f.p. Weidenfeld, 1964).

—— *Wellington, The Years of the Sword*, Panther, 1969 (f.p. Weidenfeld, 1961).

—— *Wellington, Pillar of State*, Panther, 1974 (f.p. Weidenfeld, 1972).

—— *A Pilgrimage of Passion. The Life of Wilfrid Scawen Blunt*, Weidenfeld, 1979.

LONGMATE, Norman, *How We Lived Then, A History of Everyday Life during the Second World War*, Hutchinson, 1971, Arrow, 1973 and later editions.

—— *If Britain Had Fallen*, BBC and Hutchinson, 1972, Arrow, 1975.

—— *The Real Dad's Army. The Story of the Home Guard*, Arrow, 1974.

—— *The Doodlebugs. The Story of the Flying-Bombs*, Hutchinson, 1981, Arrow, 1986.

—— *Hitler's Rockets, The Story of the V-2s*, Hutchinson, 1985.

—— *Defending the Island. From Caesar to the Armada*, Hutchinson, 1989. Grafton Books, 1990.

LOW, Sidney and SANDERS, Lloyd C., *The History of England during the Reign of Queen Victoria (1837-1901)*, Longmans, 1907.

MAC ALLESTER, Oliver, *A Series of Letters Discovering the Scheme Projected by France in MDCCLIX [i.e. 1759] for an Intended Invasion upon England*, 2 vols, n.d. but *c.*1759.

MACDONALD, John, 'Return of the Warrior', *Sunday Telegraph Magazine*, 22 June 1986. (On HMS *Warrior* and iron warships in general.)

MACKAY, Janet, *Little Madam. A Biography of Henrietta Maria*, Bell, 1939.

MACKSEY, Kenneth, *Invasion. The German Invasion of England July 1940* (fiction), Arms and Armour Press, 1980.

MCLYNN, Frank, *The Jacobites*, Routledge, 1985.

—— *Invasion. From the Armada to Hitler, 1588-1945*, Routledge, 1987.

MAHON, Alfred T., *The Influence of Sea Power upon History 1660-1783*, Methuen, 1965 (f.p. Boston, 1890).

MALLORY, Keith and OTTAR, Arvid, *Architecture of Aggression. A History of Military Architecture in North West Europe, 1900-1945*, Architectural Press, 1973. (Exceptionally informative on South Coast defences, including the sea forts built in the Second World War.)

MARCUS, Geoffrey J., *A Naval History of England*, Vol. I *The Formative Centuries* [i.e. to 1790], Longman, 1861, Vol. II *The Age of Nelson*, Allen and Unwin, 1972.

MARDER, Arthur J., *From the Dreadnought to Scapa Flow, The Royal Navy in the Fisher Era, 1904-1919, Vol I., The Road to War, 1904-1914*, OUP, 1966.

— — *The Anatomy of British Sea Power, A History of British Naval Policy in the pre-Dreadnought Era, 1880-1905*, Frank Cass, 1972 (f.p. 1940).

MARLOW, Joyce, *The Life and Times of George I*, Weidenfeld, 1973.

MARRIOTT, Sir J.A.R., *England since Waterloo*, Methuen, 1946 (f.p. 1912).

MARSHALL, C.F. Dendy, *A History of the Southern Railway*, Southern Railway, 1936. (On Railway Volunteers.)

MARTIN, Kingsley, *The Triumph of Lord Palmerston*, Allen and Unwin, 1924.

MARTIN, Sir Theodore, *Life of the Prince Consort*, Vol. IV, 1880.

MAUDE, Captain, *The Invasion and Defence of England*, 1888.

MAURICE, Sir Frederick, *Haldane 1856-1915*, Faber, 1937.

MAURICE, Baron, P.E. (pseudonym for Maurice de Sellon), *On National Defence in England*, 1852.

MAURICE-JONES, Colonel K.W., *The History of Coast Artillery in the British Army*, Royal Artillery Institution, 1959.

MELVILLE, Lewis, *The First George in Hanover and England*, 2 vols, Pitman, 1903.

MIDDLETON, Richard, 'Pitt, Anson and the Admiralty, 1756-1761', *History*, Vol.55, No. 184, June 1970.

MILLER, John, *The Life and Times of William and Mary*, Weidenfeld, 1974.

MONMOUTH. See WATSON.

MONTAGUE, F.C., *The History of England from the Accession of James I to the Restoration (1603-1660)*, Longmans, 1911.

MONTGOMERY. See HAMILTON.

MOON, Howard Roy, *The Invasion of the United Kingdom. Public Controversy and Official Planning 1888-1918*. (Unpublished manuscript thesis in the library of the University of London.)

MORGAN, Ted, *Churchill 1874-1915*, Cape, 1983.

MORRAH, Patrick, *A Royal Family. Charles I and his Family*, Constable, 1982.

MORRISS, A.J. Anthony, Haldane's Army Reforms 1906-8: 'The Deception of The Radicals', *History*, Vol.56, No. 186, Feb. 1971.

MOWAT, Charles L., *Britain Between the Wars 1918-1940*, Methuen,

1959 (f.p. 1955).

MOYNIHAM, Michael (ed.), *People at War 1914-1918*, David and Charles, 1973. (For the diary of the Town Clerk of Southwold.)

MUNRO, H.H. [also under pseudonym SAKI], *When William Came* (fiction), Penguin, 1941 (f.p. 1913).

MYATT, Frederick, *The British Infantry 1660-1945*, Blandford Press, Poole, 1983.

NAPOLEON III. See RIDLEY.

O'BRIEN, Terence, *Civil Defence*, an official *History of the Second World War* series, HMSO and Longmans, 1955.

OGG, David, *England in the Reign of Charles II*, OUP, 1984 (f.p. 1934).

— — *England in the Reigns of James II and William III*, OUP, 1984 (f.p. Clarendon Press, 1955).

OGLANDER, Sir John, *The Oglander Memoirs* (ed. W.H. Long), 1888. (A first-hand account of the Isle of Wight under Elizabeth and James I.).

OMAN, Carole, *Henrietta Maria*, Hodder, 1936.

— — *Britain against Napoleon*, Faber, 1942.

OSMOND, Lieut.-Colonel J.S., *Parliament and the Army, 1642-1904*, Cambridge University Press, Cambridge, 1933.

PALLISER, Major W., *The Use of Earthen Fortresses for the Defence of London and as a Preventive against Invasion*, 1871.

PALMERSTON. See ASHLEY, MARTIN, RIDLEY

PALMER, Alan, *The Life and Times of George IV*, Weidenfeld, 1972

— — *The Kaiser. Warlord of the Second Reich*, Weidenfeld, 1978.

PATRIOT A. [pseudonym for Guy du Maurier], *An Englishman's Home* (Drama), Edward Arnold, 1909. (For review see *The Times*, 28 January 1909.)

PATTERSON, A. Temple. *The Other Armada. The Franco-Spanish Attempt to Invade Britain in 1779*, Manchester University Press, Manchester, 1960.

PEARSE, Henry H.S., 'The Volunteers', *The Graphic*, 8 July 1899.

PEGDEN, B.K., 'The Purchase of Bricks for Martello Towers in the Year 1804', *Fort*, Vol. 8, 1980.

PEPYS, Samuel, *The Diary of Samuel Pepys* (ed. Robert Latham and William Matthews), Vol. VIII, 1667, Bell and Sons, 1974. See also BRYANT.

PINSENT, Margaret, 'The Defences of the British Channel in the last Two Centuries', *Fort*, Vol. II, 1983.

PITT, William, the Younger. See EHRMAN.

PORTSMOUTH. 'The Siege of Portsmouth'. Serial in *The Mail*, Portsmouth, 17-20 June 1895.

POSTERITAS (pseudonym), *The Siege of London*, 1885.

POWELL, J.R., *Robert Blake, General at Sea*, Collins, 1972.

POWNALL, Henry. *Chief of Staff. The Diaries of Lieut.-General Sir Henry Pownall, Vol. II, 1940-1944* (ed. Brian Bond), Leo Cooper, 1974.

POWTER, Andrew, 'Concrete in Nineteenth Century Fortifications Constructed by the Royal Engineers', *Fort*, Vol. 9, 1981.

REESON, Eric, 'When Dorset Prepared for Invasion . . .' [i.e. by Napoleon], in *Dorset County Post Magazine*, Vol. I, No. 8, Dorchester 1984.

REILLY, Robin, *Pitt The Younger, 1759-1806, Cassell, 1978.*

RICHMOND, Admiral Sir Herbert W., *The Invasion of Britain*, Methuen, 1941.

RIDLEY, Jasper, *Napoleon III and Eugenie*, Constable, 1979.

— — *Lord Palmerston*, Granada, 1972 (f.p. Constable 1970).

ROBB, Nesca A., *William of Orange. A Personal Portrait, Vol. II, The Later Years 1674-1702*, Heinemann, 1966.

ROBERTSON, Sir Charles Grant, *England under the Hanoverians*, Methuen, 1934 (f.p. 1911).

ROBERTSON, Field Marshal Sir William, *From Private to Field Marshal*, Constable, 1921.

ROGERS, P.G., *The Dutch in the Medway*, OUP, 1970.

ROOTES, Andrew, *Front Line County. Kent at War, 1939-45*, Robert Hale, 1988 (f.p. 1980).

ROSE, J. Holland, *Dumouriez and the Defence of England against Napoleon*, John Lane, 1909.

ROSKILL, Stephen, *Hankey. Man of Secrets*, 2 vols: Vol. I, 1877–1918, Vol. II, 1919–1931, Collins, 1970 and 1972.

SAKI. See MUNRO.

SAUNDERS, Andrew, *Fortress Britain. Artillery Fortification in the British Isles and Ireland*, Beaufort Publishing, Liphook, 1989.

SCOTT, A.F., *Every One a Witness. The Stuart Age*, White Lion, 1974. (A useful collection of contemporary accounts.)

SCOTT, Sir Sibbald D., Bart, *The British Army. Its Origins, Progress and Equipment*, 1868.

SELBY, John, *Over the Sea to Skye. The Forty-Five*, Hamish Hamilton, 1973.

SHAND, Innes Alexander, *The Life of General Sir Edward Bruce Hamley*, 2 vols, Blackwood, 1895. See also HAMLEY.

SHEPPARD, Alan, *The Royal Military Academy Sandhurst*, Country Life, 1980.

SHERRARD, O.A., *Lord Chatham. Pitt and the Seven Years War*, Bodley Head, 1955.

SMITH, Victor, R.C., 'Chatham Siege Operations: 1907', *Fort*, Vol. 5, 1977.

— — 'Chatham and London: 'The Changing Face of English Land

Fortifications, 1870-1918', *Post Medieval Archaeology*, Vol. 19, Summer 1986.

SOMERSET, Anne, *The Life and Times of William IV*, Weidenfeld, 1980.

SPECK, W.A., *The Butcher. The Duke of Cumberland and the Suppression of the '45*, Blackwell, Oxford, 1981.

STANHOPE, Earl, *History of England comprising the Reign of Queen Anne until the Peace of Utrecht, 1701-1713*, 1870.

STEEHOLM, Clara and Hardy, *James I of England*, Michael Joseph, 1938.

STOCQUELER, J.R., *The British Soldier. An Anecdotal History of the British Army from its Earliest Formation to the Present Time*, 1857.

STRACHAN, Hew, *Wellington's Legacy. The Reform of the British Army, 1830-54*, Manchester University Press, Manchester, 1984.

SUTCLIFFE, Sheila, *Martello Towers*, David and Charles, 1972.

TAYLOR, A.J.P., *English History 1914-1945*, Clarendon Press, 1965.

TAYLOR, I.A., *The Life of Queen Henrietta Maria*, 2 vols, Hutchinson, 1905.

TAYLOR, William, *The Military Roads in Scotland*, David and Charles, 1976.

TEIGNMOUTH: See separate bibliography.

TELEGRAPH, Daily, Report 'The Mighty Ocean Queen', 25 July 1887, reprinted in '100 Years Ago' feature, 25 July 1987.

— — 'Offering on the Altar of Patriotism', 11 July 1887, reprinted 11 July 1987.

THRUSH, Andrew, 'In Pursuit of the Frigate 1603-40', *Historical Research*, Vol. 64, 1991, pp.29-45.

TITMUSS, Richard M., *Problems of Social Policy* in Official *History of the Second World War*, HMSO and Longmans, 1950.

TRENCH, Charles Chenevix, *The Western Rising. An Account of Monmouth's Rebellion*, Longmans, 1969.

— — *George II*, Allen Lane, 1973.

TREVELYAN, George M., *England under the Stuarts*, Methuen, 1947 (f.p. 1904).

TREVOR, Meriol, *The Shadow of a Crown. The Life Story of James II of England and James VII of Scotland*, Constable, 1988.

TUNSTALL, Brian, *William Pitt, Earl of Chatham*, Hodder, 1938.

TUPPER, Martin, Poster signed by him, entitled 'West Surrey Rifle Club', 16 July 1859.

— — *Martin F. Tupper on Rifle Clubs. Some Verse and Prose about National Rifle Clubs*, 1859. See also HUDSON.

URQUHART, David, *The Invasion of England*, 1860.

VICTORIA, Queen. See LONGFORD.

VINE, Paul, A.L., *The Royal Military Canal*, David and Charles, 1972.

WARBURTON, Piers, Letter on dead rabbit in the Shetlands in 1939, *Daily Telegraph*, 31 May 1990.

WARNER, Philip, *Invasion Road*, Cassell, 1980.

WATSON, D.R., *The Life and Times of Charles I*, Weidenfeld, 1952.

WATSON, J.N.P., *Captain-General and Rebel Chief. The Life of James, Duke of Monmouth*, Allen and Unwin, 1979.

WATSON, J. Steven, *The Reign of George III, 1760-1815*, Clarendon Press, 1960.

WEINSTOCK, M.B., *Old Dorset*, David and Charles, 1967. (On Napoleonic period.)

WELLINGTON, Duke of, *Memorandum* (on the invasion danger) of 20 December 1844 reprinted in *Fort*, Vol. 9 Supplement, 1981. See also LONGFORD.

WEST, Nigel, *GCHQ. The Secret Wireless War 1900-86*, Coronet, 1987 (f.p. Weidenfeld, 1986).

WHEATLEY, Ronald, *Operation Sea Lion*, Clarendon Press, 1958.

WHEELER, H.F.B. and BROADLEY, A.M., *Napoleon and the Invasion of England*, 2 vols, John Lane, 1908.

WHEELER-BENNETT, John W., *King George VI. His Life and Reign*, Macmillan, 1958.

WILKINSON, Spencer, *The Volunteers and the National Defence*, 1896.

WILLIAM III. King. See BAXTER, MILLER, ROBB.

WILLIAMS, Basil, *The Whig Supremacy 1714-1760*, Clarendon Press, 1949 (f.p. 1939).

WILLIAMS, G.H., 'The Stokes Bay Moat near Portsmouth', in *Fort*, Vol. 11, 1983.

WILLIAMS, Lloyd, 'The Great Raid. A Story of Britain's Peril', *Black and White*, 13 February–1 May 1909.

WILLS, Henry, *Pillboxes. A Study of the UK Defences 1940*, Leo Cooper, 1985.

WILLSON, D. Harris, *King James VI and I*, Cape, 1956.

WILSON, Geoffrey, *The Old Telegraphs*, Phillimore, Chichester, 1976.

WINGFIELD, W. MacDonald, *Monmouth's Rebellion*, Moonraker Press, 1984.

WODEHOUSE, P.G., *The Swoop and Other Stories*, Seabury Press, New York, 1979. (*The Swoop* f.p. separately, Alison Rivers Ltd, London, 1909).

WOLFGANG, Michael (trans. MacGregor), *England under George I*, 2 vols, Macmillan, 1936-9.

WOOD, Derek with DEMPSTER, Derek, *The Battle of Britain*, Arrow, 1969 (f.p. Hutchinson, 1961.)

WOODWARD, David, *Armies of the World 1854-1914*, Sidgwick and Jackson, 1978.

WOODWARD, E.L. [later Sir Llewellyn], *The Age of Reform 1815-*

1870, Clarendon Press, 1946 (f.p. 1938).

— — *Great Britain and the War of 1914-1918*, Methuen, 1967. (Informative about German attitudes, based on the author's visits to Germany, pre-August 1914.)

YOUNG, G.M. and HANDCOCK W.D. (eds), *English Historical Documents, Vol. XII (I)*, 1833-1864, Eyre and Spottiswoode, 1956.

YOUNG, Peter and EMBERTON, William, *The Cavalier Army*, Allen and Unwin, 1974.

INDEX

Ranks and titles given are the highest recorded in the text. People concerned may be found in some references under lower rank. Entries in italic are ships' names unless otherwise indicated.